PRESIDENTIAL PROFILES
THE CLINTON YEARS

Shirley Anne Warshaw

Facts On File, Inc.

Presidential Profiles: The Clinton Years

Copyright © 2004 by Shirley Anne Warshaw

Facts On File, Inc.
132 West 31st Street
New York NY 10001

Library of Congress Cataloging-in-Publication Data

Warshaw, Shirley Anne, 1950–
   The Clinton years / Shirley Anne Warshaw.
     p. cm.—(Presidential profiles)
   Includes bibliographical references and index.
   ISBN 0-8160-5333-2 (acid-free paper)
   1. Politicians—United States—Biography. 2. United States—Politics and government—1993–2001. 3. Clinton, Bill, 1946– —Friends and associates. 4. United States—History—1969– —Biography. 5. United States—Biography. I. Title. II. Presidential profiles (Facts On File, Inc.)
   E840.6.W37   2004
   973.929′092′2—dc22   2004040351

Facts On File books are available at special discounts when purchased in bulk quantities for businesses, associations, institutions or sales promotions. Please call our Special Sales Department in New York at (212) 967-8800 or (800) 322-8755.

You can find Facts On File on the World Wide Web at http://www.factsonfile.com

Text design by Mary Susan Ryan-Flynn
Cover design by Nora Wertz

Printed in the United States of America

VB Hermitage 10 9 8 7 6 5 4 3 2 1

This book is printed on acid-free paper.

CONTENTS

PREFACE

*T*he Clinton Years is a new volume in the *Presidential Profiles* reference series. This volume contains, among other entries, the biographies of the several hundred individuals who were most influential in shaping American public policy during the administration of President William Jefferson Clinton. The entries include all of the cabinet officers throughout the eight years of the administration, many senior White House staff and subcabinet officials,

President Clinton and Vice President Gore announce the final cabinet nominees, including (left to right) John Gibbons, Mickey Kantor, Mike Espy, Zoe Baird, Bruce Babbitt, Federico Peña, and Dr. Jocelyn Elders. *(AP Photo/James Finley)*

many foreign leaders, the House and Senate leadership, and a host of political leaders who impacted the Clinton administration.

Each biography begins with the name of the individual, his or her date of birth, and, if required, date of death, followed with the name of the most important office or offices held, or the activity or occupation for which the subject was most noted during the Clinton presidency. From there follows a detailed account of an individual's career, with greatest emphasis on the relationship to President Clinton during his presidency. Where relevant, the individual who held the post both before and after the person profiled is included. This allows the reader to track who held a position in a particular office throughout the eight years of the administration. It should be noted that some individuals having no direct relationship to President Clinton nevertheless significantly affected the decisions made within the administration.

The focus of *The Clinton Years* is on the members of the administration, members of Congress, and foreign leaders who shaped the course of the Clinton presidency. One of the major events to affect the Clinton presidency was the Whitewater investigation and then the Monica Lewinsky investigation. This volume contains biographies of all independent counsels, the House of Representatives and Senate members who led the impeachment efforts, the judge in Arkansas who oversaw the federal trials, and others both directly and indirectly involved.

The Clinton Years contains a number of appendices, including a chronology of events during the Clinton presidency. The chronology is meant to include events both in which President Clinton participated and which impacted the administration. It is meant to capture the significant events of the eight years of the Clinton presidency. There is also a list of the Clinton cabinet for both terms, of the Supreme Court, and of the leadership of the House of Representatives and Senate. In addition, there are primary documents, including a selection of speeches made by President Clinton over the course of his eight years in office. The documents also include the Articles of Impeachment for President Clinton passed by the House of Representatives in 1998 and sent to the Senate. Finally, there is a selected bibliography at the end of the volume.

—Shirley Anne Warshaw

INTRODUCTION

After winning two presidential elections, William Jefferson Clinton became the first Democrat to be elected to two terms since Franklin Delano Roosevelt nearly 50 years earlier. Of the five Democratic presidents elected after Roosevelt, only Bill Clinton succeeded in capturing a second term. In contrast, Republicans had succeeded three times in winning two-term presidencies since the Roosevelt administration.

The election of Bill Clinton was a turning point for the Democratic Party, not only because they recaptured the White House after 12 years, but because they refocused their political objectives. Clinton moved the Democratic Party away from its liberal roots to a more moderate stance on social policy during the election. In order to regain the Oval Office from the Republicans in 1992, Clinton promised to reform the welfare system by requiring work from welfare recipients, a policy that was substantially different from that of most Democrats. Clinton was keenly aware of the conservative political trends that had captivated the nation during the 1980s. Rather than ignore the trends as other Democratic candidates had, Clinton sought to incorporate some of the Republican policies such as welfare reform into his own platform. To some extent, Clinton co-opted the Republican Party's own policies.

The Clinton platform, however, was hardly conservative. Although his welfare reform policy was designed to appeal to Republicans, his support for gun control, affirmative action, and abortion was decidedly Democratic but appealed to moderate Republicans. Clinton successfully built support for his candidacy from moderate Republicans by emphasizing fiscal responsibility. He promised a balanced budget, restraint in federal spending, and reductions in the federal workforce.

In addition to his policy positions, Clinton carefully portrayed himself as part of a new generation of political leaders. During the 1992 election, Clinton distanced himself from the World War II generation of leaders such as George Bush, as a symbol of his ability to lead the nation into the 21st century. Clinton regularly was seen jogging, playing the saxophone, and talking on youth-oriented television programs.

The results of the 1992 election on November 3 did not give the Clinton-Gore ticket a resounding mandate, but did give them the election. Clinton received 43 percent of the vote, Bush won 38 percent, and Independent Party candidate Ross Perot received 19 percent. With Democrats controlling both houses of Congress, Clinton was poised to move his election platform forward.

Following the election, Clinton began a transition process that would staff the new

Bill Clinton, standing between Hillary Rodham Clinton and Chelsea Clinton, takes the oath of office of the president of the United States, January 20, 1993. *(Library of Congress)*

administration. Its principal designers were Warren Christopher, a prominent Los Angeles attorney who had served as secretary of state in the Carter administration, and Vernon Jordan, a prominent Washington, D.C., attorney who had been deeply involved in the civil rights movement. Clinton gave them one overarching direction: build an administration that "looks like America." Clinton had campaigned on the promise to build an administration that was representative of the ethnic and gender composition of the American populace, not an administration of white males. The result was a cabinet that had more women and minorities than any cabinet in history, with four African Americans, two Hispanics, and three women. Subcabinet positions were also filled with more women and minorities than in any other previous administration.

The process of bringing women and minorities into the cabinet, however, was not without its problems. The most visible female appointment was that of attorney general. President Clinton sought to name the nation's first female attorney general, but the nomination quickly ran into problems in Congress. Zoe Baird, a corporate attorney and protégé of Warren Christopher, was President Clinton's first nominee for attorney general. The nomination was derailed when it was revealed that Baird had not paid appropriate social security taxes on her nanny. President Clinton's second nominee, Kimba Wood, another corporate attorney, also was derailed after problems regarding her household help surfaced. The third nomination, Janet Reno, the Dade County, Florida, state's attorney, was finally confirmed by the Senate.

During the election, Clinton portrayed President George Bush as a man out of touch with the economy and as head of an administration that had failed to deal with economic issues. As a result, the Clinton campaign used the economy as its primary issue, with the slogan "It's the economy, stupid!" To reinforce his commitment to the economy after the election, Clinton held an economic summit in December which included labor leaders, business leaders, and state and local government leaders.

The Clinton administration was formally moved into office after the inauguration of January 20, 1993, at which time Bill Clinton became the 42nd president of the United States. The Clinton presidency began by addressing a number of issues that did not need congressional approval but could be dealt with through executive order. On January 22, 1993, President Clinton used an executive order to lift a ban against gays and lesbians in the military. The executive order caused significant unrest in the Pentagon, leading to a compromise in July in which President Clinton allowed a "don't ask, don't tell" policy, which eliminated sexual preference questions from enlistment forms but still banned homosexuals from the military. It was not the policy that President Clinton wanted, but it was the policy that the military would enforce. President Clinton also used an executive order to remove the Reagan era "gag order" that prevented abortion counseling at federally funded family planning clinics.

Soon after taking office, President Clinton announced that he was forming a task force for health care reform. One of the main issues that the Clinton campaign had addressed was the absence of affordable health care for lower-income Americans. The health care reform task force was created to design legislation that would ensure all Americans had affordable health care. The task force was placed under the leadership of the president's wife, Hillary Rodham Clinton, in the White House, rather than through the Department of Health and Human Services or another White House policy unit. Mrs. Clinton subsequently hired Ira Magaziner to work with her and the task force staff. President Clinton announced the health care reform goals to a joint session of Congress in September 1993, to reinforce his commitment.

The health care task force worked without strong collaboration with other members of the White House staff or with members of Congress. The strategy of the task force was to meet independently with citizens, providers, hospitals, insurance companies, state and local representatives, and others to create the health care package. To some extent the strategy backfired, for it alienated some key members of Congress who were not involved in the task force discussions. It also alienated the health insurance companies, which soon launched a series of television advertisements accusing the Clinton administration of trying to nationalize health care. The health care task force worked throughout 1993 and 1994 on its proposals, but did not submit a package to Congress. The package ran into serious trouble in September 1994 when Senator George Mitchell (D-Me.) announced in a press conference on Capitol Hill that the health care reform package would not pass. The package lost all hope of passage in 1995 when the Democrats lost control of the Senate and the House of Representatives. The new Speaker of the House, Newt Gingrich (R-Ga.), was adamantly opposed to the health care legislation and had frequently voiced his opposition during the midterm elections. As a result, the Clinton administration pulled back from their proposals and the health care reform task force was disbanded.

The first year did have a number of successes for administration-sponsored legislation, most notably the passage of the Family and Medical Leave Act, signed on February 5, 1993. The bill granted workers in companies with 50 or more employees up to 12 weeks of unpaid leave in a 12-month period to care for a new baby or a seriously ill family member. Congress also passed the economic stimulus package in August 1993, the Brady Handgun Violence Prevention Act in November 1993, and the North American Free Trade Agreement in December 1993.

Although policy issues were moving along well, the internal machinery of the administration met several stumbling blocks. President Clinton fired the director of the Federal Bureau of Investigation, William Sessions, for misusing FBI resources for personal use, and nominated District Court Judge Louis J. Freeh as the bureau's director. A number of staffing changes occurred in the White House, including the addition of long-time Republican adviser David Gergen.

The White House suffered the loss of Deputy Counsel Vincent Foster in July 1993, after he was found dead of a self-inflicted gunshot wound in a public park outside Washington, D.C. Foster had been a law partner of Mrs. Clinton in Little Rock, Arkansas, and was close to both President and Mrs. Clinton. His death was later investigated by the independent counsel.

The nation suffered through a number of major events in 1993, including the attack on the World Trade Center in February. A minibus loaded with over a thousand pounds of explosives was detonated in an underground garage of the World Trade Center, killing six people and injuring more than a thousand. February also saw agents from the Bureau of Alcohol, Tobacco, and Firearms (ATF) attempt to arrest David Koresh at the Branch Davidian compound in Waco, Texas. After an exchange of gunfire, four ATF agents were killed, 16 were wounded, and numerous members of the

Branch Davidian cult were killed. The standoff with the Branch Davidians continued until April, when agents from the Federal Bureau of Investigation (FBI) attempted to storm the Branch Davidian compound. A fire broke out, and Koresh and 95 of his followers died in the inferno. Attorney General Janet Reno later ordered an investigation into the use of force by the FBI agents. Reno appointed former senator John Danforth (R-Mo.) to oversee the investigation to ensure impartiality. In July 2000 Danforth issued his final report, which exonerated the FBI agents in the deaths of the Branch Davidians in Waco.

The first year of the administration also saw the first Supreme Court appointment by President Clinton, with the nomination of Ruth Bader Ginsburg. Ginsburg became the second woman in history appointed to the Supreme Court. Justice Sandra Day O'Connor had been the first woman named to the Court. Ginsburg was confirmed by the Senate on August 3, 1993. President Clinton made his second and final appointment to the Supreme Court in 1994 with the nomination and subsequent confirmation of Stephen Breyer.

Although not known as a foreign policy president at the start of the administration, President Clinton quickly moved into the forefront of the international arena. He hosted the signing of the Oslo Accords on September 13, 1993, between the Palestine Liberation Organization (PLO) and Israel. However, the triumph of the Oslo Accords in foreign policy was overshadowed in October by the loss of 18 U.S. Rangers in a firefight in Mogadishu, Somalia. The 2001 movie *Black Hawk Down* chronicled the firefight. President Clinton subsequently expanded the number of U.S. troops in Somalia, sending 5,300 new combat troops and an aircraft carrier to Somalia "to protect our troops and to complete our mission."

The second year of the administration began on a sad note for President Clinton. His mother,

Virginia Kelley, died on January 6, 1994. President and Mrs. Clinton flew to Arkansas for the funeral. The year also saw the appointment on January 20, 1994, by Attorney General Reno of an independent counsel, Robert Fiske. Fiske was asked to look into allegations that President and Mrs. Clinton used improper loans from the Madison Guaranty Savings and Loan, owned by Susan and Jim McDougal, for their Whitewater land development project in Arkansas. The project was more than a decade old but remained only a development concept.

Six months later, Fiske was replaced by Kenneth Starr as the independent counsel. During the six-month period, the independent counsel act was reauthorized by Congress, and the new act gave a three-judge federal panel, rather than the attorney general, the authority to name the independent counsel. The Republican-controlled panel believed that Fiske had not moved aggressively enough, and viewed Starr as being a more dedicated investigator.

The appointment of a new independent counsel was compounded by the filing of a sexual harassment lawsuit against President Clinton in May 1994 by Paula Corbin Jones. Jones alleged that on May 9, 1991, Governor Bill Clinton invited her to his hotel room in Little Rock and made unwanted sexual advances. The lawsuit was filed in federal court in Little Rock, Arkansas, with Judge Susan Webber Wright assigned to the case.

Problems in the management of the White House staff led President Clinton to make a number of staff changes during the summer of 1994. Thomas "Mack" McLarty was elevated from chief of staff to presidential counselor. McLarty was replaced by Leon Panetta, the director of the Office of Management and Budget and former chair of the House Budget Committee. In addition to bringing Panetta on as chief of staff, President Clinton brought in a new press secretary at the end of the year, Michael McCurry. A series of other staff changes were made to tighten the policy process in the White House and to protect President Clinton from a constant stream of staff meetings. One of the main criticisms of the Clinton White House was that it lacked order and was in perpetual chaos. Panetta was brought in to bring order and improve the overall management of the staff and of policy decision making.

During the summer of 1994, a series of Whitewater-related decisions were made. In June 1994, independent counsel Robert Fiske announced that Vincent Foster's death was a suicide and that contacts between the White House and the Treasury Department in the investigation had not broken any laws. In July 1994 both the House Banking Committee and the Senate Banking Committee began Whitewater hearings. The following month, Fiske was replaced by Kenneth Starr as the independent counsel. The escalation in 1994 of the investigations by the House, the Senate, and the independent counsel were the beginning of a constant series of investigations that

President Clinton watches as Israeli prime minister Yitzhak Rabin (left) shakes hands with Palestinian leader Yasser Arafat (right) in the Rose Garden of the White House after the signing of a deal transferring much of the West Bank to Palestinian control, September 13, 1993. *(Hulton Archive)*

were to last through the remainder of the Clinton presidency.

The fall and winter of 1994 saw President Clinton involved in a host of domestic and foreign policy issues. In September 1994 he inducted the first 20,000 volunteers into AmeriCorps, the centerpiece of the National Service Act signed into law in 1993. During the 1992 campaign, President Clinton had urged passage of the National Service Act which he called the domestic Peace Corps. Eli Segal was named director of the National Service Corporation, the federal agency created by the National Service Act. December marked two disappointments for the administration. The first was the plea of guilty to mail fraud and tax evasion by the former associate attorney general Webster Hubbell, a Clinton friend. Soon after, President Clinton fired Surgeon General Jocelyn Elders under pressure from conservatives, for remarks she made regarding adolescent sex. Elders had been a senior member of the Clinton gubernatorial cabinet in Arkansas, and was a nationally recognized expert in adolescent health.

The international front was dominated by events in Yugoslavia and in Haiti. In their continuing civil war, the Serbs rejected an international peace plan for Bosnia in July 1994. The United States had been actively involved in reaching a settlement in the escalating war between the two Yugoslavian states. As the war continued in Bosnia, President Clinton was faced with a civil war closer to home, in Haiti. Ousted president Jean-Bertrand Aristide appealed to the United States to send troops to Haiti to remove the military junta and restore him to power. In September 1994 President Clinton made a nationally televised speech announcing that the United States would lead a United Nations–authorized mission to reinstall President Aristide in Haiti.

The third year of the administration began with the election of Newt Gingrich as the new Speaker of the House of Representatives, and the reemergence of divided government. Republicans in the House of Representatives and Senate moved quickly to assert their own policy proposals, which differed significantly from Clinton's. The House, in particular, had become more conservative in its political agenda.

Only weeks after the Congress opened, Mexico was on the verge of financial crisis as the peso continued to be devalued. President Clinton authorized a $20 billion loan to Mexico as part of an international bailout. The loan was orchestrated by the new secretary of the Treasury, Robert Rubin. Rubin had been the president's economic adviser in the White House during the first two years of the administration and had been the architect of many of the administration's economic recovery programs.

War continued during the spring of 1995 in Bosnia, with the Bosnian army launching an offensive near Tusla in March 1995. In April, a United States plane carrying humanitarian supplies to Bosnia was hit by gunfire, which forced the suspension of all United Nations aid flights to Sarajevo. In May 1995 NATO forces attacked a Bosnian Serb ammunition depot as the fighting became more intense. After months of fighting, President Clinton urged the warring parties to begin peace negotiations. In November 1995 President Clinton hosted a peace conference in Dayton, Ohio, resulting in the Dayton Peace Accords signed by the presidents of Serbia, Croatia, and Bosnia-Herzegovina. On December 14, 1995, President Clinton traveled to Paris for the signing ceremony at the Elysée Palace of the Paris Agreement on Peace in Bosnia-Herzegovina, which emerged from the Dayton Accords.

The domestic front was traumatized in April 1995 by the bombing of the Alfred P. Murrah Federal Building in Oklahoma City, Oklahoma. Timothy McVeigh was arrested two days later and subsequently convicted and executed for the crime. Terry Nichols, a collaborator in the bombing but not a participant, was convicted and sentenced to life in prison.

Although not directly involved, President and Mrs. Clinton were again brought into the public eye as Jim and Susan McDougal and former Arkansas governor Jim Guy Tucker were indicted by a grand jury for fraud and conspiracy. The indictments were not directly related to the Whitewater land investigation, but the findings stemmed from Kenneth Starr's probe into the McDougals' financial dealings.

While the conflicts between the White House and the Republican-controlled Congress seemed manageable throughout most of the year, disagreements between the two branches over the budget led to intractable positions by both parties in November 1995. President Clinton vetoed the budget reconciliation bill, leading to a stalemate on the budget. Without congressional approval for funding to carry out the business of the federal government, the government shut down. On December 18, 1995, federal agencies closed their doors until a budget bill could be approved by both the president and Congress. The shutdown lasted until January 6, 1996, when Congress grudgingly approved the president's budget. President Clinton was widely viewed as the winner in the budget crisis, and Speaker of the House Gingrich was widely viewed as the loser.

Kenneth Starr was again in the news in January 1996 when he subpoenaed President Clinton to testify at the trial of Jim and Susan McDougal and Jim Guy Tucker. President Clinton's deposition was videotaped and shown to the jury in the May trial.

The administration saw its second major personnel loss in April 1996 with the death of Secretary of Commerce Ronald Brown in a plane crash in Croatia. Brown, as executive director of the Democratic National Committee, had been a key member of President Clinton's campaign team and had become part of the president's inner circle. Brown also was the most visible African American in the administration. President Clinton tapped Trade Representative Mickey Kantor to replace Brown.

By the summer of 1996, the Whitewater investigation was again dominating the front pages of the newspapers. In June 1996 Hillary Rodham Clinton provided written responses to the Senate Banking Committee looking into the Whitewater land project. Soon after, Senator Alfonse D'Amato, chairman of the Senate Banking Committee, issued a report accusing Mrs. Clinton and White House aides of obstruction of justice. Senate Democrats on the committee countered with a separate report concluding that they were not guilty of obstruction. During the same month the independent counsel, Kenneth Starr, broadened his investigation to include the White House firings of the travel office staff in 1993 and allegations of the improper use of FBI background files by White House staff.

Problems in the Middle East were brought back to the United States in June 1996, when a truck bomb was detonated in the Khobar Towers apartment complex near an American air base in Saudi Arabia, killing 19 Americans and injuring approximately 250 others. After the 1991 Persian Gulf War, the United States had maintained a large contingent of military personnel in Saudi Arabia, in spite of strong opposition from some Muslim leaders. Tensions were frequently high as Muslim leaders denounced the presence of American troops in Saudi Arabia. The bombings were attributed to fundamentalist Muslim opposition to the American troop presence.

During the summer of 1996 the Democratic Party again nominated President Clinton as their candidate for the 1996 presidential election. The Republicans nominated Senator Robert Dole (R-Kans.) as their candidate. One of the central issues for the 1996 campaign would be welfare reform, which President

Clinton had strongly supported in the 1992 campaign. In spite of his support for welfare reform, legislation had not gone through due to differences between the administration and the Congress. Congress wanted more stringent rules requiring welfare recipients to work than did the administration. Sensing that failure to support a welfare reform package could hurt his campaign, President Clinton reluctantly signed a Republican-sponsored welfare reform bill in August 1996. Although the bill did not address many of the issues the President Clinton had favored, it was a major step toward reforming a structure that first emerged in the sixties as part of the Great Society legislation of the Johnson administration.

On November 5, 1996, President Clinton and Vice President Gore were reelected to a second term. President Clinton carried 49 percent of the popular vote, Senator Dole won 41 percent of the popular vote, and Ross Perot received 8 percent of the popular vote. By 1996, Perot's independent party movement had been splintered by internal strife within the party. Neither the party nor Perot were a significant factor in the 1996 election.

Several new staff were brought into the White House for the second term, including Chief of Staff Erskine Bowles, who replaced Leon Panetta. As was to be expected, a number of the cabinet officers left or were shuffled. Some officers, such as Hazel O'Leary, left at the request of the president. Some, such as Secretary of State Warren Christopher, left at their own request. With the new term, President Clinton was afforded an opportunity to make a number of major cabinet appointments. For secretary of state, President Clinton nominated Madeleine Albright, the first woman to hold the position. Although she was born in Czechoslovakia, Albright was not the first foreign-born citizen to hold the position. Henry Kissinger, secretary of state during the early 1970s, had been born in Germany.

For secretary of labor, President Clinton nominated Alexis Herman, the first African-American woman to hold the position. Her nomination faced substantial opposition in the Senate after allegations arose of influence peddling, but she was finally confirmed after a three-month battle. President Clinton also sought to rebuild his cabinet after several high-profile departures, when independent counsel investigations had forced the resignation of Henry Cisneros of the Department of Housing and Urban Development and of Mike Espy of the Department of Agriculture. In addition, he added another high-profile Democrat, Chicago lawyer William Daley, as secretary of commerce. In May another senior position opened after the forced resignation of the director of the Central Intelligence Agency (CIA), John Deutch. President Clinton nominated his national security adviser, Anthony Lake, for CIA director, but the Senate failed to confirm him. Lake was criticized for his position on more open relations with Cuba, among other issues. President Clinton subsequently nominated George Tenet, the deputy director of the CIA, as the director. Tenet was confirmed by the Senate.

The Paula Corbin Jones lawsuit, which had been quietly winding through the legal process, resurfaced in January 1997, when the attorneys for President Clinton argued before the Supreme Court that the lawsuit should be suspended while the president was in office because it would undermine his ability to manage the executive branch. In May the Supreme Court ruled against President Clinton and allowed the Jones lawsuit to proceed.

The Starr investigation also heated up later in the year. In June 1997 the *Washington Post* reported that Starr had been interviewing Arkansas state troopers who would provide names of women that Governor Clinton may have been romantically involved with. The interviews were the result of the innuendo that, while governor, Clinton had been engaged in a number of extramarital affairs. During the 1992 presidential campaign, Gennifer Flowers described her 12-year relationship with Clinton and later sold her story to a tabloid magazine. Clinton never denied the affair, although he denied many of the details that Flowers provided.

The summer of 1997 saw a number of major international developments, including the death of Princess Diana of Great Britain in a car crash, the NATO decision to invite Poland, Hungary, and the Czech Republic to join the organization, and the reversion of the territory of Hong Kong to Chinese sovereignty. On the domestic front, the Department of Justice won a victory in a major antitrust lawsuit against Microsoft. U.S. District Judge Thomas Jackson issued a preliminary injunction ordering Microsoft to stop requiring manufacturers to install certain Microsoft programs on computers.

Although the 1996 election was over, the Justice Department began an investigation into allegations of campaign improprieties by both President Clinton and Vice President Gore for using official telephones in the White House for fund-raising. After reviewing the charges, Attorney General Reno declined to continue the investigation or seek approval for an independent counsel.

As the year ended, President Clinton traveled to Sarajevo to see how the peace process was proceeding. The trip was relatively uneventful, with little fanfare given to his visit for fear of attracting dissidents.

The new year, 1998, offered little respite for President Clinton from the independent counsel's investigations. In January 1998 Starr was given approval by the attorney general to investigate allegations of perjury concerning former White House intern Monica Lewinsky. On January 26, 1998, President Clinton publicly denied having had an affair with Lewinsky. Speaking on national television, President Clinton stated "I did not have sexual relations with that woman, Miss Lewinsky." The following day President Clinton delivered his State of the Union address, after which his public approval ratings soared to the highest of his presidency. The Lewinsky revelations had little impact on his public approval ratings. But Starr continued to press his investigation, including securing the testimony of long-time Clinton friend Vernon Jordan. Jordan was questioned by the grand jury that Starr had convened as to his participation in finding another job for Lewinsky in return for her silence about a relationship with President Clinton.

Seeking to distance themselves from the Starr investigation, President and Mrs. Clinton began an 11-day trip to Africa in March. The trip was meant to reinforce American commitment to African economic development and to assisting the fight against AIDS in Africa. Mrs. Clinton spent much of her time meeting with women's groups, including discussions on the abuse and physical harm done to many women in sub-Saharan African nations.

After returning from Africa, President Clinton learned that Judge Susan Webber Wright had dismissed the Paula Corbin Jones lawsuit as "without merit." However, Jones appealed. In November, President Clinton agreed to an $850,000 settlement, but admitting no guilt, before the Appeals Court ruled. Jones received less than a third of the money after her lawyer's fees were paid.

April brought further good news for President Clinton. Former senator George Mitchell had successfully brokered a peace agreement in Northern Ireland. Known as the "Good Friday Agreement," it was accepted by a plebiscite in an all-Ireland poll on May 22, 1998. After leaving the Senate in 1995, Mitchell had been asked by President Clinton to lead a delegation that would work toward a peace agreement in Northern Ireland. The process took nearly three years, but was finally successful.

The summer of 1998 was marred by both domestic and international events. In July 1998, Kenneth Starr pressed his investigation into the Monica Lewinsky relationship by requiring Secret Service agents to testify before the grand jury about Lewinsky's visits to the White House. The Lewinsky investigation was becoming the central part of the expanded Whitewater investigation that Starr and his growing staff were looking into. The staff and offices had expanded during 1998, with much of the staff living in Little Rock, Arkansas, where the grand jury was meeting.

In early August, the specter of terrorism resurfaced when bombs exploded at the U.S. embassies in Nairobi, Kenya, and in Dar Es Salaam, Tanzania. The bombs left major damage to the embassies and surrounding buildings, and resulted in numerous injuries. Nearly three weeks later, after federal agents had combed the embassies for evidence, President Clinton ordered air strikes on a suspected hideout of a terrorist group, al-Qaeda, in Khartoum, Sudan. The terrorist organization was also targeted by air strikes at its training camps in Afghanistan.

The international scene was further complicated by severe economic problems in Russia.

President Clinton speaks to American, British, and French troops deployed at Skopje, Macedonia, on June 22, 1999. *(Department of Defense)*

President Boris Yeltsin of Russia devalued its currency, the ruble, on August 17, 1998, after failing to receive the necessary economic sanctions from the Duma to secure loans from the International Monetary Fund (IMF). The ruble fell to about a quarter of its value by the end of the year. Questions about Yeltsin's leadership capabilities and the status of his health escalated in discussions within the U.S. administration. President Clinton met with Yeltsin in September for a summit in Moscow to discuss problems with the sagging Russian economy and to personally assess the state of Yeltsin's health. The two also signed an agreement designed to prevent nuclear accidents. Over the course of the next year, Yeltsin would routinely be ill and leave for his summer home. During his absences, little was known about where power sat in the Russian power structure. On New Year's Eve 1999, Yeltsin abruptly resigned after a series of heart and other physical problems. He handed the presidency over to his vice president, Vladimir Putin, who was subsequently elected in national elections.

The Lewinsky affair again dominated the national news in mid-August when President Clinton testified on videotape to the federal grand jury in Little Rock that had been convened by Kenneth Starr. Later in the day, in a televised address, President Clinton admitted to the nation that he and Lewinsky had a relationship and apologized for having "misled" the nation and his wife. The revelations led to a series of public denouncements by Republicans and to calls for impeachment. The calls for impeachment were not the direct result of allegations of the Lewinsky affair, but of the cover-up and the subsequent perjury. President Clinton lied to lawyers in the Jones lawsuit about the Lewinsky affair and lied to the Starr investigators, both resulting in charges of perjury. Senator Joseph Lieberman (D-Conn.) condemned the Clinton-Lewinsky affair on the Senate floor, becoming the first senior Democrat to publicly admonish President Clinton.

September brought a series of major developments in the Lewinsky investigation after the House of Representatives released the independent counsel's report on the investigation to the public. The report provided the graphic detail that Monica Lewinsky had given to Starr about her sexual encounters with President Clinton in the White House. Her evidence also included a dress she had worn that still contained President Clinton's DNA. The Starr report also listed possible grounds for impeachment, including allegations of perjury, witness tampering, obstruction of justice, and abuse of power. With the House of Representatives firmly in Republican control, impeachment appeared to be more and more likely.

During September and October 1998, President Clinton attempted to carry on the course of business as usual. He gave little public evidence that his presidency had been overtaken by the Starr report to Congress. He continued to meet with his cabinet and staff with no discussion of the Starr report. However, on October 8, 1998, the House of Representatives voted to begin an impeachment investigation of President Clinton's conduct in the Lewinsky affair.

Still trying to continue the business of the presidency in spite of the House vote for an impeachment investigation, President Clinton hosted a retreat on the Wye River on the eastern shore of Maryland for Israeli prime minister Benjamin Netanyahu and Palestine Liberation Organization (PLO) chairman Yasser Arafat. After several days of negotiations, Netanyahu and Arafat signed the Wye River Memorandum, a land-for-security agreement between Israel and the PLO. However, in December 1998, Netanyahu suspended the agreement after violence and suicide bombings increased in the Palestinian-held territories.

The midterm elections on November 3, 1998, led to modest gains for the Democrats in the House of Representatives. Although the Republicans continued to control the House, Speaker Newt Gingrich took responsibility for losing Republican seats in the election and announced he would resign as Speaker when the new Congress convened in January 1999.

In spite of turmoil in the House, its Judiciary Committee had been carefully building its evidence against President Clinton. During impeachment proceedings that began in December 1998, the committee presented charges against President Clinton stemming from his cover-up of the Lewinsky affair and the related perjury he committed. The House voted on December 19, 1998, along strictly partisan lines to impeach President Clinton on charges of perjury and obstruction of justice.

During the impeachment hearings, Republican members of the House began considering a replacement for Gingrich as Speaker. A new Speaker-elect, Robert Livingston (R-La.), was chosen by the Republican caucus. But Livingston was soon charged with marital infidelity, to which he admitted, and resigned. The House Republicans then selected Dennis Hastert (R-Ill.), who was formally elected as Speaker in January 1999. During the period that Livingston's extramarital relationships were becoming public, allegations surfaced that Newt Gingrich also had had extramarital affairs. Democrats quickly jumped on the allegations, given Gingrich's support for "family values" and his attacks against President Clinton's personal life. Gingrich subsequently resigned his seat in the House in January.

On January 7, 1999, President Clinton's impeachment trial began in the Senate. Senate President Pro Tempore Strom Thurmond (R-S.C.) swore in Chief Justice William Rehnquist as the presiding officer of the trial, as required by the Constitution. The trial went on for over a month, with the House of Representatives using Republican members of the Judiciary Committee to present their case. President

Clinton was represented in the Senate trial by the White House counsel, Charles Ruff. When he began his opening remarks on January 19, 1999, at the Senate trial, Ruff described the House charges as "a witches' brew" resting on "shifting sand castles of speculation." Ruff was never theatrical in his presentation of the president's case in the Senate trial, but remained calm, focused, and straightforward. Although the House managers often became theatrical in their arguments against President Clinton, Ruff simply rebutted the evidence that they had presented. After Ruff's presentation, the Senate did not vote to convict the president. They acquitted President Clinton of the impeachment charges on February 12, 1999.

With the impeachment trial behind him, President Clinton returned to his job as the nation's chief executive. His immediate focus turned to Serbian aggression in Kosovo, where Serbian forces had begun ethnic killings of Albanian Muslims living in Kosovo. As part of international efforts to stop the killings, President Clinton sent Secretary of State Madeleine Albright to France to meet with delegates to the Kosovo Peace Conference. However, in March 1999, after Serbian president Slobodan Milošević refused both United States and NATO demands for a settlement with Kosovo, the United States led a bombing campaign against Serb forces in Kosovo. The air strikes were part of "Operation Allied Force" to remove the Serbs from Kosovo. In June 1999 Milošević agreed to withdraw from Kosovo, and NATO peacekeepers entered the region.

The international scene continued to be volatile as India test-fired an intermediate-range ballistic missile (IRBM), and Pakistan test-fired medium-range and short-range ballistic missiles in April 1999. The two nations were posturing with their nuclear weapons as warnings to each other to contain militants. Not to be outdone by its neighbors, China test-fired an intermediate-range missile in August. Throughout the international contests, President Clinton championed the Comprehensive Test Ban Treaty. This would have barred all signatories from such tests. However, in October 1999 the Senate rejected the Comprehensive Test Ban Treaty on the grounds that American national defense could be jeopardized.

The year ended with the surprise announcement from Russian president Boris Yeltsin that he was resigning on December 31, 1999, and handing power to the vice president, Vladimir Putin. The world had not expected the Yeltsin resignation on New Year's Eve but had expected problems to emerge that day related to the new millennium. President Clinton had created a White House task force, known as the Y2K (for Year 2000) task force, to oversee the myriad problems that could arise during the millennium changeover. Issues such as computers unable to recognize the year 2000 and issues of terrorism were discussed by the task force. Although minor problems arose, no significant disorders occurred as the clock struck midnight waving in the year 2000.

During the last year of the administration, President Clinton devoted much of his time to the problems in the Middle East. In January 2000, President Clinton hosted Israeli prime minister Ehud Barak and Syrian foreign minister Farouk Sharaa in talks held at Shepherdstown, West Virginia. The remote town was chosen because of its peaceful environment outside the Washington Beltway.

Numerous federal initiatives were launched during the last year of the administration, including such diverse programs as funding firearms enforcement, AIDS research, and programs to study the environmental causes of diseases, as well as economic stimulus packages. President Clinton also had a steady stream of foreign leaders visiting the White House for both private and public meetings, and made numerous official trips abroad.

The last year of the administration also saw a strong commitment to environmental protection. In January 1999 President Clinton created three new national monuments in national parks and signed a proclamation expanding the Pinnacles National Monument. He also vetoed a bill in April that would have allowed the shipment of thousands of tons of nuclear waste to Yucca Mountain in Nevada.

In April the Paula Corbin Jones lawsuit was again in the news as Judge Susan Webber Wright found President Clinton in contempt of court for false testimony in the Jones lawsuit. In April 2000 Wright dismissed the Jones lawsuit against President Clinton, saying that her lawyers had failed to provide enough evidence in their case. "The Plaintiff's allegations," she said in her ruling, "fall far short of the rigorous standards for establishing a claim of outrage." She further said in her ruling, "While the court will certainly agree that plaintiffs' allegations describe offensive conduct, the court . . . has found that the governor's [Clinton] alleged conduct does not constitute sexual assault."

In December 2000 Wright ordered President Clinton to pay more than $90,000 in fines for giving false testimony under oath in the Paula Corbin Jones lawsuit about his affair with Monica Lewinsky. President Clinton's private attorney, Robert Bennett, responded to Webber's decision to levy fines by saying, "We accept the judgment of the court and will comply with it." The fines were used to reimburse the court and Jones's legal teams for work that stemmed from President Clinton's January 1998 deposition, in which he denied having had sexual relations with Lewinsky, testimony that Wright called "intentionally false." Wright ordered President Clinton to pay the Rutherford Institute and the law firm of Rader, Campbell, Fisher (which both represented Jones) $89,484. The U.S. District Court received $1,202.

The election of 2000 began to gain steam in the spring when the Republicans battled among themselves to find a candidate for the presidential nomination. George W. Bush finally emerged the victor in a difficult and often hotly contested primary fight and was formally nominated by the Republican Party at their convention in August 2000. The Democrats nominated Vice President Al Gore as their nominee. Gore had only a limited challenge to the nomination, mounted by former senator Bill Bradley (D-N.J.).

During the fall of 2000, Vice President Gore maintained his distance from President Clinton. Gore chose not to involve President Clinton in the election for fear of losing votes from those offended by the Lewinsky affair. President Clinton continued to manage the country, although he remained out of the presidential race.

In October 2000 the nation was rocked by another terrorist attack against U.S. citizens. The U.S. Navy destroyer *Cole* was attacked in the Yemeni harbor of Aden, killing four U.S. sailors and wounding numerous others. President Clinton immediately sent the FBI to investigate but received only minimal assistance from the government of Yemen. Tensions in the Middle East were also escalating in Israel, as continuing violence marred peace talks between the Palestinians and the Israelis. As late as December 23, President Clinton was hosting peace talks in Washington, D.C., with Palestinian and Israeli negotiators.

The November presidential election saw Vice President Gore win the popular vote but lose the electoral vote. In a bitterly contested election, the Supreme Court ultimately decided that Governor George W. Bush had won the contested votes in Florida and thus won the presidency. Throughout the court challenges on the election in November, President Clinton remained silent, stating that the courts should resolve the issue. Whether his failure to become more active in the election was due to his position as president or due to Gore's election strategy remains unknown. Both answers appear plausible.

As the inauguration of George W. Bush drew near, President Clinton exercised his constitutional prerogative of issuing pardons. On January 19, 2001, President Clinton issued more than 100 pardons, including pardons for former Secretary of Housing and Urban Development Henry Cisneros, Patty Hearst, Susan McDougal, his brother Roger Clinton, and fugitive financier Marc Rich. The last pardon brought strong opposition from law enforcement and from his own Department of Justice. Even after Clinton left office, Congress conducted hearings on the Rich pardon.

After eight years in office, President Clinton turned over the reins of government to George W. Bush on January 20, 2001, in a ceremony first held in 1797 when President George Washington passed government leadership to John Adams. The transition of power from one administration to the next continued seamlessly from Democrat Bill Clinton to Republican George Bush. Soon after the election, President Clinton invited Governor and Mrs. Bush to the White House to see the private residence and to begin an orderly transition of power. As President George H. W. Bush had done eight years earlier for President Clinton, the process was smooth and courteous.

The new year brought a series of changes for the Clinton family. Hillary Rodham Clinton was elected to the U.S. Senate from New York in the 2000 election and took office in January 2001 only days before her husband relinquished office. For a brief time in January, the nation saw both President Bill Clinton and Senator Hillary Rodham Clinton in office.

President and Mrs. Clinton purchased a home in an upscale New York City suburb, where he spent most of his time. They also purchased a large home near Washington, D.C., where Mrs. Clinton would live while in the Senate. President Clinton established his official office in Harlem, after Republicans chastised him for the lavish suite of offices he originally had in Manhattan. The Clinton Presidential Library is being built in Little Rock, Arkansas, where President Clinton will eventually be devoting much of his time.

A

Acheson, Eleanor (Eldie) Dean

(1947–   ) *assistant attorney general, Office of Policy Development, Department of Justice*

Eleanor Acheson was named by President Clinton as assistant attorney general in the Office of Policy Development of the Department of Justice in 1993. As the person overseeing judicial appointments in the U.S. Department of Justice, Acheson took charge of increasing the number of women in the federal judiciary. While in the Department of Justice, Acheson succeeded in increasing the number of women nominated to the federal bench to a record 30 percent, compared with 18 percent under President George H. W. Bush, 8 percent under President Reagan, and 16 percent under President Carter. Nearly one-half of the women serving in the federal judiciary were appointed by President Clinton during Acheson's tenure in the Department of Justice.

Her commitment to increasing the number of women in the federal judiciary was mirrored by her commitment to ethnic diversity in the judicial nomination process. She frequently noted that the Clinton administration was committed to gender and ethnic diversity throughout the federal judiciary, a commit-ment that followed the administration's overall commitment to diversity in appointments. During her eight years as assistant attorney general for policy development at the Department of Justice, she significantly raised the profile of women, African Americans, and Hispanics in the federal judiciary.

Confirmed by the Senate in August 1993, Acheson was responsible for not only judicial nominations but a broad spectrum of issues, including crime, violence against women, welfare reform, and access to justice. The National Association of Women Judges gave her their 1995 award "in grateful recognition of her invaluable efforts on behalf of excellence and gender fairness in judicial appointments." She also received the Women's Bar Association of D.C. "Woman Lawyer of the Year Award" in 2000.

Prior to joining the administration, Acheson was a partner in Ropes & Gray in Boston. Her legal practice at Ropes & Gray centered on civil litigation, including product liability, health care, antitrust, employment, and environmental issues. Acheson created the pro bono program at Ropes & Gray, and served as its administrator until she left to join the Clinton administration in 1993. Much of her pro bono work involved women and minorities. She served on the board of directors of Women, Inc., a residential rehabilitation program for drug- and alcohol-addicted women and children. In addition, she was appointed by Governor Michael Dukakis to serve as a trustee of Roxbury Community College, an inner-city Boston public college. Acheson also was on the board of the Volunteer Lawyer's Project and on committees in the Boston Bar Association that provided legal services for the poor.

Acheson had been a Democratic activist for many years prior to joining the Clinton administration. As early as 1964, she became involved with Democratic presidential campaigns and later with state and local campaigns within Massachusetts and the Boston area. During the 1992 presidential campaign, Acheson was the cochair of the Clinton-Gore New England Finance Committee. During the 1992 campaign, she founded the New England Women Leaders organization, which sought to bring women and men together to address public issues important to women and families and their communities.

Acheson graduated with a B.A. from Wellesley College, where she had been friends with Hillary Rodham Clinton, and received a J.D. from George Washington University Law School (1973). Following law school, she served as a law clerk to Judge Edward T. Gignoux of the U.S. District Court in Portland, Maine.

Achtenberg, Roberta

(1950–   ) *senior adviser to the secretary of housing and urban development; assistant secretary for fair housing and equal opportunity, Department of Housing and Urban Development*

As assistant secretary for fair housing and equal opportunity in the Department of Housing and Urban Development (HUD) from 1993 to 1995, Roberta Achtenberg sought to ensure that fair housing protections were integral to the policies developed in HUD.

For the next two years, 1996–97, Achtenberg was the senior adviser to HENRY G. CISNEROS, secretary of the Department of Housing and Urban Development. Among the fair housing issues that Achtenberg focused on were broadening low-income loans in inner cities and monitoring redlining by commercial banks. She saw fair housing as a civil rights issue in which certain segments of the population were routinely discriminated against by the lending industry.

In her role as assistant secretary for fair housing and equal opportunity, Achtenberg worked with both public and private housing lenders, builders, and rental groups to create equal opportunities in housing. In 1997, Achtenberg left the administration to return to San Francisco as the senior vice president for public policy for the San Francisco Chamber of Commerce. Later, she was appointed to the board of directors of the Federal Home Loan Bank of San Francisco.

The first openly gay member of President Clinton's administration, Achtenberg entered the federal government after having served on the San Francisco Board of Supervisors (city council). While on the board, she had been an advocate for fair housing for gays and lesbians and had served as the executive director of the National Center for Lesbian Rights. Achtenberg became the first openly gay person nominated by the president and confirmed by the U.S. Senate to a cabinet-level or subcabinet-level position.

Her work in the Department of Housing and Urban Development elevated the problems in fair housing of gays and lesbians but did not do so to the exclusion of other segments of the population. She became a tireless advocate of fair housing for the poor, seeking ways to desegregate public housing and to tear down deteriorating public housing projects.

Achtenberg's expertise in public housing stemmed from her work on the San Francisco Board of Supervisors, where she served as chair of the City Services Committee for Housing and Land. Prior to her elected position on the Board of Supervisors, Achtenberg had served as executive director of the National Center for Lesbian Rights (1989–90) and as a staff attorney for Equal Rights Advocates (1982–88). In 1985 she published a book entitled *Sexual Orientation and the Law*. Among the issues she addressed in the book were discrimination against same-sex marriages and discrimination against children in same-sex homes.

Achtenberg had been active in the Clinton-Gore campaign during the 1992 presidential election. In 1992 she was a speaker at the Democratic National Convention. In both 1992 and 1996, she was a representative from the Clinton campaign to the Democratic Party platform committee. In both 1992 and 1996, Achtenberg was deeply involved in the Clinton-Gore campaign, holding several national positions during the campaign. In addition to her roles in both city government and the Department of Housing and Urban Development, Achtenberg had a career in higher education. After graduating from the University of Utah law school in 1975, she served as a teaching fellow at the Stanford Law School (1975–76). The following year, she was asked to serve as dean and professor of law at the New College of California School of Law (1976–81). She then served six years as a staff attorney for Equal Rights Advocates (1982–88) and as executive director for the National Center for Lesbian Rights (1989–90).

Achtenberg was born on July 20, 1950, in Los Angeles, California. She received her B.A. from the University of California at Berkeley (1972) and her J.D. at the University of Utah law school (1975).

Akihito, emperor of Japan
(1933–   ) *statesman*

Akihito became the 125th emperor of Japan on January 7, 1989, after the death of his father, Emperor Hirohito (posthumously named Emperor Showa). After an official period of mourning for Emperor Hirohito, Akihito ascended the Chrysanthemum throne in an elaborate ceremony attended by representatives from 158 nations.

The first official visit of Emperor Akihito came in 1994, when the royal couple toured the United States for 16 days. President and Mrs. Clinton held a white-tie dinner at the White House. Emperor Akihito stated at their meeting, "It is my earnest hope that peaceful interchange will continue to flourish for many more years to come and that the Pacific will become a true ocean of peace."

In 1996, President and Mrs. Clinton traveled to Tokyo for meetings with Prime Minister HASHIMOTO RYUTARO. Emperor Akihito and his wife hosted a state dinner at the Imperial Palace in Tokyo for the Clintons. In a toast to Emperor Akihito and Empress Nagako, President Clinton said, "History offers very few examples of two peoples who have forged such a powerful relationship in the short period of half a century; we have traveled far together. We have created in modern times a great democratic tradition." President Clinton also spoke before the Japanese parliament, focusing on the strong trade relationship that the United States and Japan had.

Akihito was born on December 23, 1933, in Tokyo, Japan, the first son of Emperor Hirohito and Empress Nagako (the former Michiko Shoda). He was one of seven children born to the emperor, with four elder sisters, one younger brother, and one younger sister. As the eldest son, Akihito was first in line for the throne.

He graduated from Gakushuin University's Faculty of Political Science and Economics in

1956. He was married to Empress Michiko and had three children, Crown Prince Naruhito, Prince Fumihito, and Princess Sayako.

Though the emperor has no governmental power in modern-day Japan and is no longer regarded as divine, he and the imperial family play a ceremonial role in the government by hosting state functions and making goodwill trips abroad. The emperor also performs traditional rituals that are closely connected to the Shinto religion, such as taking part in the annual ceremony at the time of the rice harvest.

Albright, Madeleine Korbel
(1937–   ) *secretary of state, United Nations ambassador*

Madeleine Albright was named secretary of state by President Clinton at the beginning of his second term in January 1997. She succeeded WARREN MINOR CHRISTOPHER, who resigned to return to his law practice in Los Angeles.

Albright was first appointed to the administration as the U.S. representative to the United Nations in January 1993. She presented her credentials at the United Nations on February 6, 1993, becoming the only woman on the 15-member Security Council. In an interview with the *Los Angeles Times*, Albright said about being the only woman at the time, "It's a great thrill to represent the United States and I'm sure that whether you're male or female, you have the same feeling when you are representing the most powerful country in the world."

After serving for four years as the ambassador to the United Nations, Albright was nominated by President Clinton on December 5, 1996, as the secretary of state. She was unanimously confirmed by the Senate on January 23, 1997, and was sworn into office on the same day.

During her tenure in the State Department, Albright endeavored to build a strong working relationship with Senator JESSE HELMS (R-N.C.), chair of the Senate Foreign Relations Committee. She successfully moved through Helms's committee 19 foreign policy nominations, including new ambassadors for Russia, Germany, France, and Britain in Clinton's second term. She failed to secure the nomination of Massachusetts governor WILLIAM WELD for the ambassadorship to Mexico. Weld had openly criticized Helms, and Albright refused to work strongly on Weld's behalf after the Helms criticisms.

Her relations with her own department were sometimes strained, particularly with regard to control she insisted on with the media. She required all media interviews by State Department staff to be cleared by her, which included the ambassador to the United Nations, WILLIAM (BILL) BLAINE RICHARDSON.

Soon after taking office, Albright began dealing with the expansion of the North Atlantic Treaty Organization (NATO) alliance. In a meeting with Russian president BORIS YELTSIN in Moscow in February 1997, she tried to allay Yeltsin's fears about new countries joining the NATO alliance. She said to Yeltsin that NATO is "no longer a situation of you versus us."

Some of the most difficult issues that arose during her tenure as secretary of state were the crisis in Yugoslavia and the Balkans, and the decision to bomb in Kosovo. She became an outspoken advocate for U.S. intervention in Kosovo, arguing that the Muslim population was being slaughtered in Kosovo. She equated the slaughter to the situation in Germany when the Nazis in World War II sent Jews to concentration camps. After taking the reins of the State Department in 1997, Albright learned for the first time that she was ethnically Jewish, and that her grandparents died in the Nazi concentration camp at Auschwitz.

Secretary of State Madeleine Albright addresses UN delegates, 2000. *(UN/DPI Photo by Eskinder Debebe)*

In September 1997, Albright made her first official trip to the Middle East, where she stayed for three days. She believed that neither the Israelis nor the Palestinians were willing to move toward a peace arrangement. Declaring that "I will not come back to tread water," she vowed to stay away until Israeli prime minister BENJAMIN NETANYAHU and Palestine Liberation Organization (PLO) chairman YASSER ARAFAT could make "hard decisions."

Albright was born on May 15, 1937, as Maria Jana Korbel in Prague, Czechoslovakia. Her father was in the Czech diplomatic corps and fled in 1938 to England when the Nazis invaded Czechoslovakia. The family eventually left England and returned to Prague after World War II but fled again when the Communists took over. They were granted political asylum in the United States in 1948. Albright's father, Josef Korbel, moved to Colorado with his family and joined the faculty of the University of Denver. He became the founding dean of its graduate school of international studies.

Albright graduated with honors from Wellesley College (1959). She married Joseph Medill Patterson Albright, heir to a newspaper fortune, whom she had met while working as a summer intern at the *Denver Post*. She continued in journalism, working for a number of newspapers that her husband owned. During the 1960s Albright left journalism to raise three children at home.

In 1968 the Albrights moved to Washington, D.C., and soon after, she began commuting to New York City to work on her doctorate in international affairs at Columbia University, receiving her M.A. and Ph.D. from the Department of Public Law and Government at Columbia University. In 1976 she returned to work as the chief legislative assistant to Senator Edmund Muskie (D-Me.), where she worked for two years. In 1978 Albright was named to the national security council staff of President Jimmy Carter, working as the congressional liaison for the national security council. Zbigniew Brzezinski, her thesis adviser at Columbia University, who was the national security adviser for President Carter, brought her into the Carter White House.

After leaving the Carter administration in 1981, she was named a research professor in International Relations and director of the Women in Foreign Service Program at Georgetown University's School of Foreign Service, where she taught undergraduate and graduate courses in international affairs, U.S. foreign policy, Russian foreign policy, and Central and Eastern European politics. From 1981 to 1982, Albright was awarded a fellowship at the Woodrow Wilson Program at Georgetown University's School of Foreign Service, where she wrote about the role of the press in political changes in Poland during the early 1980s.

In 1982, Albright and her husband divorced, and she joined the faculty of Georgetown University, where she taught international relations. She began to be involved in Democratic Party politics, serving as an adviser in 1984 to the presidential campaign for Walter Mondale and as an adviser in 1988 to Michael Dukakis. After Dukakis's defeat, she became president of the Center for National Policy, a nonprofit research organization formed in 1981 by representatives from government, industry, labor, and education. Its mandate was to promote the study and discussion of domestic and international issues.

Albright was fluent in French and Czech and could read Russian and Polish. After leaving the Clinton administration in 2001, she formed her own company, the Albright Group, which advised multinational companies and nongovernmental organizations on global policy issues. She also chaired the board of the National Democratic Institute for International Affairs, which promoted the process of democratization around the world.

Alexander, Jane Quigley
(1939–   ) *chair, National Endowment for the Arts*

Nominated by President Clinton in July 1993 as chair of the National Endowment for the Arts (NEA), which provides federal funding to the arts, Jane Alexander was sworn into office in September 1993.

After unanimous confirmation in the Senate, she was sworn into office by Supreme Court Justice Sandra Day O'Connor on October 8, 1993. She became the first artist and the sixth chairperson of the commission, which was created in 1965 during the Johnson administration. She left the commission in October 1997 after continuous battles with Congress over funding, which had been severely cut while she was in office. She returned to her career as an actress after leaving the National Endowment. In 1998 she returned to Broadway in the play *Honour* and in 1999 resumed her film career in *The Cider House Rules.*

Alexander was an award-winning actress before her tenure as chair of the National Endowment for the Arts. She left her role in *The Sisters Rosenzweig* to join the Clinton administration. In addition to more than 40 films and television programs, she performed in more than 100 plays across the country. Her awards included a Tony for *The Great White Hope* and an Emmy for *Playing for Time.* She received six Tony nominations, four Academy Award nominations, and five Emmy nominations. For her portrayal of Eleanor Roosevelt in *Eleanor and Franklin: The White House Years,* Alexander received the Television Critics Circle Award. Alexander had never been involved in politics, focusing her attention on her acting career.

When Alexander took over as chair of the National Endowment for the Arts in 1993, the agency had been through considerable strife. Under the leadership of Lynn Cheney, the agency had begun to censor certain arts awards. Cheney had received substantial support for her decisions among Republicans in both the House and Senate, who began to question whether the federal government should be funding arts programs at all. When Alexander took over the reins of the National Endowment in 1993, the debate on what was appropriate for a federal agency to fund remained at the forefront of congressional concern. As a result, Alexander's four years as chair of the National Endowment included numerous battles with the Republican leadership of Congress, who began motions to close down the agency. Newt Gingrich, the Republican conservative who served as Speaker of the House, often clashed with Alexander. The funding for the agency was regularly cut by Congress during the Clinton administration,

from its 1993 authorization of $174 million to its 1998 authorization of $98 million. Although the agency was not closed, it was severely handicapped in the funding it could provide to arts organizations.

In spite of Alexander's battles with Congress over the appropriateness of funding certain arts exhibits, she took steps to use the agency as a vehicle to support the arts in society. One of the key programs during her tenure as chair was support for arts education. She organized "Art 21: Art Reaches into the 21st Century" in Chicago, which was a national conference in April 1997 on the arts and the role of artists in society. She visited more than 130 communities in all 50 states and made more than 150 public speeches on the importance of arts in the community. Alexander created partnerships with various federal agencies to encourage the arts. Among the partners were the U.S. Department of Education, for arts-education research and development, and the Corporation for National Service to create the Writers Corps.

If her emphasis on arts education rather than specific arts projects was designed to change the debate on the National Endowment for the Arts, Alexander was successful. Although the agency lost funding during her tenure, it was not dismantled by Congress as many Republicans had sought.

Alexander was active in a number of nonprofit organizations prior to joining the Clinton administration, including the National Stroke Association and the Wildlife Conservation Society.

Born October 28, 1939, in Boston, Massachusetts, her education included two years (1957–59) at Sarah Lawrence College, after which she transferred to the University of Edinburgh, Scotland. She never completed her degree. By 1961 she was acting professionally in New York City. From 1962–69 she was married to Robert Alexander and in 1975 married

Edward Sherin, producer of the television series *Law and Order*.

Altman, Roger

(1946–   ) *deputy secretary, Department of the Treasury*

Roger Altman, a former partner in the New York City banking firm of Lehman Brothers, was appointed by President Clinton as deputy secretary of the Treasury and confirmed by the Senate on August 6, 1993. He became the most senior member of the department under Treasury Secretary LLOYD MILLARD BENTSEN, JR.

Altman returned to the private sector in 1995 and formed Evercore Partners, an investment and merchant banking firm. The firm handled leveraged acquisitions and mergers, including the 1999 $37.3 billion merger of CBS Corporation with Viacom. Evercore Partners earned $10 million from its role as an adviser to CBS during the 1999 acquisition.

Altman joined the Clinton administration after successful careers in both the private and the public sector. He began his career at Lehman Brothers in 1969 after completing the University of Chicago Graduate School of Business. His interest in politics solidified after he worked for a short time on the presidential campaign of Bobby Kennedy in 1968. When Jimmy Carter was elected president in 1977, Altman left Lehman Brothers at the age of 30 to join the Treasury Department as deputy assistant secretary for domestic finance under Treasury Secretary Michael Blumenthal. During his four years in the Treasury Department during the Carter administration, Altman worked on two major issues: the government bailout of Chrysler Corporation and the continuing problems of the New York City fiscal crisis.

Altman returned to the private sector in 1981, when Ronald Reagan defeated Jimmy Carter for the presidency. Not surprisingly, Altman was welcomed back to his Lehman Brothers job by its chairman, Pete Peterson, who had been the Nixon administration secretary of commerce. Peterson, a mentor for Altman, had been instrumental in urging him in 1976 to become involved in the Carter presidential campaign. Both Altman and Peterson were interested in politics and shared a common passion for using their skills in government.

Altman's tenure in government had proved to be valuable for building both professional skills and new business relationships. Among the clients that Altman soon brought into Lehman Brothers was Chrysler Corporation. When Peterson left Lehman Brothers to form the Blackstone Group, Altman soon followed. In 1987, he was named vice chairman of the Blackstone Group and head of the firm's merger and acquisition division.

In 1993 Altman again left the private sector to join the ranks of government in his new role as deputy secretary of the Treasury. As President Clinton's point person on the tax bill in 1993, Altman successfully moved the bill through Congress and became a key adviser to the president on economic issues. However, as the Whitewater investigation began on President and Mrs. Clinton's land holdings in Arkansas, questions arose as to whether Altman had talked improperly to anyone in the White House about the investigation. He was criticized by members of the Senate Banking Committee for giving what they believed was false testimony about communications between the White House and the Treasury over the Whitewater investigation. He denied such conversations but was forced out of the department and resigned on August 10, 1995.

Two years after joining the Treasury Department, Altman reentered the private sector, and a year later formed Evercore Partners with two associates. Among the acquisitions of

Evercore Partners in recent years was American Media, which owned the tabloid newspaper, *The Enquirer*.

Born on April 2, 1946, Altman graduated with a B.A. from Georgetown University (1967) and an M.B.A. from the University of Chicago Graduate School of Business Administration (1969). He was on the board of trustees of the National Park Foundation and on the board of trustees of New Visions for Public Schools.

Ames, Aldrich Hazen
(1941–   ) *spy*

Aldrich Ames, a counterintelligence officer with the Central Intelligence Agency (CIA), was arrested in 1994 and charged with spying for the Soviet Union. Ames, a 31-year CIA officer, pleaded guilty to charges of conspiracy to commit espionage and was sentenced to life in prison without parole. He was charged with selling CIA information to the KGB, for which he was paid nearly $3 million. His wife, Maria, was also charged with espionage and received 63 months in prison. She has served her sentence and since been released.

Ames was arrested on February 21, 1994, by the Federal Bureau of Investigation (FBI) outside his home in Arlington, Virginia. His wife, Maria del Rosario Casas Ames, was arrested at their home soon after her husband. Ames had been a career employee of the CIA, spending most his career in the Directorate of Operations, the unit responsible for clandestine operations of the CIA. He spoke Russian fluently and specialized in the Russian intelligence services, particularly the KGB. Surprisingly, the fact that Ames made less than $70,000 per year but lived in a $540,000 home and drove a new Jaguar had not attracted the attention of the CIA over the years.

Ames was promoted within the CIA to counterintelligence branch chief for Soviet operations in 1983. In 1984, he was given responsibility for developing Soviet contacts in the Washington, D.C., area who would be helpful to the CIA. He began talking regularly to several sources within the Soviet embassy, including Sergey Dmitriyevich Chuvakhin. All of Ames's meetings with Soviet contacts were supposed to be reported to the CIA local field office and to the FBI.

At the same time in 1984 that Ames was developing new contacts with Soviet officials, he began a romance with Maria del Rosario Casas, who was a foreign national from Colombia. Ames was married but separated at the time, but chose to continue the romance with del Rosario. Ames had separated from his wife in 1983 but not divorced. The relationship with del Rosario led Ames's wife to file for divorce on grounds of mental cruelty. The divorce proceedings lasted for a year, then the property settlement during the divorce put Ames in debt. Ames told the Senate hearings investigating the espionage that the financial pressure from his divorce settlement led him to find outside sources of income: the KGB.

Using his relationship with Chuvakhin, Ames began to sell intelligence to the Soviet embassy in Washington, D.C. Beginning in April 1985, Ames provided certain pieces of information to the Soviets for which he demanded $50,000. On April 17, 1985, Ames received his first payment of $50,000 from Chuvakhin. By 1992, Ames had received hundreds of thousands of dollars from the Soviets, all deposited into legitimate bank accounts in his name.

Ames's role as a spy was uncovered as the CIA and FBI began to hunt for a mole within the CIA in 1991. By 1993, they had narrowed their investigation to Ames. On November 1, 1993, the FBI followed Ames and his Russian handler in Bogotá, Colombia. When Ames prepared for an official trip to Moscow in 1994, the FBI arrested him. He did not deny being a spy for the Soviet Union; rather, he acknowledged his espionage activities and provided information on those activities to the FBI and the CIA in their investigation. Instead of receiving the death penalty, as Julius and Ethel Rosenberg had for their espionage conviction in 1951, Ames received life in prison without parole. Among the revelations that were made public was that he had been paid more than $1.8 million by the KGB and that $900,000 more had been set aside for him. All proceeds from the Ameses' espionage were signed over to the U.S. government as part of their plea agreements.

Annan, Kofi

(1938–   ) winner of 2001 Nobel Peace Prize, secretary-general of the United Nations

Kofi Annan, the winner of the Nobel Peace Prize in 2001, became the seventh secretary-general of the United Nations in 1997. Annan, who held a variety of positions within the United Nations prior to his election as the secretary-general, was born in Ghana. His first five-year term began on January 1, 1997, and lasted until December 31, 2001. He was reelected by acclamation to a second four-year term, which began on January 1, 2002, and ends on December 31, 2006. He was the second secretary-general of the United Nations elected from Africa, following Boutros Boutros-Ghali of Egypt, and is fluent in English, French, and several African languages.

Although he began his undergraduate work at the University of Science and Technology in his native city of Kumasi, Ghana, Annan completed his undergraduate work at Macalester College, in St. Paul, Minnesota, in 1961. From 1971–72, he completed his graduate work as a Sloan Fellow at the Massachusetts Institute of Technology, receiving a Master of Science degree in management.

Most of Annan's professional career was spent at the United Nations and in the United Nations system. He began his career in 1962 with the World Health Organization in Geneva as a budget officer. He moved throughout a number of United Nations organizations, including the UN Economic Commission for Africa, the United Nations Emergency Force in Ismailia, Egypt, and the Office of the United Nations High Commissioner for Refugees in Geneva. In 1987 he began his role in the United Nations in New York, first as the assistant secretary-general for human resources management and security coordinator for the UN system, where he

Secretary-General Kofi Annan *(UN/DPI by Milton Grant)*

served for three years. In 1990, he was promoted again to assistant secretary-general for
programme planning, budget and finance, and
controller. While in this role, Annan took on
an additional assignment following the invasion of Kuwait by Iraq in 1990. He oversaw
the repatriation of more than 900 staff from
western countries who left Iraq. In addition,
he worked to secure the release of western
hostages in Iraq during the war. Following the
Persian Gulf War in 1991, he represented the
United Nations in negotiating with Iraq on the
details of the humanitarian aid program and
the "oil for food" program. Following the Dayton Peace Agreement, led by the Clinton
administration, which brokered a peace among
the warring factions of Yugoslavia, Annan oversaw the transition from the United Nations
Protections Force to the multinational Implementation Force (IFOR), which was led by the
North Atlantic Treaty Organization (NATO).
As the first secretary-general who was a career
staff member from the United Nations, Annan
moved the organization into the center of
international peacekeeping. His background in
peacekeeping throughout the early and mid-
1990s positioned him to understand the role
that the United Nations could play in managing conflict negotiation. From 1993 until
1997 (except for six months in 1995–96
when he served as special representative of the
secretary-general to the former Yugoslavia),
Annan served as undersecretary-general for
peacekeeping operations. As secretary-general,
Annan emphasized his commitment to using
the United Nations as a tool for preventive
diplomacy and peacekeeping.

His focus on diplomatic solutions to issues
and on peacekeeping often concerned political
leaders in the United States. During the Clinton administration, Senate Majority Leader
Robert Dole and other Republicans urged
President Clinton to insist that U.S. troops not
be placed under foreign commanders in peace-

keeping operations. During the George W.
Bush administration, the president frequently
cited the United Nations as nearly irrelevant
for its failure to support United States actions
against Iraq.

Arafat, Yasser
(Yassir Arafat)
(1929–   ) *winner of 1994 Nobel Peace Prize,*
chairman of the Palestine Liberation Organization

Yasser Arafat was named chairman of the newly
created Palestine Liberation Organization
(PLO) in 1969. Arafat, the leader of the Fatah
organization, signed an agreement brokered by
Egypt that created the PLO from a number of
factions, including Fatah. As a result of the
agreement that created the unified PLO, Arafat
became the organization's leader, referred to as
the chairman.

During his tenure as chairman of the PLO,
Arafat made repeated calls for an independent
Palestinian state. During the 1990s he was frequently accused by the United States of supporting terrorist activities, including suicide
bombings, in Israel.

In an effort to bridge the growing divisions
between Israel and the Palestinians, Prime
Minister YITZHAK RABIN and Arafat began a
series of secret peace negotiations in Norway
in January 1993. The talks were kept ultrasecret, with only a few people within each group
familiar with the talks or the material being
discussed. On September 9, 1993, Rabin and
Arafat exchanged letters in which the PLO
recognized Israel's right to exist as a nation. In
turn, Rabin recognized the PLO as the representative of the Palestinian people. On
September 13, 1993, a Declaration of Principles between Israel, signed by Israeli foreign
minister SHIMON PERES, and the PLO, signed
by a member of the organization's Executive
Council, Abou Abbas, was held in a ceremony

hosted by President Clinton in Washington, D.C. President Clinton, Rabin, and Arafat watched as Peres and Abbas signed the Declaration of Principles, which became known as the Oslo Accords.

In 2000, President Clinton called Arafat and asked him "to take immediate steps" to end the violence after constant sniper firings on Israelis by Fatah activists. On October 16, 2000, President Clinton met with Arafat and Israeli prime minister EHUD BARAK to broker an agreement to end the almost daily violence between the Palestinians and Israelis. In a statement read by President Clinton, but not signed by either Arafat or Barak, he called for immediate steps to end the violence, the reopening of the Palestinian territories and the Gaza airport, for redeployment of Israeli troops from the edges of Palestinian territories, and a commission of inquiry into the weeks of violence.

Arafat's role as chairman of the PLO stemmed from his leadership in the guerrilla group Fatah, which opposed Israel and Israeli occupation of land won in the 1967 war. In the June 1967 Arab-Israeli war, in which Israel captured the West Bank from Jordan and the Gaza Strip from Egypt, Palestinian nationalism had grown and led to increased opposition to Israel. After the cease-fire in the war, Fatah leaders worked to create a popular revolt against Israeli occupation. But the Israeli Defense Forces killed 200 suspected members of the Fatah movement and deported or imprisoned others. Arafat, who was a member of Fatah, fled to Jordan.

Under an agreement negotiated in 1969, brokered by Egyptian president Gamal Abdel Nasser, Fatah took over the fledgling PLO and other guerrilla groups fighting Israeli occupation of the West Bank and Gaza Strip. In 1974 at the Arab League meeting, the PLO was formally recognized as "the sole legitimate representative of the Palestinian people."

Although the PLO had become a designated representative, it remained an umbrella organization that continued to have myriad factions included. When President Carter took office in 1977, Arafat sought to become a voice in any peace discussions regarding the Middle East. However, Egyptian president Anwar Sadat refused to include Arafat and pushed for direct discussions with Israel. The Camp David Accords emerged from the Egyptian-Israeli peace agreement.

Throughout the 1980s Arafat remained a spokesman for a separate Palestinian state. When the George H. W. Bush administration came to the aid of Kuwait in 1990 and 1991 after Iraq's invasion, Arafat stood firmly behind SADDAM HUSSEIN and Iraq.

Yasser Arafat was born on August 24, 1929, in Cairo, Egypt. He considers his nationality Palestinian. He shared the 1994 Nobel Peace Prize with Shimon Peres and with Yitzhak Rabin.

Aristide, Jean-Bertrand
(1953–) *president of Haiti*

Jean-Bertrand Aristide was president of Haiti on September 30, 1991, when the Haitian military overthrew the government. Lieutenant General Raoul Cedras led a military coup to remove Aristide from office. Aristide fled first to Venezuela, then to Washington, D.C., where he spent two and half years in exile. During his exile, President Clinton and heads of other countries continued to recognize Aristide as the democratically elected leader of Haiti.

Following Aristide's ouster by the military junta, a wave of violence overtook Haiti. Two of Aristide's top supporters, Justice Minister Guy Malary and Father Jean-Marie Vincent, were assassinated. By 1994, Haiti was growing increasingly unstable, and the United States became actively involved in restoring Aristide to power. Using diplomacy as the means of choice in dealing with Haiti's junta, President Clinton sent a variety of experienced diplomats, including former president Jimmy Carter, General COLIN L. POWELL, and Senator Sam Nunn (D.-Ga.), into the country. The junta agreed to step down, but chaos took over the country as soon as the government was disbanded. A reign of terror began, with 5,000 Haitians losing their lives over the next three years and hundreds of thousands forced into hiding.

President Clinton subsequently sent U.S. troops into Haiti in 1994 to reestablish order and then to reinstate Aristide in office. On September 19, 1994, Clinton ordered several thousand U.S. troops into Haiti to retake the nation from the military junta. Within a short time, the number of U.S. troops had risen to 20,000.

For nearly a month, Haiti was a nation under military siege by military forces, largely U.S. forces. Although the junta had given up power, many of its supporters continued to fight against Aristide. After numerous firefights with opposition supporters, U.S. troops regained control of Haiti. On October 15, 1994, Jean-Bertrand Aristide returned to Haiti accompanied by U.S. secretary of state WARREN MINOR CHRISTOPHER, political activist JESSE JACKSON, and members of the Congressional Black Caucus.

Born on April 15, 1953, Aristide attended elementary and high school at Catholic institutions run by the Salesian Fathers of Haiti. In 1974, he graduated from the College Notre Dame in the town of Cap Haitien and then entered the Salesian seminary in La Vega in the Dominican Republic. On July 3, 1983, Aristide was ordained in Haiti as a Roman Catholic priest and began serving as a parish priest in Port-au-Prince. He quickly became an outspoken critic of President Jean-Claude Duvalier in Haiti and a leader in the prodemocracy movement. Duvalier, known for his brutal tactics against political opposition, lost power in 1986 as the movement for democratic elections was building.

Aristide became widely known during this period for his impassioned sermons on Radio Soleil, the Catholic Church radio station, on behalf of the poor and underprivileged. These broadcasts became a galvanizing point for the prodemocracy movement. Following the fall of Duvalier, a military junta governed, promising democratic elections. For the next three years, the nation tried to hold elections which only ended in violence. In 1987, supporters of Duvalier massacred voters at one location. In 1990, elections were again called, with Aristide announcing his candidacy on the last day of registration for candidates. In a field of 13 candidates, Aristide won with 67 percent of the vote. In 1994 Aristide resigned from the priesthood and, in 1996, married. In 1995, Aristide was replaced as president in national elections by René Préval. Aristide was barred by law from serving another term. But he was again elected president in 2000.

Armey, Richard Keith
(1940–   ) *member of the House of Representatives*

Richard Armey, the powerful Republican majority leader from Texas, retired from the House of Representatives in 2003 after serving 18 years representing the 26th congressional district. One of the few academics in the House, Armey held a Ph.D. in economics from the University of Oklahoma and had taught economics at the University of North Texas from 1972 until he ran for Congress in 1984.

Armey, who had never served in public office before his election to Congress, moved quickly up the Republican leadership ladder. In 1990, after only three terms in the House,

Armey opposed President GEORGE HERBERT WALKER BUSH for breaking his "no new taxes" pledge, made during the 1988 presidential election. Armey introduced a resolution into the Republican Conference of the House, which passed overwhelmingly, that congressional Republicans would oppose any increase in federal taxes or tax rates. As a reward for his tax position, the Republican leadership in the House named him the ranking Republican on the Joint Economic Committee. This gave Armey his first national exposure, allowing him to attack any proposals for tax increases made by the Democrats or by other Republicans.

In June 1992 Armey announced his candidacy for the Republican Conference chairmanship as a way to focus Republicans in the House around his positions on taxes and other economic issues. On December 8, Armey won by a fragile margin of 88 to 84 within the caucus. Throughout his tenure in the House, Armey had been part of the minority party. With Democrats controlling the House, Armey's victory made him conference chair of the minority party.

When President Clinton entered office in 1993, Armey led the Republicans in the House to oppose the tax increase and the health care proposals offered by the administration. However, Armey broke ranks with his fellow Republicans in 1994 when President Clinton sought approval for the North American Free Trade Agreement (NAFTA). Armey heavily lobbied Republicans to support NAFTA. In 1996, he became a key supporter of the Freedom to Farm Act, in spite of opposition from many Republicans. The bill was strongly supported in his home state of Texas.

The 1994 election dramatically changed Armey's fortunes. The Republicans gained control of the House of Representatives. NEWTON (NEWT) LEROY GINGRICH and Dick Armey had led a movement of conservative Republicans to regain party control of the House, using a document which the two authored called "Contract with America." The contract was a collection of 10 bills that the Republicans would move through the House within the first 100 days of the new Congress.

Once the Republicans took control of the House in January 1995, they elected Newt Gingrich as Speaker and Dick Armey as majority leader. Armey sought a major overhaul of the tax code, including a 17 percent flat tax, during his tenure as majority leader, but the legislation never saw fruition.

During his last year in office, Armey became a vocal critic of how the United States was dealing with the Israeli-Palestinian issue. Although no stranger to opposing President Clinton on issues, Armey rarely publicly opposed President George W. Bush on issues. However, in May 2002 as the suicide bombings in Israel escalated, Armey called for Palestinians to be moved from the West Bank and Gaza and generally expelled from Israel. A longtime supporter of Israel, Armey urged the administration to take a stronger stand against Palestinians and YASSER ARAFAT. In general, the Bush administration remained silent to Armey's proposals and maintained support for a separate Palestinian state in the future.

Born on July 7, 1940, in Cando, North Dakota, Armey received a B.A. from Jamestown College in Jamestown, North Dakota (1963), an M.A. from the University of North Dakota (1964), and a Ph.D. from the University of Oklahoma (1969). He served in the House of Representatives from January 3, 1985, to January 3, 2003, serving as majority leader for three terms.

Aspin, Leslie (Les), Jr.
(1938–1995) *secretary of defense, member of the House of Representatives*

Leslie (Les) Aspin, nominated by President Clinton as secretary of defense, was confirmed

Les Aspin, secretary of defense, shaking hands with General Colin Powell, chairman of the Joint Chiefs of Staff *(NATO Library)*

by the Senate on January 21, 1993. After a series of decisions that often conflicted with the opinions of career staff within his own department, Aspin announced his resignation on December 15, 1993, effective on February 3, 1994. Although he never acknowledged that the White House had urged his resignation, it appeared clear that he resigned under pressure from the president. Aspin, who had represented Wisconsin in the House of Representatives from 1971 to 1993, was the only member of President Clinton's original cabinet to have served in Congress. Aspin was replaced by WILLIAM J. PERRY.

During his tenure in the House of Representatives, Aspin had often opposed actions within the Department of Defense. During the

war in Vietnam, he had been one of the most outspoken critics of the administration's actions and opposed U.S. continued involvement in the war. He was elected chairman of the House Committee on Armed Services in 1985 and was widely praised as an expert on defense matters.

During the Reagan administration, Aspin voted to support the MX missile and aid to the Nicaraguan contras, in spite of opposition by his Democratic colleagues. He remained opposed, however, as did most Democrats in the House, to the Strategic Defense Initiative. His efforts to support key Reagan policies, however, led to his temporary removal from committee duties in 1987 by the Democratically controlled committee. He was soon returned to his role as chair but continued to support Republican policies at times. In January 1991 he again supported a Republican, President GEORGE HERBERT WALKER BUSH, and supported military force to remove Iraqi forces from Kuwait. He accurately predicted that the U.S. military could easily defeat Iraqi forces and could win with minimal casualties. His prediction of a U.S. victory led to support from both Republicans and Democrats as Aspin became the leading military authority within the House of Representatives.

Although Aspin had publicly opposed the Vietnam War in the early 1970s, he had not been actively involved in presidential campaigns until 1992. When Bill Clinton asked him to serve as an adviser to his campaign in 1992, Aspin accepted. Aspin had long-standing views of the military which he brought to the campaign, including a proposal to reduce U.S. forces in Europe, create a smaller navy, and continue reductions in military personnel strength. These views caused significant concern among the career staff in the Department of Defense, who saw Aspin as advocating reductions in the military budget. For Aspin, the end of the cold war and the declining military budget of the former Soviet Union allowed the United States to refocus its defense expenditures. Aspin sought to reposition the military within a smaller, more modern department in a changing world.

In addition to his positions on the military budget and the strength of military forces, Aspin favored new regulations on homosexual conduct in the armed forces. Such new regulations were largely the product of others in the Clinton campaign, who saw the armed forces leadership as creating significant obstacles for gays and lesbians in the military. Aspin proposed that homosexual orientation not be considered for new applicants and that current military personnel would be judged on suitability for service, not sexual orientation. The regulations never were formally put into oper-

ation due to strong opposition within the military. Rather, a "don't ask, don't tell" policy went into effect through informal channels.

Another policy area in which Aspin quickly clashed with the career staff in the Department of Defense was the issue of women in combat. In April 1993 Aspin ordered all military services to allow women to compete for assignments in combat aircraft. The navy was ordered to allow women on combat ships and the army and marine corps were ordered to broaden opportunities for women in artillery and air defense. In line with Aspin's commitment to broadening opportunities for women in the military, he supported President Clinton's nomination of Sheila E. Widnall as the first female secretary of the air force and the first female service secretary.

Yet another policy area in which Aspin faced major opposition within the career ranks of the department was the issue of base closures. Base closures were a critical part of Aspin's plan to balance the department's budget in line with the president's call for reductions in military spending. In March 1993, Aspin issued a plan to close 31 large military installations and to reduce the size of 134 additional sites. The projected savings to the military budget was more than $3 billion per year.

Aspin's brief tenure in office was also marked by two major military crises: Haiti and Somalia. In Haiti, the elected president, JEAN-BERTRAND ARISTIDE, had been overthrown by a military junta in September 1991. The military junta, under pressure from the United States, agreed to reinstate Aristide by October 30, 1993. When the date arrived, the junta refused to step down. Under orders from President Clinton to use military force to reinstate Aristide, Aspin ordered the USS *Harlan County* with 200 troops to Port-au-Prince, Haiti's capital. The ship was met by hostile mobs and left without entering the city. The president later ordered nearly 20,000 troops into Haiti to remove the junta and restore Aristide, which was accomplished in September 1994. Aspin lost support within the White House for not developing adequate plans for conducting the necessary military operations in Haiti.

Civil war in Somalia and the decisions he made regarding military action proved to be Aspin's downfall. In August 1992 during the Bush administration, the United States began to provide food through military airlifts to the people of Somalia. Six months later, in December 1992, President Bush committed 26,000 troops to Somalia to provide security as well as food. The U.S. troops joined 13,000 troops sent from more than 20 nations to restore order.

In May 1993 Aspin reduced the number of troops in Somalia to 4,000 to prevent the United States from becoming actively involved in Somalian politics. Troops would be focused in Mogadishu, Somalia's capital, until order was restored. In September 1993 General COLIN L. POWELL, chairman of the Joint Chiefs of Staff, sought Aspin's approval for a request from the commander of U.S. forces in Somalia for tanks and armored vehicles to protect his troops. Aspin refused the request, and soon after, Somalian forces overtook U.S. troops and killed 18 U.S. soldiers. Aspin quickly admitted he had made a mistake, but argued that he believed the armored vehicles were only to be used to transport humanitarian aid and not to protect U.S. troops.

His failure to support General Powell's request and the subsequent massacre of U.S. troops in Somalia soon led to an outcry in Congress for Aspin's removal. Aspin tendered his resignation on December 15, 1993, citing personal reasons. Although Aspin had made a series of miscalculations in his brief tenure as secretary of defense, his resignation was also the result of deteriorating health problems. A heart problem sent him to the hospital for several days in February 1993, and then again a month later, he reentered the hospital for a pacemaker. He continued to serve as secretary of defense following his resignation in December 1993 until February 3, 1994, when William J. Perry was confirmed by the Senate as his successor.

After leaving the administration, Aspin began teaching in the international affairs program of Marquette University's Washington semester program. In May 1994 President Clinton appointed Aspin chair of the President's Foreign Intelligence Advisory Board, a powerful oversight board for a large array of intelligence-gathering operations. Aspin died of a stroke in Washington, D.C., on May 21, 1995. Born on July 21, 1938, in Milwaukee, Wisconsin, Aspin received his B.A. degree from Yale University, summa cum laude and Phi Beta Kappa, (1960), an M.S. from Oxford University in economics, politics, and philosophy, where he was a Rhodes scholar (1962), and a Ph.D. in economics from the Massachusetts Institute of Technology (1965). After graduating from MIT, he became an officer in the army (1966–68) and served as a system analyst in the Pentagon under Secretary of Defense Robert McNamara. He briefly taught economics at Marquette University before winning his election to the House of Representatives from Wisconsin's first congressional district in 1970. He served in the House from 1971 until he was appointed by President Clinton as secretary of defense in 1993.

Babbitt, Bruce Edward
(1938–) *secretary of interior*

Bruce Babbitt was nominated secretary of the interior by President Clinton on December 23, 1992, confirmed by the Senate on January 20, 1993, and sworn into office on January 22, 1993. Babbitt remained in the administration as secretary of the interior for both Clinton terms. At one point soon after the administration took office, Babbitt was under consideration by President Clinton for nomination to the U.S. Supreme Court as a possible replacement for Justice Harry A. Blackmun. Babbitt declined to be considered.

During the transition period, Babbitt had sought the position of United States Trade Representative, a position that eventually went to MICHAEL (MICKEY) KANTOR. As trade representative, Babbitt would have been able to negotiate the North American Free Trade Agreement (NAFTA) to ensure that American companies that transferred plants to Mexico continued to maintain environmental protections.

Babbitt, who had a record from his tenure as governor of Arizona as a strong environmentalist, was encouraged by President Clinton to pursue environmental protections for the nation's public lands. During the Reagan

and Bush administrations, the Department of the Interior had become known for its pro-business management of public lands. The Interior Department had often allowed development on federal land and had given business and development interests access to logging and mining rights on federal lands.

In contrast to its Republican predecessors, the Clinton administration sought to focus the department on protecting the nation's 500 million acres of public land and rebuilding conservation programs. Babbitt went to the Department of the Interior from his job as president of the League of Conservation Voters, where he had been paid a dollar a year to advocate environmental protection programs.

Throughout his tenure as secretary of the interior, Babbitt aggressively moved to focus the department on environmental protections. During his first six months in office, Babbitt successfully worked to protect a threatened bird species in Orange County, California, from developers, protected the habitat of the spotted owl in the Pacific Northwest, and raised grazing fees for sheep and cattle ranchers who leased federal lands for their herds.

In 1994, Babbitt came under fire by the Senate Energy and Natural Resources Committee, which was dominated by senators from the plains and western states, for raising grazing fees and for more stringent land management standards. Babbitt was threatened by the committee with losing funding for his department. He subsequently scaled back on the higher grazing fees but continued to pursue broad land management policies.

During the fall of 1997, the Department of Justice held a 90-day investigation into Babbitt's rejection of three Wisconsin Indian tribes' application to open a new casino. After its investigation, the Department of Justice determined that there was reason to pursue an independent counsel investigation, and on February 11, 1998, Attorney General JANET RENO asked for an independent counsel.

On March 19, 1998, a three-judge panel appointed an independent counsel, CAROL ELDER BRUCE, to investigate Babbitt's handling of an Indian casino license. The Bureau of Indian Affairs (BIA) within the Department of the Interior was responsible for granting the permit for the casinos. Babbitt had rejected the project in July 1995, but after Babbitt's decision the three tribes donated $270,000 to the Democratic Party. The issue became of interest to investigators when Babbitt admitted telling a lawyer for the Indian tribes that Deputy White House Chief of Staff HAROLD ICKES had pressed him to make a decision in the case. The 18-month-long review by the independent counsel found that Babbitt was not guilty of any wrongdoing and had made his decision without consideration of donations to the Democratic Party. The investigation ended on October 14, 1999, when Bruce announced that she would not seek indictments against Babbitt or anyone else.

In 1999, Babbitt was the subject of a class-action suit by the Native American Rights fund that accused the federal government of mismanaging billions of dollars in Indian trust accounts. The trust funds were established in the late 1800s to compensate Indians for the use of their land. The trust funds, which include royalties from petroleum, timber, and other natural resources on the land, pay income back to the Indian tribes totaling $350 million per year. The Indians contended that the accounts were badly managed and record keeping on the amount of revenues was poor. Babbitt agreed and promised new computer systems and other improvements to track the trust accounts.

During the latter part of the administration, Babbitt was instrumental in working with President Clinton to have certain pieces of federal land in the western states designated as "federal monuments," which added more environmental protections than the status "federal lands." The designation of the new federal monuments was widely praised by environmental groups and criticized by Republicans and business groups.

Born on June 27, 1938, in Los Angeles, California, Babbitt grew up in Flagstaff, Arizona. He received his B.S. in geology, magna cum laude, from the University of Notre Dame (1960), his M.S. in geophysics from the University of Newcastle, England, as a Marshall scholar (1963), and his LL.B. from Harvard Law School (1965). He worked briefly in the oil industry for Gulf Oil before attending law school.

While he was in law school, Babbitt was active in the civil rights movement, participating with Martin Luther King, Jr., in his march in Selma, Alabama, in 1964. He also worked for the antipoverty program of the Johnson administration.

In 1974 Babbitt successfully ran for attorney general in Arizona. After just over two years in the job (1975–78), Babbitt became governor in an accident of succession. In 1978, Arizona's governor, Raul H. Castro, was named ambassador to Argentina by President Carter and the secretary of state, Wesley Bolin, became governor. When Bolin died in office five months later, Babbitt, who was next in line as attorney general, became governor. He was then elected to two full terms. After the meltdown of the nuclear power plant at Three Mile Island near Harrisburg, Pennsylvania, in 1979, President Carter appointed Babbitt to head a commission to investigate the accident. Babbitt served as Arizona governor from 1978–87.

Babbitt gained a reputation as a fiscal conservative who was fiercely dedicated to preserving Arizona's natural environment. Both President Clinton and Babbitt had served as governors at the same time and had become friends at Democratic governors' meetings. Both were members of a new wave of the Democratic Party, dedicated to moving the party to more centrist positions. After leaving the governor's office, Babbitt became president of the League of Conservation Voters, which was one of the nation's most active environmental organizations.

In 1988, Babbitt attempted a run for the presidency, but quickly was eclipsed by the other candidates in the race. Michael Dukakis eventually became the Democratic Party standard-bearer in the 1988 general election, which he lost to Vice President GEORGE HERBERT WALKER BUSH.

Baer, Donald A.
(1954–   ) *director of strategic planning and communication; director, Office of Speechwriting*

Donald Baer served as President Clinton's chief speechwriter from 1994–95, writing and editing President Clinton's major speeches. In 1995 Baer was named the director of strategic planning and communications, where he was the chief message strategist for the president, managing all communications functions of the Clinton administration. He left the administration in 1997 to join the media enterprise, DCI which owned the Discovery Channel.

Baer joined the administration after working for seven years at *U.S. New and World Report* from 1987–94. He joined *U.S. News and World Report* in 1987 and was quickly promoted to senior editor in 1988. Four years later, in 1991, he was again promoted to assistant managing editor, where he worked until 1994 when he joined the Clinton White House Staff as director of the Office of Speechwriting.

Baer received his J.D. from the University of Virginia Law School, his Master's degree in international relations from the London School of Economics, and his B.A. Phi Beta Kappa, from the University of North Carolina at Chapel Hill. He worked as a journalist at *The American Lawyer* and wrote a number of articles for publications such as *Rolling Stone* and the *New York Times*. In addition to his career as a journalist, Baer worked from 1981 to 1985 for the New York City law firm of Patterson, Belknap, Webb, and Tyler, specializing in media affairs. While at the law firm, he received the Thurgood Marshall Award from the Association of the Bar of the City of New York for his pro bono work on behalf of a Florida death row inmate who was released.

When he left the administration in 1997, Baer was named executive vice president for strategy and development of Discovery Communications, Inc. (DCI). Among properties that DCI owned were the Discovery Channel, the Learning Channel, the Travel Channel and a host of others. He was a member of the Council on Foreign Relations. After leaving the Clinton White House, he continued to work as the chief writer for the television broadcast of the Kennedy Center Honors program.

Baggett, Joan
(1952–   ) *director and deputy director, Office of Political Affairs*

Joan Baggett was named by President Clinton in January 1993 as assistant to the president and director of the Office of Political Affairs in the White House. She was elevated to the position of director in July 1993, after serving for five months as the deputy director of the Office of Political Affairs. She replaced RAHM EMANUEL in the position.

Her promotion came as a result of a reorganization of White House staff. On June 25, 1993, Chief of Staff THOMAS FRANKLIN MCLARTY III announced three senior staff changes in the White House. Effective July 6, 1993, RICKI SEIDMAN became counselor to the chief of staff, Emanuel was moved from director of political affairs to deputy communications director, and Baggett was promoted to director of political affairs.

In that position, Baggett was charged with "reaching out to Americans around the country, ensuring that their voices are heard, and their talents are mobilized in President Clinton's efforts to change the country," according to the press release announcing her new role.

She remained in the administration for two years, leaving on December 31, 1994. She was named president of the International Masonry Institute (IMI), which represented the International Union of Bricklayers and Allied Craftsmen, as well as the International Council of Employers of Bricklayers and Allied Craftsmen. The organization was a labor/management cooperative.

She had joined the staff of the Democratic National Committee in 1990 as director of congressional relations and organizational relations, and in 1991 was named chief of staff to RONALD H. BROWN, chairman of the Democratic National Committee. She remained with the committee through the 1992 presidential campaign and then was named director of political affairs for the Presidential Inaugural Committee.

Before her job at the Democratic National Committee, Baggett had been the director of communications for the International Union of Bricklayers and Allied Craftsmen (1979–90), the first woman executive of a construction union. During her 13 years at the union, she oversaw its communications, public relations, and political programs. During her tenure in the Bricklayers Union, she also served as the national labor coordinator for the Dukakis-Bentsen presidential campaign in 1988.

Born on April 5, 1952 in Repton, Alabama, she received her B.A. from the University of Alabama (1974).

Baird, Zoe
(1952–) *failed nominee for attorney general*

Zoe Baird was President Clinton's first choice for attorney general in January 1993. However, Baird withdrew her name from consideration after one day of Senate confirmation hearings. President Clinton then nominated KIMBA WOOD, who also failed to gain Senate confirmation. The third nomination by President Clinton was JANET RENO, who did win Senate confirmation. President Clinton sought to name a woman for the post of attorney general as part of his campaign pledge to bring ethnic and gender diversity to the cabinet.

Baird was recommended to President Clinton by LLOYD M. CUTLER, who served on the Clinton transition team and had served as Counsel to the President for President Carter. Baird had been an attorney with the Department of Justice in 1980 when Cutler asked for a Justice Department ruling on an issue regarding the possibility of using patronage jobs for the 1980 census. Baird wrote the legal opinion, as a staff member in the Office of Legal Counsel, stating that it would be illegal. Cutler met with her about the opinion and, over the years, remained in touch. When Cutler was asked to recommend women for the post of Attorney General, he suggested Baird.

Baird withdrew her name from the Senate confirmation hearings after her Federal Bureau of

Investigation (FBI) background check revealed that she had hired a Peruvian woman, who was an illegal alien, to work in her home as a babysitter for her three-year-old son. Baird had also failed to pay social security taxes on the woman. Payment of social security taxes was required for all employees. It is unclear whether President Clinton knew about the background check information, since there were varying statements about his knowledge of the issue. White House communications director GEORGE ROBERT STEPHANOPOULOS said President Clinton did not know, but Press Secretary DEE DEE MYERS said that he did know.

Baird first encountered questions on her nomination when she released her financial disclosure form to the Senate Judiciary Committee. Her form indicated more than $196,000 in stock holdings in Aetna Life and Casualty Co. and General Electric Co. She said that she would divest herself of those holdings and either sell off other parts of her $1.1. million portfolio or put them in a government-approved blind trust. Baird had worked for Aetna since 1990 as its general counsel and senior vice president and had earned $507,105. Prior to joining Aetna, she had been the head of the 375-member legal department of General Electric between 1986 and 1990. However, after the financial issues had been largely resolved, it was revealed to the committee that Baird had hired an illegal alien in her home and had failed to pay social security taxes for the household help. After protests from Republicans in the Senate that Baird could not be the nation's chief legal officer as attorney general after having knowingly broken the law, President Clinton withdrew her nomination. On January 22, 2003, only two days after taking office, President Clinton announced that he was withdrawing the nomination of Zoe Baird for attorney general. In a statement released by the White House press office, President Clinton said, "With

sadness, I have accepted her [Baird's] request that the nomination be withdrawn." Senator Alan Simpson (R-Wyo.), who was the Republican whip, and Senator Larry Pressler (R-S.D.) were strongly opposed to Baird's nomination. Simpson had been the author of the law that Baird violated by hiring illegal aliens as household help. One of her strongest supporters, however, was also a Republican, Senator Orrin Hatch (R-Utah).

Although her nomination for attorney general failed, President Clinton appointed her to the President's Foreign Intelligence Advisory Board.

Born in 1952 in Brooklyn, New York, Baird graduated from the University of California at Berkeley and from the U.C. Berkeley Law School, where she was the Supreme Court editor for the California Law Review. After law school, she served as a law clerk for Judge Albert Wollenberg of the Federal District Court of San Francisco. She then worked for the Department of Justice during the Carter administration. After the Reagan administration took office in 1981, Baird left Washington, D.C., and joined the legal department at General Electric Co. In 1990 she was recruited by Aetna.

Baird was married to Paul M. Gewirtz, the Potter M. Stewart professor of law at Yale Law School, a constitutional law scholar.

Baird returned to Aetna after her failed nomination, but left Aetna in 1996 to join the faculty of Yale Law School as a senior visiting scholar and senior research associate. In 1997 Baird was named the head of the John and Mary R. Markle Foundation, a New York–based philanthropy that specialized in pioneering projects in mass communication, information technology, and public policy. The Markle Foundation had $150 million in assets and awarded $7 million in grants each year, mainly to nonprofit organizations, research institutes, and universities.

Barak, Ehud
(1942–   ) *prime minister of Israel*

After serving in numerous roles within the Israeli army and in the Israeli government, General Ehud Barak was elected prime minister of Israel on May 17, 1999, in a landslide victory over Prime Minister BENJAMIN NETANYAHU. JAMES CARVILLE, JR., who managed the campaign of President Clinton in 1992, served as a campaign consultant to Barak in 1999. During Barak's brief tenure, he continued to oversee the armed forces, serving as both prime minister and minister of defense. He was voted out of office in February 2001, replaced by General Ariel Sharon.

Ehud Barak was Israel's most decorated soldier throughout his 35-year military career. Born on a kibbutz, he entered the Israeli Defense Forces in 1959 at the age of 17 and became commander of the elite commando unit. In 1972, he led the commando unit that stormed a Belgian airliner hijacked by Palestinian guerrillas at Tel Aviv airport. The following year, 1973, he again led a commando unit which overran a Palestinian group responsible for murdering Israeli athletes during the summer Olympic games in Munich in 1972.

Throughout his military career, Barak held a series of command positions, including tank brigade commander and armored division commander, and head of the Intelligence Branch. During the 1967 Six-Day War, Barak served as reconnaissance group commander, and in 1973 during the Yom Kippur War as a tank battalion commander. Over the next decade he continued his rise within the military, being promoted to major general in 1982, appointed head of the Israeli Defense Forces Planning Branch, and appointed head of the Intelligence Branch in 1983. By 1986, he had been appointed commander of the Israeli Defense Forces Central Command and in 1991 was promoted to the rank of lieutenant general, the highest in the Israeli military.

Barak's political ambitions began in 1994, when he worked closely with the Israeli leadership to finalize the peace treaty with Jordan. Prime Minister YITZHAK RABIN appointed Barak to the position of minister of interior in July 1995, the first of several political posts. Following Rabin's assassination, Prime Minister Peres moved Barak to a new position, minister of foreign affairs. However, when Benjamin Netanyahu was elected prime minister in 1996, Barak resigned.

By the mid-1990s, Barak had become comfortable in political dealings and successfully won the leadership position within the Labour Party, a moderate group within a multiparty system. Building on his growing popularity, Barak challenged Prime Minister Netanyahu and his Likud Party government and won the election on May 17, 1999. On July 6, 1999, he was sworn in as prime minister. However, after growing dissatisfaction with his leadership on providing land for Palestinians, Barak delivered a national television address on December 9, 2000, stating that he would resign and stand for early election as a referendum on his government. He was defeated by Ariel Sharon in elections on February 6, 2001, having served in office less than two years.

During Ehud Barak's brief tenure as prime minister, the country was deeply divided over the Barak government's plan to allow most of the West Bank to be governed by an independent Palestine. During the fall of 2000, tensions increased within the West Bank and Gaza over the amount of land actually being delivered to the Palestinians by the Israeli government. Hard-liners within Israel opposed any more concessions to the Palestinians over land, leading to changing coalitions within the fragile coalition government of Prime Minister Barak.

Barak was born in 1942, but no official date is available. He was born on Kibbutz Mishmar Hasharon.

Barr, Robert
(1948–) *member of the House of Representatives*

One of President Clinton's most ardent critics during the impeachment process of 1998 was Republican congressman Robert Barr from Georgia's 7th congressional district. Barr was a conservative Republican, known for his activism in the Christian Coalition and the National Rifle Association. Barr was elected to the House of Representatives in 1994 in the Republican sweep led by NEWTON (NEWT) LEROY GINGRICH. In spite of Republicans maintaining their control of the House of Representatives and gaining control of the Senate in 2002, Barr was unable to preserve his seat in 2002.

Throughout his tenure in Congress, Barr was a frequent critic of President Clinton and of the Clinton administration. In November 1997, Barr introduced legislation to start an impeachment inquiry because of irregularities that he saw in the financing of the Clinton-Gore 1996 reelection campaign. The inquiry was not pursued by the House Judiciary Committee.

Barr rose to national attention in 1998 as a member of the House Judiciary Committee. The committee investigated allegations that President Clinton had lied under oath regarding his relationship with MONICA LEWINSKY during questioning by KENNETH W. STARR, the independent counsel. Clinton denied having a relationship with Lewinsky, which Barr and other Republicans on the committee believed was a lie and therefore an impeachable offense.

The House Judiciary Committee voted out articles of impeachment against President Clinton in December 1998, and brought the articles of impeachment to the floor of the House for a vote. Barr drafted four articles of impeachment against Clinton. Thirteen Republicans on the House Judiciary Committee were assigned the role of managers on the floor of the House to present the case of the committee. The 13 Republicans, in order of their seniority on the committee, were HENRY J. HYDE from Illinois, F. James Sensenbrenner, Jr., of Wisconsin, Bill McCollum of Florida, George W. Gekas of Pennsylvania, Charles T. Canady of Florida, Steve Buyer of Indiana, Ed Bryant of Tennessee, Steve Chabot of Ohio, Bob Barr of Georgia, Asa Hutchinson of Arkansas, Christopher B. Cannon of Utah, James E. Rogan of California, and LINDSEY GRAHAM of South Carolina. Barr was among the least senior members of the managers, yet became one of the most vocal leaders of the movement to impeach the president.

During the impeachment of President Clinton in 1998, Representative Barr became an ardent advocate of removing the president from office. In a statement presented during the House floor debate on December 18, 1998, on HR 611, impeaching President Clinton for high crimes and misdemeanors, Barr maintained that the president had engaged in a pattern of obstruction of justice in violation of Title 18 of the U.S. Criminal Code. According to Barr, Clinton had misled the Congress in its investigation as to his relationship with Monica Lewinsky.

The House of Representatives, along party lines, impeached President Clinton in December 1998. The Senate refused to convict him in early 1999. However, Barr continued his attacks on President Clinton. Following the final report issued by ROBERT RAY, the independent counsel who replaced Kenneth Starr, Barr issued a statement on March 17, 2000 (and sent a letter to Ray), that the investigation had not been thorough enough. In particular, Barr believed that the White House used information it received from the FBI to discredit

Barr. Barr provided no other information to substantiate his claim. Barr enlisted the support of the conservative group, Judicial Watch, in his claims against the Clinton White House.

While in the House of Representatives, Barr served as a member of the Conservative Action Team, the Pro-Life Caucus, and the Congressional Chapter of the Civil Air Patrol. He was also on the Board of Directors of the National Rifle Association and was active in the Federalist Society. His conservative credentials were seen throughout his professional affiliations and the organizations that he supported. His defeat in 2002 was partly due to a concerted effort by the National Democratic Committee to unseat him.

Born November 5, 1948 in Iowa City, Iowa, Barr graduated with a B.A. from the University of Southern California (1970). After college, Barr joined the Central Intelligence Agency (CIA) as a lobbyist and worked there throughout the next eight years, during which he also obtained an M.A. from George Washington University (1972) and the Georgetown University Law Center (1977). He held a series of federal appointed jobs after leaving the CIA, including serving as United States Attorney for the Northern District of Georgia (1986–90); antidrug coordinator for the Department of Justice, Southeastern United States (1986–90); and as head of the Public Corruption Subcommittee for the United States Attorney General (1987–88). All of these positions were political, requiring appointment by the president or the attorney general, and all were during the administration of President Ronald Reagan. Not surprisingly, Barr was the sponsor of the 1998 law renaming Washington's National Airport Reagan National Airport. He also was the director of the Southeast Legal Foundation from 1990–92. When the Reagan administration left office, Barr moved out of the federal government into the private sector. His interest in the public sector, however, continued as evidenced by his run for the U.S. Senate in 1992. Although he lost the election in 1992, he mounted a successful candidacy for the House of Representatives in 1994, defeating the incumbent, Rep. George Darden. Barr held the seat for four terms before being defeated in the 2002 election.

Barrett, David M.

(1937–) *independent counsel investigating Henry G. Cisneros, secretary of housing and urban development*

David M. Barrett was selected by the Special Division of the U.S. Court of Appeals for the District of Columbia to investigate HENRY G. CISNEROS, secretary of housing and urban development (HUD). Cisneros was charged with failing to tell the Federal Bureau of Investigation (FBI) in its background check for his cabinet position about payments to his ex-mistress, Linda Medlar Jones.

Barrett began his investigation in May 1995 and continued it through 1999, when Cisneros pleaded guilty to a misdemeanor charge of lying to the FBI. Although the Ethics in Government Act, which created the independent counsel statute, expired on June 30, 1999, Barrett continued his investigation as he was required to do.

Cisneros became the target of a federal investigation within the Department of Justice in March 1995. Attorney General JANET RENO asked for an independent counsel to investigate charges that Cisneros lied to the Federal Bureau of Investigation (FBI) about secret payments he made to a former mistress. Cisneros was alleged to have paid Linda Medlar, a political fund-raiser, over $250,000 between 1990 and 1993 to keep their affair quiet.

In mid-1994 Medlar sued Cisneros, saying he reneged on his oral agreement to keep paying her $4,000 per month. She then charged that Cisneros lied about the payments to the FBI during his background investigation for the position of secretary of housing and urban development. On September 12, 1994, the television show *Inside Edition* broadcast excerpts of tapes that Medlar had made of telephone conversations with Cisneros.

Reno subsequently triggered the appointment of an independent counsel as required under the Ethics in Government Act of 1978 regarding allegations against senior federal officials. Barrett was named the independent counsel.

In January 1997, as the investigation by Barrett wore on, Cisneros resigned, citing financial concerns from a child in college, another in law school, and legal bills from the investigation. He returned to the private sector, becoming president of Univision, the Spanish-language television network.

Before the end of the year, a grand jury (December 1997) charged Cisneros with eighteen counts of conspiracy, false statements, and obstruction of justice stemming from the alleged payments to Medlar. Medlar had since changed her name to Linda Jones. The grand jury charged that the payments had totaled more than $250,000. On January 15, 1998, Medlar Jones pleaded guilty to 28 charges of fraud and obstruction of justice and was sentenced to three and a half years in federal prison. Cisneros was named in that case.

After a four-year investigation, jury selection was about to begin for Cisneros in September 1999. However, before the selection, Cisneros reached a plea agreement with the federal prosecutor. He pleaded guilty to a misdemeanor count of lying to the Federal Bureau of Investigation. He was fined $10,000 but did not face prison or a fine, according to the agreement. Cisneros said in a public statement that he "was not candid" with the Federal Bureau of Investigation and hoped to be remembered for his actions as secretary of housing and urban development. In one of his final acts as president, President Clinton pardoned Cisneros.

Barrett's career had been centered around Republican politics for a number of years. Barrett made a failed bid for a U.S. House seat from Indiana in 1968. He later became active in Republican politics, volunteering for Lawyers for Reagan in 1980. After working as a Republican fund-raiser and activist, Barrett became a lobbyist, concentrating on business related to the Department of Housing and Urban Development. By 1988, he had become successful enough to spend $500,000 as a one-time premium for a life insurance policy.

During the investigation into Samuel Pierce, secretary of housing and urban development in the Reagan administration, documents surfaced that named Barrett as a lobbyist and consultant for the department. As a result, Democrats in Congress opposed Barrett's appointment as the independent counsel for the Cisneros investigation. Rep. Tom Lantos (D-Calif.), who had been part of the Pierce investigation in 1989–90, denounced Barrett's appointment, stating that Barrett "clearly benefited from influence-peddling at HUD during the Reagan administration." Lantos likened Barrett's selection to "appointing the well-fed fox to investigate the missing hens in the chicken coop."

Barshefsky, Charlene

(1950–   ) *trade representative, acting trade representative, deputy trade representative*

Charlene Barshefsky was sworn in as the U.S. trade representative (USTR) on March 17, 1997, after serving as deputy trade representative from 1993 to 1996 and as acting trade representative from 1996 to 1997. President Clinton elevated the trade representative to cabinet rank in 1993, when he came into office.

As the trade representative, Barshefsky had the rank of ambassador and served as the president's principal adviser on trade policy and as the administration's chief trade negotiator. She remained with the administration until President Clinton left office in 2001. Immediately after leaving government service in 2001, she was named as a public policy scholar at the Woodrow Wilson International Center for Scholars in Washington, D.C. She then joined the law firm of Wilmer, Cutler & Pickering as a senior partner, specializing in international law.

Barshefsky's background had been in international trade law prior to joining the Clinton administration in 1993. As a partner in the Washington, D.C., law firm of Steptoe and Johnson, she specialized in international trade law and policy and cochaired the firm's international practice group.

She had been a member of the firm since 1975. Throughout her career at Steptoe and Johnson, Barshefsky had written and lectured extensively on U.S. and foreign trade law and policies and had provided testimony before Congress on trade law. She was vice chair of the International Law Section of the American Bar Association and cochaired the International Litigation Committee of the American Bar Association. Her work also included chairing the U.S. Court of International Trade Advisory Committee. In addition, she was on the board of the International Legal Studies Program at American University School of Law.

Her initial appointment as deputy trade representative gave her responsibility for trade relations primarily in the Asia-Pacific region and in Latin America. Throughout her eight years in the Office of Trade Representative, Barshefsky negotiated 300 trade agreements around the world, including 100 in Asia. Her most successful negotiations involved China. Following years of negotiation with China, Barshefsky signed an agreement in Beijing that opened China's markets to the United States. Under the agreement, U.S. companies doing business with China could own up to 50 percent of telecommunications companies in China, sell more wheat, corn, rice, cotton, and other farm commodities to China, offer financial services to Chinese companies, and provide other services and goods in China. The pact was negotiated by Barshefsky with Premier ZHU RONGJI of China, who was considered an economic reformer.

The trade agreement with China allowed China to begin the process of entering the World Trade Organization. While many praised the agreement on economic grounds, many opposed it on human rights grounds. Opponents of the agreement argued that China's dismal record in human rights should foreclose any economic agreements. Barshefsky countered that unless China was brought into the wider community of international law, little pressure could be placed on China concerning human rights.

In addition to negotiating the trade agreement with China, Barshefsky was the architect of negotiations to create a hemispheric free-trade zone called the Free Trade Area of the Americas. She also negotiated trade agreements with Vietnam, Jordan, Singapore, and Chile. Shortly before leaving office, Barshefsky negotiated a commitment from all World Trade Organization members that they would abide by "duty-free cyberspace." This agreement prevented any member of the World Trade Organization from imposing tariffs on electronic transmissions over the Internet.

Born on August 11, 1950, in Chicago, Illinois, Barshefsky graduated with a B.A. in political science from the University of Wisconsin (1972) and a J.D. from the Catholic University School of Law (1975).

Begala, Paul

(1962–) *presidential campaign consultant, counselor to the president*

One of President Clinton's closest advisers during the 1992 presidential campaign was political strategist Paul Begala. Begala and his partner, JAMES CARVILLE, JR., managed the presidential campaign and steered Clinton to victory over incumbent president GEORGE HERBERT WALKER BUSH. Their work managing Clinton's campaign stemmed from a recommendation from Governor Zell Miller of Georgia to Governor Bill Clinton when he was exploring candidates for his campaign manager. Miller had used Begala and Carville for his successful campaign for governor and, in a meeting in Atlanta with Clinton, recommended the two.

Although Begala did not join the Clinton administration in the first term, he continued to informally advise Clinton and to work with the Democratic National Committee. Begala joined the administration in July 1997, coordinating policy, politics, and media strategy, with the title "counselor to the president." He left in the spring of 1999 to teach at Georgetown University and to write a column for *George* magazine.

Throughout the 1992 presidential campaign, Begala was one of Clinton's most trusted advisers. Begala spent nearly every day of the primary and general elections with Clinton, developing political strategies for both the long and short terms. Carville and Begala were the center of the campaign, convening 7:30 A.M. daily meetings with their campaign staff to focus the activities of the day.

Once elected, Clinton brought many of his campaign staff into the administration but neither Carville nor Begala chose to join the administration. Begala continued to advise Clinton informally and did substantial polling on the administration's behalf for the Democratic National Committee. Begala was soon in demand by other clients seeking political office or seeking reelection. His reputation within Democratic political circles had reached new heights as a result of the Clinton campaign.

However, his star began to fade with President Clinton in 1994 when Begala advised one of his clients, a candidate for the U.S. Senate seeking reelection, that he should vote against the North American Free Trade Agreement (NAFTA), since it might hurt his election chances. Clinton began to shut Begala out of meetings in the White House and turned instead to political strategist DICK MORRIS for political advice.

Begala fell further from grace in the Clinton administration when he spoke with Bob Woodward, who was preparing a book entitled *The Agenda*. The book chronicled the first year of the Clinton administration and how the White House dealt with policy and political issues. In the book, Woodward quotes Begala as calling Leon Panetta, the director of the Office of Management and Budget, "the poster boy for economic constipation." When Panetta became White House chief of staff in August 1994, he effectively banned Begala from the White House. Begala left Washington, D.C., for a while following his falling out with the White House staff, and returned to his home state of Texas where he taught a course on politics and the press for the University of Texas.

Begala continued a successful political consulting business both nationally and internationally. His clients included Brazilian president FERNANDO HENRIQUE CARDOSO, Greek prime minister Constantine Mitsotakis, and Dominican Republic president Hipólito Mejía. He also became a successful political commentator on national television, serving as host on CNN's *Crossfire* and as a commentator on NBC.

During the 1998 impeachment hearings in the House of Representatives and the trial in the Senate in 1999, Begala became one of Clinton's most ardent defenders. He regularly gave television interviews supporting President Clinton and attacking members of Congress who wanted to remove Clinton from office. He also supported President Clinton throughout the investigation by Independent Counsel KENNETH W. STARR. Not surprisingly, by the end of the administration, Begala was again advising Clinton and had again become a regular within the White House.

In addition to political consulting, Begala managed communications strategy for corporate clients such as Coca-Cola, Southwest Airlines, and the San Antonio Spurs, through his firm Public Strategies. Begala was said to have inspired the character of Josh Lyman on the NBC television series, *The West Wing*.

Begala received both his B.A. degree in government and his law degree from the University of Texas in Austin.

Bellamy, Carol
(1942–) *director of the Peace Corps*

Carol Bellamy was appointed director of the Peace Corps by President Clinton in 1993. She left the Clinton administration in May 1995, when she was named the executive director of the United Nation's Children's Fund (UNICEF) for a four-year term. She was reappointed to a second, five-year term at UNICEF in 1999. Bellamy was the first former volunteer in the Peace Corps to be named its director. After graduating from Gettysburg College in 1963, Bellamy joined the Peace Corps and served in Guatemala for two years. MARK GEARAN followed Bellamy as director of the Peace Corps.

The Peace Corps, created by President John F. Kennedy, had burgeoned into an agency that provided volunteers in 90 countries. Her primary task as head of the Peace Corps was to develop programs that could be expanded into new countries around the world. After less than two years as director of the Peace Corps, Bellamy left to join the United Nations staff as the executive director of UNICEF. There, her mission appeared to be more in line with her professional skills in managing public finance. The United Nations organizations often lacked sound financial management, including UNICEF. Bellamy was brought into the organization to restore fiscal viability and to streamline its operations. She has been given high marks within the United Nations for her financial management skills, which has enabled the agency to gain greater visibility and stronger commitments from its member nations.

Carol Bellamy *(Peace Corps)*

After Bellamy returned from the Peace Corps in Guatemala, she entered New York University School of Law and began a corporate practice at a New York City law firm, Cravath, Swaine & Moore, where she stayed from 1968–71. After leaving private law practice, Bellamy entered the public sector, working for the New York City Mental Health Department from 1971–73. Her interest in public policy led her to run for and win a seat in the New York State Senate, where she served for four years (1973–77). In 1977, she successfully captured a seat on the New York City Council, where she served until 1985. Her tenure on the council included serving as president from 1978 to 1985, the first woman to do so. In 1985 Bellamy ran unsuccessfully for mayor of New York City and subsequently left city government.

After 14 years in the public sector, Bellamy returned to the private sector as a partner with the investment banking firm of Morgan Stanley & Co. from 1986–90. She changed firms in 1990, moving to Bear Stearns & Co. as the managing director of the public finance department. Her career in the private sector came to an abrupt end in 1993 when President Clinton appointed Bellamy director of the Peace Corps.

Born on January 14, 1942, in Plainfield, New Jersey, Bellamy received her B.A. from Gettysburg College (1963) and her J.D. from New York University School of Law (1968).

Bennett, Robert (Bob)
(1933–   ) *member of the Senate*

Senator Robert (Bob) Bennett (R-Utah), was a conservative Republican in the Senate who frequently opposed President Clinton on policy issues. Bennett was a frequent critic of Clinton's during the impeachment process, voting "yes" to convict in the Senate trial.

Bennett was first elected to the Senate in 1992, winning 64 percent of the vote in Utah.

Although he had not held elective office prior to 1992, Bennett had been congressional liaison in the Department of Transportation during the Nixon administration and later was the multimillionaire chief executive officer of a private company, Franklin Day Planner, in Utah. He was reelected in 1998 to a second term. Bennett's knowledge of the political system was partly the result of his exposure to politics when he ran a senate campaign for his father, Wallace F. Bennett. Wallace Bennett served in the Senate from 1951–74.

While in the Senate, Bennett focused on technology issues. He chaired the Senate Special Committee on the Year 2000 Technology Problem and the Senate Republican task force on High Technology. He became immersed in issues relating to the computer problems that might occur during the conversion to the year 2000. In 2000, Bennett began driving a gasoline-electric hybrid car that logged 60 miles per gallon. Although Bennett championed issues related to the increased use of new technologies, his conservative views frequently were seen in other issues. He was particularly critical of the Clinton administration on federal land-management programs that he argued were dominated by environmentalists. Bennett was outraged that President Clinton used executive orders to create national monuments in Utah and other western states which effectively blocked mining and ranching in these areas.

Born on September 18, 1933, in Salt Lake City, Utah, Bennett received a B.S. from the University of Utah (1957).

Bennett, Robert S.
(1939–   ) *personal attorney to president and Mrs. Clinton*

Robert S. Bennett, a partner in the Washington, D.C., law firm of Skadden, Arps, Slate,

Meagher & Flom, served as President Clinton's private attorney throughout most of his presidency, dealing primarily with matters relating to the PAULA CORBIN JONES sexual harassment lawsuit and to the impeachment proceedings. When President Clinton left office, Bennett continued as his private attorney.

Bennett was a well-known criminal defense lawyer in Washington, D.C., who had defended former House Ways and Means chairman Dan Rostenkowski, former secretary of defense Caspar Weinberger, and members of the Keating Five. Bennett's brother, WILLIAM J. BENNETT, a conservative Republican, was a frequent critic of President Clinton. William Bennett had served as chair of the National Endowment for the Humanities and as secretary of education under President Reagan, and as director of the Office of National Drug Control Policy under President GEORGE HERBERT WALKER BUSH.

In contrast to his brother, Robert Bennett had spent most of his career in private practice. His expertise in criminal law came from his role as a federal prosecutor in the 1960s, but his career was built in the Washington, D.C., law firm of Skadden, Arps, Slate, Meagher & Flom, where he became a senior partner.

Clinton hired Bennett in 1994, when Jones accused him in court documents of seeking sexual favors from her while she was an Arkansas state employee and he was governor. He denied the allegations. In the discovery process, Jones's lawyers were provided information that Clinton had been having an affair while president with MONICA LEWINSKY. Clinton denied this allegation in tape-recorded depositions. When LINDA TRIPP began making accusations against President Clinton, Bennett argued in an interview with the *Washington Post* that Clinton had been the victim of a conspiracy by his political opponents.

Although the information was somewhat obtuse, it appeared that Jones's lawyers then provided the independent counsel, KENNETH W. STARR, with information that Clinton was involved with Lewinsky. Clinton again denied it in a deposition. Bennett then was brought into the larger case in which Starr charged Clinton with lying under oath.

The Lewinsky matter eventually led to articles of impeachment in the House of Representatives accusing President Clinton of perjury in both the Jones deposition and the Starr deposition. While the White House counsel's office defended the president throughout the impeachment process, Bennett remained the president's private counsel in settling the Jones case and later dealing with the Arkansas Supreme Court, which disciplined Clinton for lying under oath.

Born in 1939 in Brooklyn, New York, Bennett graduated with a B.A. from Georgetown University (1961) and with an LL.B. from Georgetown Law Center (1964) and an LL.M. from Harvard University (1965). Following law school, Bennett served as a law clerk for Howard F. Corcoran, U.S. district judge for the District of Columbia (1965–67).

Bennett, William J.
(1943–   ) *conservative Republican*

William J. Bennett, a conservative Republican who often criticized the Clinton administration, was the brother of Clinton's personal attorney, ROBERT S. BENNETT. William Bennett served in the Reagan administration as chair of the National Endowment for the Humanities and as secretary of education, served in the Bush administration as director of the Office of National Drug Control Policy, and formed Empower America with Jack Kemp after leaving the Bush administration. Empower America was a conservative public policy institute that provided position statements on a variety of issues.

Bennett maintained a high political profile after leaving the Bush administration. When President Clinton took over the reins of government in 1993, Bennett was often seen on national television shows attacking Clinton's policies. As a former secretary of education, Bennett was particularly critical of the Clinton administration's education proposals. In 1995, when the Republicans took over the House of Representatives with NEWTON (NEWT) LEROY GINGRICH as Speaker, Empower America and Bennett gained a new role. Although orientation sessions for new members of Congress had been run by the John F. Kennedy School of Government of Harvard University for 20 years, Gingrich replaced the Kennedy School of Government with Empower America and the Heritage Foundation.

Bennett's books in the past decade have focused on issues of morality, in line with his political philosophy. In addition to his two books on virtue, he authored *The Broken Hearth: Reversing the Moral Collapse of the American Family* (2001) and *The Devaluing of America: The Fight for Our Culture and Our Children* (1994). His focus on morality and values was the dominant theme of a book attacking Clinton, *The Death of Outrage: Bill Clinton and the Assault on American Ideals* (1998).

Bennett appeared to be less focused on issues of morality once Clinton left office and after GEORGE WALKER BUSH was elected. Following the terrorist attacks of September 11, 2001, Bennett took up a new cause which supported the president's War on Terrorism. He created a unit within Empower America, entitled Americans for Victory over Terrorism (AVOT). The goals of AVOT were "to educate the public about the nature of terrorist organizations, educate the public about the nature and threat of radical Islamism, articulate American ideals in schools and campuses, and support democratic patriotism when it is questioned."

The refocus to the War on Terrorism after September 11, 2001, began a new chapter for Empower America. However, the goals of the organization remained conservative as it sought to articulate Bennett's political views.

Born on July 3, 1943, Bennett graduated with a B.A. in philosophy from Williams College (1965), a Ph.D. in philosophy from the University of Texas in Austin (1970), and a J.D. from Harvard University (1971) and served on the faculty of the University of North Carolina and North Carolina State. He is the author of 14 books, including *The Book of Virtues: A Treasury of Great Moral Stories* and *The Children's Book of Virtues*.

Bentsen, Lloyd Millard, Jr.
(1921–   ) *secretary of the Treasury, member of the Senate, member of the House of Representatives*

Lloyd M. Bentsen served as President Clinton's secretary of the Treasury following his Senate confirmation on January 20, 1993. Prior to his appointment at Treasury, Bentsen had served in the U.S. Senate (D-Tex.) continuously since 1971. He resigned as secretary of the Treasury on December 22, 1994. During the 1970 Senate election in Texas, Bentsen had faced GEORGE HERBERT WALKER BUSH. Bentsen had also served three terms, 1949–55, in the House of Representatives and then built a personal fortune as president of Lincoln Consolidated Insurance Company.

During his brief tenure in the Clinton administration, Bentsen emerged as a major proponent in the Senate of the administration's tax reform legislation and in passing the 1993 deficit reduction bill. In addition to his work on the economic plan, Bentsen worked to support the Interstate Banking and Branching Efficiency Act of 1994 which allowed interstate branching for banks. He also worked to pass the 1994 crime bill, which banned assault rifles.

He left the administration at the end of his second year as secretary of the Treasury, at which time ROBERT RUBIN, the director of the National Economic Council, was nominated to the position. Rubin took over at the Treasury in January 1995.

While there is little evidence that Bentsen was forced out of the job, it appears that he felt that Rubin had become the president's primary economic adviser. Bentsen had not been part of the Clinton campaign and had never been part of the president's inner circle. At no point was Bentsen able to gain control of the economic policy mechanism, which was always firmly held within the White House by Rubin's National Economic Council, in concert with LEON EDWARD PANETTA at the Office of Management and Budget. As a senior staffer in the White House, Rubin had constant access to Clinton and was routinely suggesting new policy initiatives that Bentsen was not involved in developing.

Bentsen left the administration with little explanation, although few doubted that Clinton preferred a more aggressive secretary of the Treasury with whom he had closer ties. Since the Clinton campaign motto had been "It's the economy, stupid," the administration was focused on economic growth. Clinton did not appear to have full faith that Bentsen could create the types of economic policies that Clinton saw as critical to economic growth.

During the 1988 presidential election, Bentsen was the Democratic vice presidential candidate with Massachusetts governor Michael Dukakis. Dukakis chose Bentsen as his running mate for both political and pragmatic reasons. On the political side, Bentsen provided geographic balance to Dukakis's New England base. Bentsen's home state of Texas also provided more electoral votes than any state except California and New York. However, it was not only Texas that Dukakis hoped to garner by adding Bentsen to the ticket, but also most of the South. Dukakis hoped that Bentsen, known as a conservative Democrat, could gain votes from the "Reagan Democrats" who had won the 1980 election for Ronald Reagan. In addition, Dukakis hoped to use Bentsen's skills in the Senate to broaden the opportunities for administration-sponsored legislation.

Although Dukakis and Bentsen failed to defeat George H. W. Bush and Dan Quayle in their quest for the presidency, Bentsen gained national prominence for the first time in his political career. Although well known in the Senate, he had not been well known on the national stage. The 1988 presidential campaign provided Bentsen the chance to hone his knowledge of national issues and to work within the national party structure, skills which would serve him well as secretary of the Treasury during the Clinton administration. One of the most memorable moments of the 1988 campaign came during the presidential debates, when the two vice presidential candidates debated alone. In response to a remark by Dan Quayle regarding how President Kennedy would have approached an issue, Bentsen firmly declared "I knew John F. Kennedy, and you are not John F. Kennedy." The statement reverberated in comments across the nation, giving Bentsen instant recognition. Not only had he established his experience as an elder statesman to Quayle, but he had identified himself with the still popular Kennedy administration.

Born on February 11, 1921, in Mission, Texas, Bentsen received his J.D. from the University of Texas at Austin (1942). During World War II, Bentsen served as a pilot in the Army Air Corps, where he was the squadron commander. He received the Distinguished Flying Cross and the Air Medal with three oak-leaf clusters. From 1945 to 1946 Bentsen practiced law before being elected as a judge in Hidalgo County, Texas. During his tenure in the Senate, Bentsen rose to chairman of the Finance Committee in 1987.

Berger, Samuel (Sandy) R.

(1945–   ) *assistant to the president for national security affairs, deputy assistant to the president for national security affairs*

Samuel "Sandy" Berger was appointed assistant to the president for national security affairs on December 5, 1996, by President Clinton. He had been the deputy assistant to the president for national security affairs since the start of the administration, working under ANTHONY LAKE. Berger, who was promoted when Lake was nominated to the position of director of the Central Intelligence Agency (CIA), was one of the few members of the White House staff who remained the entire eight years of the administration. Prior to joining the administration, Berger had been a foreign policy adviser during the 1992 presidential campaign and was assistant director for national security of the transition team.

During the second term of the Clinton administration, when Berger was national security advisor, he worked with President Clinton on a host of issues, including the normalization of trade relations with China, on the Palestinian-Israeli conflict, on the conflict in Yugoslavia, and on the North Atlantic Treaty Organization (NATO)–led bombing campaign in Kosovo. Writing in the *Washington Post* in June 2000 to explain the American participation in the Kosovo bombing over 79 days, Berger said that the United States succeeded "in ending years of violent repression that had culminated in a grotesque campaign of mass expulsion that endangered stability and peace in the region." He continued by noting, "As Elie Wiesel said a year ago, 'This time, the world was not silent.'"

Berger first met President Clinton in 1972, when both worked for George McGovern's presidential campaign. President Clinton was working in Texas as a state organizer for McGovern, and Berger was a McGovern speech writer. After the campaign, Clinton and Berger remained in touch. Berger first encouraged Clinton to run for president in 1987. In 1991, when Clinton decided to launch a presidential campaign, Berger began working for the campaign as a foreign policy adviser. Berger then brought in Lake and MADELEINE KORBEL ALBRIGHT as foreign policy advisers. He often attended dinners on foreign policy hosted by Albright at her Washington, D.C., home.

Prior to working in the Clinton White House, Berger had held a variety of positions in the federal government, in addition to serving for a short time in local politics in New York City. Berger served as special assistant to New York City mayor John Lindsay (1972), as legislative assistant to former senator Harold Hughes (D-Iowa) and to Rep. Joseph Resnick (D-N.Y.) (1971–72). In addition he was the deputy director of the policy planning staff at the Department of State during the Carter administration (1977–80). While he was at the Department of State, he often wrote speeches for Secretary of State Cyrus Vance and worked on the Strategic Arms Limitation Treaty in his role as the deputy director of policy planning. When Michael Dukakis ran for president in 1988, Berger worked in the foreign policy section under Madeleine Albright.

For most of his career, Berger had practiced law at the Washington, D.C., law firm of Hogan and Hartson (1973–77 and 1981–92). He headed the firm's international trade group. Among his clients was the Toyota automobile corporation. He was also a close adviser to Pamela Harriman, who was named ambassador to France by President Clinton.

Born on October 28, 1945, Berger received his B.A. degree from Cornell University (1967) and his J.D. from Harvard Law School (1971).

Berry, Mary Frances

(1938–   ) chair, Commission on Civil Rights; member, Commission on Civil Rights

Mary Frances Berry was appointed by President Clinton in 1993 as chair of the Commission on Civil Rights. She had been a member of the commission since 1980. She was reappointed by the president in 1999 for a second six-year term as chair. The eight Civil Rights Commission members were appointed by the president and confirmed by the Senate for six-year terms. When President GEORGE WALKER BUSH entered office in 2001, he quickly clashed with Berry over appointments to the commission. It appeared unlikely that President Bush, if elected to a second term, would reappoint Berry in 2005 when her term expires.

Berry began her tenure in government during the Carter administration. She was appointed by President Carter as assistant secretary for education in the Department of Health, Education, and Welfare (HEW) from April 1977 until January 1980. During part of her tenure in the Department of Education during the Carter administration, she served as acting U.S. commissioner on education. As assistant secretary of education, Berry oversaw the annual education budget of $13 billion and managed the National Institute of Education, the Office of Education, the Fund for the Improvement of Post-Secondary Education, the Institute of Museum Services, and the National Center for Education Statistics.

In January 1980, one month before he left office, Carter successfully nominated Berry to the Civil Rights Commission. However, Berry's activism on behalf of minorities led to serious conflict with the Reagan administration White House staff. In 1984, President Reagan dismissed her. She sued for reinstatement and won in the Federal District Court. Although absent from the commission for a brief period during the litigation, Berry is considered to have continuous service on the Civil Rights Commission for purposes of reappointment.

Among the issues that the Civil Rights Commission tackled under Berry's leadership during the Clinton administration was police brutality based on racial prejudice. In May 1999 Berry held public hearings in New York City examining the allegations of brutality within the New York City Police Department. Both Mayor Rudolph Giuliani and Police Commissioner Howard Safir defended the police department during the hearings. Disputing the response by Giuliani and Safir were Dennis Walcott, president of the New York Urban League, and Norman Siegel of the New York Civil Liberties Union. The issue of police brutality in New York City became a civil rights issue for the commission to address as a result of the torture case of a Haitian immigrant, Abner Louima, by the New York City police. Another case involved a street vendor from Guinea killed by four white police officers, who fired 41 shots at him. The commission sought to ensure that racial profiling or any issue of ethnicity was not involved in police activities.

When President George W. Bush was elected, he did not attempt to remove Berry from office but did attempt to remove her staff director. When President Clinton entered office, he had replaced the Republican staff director. President Bush sought to replace the Democratic staff director, but encountered substantial opposition from Berry.

Born on February 17, 1938 in Nashville, Tennessee, Berry received her B.A. and master's degrees from Howard University and a Ph.D. in history from the University of Michigan. In addition, she earned a J.D. from the University of Michigan Law School. She has published eight books, including *Why ERA Failed: Politics, Women's Rights, and the Amending Process of the Constitution* and *The Politics of*

Parenthood: Child Care, Women's Rights and the Myth of the Good Mother. Prior to joining the Carter administration in 1977, Berry was chancellor of the University of Colorado at Boulder, Provost of the Division of Behavioral and Social Sciences at the University of Maryland at College Park, and has held a series of faculty appointments. She currently is the Gerald R. Segal Professor of American Social Thought and professor of history at the University of Pennsylvania.

bin Laden, Osama

(1957–   ) *terrorist, exiled from Saudi Arabia, living in Afghanistan*

Osama bin Laden, a wealthy terrorist from Saudi Arabia, led a series of attacks against United States facilities and interests throughout the 1990s. In 2001 bin Laden masterminded the attacks of September 11 against the World Trade towers in New York City and the Pentagon in Washington, D.C.

In 1995 Ramzi Yousef and Wali Khan Amin Shah were tried and convicted in New York City for the 1993 bombing of the World Trade Center, which had been planned by Osama bin Laden. Bin Laden's terrorists parked a truck with a bomb in the parking lot in the basement of the World Trade Center. The bomb exploded, destroying the parking lot and damaging, but not destroying, the tower, killing six people and wounding more than a thousand. The attack on September 11, 2001, completed the attack on the World Trade towers that had failed in 1993. During the trial for the 1993 bombing, Wali Khan Amin Shah told federal investigators that bin Laden had ordered the assassination of President Clinton. Ramzi Yousef also admitted an order to assassinate President Clinton, stating that he tried at one point during a presidential motorcade, but the security was too tight.

In November 1994 President Clinton canceled a trip to the Philippines when U.S. intelligence believed that bin Laden was involved in a terrorist plot against President Clinton. In February 1998 President Clinton also canceled a trip to Pakistan because of terrorist threats from bin Laden's organization, al-Qaeda. Bin Laden had ordered an assassination of President Clinton in Islamabad.

In August 1998 President Clinton ordered retaliatory air strikes against bin Laden for his role in the bombing of two American embassies in Kenya and Tanzania that killed 257 people on August 7, 1998. The United States military fired 80 cruise missiles, from warships into Khartoum, Sudan, and the hills of Afghanistan where bin Laden's forces were hiding. Targets in Sudan, which was considered controlled by bin Laden, included a chemical weapons factory.

After the air strikes, President Clinton stated in his weekly radio address that he had signed an executive order barring U.S. companies from dealing with groups linked to bin Laden. "Our efforts against terrorism cannot and will not end with this strike," President Clinton said in the radio address, "and we must be prepared for a long battle."

At the time that President Clinton ordered the air strikes against bin Laden, independent counsel KENNETH W. STARR was interviewing MONICA LEWINSKY about her relationship with Clinton. During the same week, President Clinton also became the first sitting president to testify before a federal grand jury. Republicans charged that the air strikes were conducted to deflect public opinion away from the independent counsel's investigation. Secretary of Defense WILLIAM SEBASTIAN COHEN reacted to the charge by saying, "The only motivation was our absolute obligation to protect the American people."

In December 1999 the Clinton administration said that bin Laden's terrorist organization had direct links to a dozen suspects detained in an unnamed Mideast country on grounds that they were planning an attack on New Year's Eve of the year 2000 against Americans. The New Year's Eve attack was apparently a retaliation. Bin Laden had been indicted by a New York grand jury on charges of conspiracy and murder in the 1998 bombings of the U.S. embassies in Kenya and Tanzania.

In March 2000 President Clinton canceled a scheduled visit to a rural village in Bangladesh after U.S. intelligence revealed that bin Laden may have planned to fire a Stinger missile at President Clinton's helicopter. The intelligence revealed that the attack would strike as President Clinton flew from Dhaka, the capital of Bangladesh, to the village of Joypura, 60 miles away.

Bin Laden was born in 1957 in Riyadh, Saudi Arabia. He was one of 50 children from multiple wives of Mohammad bin Laden, a wealthy construction businessman in Saudi Arabia. When Mohammed bin Laden was killed in 1968 in a helicopter crash, his industrial empire, called the bin Laden Group, was passed to his children.

Bin Laden's Muslim fundamentalism began while he was a student in Saudi Arabia. While studying at King Abdul Aziz University in Jiddah, Saudi Arabia, bin Laden was influenced by the Muslim fundamentalist Sheik Abdullah Azzam. Azzam was dedicated to the cause of liberating Islamic lands from foreign influences and reintroducing young Muslims to the tenets of the faith. When the Soviet Union invaded Afghanistan on December 26, 1979, bin Laden joined thousands of Muslims in the jihad, or holy war, to liberate Afghanistan from the invaders. He used his family's wealth to purchase and to finance the opposition in Afghanistan to the Soviet Union. He established training camps and provided food and medical care for the Afghan resistance.

After the United States sent troops to Saudi Arabia as part of its efforts to push Iraqi troops out of Kuwait, bin Laden transferred his anger from the Soviet Union for its invasion of Afghanistan to the United States for its invasion of Saudi Arabia, as bin Laden termed it. The U.S. troops were placed in Saudi Arabia, at the invitation of the Saudi government, to prevent SADDAM HUSSEIN from invading Saudi Arabia after he had invaded Kuwait. Bin Laden believed that the Arabian Peninsula would eventually be used by the United States as a staging area to protect Israel.

In April 1991 bin Laden left Saudi Arabia with his family and moved to Sudan, where a militant Islamic government had taken power. He used his wealth, estimated at $250 million, to invest in Sudan's National Islamic Front. Soon after, the United States became the prime target of bin Laden's jihad. His first attack against the United States was the 1993 bombing of the World Trade Center.

Blair, Anthony (Tony) Charles Lynton
(1953–) *prime minister of the United Kingdom*

Tony Blair was elected leader of the Labour Party in July 1994, becoming the youngest person to head the Labour Party in history. After his party had lost four consecutive general elections, Blair began a concerted effort to restructure the party to regain control of the government from the Conservative Party. He began to focus the party on free enterprise and economic reform, coining the slogan "New Labour, New Britain." His efforts led to a dramatic increase in the membership of the Labour Party and a growing dissatisfaction with Prime Minister John Major's Conservative government. Three years after taking the helm of the Labour Party, Blair led the party to a majority in Parliament and was elected prime minister in May 1997, and reelected in

June 2001. At the age of 43, Blair was the youngest person to be prime minister since Lord Liverpool in 1812.

During the 1997 election, Blair was often compared to President Clinton. Blair, like President Clinton, was young, was married to a lawyer (Cherie Booth), and had focused the election on rebuilding the economy.

After winning the 1997 general election, Blair began to implement a series of political and economic reforms. He supported constitutional changes which established an elected post of mayor of London and removed all but 92 hereditary peers from the House of Lords. The Labour government also restructured his health and education systems with an infusion of new government funding.

As prime minister, Blair sought to end the conflict with Northern Ireland and to build on the recommendations of the U.S. mediator, GEORGE MITCHELL. In 1999, Britain joined the United States and the North Atlantic Treaty Organization (NATO) in 79 days of bombing in Kosovo to remove Yugoslav president SLOBODAN MILOŠEVIĆ's Serbian military from the country.

Blair was born on May 6, 1953, in Edinburgh, Scotland. He grew up in Durham, in the northern part of England, and attended Fettes College in Edinburgh from 1966 to 1971 before studying law at St. John's College of Oxford University (1975). While at Oxford, he was the lead singer of a rock band called Ugly Rumours. His participation in a rock band was another similarity to President Clinton, who played the saxophone.

After graduation from law school at Oxford University, Blair received an apprenticeship with Alexander Irvin, a Queen's counsel and a well-connected member of the Labour Party. Blair's interest in the Labour Party began during this period in his life when he started to meet senior members of the party.

Blair practiced law from 1976 to 1983, specializing in employment and industrial law and joined the Labour Party in 1976. After a series of labor strikes in 1978, the Tory Party, led by Margaret Thatcher, gained control of the government in 1979. The Tory, or Conservative, Party held control of the British government until Blair's Labour Party won in 1997.

In 1982, Blair made his first attempt at gaining public office. He ran for Parliament as Labour Party candidate from Beaconsfield, but lost the election. The following year, he was elected to Parliament with the Labour Party from Sedgefield, near his hometown of Durham. While in Parliament, Blair began steering the Labour Party away from its leftist base toward a more centrist orientation. He served as opposition speaker for treasury affairs from 1984 to 1987 and opposition speaker for trade and industry from 1987 to 1988. He was elected to the Labour Party's shadow cabinet in 1988, where he was responsible for energy and employment issues before becoming home secretary in 1992. As home secretary, Blair made the famous pledge that the Labour Party would be tough on crime and tough on the causes of crime, which had been stands that the Conservative Party had once taken. The Labour Party elected him to its National Executive Committee in 1992.

Blair and his wife had four children (Euan, Nicky, Kathryn, and Leo). Leo, who was born on May 20, 2000, became the first child born to a sitting prime minister in 152 years.

Following the September 11, 2001, attack on the World Trade Center and the Pentagon, Blair became a key ally to the United States in the war on terrorism. Blair joined with President GEORGE WALKER BUSH to send troops into Afghanistan in the fall of 2001 and to send troops into Iraq in the spring of 2003. The British and American forces led the coalition in both military actions.

Blumenthal, Sidney

(1948–   ) *assistant to the president*

After working as a journalist for most of his professional career, Sidney Blumenthal joined the Clinton administration on July 1, 1997, as an assistant to the president. Although nearly all senior staff in the White House had the title assistant to the president, they also had a descriptive title such as "press secretary" or "director of communications." Only Blumenthal had the simple title assistant to the president.

The lack of description in his job title reflected the lack of clear area of responsibility that Blumenthal had in the White House. He was hired to work on major speeches and develop a political message for the administration.

Blumenthal joined the administration after having worked as a staff writer for *The New Yorker* magazine for the previous five years. He had also worked for *Vanity Fair* and *The New Republic*, and had been a staff writer for the *Washington Post*. His relationship with President Clinton dated to the mid-eighties when both attended the Renaissance Weekends in Hilton Head, South Carolina, that PHILIP LADER organized. Blumenthal had then covered the 1992 presidential election as a reporter. During his years covering the Clinton administration for the press, he was at times accused of being too supportive and lacking objectivity.

By 1998 Blumenthal was spending much of his time in the White House on the Whitewater investigation, particularly as it pertained to MONICA LEWINSKY. He believed that Hillary Clinton had correctly described KENNETH W. STARR's investigation as part of a "vast right-wing conspiracy" and at one point called Starr "a prosecutor on a mad mission from God" and "a constitutional illiterate."

When the independent counsel sought his testimony with regard to his knowledge of President's Clinton's relationship with Monica Lewinsky, he refused to testify, stating that he had executive privilege. Blumenthal's argument was denied by the Supreme Court, which ruled that executive privilege only pertained to matters of state, not personal matters.

After the impeachment of President Clinton in December 1998, Blumenthal came under fire for circulating rumors that Lewinsky had stalked President Clinton. A British reporter claimed that Blumenthal had given him the information about Lewinsky. Blumenthal fervently denied it, but was subsequently called by the House managers for his deposition on February 1, 1999. He became the only White House staff member to be called to testify by the House managers. The House managers were building a case against President Clinton for the trial in the Senate. The Senate acquitted President Clinton on February 12, 1999.

Blumenthal left the White House at the end of 1999, but was never a popular member of the White House staff. His political enemies referred to Blumenthal as "Sid Vicious." He later wrote an 800-page book about the Clinton administration entitled *The Clinton Wars* (2003), which focused primarily on the Whitewater and Monica Lewinsky investigations by Kenneth Starr.

Born on November 6, 1948, in Chicago, Illinois, Blumenthal received his A.B. from Brandeis University (1969).

Bonior, David Edward

(1945–   ) *member of the House of Representatives*

One of President Clinton's strongest advocates in Congress was Representative David Bonior of the 10th Congressional District in Michigan. Bonior was first elected to Congress in 1977, following in the Democratic sweep that brought Jimmy Carter into office. Bonior served in the House until 2003, when he left to mount a campaign for governor of Michigan.

By the time he left the House, Bonior had risen to the post of House minority whip, elected in 1991.

Bonior was an important ally of the Clinton administration in the House, frequently supporting major pieces of legislation that the administration introduced. Bonior actively worked to raise the minimum wage, a proposal championed by Senator EDWARD MOORE KENNEDY in the Senate and supported by the Clinton administration. In his role as minority whip, Bonior became the vote counter for the administration. Bonior worked closed with the White House to determine which members could be swayed to administration proposals. The administration and Bonior supported passage of the Violence Against Women Act in 1994, continuation of Title IX which bars sex discrimination in women's sports, and the Family Medical Leave Act of 1994.

One of the few times that Bonior clashed with the Clinton administration was over passage of the North American Free Trade Agreement (NAFTA). Bonior opposed NAFTA, arguing that the trade agreement would not protect workers' rights and could weaken environmental protections. The bill passed, in spite of Bonior's opposition, but this did not destroy the strong working relationship between Clinton and Bonior.

Part of the reason that Bonior remained popular with the administration was his strong voting record for civil rights and for labor issues. Both issues were important to Clinton and high on the administration's priorities for legislative action. Both the NAACP and the AFL-CIO gave Bonior a 100 percent rating on his voting in the House. Clinton was also dependent on these two organizations for support in his 1996 reelection campaign, which was a pragmatic reason to maintain strong relations with Bonior.

During the impeachment in the House in December 1998, Bonior remained a staunch defender of Clinton. He voted against impeachment, as did most Democrats in the House. Bonior and Clinton were both moderates, supporting traditional Democratic causes such as civil rights, labor, education, and women's issues. Their relationship during the eight years of the Clinton presidency was one of the strongest between any member of Congress and the president.

As a representative of the state of Michigan, which has the largest Muslim population in the United States, Bonior frequently sought to build bridges to the Muslim community. Dearborn, Michigan, has the largest Muslim population of any city in the United States. In 1998, Bonior was the keynote speaker at the American Muslim annual national convention in Hempstead, New York. He was also a speaker at the national convention of the Islamic Society of North America in St. Louis, Missouri. Not surprisingly, Bonior often was involved in issues regarding immigration. In 1996 Bonior voted for the Chrysler-Berman Amendment to H.R. 2202. The bill allowed immigrants to bring their adult relatives to the United States. He successfully blocked efforts to ban "chain migration," allowing relatives into the country, in spite of efforts by the administration to halt the practice. The Department of Commerce, Bureau of the Census, projected that this practice would result in a doubling of the United States population during the 21st century. This was one of the few conflicts that Bonior had with the Clinton administration and one he prevailed in.

Born June 6, 1945, in Detroit, Michigan, Bonior received his B.A. from the University of Iowa (1967) and his M.A. from Chapman College in Orange, California (1972). Prior to running for Congress, Bonior served in the Michigan House of Representatives from 1973–77. He served in the U.S. House of Representatives from January 3, 1977, to January 3, 2003.

Boren, David Lyle

(1941–) *member of the Senate*

David Boren, a conservative Democrat, served in the Oklahoma House of Representatives (1967–75), as Oklahoma's governor (1975–79), and U.S. senator (1979–94) before resigning from the Senate to become president of the University of Oklahoma. Boren was the son of Lyle H. Boren, who served in the U.S. House of Representatives (D-Okla.) and was a protégé of Speaker Sam Rayburn.

As governor of Oklahoma, David Boren was the youngest governor in the nation. In 1979, he was named by *Time Magazine* as one of America's most promising young leaders. After serving two terms in the state House of Representatives and one term as governor, Boren successfully ran for the U.S. Senate in 1979, then rewarded his state for its electoral support with a host of special-interest legislation, including funding for the Oklahoma Summer Art Institute and the Oklahoma Foundation for Excellence. In 1990, Boren was reelected to the Senate with 83 percent of the vote against Republican challenger Stephen Jones.

During his tenure in the Senate, Boren served on the finance committee and the agriculture committee. He rose to chair of the Subcommittee on Tax Policy of the Committee on Finance. However, he gained the most attention as the chair of the Senate Select Committee on Intelligence, where he was known as a military hawk.

Boren gained national attention over several of his votes in the Senate. During the Senate hearings over the confirmation of Clarence Thomas for the U.S. Supreme Court during the GEORGE HERBERT WALKER BUSH administration, Boren actively supported Thomas. He was one of the few Democrats in the Senate to do so. Boren's father, who remained active in Oklahoma Democratic politics, lobbied his son to oppose the Thomas nomination. During the

Clinton administration, Boren became the swing vote on the 1993 energy tax bill. Major energy corporations, many of which had operations in Oklahoma, opposed the tax. They mounted a campaign in Oklahoma to oppose the legislation, including radio and television advertisements and rallies across the state. Their message in the state was "write, phone, or fax Senator Boren and tell him that you oppose this unfair tax that will cost Oklahoma thousands of jobs." One of the groups that targeted Boren, Citizens for a Sound Economy, was heavily supported by Exxon, General Motors, and General Electric, which would have lost profits had the tax been imposed. Boren voted against the bill in the Senate Finance Committee, effectively blocking it from further action.

Boren opposed the Clinton administration on other issues, including the administration's proposal for most-favored-nation trade status for China. Although the administration was committed to gaining its approval in the Congress, Boren became a leading opponent within his own party. Boren argued that the human rights violations within China should deny them any trade benefits. His views on most-favored-nation status for China were not new to the Clinton administration, given Boren's long-standing opposition. In 1992, Boren had joined a U.S. Senate delegation (consisting of Sen. Claiborne Pell, D-R.I., and Sen. Carl Levin, D-Mich.) to Beijing, China, to discuss problems with human rights violations.

Throughout Boren's tenure in the U.S. Senate, rumors of his homosexuality followed him. During his 1978 campaign for the Senate, he was forced by the continuing rumors to swear on a Bible that he was not homosexual. He repeatedly denied the allegation, noting that he was married with children.

Born on April 21, 1941, Boren received a B.A. degree from Yale University (1963), a master's degree from Oxford University as a

Rhodes scholar (1965), and a J.D. from the University of Oklahoma College of Law (1968). He spent four years on the faculty of Oklahoma Baptist University, where he was chairman of the Department of Political Science and chairman of the Division of Social Science.

Bowles, Erskine B.

(1945–) *White House chief of staff; White House deputy chief of staff; administrator, Small Business Administration*

Erskine Bowles was named assistant to the president and White House chief of staff after the departure of chief of staff LEON EDWARD PANETTA at the end of the first term.

Bowles joined the administration in 1993 as the administrator of the Small Business Administration, but in July 1994 President Clinton made a number of changes in the senior White House staff. Chief of Staff THOMAS FRANKLIN McLARTY III was moved to the position of counselor to the president, and Office of Management and Budget (OMB) director Leon Panetta was moved to the position of White House chief of staff. When President Clinton named Panetta as his new chief of staff, he also named Bowles as his deputy. Bowles left that position in December 1995 to return to Charlotte, North Carolina, and helped to found Carousel Capital. One year later, in December 1996, President Clinton asked Bowles to return to the White House as chief of staff.

Throughout the 1992 presidential campaign, Bowles had been a major fund-raiser for the Clinton-Gore campaign. During the presidential transition, Bowles organized the December 1992 economic summit in Little Rock, Arkansas, for President-elect Clinton. Bowles, a North Carolina investment banker, had known President and Mrs. Clinton for a number of years, having met them at PHILIP

LADER's Renaissance Weekends on Hilton Head Island, South Carolina. Lader, who had been McLarty's deputy chief of staff in the White House, was named administrator of the Small Business Administration in October 1994, replacing Bowles.

In his role as chief of staff, Bowles continued to bring to the White House a strong sense of organization and structure, as had Panetta. All correspondence and all meetings with the president were managed through the chief of staff's office. Bowles tried to minimize the number of staff and cabinet officers who sought to meet with the president and keep the agenda focused. One of the management problems that chief of staff McLarty faced in the first year of the administration was the constant flow of people in and out of President Clinton's office. Both Panetta and Bowles sought to control the flow of people and to keep the president's schedule less hectic. Bowles became particularly effective at ensuring punctuality at meetings. Meetings that he conducted and that the president conducted would start and end on time, which had failed to happen during the first year and half of the administration. As chief of staff, Bowles also oversaw the congressional liaison office, scheduling, personnel, the counsel's office, and the National Security Council.

Although Bowles had little involvement with the Whitewater land deal investigation by the independent counsel, he was brought in after he helped WEBSTER HUBBELL find legal work, after Hubbell was convicted of improper billing of clients at the Rose Law Firm in Little Rock, Arkansas. In 1997 Bowles also became involved in responding to the independent counsel's investigation of the 1996 Clinton-Gore campaign finances. Bowles had originally told President Clinton that he would stay on the job as chief of staff only one year, but at the end of 1997 he was persuaded by the president to remain for another year. As 1998 began, the independent counsel, KENNETH W.

STARR, aggressively pursued the Monica Lewinsky investigation. Bowles then acted as the investigation liaison, while President Clinton and other members of the White House staff focused their energies on the president's response and on damage control.

During 1998, Bowles tried to remain out of the White House discussions on the Monica Lewinsky investigation, leaving the White House counsel's office and a select group of political advisers to deal with the Starr investigation. Bowles kept the majority of White House staff directed at policy issues and completely out of the Starr investigation. According to Bowles, "Nobody else spends time on it—none—and that's a plus."

During the spring of 1998, Bowles devoted much of his time to moving forward antismoking legislation being considered in Congress. He worked closely with both Democratic and Republican leaders in Congress to have the bill passed. In the end, the bill failed. Bowles believed that it had been defeated by Senate Majority Leader CHESTER TRENT LOTT (R-Miss.), who had given Bowles assurances that it would pass, but then failed to support it. According to one White House staffer, "Erskine felt double-crossed."

Bowles resigned in November 1998 as chief of staff. After leaving the White House, he considered running in the 2000 gubernatorial race in North Carolina. Governor James B. Hunt, Jr., the popular four-term Democratic governor, did not seek another term in 2000. However, Bowles decided against the race for governor and chose instead to run for a Senate seat in 2002. He won the Democratic nomination and ran against Republican ELIZABETH HANFORD DOLE, wife of former senator ROBERT (BOB) JOSEPH DOLE. Dole won the election.

Bowles's father, Hargrove "Skipper" Bowles, who died at the age of 66 of Lou Gehrig's disease in 1986, had run in 1972 as the Democratic nominee for governor, but lost in a tight election. Many Republicans around the country won as part of the Republican sweep on the coat tails of President RICHARD MILHOUS NIXON's 1972 landslide victory. Erskine Bowles had been his father's campaign manager.

Born on August 8, 1945, in Greensboro, North Carolina, Bowles graduated with a B.A. in business administration from the University of North Carolina (1967) and a M.B.A. in business administration from Columbia University (1969). From 1969 to 1972 he was an associate with Morgan Stanley & Co. in New York City, and left in 1972 to run his father's unsuccessful campaign for governor. From 1973 to 1975 Bowles was vice president of corporate finance for Interstate Securities Corporation in Charlotte, North Carolina. In 1975 he founded Bowles Hollowell Conner & Co. in Charlotte, North Carolina, where he served as chairman and chief executive officer (1975–93).

Soon after leaving the White House in 1998, Governor James Hunt of North Carolina named Bowles to head a blue ribbon commission, the Rural Prosperity Task Force, to study the economic conditions of rural North Carolina. He also returned to Charlotte, North Carolina, as the managing director of Carousel Capital. In January 1999 Bowles was named a general partner in the New York equity firm Forstmann Little.

During his tenure as chief of staff, Bowles accepted only a nominal salary of $1.00 per year, saying that he viewed his work in the White House as a public service.

Bradley, William (Bill) Warren

(1943–) *challenged Vice President Al Gore in 2000 primaries for the Democratic Party's nomination for president, member of the Senate*

Former senator Bill Bradley challenged Vice President ALBERT (AL) GORE, JR., in the primaries for the Democratic Party's nomination for president in 2000. Gore won the nomination, easily beating Bradley.

Born on July 28, 1943, in Crystal City, Missouri, Bradley graduated as an all-star basketball player from Crystal City High School, where he was twice named an All-American. He scored over 3,000 points in his high school basketball career. He was also president of the Missouri Association of Student Councils his senior year in high school. After receiving scholarship offers from 75 colleges, he chose Princeton University. He graduated from Princeton University (1965) and then received his M.A., with honors, from Oxford University as a Rhodes scholar (1968). In 1964, he was captain of the U.S. Olympic basketball team that won a gold medal in Tokyo.

When Bradley returned from England, he joined the U.S. Air Force Reserve, and was on active duty for six months. He remained in the reserves until 1978, rising to the rank of first lieutenant.

After his initial tour on active duty in the Air Force Reserve, Bradley returned to basketball. He then began a career as a star forward for the New York Knickerbockers basketball team. In 1976 Bradley wrote a book, *Life on the Run*, describing his experience with the team. After his basketball career, Bradley opted for a political career and in 1978 successfully ran as a Democrat for the U.S. Senate from New Jersey. When asked whether a former basketball player was qualified to serve in the Senate, Bradley responded, "The question is not whether a professional basketball player can be a good United States senator, but whether he can work with people. Does he have the qualities of character is the question—and they are as likely to be found among electricians, lawyers, doctors, businessmen." In the middle of his third term in the Senate, he announced his retirement. In a speech in August 1995, Bradley stated that he would not seek a fourth term to the Senate. In early 1996, he released another book, *Time Present, Time Past*, describing his career in the Senate. When Bradley announced his retirement from the Senate, President Clinton issued a statement calling Bradley "a voice for civility." Bradley left the Senate in January 1997.

When Bradley announced his retirement from the Senate, he criticized the political system in general and explained his retirement by stating that "politics is broken." But he noted in an interview that he would remain involved in causes. "The mistake is to assume that to be in public life today you have to be in elected office. I'm leaving the Senate, but I'm not leaving public life." Many believed that he had left the Senate to run for the presidency, but he denied it.

By 1998 Bradley appeared to be planning a run for the presidency, and in 1999 he declared that he would run. By August 1999 Bradley had successfully raised over $9 million for his campaign, only $2 million less than the $11 million that Gore had raised. Bradley was endorsed by Senators Bob Kerrey (D-Neb.), Paul Wellstone (D-Minn.), and DANIEL PATRICK MOYNIHAN (D-N.Y.).

In December 1999, the *Washington Post* headlined a story on Bradley called "Bradley: Meandering toward a Candidacy," which detailed how Bradley had left the Senate with the full intention of running for the presidency in 2000. As the spring of 2000 began, Bradley tried to build momentum in the primaries to take the Democratic Party nomination from Vice President Al Gore. Bradley was the only serious challenger to Gore in the 2000 primaries. The two held a series of debates during the primaries, in which Bradley's key issues became campaign finance reform, universal health care, gun control, and fighting child poverty. But Bradley's campaign never caught fire with most Democrats.

Bradley received substantial criticism from many Democrats for his position on health care reform during the 2000 campaign. While he advocated universal health care in the 2000 campaign, he had failed to support it during the health care debate in 1993 and 1994, while he was in the Senate. His lack of support for the Clinton administration health care reform plan was considered by many Democrats a serious problem for his candidacy. Bradley pursued the Democratic nomination on a platform of political independence from the White House and as a politician who supported bipartisanship. However, many Democrats viewed Bradley as a political outsider who failed to support party positions on major policy initiatives. As a result, he lost the Democratic Party nomination to Al Gore.

Breaux, John Berlinger
(1944–) *member of the Senate*

John Breaux, a moderate Democrat from Louisiana, first entered the U.S. Senate in 1987 after serving in the U.S. House of Representatives from 1972–87 representing the 7th Congressional District. Breaux was elected to the House in a special election, September 30, 1972. His experience in the House of Representatives began as a staff assistant to Congressman Edwin W. Edwards, where he was both a district assistant (1969–72) and legislative assistant (1968–69).

Breaux served on the Senate Commerce, Science and Transportation Committee and the Senate Finance Committee. He also served on the Rules and Administration Committee and the Special Committee on Aging. Breaux served as chairman of the Subcommittee on Social Security and Family Policy on the Finance Committee.

During his tenure in the Senate, Breaux built a record as a centrist, seeking to build coalitions of Democrats and Republicans. In 1992 Breaux succeeded President Clinton as chairman of the Democratic Leadership Council (DLC), which was a group of moderate Democrats who sought to move the Democratic Party from a liberal to a moderate political stance. Breaux had been one of the founding members of the DLC in 1985. President Clinton had been another of the founding members. In 1993 Breaux was elected Chief Democratic Whip in the Senate.

In the Senate, Breaux and Senator John Chafee (R-R.I.) founded the Senate's Centrist Coalition in 1995, which was a bipartisan caucus to seek broad support for major policy initiatives. By 2003, the Centrist Coalition had 33 senators involved. The coalition sought bipartisan agreements on the balanced budget, welfare reform, and health care reform. The Centrist Coalition, however, often became an obstacle for the Clinton administration, as did Breaux himself.

Although Breaux had been aligned with Clinton while at the Democratic Leadership Council, he often opposed or sought compromise solutions with Republicans to Clinton-sponsored legislation. For example, Breaux opposed the 1993 energy bill which included a British thermal unit (Btu) tax. As had DAVID LYLE BOREN (D-Okla.), Breaux opposed the energy bill fearing that the large oil and gas industry in Louisiana would be adversely affected. Breaux received substantial funds for his Senate campaigns from the energy industry. He was Senate cochair, along with Senator Kay Bailey Hutchison (R-Tex.) of the Congressional Oil and Gas Caucus. In addition to his opposition to the energy tax, Breaux regularly opposed strengthening environmental protection laws on industrial emissions. In 1996 when the Environmental Protection Agency (EPA) proposed regulations to strengthen pollution standards, Breaux opposed them as too costly.

In 1998, Breaux was named by the White House and House and Senate leaders to chair the National Bipartisan Commission on the

Future of Medicare. However, when the Clinton administration tried to broaden Medicare coverage in 1999 to include universal drug benefits, Breaux proved to be an obstacle. As he often did, Breaux opposed the initial bill that the Clinton administration introduced on drug benefits within the Medicare program. Rather than lobbying on behalf of the Clinton bill, Breaux lobbied for a new bill that Republicans preferred. Breaux developed a compromise, less costly proposal on drug benefits with Senator Bill Frist (R-Tenn.). However, the proposal ultimately failed.

The issue of amending the Individual Retirement Act (IRA) provided another conflict between the Clinton administration and Breaux. When the Republicans in the Senate tried to expand the legislation governing how Individual Retirement Act (IRA) accounts could be used, the Clinton administration opposed the legislation as too costly but Breaux supported the legislation.

Born on March 1, 1944, in Crowley, Louisiana, Breaux received his B.A. from Southwestern Louisiana University (1964), now the University of Louisiana at Lafayette, and his J.D. from the Louisiana State University School of Law in Baton Rouge (1967). He practiced law with the firm of Brown, McKernan, Ingram & Breaux from 1967–68. Louisiana State University's Reilly Center for Media & Public Affairs created the annual John Breaux Symposium. The symposium focuses on the role of politics and the media.

Breyer, Stephen Gerald

(1938–) *associate justice of the Supreme Court*

Stephen Breyer was one of President Clinton's two nominees, along with RUTH BADER GINSBERG (appointed in 1993), to the United States Supreme Court. Breyer was nominated on May 17, 1994, and confirmed by the Senate on July 29, 1994, by a vote of 87 to 9. He was sworn into office on August 2, 1994, as the 108th Supreme Court justice.

Breyer replaced Justice Harry A. Blackmun. Prior to his nomination on the Supreme Court, Breyer served on the U.S. Court of Appeals for the First Circuit. From 1990–94 Breyer was chief judge of the court. He had served on the U.S. Court of Appeals since his confirmation by the Senate on December 10, 1980. He was appointed by President Jimmy Carter on November 13, 1980. The position on the U.S. Court of Appeals had been a new seat created by an expansion of the federal courts, in legislation sponsored by the Carter administration.

Born on August 15, 1938, Breyer received his A.B. degree from Stanford University (1959), his B.A. degree from Oxford University where he was a Marshall scholar (1961), and a J.D. from Harvard Law School (1964). After graduating from law school, Breyer became a law clerk to Arthur J. Goldberg, associate justice, United States Supreme Court (1964–65). He served in the U.S. Army in 1957.

After his work as a law clerk to Justice Goldberg, Breyer moved to the Department of Justice. There he was special assistant to the assistant attorney general, Donald Turner, in the Antitrust Division. In 1967 he left the Department of Justice to join the faculty of Harvard Law School. He was assistant professor of law from 1967 to 1970 and professor of law from 1970–80. In addition to his appointment at Harvard Law School, he was on the faculty at the Kennedy School of Government at Harvard University from 1977–90. He was also a visiting professor at the College of Law in Sydney, Australia, in 1975 and at the University of Rome in 1993. Breyer remained involved with the Harvard Law School during his tenure on the U.S. Supreme Court, as one of three judges evaluating student arguments in the finals of Harvard Law School's Ames Moot Court Competition.

In addition to his faculty role, Breyer was assistant special prosecutor of the Watergate Special Prosecution Task Force in 1973, special counsel on the Subcommittee on Administrative Practices of the U.S. Senate Judiciary Committee in 1974–75, and chief counsel of the Senate Judiciary Committee in 1979–80. Breyer also served as a member of the Judicial Conference of the United States from 1990–94, and as a member of the United States Sentencing Commission from 1985–89. He was a trustee of the University of Massachusetts from 1974–81, and has been a trustee of the Dana Farber Cancer Institute since 1977.

During his confirmation hearings, Breyer noted that the role of a jurist in interpreting the law was to examine the legislative history. His positions while on the Supreme Court have been moderate. His decisions on the Court included a requirement that Boy Scouts should accept gay scoutmasters (2000), disabled people could sue states under the federal ADA law (2000), a finding that *Roe v. Wade* is settled law (1998), Congress could regulate guns in school under the commerce clause, and states could restrict cigarette ads beyond federal rules (2001). He consistently sided with the moderate and liberal wing of the Court, often firmly disagreeing with Justices Rehnquist, Scalia, and Thomas. Some have noted that President Clinton appointed Breyer to be an intellectual counterweight to Justice Antonin Scalia, a conservative on the Court.

Brown, Jesse

(1944–2002) *secretary of veterans affairs*

Jesse Brown was named secretary of veterans affairs by President Clinton, and sworn into office on January 22, 1993. Brown served until July 1997, when he resigned for health reasons. He died in 2002 of amyotrophic lateral sclerosis, commonly known as Lou Gehrig's disease. TOGO WEST succeeded Brown after HERSHEL GOBER, deputy secretary of veterans affairs, failed to win Senate confirmation.

After graduating from Hyde Park High School in Detroit in 1963, Brown enlisted in the marines. He was soon sent to Vietnam, during some of the fiercest fighting of the war. During a firefight in Da Nang in 1965, Brown's right arm was shattered, paralyzing it for life. He returned to the United States for medical treatment, spending a year of physical therapy at Great Lakes Naval Hospital near Chicago.

Brown found that there were few jobs in the late 1960s for African-American men with one arm. He sought assistance from the Disabled American Veterans (DAV) Association, which offered Brown a job as a national service officer in its Chicago office. As a staffer in the DAV from 1967–73, Brown handled the interview process for veterans seeking assistance in their veterans benefits. This role became critical to his understanding of the bureaucracy within the Veterans Administration, an agency he would later head.

During his long association with the Disabled American Veterans Association, Brown held increasingly powerful jobs. After working in the Chicago office for six years, Brown moved to Washington, D.C., in 1973 to the national office. There he worked in the legislative section, lobbying for changes and improvements to various programs affecting veterans. Nine years later, in 1982, he assumed the position of executive director of the association.

Under Brown the DAV became part of a coalition of veterans groups that sought to have the Veterans Administration elevated to cabinet rank. Partly due to his aggressive lobbying of President Ronald Reagan's administration, Reagan sought and received congressional authorization to create the Department of Veterans Affairs. The department became a cabinet-level agency in 1989, assuming the functions of the Veterans Administration.

The centerpiece of Brown's agenda for the Department of Veterans Affairs was increasing health care benefits for veterans. He argued that a core group of veterans with severe disabilities was the priority clientele of the veterans health care system, including veterans hospitals. He sought a broader use of veterans hospitals for all veterans. To support the costs of increasing the clientele in veterans hospitals, Brown proposed that Medicare and Medicaid reimburse the hospitals for treatment, as they did private hospitals.

One of Brown's most aggressive projects was seeking answers to why so many veterans of the Persian Gulf War in 1991 had unexplained illnesses. He used the research facilities within the Department of Veterans Affairs to explore possible sources of the illnesses, including the weapons and materials that were used by the soldiers, and the desert environment in which they lived for several months. Although no specific cause was ever found for the illnesses, Brown succeeded in gaining enactment of laws that provided benefits to Persian Gulf War veterans who had such unexplained illnesses.

Brown was one of four African Americans brought into the Clinton cabinet in 1993. The others were RONALD H. BROWN, Department of Commerce; ALPHONSO MICHAEL (MIKE) ESPY, Department of Agriculture; and HAZEL O'LEARY, Department of Energy. Clinton had the greatest ethnic diversity of any cabinet in history, as part of his commitment to make the cabinet "look like America." Since Lyndon Johnson appointed the first African American to his cabinet in 1966, only one African American has been part of the president's cabinet at any given time. Clinton became the first president to have more than one African American in his cabinet, and he appointed African Americans to departments that had not had minority cabinet officers before.

Brown was born on March 27, 1944, and died on August 17, 2002. He received his NSO training certificate from the Catholic University of America (1967), his Associate's Degree with honors from Chicago City College (1972), and attended Roosevelt University in Chicago from 1972–73.

Brown, Lee Patrick
(1947–) *director, Office of National Drug Control Policy*

Lee Brown was appointed by President Clinton to the cabinet-level position of director of the Office of National Drug Control Policy (ONDCP), a position widely referred to as "drug czar." He was confirmed by unanimous vote in the U.S. Senate and was sworn into office on June 21, 1993. Brown was one of several cabinet-level appointments of African Americans by President Clinton. Within the cabinet, appointments of African Americans also included JESSE BROWN, secretary of veterans affairs; RONALD H. BROWN, secretary of commerce; ALPHONSO MICHAEL (MIKE) ESPY, secretary of agriculture; and HAZEL O'LEARY, secretary of energy.

Lee Brown left the administration in 1997 to run for mayor of Houston, Texas. Elected on December 6, 1997, Brown was inaugurated on January 2, 1998, and was reelected in 1999 and again in 2001 to his third and final term.

As director of the Office of National Drug Control Policy, a White House staffing unit created during the Reagan administration, Brown was responsible for creating strategies for ending illegal drug use within the United States. In addition, the office was responsible for creating strategies to break the illegal drug trade in the United States, particularly from Latin American countries. Brown had relatively low visibility during his tenure in the Clinton administration, largely due to other priorities of the White House.

Born on October 4, 1947, in Wewoka, Oklahoma, Brown graduated with a B.S. from Fresno State University (1964). Brown became a patrolman in 1960 with the local police department, where he worked for eight years. After completing his degree at Fresno State University, Brown pursued a master's degree in sociology at San Jose State University (1968) and a Ph.D. in criminology from the University of California at Berkeley (1970). While working on his doctorate, Brown left the police force in San Jose and established the Department of Administration of Justice at Portland State University. In 1972 he joined the faculty of Howard University, becoming associate director of the Institute for Urban Affairs and Research, and professor of public administration. He served as director of criminal justice programs.

Fifteen years after first joining a police force, Brown returned to law enforcement (1975–82) as the sheriff of Multomah County, in Portland, Oregon. He left Oregon after being offered the position in Atlanta, Georgia, as the public safety commissioner (police commissioner), where he worked from 1982–90. In 1990 he was offered and accepted the top position in law enforcement as New York City's police commissioner, where he stayed until 1992. After leaving New York City, Brown became a Distinguished Professor at Texas Southern University, and director of the university's Black Male Initiative Program. Noteworthy among his roles in law enforcement was his election as president of the International Association of Police Chiefs.

Brown, Ronald H.
(1941–1996) *secretary of commerce*

Ronald Brown was nominated by President Clinton on December 12, 1992, and confirmed by the Senate on January 21, 1993, as secretary of commerce. He was sworn into office on Jan-

Ronald H. Brown *(Department of Commerce)*

uary 22, 1993. Brown joined three other African Americans in the president's cabinet: ALPHONSO MICHAEL (MIKE) ESPY, secretary of commerce; HAZEL O'LEARY, secretary of energy; and LEE PATRICK BROWN, secretary of veterans affairs. Ronald Brown became the first African American to serve as secretary of commerce. MICHAEL (MICKEY) KANTOR replaced Brown as secretary of commerce.

Brown was killed in an airplane crash during a storm near Dubrovnik, Croatia, on April 4, 1996. Thirty-four members of an official delegation from the United States were killed when their airplane crashed on a fog-shrouded mountainside in Croatia. The delegation on the plane included representatives of the Department of State, the Department of Defense, the National Security Council, and business leaders. Brown had been on a tour of

Croatia and Bosnia and Herzegovina with U.S. government officials and business leaders, exploring investment opportunities within the Balkans region.

Brown and his delegation began their tour on April 2, when they flew to Tuzla, the base for American soldiers taking part in the North Atlantic Treaty Organization (NATO) peace-keeping mission in Bosnia. The group met with Bosnia businessmen on April 3, then flew to Dubrovnik, Croatia, to meet with Croatian officials. Using a Boeing T-43A aircraft, a military plane similar to a commercial 737 Boeing aircraft, the group headed for Cilipi Airport, located southeast of Dubrovnik. However, heavy rains and strong winds brought the plane down near the top of Mount Sveti Ivan. Some suggested that pilot error, not the storm, brought the plane down, suggesting that the pilot made a wrong turn descending to the airport.

Prior to joining the Clinton administration, Brown had been a partner with the Washington, D.C., law firm of Patton, Boggs and Blow since 1981. At Patton, Boggs and Blow Brown focused most of his work as a lobbyist for foreign governments. He served as chairman of the Democratic National Committee while at the law firm, from 1989–93. Brown's political career began in 1979, when he was deputy campaign manager for Senator EDWARD M. KENNEDY's campaign for president, deputy chairman of the Democratic National Committee (1981–85), and convention campaign manager for Jesse Jackson in 1988.

Brown's tenure as secretary of commerce included a variety of trade missions, which often included representatives of large corporations seeking investment opportunities in other countries. Among the trade missions that Brown led were those to South Africa (1993); Mexico (1993); Saudi Arabia, Jordan, Israel, West Bank and Gaza, and Egypt (1994); Russia (1994); Brazil, Argentina, and Chile (1994); China and Hong Kong (1994); Ireland (1994); India (1995), and Senegal (1995). Brown was on a trade mission to Yugoslavia in 1996 when he was killed in the plane crash.

Brown actively encouraged representatives of large corporations to join the trade missions, for which they paid all of their expenses including costs on government planes. However, the trade missions became controversial when allegations arose that companies that had made contributions to the Democratic Party were given priority on the trips. Brown denied the allegations, arguing that companies routinely donated to both parties, and no priority had ever been given for political reasons.

Born on August 1, 1941, in Washington, D.C., Brown was raised in New York City. Brown received his B.A. from Middlebury College (1962), his J.D. from St. John's University (1970), and served four years in the U.S. Army between college and law school. After graduating from law school, Brown became general counsel to the National Urban League (1971) in New York City. After five years in New York City, he became the National Urban League's vice president for Washington, D.C., operations (1976–79). In 1980, Brown became an attorney for the Senate Judiciary Committee and in 1981 was named its first African-American chief counsel.

Browner, Carol M.
(1955–   ) *administrator, Environmental Protection Agency*

Carol Browner was nominated by President Clinton in January 1993 as the administrator of the Environmental Protection Agency (EPA) and remained at EPA throughout the administration. She became the longest-serving administrator in the history of the agency after completing two terms in the position.

Browner, who had worked for two years in ALBERT (AL) GORE, JR.'s Senate office, was brought into the administration by Gore. During the transition after the 1992 election, Gore was responsible for creating the administration's environmental focus and for developing candidates for senior positions that oversaw environmental issues. Both Browner and KATHLEEN MCGINTY, director of the Office of Environmental Policy in the White House, were former Gore staffers.

Among the issues that Browner dealt with in the Environmental Protection Agency was the Superfund cleanup, in concert with the Department of Energy. The Clinton administration was committed to increasing the EPA's work on the numerous locations where the federal government was overseeing toxic cleanups. She also aggressively moved to increase fines on business and industry that violated the Clean Water Act and the Clean Air Act.

In testimony before the House of Representatives Subcommittee on Energy and Environment of the Committee on Science in May 1997, Brown described the Clinton administration's efforts to reduce pollution and improve air quality. "The Clinton administration views protecting public health and environment as one of its highest priorities," she said. "We have prided ourselves on protecting the most vulnerable among us, especially our children, from the harmful effects of pollution. When it comes to the Clean Air Act, I take very seriously the responsibility that Congress gave me to set air quality standards that protect public health." The Clean Air Act gave the Environmental Protection Agency the authority to set national standards for air pollutants.

Browner's experience in regulatory issues stemmed from her role as secretary of the Department of Environmental Regulation in Florida from 1991 to 1993. She had been appointed to the position by Governor Lawton Chiles. Prior to her role in Florida state government, Browner had worked in Washington, D.C., for Senator Lawton Chiles (D-Fla.) from 1986 to 1988. She had also been the legislative director for then-senator Al Gore (D-Tenn.) from 1989 to 1991.

Born on December 16, 1955, in Miami, Florida, Browner graduated with an Associate's Degree from Miami Dade Community College (1974), with a B.A. from the University of Florida (1977), and a J.D. from the University of Florida Law School (1979). After law school, she served as the general counsel for the Florida House of Representatives Government Operations Committee (1980) and then worked for Citizen Action, a grassroots consumer group in Washington, D.C.

Bruce, Carol Elder

(1949–   ) *independent counsel investigating Bruce Babbitt, secretary of interior*

Carol Elder Bruce was appointed by a three-judge panel on March 19, 1998, to investigate BRUCE EDWARD BABBITT, secretary of interior, for his handling of an Indian casino license. Charges were brought against Babbitt for his denial of a license for a casino by three bands of the Chippewa Indian tribe after allegations were brought that the denial was based on a donation to the Democratic National Committee by rival Indian tribes.

During the fall of 1997, the Department of Justice held a 90-day investigation into Babbitt's rejection of the Chippewa's application to open a new casino. The Chippewa had applied for a license in 1995 to establish a casino at a pari-mutuel racetrack in Hudson, Wisconsin, an hour's drive from Minneapolis. Babbitt rejected the application in July 1995. The application also needed the approval of Governor Tommy Thompson, who had objected to any expansion of gambling in Wisconsin.

After Babbitt announced the application's rejection, several casino-operating Indian tribes in Minnesota and Wisconsin donated $270,000 to the Democratic National Committee because they did not want the competition. After its investigation, the Department of Justice determined that there was reason to pursue an independent counsel investigation, and on February 11, 1998, Attorney General JANET RENO asked for an independent counsel. Babbitt and the Bureau of Indian Affairs in the Department of Interior insisted that their decision had not been made for political reasons but because the community of Hudson did not want the casino.

On March 19, 1998, the three-judge panel appointed an independent counsel, Carol Elder Bruce, to investigate Babbitt's handling of the license. The issue became of interest to investigators when Babbitt admitted telling a lawyer for the tribes that then-deputy White House Chief of Staff HAROLD ICKES had pressed him to make a decision in the case. The 18-month-long independent counsel investigation found that Babbitt was not guilty of any wrongdoing and had made his decision without consideration of any donation to the Democratic Party. The investigation ended on October 14, 1999, when Bruce announced that she would not seek indictments against Babbitt or anyone else.

Bruce was a former associate of CHARLES F. C. RUFF, who was at the time the counsel to the president. She and Ruff defended Senator John Glenn (D-Ohio) during a Senate Ethics Committee investigation of allegations that Glenn did favors for wealthy campaign contributor Charles Keating, Jr., in connection with the savings and loan scandal. Both Ruff and Bruce were members of the Washington, D.C., law firm of Covington and Burley at the time.

Born on June 7, 1949, in East Orange, New Jersey, Elder graduated with a B.A. from George Washington University (1971) and with a J.D. from George Washington University Law School (1974). She was an assistant U.S. attorney for the District of Columbia from 1975 to 1985. During her 10 years in the U.S. attorney's office, she helped to prosecute Edwin P. Wilson and Frank E. Terpil, former Central Intelligence Agency (CIA) agents accused of assisting Libyan terrorists. In 1988, she served as the deputy independent counsel investigating Attorney General Edmund Meese. Meese was never charged by the independent counsel's office.

After the Babbitt investigation, she was named an international criminal law specialist for the Bosnian War Crimes Tribunal for the Coalition for International Justice (1996).

Bruce was a partner in the law firm of Tighe Patton Armstrong and Teasdale in Washington, D.C.

Burton, Danny (Dan) Lee
(1938–) *member of the House of Representatives*

Dan Burton, a conservative Republican from Indianapolis, Indiana, was first elected to the House of Representatives for the 6th Congressional District in 1982. As chairman of the House Government Reform Committee, Burton aggressively pursued President Clinton's campaign finances throughout 1997 and 1998. He was also a supporter of the impeachment movement in the House in 1998.

On September 4, 1998, Burton admitted to having an affair in 1983 that produced a son, but he provided no names. Burton revealed his affair after being told that *Vanity Fair* magazine was doing an exposé on him and would discuss the issue. The magazine never published the story, but it did appear on the Salon.com Web site. The admission seemed to have little effect on his political career, for he was reelected in November 1998, with 70 percent of the vote.

Burton served in the U.S. Army for two years, 1956–57 and the Army Reserves from 1957–62. Prior to running for office, in 1968

Burton established an insurance company called the Dan Burton Insurance Agency. Burton won a seat in the Indiana House of Representatives from 1967–69, then pursued a seat in the Indiana Senate. In 1968 he won a Senate seat that he held from 1969–71.

In 1970 he set his sights on the U.S. House of Representatives and ran for the seat held by the incumbent Democratic representative, Andy Jacobs, Jr., but Burton lost. He tried again in 1972 to capture Jacobs's seat, but lost in the Republican primary. Not content to stay out of politics, Burton again tried his hand at elective office and won a seat in the Indiana Senate, which he held for one term (1981–83). Two years after his move to the Indiana Senate, he sought to move to Washington, D.C., and ran for the U.S. House of Representatives. Burton was elected to the House in 1982 and has been continuously reelected since then.

Burton was a born-again Christian and outspoken conservative. When the Democrats controlled the House, Burton was often overshadowed by more moderate members of the Republican Party. However, following the 1994 Republican "revolution," in which conservative Republicans gained control of the House under the leadership of NEWTON (NEWT) LEROY GINGRICH, Burton became a leader of the conservative faction. He often introduced legislation that was primarily supported by conservative Republicans in the House.

For example, in 1995 Burton introduced legislation, known as the Burton Bill, that allowed foreign companies to be sued in American courts if they acquired assets formerly owned by Americans. Conservatives such as Burton supported the economic embargo of Cuba and punishment of any foreign company that did business with Cuba. The bill passed the House and the Senate after Cuba shot down two small planes piloted by Cuban Americans in 1996. President Clinton reluc-

tantly signed the Burton Bill into law following the public outcry against Fidel Castro and his attack on unarmed planes.

When Burton was appointed chairman of the Government Reform and Oversight Committee, he immediately began an investigation into allegations of illegal Democratic Party fund-raising for the 1996 election. Burton used his powerful committee for other investigations of the Clinton administration, including that of WEBSTER HUBBELL, a former law partner of Hillary Rodham Clinton in Little Rock, and that of the suicide of White House deputy counsel VINCENT W. FOSTER, JR. Burton was known for his intense dislike of President Clinton, at one point calling the president a "scumbag."

After President Clinton left office, he remained a favorite target of Representative Burton and his Government Reform Committee. Burton began an investigation into Clinton's pardon in the final days of the administration of financier Mark Rich. Burton routinely issued statements questioning the constitutionality of the pardon and attacking Clinton's reputation for months after Clinton left office.

Born on June 21, 1938, in Indianapolis, Burton attended Indiana University from 1958–59 and the Cincinnati Bible Seminary 1959–60.

Bush, George Herbert Walker
(1924–   ) *president, vice president*

George H. W. Bush served as the 41st president of the United States from 1989–93. Prior to his service as president, Bush had served as vice president of the United States from 1981–89 under President Ronald Reagan.

Born on June 12, 1924, Bush was a member of a wealthy New England family with strong ties to the New York banking community. His father, Prescott Bush, had served in the U.S. Senate from Connecticut from 1953–63, first defeating Abraham Ribicoff for the vacancy caused by the death of James O'Brien McMahon. Prescott Bush had been a partner in the Wall Street firm of Brown Brothers, Harriman and Company both before and after his decade in the Senate. The family lived in Greenwich, Connecticut.

Bush left New England after college rather than joining his father's banking firm. He moved to Texas where he joined Dresser Industries, an oil-field supply company. In 1953, he became the cofounder of the Zapata Petroleum Corporation and in 1954 became president of its subsidiary, Zapata Off-Shore Company. When Zapata Off-Shore Company became an independent company, Bush moved the firm from Midland, Texas, to Houston. He served as president of the company until 1964 and as chairman from 1964–66. He sold his interest in the company in 1966, when he ran for a seat in the U.S. House of Representatives.

His entrance into politics came two years prior, in 1964, when he ran for the U.S. Senate. As an active Republican within Harris County, Bush sought and won the state Republican nomination for the Senate seat. Although he won the nomination, he lost the election to Ralph Yarborough, the incumbent Democrat. Two years later he successfully ran for the U.S. House of Representatives and was reelected in 1968. He became the first Republican to win a House seat representing Houston.

During his two terms in the House, Bush had a mixed voting record, supporting positions that had both conservative and liberal sponsors. He opposed the public accommodations provision of the 1964 Civil Rights Act, arguing that moral persuasion at the local level was more often effective. During the brief period that Bush was in office during the Nixon administration, he publicly supported President Nixon on the Vietnam War. Yet he supported open-housing legislation and birth control programs, positions supported by moderate Republicans and Democrats.

In 1970, after four years in the House, Bush ran again for the U.S. Senate but lost to the Democratic candidate, Lloyd M. Bentsen, Jr. His loyalty to the Nixon administration was rewarded by his appointment as ambassador to the United Nations. He was confirmed unanimously by the U.S. Senate in February 1971. One of the most difficult tasks that Bush faced while at the United Nations was trying to preserve a General Assembly seat for the Republic of China (Taiwan). The United Nations denied these efforts and recognized the People's Republic of China (mainland China) as the sole representative of China. He was considered a strong negotiator and was widely praised within the Nixon administration for his work on the China issue.

Following the 1972 presidential election, Nixon asked Bush to take over as chair of the Republican National Committee. Bush assumed the role in early 1973, soon after Nixon was inaugurated for his second term. As the charges of involvement in the break-in at the Democratic National Committee's headquarters in the Watergate office building mounted against Richard Nixon, Bush continued to defend him. Not until the evidence proved overwhelming in early August 1974 did Bush write to Nixon seeking his resignation. Nixon resigned on August 8, 1974.

When Vice President Gerald Ford took over the reins of government following Nixon's resignation, he asked Bush to join the Ford administration. Ford gave Bush a blank check regarding the position he would like, and Bush chose the role of head of the U.S. Liaison Office in the People's Republic of China. Since the United States did not have formal diplomatic relations with China in 1974, the U.S. Liaison Office was the equivalent of the U.S.

embassy. Bush spent 14 months in Beijing during 1974 and 1975.

In 1975 Ford assigned Bush a new job, that of director of the Central Intelligence Agency (CIA). Congress had become increasingly distrustful of covert activities being conducted by the CIA and sought to rein in the agency. Most important, Congress accused the CIA of violating its own legislative mandate. Bush accepted the job and served from 1975 until 1977, when Gerald Ford left the White House.

Bush returned to Texas after the failed 1976 Ford reelection campaign. He became chairman of the First National Bank in Houston. But his interest in politics had not dimmed and he soon began to plan for a 1980 campaign for the presidency. He formally entered the race in May 1979. Bush stressed his broad experience in government during the primaries of 1980 and took generally moderate positions on issues. He stood in contrast to another Republican candidate, Ronald Reagan, who routinely expressed conservative positions on issues. At one point during the Republican primaries, Bush criticized the Reagan plan of cutting taxes while increasing military spending, arguing that this was tantamount to "voodoo economics." This description of Reagan's economic plan would become a problem for him both during the Reagan administration and during his own administration.

After Reagan won the primaries in 1980, he selected Bush as his vice presidential running mate. Bush brought geographic balance to the ticket (Reagan was from California), added substantial electoral support if he could deliver Texas, and brought political balance with his moderate credentials. The Reagan-Bush ticket won 44 states in the 1980 presidential election, beating the incumbent president Jimmy Carter and his vice president, Walter Mondale.

Reagan relied heavily on his White House staff for policy assistance, giving George H. W. Bush little substantive policy role. When John Hinckley shot President Reagan on March 30, 1981, Bush worked closely with the White House staff but did not assume the position of acting president. There was no transfer of power under the Twenty-fifth Amendment. However, four years later when President Reagan underwent surgery for colon cancer, he authorized Vice President Bush to serve as acting president while he was in surgery. Reagan did not assign power to Bush through the amendment, but stated they had a "long-standing arrangement." Bush served as acting president on July 13, 1985, from 11:28 A.M. until 7:22 P.M.

As vice president, the only constitutional role that Bush had was to preside over the Senate and to break ties, when necessary. Most of the assignments that the president gave to Bush involved international travel. As vice president, Bush traveled to more than 60 countries. He also served as chairman of the National Security Council's "crisis management" team, which encompassed task forces that looked at crime, terrorism, and drug smuggling. When Reagan became the 1984 nominee of the Republican Party, Bush became the administration's primary campaigner. The Reagan-Bush ticket won 49 states in the 1984 reelection campaign.

The most serious crisis of the Reagan administration was the Iran-contra affair, which Oliver North managed from his position in the National Security Council. Following the 1984 election, the issue heated up and by 1986 dominated the front pages of the newspapers. Reagan denied that he knew about the transfer of funds from the arms sale to Iran to the Nicaraguan contras, which violated the law. Bush also denied any involvement in the scheme or having attended meetings in which the issue was discussed. Several members of the Reagan administration were convicted of complicity in the Iran-contra affair. When Bush became president himself, he pardoned those convicted.

Barred by the Constitution from seeking a third term in office, Ronald Reagan returned to California in 1989. The 1988 election had provided George H. W. Bush the opportunity he had sought for many years: the chance to grab the golden ring of the presidency. In October 1987 Bush entered the presidential race. During the Republican primaries, he soon captured New Hampshire and then the southern states. At the Republican National Convention in August 1988 in New Orleans, Bush was unanimously nominated. As his running mate, Bush chose Senator Dan Quayle (R-Ind.). The theme of the campaign became a call for a "kinder, gentler nation."

The Democratic Party chose Governor Michael Dukakis of Massachusetts as its presidential contender, with Senator Lloyd Bentsen of Texas as his running mate. The campaign became surprisingly bitter, as Bush accused Dukakis of being a liberal with little connection to the current political orientation of America. Bush asserted that Dukakis would increase taxes, but that he would not, repeating often the pledge "Read my lips, no new taxes."

Bush ran a series of attack ads against Dukakis, including the famous Willie Horton ad suggesting that Dukakis was soft on crime. Following a bitter election, Bush won with 40 states and 53.4 percent of the popular vote. For the first time in his political career, Bush had taken on a decidedly negative bearing.

Following his inauguration in 1989, Bush became less combative with the Democrats in Congress than he had been with his Democratic opponent in the presidential election. With the Democrats controlling both houses of Congress, Bush sought few legislative initia-

tives and often allowed compromise positions on bills.

His greatest conflict with Congress came in 1990 when he needed to solve an impending federal budget crisis by raising taxes. Republicans tried to hold him to his pledge of "no new taxes," but his own budget director recommended supporting tax increases. His relationship with Republicans in Congress was forever damaged by his decision to raise taxes, and Democrats used the flip-flop as a campaign issue.

During his tenure, Bush filled two Supreme Court vacancies. The first came in 1990 when he nominated David H. Souter, a federal judge from New Hampshire. In 1991 Bush nominated Clarence Thomas to the Court. Thomas, an African American, was nominated to replace Thurgood Marshall, who had retired. Thomas was an ardent conservative, who was opposed by a broad coalition of activists. The most serious threat to his nomination came from a former staff member, Anita Hill, who accused Thomas of sexual harassment. After nationally televised and graphic testimony by Hill, the Senate confirmed Thomas by a 52-48 vote.

Two major military incursions took place during the four years of the Bush administration. The first was in December 1989 when Bush ordered U.S. troops into Panama to arrest General Manuel Noriega, the nation's dictator. Noriega was accused of masterminding a significant drug trade into the United States. The troops captured Noriega and brought him to Florida for trial. He was found guilty during the trial and sentenced to prison, where he currently is incarcerated.

The second military event occurred in 1990 when Iraq invaded Kuwait. The United States led a coalition of troops from other countries in early 1991 to remove Iraq from Kuwait. Bush worked closely with his secretary of state, James Baker, and his secretary of defense, Dick Cheney, in developing the military strategy to oust Iraqi troops from Kuwait. They also stationed thousands of U.S. troops in Saudi Arabia to prevent Iraq from also invading that nation. Bush's popularity rating rose to over 80 percent, which seemed to indicate an easy reelection campaign in 1992.

However, the economy continued to slump throughout the Bush presidency. Patrick Buchanan, a speechwriter for President Nixon and conservative talk show host, challenged Bush during the Republican primaries in 1992. Buchanan, although defeated in the primaries, forced Bush to move to a more conservative agenda.

Although the Bush-Quayle ticket was nominated by the Republican Party, it had become more vulnerable as a result of the Republican primaries. No longer was the president riding high from the success of liberating Kuwait, but was facing challenges within his own party on his economic policies. Buchanan attacked Bush for violating his own promise not to raise taxes.

When Bill Clinton was nominated by the Democratic Party in 1992 as its presidential candidate, he immediately realized that Bush was vulnerable on economic issues. The Bush administration had made its name through successful military decisions, not successful economic decisions. Unemployment was growing and the economy was sinking in 1992. The Clinton campaign motto became "It's the economy, stupid."

The 1992 campaign was complicated by the addition of HENRY ROSS PEROT as a candidate. Perot, who advocated a balanced budget and focused on economic issues, primarily attacked Bush for his failure to lift the economy. Clinton was relatively unscathed by Perot's candidacy. On November 3, 1992, Clinton successfully overcame both Bush and Perot to capture the presidency. Exit polls indicated that most of those who voted for Perot were Republicans. Perot had effectively denied Bush the presidency. Clinton won with 43 percent, with Bush garnering 38 percent and Perot 19 percent of the vote.

Bush, George Walker
(1946–   ) *president of the United States*

George Walker Bush, the 43rd president of the United States, succeeded Bill Clinton as president. Bush defeated Vice President Al Gore in the 2000 election to capture the Oval Office.

Bush was the son of GEORGE HERBERT WALKER BUSH, the 41st president of the United States. The Bush family became the second family in American history to have both a father and a son serve as president, with John Adams and his son John Quincy Adams being the other father and son to serve. Both John Adams (1797–1803) and his son John Quincy Adams (1825–29) served only one term each.

Before entering the national limelight, George W. Bush had held elective office as governor of Texas. Bush, first elected as governor in 1994, was reelected to a second term with 65 percent of the vote. He left in midterm after winning the presidency, turning over the office in Texas to the lieutenant governor who by law became governor.

Bush was born on July 6, 1946, in New Haven, Connecticut, where his father and grandfather lived. Prescott Bush, Bush's grandfather, had been the U.S. senator from Connecticut. Bush, the eldest of six children of George and Barbara Pierce Bush, had five siblings: Jeb, Neil, Marvin, Dorothy, and Robin. Robin died of leukemia in 1953 at the age of three. The family moved to Midland, Texas, in the mid-1950s when George H. W. Bush formed an oil company there. George W. Bush, however, returned to the northeast for his education. Following in his father's footsteps, Bush attended Philips Andover Academy in Massachusetts and Yale University (1968). While his father had pursued a law degree, George W. Bush pursued an M.B.A. at Harvard Business School (1975).

After graduating from Yale with a bachelor's degree in 1968, Bush joined the Texas Air National Guard and learned to fly fighter jets. He attained the rank of lieutenant while in the Texas Air National Guard, but was not called to fight in the Vietnam War. After leaving the Air National Guard he held a series of jobs near Midland and entered Harvard Business School in 1972.

As his father had done, Bush began an oil and gas exploration company in Midland. His company was named Arbusto, the Spanish word for "bush." In 1977 he married Laura Welch, a teacher and librarian, and in 1981 she gave birth to twin daughters, Barbara and Jenna. His oil company was later renamed Bush Exploration.

The political career of George W. Bush began in 1978 when he made an unsuccessful race for the U.S. House of Representatives. Bush won in the primary election but lost in general election to Democratic state senator Kent Hance. Bush had raised significant amounts of money during the race and became known as a prodigious fund-raiser.

Bush remained in the oil business, merging his company with an oil investing fund named Spectrum 7. He became chairman of the new corporation. As the economy collapsed in the mid-1980s, Bush sold Spectrum 7 to Harken Energy. He made a significant profit from his holdings.

In the fall of 1987, Bush moved his family to Washington, D.C., to work on his father's presidential campaign. Bush had no official title with the presidential campaign, although considered one of his father's closest advisers.

Among his roles within the campaign was serving as the liaison to the Christian Coalition and other conservative groups.

After the election of 1988 in which his father captured the White House, Bush left Washington and returned to Texas with his family. There he organized a group of investors and together they purchased the Texas Rangers baseball team. He became the investment group's managing partner and supervised the day-to-day activities of the team. When he sold the team in 1998 as he prepared to run for president, he turned his initial investment of $606,000 into a profit of $15,000,000.

His first successful run for elected office came in 1994 when he defeated incumbent Democrat Ann W. Richards for Texas governor by 350,000 votes. He was reelected in 1998 with 65 percent of the state's vote. His greatest success as governor was to woo the Hispanic and minority voters into the Republican Party, which partly explained the significant voter edge he had in 1998.

In June 1999 Bush announced his candidacy for president of the United States. He pledged during his campaign to restore dignity to the presidency, improve education, rebuild the military, and cut taxes. He called himself a "compassionate conservative." During a long primary season, Bush's strongest opponent proved to be Senator John McCain (R-Ariz.). McCain, who had been a prisoner of war in Vietnam and had a strong following, was not able to stop Bush's campaign for the nomination.

In a surprise move, Bush nominated one of his top campaign advisers as his vice presidential nominee. Dick Cheney, who had served as chief of staff in the Ford administration and as secretary of defense in the George H. W. Bush administration, was named the vice presidential nominee. The Bush-Cheney ticket was formally nominated by the Republican National Committee on August 2, 2000.

Butler, Richard

(1942–   ) *executive chairman, United Nations Special Commission on Iraq*

Richard Butler served as executive chairman of the United Nations Special Commission on Iraq (UNSCOM) from 1997 to 1999. Butler took over his role at UNSCOM from Swedish diplomat Rolf Ekeus in July 1997. UNSCOM was established by the United Nations Security Council in 1991, following the Persian Gulf War in which Iraq invaded Kuwait. UNSCOM was charged with ensuring that Iraq destroyed its chemical and biological weapons and certain ballistic missiles. In addition, UNSCOM was charged with monitoring Iraq to ensure that it did not reactivate its weapons programs. Butler and his team of inspectors went to Iraq soon after his appointment to ensure that Iraq was disposing of weapons of mass destruction (as they became known).

In November 1997, a breakdown in negotiations between Butler and Iraq led Iraq to call for his removal as UNSCOM chairman and the lifting of the United Nations oil embargo. The United States, which supported UNSCOM and Butler, threatened air strikes if Iraq did not comply with Butler's demands. On November 11 Butler withdrew UNSCOM inspectors in Iraq, fearing an American air strike. Butler, however, failed to consult with members of the United Nations Security Council before he ordered the inspectors to leave Iraq. This decision drew heated protests from China, France, and Russia in the Security Council.

Butler soon returned to Iraq with his inspectors after air strikes from the United States were averted. Two weeks later, the UNSCOM team accused Iraq of failing to hand over a file of chemical weapons documents before the UNSCOM deadline. During November and December 1997 the UNSCOM teams visited or revisited hundreds of sites with the cooperation of Iraqi officials. The possibility of air strikes by the United States occurred again on December 9 when the UNSCOM team attempted to enter the headquarters of the ruling Ba'ath Party but was blocked. The following day, the U.S. secretary of defense notified Iraq that, unless Butler's team was given access, Iraq would be subject to U.S. air strikes.

Five days later, on December 15, Butler presented a report to the United Nations Security Council claiming a lack of cooperation by Iraqi officials. Russia's United Nations representative, Sergei Lavrov, described the report as inaccurate. Russia, China, and France subsequently called for Butler's removal. Throughout the day, the debate on the report continued.

On December 16, 1997, before the United Nations debate on the report had concluded, Butler ordered the withdrawal of UNSCOM inspection teams. Butler had been forewarned that British and American air strikes were to begin, and so ordered the teams out of Iraq. The air strikes began by the United States soon after. In spite of the air strikes, several members of the United Nations Security Council demanded Butler's resignation for not having consulted them before he ordered the teams to leave Iraq. Again, Russia, China, and France were outraged at Butler.

Butler, a member of Australia's Labor Party, was fully supported in his actions by his government. Australian prime minister John Howard was one of the few national leaders to unequivocally endorse the United States air strikes on Iraq.

Born in Sydney, Australia, Butler was a graduate of the University of Sydney and the Australian National University. He entered the Department of Foreign Affairs in 1965. During his early career in the Australian foreign service, he had postings in Vienna, where he was the deputy permanent representative of Australia to the International Atomic Energy Agency, to

Singapore, to Bonn, and to the Organization of Economic Cooperation and Development in Paris. Butler also held a number of high-level positions in the Australian foreign service, including serving as Australia's first secretary at the United Nations from 1970–73.

Butler had throughout his career significant political ties to Australia's Labour Party. When the Labour Party won the government in 1983, Butler was appointed Australia's first ambassador for disarmament. He subsequently was appointed ambassador to Thailand in 1989 and ambassador to the Supreme National Council of Cambodia in 1991. While at the Supreme National Council, he became deeply involved in the negotiation of the Cambodian peace accords.

In 1992 Butler was named Australia's ambassador to the United Nations, a position he held until 1995. While at the United Nations, he was elected chairman of the United Nations Preparatory Commission Committee for the 50th Anniversary of the United Nations, celebrated in 1995. He was also chairman of the World Summit on Social Development, held in Copenhagen in March 1995. In November 1995 the prime minister of Australia appointed him convener of the Canberra Commission on the Elimination of Nuclear Weapons.

After leaving the United Nations in 1999, Butler was named diplomat in residence at the Council of Foreign Relations in New York. In January 2002 he published a book, *Fatal Choice: Nuclear Weapons and the Illusion of Missile Defense.*

Byrd, Robert Carlyle
(1917–   ) *member of the Senate*

Senator Robert Byrd of West Virginia was one of the Senate's most powerful Democratic leaders during the terms of President Clinton. Byrd was elected president pro tempore of the Senate in 1989. His term lasted until January 2001, when the Republicans gained control of the Senate. However, in June 2001, when Senator James Jeffords of Vermont defected from the Republican Party, the Democrats regained control of the Senate. Byrd was elected president pro tempore again in June 2001, a position he maintained until January 2003 when the Senate was returned to Republican control.

During the impeachment trial of President Clinton in 1999, Senator Byrd voted to acquit. However, he publicly noted that he believed that President Clinton was guilty of the charges against him, as defined in the House of Representatives articles of impeachment. In his interview on the ABC television program, *This Week with Sam Donaldson and Cokie Roberts*, Byrd said "The question is, does this rise to the level of high crimes and misdemeanors? I say 'yes,' no doubt about it in my mind . . . I have no doubt that he has given false testimony under oath, and that he has misled the American people, and that there are indications that he did, indeed, obstruct justice." Despite his misgivings about President Clinton, Senator Byrd indicated at that point that he intended to vote for acquittal because "conviction carries with it removal, and the American people want him to remain in office."

Byrd was born November 20, 1917, in North Wilkesboro, North Carolina, but left an orphan at age one when his mother died. His mother, Ada Kirby Sale, died of influenza in the epidemic of 1918. He was taken in by his aunt and uncle to their home in West Virginia where he was raised. Titus Dalton Byrd adopted Cornelius Calvin Sale, Jr., the child of Ada Sale, who was renamed Robert Carlyle Byrd. Byrd emerged as the valedictorian of his high school class but found few jobs in West Virginia during the war. He subsequently left his home state during World War II to work as a welder in the construction yards of Baltimore, Maryland, and Tampa, Florida.

Following the war, he returned to West Virginia and made his first run for political office in 1946. He was elected to the West Virginia House of Delegates that year. After two terms in the West Virginia House of Delegates, Byrd was elected to the West Virginia Senate. He then served three terms in the U.S. House of Representatives and in 1958 was elected to the United States Senate. Byrd has served continuously in the Senate since he was first elected in 1958.

Byrd's political career in the Senate included serving as secretary of the Democratic Conference (1967) and as Democratic Whip in 1971. In 1977 he was elected Senate Majority Leader, a role he held from 1977–80 and 1987–88. For six years when the Democrats were in the minority in the Senate, he was elected Senate Minority Leader (1981–86). When Byrd left his leadership position in 1989, he took over as chairman of the powerful Senate Appropriations Committee. He served as chair of the committee until 1994.

Throughout his career in the Senate, Byrd successfully brought millions of dollars of federal funding to West Virginia. He moved a host of federal offices there, including the Federal Bureau of Investigation, numerous special interest packages, and enormous federal highway projects for the state. He donated his personal papers to Shepherd College, the elite public university within the state which also received federal funding for the Robert Byrd Library to house the papers.

Byrd was best known in the Senate for his mastery of parliamentary detail. He could block motions that he opposed with ease. He focused on the intricacies of the parliamentary rules as a freshman senator in 1959, which brought him to the attention of the Democratic leadership and gave him a separate identity within the large party membership. When Robert Dole served as majority leader before his run for the presidency in 1996, Byrd frequently tied up legislation with parliamentary moves.

In addition to his expertise in parliamentary detail, Byrd was a gifted speaker. He often gave eloquent speeches on the floor of the Senate, quoting Shakespeare or Plato. His knowledge of history was well known, as he wove tales of American history throughout his often lengthy floor speeches.

Byrd earned a J.D. from American University (1963). He took 10 years of night classes at the law school at American University before finally graduating.

Cardoso, Fernando Henrique
(1931–) *president of Brazil*

Cardoso was elected president of Brazil on October 3, 1994, overcoming his opponent Luiz Inácio Lula da Silva. Cardoso was inaugurated on January 1, 1995, and was reelected in 1998 for a second term, again overcoming Lula at the polls. JAMES CARVILLE, JR., who managed President Clinton's 1992 presidential campaign, managed Cardoso's 1994 campaign.

The major issue that Brazil faced when Cardoso was first elected in 1994 was hyperinflation and a faltering economy. Cardoso's Social Democratic Party focused its energies on domestic economic issues throughout his tenure in office. During the 1994 campaign he made it clear that the next four years for the nation would be difficult ones. He made few promises, but did state that the nation would have to deal with the International Monetary Fund (IMF) in order to gain control of the economy. The package of economic reforms that Cardoso set in motion included privatizing many state-owned operations, including state-owned banks. However, he faced substantial opposition to his privatization of the nation's banks in the Brazilian Congress.

Cardoso succeeded in obtaining financial assistance from the IMF to stabilize the economy in 1995. President Clinton supported the loan and economic reforms of the Cardoso administration. In 1995 Cardoso visited the United States and in 1997 President Clinton traveled to Brazil.

Cardoso was born June 18, 1931, in Rio de Janeiro, into a wealthy military family. He joined the faculty of the University of São Paulo as a sociologist but fled his academic position in 1964 for exile in Chile. He returned to the University of São Paulo in 1968, but was not reappointed to the faculty. Rather, he was arrested and barred from teaching in Brazilian universities because of his left-of-center positions on political issues. Cardoso founded the Brazilian Analysis and Planning Center, a research center which became known for its affiliation with blacklisted academics. Viewed by the military as a center for left-wing intellectuals, the research facility was frequently bombed by right-wing activists during the 1970s. Cardoso then fled from Brazil into exile again, teaching at a series of universities including Oxford, Princeton, Yale, Berkeley, and Stanford.

He returned in 1978 to run for the Brazilian Senate. He was elected as an alternate. In 1979, he gained the vice presidency of the

Brazilian Democratic Movement Party (Partido do Movimento Democratico Brasileiro, or PMDB) and was elected to the Senate in 1983. In 1985 Cardoso ran unsuccessfully for mayor of São Paulo. In 1988, he helped to create the Brazilian Social Democratic Party (Partido do Social Democracia Brasileira, or PSDB), which had a left-of-center political orientation.

Four years later, in 1992, he joined the cabinet of the newly elected president, Itamar Franco, as foreign minister. Soon after joining the cabinet, Franco moved Cardoso to finance minister. During his tenure as finance minister, Cardoso developed an economic stabilization plan that was necessary to restructure the nation's international debt. The plan was approved by the Congress and became effective in July 1994. The economic stabilization plan allowed Brazil to renegotiate the payment of its foreign debt on favorable terms. Within three months after the plan took effect, Brazil's inflation was reduced from 50 percent to less than 2 percent. The success of the economic program led to Cardoso's ambitions for the presidency as the candidate from the Social Democratic Party.

Carns, Michael

(1937–) *failed nominee for director, Central Intelligence Agency*

Air Force General (retired) Michael Carns was nominated by President Clinton on February 8, 1995, as the director of the Central Intelligence Agency (CIA). He failed to be confirmed in the Senate after allegations arose that he failed to properly pay a young Filipino man who worked for the family. Carns withdrew his name from consideration as CIA director on March 11, 1995. President Clinton then successfully nominated JOHN DEUTCH as CIA director.

Carns graduated from the Air Force Academy in 1959. As an air force pilot in Vietnam, Carns flew more than 200 combat missions, for which he earned a Silver Star and the Distinguished Flying Cross. Carns then rose in the ranks of the air force. He served as director of operations for the Rapid Deployment Task Force, deputy commander in chief of the U.S. Pacific Command, and vice chief of staff of the air force before retiring in September 1994.

On March 11, 1995, Carns was forced to withdraw his name after allegations arose that a Filipino employee of the family did not have a proper visa nor had been adequately paid. The allegations were somewhat similar in nature to those Republicans in the Senate made against ZOE BAIRD and KIMBA WOOD, failed nominees for attorney general in 1993.

When President Clinton accepted Carns's withdrawal from the nomination, he said, "General Carns' decision to withdraw is our country's loss. This man, who flew more than 200 combat missions over southeast Asia and distinguished himself as a military commander and innovative manager was prepared to come out of retirement to serve for one more time in a vital mission." Carns had retired from active duty in the air force in September 1994.

Carville, James, Jr.

(1944–) *presidential campaign consultant*

James Carville managed President Clinton's successful 1992 presidential campaign. After Clinton won the election in 1992, Carville returned to private campaign consulting. Unlike many members of Clinton's campaign team in 1992, Carville did not join the administration but did remain an informal adviser to the president. Not surprisingly, Carville was honored as the campaign manager of the year by the American Association of Political Consultants in 1993.

Carville was widely credited for developing the campaign strategy that won Clinton the presidency. He centered the campaign on economic issues, using the slogan "It's the economy, stupid" to energize the campaign staff. Clinton, who was known for being disorganized and often involved in too many issues, was forced to master a series of economic plans, economic data, and economic position papers that Carville gave him. Carville's demands on Clinton succeeded, for exit polls showed that the voters viewed Clinton as the better candidate to deal with the nation's economic problems. Although GEORGE HERBERT WALKER BUSH had been viewed as a successful war president, with a 91 percent approval rating, he had not been viewed as a successful economic president.

Carville also developed the campaign message for Clinton that had centered on universal health care. He had developed the same

James Carville *(Courtesy of the Office of James Carville)*

strategy in 1991 for HARRIS WOFFORD's Senate race. Wofford, a relative unknown within the state of Pennsylvania, fought former governor Richard Thornburgh in the 1991 election. Thornburgh, a popular two-term governor of Pennsylvania, had served as George H. W. Bush's attorney general. Wofford appeared to have an uphill battle against Thornburgh, but Carville created a theme for Wofford around universal health care. The strategy worked and Wofford was elected. Carville then devised a similar strategy for Clinton during the 1992 election, which became a centerpiece of his campaign.

Throughout the Clinton presidency, Carville maintained a relatively low profile, focusing on his political consulting for a series of international candidates. He returned to public view during the impeachment of President Clinton in 1998. Carville became an outspoken defender of Clinton's in the media. He was a frequent guest on television talk shows, challenging the independent counsel, Kenneth Starr, and others who were attacking Clinton. Carville became particularly aggressive about Starr, who he felt had misused his position and had a personal vendetta against Clinton. At no point did Carville stop defending Clinton and routinely sought platforms to pursue his support for Clinton.

One of the more interesting notes about Carville's defense of Clinton was that Carville was married to Mary Matalin, who was a Republican campaign strategist and deputy campaign manager for GEORGE WALKER BUSH's presidential campaign. During the George W. Bush administration, Matalin joined the staff of Vice President Dick Cheney. Matalin and Carville often did television appearances together, clashing on their views of the Clinton presidency.

Carville's professional career as a campaign consultant began in 1982 when he created a professional campaign management company and managed his first campaign. The following year, while working on Lloyd Doggett's unsuccessful bid for the governorship of Texas, Carville formed a professional collaboration with another political consultant, PAUL BEGALA. In 1989 they created the Carville and Begala political consulting firm, specializing in campaign management.

Carville had worked on a number of successful campaigns before taking over the Clinton campaign in 1992. His list of successes included the 1986 gubernatorial victory of Robert Casey in Pennsylvania; the 1987 gubernatorial victory of Wallace Wilkinson in Kentucky; the 1988 reelection of Senator Frank Lautenberg in New Jersey; the 1990 gubernatorial elections of Zell Miller in Georgia and Robert Casey in Pennsylvania; and the U.S. Senate election of Harris Wofford over Richard Thornburgh in 1991 in Pennsylvania. The election of Robert Casey to the governorship in 1986 was perhaps the turning point in Carville's career. Casey had run three times before but had always lost. Carville guided Casey to a victory over the popular Lieutenant Governor William Scranton, Jr., who was considered the shoo-in candidate.

After his string of successes in domestic politics, Carville began to focus on foreign consulting. Among his clients were Greek prime minister Constantine Mitsotakis, Brazilian president FERNANDO HENRIQUE CARDOSO, President Jamil Mahuad of Ecuador, Honduran prime minister Carlos Flores, British prime minister ANTHONY (TONY) CHARLES LYNTON BLAIR, São Paulo mayor Celso Pitta, Argentine economic minister Domingo Carvallo, Francisco Labastida of Mexico, and President Hipólito Mejía of the Dominican Republic. In 1999, Carville managed the successful campaign of EHUD BARAK as prime minister of Israel.

Born on October 25, 1944, Carville entered Louisiana State University in 1962, but after four years had not completed his degree.

As a result, he entered the marine corps. After serving for two years at San Diego's Camp Pendleton, Carville returned to Louisiana State University where he finished his undergraduate degree at night. He then completed his law degree at Louisiana State University and practiced law from 1973–79.

Chavez, Linda
(1947–   ) *lobbyist against bilingual education*

Linda Chavez was a conservative Hispanic Republican who lobbied the Clinton administration against bilingual education and against affirmative action. Prior to her role as a lobbyist, Chavez had served in the Reagan administration as the White House director of public liaison (1985). Prior to joining the White House staff, she had been staff director of the U.S. Commission on Civil Rights (1983–85) and was a member of the Administrative Conference of the United States (1984–86).

As president of the Center for Equal Opportunity, Chavez began a lobbying campaign against bilingual education, opposing any efforts to create bilingual programs in the public schools. Hispanics, Chavez believed, should assimilate into the American culture and not remain a separate community through language. Chavez also opposed affirmative action and the federal programs that supported those goals.

On December 19, 1997, President Clinton held a meeting at the White House that Chavez attended. He met with Chavez once when he discussed his affirmative action plans with members of conservative groups who opposed the plan. Included in the meeting with Chavez were Ward Connerly, a leading backer of California's 1996 ban on affirmative action in state government; Abigail and Stephan Thernstrom, coauthors of book on the state of race relations in the United States; and Representative Charles T. Canady (R-Fla.).

In her role as White House director of public liaison during the Reagan administration, Chavez reported to Communications Director Patrick Buchanan. Buchanan urged her to seek elective office, noting that Republican senator Charles Mathias was vacating his Senate seat in Maryland and she currently lived in Maryland. In 1986, Chavez captured the Republican nomination for the Mathias seat and battled a 10-year veteran of the House of Representatives, Barbara Mikulski, the Democratic nominee. Mikulski, who attacked Chavez as a carpet-bagger, noted that Chavez had only lived in the state for two years. Mikulski also had a significant voter edge, in a state with twice as many Democrats as Republicans. Chavez lost the race with 39 percent of the vote to Mikulski's 61 percent.

After her failed Senate race, Chavez served as president of U.S. English, a group that lobbied federal, state, and local governments to make English the official language of the nation. In 1989 she became a senior fellow of the Manhattan Institute, a conservative think tank in New York City focusing on social issues. Her work at the Manhattan Institute led to publication of her first book, *Out of the Barrio: Toward a New Politics of Hispanic Assimilation* (1991). She argued in the book for policies that allowed Hispanics to assimilate into the American society. She argued against affirmative action and bilingual programs in her book.

She remained with the Manhattan Institute during the early years of the Clinton administration. During this period she was a frequent commentator on television shows and a syndicated weekly columnist for *USA Today*. However, she left the Manhattan Institute in 1995 to found her own organization, the Center for Equal Opportunity, which opposed affirmative action and similar programs that prioritized certain ethnic groups. Her primary role was to draw public attention to the problems of affirmative action, using such forums as conferences, congressional testimony, and articles.

Born June 17, 1947, Chavez earned her B.A. degree from the University of Colorado at Boulder (1970) and did postgraduate work at the University of California, Los Angeles (1970–72).

President-elect George W. Bush nominated Chavez as his secretary of labor in January 2001. However, Chavez withdrew her name from nomination after a background check by the Federal Bureau of Investigation (FBI) found that she had hired an illegal immigrant from Guatemala for housecleaning. She failed to pay social security taxes for the woman, which led to challenges from Democrats. Democrats did not want to see Chavez confirmed after Republicans had challenged ZOE BAIRD's and KIMBA WOOD's nomination for attorney general in 1993 and BOBBY RAY INMAN's nomination for secretary of defense in 1993 on similar grounds.

Chavez-Thompson, Linda

(1944–) *vice president, American Federation of Labor–Congress of Industrial Organizations (AFL-CIO)*

Linda Chavez-Thompson was elected executive vice president of the American Federation of Labor–Congress of Industrial Organizations (AFL-CIO) in 1995 with the strong backing of AFL-CIO president John Sweeney, and American Federation of State, County and Municipal Employees (AFSCME) international vice president Gerald W. McEntee for her candidacy.

President Clinton appointed her to the President's Race Advisory Board. As the only Hispanic on the board, she attempted to draw attention to issues regarding Hispanics as well as African Americans. Her political role within the Clinton administration was furthered by her selection as the vice chair of the Democratic National Committee.

Her most successful political role, however, came when she successfully campaigned for a senior elected office within the powerful AFL-CIO in 1988. Her campaign for the vice presidency of the union centered on increasing opportunities for women and for minorities within the union, particularly in the leadership roles of the union. She emphasized the need to rebuild the union's strength, which had dwindled to 15 percent of the workforce. One of her strategies was to target the service sector, which was relatively nonunion and composed primarily of women and minorities.

Chavez-Thompson is a second-generation Mexican-American, born on August 1, 1944, in Lubbock, Texas. She was one of eight children of sharecropper parents. At the age of 10, she began to work in cotton fields in west Texas. She dropped out of school in the ninth grade and began to clean houses to help support her family.

In 1967 she became involved with her first union. She joined the Laborer's International Union, a labor group to which her father belonged. In 1971 she became a representative for the American Federation of State, County, and Municipal Employees (AFSCME), working her way through a variety of leadership positions. In 1988, Chavez-Thompson was elected AFSCME vice president and in 1995 the executive director of the AFSCME in Texas. Her election to the position in the AFL-CIO was the result of her leadership position in AFSME, which is an affiliate of the AFL-CIO.

Chirac, Jacques
(1932–) *president of France*

Jacques Chirac, the former mayor of Paris, was inaugurated as president of France, on May 18, 1995, replacing FRANÇOIS MITTERRAND. The election of 1995 was generally a repudiation of Mitterrand's socialist agenda, which had created a sagging economy and discontented workers in France. Chirac served continuously as president of France through the end of President Clinton's first term and all of his second term. He was reelected president of France in 2002.

When Chirac took over the presidency in 1995, he had strong support for his conservative agenda within the national government. Conservatives controlled 80 percent of the seats in the National Assembly, 67 percent of the seats in the Senate, and 20 of 22 regional councils. The election of Chirac to the presidency was a major turnaround for the nation's leadership after the domination of Mitterrand and his Socialist Party from 1981 to 1995.

The economy became the central issue during his tenure as president. Chirac faced substantial economic problems, particularly high unemployment, both within France and across Europe (which was France's strongest trading partner). In 2000, Chirac led the European community to have all of the members of the European Union convert to a new currency, the euro, to restart the European economies.

When war broke out in the Balkans, in Yugoslavia, France became the lead nation in ending the conflict. France had the largest contingent of troops in the United Nations peacekeeping forces on the ground in Bosnia and Serbia. Chirac argued for stronger peacekeeping participation from the United States and Britain. In response, President Clinton increased the number of U.S. troops. American armed forces later took the lead in military action in Kosovo when Serbian forces were attacking and killing Muslims there. Clinton argued that the Serbian forces had engaged in ethnic cleansing, which the U.S. would not allow. Secretary of State MADELEINE KORBEL ALBRIGHT became the lead member of the Clinton administration in the Kosovo conflict, comparing the ethnic cleansing to that during the German occupation of much of Europe in World War II.

The economy, however, became Chirac's greatest problem. Support for Chirac's conservative economic agenda waned over the next two years and the Socialist Party gained substantial seats in the national government. Chirac's popularity tumbled during 1997 as the economy continued to fail. Months of riots shook the nation as workers sought relief. Chirac reformed the leadership in his government and was forced to join a coalition with the Socialist Party. The Socialist Party leader, Lionel Jospin, was named prime minister. Jospin remained prime minister until the elections of 2002, when Chirac won without needing a coalition government. Throughout the five years in which Chirac and Jospin shared power, Chirac battled with Jospin.

Chirac's government service began immediately after graduate school in Paris. After holding several positions in the French civil service, Chirac joined the General Secretariat of the Council of Ministers in 1962, quickly moving to the staff of Prime Minister Georges Pompidou. Chirac left Pompidou's staff in 1965 to run for local elected office, which he won, in his hometown of Sainte-Fereole. Two years later Chirac returned to national politics and was named by Pompidou as the undersecretary of state for political affairs. The following year Chirac was named to a more senior position, secretary of state for Economic Affairs and Finance.

When Charles de Gaulle resigned from the presidency in 1969, Pompidou was elected to the presidency and continued Chirac in his role in economic affairs and finance. When Pompidou died in office in April 1974, Chirac was instrumental in the victory of Valéry Giscard d'Estaing in his presidential election. Giscard d'Estaing subsequently appointed Chirac as prime minister in 1974 as a reward for his support. Chirac only lasted two years in the role of prime minister before a conflict with Giscard d'Estaing forced Chirac's resignation.

After his resignation from the government, Chirac was elected president of the Rally for the Republic (Rassemblement pour la République, or RPR) a conservative political party of which he had been undersecretary since 1974. The party under Chirac's leadership had moved to the political right and changed its name from l'Union de démocrates pour la République. He subsequently ran for and won the office of mayor of Paris.

During the election of 1981, Chirac ran for president but finished third behind Giscard and the socialist candidate, François Mitterrand. In the run-off election, Chirac supported Mitterrand over Giscard, and Mitterrand won the election. Chirac returned to his role as mayor of Paris but continued as a national political figure, building conservative coalitions. President Mitterrand appointed Chirac prime minister in 1986 when Mitterrand was facing numerous attacks from conservatives.

Chirac left government in 1989 but continued as the party leader. In March 1989 he was again elected mayor of Paris. Chirac had become a national force by this time, and led passage in the 1992 national referendum of the Maastricht Treaties on the European Union.

In 1995 Chirac sought the presidency of France to replace the retiring François Mitterrand. In the first round of balloting on April 23, 1995, Chirac finished in second place with only 20 percent of the national vote in a broad field of candidates. Since federal law requires a run-off between the top candidates, a second ballot was held on May 7, 1995. He won, with 52 percent of the vote, defeating the socialist candidate.

Chirac was born on November 19, 1932, in Paris, attending the Lycée Carnot throughout his youth. He enrolled in the Institut d'Etudes Politiques (Institute for Political Studies), a university that trained those interested in careers in politics and diplomacy, and graduated in 1953.

He then spent the summer studying at Harvard University. After serving in the French military with active duty in Algeria, he entered the graduate program at the Ecole nationale d'administration (National School of Administration) in 1958 and graduated in 1959.

Chrétien, Jean Joseph-Jacques
(1934–) *prime minister of Canada*

Jean Chrétien was the prime minister of Canada throughout most of President Clinton's eight years of office. Throughout his tenure, Chrétien built strong diplomatic relations with Clinton on most issues. Cuba proved to be one of the few areas of policy that the two leaders disagreed on, with Chrétien opposed to any trade embargo against Cuba.

During his tenure in office, Chrétien pursued a moderate to conservative agenda, in contrast to the more progressive policies of his predecessor, prime minister Brian Mulroney. The major issue that faced Chrétien while in office was the Quebec separatist movement. As a native of Quebec, Chrétien chose not to directly oppose the separatist movement but to transfer greater power to the provinces as a way to mollify Quebec.

Chrétien, whose native language was French, did not learn to speak English until he was 28. As a child Chrétien had had polio, which left him with a distorted mouth and deafness in his right ear.

Born on January 11, 1934, Chrétien graduated from high school and went to law school as a means of building his credentials for a run at elected office in the House of Commons. At Laval Law School in Quebec, he first entered politics by running the school's Liberal Club, which advocated policies similar to those of the Liberal Party in Canada. He passed the bar exam in 1958, practiced law briefly with the firm of Chrétien, Landry, Deschenes, Trudel

and Norman in Shawinigan, and in 1963 won a seat in the House of Commons.

Soon after he entered parliament, he was named parliamentary secretary to prime minister Lester Pearson (1965) and held a series of positions related to the Pearson government. In 1968, following the election of Prime Minister Pierre Trudeau, he was named minister of Indian affairs and northern development and in 1974 was appointed president of the Treasury Board. In 1976 he became minister of industry, trade and commerce and in 1977 became minister of finance.

When Trudeau resigned as prime minister in 1984, Chrétien ran for the leadership position of the Liberal Party but lost to John Turner. Two years later, Chrétien left parliament when the Conservative Party swept the elections.

He returned to the practice of law with the firm of Lang Michener Lawrence and Shaw from 1986 to 1990 but soon returned to public life. When Turner suddenly left government in 1990, Chrétien ran again for the leadership of the Liberal Party and won. He then led the party to a landslide victory in the national elections in the House of Commons. As leader of the majority party in the House of Commons, Chrétien was sworn into office as prime minister on November 4, 1993. He was reelected in 1997 and on November 27, 2000, for a third term. Throughout his tenure, Chrétien battled the Quebec separatists who actively pursued their cause in spite of having lost the battle in 1980. The issue remained central to the administration, including a major political confrontation in 1995 over separatism.

The prime minister of Canada is appointed formally by the governor general of Canada. Traditionally, although not by law, the prime minister is a member of the majority party of the House of Commons. The prime minister remains in office as long as his/her party holds the majority.

Christopher, Warren Minor
(1925–) *secretary of state*

Warren Christopher was confirmed as secretary of state in January 1993 and remained throughout President Clinton's first term in office. Christopher did not seek reappointment for the president's second term and was replaced by MADELEINE KORBEL ALBRIGHT in 1997.

Prior to joining the Clinton administration, Christopher spent four years in the State Department as deputy secretary of state during the Carter administration, a position he held from February 26, 1977, until January 20, 1981. As deputy secretary under Secretary of State CYRUS R. VANCE, Christopher oversaw the negotiations for the 52 hostages held in Iran, who were finally released on the day that President Reagan took office. Christopher also oversaw the normalization of diplomatic relations with China and ratification of the Panama Canal treaties. He was awarded the Medal of Freedom by President Carter, the nation's highest civilian award, for his diplomatic work in the State Department.

Christopher had been involved in Democratic Party politics since entering private law practice in Los Angeles in 1950, particularly in Los Angeles and California. On two separate occasions, he was tapped by local and state officials to investigate problems in Los Angeles. In 1965 he was named vice chairman of the Governor's Commission on the Los Angeles Riots and in 1991 was named chairman of the Independent Commission on the Los Angeles Police Department.

His expertise, however, in the practice of law focused on international issues. As a result, during Clinton's presidential campaign in 1992, he became a key foreign policy and campaign adviser. Christopher was one of the few members of the Clinton campaign who had deep roots within the Democratic Party. When Clinton won the election, he tapped

U.S. Secretary of State Warren Christopher speaking at a NATO press conference, May 6, 1993 *(NATO Library)*

Christopher to oversee the transition and bring a broad range of Democrats into the administration. Christopher also was not a member of the Arkansas team that Clinton had often surrounded himself with during the campaign. He was selected to give the transition team greater credibility within the Democratic establishment.

As transition director, Christopher recommended nominees for cabinet positions. Among those that Christopher personally recommended were ZOE BAIRD and KIMBA WOOD for attorney general. Clinton had asked that the transition team include broad gender and ethnic representation in its nominees for the cabinet and specifically asked that the job of attorney general be given to a woman. Baird and Wood, both prominent attorneys in the private sector, had worked with Christopher at various times. Both, however, were stalled in their nomination process by their "nanny-tax" problems and both withdrew their nominations. Christopher eventually recommended JANET RENO for attorney general. Reno, a local prosecutor from Dade County, Florida, had not been married and had no children, and so did not have problems with the "nanny tax" that plagued Baird and Wood.

During his four years in the Clinton administration, Christopher managed a series of international conflicts in which the president saw a diplomatic role for the United States. Christopher was deeply involved in the Middle East negotiations, often meeting with leaders from Israel, Jordan, Egypt, and other nations in the region. He also oversaw the barrage of diplomatic issues that arose in the Balkans in Bosnia, Serbia, and Kosovo. Christopher was instrumental in setting up the international court that tried SLOBODAN MILOŠEVIĆ for crimes against humanity in Bosnia and Kosovo. Christopher left the administration in 1997 to rejoin his law firm in Los Angeles.

From October 1949 to September 1950, Christopher had served as a law clerk to Justice William O. Douglas of the U.S. Supreme Court. He practiced law with the firm of O'Melveny & Myers in Los Angeles from October 1950 to June 1967, becoming a partner in 1968. Christopher was appointed deputy attorney general from 1967 through 1969. As a political appointee of President Johnson, he resigned when President Nixon was sworn into office.

Christopher was a member and then president of the Board of Trustees of Stanford University; chairman, Carnegie Corporation of the New York, Board of Trustees; director and vice chairman of the Council of Foreign Relations; director of the Los Angeles World Affairs Council; vice chairman of the Governor's Commission on the Los Angeles Riots, 1965–66; special consultant to Undersecretary George W. Ball on foreign economic problems; and president, Coordinating Council for Higher Education in the State of California. In 1991, Christopher was named chairman of the Independent Commission on the Los Angeles Police Department, which investigated police brutality in the wake of the Rodney King beating by the police.

Born on October 27, 1925, in Scranton, North Dakota, Christopher received his B.S. from the University of Southern California (1945) and his J.D. from the Stanford University School of Law (1949). From July 1943 to September 1946 he served in the naval reserve, with active duty as an ensign in the Pacific theater.

Chung, Johnny

(1954–) *Taiwanese-born businessman, involved in 1996 campaign finance investigation*

Johnny Chung was a Taiwanese-born American citizen who was charged with illegal contributions to the 1996 Clinton-Gore campaign. The charges stemmed from funds that he gave to the Democratic National Committee as a middleman for Chinese companies. Allegations arose that the Chinese government and Chinese companies were trying to buy influence with the Clinton administration, using the contributions that they funneled through Chung to the Democratic National Committee.

Chung was an immigrant to California from Taiwan. In the early nineties he opened a company, Automated Intelligent Systems, Inc., that provided mass fax distributions for Chinese businesses. He regularly traveled to China to build business for his company and while in China was approached by members of the Chinese government to serve as an intermediary for donations to the Democratic National Committee.

During 1995 and 1996, Chung became a regular contributor to the Democratic National Committee using the Chinese funds and was often invited to the White House. According to the records of the Federal Election Commission (FEC), Chung began donating to the Democratic National Committee in August 1994 and continued making contributions until August 1996. His contributions to the Democratic National Committee led to invitations to the White House on 49 occasions between February 1994 and February 1996. He testified to federal investigators that he sought the invitations as a means of entertaining foreign clients. He noted, for example, that he had brought the chairman of Tangshan Haomen Group, the second largest beer manufacturer in China, to the White House. At the time that Chung was making the contributions to the Democratic National Committee, there was no evidence that he was a middleman for either the Chinese government or Chinese companies.

In 1997 the Department of Justice began to investigate several irregularities in the campaign finances of the Clinton-Gore 1996 campaign, which included the donations by Chung. After the investigation, Chung was charged by the Department of Justice with providing $366,000 in illegal donations to the Democratic National Committee. According to his testimony, in August 1996, Chung had dinner in Hong Kong with General Ji Shengde, who was then the chief of China's military intelligence. The general arranged with Chung to donate $300,000 to the Democratic National Committee, which was handled through an official of a state-owned aerospace company.

One of the questioned donations was a $50,000 check to the Democratic National Committee which Chung gave to MARGARET A. WILLIAMS, Mrs. Clinton's chief of staff, in the White House. Williams was investigated by the Justice Department for accepting the $50,000 gift from Chung. The federal Hatch Act barred political contributions from being solicited or received on federal property.

Several Republicans in Congress had asked Attorney General JANET RENO to appoint an independent counsel for the investigation, but she refused, stating that the Justice Department had not found enough evidence to lead to such an appointment. While Chung had been found to have illegally donated funds, the Clinton-Gore '96 Committee and the Democratic National Committee were cleared of any knowledge of Chung's backers for the donations.

Chung agreed to a plea bargain with federal prosecutors in 1998 and testified that he funneled money from state-controlled businesses in China to the Democratic National Committee. The issue, which was never discussed in public, but which was at the heart of the investigation, was whether Chung's associates in China were government agents or businessmen seeking to influence American policy toward China.

Cisneros, Henry G.

(1947–   ) *secretary of housing and urban development*

Henry Cisneros served as President Clinton's secretary of housing and urban development from 1993 to 1997. He was confirmed unanimously by the Senate on January 21, 1993, and was sworn into office by Chief Justice William H. Rehnquist on January 22, 1993. He resigned in 1997 following an investigation by the independent counsel into charges of lying to the Federal Bureau of Investigation in his background check.

Cisneros was selected by Clinton for a number of reasons. He offered geographic balance to the cabinet, representing the southwest, and was an elected official of a large urban population who understood complex urban matters. Perhaps most important to Clinton, Cisneros represented the growing Hispanic population in the nation. Clinton had sought to have a cabinet that was diverse in both ethnicity and gender, one "that looked like America." Cisneros, who was Hispanic, filled a role in the cabinet by broadening its ethnic diversity. A Democrat, Cisneros had been an active campaigner for President Clinton during the 1992 election, particularly courting the Hispanic vote.

As secretary of housing and urban development, Cisneros was responsible for administering the nation's housing laws, including overseeing federally assisted housing and economic development programs in urban areas. When Cisneros took over the reins of the department, he focused, among other areas, on the problems of the homeless. Cisneros made the elimination of homelessness the top priority of the Department of Housing and Urban Development.

Cisneros became the target of a federal investigation in March 1995. Attorney General JANET RENO asked for an independent counsel to investigate charges that Cisneros lied to the Federal Bureau of Investigation (FBI) about secret payments he made to a former mistress. Independent counsel DAVID M. BARRETT was appointed by the three-judge federal panel in May 1995.

Cisneros was alleged to have paid Linda Medlar, a political fund-raiser, more than $250,000 between 1990 and 1993 to keep their affair quiet. In mid-1994 Medlar sued Cisneros, saying he reneged on his oral agreement to keep paying her $4,000 per month. She then charged that Cisneros lied about the payments to the FBI during his background investigation for the position of secretary of housing and urban development. Reno triggered the

appointment of the independent counsel as required under the Ethics in Government Act of 1978 regarding allegations against senior federal officials.

In January 1997, as the investigation wore on, Cisneros resigned from office citing financial concerns arising from having a child in college, another in law school, and legal bills from the investigation. He returned to the private sector, becoming president of Univision, the Spanish-language television network.

Before the end of the year, a grand jury (December 1997) charged Cisneros with 18 counts of conspiracy, false statements, and obstruction of justice stemming from the alleged payments to Medlar. Medlar had since changed her name to Linda Jones. The grand jury charged that the payments had totaled

Henry G. Cisneros *(Department of Housing and Urban Development)*

more than $250,000. On January 15, 1998, Medlar Jones pleaded guilty to 28 charges of fraud and obstruction of justice, and was sentenced to three and a half years in federal prison. Cisneros was named in that case.

After a four-year investigation, jury selection was about to begin for Cisneros in September 1999. However, before the selection began, Cisneros reached a plea agreement with the federal prosecutor. He pleaded guilty to a misdemeanor count of lying to the Federal Bureau of Investigation. He was fined $10,000, but did not face prison according to the agreement. Cisneros said in a public statement that he "was not candid" with the Federal Bureau of Investigation and hoped to be remembered for his actions as secretary of housing and urban development. In one of his final acts as president, Clinton pardoned Cisneros.

Cisneros entered public service as an administrative assistant in the San Antonio City Manager's Office. In 1971, he was selected as a White House Fellow and worked as an assistant to Eliot Richardson, the secretary of health, education and welfare.

Four years later, in 1975, Cisneros was elected to the San Antonio City Council, where he served until 1981. That year, he ran successfully for mayor, becoming the first Hispanic in that post. During his tenure as mayor (1981–89) he was elected president of the National League of Cities for a one-year term. He was also given a citation in 1982 from the United States Jaycees as one of the "Ten Outstanding Young Men of America."

After his eight years as mayor of San Antonio, Cisneros left public service to head the newly created Cisneros Asset Management Company, a national fixed-income asset management firm for tax-exempt institutions. During this time in private life, Cisneros also hosted a one-hour television show, *Texans*, produced quarterly in Texas, and *Adelante*, a national daily Spanish-language radio show.

During this period his son, John Paul, who was born in 1987, had serious health problems from a heart defect at birth. Cisneros was urged by Democrats within the state to run for governor in 1990, but he turned down the offer to remain close to his ailing son. The son later recovered through surgery in 1993.

Although not serving in elected office, Cisneros remained active in the public sector during this period. He was chairman of the National Civic League and chairman of the Advisory Committee on the Construction of San Antonio's Alamodome. In addition, he was a board member of the Rockefeller Foundation.

Born June 11, 1947, Cisneros earned his B.A. from Texas A&M University (1968) in urban and regional planning, a master's degree in urban planning from Texas A&M University (1970), another master's in public administration from the John F. Kennedy School of Government at Harvard University, and his Ph.D. in public administration from George Washington University (1975). Cisneros was one of five children born in a middle-class Hispanic section of San Antonio to Elvira and George Cisneros.

Clark, Wesley K.
(1944–) *supreme allied commander*

From 1997 to 2000 General Wesley Clark served as the supreme allied commander, responsible for the air strikes in Kosovo and Belgrade, Yugoslavia, in 1999. He was named supreme allied commander and commander in chief of the United States European Command on July 11, 1997. He was headquartered in Brussels, Belgium, at the NATO command offices.

In an interview in March 1999 for the Public Broadcasting System (PBS), Clark discussed the conditions in Kosovo that led to the air strikes by the North Atlantic Treaty Organization (NATO), led by U.S. forces. Conditions in Yugoslavia deteriorated when Serbian forces, under the direction of President SLOBODAN MILOŠEVIĆ, entered Muslim-dominated Kosovo and began what the United States charged was ethnic cleansing. Kosovo was a semiautonomous part of Yugoslavia.

Clark said of the Serbian forces entering Kosovo, "We're taking about civilians who are living in villages being surrounded by [Serbian forces], being told they have to stay in their homes. Snipers are placed on the rooftops to shoot people who try to get out. And then the hit squads come through, pick out the people they want to kill, everybody else is beaten up, robbed, kicked out of their homes, and the homes are burned." The operation in Kosovo under General Clark was called Operation Allied Force.

Although the air strikes succeeded in routing the Serbs from Kosovo, Clark faced a number of problems during Operation Allied Force. During one air raid, American planes mistakenly bombed the Chinese embassy in Belgrade. Clark also had a number of disagreements with General Sir Mike Jackson, who commanded the British forces.

Clark was an advocate of stronger intervention by the United States, including a commitment of ground forces. He sought authority from President Clinton to commit the ground troops, but the authority was denied. President Clinton and the national security team in Washington, D.C., wanted to keep ground troops out of the area and to rely on air strikes to remove the Serbs from Kosovo. Clark constantly lobbied both the White House and NATO for ground troops for the war in Kosovo. However, neither the Clinton administration nor the Europeans wanted to support a land war. As a result, just one month after the end of the air strikes, White House officials leaked news that Clark would retire early and

General Wesley K. Clark *(Department of Defense)*

would vacate the position of supreme allied commander. He was replaced at NATO a month earlier than he had planned.

In May 2001 Clark published a book, *Waging Modern War*, which argued for ground troops, which he called "boots on the ground," in future armed conflicts.

Clark served as the commander in chief of the Southern Command, Panama, from June 1996 to June 1997, where he commanded all U.S. forces and was responsible for military activities and interests in Latin America and the Caribbean. His previous assignment was director, strategic plans and policy for the Joint Staff (1994–96). He was responsible for worldwide politico-military affairs and the U.S. military strategic planning. He also led the military negotiations for the Bosnian Peace Accords at Dayton, Ohio, with RICHARD C. HOLBROOKE, who was the chief U.S. negotiator for the accords.

In addition to his work on the Joint Staff, he served as deputy chief of staff for concepts, doctrine, and developments, U.S. Army Training and Doctrine Command, Fort Monroe, Virginia (1991–92), as chief of the army's study group, Office of the Chief of Staff of the Army (1983–84), and a chief of plans and integration division, Office of the Deputy Chief of Staff for Operations and Plans, U.S. Army (July–September 1983).

Born on December 23, 1944, Clark grew up in Little Rock, Arkansas. He graduated first in his class from the United States Military Academy at West Point, New York (1966), and was named a Rhodes scholar. He graduated with a master's degree from Oxford University (1968). He was a White House Fellow in 1975–76 and served as a special assistant to the director of the Office of Management and Budget.

After leaving the military in May 2000, he was awarded the Presidential Medal of Freedom, the nation's highest civilian honor. He began to work for the Stephens Group, a high-technology venture-capital company. He also served as a senior adviser for the Center for Strategic and International Studies, a Washington, D.C., think tank.

Clinton, Chelsea Victoria
(1980–) *daughter of President and Mrs. Clinton*

Chelsea Clinton, the daughter of President and Mrs. Clinton, was born on February 27, 1980, in Little Rock, Arkansas. The Clintons reportedly named their daughter in honor of the Joni Mitchell song, "Chelsea Morning."

She was only nine years old when her father was elected president and became the first adolescent in the White House since Amy Carter during the administration of President Jimmy Carter (1977–81).

During his presidency, President and Mrs. Clinton were fiercely protective of their daughter and asked the press to leave her alone. The press was generally supportive of their request and rarely ran stories about Chelsea. She attended a private school in Washington, D.C., while living there and rarely was seen in public by the press.

While her father was in office, Chelsea often traveled with her parents on international trips. Once the independent counsel's office broke the story of President Clinton's relationship with MONICA LEWINSKY, Chelsea Clinton appeared to be a buffer between her parents.

She enrolled in Stanford University in 1997, where she majored in history. After graduation from Stanford University in the summer of 2001, she pursued a two-year program at University College at Oxford University, where her father studied as a Rhodes scholar from 1968–70. Although she did not attend Oxford University as a Rhodes scholar, she successfully graduated in 2003 with a master of philosophy degree in international relations.

After graduation in June 2003, she accepted a position in New York City with McKinsey & Company. McKinsey & Company is an international consulting firm with more than 5,000 employees worldwide.

Clinton, Hillary Diane Rodham
(1947–) *first lady, wife of President Bill Clinton*

Hillary Rodham Clinton, wife of President Bill Clinton, served as first lady from January 20, 1993, until January 20, 2001.

The Clintons were married October 11, 1975. During her husband's first term as governor in 1978 she did not take her husband's name and was known as Hillary Rodham. Not until her husband was elected in 1982, after losing the 1980 election, did she formally become known as Hillary Rodham Clinton. Throughout the remainder of his tenure as governor (1983–93) and throughout his presidency (1993–2001), Mrs. Clinton was known as Hillary Rodham Clinton.

Hillary Diane Rodham was born on October 26, 1947, in Chicago, Illinois, and raised with her two brothers, Hugh and Tony, in a Chicago suburb, Park Ridge, Illinois. In her senior year in high school, she was class president. Mrs. Clinton graduated with a B.A., with honors, from Wellesley College in 1969, where she was president of the student government and the school's first student graduation speaker. The speech drew a standing ovation and a mention in an article in *Life* magazine. Her speech was so well crafted that she was asked to join the Board of Junior Advisors of the League of Women Voters and became a sought-after speaker by various organizations.

After graduating from Wellesley College, she entered Yale Law School. The League of Women Voters asked her to speak at their annual meeting and she met Marian Wright Edelman, who was the keynote speaker of the meeting. She approached Mrs. Edelman for a job at the Children's Defense Fund, which she was given if she could find her own funding. Mrs. Clinton did find the funding to support her through the law school civil rights fund and worked for Edelman over the summer. The exposure to children's issues and the relationship to Edelman would influence her throughout her service in the Clinton administration.

While at Yale Law School, Hillary Rodham, who was an editor of the *Yale Law Review*, met Bill Clinton. After graduating from law school in 1973, Hillary Rodham returned to work for the Children's Defense Fund as a staff attorney in Cambridge, Massachusetts. She was then recruited to work for the House of Representatives judiciary committee which was investigating impeachment charges against President RICHARD MILHOUS NIXON.

She remained on the staff of the judiciary committee through 1974 and moved to Arkansas to join Bill Clinton. She joined the faculty of the University of Arkansas Law School, where he also taught, and they were married in October 1975. She joined the Rose Law Firm in 1977 when he was elected state attorney general. Their daughter, Chelsea Victoria, was born in 1980.

Mrs. Clinton remained at the Rose Law Firm in Little Rock, Arkansas, throughout her husband's political career in Arkansas. She served as first lady of Arkansas for 12 years, during which she continued her law practice and became involved with a number of children's organizations. Among the organizations were the Arkansas Educational Standards Committee, which she chaired, and the Arkansas Advocates for Children and Families, which she cofounded. She served on the boards of the Arkansas Children's Hospital, Legal Services, and the Children's Defense Fund (which Marion Wright Edelman founded).

When President Clinton began his race for the presidency in 1991, Mrs. Clinton became deeply involved in the campaign. She not only campaigned for her husband, but was a key political strategist. At one point in the primary process in 1992, GENNIFER FLOWERS announced that she had had a 12-year relationship with Governor Clinton. Mrs. Clinton joined her husband on the CBS television program *60 Minutes* to deny the charges. She remained steadfastly at his side throughout the allegations by Flowers.

After the election in November 1992, Mrs. Clinton continued to be deeply involved in the decision-making process and was part of the inner circle that chose key White House staff and cabinet officers.

Once the administration was in office, Mrs. Clinton was named the chair of the Task Force on National Health Care Reform. The goal of the task force, which also included IRA

MAGAZINER of the White House staff, was to propose legislation in 1994 for health care reform. During 1993, Mrs. Clinton and Magaziner met with members of Congress, the health care industry, and a host of others to fashion a health care reform initiative.

Their efforts were vehemently opposed by the health care insurance industry and by many Republican members of Congress. In addition, they failed to build bridges to key members of the Democratic leadership in Congress throughout the process. The result was a complete failure for the health care initiative during 1994. When the Republicans took control of Congress in the elections of November 1994, many analysts believed that Mrs. Clinton's handling of health care reform had alienated voters. Their alienation stemmed both from her

First Lady Hillary Rodham Clinton *(Library of Congress)*

activism as first lady in the health care reform process but also from the perception that health care would be nationalized. After the failed health care initiative and the takeover of the Congress by Republicans in 1994, Mrs. Clinton refocused her attentions on more traditional roles for the first lady. In the spring of 1995, Mrs. Clinton completed a 12-day goodwill tour of southern Asia. Among the issues that she discussed on the trip were women's and children's issues. In September 1995, Mrs. Clinton served as the honorary chairperson of the American delegation to the fourth United Nations international conference on women held in Beijing, China.

During the second term of the administration, Mrs. Clinton traveled extensively, often with her daughter, Chelsea, around the world. She became the most traveled first lady in history. She often met with women who were poor and lacked health care and educational facilities. Among the issues she raised in foreign countries were ways to improve the conditions of women and children. In 1997, Mrs. Clinton chaired a White House conference on the issue of child care.

In 1999, two years before her husband was to leave office, Mrs. Clinton began to consider running for a Senate seat from New York, after Senator DANIEL PATRICK MOYNIHAN announced his intention to retire. Before she formally announced her candidacy, she traveled across New York in what she called a "listening campaign." President and Mrs. Clinton purchased a home in Chappaqua, New York, in order to establish residency. Prior to purchasing the home, in Chappaqua, the Clintons did not have New York residency.

At the time that she began to consider the race for the Senate, her likely opponent was New York City mayor Rudolph Giuliani. However, he withdrew from the race after a diagnosis of prostate cancer. Once she decided to pursue the race for the New York Senate seat, she formally declared her candidacy early in 2000. Representative Nita Lowey (D-N.Y.), who had intended to run for Moynihan's Senate seat, bowed out of the race in favor of Mrs. Clinton.

The Senate campaign between Mrs. Clinton and Representative Rick Lazio (R-N.Y.) ended in a victory for Mrs. Clinton in the election on November 7, 2000. She was sworn into office on January 3, 2001, for a term to end on January 3, 2007. For a brief period between January 3 and January 20, 2001, Mrs. Clinton was both the first lady and a U.S. senator.

In 1997, Mrs. Clinton wrote the best-selling book *It Takes a Village and Other Lessons Children Teach Us*. She also wrote *Dear Socks, Dear Buddy: Kids' Letters to the First Pets*. In 2003 she published her memoirs, *Living History*.

Clinton, Roger, Jr.

(1956–) *half brother of President Bill Clinton*

Roger Clinton, Jr., the half brother of President Bill Clinton, was born to Virginia Cassidy Clinton and Roger Clinton in 1956. He never graduated from college and until his brother became president, made his living as a member of a band. After his brother became president, Roger Clinton tried to capitalize on President Clinton's position in a variety of ways. He was regularly in trouble or in the news for his actions throughout the eight years of the Clinton presidency.

President Clinton's father, William Jefferson Blythe, was killed in a car accident in 1944. However, there is conflicting material on this information. According to a biography by David Maraniss entitled *First in His Class*, Blythe was serving in Italy with the army for the nine months before Bill Clinton's birth. According to Maraniss, it was unlikely that Blythe was the father, although VIRGINIA KELLEY firmly stated he was. President Clinton's name at birth was William Jefferson Blythe, IV.

Bill Clinton was born on August 19, 1946. After his birth, Virginia Cassidy Blythe went to live with her parents. She left soon after to attend school in New Orleans and left Bill with his grandparents. He remained with them for four years. On June 19, 1950, she married a car salesman, Roger Clinton, whom she had met in New Orleans. The three then moved to Hot Springs, Arkansas, where Roger Clinton ran the parts department of his brother's car dealership. Virginia and Roger Clinton had one child, Roger, Jr.

Roger Clinton, Sr., was an alcoholic and was abusive to Virginia Clinton and to the two boys. Roger and Virginia divorced when Bill Clinton was 15 years old, but they quickly reconciled and were remarried. Bill then legally changed his name to Clinton. Roger Clinton, Sr., died of cancer in 1968.

Virginia Clinton then married Jeff Dwire, who ran a beauty shop in Hot Springs. Dwire died of diabetes in 1974, and she married Richard Kelley, a food broker. Virginia Clinton Kelley died on January 6, 1994, of breast cancer.

Although there was 10 years' difference in age between Roger, Jr., and Bill Clinton, they were close while growing up. Their closeness stemmed from the problems that Roger Clinton, Sr., brought to the family. He was frequently abusive, leading Bill Clinton to serve as the protector to his mother and younger brother.

Young Roger's problems began when Bill Clinton was governor of Arkansas. Roger was arrested for selling cocaine. When state police came to Governor Clinton with the information that his brother was involved with drugs, Clinton approved a continuation of the investigation of his brother. As a result, Roger was arrested, convicted, and served more than a year in prison in 1985. Bill Clinton, Hillary Clinton, and Virginia Kelley were all in the courtroom when Roger Clinton was sentenced in January 1985.

Both before and after his prison term, Roger Clinton had been involved in a band. By the time he was 10 years old he had formed his own band, called the Hundred Millimeter Banana. His band played in local clubs in Arkansas while he was a teenager, and then after he was released from prison.

After Bill Clinton's election to the presidency, Roger started a band called Politics, and in 1994 released a compact disk entitled "Nothing Good Comes Easy." He also had a number of cameo roles in movies during his brother's presidency and was interviewed on a number of programs, including *Larry King Live* on CNN on August 28, 1999.

Roger Clinton married Molly D'Ann Martin on March 26, 1994, in an outdoor ceremony at the Dallas Arboretum in Texas. President Clinton was the best man. Molly was nearly eight months pregnant when they married, and on May 12, 1994, their son, Tyler Cassidy Clinton, was born.

Throughout the Clinton presidency, Roger Clinton was often in the news. In December 1998, a California judge ordered Roger Clinton to pay $1,258 to a former neighbor who said he was bitten by Clinton's black Labrador as he passed Clinton's house in Redondo Beach, California.

In December 1999, Roger Clinton joined a cultural exchange of entertainers and traveled to Pyongyang, North Korea. Clinton and his rhythm and blues band joined South Korean pop stars for a concert, sponsored by the semiofficial Korean Asia-Pacific Peace Committee. The band played in a 2,000-seat arts theater in Pyongyang. During the visit, Roger Clinton laid flowers at the statue of North Korea's late leader Kim Il Sung. In an interview with CNN news, Roger Clinton said, "You don't have to be a politician to do something worthwhile. I'm hoping to use my position as first brother to . . . just show people what good people really want and that people just want to get along."

The State Department made a point of stating that Roger Clinton did not have any official support from the United States. James Rubin, the State Department spokesman, said of Clinton's visit to North Korea, "As a rule, we do not oppose cultural exchanges with North Korea. As far as what he's going to do and not do, I urge you to contact him directly. We have no official connection with this event in any way, shape or form." During the last days of the Clinton presidency, in January 2001, Roger Clinton was again in the news when President Clinton pardoned him for his 1985 drug conviction. But the pardon for Roger Clinton drew relatively little attention next to the attention drawn from Roger Clinton's lobbying for pardons for a number of other people. According to Julia Payne, an aide to President Clinton, Roger Clinton sought pardons for a list of "five or six people." According to Payne, however, he did "not lobby the president. He personally asked his brother and asked just once if he could look at a list of names."

President Clinton did not pardon any of the people on Roger Clinton's list. After the list was published, Roger Clinton stated that he had not received any money for his efforts. However, Roger Clinton was allegedly paid $10,000 to help obtain diplomatic passports for two businessmen. Roger Clinton denied the allegations, although admitted to receiving $35,000 in cash and checks from the businessmen for consulting services.

Roger Clinton was then subpoenaed on April 20, 2001, to testify before U.S. Attorney Mary Jo White's investigation of whether pardons were given by President Clinton in exchange for any financial rewards to his presidential library or to his brother. A Texas man claimed that Roger Clinton sought more than $200,000 in exchange for an effort to secure a pardon for a member of his family. They alleged that Roger Clinton took the money but did nothing to try to secure the pardon. He denied the allegation and no charges were ever brought against him.

Roger Clinton was also being investigated by the Federal Bureau of Investigation for his involvement with organized crime figures. The investigation began in 1998.

In mid-February 2001, Roger Clinton was charged with driving while intoxicated and with disorderly conduct after an incident in Hermosa Beach, California. In August 2001, Roger Clinton pleaded guilty to a nonalcohol-related charge of reckless driving. The initial charges of drunken driving and disturbing the peace were dismissed. Roger Clinton received 24 months probation and a fine of $1,351.

Clinton, William (Bill) Jefferson
(1946–   ) *president of the United States*

Bill Clinton served as the 42nd president of the United States from 1993–2001. Clinton defeated President GEORGE HERBERT WALKER BUSH on November 3, 1992, garnering 43 percent of the vote. Bush received 38 percent of the vote and third-party challenger HENRY ROSS PEROT received an unprecedented 19 percent of the vote. Clinton was reelected on November 5, 1996, for a second term, garnering 49 percent of the popular vote. The Republican challenger, Senator ROBERT (BOB) JOSEPH DOLE, received 41 percent of the vote and Ross Perot, again in the race, received 8 percent of the vote.

When he ran for president in 1992, Clinton was the governor of Arkansas, where he had been the nation's longest-serving governor. Clinton first ran for governor in 1978, after having served as Arkansas attorney general for two years (1976–78). He was governor for only two years, losing the election in 1980, but recapturing the office in 1982. He was then reelected for five consecutive terms.

During his tenure as governor of Arkansas from 1982 to 1993, Clinton served as chair-man of the Democratic Leadership Council (1990–91), an organization that he had helped to create; chairman of the National Governors' Association (1986–87); chairman of the Educational Commission of the States (1986–87), and chairman of the Mississippi Delta Development Commission (1988–90). In addition he cochaired the National Governors' Association Task Force on Health Care (1990–91).

In 1988, Clinton led a major effort by the nation's governors to restructure national welfare laws and to secure congressional support for the Family Support Act. The Family Support Act proposed to change the welfare system to require that welfare recipients work while receiving support from the federal government. The act was finally passed, in a somewhat altered form, during his first term as president.

Clinton announced his candidacy for president on October 3, 1991, while President George H. W. Bush was still receiving strong public support after defeating Iraq in the Persian Gulf War. As a result of Bush's high polling numbers, many Democratic contenders chose not to enter the 1992 presidential race.

Convinced that he could win the presidency, Clinton actively sought the Democratic nomination, entering the 1992 Democratic primary elections. He focused his fledgling campaign around the nation's economy, constantly using the state of the economy as the theme of his campaign. He hired political strategists JAMES CARVILLE, JR., and PAUL BEGALA to manage the campaign. The major setback to the campaign came when GENNIFER FLOWERS asserted that she had had a 12-year relationship with Clinton, which he denied. Clinton and his wife, HILLARY DIANE RODHAM CLINTON, chose to be interviewed on the national news program *60 Minutes* and fervently denied Flowers's assertions. When she sold her story to a national tabloid, her credibility was further diminished.

By June 1992, the Clinton campaign had won enough primary states to secure the Democratic Party's nomination. In mid-July, at the Democratic National Convention in New York City, Clinton was elected the party's candidate and he then chose Senator ALBERT (AL) GORE, JR. (D-Tenn.), as his running mate. On Tuesday, November 3, 1992, Clinton was elected president and sworn into office on January 20, 1993.

The first year of the presidency was marked by a series of missteps on the part of President Clinton. He was unable to secure the confirmation of his first two nominations for attorney general, ZOE BAIRD and KIMBA WOOD, finally securing the nomination of JANET RENO for attorney general in March 2003. His White House staff underwent a series of staff changes when he brought in DAVID GERGEN, a former Republican speechwriter, to advise him on policy, and moved a number of senior staff, including GEORGE ROBERT STEPHANOPOULOS, to new positions.

He also drew significant criticism from Republicans when he reversed federal abortion policy. On January 22 he issued an executive order that lifted a "gag rule" barring abortion counseling by clinics that received federal funding. He also abolished a prohibition against performing abortions at U.S. military hospitals overseas.

His efforts in the first half of the year to lift a ban against gays and lesbians in the military was marked by opposition from both Republicans in Congress and many in the military. In July 1993, he agreed to a compromise policy called the "don't ask, don't tell" policy which eliminated sexual preference questions from enlistment forms but still banned homosexuals from the military.

The first bill passed by Congress in 1993 was the Family and Medical Leave Act, which had been a key part of the Clinton presidential campaign. The bill granted workers from companies with 50 or more employees up to 12 weeks of unpaid leave in a 12-month period to care for a new baby or a seriously ill family member.

After months of debate, Congress finally passed the economic stimulus package in August 1993 that President Clinton had sought. While some income taxes were raised, as the president had wanted, he dropped an energy tax in favor of a 4.3-cent-per-gallon increase in the federal gasoline tax. The goal of the tax bill was to reduce federal budget deficits over five years.

On May 19, 1993, seven members of the White House travel office were dismissed on the grounds of financial mismanagement. The firings, called "Travelgate," were eventually part of the investigation by independent counsel KENNETH W. STARR. No charges were ever filed against President or Mrs. Clinton for the firings, which Starr alleged were made in order to hire an outside firm with political ties to a Clinton supporter, HARRY THOMASON.

Throughout 1993 Mrs. Clinton worked to create a policy proposal for national health care reform. As head of the White House Task Force on Health Care, Mrs. Clinton met with members of Congress, health care professionals, and others to design legislation throughout the year. Their goal was to introduce legislation in the 1994 legislative session. However, the legislation was attacked in Congress in 1994 both by Republicans and by the health insurance industry. Many Democrats also opposed the health care reform package, which required that employers pay 80 percent of their workers' insurance cost. As a result, the health care reform package never moved forward and essentially died during 1994 in Congress.

The major foreign policy legislation that was passed during the first year of the administration was the North American Free Trade Agreement (NAFTA), which called for the creation of a free trade zone encompassing

Canada, Mexico, and the United States. Although it was not widely supported in Congress, including by Majority Leader RICHARD (DICK) A. GEPHARDT (D-Mo.) in the House of Representatives, Clinton lobbied for the bill and finally secured its passage on November 18, 1993. The legislation took effect on January 1, 1994.

In 1994, the Clinton administration successfully moved its crime bill through Congress, including a $30.2 billion appropriation to pay for more police, to build new prisons, and to ban certain assault weapons.

Foreign policy had its successes and failures. He failed to win European support for intervening militarily in the former Yugoslavia to stop Serbian aggression against Muslims in Bosnia-Herzegovina. In October 1993 U.S. Army forces suffered major losses in Mogadishu, Somalia, after attacks by forces loyal to rebel leader Mohammed Farah Aideed.

The major foreign policy success during the first year came on September 13, 1993, when Clinton brought together Israeli prime minister YITZHAK RABIN and Palestine Liberation Organization (PLO) chairman YASSER ARAFAT for the signing ceremony of a "declaration of principles," more commonly referred to at the time as the Oslo Accords. Israel and the PLO signed an agreement which called for Palestinian self-rule in the Gaza Strip and the West Bank of Israel. In the summer of 1994, President Clinton continued his efforts to bring peace to the Middle East when the Israel-Jordan peace agreement was signed at the White House between Rabin and King Hussein of Jordan. During the second year of the administration, President Clinton signed a nuclear missile agreement with Russian president BORIS YELTSIN that pledged that their nuclear arsenals would not be aimed at each other's countries. President Clinton also lifted the 19-year-old trade embargo on Vietnam in 1994 and renewed China's most-favored-

nation status for trade purposes. In 1995, President Clinton reestablished normal diplomatic relations with Vietnam.

However, in a policy reversal from previous administrations, President Clinton changed the status of Cuban refugees by limiting the number that would be allowed into the United States each year. While all Cuban refugees had been previously allowed to remain in the United States, the new policy stated that only 20,000 would be allowed to stay.

On October 15, 1994, President Clinton sent 20,000 U.S. troops into Haiti to restore President JEAN-BERTRAND ARISTIDE to power. Aristide, who had been ousted in 1991 by a military takeover, returned to Haiti after former president Jimmy Carter arranged for the military junta to peacefully give up their power before the troops removed them. In April 1996 President Clinton withdrew U.S. troops from Haiti after the government seemed to be stabilized.

The Whitewater investigation began in January 1994 when Attorney General Janet Reno named an independent counsel, ROBERT FISKE, to investigate the financial dealings of President and Mrs. Clinton and their Whitewater Land Development project in Arkansas. In August 1994, after the independent counsel law had been reauthorized by Congress, Fiske was replaced by Kenneth Starr, who was appointed by a three-judge federal panel. The legal problems of President and Mrs. Clinton escalated in 1994 when PAULA CORBIN JONES filed a sexual harassment lawsuit in federal court in Arkansas against President Clinton for actions during his tenure as governor of Arkansas.

In November 1994 the Republican Party captured control of the House of Representatives and the Senate for the first time in 40 years. The House, led by NEWTON (NEWT) LEROY GINGRICH (R-Ga.), moved not only to a Republican majority but to a decidedly conservative posture. When the new members took office in January 1995, the Congress actively opposed most of the Clinton administration legislation. Gingrich, who was elected Speaker of the House, became the leading spokesman for the Republicans, frequently criticizing President Clinton and the administration.

In November 1995, President Clinton vetoed the Republican-sponsored budget, which led to a partial shutdown of the federal government for six days in November. President Clinton refused to accept Republican conditions on a temporary spending bill, forcing the furlough of 800,000 federal employees on November 14 until a compromise was reached on November 20 to reopen the government. In December a second government shutdown occurred as President Clinton and Republican leaders in Congress battled for control of the budget. When the government reopened on January 6, 1996, President Clinton claimed the upper hand, leading to a loss of some political clout for Newt Gingrich.

In January 1995, President Clinton authorized a $20 billion loan of federal funds to Mexico as part of a $49.5 billion international loan package to stabilize the peso. The action had been strongly supported by the newly appointed treasury secretary, ROBERT RUBIN.

As 1995 progressed, the Whitewater investigation intensified. On April 22, 1995, both President and Mrs. Clinton were interviewed by the independent counsel, Kenneth Starr. In June 1995, the Resolution Trust Corporation, which was investigating the failure of Madison Guaranty Savings and Loan, owned by JAMES (JIM) and SUSAN McDOUGAL, concluded that the Clintons did not know about a loan made by McDougal's bank to the Whitewater Land Development project, of which they were investors with the Clintons. The report by the Resolution Trust Corporation cleared the Clintons and noted that they lost $42,000 on their investment in the project.

In spite of the report, Starr continued his investigation into whether then attorney general Clinton had pressured one of the lenders into a loan for Madison Guaranty Savings and Loan. Starr also pursued his investigation into the 1993 death of VINCENT W. FOSTER, JR., the deputy White House counsel, and into the Travelgate and Filegate matters within the White House. Starr also secured a conviction against former deputy attorney general WEBSTER HUBBELL on tax evasion and mail fraud for cheating his former law firm's expense account. Hubbell was a partner of Hillary Clinton at the Rose Law Firm in Little Rock, Arkansas.

After new aggressions by SLOBODAN MILOŠEVIĆ in Bosnia, President Clinton announced in November 1996 that U.S. troops would be sent to Bosnia for an additional 18 months. The troops had been originally deployed by President Clinton in November 1995. The issue remained volatile within the United States, with President Clinton vetoing legislation in August 1995 to lift the Bosnian arms embargo. President Clinton sent RICHARD C. HOLBROOKE to Bosnia to try to negotiate a peace accord. In November 1995, during intense negotiations in Dayton, Ohio, Holbrooke succeeded in having a peace agreement signed between Bosnia and Herzegovina, Croatia, and Yugoslavia that "respected the sovereign equality" of each of the countries.

The issue of welfare reform, which had been a leading issue during the presidential campaign, but which failed to move forward under the Democrat-controlled Congress, finally reached fruition in 1996. In August, President Clinton signed a welfare reform bill that ended federal cash assistance for lower-income families with certain conditions, such as employment, being imposed. Clinton was forced to sign the bill, even though it did not meet his goals for welfare reform, since it was an election year. In the 1992 campaign he had promised to "end welfare as we know it," which meant he had to support some form of welfare reform before the next election. In another move toward fulfilling a campaign promise in 1992, President Clinton signed a bill in August 1996 that raised the minimum wage from $4.15 an hour to $5.15 an hour.

The Middle East continued to be a constant problem for the administration as factions within Israel failed to agree on how to deal with the Palestinians. In elections on May 19, 1996, BENJAMIN NETANYAHU overwhelmed Prime Minister SHIMON PERES at the polls to become the new prime minister of Israel. The result was a setback to peace negotiations between Israel and the Palestine Liberation Organization which the Clinton administration had been moving forward.

Iraq also continued to be a thorn among the problems within the Middle East. In September 1996, President Clinton ordered missile attacks on Iraq's military forces in retaliation for SADDAM HUSSEIN's failure to abide by the terms of the peace agreement at the end of the Persian Gulf War.

Following the election in 1996, President Clinton moved a number of his White House staff to new positions and a number of his cabinet members were either replaced or moved to new cabinet positions. Included among the changes were the resignation of Secretary of State WARREN MINOR CHRISTOPHER, who was replaced by MADELEINE KORBEL ALBRIGHT, and the resignation of White House chief of staff LEON EDWARD PANETTA, who was replaced by ERSKINE B. BOWLES.

Although President Clinton succeeded in moving relatively little of his domestic agenda through Congress after the Republican takeover in 1995, he was able to continue policies that produced a strong economy. The 1998 fiscal year ended with a federal budget surplus of $70 billion, the largest surplus since the Eisenhower administration.

Foreign policy dominated the administration's major actions in 1998, partly due to the Whitewater investigation and partly due to the Republican-dominated Congress. President Clinton mediated a peace agreement in Northern Ireland as part of his efforts to end the continuing battles between Protestant militants and the Irish Republican Army (IRA). The issue of Iraq arose again in 1998 when Saddam Hussein consistently placed stumbling blocks in the way of United Nations weapons inspectors. On December 16, 1998, President Clinton and Prime Minister ANTHONY (TONY) CHARLES LYNTON BLAIR of Great Britain authorized renewed air strikes against Iraq.

Most of the winter and spring of 1998 was dominated by the investigation by independent counsel Kenneth Starr into the relationship that President Clinton had with MONICA LEWINSKY. In January 1998, President Clinton was called to testify in the sexual harassment suit of Paula Corbin Jones. In his testimony, Clinton denied that he had a sexual relationship with Lewinsky and that he had attempted to cover it up. Although President Clinton denied the relationship, Lewinsky provided Starr detailed information that confirmed the relationship. In August 1998 President Clinton admitted to an "inappropriate relationship with Lewinsky." Because President Clinton had testified under oath in the Paula Corbin Jones lawsuit that he had not had a relationship with Lewinsky, he was then subject to the charge of perjury.

On September 9, 1998, Starr delivered his report on the Whitewater investigation and the Lewinsky-Clinton relationship to the House of Representatives in what became known as the Starr Report. In November, the House Judiciary Committee began impeachment hearings based on the perjury issue, obstruction of justice, and issues related to abuse of power. Four articles of impeachment were drafted by the judiciary committee. All of the impeachment articles were related to the

William Jefferson Clinton *(Library of Congress)*

Lewinsky case and none to the original Whitewater investigation.

On December 19, 1998, after the judiciary committee had reported out the Articles of Impeachment, the full House approved two of the four articles (perjury and obstruction of justice). President Clinton became the second president in history to be impeached. President Andrew Johnson had been impeached in 1868 but not convicted. President Nixon, although the House was poised to impeach him, resigned before the vote.

On January 7, 1999, the Senate began to sit as a court of impeachment to consider the articles of impeachment brought against President Clinton. Chief Justice William Rehnquist presided over the trial. The trial ended on February 12, 1999, with neither article gaining the majority of votes needed: the Senate voted 46-54 on the first article (perjury) and 50-50 on the second article (obstruction of justice). The Constitution required 67 votes to remove President Clinton from office.

Although the congressional impeachment process was over, President Clinton continued to deal with other issues related to the Jones lawsuit and to the independent counsel investigation. He settled the Jones suit for $850,000, although most of the money went to her lawyers.

President Clinton also signed a consent order on January 19, 2001, the day before he left office, with independent counsel ROBERT RAY, who replaced Kenneth Starr. The agreement called for Ray not to prosecute President Clinton after he left office. In return, President Clinton agreed to accept a five-year suspension of his law license in Arkansas and to pay a $25,000 fine. Clinton also agreed not to seek any legal fees incurred from the Lewinsky investigation to which he might be entitled under the independent counsel act.

In the spring of 1999, President Clinton and Prime Minister Tony Blair supported the intervention of the NATO alliance in the ethnic cleansing of Kosovo by Serbia. The United States led a 78-day bombing campaign that began in March against Serbian troops in Kosovo. President Slobodan Milošević of Serbia finally agreed to withdraw his troops and sign a peace treaty on June 9, 1999.

During 2000, President Clinton maintained a relatively low profile as his wife, Hillary Rodham Clinton, began a race for the U.S. Senate, and Vice President Gore began his race for the presidency. Mrs. Clinton won her race for the Senate but Vice President Gore lost to GEORGE WALKER BUSH in a bitterly contested election.

During the last few days of his administration, President Clinton issued a series of pardons. One of the pardons was for Marc Rich, a financier who had fled to Europe. The pardon was opposed by the Department of Justice and was challenged by Republicans as a reward for a donation to the Clinton Presidential Library in Little Rock, Arkansas. The issue continued to haunt President Clinton after he left office, with hearings held in Congress questioning the appropriateness of the Rich pardon. House Government Reform Committee chairman DANNY (DAN) LEE BURTON held a series of hearings on the pardon issue in the spring of 2001.

President Clinton pardoned a total of 140 people, including his half brother, ROGER CLINTON, JR., for a 1985 drug conviction. In addition, he commuted the sentences of 36 people.

After leaving office, President Clinton moved into spacious offices in Manhattan, but the cost of the offices was attacked by Republicans. Since his wife had just been elected to the U.S. Senate in New York, President Clinton chose to move to less expensive offices. At the suggestion of Representative CHARLES BERNARD RANGEL (D-N.Y.), who represented Harlem, in New York City, President Clinton moved his official offices to Harlem. President and Mrs. Clinton also purchased a home in Chappaqua, New York, and a home in Washington, D.C. His memoirs, entitled *My Life*, were published in June 2004.

President Clinton was born on August 19, 1946, in Hope, Arkansas. His mother, Virginia Cassidy, married William Blythe, but Blythe died in an automobile accident before his son's birth. The son, William Jefferson Blythe IV, was later adopted by Roger Clinton, Virginia Blythe's second husband. The young Bill Blythe took Clinton's surname and became William Jefferson Clinton when he was 15 years old.

Clinton graduated from Georgetown University in international affairs in 1968, after serving as an intern during college for Senator J. William Fulbright (D-Ark.). After winning a Rhodes scholarship, Clinton attended Oxford University from 1968–70. He returned to the United States and entered Yale Law School, graduating in 1973. While at Yale Law School, Clinton met another law student, Hillary Rodham, whom he married on October 11, 1975.

After graduating from law school, Clinton returned to Arkansas to teach law at the University of Arkansas at Fayetteville (1974–76). In 1974 he made his first run for public office by challenging Republican incumbent John Paul Hammerschmidt for a seat in the U.S. House of Representatives. He successfully ran for state attorney general in 1978 and for governor in 1980.

Cohen, William Sebastian

(1940–   ) *secretary of defense, member of the Senate*

William Cohen became President Clinton's third secretary of defense in 1997. Cohen was nominated by Clinton on December 5, 1996, confirmed by the Senate on January 22, 1997, and sworn into office on January 24, 1997.

Cohen, a Republican, served as secretary of defense throughout the entire second term of the Clinton administration (1997–2001). Clinton's first secretary of defense, Congressman LESLIE (LES) ASPIN, JR., resigned after two years and was replaced by WILLIAM J. PERRY, a career executive in the Department of Defense. Neither Aspin nor Perry had developed a coherent defense policy for the United States, which left Cohen a broad opening to promote a new foreign policy agenda. However, Cohen never became the leading foreign policy spokesman for the administration. Secretary of State MADELEINE KORBEL ALBRIGHT, who also took office in 1997, dominated foreign policy issues. In the major foreign policy crisis of the second term, the Balkans and Kosovo, Albright became the administration's lead player.

During the impeachment process, Cohen remained silent. Unlike Secretary of State

Albright, who became an ardent defender of Clinton, Cohen offered no public statement. Cohen's failure to defend the president may have led to his secondary role in the Clinton cabinet. In general, Cohen had a low profile throughout his four years in the administration. He was not considered a policy insider nor a member of the president's inner circle.

Issues that Cohen faced while in office included problems of sexual harassment in the military. He appointed a panel to investigate the military's policy of having both male and female recruits mixed during their first 12 weeks of training. Cohen supported the recommendation of the panel to segregate the recruits during basic training.

Secretary of Defense William S. Cohen
(Department of Defense)

Cohen became an advocate for removing land mines. He successfully moved to have all U.S.-placed land mines removed around the world and initiated training programs for militaries from other nations to remove their mines.

He also took an active role in ensuring security in the Middle East, particularly as it related to escalating military threats from Iran and Iraq. When the United States's embassies were attacked in Africa, Cohen ordered air strikes against al-Qaeda in Afghanistan. Cohen was one of Clinton's strongest supporters in the decision to send troops into the Balkans and to order air strikes in Kosovo.

Cohen became the first Republican in President Clinton's cabinet. Clinton had sought to build a cabinet that was diverse in ethnicity and gender in the first administration, but it did not emphasize political diversity. During his second term in office, Clinton included political diversity as part of his cabinet-building strategy, and chose Cohen, a Republican, as his secretary of defense. Clinton's choice of Cohen was not surprising, given his admiration for the Kennedy presidency. President John F. Kennedy had included a Republican, Robert McNamara, in his cabinet as his secretary of defense.

When Cohen accepted the nomination to President Clinton's cabinet, it ended a 25-year career in the Congress. First elected to the 2nd Congressional District of Maine in 1972, Cohen served three terms in the House before being elected to the U.S. Senate in 1978. He served continuously in the Senate (R-Me.), winning three consecutive elections before accepting President Clinton's nomination to the cabinet as secretary of defense in 1997. Cohen, an expert in defense issues, served on the Senate Armed Services Committee and the Senate Select Committee on Intelligence.

As a freshman representative, Cohen gained a seat on the prestigious House Judiciary Committee. When the Watergate hearings thrust the committee to national attention, Cohen joined the Democrats on the committee in seeking a vote in favor of the impeachment of President RICHARD MILHOUS NIXON. Building on the strength of his Watergate prominence, Cohen sought and won the U.S. Senate seat in 1978 after three terms in the House. Cohen defeated a moderate incumbent Democratic senator, William Hathaway.

Cohen entered the Senate in 1979 when the Democrats controlled the White House and both houses of Congress. As a member of the Senate Armed Services Committee, Cohen quickly became engaged in questioning the administration on foreign policy issues. He gained a reputation as a conservative on defense issues, attacking the Carter administration for the Panama Canal treaties and the Strategic Arms Reduction Talks (START) with the Soviet Union. During the Reagan administration, Cohen became one of the most vocal critics of the administration's handling of the Iran-contra affair.

Born on August 18, 1940, Cohen received his B.A. from Bowdoin College (1962) and his LL.B. from Boston University Law School (1965).

Crowe, William J., Jr.
(1925–) *ambassador to the United Kingdom, chairman of the Joint Chiefs of Staff*

Admiral William J. Crowe, a four-star admiral, served two terms as chairman of the Joint Chiefs of Staff (1985 to 1989). On May 22, 1994, Crowe was nominated by President Clinton as ambassador to Great Britain, confirmed by the Senate on May 12, 1994, and sworn in as ambassador on May 19, 1994. He left the position in 1997. On August 9, 2000, Crowe was awarded the Presidential Medal of Freedom, the nation's highest civilian honor, by President Clinton. The Presidential Medal

of Freedom is awarded for a lifetime of service to the country or at the conclusion of a distinguished career.

Crowe had been appointed chairman of the Joint Chiefs of Staff by President Reagan on October 1, 1985, a position to which he was reappointed in 1987 for another two-year term. He held the position until his retirement from the navy in 1989. Prior to his appointment as ambassador to Great Britain, Crowe had chaired the President's Foreign Intelligence Advisory Board during the first two years of the Clinton administration (1993–94).

Crowe's various positions in the Clinton administration were partly a reward for his support for the Clinton candidacy in 1992. Clinton, who had not served in the military, was often eschewed by the military establishment. Crowe's endorsement of Clinton was considered important to the campaign in 1992, since it represented a strong endorsement from the former chairman of the Joint Chiefs of Staff during a Republican administration and an endorsement from a senior member of the military establishment.

In a press release issued by the Clinton campaign on October 12, 1992, Crowe said, "This is the first time in my life that I have publicly endorsed a candidate for any political office, [because] I believe that the stakes in this election are considerable, both for the national security of this nation and for the prospects of stability throughout the world." Crowe joined a list of 21 retired military officers in a published list who endorsed the Clinton candidacy.

Following his retirement from the navy in 1989, Crowe served as a counselor at the Center for Strategic and International Studies (CSIS) in Washington, D.C., and a professor of geopolitics at the University of Oklahoma. He remained with CSIS until his appointment in 1994 by President Clinton as ambassador to Great Britain.

Crowe's career in the navy began when he was a cadet at Annapolis during World War II. Following his commission in the navy, he held a series of jobs including executive officer of the USS *Wahoo* (1956–58), commander of the USS *Trout* (1960–62), and 10 months in Vietnam in charge of river forces in the Mekong Delta.

In 1962, Crowe was accepted at Princeton University for his doctorate. While most officers in the navy pursued graduate work in engineering, Crowe pursued his degree in political science and international relations. In 1965, Crowe returned to the navy with his Ph.D. from Princeton University. Crowe also held a master's degree in education from Stanford University.

Cuomo, Andrew M.
(1957–   ) *secretary of housing and urban affairs, assistant secretary of housing and urban affairs*

Andrew Cuomo was nominated by President Clinton as his second secretary of housing and urban development (HUD), replacing HENRY CISNEROS. He was sworn into office on January 27, 1997, and served as secretary of housing and urban development from 1997–2001. During the first term of the Clinton administration, Cuomo had served as assistant secretary of housing and urban development (1993–97).

Cuomo's background in urban affairs included directing a private organization that provided support for the homeless, and working as an assistant district attorney in Manhattan. He founded the Housing Enterprise for the Less Privileged (H.E.L.P.) in 1986, which provided transitional housing for the homeless. In 1991 Mayor David Dinkins appointed him director of the New York City Commission on the Homeless, while he continued to run H.E.L.P. Prior to creating H.E.L.P., he

Andrew M. Cuomo *(Department of Housing and Urban Affairs)*

had worked in the district attorney's office in Manhattan (1984–85) and as a partner in the New York City law firm of Blutrich, Falcone and Miller (1985–88).

His involvement in Democratic Party politics began when his father, MARIO M. CUOMO, entered the 1982 race for governor of New York. Andrew Cuomo spent a year as campaign manager, with an annual salary of $1, developing campaign strategies and working as a key adviser to his father. Mario Cuomo was elected governor of New York and became a major voice in both the state and the national Democratic Party.

In 1994 Mario Cuomo again ran for governor of New York against Republican George Pataki but lost the election. After leaving the Clinton administration, Andrew Cuomo entered the governor's race in New York, running for the Democratic nomination in 2002, but losing in the primary election to New York state comptroller Carl McCall. McCall faced Pataki in the general election, but lost, giving the Republican Party the state house again. Pataki won a third term as governor.

Born on December 6, 1957, in Queens, New York, Cuomo received his B.A. from Fordham University (1979) and J.D. from Albany Law School of Union University (1982). He married Kerry Kennedy, the daughter of Senator Robert Kennedy of New York, who had been assassinated in June 1968, after winning the California primary in his run for the Democratic nomination for president. When Andrew Cuomo became secretary of housing and urban development, he was the second-youngest cabinet officer in history. Only Robert Kennedy, appointed attorney general by his brother, President John F. Kennedy, was younger while serving in the cabinet.

Cuomo, Mario M.
(1932–) *governor of New York*

First elected governor of New York in 1982, Mario Cuomo was reelected in both 1986 and 1990. Cuomo became the longest-serving Democratic governor in New York history. He was defeated in 1994 for a fourth term by the Republican candidate for governor, George Pataki. During the period in which President Clinton served, Cuomo was considered by the White House as a nominee for the U.S. Supreme Court, but quietly told the president he was not interested. There was no public explanation as to why he declined the nomination. Cuomo remained a national figure in Democratic politics but was never considered an insider within the Clinton camp.

The explanation for Cuomo's failure to become a close adviser to President Clinton was twofold. First, Cuomo remained a constant challenge to Clinton's control of the Democratic Party machine, particularly in New York State and in New York City. Second, Cuomo tended to have more liberal views than Clinton on domestic policy issues. While Clinton was trying to move the Democratic Party closer to the political center to capture the Reagan Democrats, Cuomo was continuing to support traditional Democratic views on social policy. Some have suggested that President Clinton considered Mario Cuomo for the Supreme Court in order to remove Cuomo from the Democratic Party. By appointing Cuomo to the Supreme Court, Clinton would also have removed a potential rival in the 1996 presidential election.

Mario Cuomo's son, ANDREW M. CUOMO, was appointed to the Clinton cabinet in 1993 as assistant secretary of housing and urban development. In 1997, at the beginning of the president's second term, Andrew Cuomo was named secretary of housing and urban development and remained in the position throughout the second term. Andrew Cuomo was closely aligned with his father, having been campaign manager for his father's 1982 successful candidacy for governor.

Mario Cuomo rose to national prominence in 1982 as governor of New York as a liberal Democrat, often challenging the conservative agenda of the administration of President Ronald Reagan. In 1984, Cuomo was chosen by the Democratic National Committee to deliver the keynote address at the Democratic National Convention in San Francisco. By 1992, he had become one of the nation's most prominent Democratic governors, often speaking out on issues affecting the nation's cities and states. Many members of the national Democratic Party urged Cuomo to run for president in 1992, but he declined. Cuomo never seriously pursued the Democratic nomination in 1992 that Governor Bill Clinton of Arkansas finally captured. For whatever reason, Cuomo never explained why he chose not to pursue the nomination for president.

During his tenure as governor of New York, Cuomo appointed 112 judges, including all of the judges of the Court of Appeals, as well as the first and second women judges, the first African-American judge, the first Hispanic judge, and the first woman to serve as chief judge.

Born June 15, 1932, Cuomo received his B.A. degree summa cum laude from St. John's College (1953) and his LL.B. summa cum laude from St. John's University (1956). His career began when he was a law clerk for Judge Adrian P. Burke of the New York Court of Appeals. He then entered private practice in 1958 with the law firm of Corner, Weisbrod, Froeb, and Charles. In 1975 Cuomo left his law practice following his appointment by Governor Hugh Carey as New York's secretary of state. His political career took another turn in 1978 when he was elected lieutenant governor, a position he held until being elected governor in 1982.

After leaving the governor's office, Cuomo returned to the practice of law as a partner in the New York law firm of Willkie, Farr, & Gallagher. His job in the law firm focused on advising public companies on issues of corporate governance and financial reporting and other aspects of corporate law. Cuomo also joined the lecture circuit after leaving the governor's office and became a popular speaker.

Currie, Betty

(1939–   ) *secretary to President Clinton*

Betty Currie served as President Clinton's personal secretary throughout his two terms in the White House (1993–2001). Currie, who maintained a low profile as the president's secretary, was thrust into the public limelight during the investigation by independent counsel KENNETH W. STARR into the MONICA LEWINSKY scandal.

Starr contended that Currie had sought the help of VERNON EULION JORDAN, JR., in December 1997 in finding Lewinsky a position in the private sector in New York City. Starr also contended that Lewinsky sent packages to President Clinton using Currie as the recipient on the address given to courier services. Starr had receipts from a Washington, D.C., messenger service showing that Lewinsky sent packages to Currie in the White House on nine separate occasions between October 7 and December 8, 1997. In addition to questions from Starr as to the gifts, Currie was also questioned about the number of times that Lewinsky visited Clinton in the Oval Office. Currie's recollection of the number of visits varied from the number given by Lewinsky.

When the House of Representatives handed down articles of impeachment against President Clinton in December 1998, the ninth of 11 impeachable offenses was that Clinton had tried to persuade Currie to lie in his behalf with regard to Monica Lewinsky. Clinton and Currie denied any effort to change her testimony or for her to lie about Lewinsky.

Currie first joined the federal government in 1959 with the Navy Department after moving from Illinois to Washington, D.C. She worked in various positions within the federal government throughout her career. During the Carter administration, she worked in the Agency for International Development and later worked at the Peace Corps. In 1984 she volunteered on the campaign of vice presidential candidate Geraldine Ferraro. Four years later, she again volunteered for a presidential campaign, working on the campaign of Massachusetts governor Michael S. Dukakis.

When Governor Bill Clinton of Arkansas sought the presidency in 1992, Currie signed on to work in the presidential campaign. She became the office manager of the "war room" in the Clinton campaign headquarters in Little Rock, Arkansas.

Following the election, Currie became the personal secretary to Warren Christopher, who was cochair of the Clinton transition team. Currie, who had not known Clinton prior to the campaign, was selected as his personal secretary after having worked for Christopher during the transition.

Currie was raised in Waukegan, Illinois, and graduated in 1957 from Waukegan Township High School in Illinois. After graduation from high school, she became a secretary. In 1959, she moved to Washington, D.C., and began working as a secretary first in the Navy Department and then in the postal service. In 1969, Joseph Blatchford, who headed the Peace Corps, hired Currie as his secretary. When Blatchford moved to ACTION, the federal agency created to oversee the Peace Corps, Currie went with him.

She remained with ACTION throughout the seventies and served as the administrative assistant to three directors. During this period, she married, divorced, and began dating Robert Currie, an ACTION executive. They were married in 1988. When Ronald Reagan was elected in 1980, he appointed Dallas lawyer Thomas Pauken as the head of ACTION, and Pauken promptly demoted Currie. Pauken, who believed the agency was too liberal in its orientation, demoted many of the existing staff. Currie retired from the federal government in 1984 and began to work for Geraldine Ferraro's campaign for vice president. In 1988 she worked for Michael Dukakis's presidential campaign and in 1992 moved to Little Rock, Arkansas to work for JAMES CARVILLE, JR., the campaign manager for the Clinton campaign. After the election, she remained in Little Rock and became the secretary to WARREN MINOR CHRISTOPHER, who became the presidential transition director. When President Clinton's secretary decided not to leave Little Rock and move to Washington, D.C., with the new administra-

tion, Currie was asked to take the job as secretary to the president.

Cutler, Lloyd N.
(1917–   ) *White House counsel*

Lloyd Cutler was named White House counsel as the Whitewater investigation began to broaden under independent counsel ROBERT FISKE. Cutler, a partner in the Washington, D.C. law firm of Witmer, Cutler, and Pickering, replaced BERNARD NUSSBAUM who had abruptly resigned in April 1994. Nussbaum had dealt with three nominations for attorney general, including the failed nominations of ZOE BAIRD and KIMBA WOOD, and had been deeply involved in the Fiske investigation of the death of deputy White House counsel VINCENT W. FOSTER, JR.

Cutler was brought into the White House as counsel in March 1994 to enhance the position's stature among the White House staff, many of whom were young and had been involved with the 1992 presidential campaign. Cutler was known for his political expertise, having served as White House counsel to President Carter. A former White House counsel to President Nixon, Leonard Garment, described the decision to bring Cutler into the Clinton administration. "He's old enough and has enough gray hair and character security to understand what to do for a president in trouble," Garment said. Not everyone in the White House approved of Cutler's appointment. Some White House staff believed that they had been elected because they were not from the Washington community and were independent of the establishment.

Chief of Staff THOMAS MCLARTY and President Clinton chose Cutler from among a small list of possible replacements for Nussbaum. Cutler, who did not know President Clinton well, had become friends with members of the

White House staff during the nomination process for Zoe Baird, whom he had recommended for attorney general, and for his support of President Clinton during the Whitewater investigation.

Once President Clinton had made the decision, he called Cutler and offered him the position. Two days later, Cutler was at the White House. When President Clinton announced the appointment of Cutler, he said that he wanted "to bring someone of unquestioned integrity, and a lot of experience in dealing with the kinds of issues that have to come into the White House." He also said that he wanted "someone who will inspire confidence in me and in you, the press, and most importantly, in the American people, and that we are going the extra mile to deal with all matters in the appropriate way."

However, Cutler, who was 76 years old, agreed only to serve for 130 days, until the White House had time to find a permanent replacement. Cutler did not accept any salary for his position as White House counsel. The 130 days was determined by a rule in the federal government that allowed for a "special government employee," but the employee was limited to working for 130 days. Cutler was replaced by ABNER MIKVA.

One of the roles that Cutler played in the White House with regard to the Whitewater investigation, which was expanded by independent counsel KENNETH W. STARR, was to develop the legal defense fund for President and Mrs. Clinton, which would be supported by private contributions. The legal defense fund would pay for private attorneys.

Cutler served as special counsel to the president on the ratification of the SALT II treaty (1970–80), as the president's special representative for maritime and boundary negotiations with Canada (1977–79), and as a senior consultant of the President's Commission on Strategic Forces (also known as the Scowcroft Commission) in 1983–84.

Born on November 10, 1917, Cutler graduated from Yale University (1936) and Yale Law School (1939).

Cutter, W. Bowman
(1943–   ) *deputy director of the National Economic Council*

W. Bowman Cutter served as deputy assistant to the president for economic policy, and as deputy director of the National Economic Council from 1993, when the administration came into office, until 1996. In March 1996, Cutter joined E. M. Warburg, Pincus & Co. as a managing partner. E. M. Warburg, Pincus & Co. is a private equity investment firm.

The National Economic Council was chaired by ROBERT RUBIN, who served as assistant to the president for economic policy, and as director of the National Economic Council. Rubin had two deputies: Cutter and GENE SPERLING. Sperling was responsible for domestic issues and coordination of policy and "message," and Cutter was responsible for the international economic policies of the National Economic Council.

One of Cutter's key duties was to oversee the National Economic Council deputies group, which coordinated interagency international economic policy. Among the major projects undertaken by the deputies group was coordinating the U.S.-Japanese framework trade talks during 1994. Cutter also was the key White House staffer in charge of crafting legislation to revamp the superfund toxic waste cleanup program through the deputies group.

Cutter was widely praised during his tenure in the Clinton administration for building strong personal relationships among the departmental deputies responsible for international policy. As I. M. Destler wrote in his study of the National Economic Council, the relationships that Cutter fostered among agency deputies "made it easy for individual deputies to 'pick up the phone' and settle lower-level disputes between agencies." (See I. M. Destler, *The National Economic Council: A Work in Progress,* 1996, page 62.)

Prior to joining the Clinton administration, Cutter worked with Coopers & Lybrand as the managing partner of the firm's strategic services division. One of Cutter's roles at Coopers & Lybrand had been to work with the National Aeronautics and Space Administration (NASA) to sell U.S. corporations on using the space shuttle for research and development. According to Cutter in an October 10, 1983, article in *Forbes* magazine, the idea was to help NASA sell "the concept of space" as a place for experimentation.

During the Carter administration, Cutter had been executive associate director of the Office of Management and Budget. Harold Brown, former secretary of defense during the Carter administration, is currently a director of E. M. Warburg, Pincus & Co.

Cutter, frequently referred to as "Bo," held economics degrees from Harvard University, Princeton University, and Oxford University, where he was a Rhodes scholar. He served on the Council of Foreign Relations, the Advisory Board of the Woodrow Wilson School of Princeton University, the board of directors of the Immigration and Refugee Services of America, and the board of directors of CARE and the board of directors of VITA (Volunteers in Technical Assistance).

Daley, Richard Michael
(1942–) *mayor of Chicago*

Richard M. Daley was elected to his first term as mayor of Chicago on April 4, 1989, to complete the term of the late Harold Washington. Daley, a Democrat, was reelected in 1991, 1995, and 1999 by overwhelming margins.

Daley, the son of former Chicago mayor Richard J. Daley, was a key supporter of President Clinton in the 1992 presidential election and delivered Chicago for the Democratic ticket of Clinton-Gore. Daley's brother, WILLIAM MICHAEL DALEY, was also a key supporter of President Clinton in the 1992 presidential election and served as Clinton's Illinois chair for the presidential campaign. William Daley, a Chicago lawyer, was named secretary of commerce in 1997, after serving as special counsel to President Clinton on the North American Free Trade Agreement in 1993. William Daley also was chairman of Vice President Al Gore's presidential campaign in 2000 and was appointed president of SBC Communications in 2001.

In June 1996 Mayor Richard Daley was elected president of the national conference of mayors, a position his father had been elected to in 1959. Richard Daley served a one-year term as president.

Daley was able to build strong coalitions within the racially charged city throughout his tenure in office. According to the 1990 census, Chicago's 2.8 million citizens were 39 percent African-American, 38 percent white, and nearly 20 percent Hispanic. Although race relations was continually an issue in Chicago, Daley was considered a strong advocate for the city's minority populations. But he was equally respected and supported by the business establishment in Chicago. As the *New York Times* noted in an article on April 1, 1995, "Black ministers pray and pass the plate for him. Gay and Hispanic groups endorse him. Business leaders, real estate developers, and lots of Republicans support him."

Daley's strength was that he reached out to both Democrats and Republicans in the election process and as mayor. Unlike his father, who had been chairman of the Cook County Democratic Party, Richard Daley sought to build coalitions for his administration among both political parties in Chicago. Daley's decision to use the Cook County Democratic Party as the centerpiece of his political decision making was largely a pragmatic decision. The Democratic Party political machine that his father had overseen, which had grown as the Daley administration used city jobs for political rewards, was largely disbanded by a series of court decisions that abolished patronage in most city jobs. Civil service replaced patronage in the years between the two Daley administrations.

Daley had strong support within the Illinois legislature. In 1995 the state of Illinois took over the troubled Chicago public school system, fired its elected board, and handed the system over to Mayor Daley to restructure. He handpicked a five-member team to run the school district and became directly involved in its decisions. His experience in actively working with the school district received such accolades that the National Board for Professional Teaching Standards nominated Daley to its board of directors. Daley became the first mayor to serve on the governing board, which was composed of governors, state legislators, teachers, and teacher organizations.

Born in Chicago in 1942, Richard M. Daley served as state's attorney for Cook County before being elected mayor of Chicago in 1989. He graduated with a B.A. and a J.D. from DePaul University.

Daley, William Michael
(1948–   ) *secretary of commerce, special counsel to the president*

William M. Daley, brother of Chicago's mayor RICHARD MICHAEL DALEY, served as secretary of commerce from 1997 to 2000. Daley was nominated by President Clinton on December 13, 1996, at the end of Clinton's first term in office, and sworn into office on January 30, 1997, following his Senate confirmation by a 95-2 vote. Daley succeeded MICHAEL (MICKEY) KANTOR, who had served as acting commerce secretary from 1996–97 following the death in a plane crash in Bosnia of Secretary of Commerce RONALD H. BROWN. Prior to joining the administration, Daley had been president and

chief operating officer of Amalgamated Bank of Chicago (1990–93).

Daley resigned his post as secretary of commerce in June 2000 to serve as chairman of Vice President Al Gore's unsuccessful presidential campaign. Following Vice President Gore's defeat in the 2000 election, Daley returned to Chicago as president of SBC Communications in 2001.

Daley, whose father was the legendary mayor Richard J. Daley of Chicago (1955–76), served as chairman of the Illinois Clinton campaign during the 1992 presidential election. In August 1993, Daley was named special counsel to President Clinton to lead the congressional lobbying effort to gain passage of the North American Free Trade Agreement (NAFTA). During the 1996 presidential campaign, Daley

William M. Daley *(Department of Commerce)*

was named as the cochairman of the Democratic National Convention host committee. Daley, active in state and local Democratic politics, helped to deliver Chicago (80 percent of the vote) and Illinois (55 percent of the vote) to Clinton in 1996.

Following the 1992 election, Daley was rumored to be Clinton's nominee for the position of secretary of transportation. However, Clinton chose FEDERICO PEÑA, the mayor of Denver, for that post. Daley, a Chicago lawyer at the time, continued to support Clinton, and in 1993 was named special counsel on NAFTA. Daley commuted to Washington from Chicago to lobby Congress for passage of NAFTA.

As secretary of commerce, one of Daley's assignments from President Clinton was to lead the campaign to have Congress grant normal trading relations to China. Congress was generally opposed to the trading agreement, since China had a poor human rights record. In addition, Daley oversaw the 1990 census. The census bureau, a division of the Commerce Department, sought to implement a statistical sampling process for the census but the Supreme Court ruled that the bureau could not use sampling for purposes of apportioning seats for the House of Representatives. Complete counts were required.

William M. Daley, born August 9, 1948, was one of seven children (four boys and three girls) born to Richard and Eleanor Daley. He grew up in the South Side Bridgeport neighborhood, attending De La Salle High School. He received his B.A. degree from Chicago's Loyola University and obtained his LL.B. from the John Marshall Law School in Chicago. In 1975 Daley began to practice law in Chicago. Although Daley served in elected public office, he worked on the presidential campaigns of Walter Mondale (1984) and Michael Dukakis (1988) and on the Senate campaign of Carol Moseley-Braun (1992).

Daley was on the board of the Federal National Mortgage Association and the board of Chicago's Field Museum. He also was on the board of directors of Electronic Data System Corporation.

D'Amato, Alfonse (Al) Marcello
(1937–   ) *member of the Senate*

Alfonse D'Amato (R-N.Y.) served as the U.S. senator from New York from 1981–99, losing his seat in a bitter election to Democrat Charles Schumer. Schumer won with 54 percent of the vote. D'Amato had originally defeated Democrat Elizabeth Holtzman in the 1980 Senate race.

D'Amato was chair of the powerful Senate Committee on Banking, Housing and Urban Development. In addition, D'Amato chaired the Senate Whitewater Committee, which investigated the Whitewater holdings of President and Mrs. Clinton in Arkansas and other issues. Among the issues the committee looked into was the death of VINCENT W. FOSTER, JR. Most Democrats in the Senate, particularly committee member Senator Paul Sarbanes (D-Md.), accused D'Amato of using the committee for partisan reasons.

After Senator ROBERT (BOB) JOSEPH DOLE lost the 1996 presidential election to President Clinton, D'Amato abruptly ended the Senate Whitewater Committee's investigation. D'Amato had been cochairman of Dole's presidential campaign. On November 8, 1996, D'Amato announced that the committee had concluded its work. President Clinton won 59 percent of the vote in New York, in spite of D'Amato's constant criticism during the election.

D'Amato realized that his seat would be up for reelection in 1998 and he could not afford to be viewed in New York as a partisan who was attacking President Clinton. If he was going to win reelection in 1998, he needed the support of Democrats in New York. D'Amato was subsequently defeated.

Not only had he failed to capture Democratic support in the mid-1990s, but D'Amato had also failed to build support among conservative Republicans. He publicly called for Speaker of the House of Representatives NEWTON (NEWT) LEROY GINGRICH (R-Ga.) and House Republicans to moderate their message. In an interview with CNN television anchor Judy Woodruff on May 3, 1996, D'Amato noted that Gingrich had focused too heavily on a small portion of the Republican Party. "Less than 10 percent of the people," D'Amato said to Woodruff, "knew anything about the Contract with America," Gingrich's 1994 campaign platform for House Republicans. D'Amato's efforts to move the Republican Party away from Gingrich's conservative agenda became controversial after he chaired the Senate Whitewater Committee.

He graduated in business administration from Syracuse University (1959) and received his J.D. from Syracuse University (1961).

Danforth, John
(1936–) *special counsel, Department of Justice, into deaths of Branch Davidians at Waco, Texas; member of the Senate*

John Danforth (R-Mo.) served in the U.S. Senate for three terms (1977–95). After he left the Senate, Attorney General JANET RENO appointed Danforth as the special counsel for the investigation into the FBI's 1993 assault on the Branch Davidian compound in Waco, Texas. Reno appointed Danforth on September 9, 1999, to lead the Department of Justice investigation into the April 19, 1993, stand-off. As special counsel, Danforth was charged by the attorney general with determining whether the government had made mistakes when it confronted DAVID KORESH and the Branch

Davidians, and whether any government employee had used incendiary devices or engaged in gunfire at the Mt. Carmel compound of the Branch Davidians. He was also charged with determining if any federal employees, particularly the FBI agents, had committed perjury during the initial investigation or destroyed evidence.

Danforth was a moderate Republican, known in the Senate for his strong sense of personal ethics, his thoughtful speeches, and his consistent efforts to find compromise on difficult decisions that members of the Senate were faced with. During the 1997 and 1998 investigation of President Clinton's relationship with MONICA LEWINSKY, Danforth called for Clinton's impeachment. In a January 1998 interview on PBS's *NewsHour with Jim Lehrer*, Danforth said, "It would be a very bad thing for our country if we came out of all of this and said, in effect, well, it's okay . . . to obstruct justice."

Danforth had made a name for himself in 1991 as a staunch defender of Clarence Thomas, President GEORGE HERBERT WALKER BUSH's nominee for the U.S. Supreme Court. Thomas had once served as assistant attorney general to Danforth in Missouri, worked for Monsanto Chemical Corp. based on Danforth's recommendation, and later worked as a staff member in Danforth's Senate office. Following the hearings, Danforth wrote a book, entitled *Resurrection*, about the hearings.

During the 2000 election, GEORGE WALKER BUSH was said to be considering Danforth as his vice presidential choice. As a pro-life Episcopal minister, who remained popular in the battleground state of his native Missouri, Danforth's popularity among moderate Republicans recommended him to Bush.

Although Bush did not name Danforth to the vice presidency, he did name him as his envoy for peace in the Sudan on September 6, 2001. Danforth had two missions to Sudan and the surrounding region, one in November

2001 and one in January 2002. His recommendation to President Bush was to continue humanitarian assistance to Sudan as a high priority for U.S. foreign policy, and work to find a negotiated settlement for the warring parties in the Sudan.

Prior to his election to the U.S. Senate, Danforth served two terms as Missouri's attorney general. Born September 5, 1936, Danforth received an undergraduate degree in divinity and a law degree from Yale University and was a lawyer in New York and St. Louis before running for political office.

Danforth was independently wealthy as a result of his family fortune in the Ralston Purina conglomerate.

Daschle, Thomas Andrew

(1947–   ) *member of the Senate, member of the House of Representatives*

Tom Daschle was elected to the Senate from South Dakota in 1986 and reelected in 1992 and in 1998. He was elected minority leader for the session beginning in 1995 and remained minority leader until mid-2001, when he was elected majority leader. Following the Republican takeover of the Senate in 2003, he lost his role as majority leader but was elected again as minority leader.

His ascent to the position of minority leader during his second term in office began when Senator GEORGE JOHN MITCHELL (D-Me.) announced his retirement in 1994. Soon after Mitchell's announcement, Daschle began campaigning for the job of minority leader. Budget Committee chairman James Sasser (D-Tenn.) also announced his candidacy for minority leader, but lost his seat in the November elections. Senator CHRISTOPHER JOHN DODD (D-Conn.) emerged as a candidate for minority leader only after Sasser withdrew in November. On December 2, 1994, in a caucus

vote, Daschle was elected minority leader, defeating Dodd by a vote of 24–23.

Daschle remained minority leader for five and a half years before the Senate unexpectedly changed majority control in mid-2001. On June 6, 2001, following the defection of Senator James Jeffords (R-Vt.), who left the Republican Party and became an independent, Daschle was elected majority leader. Daschle said, "This will be America's first 50-49-1 Senate. What does not change with this new balance of power is the need for principled compromise. Bipartisanship, or I guess I now should say tripartisanship, is still a requirement."

Daschle moved into the Democratic hierarchy at a relatively early age by supporting the Democratic leadership. After his election to the Senate in 1986, but before he had been sworn into office in January 1987, Daschle publicly endorsed Senator ROBERT C. BYRD of West Virginia for majority leader. After being elected majority leader, Byrd assigned Daschle to the Finance Committee, one of the most prestigious committees in the Senate. When George Mitchell was elected majority leader, Daschle became one of his key supporters.

As cochair of the Vietnam-Era Veterans in Congress, Daschle supported legislation for compensation for Agent Orange–afflicted veterans in 1991. He also supported the Veterans Benefits Improvement Act of 1994, which authorized disability payments to Persian Gulf War veterans suffering from undiagnosed war-related illnesses.

During the Clinton administration, Daschle became the Senate coordinator of the effort to pass the health care reform bill in 1994. He held weekly policy meetings of congressional leaders and administration officials and convened a two-day policy briefing for members of Congress interested in the issue.

Although Daschle was the leader of the Democrats in the Senate, he remained low-key throughout the events surrounding the MON-

ICA LEWINSKY investigation by the independent counsel, KENNETH W. STARR. When one high-profile member of the Senate, Senator Joseph Lieberman (D–Conn.), said of President Clinton that his behavior was "immoral" and "disgraceful," Daschle remained silent. Daschle said simply, "This has been a very troubling matter to me." However, Daschle later denounced President Clinton for his behavior.

Months before the impeachment articles reached the Senate, President Clinton called Daschle to ask if it might be possible to find 34 Democrats who would sign a letter saying they would not convict if the House were to impeach the president. Daschle would not provide such a letter to President Clinton. During the Senate trial, Daschle joined Senate majority leader CHESTER TRENT LOTT (R–Miss.) to develop the process for the proceedings. He never fought Lott on the process and allowed Lott considerable authority, much to Clinton's dismay.

When the Republicans regained control of the Senate in January 2003, Daschle was again elected minority leader. Daschle replaced Lott as majority leader in 2001 and, in a game of musical chairs, was replaced by Lott as majority leader in 2003.

Born on December 9, 1947 in Aberdeen, South Dakota, Daschle became the first member of his family to graduate from college when he graduated from South Dakota State University (1969). After serving for three years as an intelligence officer in the U.S. Air Force Strategic Air Command (1969–72), he spent five years as an aide to South Dakota senator James Abourezk.

In 1978 Daschle returned to South Dakota to run for a seat in the House of Representatives. He was elected by a slim margin of 139 votes and served until 1986, when he successfully ran for the Senate.

Following the terrorism attacks of September 11, 2001, a letter was sent to Daschle's office in October 2001 that contained anthrax. Twenty staff members of Daschle's were exposed to the anthrax and rushed to the hospital. All survived. As a result, however, Daschle was forced to vacate his office for months and use temporary offices while his was decontaminated.

Days, Drew S., III
(1941–   ) *solicitor general, Department of Justice*

Drew Days III was named solicitor general in the Department of Justice by President Clinton in 1993. Days easily moved through the confirmation process in the Senate and was sworn into office in May 1993. Among Days's supporters in the Senate was Senator Alan Simpson (R–Wyo.) who praised Days for his "ability to be terribly forceful and keep [his] head . . . steadiness . . . and humor." Days left the administration in 1996.

President Clinton's success in moving Drew Days through the appointment process with relative ease was important given the problems that other nominees in the Department of Justice faced in their confirmation hearings. Two nominees for attorney general, ZOE BAIRD and KIMBA WOOD, had been withdrawn by President Clinton after problems arose in their hearings. In addition, LANI GUINIER, nominated by President Clinton as assistant attorney general for civil rights (a position that Days held in the Carter administration), faced such stiff opposition in her Senate confirmation hearings that her name was also withdrawn by President Clinton.

Born on August 29, 1941, Days received his B.A. degree (English literature), cum laude, from Hamilton College (1963) and his LL.B. from Yale Law School (1966). After leaving law school, he joined the Illinois Civil Liberties Union as an attorney and soon moved to the Chicago law firm of Cotton, Watt, Jones, King, and Bowlus. From 1967–69 Days served as a Peace Corps volunteer in Honduras and, after leaving the Peace Corps, became an attorney for the National Association for the Advancement of Colored People (NAACP) Legal Defense and Education Fund as first assistant counsel (1970–76). While at the NAACP Legal Defense and Education Fund, Days also taught at Temple University School of Law, where he became an associate professor of law.

When the Democrats regained the White House, Days joined the Carter administration, serving in the Department of Justice as the assistant attorney general for civil rights (1977–81). He became the first African American to hold the position. Days's tenure in the Department of Justice was largely due to Attorney General Griffin Bell, who as a private attorney had met Days while he was working for the NAACP. Bell brought Days into the Department of Justice.

When President Reagan took office in 1981, Days left the Department of Justice to join Yale University Law School as a professor of law (1981–present). He focused on areas of civil procedure, federal jurisdiction, Supreme Court practice, antidiscrimination law, comparative constitutional law, and international human rights. Days was the first African American on the Yale University Law School faculty and the first African American to gain tenure at the law school.

Although out of the public eye, Days remained involved in public issues. During the George H. W. Bush administration's fight to have Clarence Thomas confirmed on the Supreme Court, Days was one of three African-American law professors to testify against Thomas. Days noted that Thomas had not been supportive of affirmative action programs. In spite of substantial opposition among supporters of affirmative action programs, Thomas was confirmed by the Senate.

Days returned to the Clinton administration for eight years as solicitor general (1993–2001). Days argued for federal set-asides for minorities and women in *Adarand v. Pena*. Although Days had argued in 1980, as Jimmy Carter's assistant attorney general for civil rights, that federal set-asides should be continued under the Public Works Employment Act, he wrote in 1987 in the *Yale Law Journal* that he may have argued too strongly for such set-asides for certain minorities. He said in the *Yale Law Journal*, "One of the major flaws in the set-aside upheld in *Fullilove*, one that subsequent federal, state, and local programs have replicated, is that the record did not explain why six racial groups were selected to receive the 10 percent preference." However, in *Adarand*, Days noted that the Clinton administration supported federal set-asides for minorities without classifying any racial groups into or out of the classification.

The role of the solicitor general is to represent the United States government before the Supreme Court. Not only does the solicitor general argue cases before the Supreme Court, but the solicitor general's office determines which Supreme Court cases the government will take a position on and which cases the government will argue in the Court.

After leaving the Clinton administration, Days joined the Washington, D.C., law firm of Morrison & Foerster.

DeLay, Thomas Dale
(1947–   ) *member of the House of Representatives*

Tom DeLay, a conservative Republican in the U.S. House of Representatives from the 22nd Congressional District in Texas, was one of the most outspoken critics of President Clinton during the impeachment process in 1998.

DeLay maintained a "Family Values" Web site and repeatedly criticized Clinton's involvement with MONICA LEWINSKY, a White House intern. Although DeLay was a critic of Clinton's involvement with Lewinsky and his failure to be forthcoming in the depositions, DeLay himself had faced legal issues regarding the truthfulness of his depositions. DeLay came under scrutiny in 1994 as a result of a civil lawsuit involving fraud of his defunct extermination business, Albo Pest Control, Inc. DeLay was at one point criticized for making conflicting statements under oath. The case was settled before it went to trial. During the impeachment proceedings against President Clinton, DeLay did not become a central figure within the conservative Republican leadership. He allowed others, such as ROBERT BARR and LINDSEY GRAHAM, to take the leadership roles.

DeLay developed a strong bond with Dick Cheney, who served in the House as the Republican whip from 1988 to 1989. During the 1988 Republican presidential convention, DeLay asked Cheney to be part of the whip's House organization. Cheney asked DeLay to help persuade the rules committee of the convention to allow members of Congress to have floor privileges. The request had been repeatedly turned down by previous Republican presidential conventions. DeLay succeeded in his mission and Cheney gave him a major role within the whip organization of the House.

Following the Republican takeover of the House of Representatives in 1994, DeLay followed in Cheney's footsteps and was elected House majority whip, the third highest leadership position within the majority party in the House. DeLay had carefully planned for his run at the leadership post, hiring political consultant Mildred Webber in 1993 to work with him. Webber's job was to assess Republican candidacies for the House in the 1994 election and to offer DeLay's help for those candidates with a strong chance of winning the seat. When DeLay challenged the incumbent whip, Robert S. Walker, following the 1994 elections, he won. NEWTON (NEWT) LEROY GINGRICH, who became Speaker of the House in 1995, had been a close friend of Robert S. Walker

and never became a close ally of DeLay's in the House. Gingrich's distrust of DeLay also stemmed from a political battle for House minority whip in 1989 when Gingrich defeated Edward Madigan. DeLay had managed Madigan's campaign for the post.

In 1997 DeLay joined 18 conservative Republicans in the House to oust Gingrich as Speaker of the House. Representative Lindsey Graham was at the center of the movement to oust Gingrich. The coup to oust Gingrich failed, but DeLay had lost significant power in the process with the established leadership of the House Republicans, led by Gingrich.

DeLay routinely voted for legislation that supported conservative positions and subsequently earned a 100 percent voting rating from the *Christian Voice* magazine and the *New American* magazine. He routinely supported business interests over environmental interests, such as repealing the 1990 amendments to the Clean Air Act, reducing the budget of the Environmental Protection Agency, and environmental deregulation. His opposition to environmental legislation stemmed partly from the need to protect the industrial plants located in his Houston congressional district, such as Monsanto, BASF, and Dow chemical plants.

Although DeLay was a supporter of free markets and often opposed government regulation, he made an exception at one point. When the National Football League's Houston Oilers were planning to move to Nashville, Tennessee, over DeLay's strong objections, he cosponsored a bill that limited the ability of privately owned sports franchises to move to new cities.

When George W. Bush was elected president, DeLay remained outside the White House inner circle. Although DeLay had close ties to Cheney, he never became close to Bush. To some extent, the lack of a close relationship stemmed from their Texas roots. While Bush was governor, DeLay never became a close adviser and never built a strong rapport with Bush.

Born April 8, 1947, in Laredo, Texas, DeLay entered Baylor University in 1965 immediately after high school where he stayed for two years. He completed his B.S. degree in biology in 1970 at the University of Houston.

After settling in a Houston suburb, Sugar Land, DeLay established a successful pest control business called Albo Pest Control, Inc. In 1979 he was elected to the Texas House of Representatives where he served until 1984. In 1984 he was elected to the U.S. House of Representatives and has been reelected every term since then.

Deng Xiaoping

(1904–1997) *chairman, Central Advisory Committee (Communist Party), China*

Deng Xiaoping led China's Communist Party during most of the 1980s, as head of the newly created party Central Advisory Commission. A series of his protégés were named chairman of the Communist Party, giving Deng unparalleled power within the party structure. Deng sought to loosen government control of the economy in order to promote development. However Deng refused to relax party control of the government and the political process.

Deng resigned from his last party post in 1989, designating Jiang Zemin his successor, after supporting the use of military force to suppress the Tiananmen Square marchers.

Following his death on February 20, 1997, from advanced Parkinson's disease, Deng's ashes were placed in the Great Hall of the People in Beijing. Ten thousand of China's Communist Party elite stood silently, bowing before Deng's ashes. At the same time across China, billions of people paused briefly to commemorate the passing of Deng, whose economic reforms changed the nation. For three min-

utes, sirens and horns were sounded nationwide. Work was stopped in factories and offices. The memorial ceremony at the Great Hall of the People was broadcast live on giant screens throughout the country. President Jiang Zemin read the eulogy for Deng.

In a lengthy state of the union address following Deng's funeral, President Jiang urged China to continue the economic reforms started by Deng and to maintain an open door to the outside world. He said reform was the only way to achieve modernization. "We must continue under the guidance of Comrade Deng Xiaoping," said Jiang, "to follow the road of reform and socialist modernizations."

President Clinton led world tributes to Deng's reforms and the opening of China to the outside world.

Born in Sichuan Province, China, on August 22, 1904, Deng joined the Chinese Communist Party in 1924 while studying in France. He later studied in the Soviet Union in Moscow. In 1927, Deng became a party organizer in southwest China. By 1934 he had become so involved in party affairs that he joined the Long March. By 1973 Deng had risen to the position of vice chairman of the party. His rise to power ended in 1976 when he was purged by the Maoist Gang of Four. In 1977 he was considered rehabilitated and launched a successful bid for power within the party. As a senior member of the Chinese power structure, Deng concluded a deal in 1989 for the return of Hong Kong to China in 1997.

Deutch, John Mark

(1938–   ) *director, Central Intelligence Agency*

John Deutch served as the director of the Central Intelligence Agency (CIA) from 1995–96. On May 10, 1995, Deutch was sworn into office after a unanimous vote in the Senate, and served in the position until December 15,

1996. Deutch replaced CIA director R. JAMES WOOLSEY, who had suddenly resigned. Deutch was nominated for the position in March 1995 when General MICHAEL CARNS failed to win Senate confirmation.

After Deutch resigned, President Clinton nominated ANTHONY LAKE as director of the CIA, but Lake failed to win Senate confirmation. President Clinton subsequently nominated GEORGE JOHN TENET in March 1997 to succeed Deutch. Tenet was confirmed by the Senate and sworn into office in July 1997.

Prior to his position at the CIA, Deutch had been deputy secretary of defense from 1994–95 and under secretary of defense for acquisitions and technology from 1993–94. His role in the Department of Defense included finding the cause of the exposure that soldiers suffered during the Persian Gulf War. Deutch classified many of the documents that Gulf War veterans were seeking to explain a variety of illnesses that they suffered from the war. As a result, many Gulf War veterans opposed his confirmation in the Senate for the director of the CIA. In spite of their opposition, Deutch won Senate confirmation.

Deutch's career in government began in the Carter administration, where he served in a number of positions in the U.S. Department of Energy, including director of energy research, acting assistant secretary for energy technology, and undersecretary of the Department of Energy.

In addition to his work at the Department of Energy, Deutch served on a host of commissions throughout several administrations. He served on the President's Nuclear Safety Oversight Committee (1980–81); the President's Commission on Strategic Forces (1983); the White House Science Council (1985–89); the President's Committee of Advisors on Science and Technology (1997–2001); the Presidents Intelligence Advisory Board (1990–93); the President's Commission on Aviation Safety

John Mark Deutch *(National Archives)*

and Security (1996); the Commission on Reducing and Protecting Government Secrecy (1996); and as chairman of the Commission to Assess the Organization of the Federal Government to Combat the Proliferation of Weapons of Mass Destruction (1998–99).

Deutch was pardoned by President Clinton on January 20, 2001, as part of a series of last-minute pardons before the inauguration of GEORGE WALKER BUSH. Deutch had been accused by the Department of Justice of maintaining highly classified documents on unsecured home computers linked to the Internet. Deutch told investigators that he routinely took work home from CIA headquarters but used his unsecured personal computer to review documents. The presidential pardon came as a surprise to officials in the Department of Justice.

The day before the pardon Deutch had signed a plea agreement with the Department of Justice in which he admitted to a misdemeanor and agreed to pay a $5,000 fine.

When George John Tenet took over as CIA director, he stripped Deutch of his security clearances. Deutch had cooperated with the CIA probe into his use of his home computer for official documents and apologized for the problems he had caused.

Born July 27, 1938, Deutch received his B.A. in history and economics from Amherst College (1961), his B.S. in chemical engineering from Massachusetts Institute of Technology (MIT) (1961), and Ph.D. in physical chemistry from MIT. His career included tenure at MIT as a professor of chemistry and as provost. In 1990, after leaving the Central Intelligence Agency, Deutch was named Institute Professor at MIT, a rank that recognized distinguished accomplishment in scholarly, educational service, and leadership.

Dodd, Christopher John
(1944–) *member of the Senate*

A supporter of President Clinton in the Senate, Senator Chris Dodd (D-Conn.) served as the chairman of the Democratic National Committee during 1995 and 1996. President Clinton, as party leader, had selected Dodd for the position. During the 1996 Democratic National Convention in Chicago, Dodd placed President Clinton into official nomination before the delegates.

Dodd was named chairman of the Democratic National Committee after he lost the election for the position of Senate minority leader to Senator THOMAS ANDREW DASCHLE (D-S.D.). When Senator GEORGE JOHN MITCHELL (D-Me.) announced his retirement in 1994, Daschle began campaigning for the job of minority leader. Budget Committee

chairman James Sasser (D-Tenn.) also announced his candidacy for minority leader, but lost his seat in the November election. Dodd emerged as a candidate for minority leader only after Sasser withdrew in November. On December 2, 1994, in a caucus vote, Daschle was elected minority leader, defeating Dodd by a vote of 24-23.

During the Clinton administration, Dodd was an active supporter of legislation involving children and families. His work in this area stemmed from his tenure as a senior member of the labor and human resources committee and the senior Democrat on the subcommittee on children and families. In 1993, Dodd was a prime sponsor of the Family and Medical Leave Act. This was the first piece of legislation signed into law by President Clinton in January 1993. The bill was strongly supported by President Clinton and was frequently touted as one of the most important pieces of legislation during the administration's first term in the 1996 reelection campaign.

As an ally of President Clinton throughout his presidency, Senator Dodd became one of the most vocal supporters of President Clinton during the impeachment process of 1998. Dodd regularly went on national talk shows to support President Clinton. Dodd never criticized Clinton after the MONICA LEWINSKY issue subsided, remaining a steadfast defender of the president.

Born on May 27, 1944, Dodd was the son of the late senator Thomas J. Dodd. After graduating from Providence College in 1966, Dodd joined the Peace Corps and spent two years in the Dominican Republic. He was assigned to the Dominican Republic partly because he was fluent in Spanish. After his work in the Peace Corps, Dodd enlisted in the army and served in the army reserves. He later attended law school at the University of Louisville, where he received his law degree in 1972. He practiced law for two years in Connecticut before his election to the U.S. House of Representatives in 1974. He was reelected in 1976 and 1978 and then was elected to the U.S. Senate in 1980. He was reelected in 1986, 1992, and 1998.

Dole, Elizabeth Hanford
(1936–   ) *president, American Red Cross*

Throughout most of the Clinton presidency, Elizabeth Dole served as president of the American Red Cross. First elected by the board of directors of the American Red Cross in 1991, Dole remained in the position until she resigned in 1997 and announced her candidacy for president in the 2000 election.

Throughout her tenure at the American Red Cross, Dole oversaw the organization's efforts to create more stringent blood screening tests and led the organization through a number of major disasters, including Hurricane Andrew and the floods throughout the Midwest.

In addition, Dole oversaw the restructuring of the Red Cross to focus on improving the accountability of the organization's finances. In 1996, *Money Magazine* named the American Red Cross as the nation's "Top-Rated Charity" for providing 92 percent of its income directly to services. Dole was credited with transforming the Red Cross into a well-managed business rather than simply a well-funded charity. As a result of her efforts at the Red Cross, Dole became nationally recognized and gained expertise in fund-raising activities. Both of these skills became essential assets in her unsuccessful bid for the presidency in 2000 and her successful bid for the U.S. Senate in 2002.

In the 2000 presidential election, Dole became the first woman to seek the nomination for president of the Republican Party. Dole did not fare well in the nomination process, losing the party's nomination to GEORGE WALKER BUSH. She often supported gun control, refused to endorse an antiabortion platform,

and failed to garner the core voters, who tended to be conservative, during the primaries. In 2002, she ran successfully for the Senate from her home state of North Carolina, defeating the Democratic candidate, former White House chief of staff ERSKINE B. BOWLES.

Elizabeth Dole's candidacy for the presidency followed that of her husband, Senator ROBERT (BOB) JOSEPH DOLE (R-Kans.) who had successfully sought the nomination in 1996. Robert Dole, the Republican nominee for president, faced President Clinton in his reelection campaign. Robert Dole, as did his wife four years later, failed to capture the Oval Office.

Dole began her career in government in the Johnson administration as a Democrat in the new consumer affairs bureau in the White House. During the Nixon administration she switched parties to become a registered independent and later became a Republican when she married Robert Dole in 1975.

She remained in the Nixon White House in the office of consumer affairs as a protégé of Virginia Knauer. Nixon then appointed Dole to the Federal Trade Commission, after Knauer had strongly supported her. She held the position at the Federal Trade Commission from 1973–79. During the 1976 presidential campaign, in which her husband was Gerald Ford's vice presidential nominee, Elizabeth Dole became a frequent speaker on behalf of the Ford-Dole ticket at political events.

An active Republican by the time of the Reagan campaign, Dole returned to public service after Ronald Reagan won the presidency in 1980. She served on the transition team for the Department of Health and Human Services for Reagan and became a White House staff member in 1981 as director of the White House Office of Public Liaison. Two years later (1983), Dole was appointed by Reagan as the secretary of transportation, a position she held until 1987. Dole's appointment to a cabinet position was to some extent due to the Reagan administration's decision to court women for the 1984 reelection.

In 1987 Dole moved from her Methodist roots into the evangelical movement. In 1987 she "gave witness" at the National Prayer Breakfast in Washington, D.C., where, as she describes, "you explain what Christ has meant in your life." Since 1987, Dole has been a frequent speaker for religious organizations. In October 2002, Dole appeared on the *Hour of Prayer* national television program with evangelist Robert Schuller, broadcast from the Crystal Cathedral in Anaheim, California. Dole appealed for both money and blood donations for the American Red Cross and then read a psalm from the Bible.

When GEORGE HERBERT WALKER BUSH entered office in 1989, Dole again returned to the president's cabinet as secretary of labor. Dole successfully intervened in the United Mine Workers strike against the Pittson Coal Company in 1989. She remained in this position until 1991 when she was named president of the American Red Cross.

Born on July 29, 1936, Elizabeth Hanford Dole received her B.A. from Duke University in 1958, where she was elected women's student government president in 1957. During her four years at Duke University, the campus was divided into a men's and a women's campus. She received her law degree from Harvard University in 1965, where she was in the first class of women at the formerly all-male law school. She married Robert Dole in 1975 after his divorce and became stepmother to his daughter, Robin.

Dole, Robert (Bob) Joseph

(1923–   ) *Republican candidate for president, member of the Senate*

Robert (Bob) Dole (R-Kans.), Senate majority leader from 1984–87 and from 1995 until his resignation from the Senate in 1996, chal-lenged President Clinton for the presidency in the 1996 election. Dole ran as the Republican Party's presidential candidate. Dole lost the election, carrying 19 states and 41 percent of the popular vote. Clinton carried 31 states and 49 percent of the popular vote. Reform Party candidate HENRY ROSS PEROT garnered 8 percent of the vote, less than the 19 percent he had in the 1992 presidential election. Although Dole did not capture the White House, the Republicans maintained control of both the House and the Senate and elected a majority of the nation's governors in 1996.

Dole resigned from the Senate in June 1996 before the Republican nominating convention. Although he had originally not intended to resign, he was pressured by both Senate colleagues and other Republicans. They argued that he could not successfully run the Senate and run for office. During the 1996 Republican primaries, Dole fended off a challenge by Steve Forbes, who ran a $25 million advertising campaign against Dole, and by Patrick Buchanan. Dole had the nomination locked up by the end of March 1996.

Dole's 1996 presidential campaign never gained momentum. He was frequently criticized by Democrats, although never by President Clinton, as being too old to handle the presidency. He also faced an incumbent president who had strengthened the national economy and was rapidly moving toward federal surpluses rather than federal deficits.

After the election, Dole began to increase his income through a number of product endorsements, including Pepsi and Viagra. In 1997, Dole and his wife, ELIZABETH HANFORD DOLE, earned in excess of $1 million from her salary as executive director of the American Red Cross, and from his speaking engagements and product endorsements, and from their pensions. Dole also advanced former House Speaker NEWTON (NEWT) LEROY GINGRICH $300,000, which Gingrich owed the House of

Representatives as a fine for violating House ethics rules. Gingrich agreed to repay the loan over 10 years at 10 percent interest.

Dole's involvement in presidential politics began in 1976, when President Gerald R. Ford tapped him as his vice presidential running mate. Vice President Nelson Rockefeller, a liberal Republican, was dropped from the 1976 ticket in favor of the more conservative Dole. Ford's election committee was concerned that Ronald Reagan, a conservative, would win the Republican nomination if Ford did not balance the ticket with a more conservative running mate. The Ford-Dole ticket lost the election in 1976 to Jimmy Carter and his running mate, Walter Mondale.

Born on July 22, 1923, in Russell, Kansas, Dole graduated from Washburn University where he earned both a B.A. and a law degree after serving in the army during World War II. In 1945 Dole was a platoon leader with the 10th Mountain Division in Italy, was wounded, and was hospitalized for more than three years. He was left with a permanently disabled right arm.

After a single term in the Kansas House of Representatives (1951–53), Dole won a seat as the Russell County prosecutor, a post he held for seven years until his successful 1960 race for the U.S. House of Representatives. He served eight years in the House (1961–69) before running for a Senate seat. In 1968, Dole defeated moderate Democrat William

Senator Robert J. Dole *(Department of Defense)*

Robinson, winning more than 60 percent of the vote. Dole remained in the Senate for two years, 1969 to 1971, when President Nixon tapped him to serve as chair of the Republican National Committee. He helped orchestrate Nixon's landslide election in 1972 against Democratic challenger Senator George McGovern (D-S.D.), but chose not to join the Nixon administration as the Watergate scandal grew larger.

Dole ran successfully for the Senate from Kansas again in 1974. In August 1976 President Gerald Ford named Dole his running mate at the Republican national convention in Kansas City, Missouri. Dole and Mondale participated in the first vice presidential debate in October 1976, held in Houston, Texas.

Dole divorced his first wife in 1972, and in 1975 married Elizabeth Hanford. Elizabeth Hanford Dole was named secretary of transportation in January 1985, and Robert Dole was elected Senate majority leader in January 1985. The Doles later created the Dole Foundation to raise funds to assist disabled Americans.

During the 1980 Republican primaries, Dole briefly entered the presidential race but was quickly overtaken by Ronald Reagan. When Reagan swept into office in November 1980, the Republicans also gained control of the Senate. Dole became chair of the Senate Finance Committee in January 1981 and became majority leader in late 1984. In November 1986 the Democrats regained the Senate, and Dole became minority leader with the new session in 1987.

Dole tried again for the Republican nomination for president in 1988, after Reagan's two terms ended. Vice President GEORGE HERBERT WALKER BUSH fought Dole for the nomination and ultimately captured it. Bush won the presidency in the 1988 election, defeating Democratic candidate Michael Dukakis.

When the Republicans gained control of the House and the Senate in the 1994 elections, Dole was again elected majority leader in January 1995. He remained majority leader until resigning his seat in the Senate to run for president in the fall of 1996.

E

Edelman, Marian Wright
(1939–) *founder and president, Children's Defense Fund*

Marian Wright Edelman was a friend of Hillary Clinton's, who had served as the chairman of the board of directors of the Children's Defense Fund, which Edelman founded. Mrs. Clinton had first worked for Edelman as a staff attorney for the fund in 1973, and had remained friends with Edelman. Both worked for a variety of children's programs and causes.

The relationship between Mrs. Clinton and Edelman deteriorated in 1996 when President Clinton supported the welfare reform bill, which Edelman opposed. Although Mrs. Clinton was friends with Edelman, their friendship may have been compromised during the Clinton administration. The *Washington Post* reported that Peter Edelman, a lawyer at the Georgetown University Law Center and Mrs. Edelman's husband, was in line to be considered for a seat on the District of Columbia Circuit Court of Appeals and for a seat on the U.S. District Court, but in both cases his name was never put forward to the Senate by the administration. The administration apparently feared that conservatives would oppose his nomination due to the liberal nature of his legal writings. Peter Edelman served for a time in the Department of Health and Human Services as acting assistant secretary for children and families, but resigned in September 1996. Edelman's resignation was in protest against the welfare reform bill that President Clinton signed.

When President Clinton signed the welfare reform bill, Marian Wright Edelman issued a statement that reflected the downhill spiral of her relationship with President and Mrs. Clinton: "President Clinton's signature on this pernicious bill makes a mockery of his pledge not to hurt children." Under Edelman's leadership, the Children's Defense Fund had been an advocate for children and families. In 1992 the Children's Defense Fund began a campaign called "Leave No Child Behind," which sought increased funding for programs such as Head Start and sought to ensure that every child had access to vaccinations and medical insurance. Edelman's goals for the Children's Defense Fund was to be a voice for children in the legislative process. In an interview with the CBS television program *60 Minutes*, Edelman said, "Everybody loves children. Everybody is for them in general. . . . But when they get into the budget rooms or behind closed doors—to really decide how they're going to carve up money—children get lost in the process."

Marian Wright Edelman's advocacy for children began when she worked for the National Association for the Advancement of Colored People (NAACP) and became an advocate for poor rural children in the South. Following graduation from law school, Edelman worked in New York City as a staff attorney for the NAACP Legal Defense and Education Fund, and then in Jackson, Mississippi, from 1964–68 as director of the NAACP office in Jackson. She became the first African-American woman to practice law in Mississippi. In 1967 she testified before a Senate subcommittee hearing in Jackson, on poverty in the rural South. While the subcommittee was in Mississippi, Edelman took Senator Robert Kennedy and Senator Joseph Clark on a tour of the slum areas of the Mississippi Delta.

Edelman then moved to Washington, D.C., to be nearer to Peter Edelman, a Kennedy staffer whom she later married. They had three children. In 1971 she helped to establish a coalition of groups to support a comprehensive child care bill. The bill passed in the House and in the Senate, but was vetoed by President RICHARD MILHOUS NIXON. Her experience in working to move this bill through Congress led to her creation of the Children's Defense Fund in 1973.

The Children's Defense Fund was created to protect the interests of children. Supported by private foundations, the fund developed studies on the conditions of children and then lobbied Congress for legislation to improve those conditions. The agenda of the fund included issues such as foster care, teen pregnancy, and child care. In 1984 the Children's Defense Fund successfully lobbied for increased Medicaid coverage for poor children.

Born on June 6, 1939, in Bennettsville, South Carolina, Wright graduated with a B.A. from Spelman College (1960) and with a LL.B. from Yale University (1963).

Elders, Joycelyn
(1933–   ) *U.S. surgeon general*

Dr. Joycelyn Elders was named U.S. surgeon general by President Clinton in 1993 soon after taking office. Elders, an African American, had been the director of the Arkansas Department of Health under then-governor Clinton.

Elders was confirmed after difficult hearings in the Senate, in which her views on sex education were attacked, primarily by conservative Republicans. Conservative groups disapproved of her efforts in Arkansas to create school-based health clinics that dealt with a broad range of health care issues, including sex education. They particularly objected to having public schools provide condoms, yet only a fraction of public schools had done so. Conservative Christian groups also objected to Elders's pro-choice position.

Elders was finally confirmed by the Senate but lasted less than two years in the position. In the fall of 1994, Elders spoke at the United Nations's World AIDS day. A question was posed to her at the conference asking if she thought that masturbation could serve as a useful tool to help discourage schoolchildren from becoming sexually active too early. Elders responded by saying, "With regard to masturbation, I think that is something that is part of human sexuality and a part of something that perhaps should be taught." Her conservative opponents argued that she supported masturbation for children. As the controversy grew, Elders was forced to resign.

She returned to the University of Arkansas School of Medicine to continue her practice after leaving the Clinton administration at the end of 1994. On February 2, 1995, President Clinton nominated Dr. HENRY FOSTER as U.S. surgeon general, but he failed to gain confirmation when conservatives opposed his prochoice position. Dr. DAVID SATCHER was finally confirmed as U.S. surgeon general in 1995 to replace Elders.

Elders was born on August 13, 1933, the eldest of eight children, with the name Minnie Lee Jones. She changed her name to Joycelyn Jones in college. After marrying her second husband, Oliver Elders, in 1960, she became Joycelyn Elders.

Born in Schaal, Arkansas, Elders graduated with a B.A. from the segregated Philander Smith College in Little Rock, Arkansas. After graduation from college, Elders joined the U.S. Army Women's Medical Specialist Corps. In 1956 she entered the University of Arkansas School of Medicine on the G.I. bill. Although *Brown v. Education* in 1954 had mandated equality in education, segregation still remained in many parts of the educational system. While at medical school, Elders was required to use a separate university dining room, where the cleaning staff ate.

After an internship in pediatrics at the University of Minnesota, Elders returned to Little Rock in 1961 for her residency and was soon appointed as the chief pediatric resident. Over the next 20 years, Elders remained at the University of Arkansas to practice medicine, focusing on a career with pediatric endocrinology and juvenile diabetes. In 1987, Governor Bill Clinton named Elders the director of the Arkansas Department of Health. In that position, she lobbied the state legislature for more education in the public schools on hygiene, substance abuse prevention, sexual responsibility, and improving self-esteem among teenagers. One of her major goals was to reduce the rising rate of teenage pregnancies.

Emanuel, Rahm

(1959–) *special adviser to the president for policy and strategy, and executive assistant to the chief of staff for policy; deputy director, Office of Communications; director, Office of Political Affairs*

Rahm Emanuel was named assistant to the president and director of the White House Office of Political Affairs in January 1993. Emanuel had been one of the earliest members of the Clinton advisory team, having moved from Chicago to Little Rock, Arkansas, in the fall of 1991 to work on the Clinton for President campaign.

Five months after taking office, Emanuel was given a new assignment in the White House. In July 1993 Chief of Staff THOMAS MCLARTY announced a reorganization of White House staff, including three senior staff changes. Effective July 6, 1993, RICKI SEIDMAN became counselor to the chief of staff, Emanuel was moved from director of political affairs to assistant to the president and deputy director of communications, and JOAN BAGGETT was promoted from deputy director to director of political affairs, replacing Emanuel. After the departure of GEORGE ROBERT STEPHANOPOULOS at the end of the first term, Emanuel took over Stephanopoulos's job as special adviser to the president for policy and strategy.

Emanuel was born four months after his parents moved to the United States from Israel in 1959. His parents moved to Chicago, Illinois, where his father was a pediatrician and his American-born mother was a psychiatric social worker. Every summer during his childhood, Emanuel and his brothers went to camp in Israel. He maintained dual citizenship, in Israel and the United States, until he was old enough to be subject to the Israeli draft. He then dropped his Israeli citizenship.

While he was growing up, Emanuel's mother insisted that her three sons take ballet lessons. Emanuel became so proficient at the ballet that he was offered a scholarship to the Joffrey Ballet School, but he declined it. Throughout his adult life, however, he continued to practice ballet and to train at dance classes.

Emanuel graduated from Sarah Lawrence College, in Bronxville, New York, with a B.A. degree in 1981, and earned an M.A. degree from Northwestern University in speech and communications in 1985. His first political job came in 1980 while he was in college, when he worked on the congressional campaign of David Robinson of Illinois. The campaign manager for Robinson was DAVID WILHELM, who later was named national campaign manager for the Clinton-Gore campaign in 1992. Wilhelm was named chairman of the Democratic National Committee in 1993, and remained until 2001.

After working as the Midwest field director for the Democratic Congressional Campaign Committee in 1989, and then as the committee's national campaign director, he established his own Chicago-based consulting firm. His clients included Mayor RICHARD MICHAEL DALEY of Chicago and Virginia governor Douglas Wilder.

In November 1991, Emanuel was hired as the national finance director for the fledgling Clinton for President campaign. When he began working, the campaign had $600,000 in the bank. He organized 26 fundraising events between Thanksgiving and Christmas 1991, and raised more than $3 million for the campaign. During the following year, Emanuel raised over $71 million for the campaign.

After the November election, Emanuel was named codirector of the Presidential Inaugural Committee. Working with a 300-member staff, Emanuel set up five days of events, including a Clinton-Gore bus tour, 11 inaugural balls, several concerts, and the opening to the public of the White House after the inauguration.

Once in office, President Clinton named Emanuel to the position of director of the Office of Political Affairs. But Emanuel often clashed with staff in the White House, particularly those who had worked closely with President Clinton in the Little Rock campaign headquarters.

After the reorganization of the White House staff by McLarty in July 1992, Emanuel was moved from the Office of Political Affairs to the Communications Office. His title was somewhat misleading, however, for his role was to manage special projects. His first assignment in the Communications Office was to work with a task force trying to secure passage of the North American Free Trade Agreement (NAFTA). Emanuel worked with WILLIAM MICHAEL DALEY, who had been named special counsel for NAFTA by President Clinton in August 1993. Daley was a fellow Chicagoan and brother of Mayor Richard Daley, whom Emanuel knew well.

Once NAFTA had passed, Emanuel became involved in the welfare reform and immigration reform bills of 1996. At the beginning of the second term, Emanuel moved out of the Communications Office to the chief of staff's office, with the title senior adviser to the president for policy and strategy, and executive assistant to the chief of staff for policy. He was largely responsible for developing political strategies for moving legislation through Congress. He replaced George Stephanopoulos, who left after the first term, as the primary political expert in the White House. Emanuel was even given Stephanopoulos's old office, next to the private dining room adjoining the Oval Office.

Emanuel left the White House on October 19, 1998. The week before he left the White House, President Clinton had a farewell dinner in the State Dining Room for Emanuel, which was described as the end of an era. Emanuel had been among the last of the original campaign team that joined the White House staff in 1993.

In an October 1998 article in the *Washington Post* that chronicled his tenure in the White House, Emanuel was described as both persistent and as "a popular figure among his White House colleagues." Emanuel returned to Chicago to become managing director of Dresdner Kleinwort Wasserstein, a global investment bank. He then became the managing director of Wasserstein Parella & Co. in Chicago.

In 2002 Emanuel was elected to the U.S. House of Representatives from the 5th District in Illinois.

Espy, Alphonso Michael (Mike)

(1953–) *secretary of agriculture, member of the House of Representatives*

Mike Espy served as President Clinton's first secretary of agriculture, one of four African Americans appointed to the cabinet in January 1993. Espy, sworn into office on January 22, 1993, presided over the fourth-largest federal agency, with 14,000 offices around the country serving over 2.1 million farmers. He became the first African American to hold the position of secretary of agriculture.

Espy resigned from office on October 3, 1994, after an August 27, 1994, indictment on 37 criminal counts by independent counsel DONALD C. SMALTZ. Espy was replaced as secretary of agriculture by DANIEL GLICKMAN.

Espy, a former member of the House of Representatives, had worked with President Clinton while he was governor of Arkansas, when Clinton and Espy were both involved with the Democratic Leadership Council (DLC). Although most African-American members of Congress, who generally represented urban areas, shied away from the centrist DLC, Espy became an active member

of the DLC. During the 1992 presidential election, Espy was one of the first African-American members of Congress to endorse Clinton, and coauthored the campaign plan to overhaul the welfare system. When Clinton won the election, Espy lobbied for a cabinet post. His first choice for a cabinet position was secretary of housing and urban development. When that position did not develop, Espy sent Clinton a handwritten note that said "Ten Reasons Why Mike Espy Should Be Your Agriculture Secretary."

Espy had a short tenure in the Department of Agriculture, after being charged with accepting illegal gratuities for himself, his girlfriend, and his relatives. Attorney General JANET RENO announced in August 1994 that the Justice Department had begun an investigation into allegations against Espy. The White House demanded that Espy resign after the announcement by the attorney general.

A three-judge federal panel appointed Donald C. Smaltz, a Los Angeles attorney, on September 9, 1994, to head the investigation. Smaltz was named the independent counsel under the requirements of the 1988 Ethics in Government Act. Smaltz subsequently hired a staff of 35 to investigate Espy. The staff was headquartered in Alexandria, Virginia, outside of Washington, D.C.

In a 38-count indictment on August 27, 1997, a federal grand jury said that Espy violated the Meat Inspection Act of 1907, which prohibits Agriculture Department employees from taking anything of value from companies they are supposed to regulate, and that he lied to the FBI and the department's inspector general. Espy was charged with receiving $35,458 in illegal gifts, including a $1,200 scholarship for his girlfriend, Patricia Dempsey, from a foundation affiliated with Tyson Foods. Among the allegations, Espy was charged with accepting free travel, meals, and tickets to sporting events from Tyson Foods, including sky-box seats at a Dallas Cowboys game and tickets to a Chicago Bulls play-off game. White House chief of staff LEON EDWARD PANETTA testified at the trial in 1998 that Dempsey's scholarship from Tyson Foods created an appearance of impropriety and led to his demand that Espy resign from the Department of Agriculture.

In November 1998, U.S. District Judge Ricardo M. Urbina dismissed eight of the most serious charges against Espy. Urbina ruled that federal prosecutors had failed to show criminal conduct in Espy's acceptance of Super Bowl tickets and a Waterford crystal bowl from two corporations that did business with the USDA. In a trial on the remaining counts in December 1998, Espy was acquitted of 30 corruption charges brought against him by Smaltz. The jury acquitted Espy of taking tickets to sporting events and other benefits from Tyson Foods, Sun-Diamond Growers of California, Oglethorpe Power Corp. of Georgia, Smith Barney, EOP Group, and Quaker Oats Co. of Chicago. Jurors also acquitted him of charges that he lied to investigators and on financial disclosure forms. Espy was represented by defense lawyers Ted Wells and Reid H. Weingarten.

In a statement issued by the White House following the acquittal, President Clinton said of Espy, "I am heartened that he has, as he said, emerged from this ordeal stronger. I hope that as he moves forward he will continue his notable record of service to his country."

Born November 30, 1953, in Yazoo City, Mississippi, Espy received a B.A. degree in political science from Howard University (1975) and a J.D. from the University of Santa Clara School of Law (1978). Espy's father, John Espy, had been a county agent for the U.S. Department of Agriculture (USDA) in Yazoo City, Mississippi, during the 1930s and 1940s.

After graduating from the University of Santa Clara School of Law in 1978, Espy returned to his native state of Mississippi to practice law with the Central Mississippi Legal Services until 1980. He soon entered Mississippi state government, serving as assistant secretary of state for the Public Lands Division. In 1983 he began working for the election of Ed Pittman for state attorney general in Mississippi. After Pittman was elected, Espy served as assistant attorney general for consumer protection from 1984–85.

Espy won a seat in the U.S. House of Representatives in 1986 from the 2nd District of Mississippi, which included the Delta cities of Yazoo City, Greenville, Vicksburg, and Clarksdale. His opponent was the two-term incumbent, Webb Franklin. Although Espy beat Franklin by fewer than 5,000 votes, he received 98 percent of the African-American vote, but only 12.5 percent of the white vote.

While in the House of Representatives, Espy served on the Agriculture Committee, the Budget Committee, and the Select Committee on Hunger. His positions on issues were often controversial, and not in step with the more liberal Democrats who controlled the House. Espy supported the death penalty, opposed much of the gun control legislation, and supported U.S. funding for the Nicaraguan contras. He also became the first member of Congress to appear in an advertisement for the National Rifle Association, of which he had been a member since 1974.

Fiske, Robert Bishop, Jr.
(1930–) *independent counsel, Whitewater investigation*

Robert B. Fiske was named the independent counsel in January 1994 by Attorney General JANET RENO to investigate President and Mrs. Clinton's dealings in the Whitewater land development project. Fiske was named by Reno after the Ethics in Government Act had expired, which allowed the attorney general to investigate the president. When the act was renewed by Congress in August 1994, the three-judge panel empowered by the law to name an independent counsel replaced Fiske with KENNETH W. STARR. Many Republicans had urged the three-judge panel to replace Fiske, who they believed had not been aggressive enough in his investigation. Starr, a conservative Republican, was viewed as a more thorough investigator.

Fiske was charged by the attorney general with investigating the relationship of President and Mrs. Clinton to the Whitewater Development Corp. The Whitewater Development Corp. was a partnership in 1978 between the attorney general of Arkansas, Bill Clinton, and his wife, Hillary, with JAMES (JIM) and SUSAN McDOUGAL. They purchased 220 acres of riverfront land to sell for vacation homes.

The McDougals funded the land purchase through a savings and loan association which they owned, the Madison Savings and Loan. James and Susan McDougal were subsequently found guilty of fraud in their loans through Madison Savings and Loan. Their loans included a $300,000 loan to the Whitewater Development Corp.

As independent counsel, Fiske sought to determine the degree of involvement of President and Mrs. Clinton with any fraudulent loans made by Madison Savings and Loan. The original investigation, however, took several turns as Fiske expanded into what his office believed were further cases of improper or illegal behavior by President and Mrs. Clinton.

His investigation was expanded into other areas, including the firing of seven members of the White House travel office in 1993 for allegedly political reasons. This investigation became known as Travelgate. A friend of the Clintons, HARRY THOMASON, admitted to the FBI that he had urged the Clintons to fire the staff in the Travel Office and replace them with staff from a company he was financially involved with. No evidence of wrongdoing by the Clintons was found by Fiske.

Fiske further expanded the Whitewater investigation into the 1993 suicide of White

House deputy counsel VINCENT W. FOSTER, JR. Fiske examined whether Foster had committed suicide or died as a result of foul play. Fiske concluded that Foster had committed suicide.

In another expansion of his role as independent counsel, Fiske investigated whether White House staff should have access to FBI files on certain Republicans. This investigation became known as Filegate. The White House acknowledged that Craig Livingstone, a lower-level staffer without a security clearance, had improperly asked for the files. The White House denied using the files, noting that Livingstone had told few that he had the files. Fiske found no evidence that anyone other than Livingstone was involved.

In a further expansion of his role as independent counsel, Fiske looked into the more than $700,000 that former associate attorney general WEBSTER HUBBELL collected for legal work after resigning from his position in the Department of Justice. Allegations arose that he did little legal work but received substantial fees from clients. Most of the fees were generated from friends of President Clinton and the Democratic Party. Fiske found no evidence that Hubbell had not performed the required legal work for his clients, as had been alleged.

Throughout the various investigations by Fiske and his staff, President and Mrs. Clinton were never charged with improper actions. Not until Kenneth Starr took over the Whitewater investigation and expanded it into the MONICA LEWINSKY case did any charges arise from either the Fiske or Starr investigations of the president.

Born December 28, 1930, Fiske received his B.A. from Yale University (1952), his J.D. from the University of Michigan (1955), and an honorary LL.D. from the University of Michigan in 1997. After graduating from law school, he joined the law firm as an associate of Davis, Polk, Warwell, Sunderland, & Kiendl (1955–57). He left the firm to join the U.S. attorney's office of the Southern District of New York (1957–61), returning to the firm in 1961. He became a partner in the firm in 1964, and remained until 1976. At that time, he was named U.S. attorney for the Southern District of New York (1976–80). He returned to the firm in 1980 until he was named independent counsel for the Whitewater investigation in 1994.

Fleming, Patricia (Patsy) S.
(unknown) *national AIDS policy coordinator*

Patricia Fleming replaced KRISTINE GEBBIE as the national AIDS policy coordinator. When Gebbie resigned in July 1994, Fleming was named as the interim AIDS policy coordinator.

In making the announcement, President Clinton said on August 2, 1994, "This administration has made significant strides in the fight against the terrible epidemic. We've increased our budget on AIDS research, treatment, and prevention and have fought hard to provide health insurance for all Americans, regardless of preexisting conditions. Patsy Fleming will make sure we don't lose our momentum."

Fleming had been the chief adviser on HIV/AIDS to Secretary of Health and Human Services DONNA SHALALA during the first year of the administration. When President Clinton announced Fleming's appointment as the National AIDS Policy Coordinator in August 1994, she stated that she would serve as interim coordinator until a permanent replacement could be found. She then intended to return to the Department of Health and Human Services.

Part of the momentum to name an interim AIDS policy coordinator was to have an official representative at the 10th International Conference on AIDS in Yokohama, Japan, in mid-August 1994.

After she had served as the interim coordinator for six months, President Clinton named Fleming the National AIDS Policy Coordinator in January 1995. In accepting the position, Fleming said, "As an African American, as a woman, and as a mother of three sons, I know all too well the threat that HIV poses for every American family."

She was strongly supported for the position by AIDS activists. The executive director of the AIDS Action Council said of her, "Fleming's dedication to the fight against AIDS is unparalleled."

Prior to joining the Clinton administration, Fleming had been the administrative assistant to Ted Weiss (D-N.Y.), specializing in AIDS and public health issues.

Flowers, Gennifer

(1950–) *announced in 1992 primaries a past extramarital affair with Bill Clinton*

Gennifer Flowers, an Arkansas state employee and part-time cabaret-lounge singer in Little Rock, Arkansas, announced in 1992 that she had had a 12-year relationship with Bill Clinton. At the time, President Clinton was seeking the Democratic nomination for president. President Clinton denied the relationship.

On January 1992, President and Mrs. Clinton were interviewed by Steve Kroft of the television program *60 Minutes* about Flowers. President Clinton stated, "She was an acquaintance, I would say a friendly acquaintance." When Kroft responded, "She is alleging and has described in some detail in the supermarket tabloid what she calls a 12-year affair with you." President Clinton replied, "That allegation is false. . . . It was only when money came out, when the tabloid went down there offering people money to say that they had been involved with me, that she changed her story. There's a recession going on."

However, during depositions in the PAULA CORBIN JONES lawsuit in which Jones charged President Clinton with sexual harassment while he was governor, President Clinton reversed his earlier statements and acknowledged his relationship with Flowers. The questions about Flowers were asked of President Clinton by the Jones lawyers to prove a pattern of sexual misconduct by the president. The Jones lawyers also tried to prove that President Clinton rewarded those who accepted his sexual advances, as Flowers received a job with Arkansas state government during her relationship with President Clinton. President Clinton settled with Jones for $850,000.

In November 1999, Flowers sued Mrs. Clinton, GEORGE ROBERT STEPHANOPOULOS, and JAMES CARVILLE, JR., for defamation of character. Flowers accused Mrs. Clinton of orchestrating burglaries of her home, defaming her, and invading her privacy. The lawsuit also contended that Carville and Stephanopoulos libeled and slandered Flowers continuously since 1992. DAVID KENDALL represented Mrs. Clinton in the lawsuit.

The case was dismissed by the U.S. District Court Judge Phillip Pro in Las Vegas. Arguments in the case had been heard in February 2002 in the 9th U.S. Circuit Court of Appeals in San Francisco.

Foley, Thomas Stephen

(1929–) *ambassador to Japan, Speaker of the House of Representatives, member of the House of Representatives*

Representative Thomas (Tom) Foley (D-Wash.) served as Speaker of the House during the first two years (1993 and 1994) of the Clinton presidency. Foley lost his seat after 30 years in the House, in the 1994 elections, to the Republican challenger George Nethercutt, who promised not to seek more than three terms if elected. Foley was replaced as speaker by NEWTON (NEWT) LEROY GINGRICH (R-Ga.) in 1995.

In November 1997, Foley was nominated by President Clinton and confirmed by the Senate as ambassador to Japan. He remained ambassador to Japan until 2001, when he joined a Washington, D.C., law firm.

Foley was never considered a close friend of the Clinton administration during his tenure in the House of Representatives. Although President Clinton was a Democrat, Foley never became part of the inner circle of the Clinton decision makers. To some degree, the often difficult relations between the White House and Foley were due to a perception that public opinion could sway the Congress and that the White House did not need to build strong, direct relations. The view in the White House was often that if the president could convince the public on an issue, the public would convince Congress. In addition Foley and others, particularly Democrats, were unhappy that the Health Care Task Force, headed by HILLARY DIANE RODHAM CLINTON and IRA MAGAZINER, often bypassed the Democratic leadership in its deliberations.

The "Republican Revolution" of the 1994 elections was based in part on a move to create term limits in the House of Representatives. The move was led by Gingrich, who supported the 10-point "Contract with America" and term limits. Foley, who had been in Congress since 1965, was vulnerable to the charge that he had been in office too long. After the 1994 elections, the Republicans gained control of the House and elected Gingrich as the Speaker.

Foley's rise to power in the House had begun when he began work in Washington, D.C., as a committee lawyer. In 1961, Senator Henry (Scoop) Jackson (D-Wash.), who was a friend of Foley's father, hired him as special counsel to the Senate Interior and Insular Affairs Committee. Foley remained at the Senate committee for three years, and in 1964 won a seat in the House from the 5th District of Washington. Although the district was primar-

ily Republican, Foley had the support of Jackson and of organized labor, and was helped by the landslide victory of Lyndon Johnson.

During his tenure in the House, Foley took pro-choice positions, supported the Great Society legislation of President Johnson, and pushed for passage of the Equal Rights Amendment. He opposed many of the policies put forth during the Nixon and Ford administrations and again during the Reagan and Bush administrations.

In 1981 he was elected chair of the House Agriculture Committee, where he tried to orient the committee away from livestock and grain issues into issues concerning health and nutrition and consumer interests. He became the youngest chair in history of the Agriculture Committee. In 1987 he was elected House majority leader, after Jim Wright (who had been majority leader) became Speaker of the House, a position Wright held until 1989. In 1989, when Wright resigned as Speaker over questions about his outside income from a book he had written, Foley was elected Speaker on June 6, 1989.

During the early 1990s, the House banking scandal broke, in which a number of House members were charged with writing checks at the House bank with insufficient funds in their accounts. The checks were covered by the House and then the members repaid the House bank. In another scandal, several members were caught purchasing stamps at the House post office with official funds and returning the stamps for cash, which they received.

Foley was accused by many in the House and by the media of ignoring the problems, particularly the banking scandal, for several years as it emerged. Rather than immediately trying to discipline members, he did little. When Nethercutt challenged Foley in 1994, all of the scandals in the House under Foley's leadership were brought out. In addition, Foley joined President Clinton in his effort to pass an assault weapons ban. The National Rifle Association (NRA) led an advertising drive to defeat Foley for his vote on the assault weapons as a violation of the Second Amendment.

Born on March 6, 1929, in Spokane, Washington, Foley received his A.B. (1951) and his LL.B. (1957) from the University of Washington. After graduation he practiced law in Spokane with his cousin, Henry Higgins. Two years later, he became an assistant attorney general for the state of Washington and in 1964 won a seat in the House of Representatives. He remained in the House until 1995.

After leaving the House of Representatives in 1995, Foley joined the law firm of Akin, Gump, Strauss, Hauer, & Feld, LLP, where he specialized in international affairs. He returned to the law firm in 2000 after serving as ambassador to Japan.

Ford, Wendell Hampton
(1924–   ) *member of the Senate*

Wendell Ford (D-Ky.) served in the U.S. Senate for 25 years, before retiring in 1999 (1974–99). Prior to winning the Senate seat, Ford had been governor of Kentucky, from 1971–74.

Ford successfully ran for the Senate in 1974, defeating the incumbent, Republican Marlow Cook. Cook resigned his seat in December 1974 to allow Ford to gain an advantage in committee seniority. Ford then resigned the governorship on December 28, 1974, and was then appointed to the Senate seat by his lieutenant governor, Julian Cornel. He was reelected in 1980, 1986, and 1992. He did not seek reelection in 1998.

Born on September 8, 1924, Ford attended the University of Kentucky from 1942–43 but left to join the U.S. Army (1944–46). He returned to school after World War II and graduated from the Maryland School of Insur-

ance in 1947. Soon after, he began in the insurance business in Kentucky. His political career began in 1959, when he was asked to become the chief assistant to the governor of Kentucky. He successfully ran for the state Senate in 1965–67, lieutenant governor 1967–71, and governor 1971–74. During his tenure in the Senate, Ford spent eight years as Democratic whip (1991–99).

Foster, Henry Wendell, Jr.
(1933–   ) *failed surgeon general nominee*

Henry Foster was nominated for U.S. surgeon general by President Clinton on February 2, 1995, but did not receive Senate confirmation. Foster had been nominated to replace JOYCELYN ELDERS, the first African American in the position. Elders had resigned under pressure for remarks she made concerning adolescent sexual activities.

Because of Foster's support for abortion, abortion foes strongly opposed his confirmation in the Senate. Senators ROBERT (BOB) JOSEPH DOLE (R-Kans.) and Phil Gramm (R-Tex.) led the fight against Foster in the confirmation hearings. Foster won support in the committee and his name was reported out to the full Senate with a favorable vote. However, the Republicans in the Senate refused to allow the nomination to be approved. At one point in the debate over Foster's nomination, Senator Bob Smith (R-N.H.) brought a plastic fetus, an easel, and six posters into the Senate chamber. For 30 minutes, Smith gave a detailed description of a "partial-birth" abortion. Although Smith never suggested Foster had actually performed such a procedure, he indicated that Foster might perform one and might support those who do.

The final vote in the Senate, on June 22, 1995, failed to confirm Foster. The Republicans led a filibuster against confirmation A filibuster required 60 votes to terminate while confirmation required 51 votes. The vote on June 22 was 57-43 to confirm, three votes short of the required 60 votes to end the filibuster. The final tally included all 46 Democrats plus 11 Republicans in favor of confirmation.

Seven months after the failed confirmation hearing, President Clinton named Foster as his senior adviser on teen pregnancy reduction and youth issues. In 1997, President Clinton submitted DAVID SATCHER's name for confirmation as U.S. surgeon general.

Born on September 8, 1933, Foster graduated with a B.S. in biology from Morehouse College (1954) and with his M.D. from the University of Arkansas Medical School (1958), where he was the only African American in a class of 96 students. He became the first African-American student to be elected into Alpha Omega Alpha, the school's honor society in medicine. He began an internship following graduation from medical school at Detroit Receiving Hospital, which was connected to Wayne State University.

In 1959 Foster entered the air force. Because the air force had a shortage of obstetricians, Foster began a three-month course in obstetrics and gynecology. After completing the training program at Carswell Air Force Base in Texas, Foster was sent to Moses Lake, Washington, where he worked with a local obstetrician. While in the air force, Foster delivered 500 babies.

After serving in the air force until 1961, Foster moved to Boston for a year of general surgical training at Malden Hospital and then completed his residency at Hubbard Hospital of Meharry Medical College in Nashville, Tennessee. After completing his residency in 1965, he accepted a position at the John A. Andrew Memorial Hospital at the Tuskegee Institute in Alabama where he worked from 1965–70. While at Tuskegee Institute, Foster served a rural population that was primarily African American and poor. His understanding of rural health care led to substantial changes in rural health care delivery at the hospital.

In 1970 Foster returned to Nashville as chair of the Department of Obstetrics and Gynecology at John A. Andrews Memorial Hospital. From 1973 to 1990 he was professor and chair in the Department of Obstetrics and Gynecology at Meharry Medical College, and in 1975 he joined Vanderbilt University as a clinical professor of obstetrics and gynecology. In 1990, he was named dean of the School of Medicine and vice president for health affairs at Meharry.

When Meharry president David Satcher was named head of the Centers for Disease Control in Atlanta in 1993 by President Clinton, Foster was named acting president of Meharry Medical College. After a new president was appointed in 1994, Foster took a sabbatical leave for a year to work at the Association of Academic Health Centers in Washington, D.C. He focused on "Gender Shift in the Physician Work Force" during his sabbatical. During Foster's sabbatical in 1995, President Clinton nominated him as U.S. surgeon general.

Foster, Vincent W., Jr.
(1945–1993) *White House deputy counsel*

Vincent Foster was White House deputy counsel during the first year of the Clinton administration. Foster had been a friend of President and Mrs. Clinton from Little Rock, Arkansas, where he practiced in the same law firm (the Rose Law Firm) as had Mrs. Clinton. Foster served as deputy counsel to BERNARD NUSSBAUM, White House counsel.

Foster committed suicide on July 20, 1993. He died of a self-inflicted gunshot wound in Fort Marcy Park, Virginia, along the George Washington Memorial Parkway, after leaving the White House following morning meetings, a Rose Garden ceremony announcing the nomination of LOUIS J. FREEH to be director of the FBI, and lunch at his desk. He left his office soon after lunch and was found in the park at 6:00 P.M. by a passing motorist. The autopsy determined that Foster's death was caused by a gunshot wound to the head.

Foster's death was investigated for three years by the office of Whitewater independent counsel KENNETH W. STARR, to determine whether the death was suicide or whether Foster was a victim of foul play due to the sensitivity of his White House work. No allegations were raised during the investigation as to who would have been threatened by Foster's work.

The investigation was begun by Starr's predecessor, ROBERT B. FISKE, JR. Fiske concluded in a June 1994 report that Foster, who was reportedly depressed at the time, had taken his own life. Two congressional panels drew the same conclusion. Starr continued to pursue Fiske's investigation. According to Starr's report, Foster was clinically depressed and concerned about mistakes he may have made with regard to the handling of legal issues in the counsel's office in the White House. Both Fiske and Starr investigated the death of Foster with regard to his dealings with the Whitewater investigation of President and Mrs. Clinton by the independent counsel's office.

When the independent counsel's office began to investigate the firing of existing staff in the White House travel office for new hires by the Clinton White House, Foster was also in charge of reviewing and releasing documents for the investigation. As deputy counsel, Foster's role in the White House was to secure the documents that Fiske and then Starr needed for the independent counsel's investigation into the Whitewater land deal and into the travel office firings.

Following Foster's death, the independent counsel's office sought to interview Foster's lawyer, James Hamilton. The independent counsel wanted to secure all notes that Hamilton had taken with regard to discussions with Foster. Hamilton refused, arguing that the attorney-client privilege is not lost after the death of the client. The case went to court, and five years later reached the Supreme Court in *Swidler & Berlin v. United States* (1999). The Supreme Court ruled that Hamilton did not have to provide the independent counsel with information since the attorney-client relationship remained intact in spite of Foster's death.

Born on January 15, 1945, Foster graduated from the University of Arkansas School of Law in 1971, ranked first in his class. He had served as managing editor of the law review. After law school, he joined the Rose Law Firm in Little Rock as an associate, rising to partner in the firm in 1974. He remained with the law firm until he accepted a position in the Clinton White House as deputy counsel.

Fox, Vicente
(1942–   ) *president of Mexico*

On July 2, 2000, Vicente Fox, a member of the National Action Party (Partido Acción Nacional, or PAN), won the presidency of Mexico and toppled the Institutional Revolutionary Party (Partido Revolucionario Institucional, or PRI). The PRI had held power in Mexico for more than 70 years. Fox replaced President ERNESTO ZEDILLO, who had held the office since his election in 1994.

During the six months he was in office at the end of the Clinton administration, Fox met once with President Clinton. Fox sought to build closer relations between the United States and Mexico on issues relating to immigration, trade, and controlling the drug trade.

Fox ran for his first political office in 1988, winning a seat in the Chamber of Deputies, the lower house of the Mexican Congress, as a member of the conservative National Action

Party. He ran unsuccessfully for governor of Guanajuato in 1991 but succeeded in 1995. Fox began to gear up for the 2000 presidential election in 1998, delivering speeches around the country condemning the ruling Institutional Revolutionary Party. During the 2000 presidential elections, Fox won a convincing victory with 42.5 percent of the vote against that of his main opponent, Francisco Labastida, with 36.1 percent of the vote.

During Fox's presidential campaign, he visited the United States and met with representatives of the Clinton administration, asking them to remain noncommittal in the Mexican elections. He also met with the administration's drug policy director, Barry McCaffrey, and argued for closer relations between the two countries in dealing with the drug trade. He urged that a plan be developed to deal with drug operations but that the plan not include drug agents within Mexico from the United States. During his campaign, Fox declared that he was an admirer of President Clinton and of British prime minister Tony Blair.

Once in office, Fox began to promote a series of new policies between the United States and Mexico. Among those new policies was a proposal that the United States allow 250,000 visas per year for Mexican immigrants. He argued that the Mexicans provided needed workers in a variety of industries, such as agriculture and the hotel industry. In exchange, Fox promised to police the border to stop illegal immigration and to cut off social programs in Mexico if a member crosses the border to work illegally.

In August 2000, Fox traveled to Washington, D.C., for a two-day trip. He met first with Vice President ALBERT (AL) GORE, JR. in a private meeting at the vice president's residence at the Naval Observatory. He later met privately with President Clinton and then secretary of state MADELEINE KORBEL ALBRIGHT. Following his trip to Washington, D.C., Fox left for Dallas, Texas, where he met with Governor GEORGE WALKER BUSH, the Republican presidential candidate.

Born July 2, 1942, in Mexico City, Fox (whose full name is Vicente Fox Quesada) was raised in Guanajuato near León. His father was a rancher of Irish descent and his mother was from Spain. After studying business management at Mexico City's Iberoamerican University, Fox was hired by Coca-Cola in 1964. By 1974, Fox had advanced to president of Coca-Cola of Mexico. In 1979, rather than accept a promotion to head of Latin American affairs for Coca-Cola, which would have meant a transfer to Miami, Fox left the company and returned to his family farming business in Guanajuato.

Frampton, George T., Jr.

(1944–) *chair, Council of Environmental Quality; assistant secretary for fish and wildlife and parks, Department of Interior*

George Frampton, the former president of the Wilderness Society, was named by President Clinton as chair of the Council of Environmental Quality (CEQ) on October 30, 1998. Frampton replaced KATHLEEN McGINTY.

In making the announcement of Frampton's nomination to chair the Council of Environmental Quality, President Clinton said he would nominate Frampton as acting chair of the Council of Environmental Quality until he could send his nomination forward following the midterm election recess.

Prior to his nomination, he had since 1993 been the assistant secretary for fish and wildlife and parks at the Department of Interior. He was confirmed by the Senate on June 30, 1993.

Frampton had held a number of roles in the federal government during his career, including Supreme Court law clerk, assistant special prosecutor during Watergate, and part of the investigative team for Three Mile Island. However, he gained the most attention during his career as a successful lobbyist for environmental programs as president of the Wilderness Society.

Frampton served as law clerk to Justice Harry A. Blackmun of the U.S. Supreme Court during the early 1970s. From 1973 to 1975 he served as an assistant special prosecutor in the Watergate investigation. From 1979 to 1980, he served as deputy director and chief of staff for the Nuclear Regulatory Commission's Special Inquiry into the nuclear accident at Three Mile Island near Harrisburg, Pennsylvania.

In 1976, Frampton joined the Washington, D.C., law firm of Rogovin, Huge, and Lenzer, where he worked until 1985. He left the law firm in 1986 to become the president of the Wilderness Society, headquartered in Washington, D.C. Under Frampton's leadership, the Wilderness Society's budget increased threefold and membership increased fourfold.

Born on August 24, 1944, in Washington, D.C., Frampton was raised in Urbana, Illinois. He received his B.A. from Yale University in physics and philosophy (1965), a master's degree in advanced economic theory from the London School of Economics, and a J.D. from Harvard Law School, where he was managing editor of the *Harvard Law Review* (1969).

Louis J. Freeh *(AP Photo/J. Scott Applewhite)*

Freeh, Louis J.
(1950–) *director, Federal Bureau of Investigation*

Nominated by President Clinton to replace WILLIAM SESSIONS on July 20, 1993, Louis Freeh was confirmed unanimously without debate by the Senate on August 6, 1993, as director of the Federal Bureau of Investigation (FBI). His first day on the job, however, was September 1, 1993. Freeh retired from the Federal Bureau of Investigation on May 1, 2001, during the first year of the Bush administration.

Freeh had been a federal judge for the U.S. District Court for the Southern District of New York prior to accepting the position as director of the Federal Bureau of Investigation. He had been nominated by President GEORGE HERBERT WALKER BUSH on April 9, 1991, to the court and confirmed by the Senate on May 24, 1991, but resigned on August 31, 1993, following his Senate confirmation as director of the Federal Bureau of Investigation.

After graduating from law school, Freeh went into private practice (1974–75). His tenure in private practice lasted two years. He then decided to enter the FBI Academy in Quantico, Virginia, where he underwent 16 weeks of training to become an agent. He completed the course in Quantico in 1976 and was assigned to New York City. He spent five years investigating organized crime on New York City's waterfront docks, leading to the prosecution of 125 people. His undercover work on the docks led to a commendation from FBI director William S. Sessions in 1980. As a result, he was promoted in 1980 from investigative activities to a supervisory role in the FBI, but he soon left the FBI complaining about the bureaucratic nature of the new role. He was soon after hired as an assistant United States attorney for the Southern District of New York.

One of his high-profile cases came when he led the prosecution team against a heroin operation that used pizza restaurants as a front. In the "Pizza Connection" case, Freeh secured convictions for 18 of the defendants. According to a *New York Times* article (July 21, 1993), Freeh "masterminded the prosecution, at times traveling to Turkey and Switzerland to interview witnesses and take depositions." He was promoted to the rank of deputy and associate United States attorney in 1989, and named interim second-in-command when Rudolph Giuliani, then the United States attorney in the Southern District of New York, resigned to run for mayor of New York City. Freeh left the U.S. Attorney's office in 1991 when President Bush nominated him for the U.S. District Court of the Southern District of New York.

When President Clinton was seeking a new FBI director in 1993 following his dismissal of William S. Sessions, Freeh's name was prominently mentioned. On July 16, 1993, Freeh was called to the White House where President Clinton and Attorney General JANET RENO offered him the job. Freeh sought two guarantees from President Clinton: that he would have complete independence and that he would have time to spend with his family. Clinton agreed to both requests, and Freeh accepted the nomination.

When Freeh took over the FBI in September 1993, he moved to reorganize the bureau's internal operations. Among his actions to streamline the FBI were eliminating positions

and demoting others. He worked closely with Congress during his first two years in office to increase the FBI's budget and to strengthen federal wiretapping laws.

Although Freeh built a strong relationship with Congress during his first two years in office, the relationship was severely tested during Senate hearings into the August 21, 1992, shoot-out in Ruby Ridge, Idaho. Federal marshals and the FBI were trying to arrest Randall C. Weaver, a white separatist, on weapons charges at their isolated home near Ruby Ridge, Idaho. During a gun battle, Weaver's 14-year-old son and a federal agent were killed. The next day, an FBI sharpshooter wounded Weaver and killed his unarmed wife, who was carrying an infant. Weaver surrendered on August 31.

Freeh's handling of the investigation into the shootings at Ruby Ridge was subsequently investigated by Congress. In an October 1995 hearing at the Senate Judiciary Committee's Subcommittee on Terrorism, Technology, and Government Information, Freeh said, "Ruby Ridge was a series of flawed mistakes." Although Freeh was not rebuked by the committee, his reputation with Congress began to suffer after the Ruby Ridge investigations.

The lessons of Ruby Ridge were not lost on Freeh. In March 1996 when a small antigovernment group locked themselves into a house on a Montana ranch and refused to surrender, Freeh worked for a peaceful settlement. The FBI remained at the ranch for 81 days until the group surrendered.

One of the highest-profile cases under Freeh was the Oklahoma City bombing of the Alfred P. Murrah Federal Building in April 1995. Although Timothy McVeigh was tried, convicted, and executed for his role in the bombing, Freeh's office came under fire in 2001 (after McVeigh's execution) for witholding 3,000 pages of documents from McVeigh's attorneys.

Another high-profile case under Freeh's tenure was the Unabomber case. The FBI arrested, after 17 years of investigation, Theodore Kaczynski, a Montana recluse, who had sent letter bombs that killed three people. He also was deeply involved in the investigation of the backpack bomb that exploded in Atlanta during the summer Olympics in 1996.

The FBI also suffered several setbacks during Freeh's tenure. In 2000 nuclear scientist Wen Ho Lee pleaded guilty to one of 59 felony counts of mishandling classified data at the Los Alamos National Laboratory. The FBI led the investigation but was never able to secure a significant jail sentence for Lee, who served nine months in prison. Lee was a Taiwan-born naturalized citizen who the FBI believed had delivered sensitive nuclear documents to Taiwan. The case was never proven in court. In 2001, only months before Freeh left office, FBI agent Robert Hanssen was arrested and charged with spying for the Russians.

Although Freeh acted independently of President Clinton and Attorney General Reno, he needed Reno to approve his request for an independent counsel to investigate fund-raising by the Clinton-Gore presidential campaign in 1996. She refused, citing lack of evidence to support the need for an independent counsel.

The FBI's relationship with the White House during the tenure of Louis Freeh was never strong. In 1996, when newspaper reports indicated that several members of the Clinton White House had received FBI background reports on employees of previous Republican presidents, Freeh argued that he had been "victimized" by the White House.

Although many close to President Clinton urged him to dismiss Freeh, Clinton never did. Clinton chose, instead, to distance himself and the White House from the FBI.

Born January 6, 1950, in Jersey City, New Jersey, Freeh received his B.A. degree, Phi Beta Kappa, from Rutgers College (1971) and his J.D. from Rutgers University School of Law (1974). He also received a LL.M. from New York University School of Law in 1984.

From, Al

(1943–   ) chief executive officer, Democratic Leadership Council

Al From was a founding member and chief executive officer of the Democratic Leadership Council (DLC). From met Governor Bill Clinton in 1985 when a group of centrist Democrats formed the DLC. Vice President ALBERT (AL) GORE, JR., also had been a central figure in the DLC, and both formed a lasting bond with President Clinton while working with the DLC.

Clinton served as DLC chairman from March 1990 to October 1991, when he resigned to run for president. During his tenure as chairman, Clinton worked with From to prepare a 44-page agenda for the nation, entitled "The New American Choice." The agenda emphasized private-sector growth, personal responsibility, and community service. Many of the proposals outlined in this agenda were incorporated into the Clinton campaign for president.

During the 1992 presidential campaign, the DLC created numerous position papers for the Clinton campaign. From became a key Clinton-Gore campaign adviser and, after the election, was the Clinton-Gore transition team head overseeing domestic policy issues. Although From did not accept a position in the White House or the cabinet, following Clinton's successful election in 1992, he did accept an appointment in 1999 to the U.S. Naval Academy Board of Visitors.

Several staffers from the Democratic Leadership Council did receive jobs in the Clinton White House, including Elaine Kamarck, who handled campaign finance issues; BRUCE REED, who was issues director;

and WILLIAM GALSTON, who handled family and children's issues. By placing former DLC staffers into White House positions, President Clinton sent a signal to the Democratic Party that his administration would be run by centrists.

From remains the chief executive officer of the DLC and frequently discusses in interviews and speeches the need for the Democratic Party to remain moderate in its positions and not return to liberal or left-wing positions.

Born on May 31, 1943, From graduated from Northwestern University with a B.S. (1965) and an M.A. (1966) in journalism. He served as director of the U.S. Senate Subcommittee on Intergovernmental Relations (1971–79), deputy adviser on inflation to President Carter (1979–81), and executive director of the House Democratic Caucus (1981–85). From left the House of Representatives in 1985 to help found the DLC and to serve as its president.

Galston, William A.

(1946–) deputy assistant to the president for domestic policy

William A. Galston was named deputy assistant to the president for domestic policy in January 1993. He resigned in 1995 to become executive director of the National Commission on Civil Renewal. Galston had served as a domestic policy adviser for the 1992 presidential campaign and for the presidential transition team.

While in the White House, Galston became involved in a wide variety of domestic policy initiatives that the Clinton administration sought to move through Congress, including the overhaul of the welfare system. Galston worked in the White House with CAROL RASCO, the assistant to the president for domestic policy, and with BRUCE REED, who also held the title deputy assistant to the president for domestic policy. Rasco had held numerous positions in Clinton's gubernatorial administration in Arkansas, and Reed had served as policy director for the Democratic Leadership Council.

Clinton's relationship to Galston began before the campaign, when both were deeply involved with the newly created Democratic Leadership Council. Founded in 1985 by AL FROM, the Democratic Leadership Council

brought together moderate Democrats seeking to move the Democratic Party away from its liberal traditions into a more moderate series of positions. Galston began in 1989 to work with the Democratic Leadership Counsel as a senior adviser on domestic policy issues.

Galston's work in Democratic political circles had spanned more than a decade. He had worked for a number of presidential campaigns before the Clinton-Gore campaign. In 1980, Galston was a speechwriter for independent presidential candidate John Anderson, was an issues director in 1984 for Walter Mondale's presidential campaign, and was an issues adviser to Senator Al Gore's 1988 presidential campaign during the primaries.

After leaving the Clinton administration in 1995, Galston became executive director of the National Commission on Civic Renewal, chaired by Sam Nunn and William Bennett. The National Commission on Civic Renewal was funded though a $950,000 grant from the Pew Charitable Trusts of Philadelphia.

Born on January 17, 1946, Galston received his B.A. from Cornell University (1967), and his M.A. (1969) and his Ph.D. (1973) from the University of Chicago. Galston was an assistant professor in the department of government at the University of Texas at Austin from 1973–80, a visiting fellow at

Yale University from 1980–81, an associate professor at the University of Texas from 1980–84, and director of economic and social programs, Roosevelt Center for American Public Policy Studies, in Washington, D.C., from 1985–88. In 1988, he became professor of the School for Public Affairs at the Institute for Philosophy and Public Policy at the University of Maryland. Among his books is *Liberal Purposes: Goods, Virtues, and Diversity in the Liberal State* (1991).

Galston was cofounder of *The Responsive Community*, a journal that explored the issues of community, responsibility, and the common good in public policy. His writings often reflected his academic training as a political theorist.

Gearan, Mark D.

(1957–) *director of the Peace Corps, director of communications, deputy chief of staff*

Mark Gearan was named by President Clinton as deputy chief of staff under Chief of Staff THOMAS McLARTY in January 1993. Five months into the administration, McLarty made a series of changes among the senior White House staff, moving staff from one position to another. Gearan was shifted in June 1993 from deputy chief of staff to assistant to the president and communications director. GEORGE ROBERT STEPHANOPOULOS, who had been communications director, was moved to the position of senior adviser to the president for policy and strategy. As communications director, Gearan traveled extensively with President Clinton, including trips to Russia, Japan, the Middle East, Germany, Italy, and Ireland.

After two years on the White House senior staff, Gearan was nominated to be director of the Peace Corps, replacing CAROL BELLAMY, who was named director of UNICEF at the United Nations. When President Clinton nominated Gearan on June 21, 1995, he said, "I think it would be fair to say that if we had a secret ballot for who was the most popular person working in the White House, Mark Gearan would probably win it in a walk. He has the understanding and the ability to build bridges and the tenacity to cross them." Gearan was confirmed by the Senate on September 26, 1995, and remained on the job until August 11, 1999.

As director of the Peace Corps, Gearan established the Crisis Corps, which was a program within the Peace Corps. The Crisis Corps sent former Peace Corps volunteers to countries for short-term assignments, generally six months or less. Volunteers in the Crisis Corps return to the country that they originally served in to assist in natural disaster relief or other crises. When the program was created in 1999, Gearan noted that he expected approximately 100 volunteers to be part of the Crisis Corps. Under Gearan, the Peace Corps had 6,700 volunteers in 80 countries and he was working toward a growth to 10,000 volunteers.

Gearan left the Peace Corps to accept the appointment as president of Hobart and William Smith Colleges in 1999, becoming one of the youngest college presidents in the nation. He also was confirmed by the Senate to serve on the board of directors of the Corporation for National and Community Service, after leaving the Peace Corps.

Born in 1957 in Gardner, Massachusetts, Gearan graduated with a B.A., cum laude, in government from Harvard College (1978) and with a J.D. from Georgetown University Law Center (1991). In 1978 he served as press secretary for the reelection campaign of Representative Robert F. Drinan (D-Mass.) and also as press secretary in 1978 for a Massachusetts ballot initiative. Gearan met his wife, Mary Herlihy, while working in Drinan's office. A Roman Catholic priest, Drinan married them.

Gearan then joined the staff of the *Fitchburg-Leominster Sentinel* (1978–80). In 1980 he was named press secretary and then chief of staff for Representative Berkley Bedell (D-Iowa) from 1980 to 1983. When he left Congressman Bedell's staff, he was named the director of the Massachusetts Office of Federal Relations for Governor Michael Dukakis (1983–87). When Governor Dukakis ran for president, Gearnan joined his staff as press secretary, 1988–89. He returned to his position as director of the Massachusetts Office of Federal Relations after Dukakis failed to win the 1988 presidential election. In 1989 Gearan was named executive director of the Democratic Governor's Association, and in 1992 became a senior adviser to the Clinton-Gore presidential campaign.

During Gearan's tenure at the Democratic Governors Association, the association doubled its yearly budget and created a new policy unit. In 1992 he took a leave of absence from the association to work for the Clinton-Gore presidential campaign. At the Democratic National Convention in New York City, Gearan worked closely with vice presidential nominee ALBERT (AL) GORE, JR. He then was named Gore's campaign manager for the remainder of the election, traveling with Gore and advising him on strategy issues. Following the election, Gear was named deputy director of the transition team, working with transition director WARREN MINOR CHRISTOPHER. Gearan's role was director of Washington operations.

Gebbie, Kristine M.

(1943–   ) *national AIDS policy coordinator*

President Clinton appointed Kristine M. Gebbie on June 18, 1993, as the national AIDS policy coordinator. The position was part of the White House Domestic Policy Office under CAROL RASCO. Gebbie resigned on July 8, 1994 (effective August 2, 1994), due to a frustration that the White House had not allowed her greater latitude in lobbying Congress as an advocate for AIDS funding. PATRICIA FLEMING was named as her replacement.

As the Clinton point person for AIDS policy, Gebbie was charged with coordinating programs in the Department of Health and Human Services, the Centers for Disease Control, and other federal agencies. In addition, she was responsible for lobbying Congress for a proposal to spend $500 million on AIDS.

In addition, Gebbie worked on the administration's "condom campaign," which was a series of television commercials advocating the use of condoms to prevent the spread of AIDS. The ads drew criticism from the Christian right, adding to the political difficulties that Gebbie faced in lobbying activities for AIDS funding in Congress.

In an interview for the *New York Times* following her resignation, Gebbie complained that she had been frustrated by her inability to lobby Congress actively for greater funding for AIDS. In part, the AIDS community had been unhappy with her failure to support their lobbying activities in Congress. She told the *New York Times* that "it's time for someone else to try" (July 9, 1994).

Her appointment as AIDS czar stemmed from her public health background and her experience working with AIDS policy. She was a member of the HIV Committee of the Association of State and Territorial Health Officials, and she chaired the Centers for Disease Control's Advisory Committee on the Prevention of HIV Infection.

Born on June 23, 1943, Gebbie received her B.S. in nursing from St. Olaf's College (1965), an M.A. degree from the California School of Nursing (1968), and a Ph.D. in public health from the University of Michigan. Throughout most of her professional career, she worked as a community nurse. In 1979, she became the director of the Oregon Division of Health, where she remained until 1990. Then she became secretary of the Department of Health in the state of Washington. She had also been a member of the Presidential Commission on AIDS during the Reagan administration.

After leaving the White House, she was named the Elizabeth Standish Gill Associate Professor of Nursing, and director, Center for Health Policy, at Columbia University School of Nursing.

Gephardt, Richard (Dick) A.
(1941–) *member of the House of Representatives*

Richard (Dick) Gephardt was elected to Missouri's 3rd Congressional District in the U.S. House of Representatives in 1976. After taking office in 1977, he rose rapidly in the leadership ranks of the Democratic Party within the House. He was first elected in 1984 as chairman of the House Democratic Caucus (the fourth-ranking leadership post in the U.S. House), as majority leader in 1989, and as minority leader in 1995. He did not seek reelection as minority leader in 2003 to mount a campaign for the Democratic presidential nomination in 2004. Gephardt failed in his presidential bid, withdrawing from the race after losing in the early primary states. After losing in his home state of Missouri, Gephardt announced he would not run for reelection in 2004 and would end his political career at the end of his term.

Gephardt's rise to the top position began when the House Democrats underwent a major shake-up in 1989 when Jim Wright resigned as Speaker of the House. Gephardt successfully ran for the majority leader post as Democrats were carving out new roles within the leadership structure. In 1989 Gephardt was elected majority leader, a position he maintained until 1995 when the Republicans gained control of the House. He was then elected by

the Democratic members of the House as minority leader, a position he maintained until 2003. Gephardt did not run for minority leader in 2003, instead focusing his energies on his presidential campaign for 2004 while remaining in the House.

Gephardt's 2004 run for the presidency was not his first attempt. In 1988, he was among a field of Democrats that sought to recapture the Oval Office for the Democrats. He had been the first Democrat to enter the primary contests in 1987. Democrats believed that Vice President George Bush, the likely Republican candidate, could be defeated, which provided for a large field of candidates in the Democratic primaries. Governor Michael Dukakis of Massachusetts ultimately became the nominee.

In the 1988 Democratic primaries, Gephardt won the Iowa caucus, finished second in the New Hampshire primary, but was forced to drop out of the campaign by Super Tuesday because his funding had dried up. Twelve years later, he considered challenging Vice President Al Gore in the primaries in 2000, but chose not to. Gore was considered the strongest candidate among the Democratic funding sources, leaving Gephardt few places to raise money.

During his long tenure in the House of Representatives, Gephardt often joined forces with traditional Democratic constituencies such as minorities, the poor, and organized labor. To some extent, his activism among these constituencies stemmed from his own political base which was 98 percent white, conservative, and blue-collar. During the Reagan administration, he often supported positions that protected his blue-collar district.

Gephardt continued to support organized labor once the Clinton administration entered office, in spite of conflicts within the Democratic Party on a key piece of trade legislation. Gephardt opposed President Clinton on the

North American Free Trade Act (NAFTA), arguing that the bill would hurt labor's interests. When NAFTA passed in Congress, Gephardt lost considerable political clout within the White House.

Gephardt's support for organized labor paid off in the form of campaign contributions. Between 1993 and 1995, Gephardt received the most political action committee (PAC) money in the House, and the second-most PAC money in Congress, following Senator Kay Baily Hutchison (R-Tex.). Gephardt's leading donors included labor unions, lawyers, and the tobacco and insurance industries. Gephardt also received substantial PAC contributions from McDonnell Douglas, a St. Louis-based company that received substantial weapons contracts that Gephardt protected.

One of the more surprising aspects of Gephardt's coalition-building among the liberal wing of the Democratic Party was that he was one of the early members of the centrist Democratic Leadership Council with then-governor Bill Clinton. Gephardt became the first head of the DLC in 1985, a position Clinton would later have in 1990.

By 1997, after Clinton had won the 1996 presidential election, the relationship between Clinton and Gephardt had moved to new lows. When a bipartisan balanced budget agreement passed in Congress, President Clinton failed to mention Gephardt on May 16, 1997, when he was congratulating congressional leaders for their work on the bill. Senate Minority Leader Tom Daschle (D-S.D.), Senate Majority Leader Trent Lott (R-Miss.), and House Speaker Newt Gingrich (R-Ga.) were mentioned during a press briefing, but Gephardt was not mentioned.

Gephardt had been critical of the balanced budget agreement because of its Medicare cost savings and business tax cuts. Representative John M. Spratt Jr. (D-S.C.) was the only House Democrat noted by the Clinton White House

for his work on the balanced budget bill. Clinton went on to note "the Congressional leadership who supported this process," without mentioning Gephardt by name.

Gephardt, a St. Louis native who continued to represent St. Louis in the House, brought a wide variety of federally funded projects to the area. A devoted Cardinals baseball fan, he is credited with the effort that brought the Rams football team to St. Louis.

Born on January 31, 1941, in St. Louis, Gephardt graduated with a B.S. from Northwestern University (1962) and a J.D. from the University of Michigan Law School (1965). Eager to become involved in political activities, Gephardt became a Democratic precinct captain for the 14th ward of St. Louis. He practiced law in St. Louis from 1965–71 before being elected as an alderman (1971–76). In 1976 he again successfully ran for public office in the U.S. House of Representatives. He served in that role continuously throughout his career.

Gergen, David

(1942–   ) *special adviser to the secretary of state, counselor to the president*

David Gergen, a Republican who had worked on the White House staffs of Presidents Nixon, Ford, and Reagan, was asked by President Clinton in May 1993 to cross party lines to join the White House staff as counselor to the president. Gergen's role was described as planning long-range policy, although he became involved in a broad range of communications issues. At the same time that President Clinton announced that Gergen had been hired for the White House staff, he announced that GEORGE ROBERT STEPHANOPOULOS would be moving from communications director to a new position as policy adviser to the president.

Gergen later moved to the Department of State where he served as a special adviser to the secretary of state, WARREN MINOR CHRISTO-PHER, for six months. Gergen left in 1995 to return to his job as editor at *U.S. News and World Report*. In 1999 Gergen was appointed a professor of public service at the John F. Kennedy School of Government and director of the Center for Public Leadership.

Gergen's relationship with Clinton began in 1985 after a meeting of the private Renaissance Weekend in Hilton Head, South Carolina, created by PHILIP LADER, over New Year's weekend. Throughout the following years, Clinton and Gergen saw each other at the annual Renaissance Weekends and kept in touch. When Clinton delivered a long-winded speech at the 1988 Democratic convention, Gergen sent a note to his hotel room. When Clinton announced his presidential bid in 1991, he spent 90 minutes on the phone with Gergen.

Gergen's primary role in the Clinton White House was to bring experience to a relatively inexperienced White House staff. Only Gergen of the senior White House staff had served previously on a White House staff. In an interview with *ABC News* in 2001 after leaving the White House, Gergen was asked why he joined the Clinton administration. He answered that President Clinton indicated to him that he wanted to bring a bipartisan approach to reforms in education, health care, and other fields, and that Gergen could help with planning those initiatives. Gergen added in the interview, "I made it clear I could not participate in campaigns, or remain there long enough to participate in campaigns against friends in the Republican Party."

As a former White House communications director, Gergen believed in using the press to put forward the president's policies. Gergen often brought in members of the press to meet with Clinton in one-on-one sessions. Rather than avoid the press, Gergen sought to use the press to Clinton's benefit.

Although he was a Republican in a Democratic White House, Gergen worked to build strong relations with staff. His first move was to keep a low profile in the White House, choosing a smaller office on the second floor of the west wing. He also tried to build rapport with staffers, such as by supporting an increase in the speechwriting staff when he learned there were only three speechwriters.

Prior to joining the Clinton administration, Gergen had spent much of his professional career in Republican administrations. He first joined the Nixon administration's White House staff in 1971, rising to the position of special assistant to the president and chief of the White House speechwriting office by 1973. In 1975, after President Ford had taken over the government, Gergen became special assistant to the president and director of the White House Office of Communications.

He returned to the White House in the Reagan administration as assistant to the president for communications, where he worked from 1981–83. He left in 1983 to be a Fellow at the John F. Kennedy School of Government, Harvard University, where he stayed for two years. In 1985 he assumed the position of managing editor of *U.S. News and World Report*, and in 1986 became its editor, until he joined the Clinton White House in 1993. In 1980, Gergen had worked for Republican candidate GEORGE HERBERT WALKER BUSH in his bid for the presidency.

After leaving the Clinton White House, Gergen worked with the Aspen Institute, chairing a domestic policy group. The Aspen Institute included among its directors former senator WILLIAM (BILL) WARREN BRADLEY (D-N.J.) and former education secretary (under both Reagan and Bush) WILLIAM J. BENNETT.

Born on May 2, 1942, Gergen received his A.B. degree from Yale University, with honors (1963), and his LL.B. from Harvard Law School (1967).

Gibbons, John (Jack) H.

(1929–   ) director, White House Office of Science and Technology

John (Jack) Gibbons, an internationally known scientist, was appointed by President Clinton as the assistant to the president for science and technology, and director of the White House Office of Science and Technology, on February 2, 1993. Gibbons also cochaired the President's Committee of Advisors on Science and Technology (PCAST) and managed the National Science and Technology Council (NSTC). Gibbons left the White House in 1998.

While on the White House staff, Gibbons also was a member of the National Security Council, the Economic Council, and the Domestic Policy Council, in addition to his role on the Science and Technology Council. He advocated science and technology policy interwoven throughout the administration's policy decisions.

As cochair of PCAST, Gibbons provided the staff support for the committee. The committee gave the president information from outside the federal sector on science and technology issues. Members of PCAST included three Nobel Prize winners, and individuals from industry, education, and research institutions. Among the PCAST reports to President Clinton was an examination of how to improve U.S.-Russian cooperation on weapons-usable nuclear material.

As the president's adviser on science and technology, Gibbons established six goals for the administration:

1. maintain world leadership in science, engineering, and mathematics,
2. promote long-term economic growth that creates jobs,
3. sustain a healthy, educated citizenry,
4. harness information technology,
5. improve environmental quality,
6. enhance national security.

One of the initiatives under Gibbons was the Next General Internet (NGI), created in 1996 to foster partnerships among academia, industry, and federal laboratories to develop and experiment with technologies that would enable more powerful information networks in the 21st century.

Born January 15, 1929, Gibbons received a B.S. from Randolph-Macon College, Phi Beta Kappa (1949), and a Ph.D. from Duke University (1954). After graduating from Duke University, Gibbons began as a research associate in nuclear physics at the university. He left in 1954 to join the Oak Ridge National Laboratory in Oak Ridge, Tennessee, as a physicist and group leader in nuclear geophysics (1954–69). In 1969 he became director of the Environmental Program at Oak Ridge. For a brief period (1973–74) Gibbons went to the Federal Energy Administration, Washington, D.C., as the first director of the Office of Energy Conservation.

He returned to academia in 1974 at the University of Tennessee, Knoxville, as professor of physics and director of the Energy, Environment and Resources Center (1974–79). In 1979 he returned to Washington, D.C., and to public service as director of the Office of Technology Assessment within the Congress (1979–93).

Gingrich, Newton (Newt) Leroy

(1943–   ) Speaker of the House, member of the House of Representatives

Newt Gingrich (R-Ga.) led the Republican Party in capturing the majority in the House of Representatives in the 1994 elections. As a result, Gingrich was elected Speaker of the House in 1995 and named by *Time* magazine as the "Man of the Year." *Time* stated in its article that "Leaders make things possible. Exceptional leaders make them inevitable. Newt Gingrich belongs in the category of the exceptional."

Although Gingrich had led the House for two terms, he was disappointed by the elections of 1998 and announced on November 6, 1998, "that I will not be a candidate for Speaker of the 106th Congress." The Republican caucus subsequently elected ROBERT LIVINGSTON as Speaker for the new term.

However, on December 16, 1998, during the impeachment proceedings against President Clinton, *Hustler* magazine revealed that Livingston had had an extramarital relationship. Livingston announced on December 19, 1998, that he would not accept the position of Speaker. DENNIS HASTERT was then nominated as Speaker by the Republican majority, to be formally elected by the entire House in January 1999. Only days after Livingston made the announcement, Gingrich abruptly resigned his seat in December 1998 when it was revealed that he had been having an extramarital affair.

Prior to his tenure as Speaker, Gingrich supported President Clinton on the North American Free Trade Agreement (NAFTA) but opposed him on health care reform. Once he was elected Speaker, Gingrich rarely supported administration-sponsored legislation. Gingrich led the opposition against the administration's 1995 budget, leading to a government shutdown in the fall, before the budget was resolved between Congress and the White House. In July 1996 Gingrich restarted the Clinton administration's welfare reform package, forcing the administration to compromise on certain parts to secure its passage before the November presidential election.

Although Gingrich had been a powerful force in the House during his first term as Speaker, moving forward to enact his 10-point

"Contract with America," Gingrich's second term was plagued with controversy. When he ran for his second term as Speaker of the House, Gingrich won by only three votes. His fall within the Republican Party stemmed from an ongoing ethics investigation into his financial dealings. The Ethics Committee began an investigation on allegations that he violated the tax code with regard to raising funds for a college course he was teaching in Georgia. He was also criticized for a book advance of $4.5 million from publisher HarperCollins. He subsequently chose to decline the advance and accept only the royalties. However, his support in the House was eroding.

The Ethics Committee voted on January 21, 1997, to acquit him on 74 of the 75 charges against him. On the one charge for which he was found guilty, he was ordered to pay a $300,000 fine. Senator ROBERT (BOB) JOSEPH DOLE lent him the $300,000, at an interest rate of 10 percent to be repaid over 10 years. Gingrich had dealt with the Ethics Committee in 1987, when he led accusations of ethics violations against Speaker Jim Wright for a scheme to circumvent ethics rules in book sales from which Wright profited. Since Wright resigned before a verdict was delivered, Gingrich became the first Speaker to have a verdict against him for ethics charges.

Gingrich was reelected in 1998 but announced on November 6 that he would not run for Speaker again. House Republicans had voiced strong opposition to his leadership, and a number of Republicans announced after the November 1998 elections that they would not support Gingrich for Speaker. He resigned from his House seat in December.

However, his resignation was largely tied to his personal life. Throughout his tenure in the House, Gingrich had been an outspoken supporter of "family values" and became the leading spokesman for conservatives in Congress. During the independent counsel's investigation of President Clinton with regard to his relationship with MONICA LEWINSKY, Gingrich repeatedly supported the investigation and criticized President Clinton for lying about the relationship. In December 1998 it was revealed in the media that Gingrich, who was married, had been involved in a relationship with a House staff member. Gingrich resigned soon after. He divorced his wife in August 1999 and married Callista Bisek, who he said he had been dating since 1993. This was Gingrich's third marriage.

Gingrich's rise to power in the House began in 1989 when he was elected minority whip in a close vote, 87-85. His election as Speaker on January 4, 1995, came after he had successfully campaigned for candidates who strongly supported him and his "Contract with America."

Gingrich was born on June 17, 1943, in Harrisburg, Pennsylvania, to 19-year-old Newton McPherson and 16-year-old Kathleen Daugherty. Gingrich's parents divorced soon after their marriage. His mother remarried Robert B. Gingrich, a career soldier, three years later. Gingrich's father was transferred frequently as an army officer and was stationed at Fort Benning, Georgia, when Gingrich began college at Emory University. Gingrich's first foray into politics began at Emory University, when he founded a Young Republicans Club. He graduated with a B.A. from Emory University (1965), an M.A. from Tulane University (1968), and a Ph.D. from Tulane University (1971). He began his career as an assistant professor of history and environmental studies at West Georgia College in Carollton (1970–78), and then ran successfully for the House of Representatives from the 6th Congressional District of Georgia. He had lost two races for the House before winning a seat in 1978.

After leaving office, Gingrich formed the Gingrich Group and was named as a Distin-

guished Visiting Fellow at the Hoover Institution of Stanford University. The Gingrich Group was established, according to their literature, to "develop strategic initiatives with national and global employers on a broad range of economic issues, including issues related to health and health care, the environment, information systems, international finance, international relations and trade." The Gingrich Group was allied with Pricewaterhouse-Coopers, the financial consulting firm. In addition, Gingrich was a member of the congressionally chartered National Strategic Study Group. He also created his own Web site, www.newt.org.

Ginsburg, Ruth Bader
(1933–) *justice of the Supreme Court*

Ruth Bader Ginsburg was one of President Clinton's two appointees to the U.S. Supreme Court. STEPHEN BREYER was the second appointment made by President Clinton to the Court during his tenure in office.

On August 3, 1993, the Senate confirmed Ginsburg's nomination by a vote of 96-3, after relatively little debate. Republicans in the Senate viewed Ginsburg as a conservative or moderate on the U.S. Court of Appeals and were delighted that President Clinton had not nominated a liberal for the Supreme Court. She became the 107th Supreme Court justice, the second female jurist, and the first justice to be named to the Supreme Court by a Democratic president since Lyndon Baines Johnson.

Ginsburg was nominated by President Clinton on June 14, 1993, to replace the retiring Justice Byron R. White and took her seat on the Supreme Court on August 10, 1993. Prior to her nomination to the Supreme Court, she had served on the U.S. Court of Appeals, District of Columbia Circuit, since 1980, having been appointed by President Jimmy Carter.

She had been sworn into the Court of Appeals on June 30, 1980.

When an opening appeared in 1993 on the Supreme Court for President Clinton to fill, the White House considered several nominees. The front-runner was New York governor MARIO M. CUOMO, but he declined. The next choice appeared to be Secretary of Interior BRUCE EDWARD BABBITT. However, environmental groups successfully lobbied President Clinton to keep Babbitt at the Department of Interior, given his strong record of environmental activism. Judge Stephen Breyer was also on the list but apparently did not have a positive interview at the time with President Clinton. As a result, Clinton returned to the short list of nominees and asked to meet with Judge Ginsburg.

Prior to her appointment to the Court of Appeals in 1980, Ginsburg had been on the faculty of Columbia University School of Law. As a professor of law, Ginsburg became an activist for the rights of women and against gender discrimination. Having won five of the six cases she argued before the U.S. Supreme Court on equal protection issues, she became known as an advocate for women's issues. However, once on the Court of Appeals, she did not pursue the same degree of activism she had in the private sector. Her view was that the role of the courts was to interpret the law rather than to become active in policy making. Her tenure on the Court of Appeals was marked by her conservative approach to decisions.

Born on March 15, 1933, Ginsburg was raised in the Flatbush section of Brooklyn, New York, graduating from James Madison High School. She received her B.A. from Cornell University, Phi Beta Kappa (1954) and then began law school at Harvard Law School (1956–58), where she was one of nine women in a class of 500 students. She left Harvard Law School when her husband, also at Harvard Law School, accepted a job with a law firm in New York City. Ginsburg transferred to Columbia University Law School where she finished her law school education (1959). At Columbia University Law School, she tied for first place in her graduating class. Ginsburg had been an editor of the law review at both Harvard and Columbia Law Schools. Although she had graduated at the top of her class, law firms refused to hire her because she was a woman.

After clerking for Judge Edmund L. Palmieri, U.S. District Court, Southern District of New York, from 1959 to 1961, and working on an international law project, she accepted a position in 1963 at Rutgers University School of Law in Newark, New Jersey. She remained at Rutgers from 1963 to 1972, where

Ruth Bader Ginsburg *(United States Supreme Court)*

she was only the second female law professor in the law school's history, and one of only 20 female law professors nationally at the time.

She later accepted a position at Columbia University School of Law (1972–80) and became the first female tenured faculty member. Throughout her legal career, Ginsburg was active in gender equality issues, including heading the American Civil Liberties Union's women's rights project. She argued six cases before the U.S. Supreme Court on gender discrimination during the 1970s, winning five of the six cases.

Glickman, Daniel Robert
(1944–) *secretary of agriculture, member of the House of Representatives*

Daniel Glickman was nominated by President Clinton as secretary of agriculture in March 1995 and confirmed by the Senate following the resignation of ALPHONSO MICHAEL (MIKE) ESPY. Ethics charges were filed against Espy by independent counsel DONALD C. SMALTZ.

Although Glickman had not been part of the original team chosen for the cabinet, he built a strong relationship with the Clinton White House while in office. His long tenure on the House Agriculture Committee had given him an expertise in federal farm policy, the constituent players, and the legislative hurdles that the administration needed to overcome to move their policies forward. His expertise on both farm issues and legislative maneuvering made Glickman a valuable asset to the administration.

Glickman had served in the House of Representatives for 18 years, representing the 4th Congressional District in Wichita, Kansas. He was first elected to the House in 1976 and served continuously until his defeat in the 1994 elections. Glickman was among a host of Democrats who were defeated in the 1994

elections, which gave the Republicans control of the House of Representatives in what became known as the "Republican Revolution." NEWTON (NEWT) LEROY GINGRICH, who led the 1994 election strategy to defeat Democratic incumbents, was elected Speaker of the House in 1995.

While in the House of Representatives, Glickman was a member of the Agriculture Committee, including six years as chairman of the subcommittee that had jurisdiction over most federal farm policy issues.

During his tenure as secretary of agriculture, Glickman refocused departmental policy on consumer information regarding nutrition. The Department of Agriculture began requiring packages of meat and poultry products to display nutritional information, such as those required from processed foods. On May 17, 2000, President Clinton announced the proposal during his weekly radio address. As part of his effort to increase information on nutrition, Glickman worked with the White House to sponsor a national summit on nutrition, which was the first such summit in 30 years. Glickman also published new dietary guidelines, which added information that children and adults should exercise at least 30 minutes per day to reduce the risk of heart disease, colon cancer, and diabetes.

Born on November 24, 1944, Glickman graduated with a B.A. from the University of Michigan (1966) and a J.D. from the George Washington University School of Law (1969). After law school, Glickman was a partner in a private law firm and a trial attorney for the U.S. Securities and Exchange Commission.

After leaving the Clinton administration in 2001, Glickman became the director of the Institute of Politics at the John F. Kennedy School of Government at Harvard University (appointed August 1, 2002). The Institute of Politics began operation in 1966 with an endowment from the Kennedy Library Corporation, seeking to unite students with academics and policymakers on a nonpartisan basis and to encourage their interest in public service.

He remained a partner at Sedgwick Co. in Wichita, Kansas.

Gober, Hershel W.

(1936–   ) *nominated, but nomination withdrawn, as secretary of veterans affairs; deputy secretary of veterans affairs*

Following the resignation of JESSE BROWN as secretary of veterans affairs, President Clinton nominated Hershel Gober to replace Brown. Brown resigned for health reasons related to Lou Gehrig's disease, from which he died in 2002.

Gober was nominated on July 3, 1997. However, Clinton withdrew Gober's name from nomination on October 24, 1997, after charges of sexual harassment were levied against him. He firmly denied the charges. It appeared that Gober would have easily gained Senate confirmation. Senate Minority Leader Tom Daschle called Gober "the right person with the right background at the right time," prior to the allegations lodged against him.

When Gober's name was withdrawn as secretary of veterans affairs, President Clinton nominated TOGO WEST, who was successfully confirmed by the Senate.

Gober, the deputy secretary of veterans affairs under Jesse Brown, became acting secretary when Brown resigned on July 1, 1997, after he was diagnosed with amyotrophic lateral sclerosis (commonly known as Lou Gehrig's disease). He died on August 17, 2002.

During his tenure as deputy secretary of veterans affairs, Gober pressed for the expansion of benefits for veterans who were prisoners of war, for those who were exposed to Agent Orange, and for Persian Gulf war veterans suffering from unexplained illnesses. Gober

was named to the President's Management Council and led presidential missions to Vietnam, seeking resolution of POW and MIA issues. The Department of Veterans Affairs provides services for over 26 million veterans.

Prior to his professional career, Gober served in the U.S. Marine Corps (1956), rising from private to major. He served two tours of duty in Vietnam and earned a Purple Heart, Bronze Star, and Soldier's Medal.

Born on December 21, 1936, Gober received his B.A. in history, cum laude, from Alaska Pacific University, Anchorage, Alaska (1975). From 1978–83 he was director of land acquisition and permits for the Alaska Pipeline Co., in Fairbanks. He then moved to Arkansas as an instructor for Junior ROTC in Warren, Arkansas (1983–85). In 1985 he became director of the Arkansas Veterans Welfare Services in Little Rock (1985–87) under then-governor Bill Clinton. During the 1992 presidential election, Gober was the campaign manager for veterans affairs for the Clinton-Gore campaign. His work on behalf of veterans affairs during the campaign led to his nomination by President Clinton as the second in charge of the Department of Veterans Affairs.

Goldin, Daniel Saul

(1940–   ) *administrator, National Aeronautics and Space Administration (NASA)*

Daniel Goldin was named by President GEORGE HERBERT WALKER BUSH as the administrator for the National Aeronautics and Space Administration (NASA) on April 1, 1992. He resigned on October 17, 2002, effective November 17, 2001.

Goldin was the longest-serving administrator in NASA's history. During his tenure in office, NASA had 171 space missions, launched the Hubble Space Telescope and the Mars Pathfinder, and kept the International Space

Station as a viable part of NASA's programs. The space station was launched on November 2, 2000.

Although Goldin entered office in 1987 with a challenge to reduce what was perceived as NASA's bloated bureaucracy, he could not stop Congress from continually reducing NASA's annual budget. By 1998, the budget for NASA had been cut by $1 billion since he took office in 1987.

Prior to joining NASA, Goldin had had a 25-year career as vice president and general manager of the TRW Space & Technology Group in Redondo Beach, California. He began his career in 1962 at NASA's Lewis Research Center in Cleveland, Ohio, where he worked on electric propulsion systems for human interplanetary travel.

Goldin was born on July 23, 1940, in New York, New York. He graduated from Hunter College in New York City.

Albert Gore, Jr. *(Office of the Vice President)*

Gore, Albert (Al), Jr.

(1948–   ) *Democratic Party candidate for president, vice president of the United States, member of the Senate, member of the House of Representatives*

Albert Gore, Jr., was vice president throughout President Clinton's two terms in office (1993–2001). Gore ran unsuccessfully for president in 2000, losing to Governor GEORGE WALKER BUSH of Texas.

First elected to the U.S. House of Representatives in 1976 from Tennessee, Albert Gore, Jr., won reelection in 1978, 1980, and 1982. While in the House, Gore served on the House Intelligence Committee. He became an expert on arms control after poring over the literature, and in February 1982 published a comprehensive report of arms control issues in the *Congressional Quarterly*, which became known as the Gore Plan. Several months later

when a group of American arms experts went to Moscow, Soviet arms control experts wanted to discuss the "Gore Plan."

In 1984 Gore ran for and won a Senate seat, becoming the first statewide candidate in modern history to carry all 95 Tennessee counties. He took office in January 1985 and was reelected to the Senate in 1990.

In 1987, having served two years in the Senate, Gore launched a bid to win the Democratic nomination for president. On Super Tuesday, 1988, he won primaries in five southern states but won only two other primaries. He subsequently dropped out of the race, which Governor Michael Dukakis went on to run. Dukakis became the 1988 nominee of the Democratic Party against the Republican candidate, Vice President GEORGE HERBERT

WALKER BUSH. Bush won the election and Gore returned to the Senate.

In 1992 Governor Bill Clinton of Arkansas selected Gore to be his vice presidential running mate. After winning the election, Gore was sworn into office on January 20, 1993, as the 45th vice president of the United States. The Clinton-Gore ticket was reelected in 1996, and Gore was again sworn into office on January 20, 1997.

After serving two terms as vice president, Gore became the Democratic Party's nominee for president in 2000 after winning the primary contest against former senator WILLIAM (BILL) WARREN BRADLEY (D-N.J.). Gore chose as his vice presidential nominee Senator Joseph Lieberman of Connecticut. The battle between Gore and GEORGE WALKER BUSH was consistently close throughout the general election cycle, with polls showing the election too close to call. During the last month of the campaign, both Gore and Bush were considered "neck and neck," with pollsters showing a 50-50 voter split.

During the presidential debates between Gore and Bush, Gore often was seen as "wooden" in his demeanor and condescending to Bush. Although Gore was well versed in material for all of the questions, Bush often stumbled over his answers. While Gore thought that he had routinely won the debates, the American public seemed to view Bush as the more human candidate and not as much of a professional politician. The edge that Gore had in September was eroded by November, in part due to the public's changing perception of the candidates during the nationally televised debates.

Another reason that Gore failed to capture the election was his failure to include President Clinton in his campaign strategy. Throughout the campaign, Gore focused on the success of the economy during the administration's eight years in office, but distanced himself from President Clinton's impeachment issues and his relationship with MONICA LEWINSKY. He rarely discussed President Clinton and rarely asked him to campaign rallies. Gore referred to the Lewinsky affair as "inexcusable" and "awful."

The Gore-Lieberman campaign also focused on family values during the election and believed that President Clinton's presence at campaign events would hurt their efforts. The strategy to exclude Clinton from the campaign was considered a central reason why the Republican candidate won the election, since Clinton remained popular with the electorate. Gore won the popular vote by 539,947 votes in the 2000 election but lost the electoral vote to Governor Bush.

The 2000 election was not easily resolved on election day. Gore challenged the final outcome of the election, arguing that the Florida vote, which was decided in Governor Bush's favor, should have gone to Gore. The Florida vote count determined which candidate, Gore or Bush, would win the election. Gore argued that many ballots, tallied on "butterfly" ballots, were improperly counted or even thrown out when the vote-counting machines could not read them. Gore also argued that many minorities were denied their civil rights by being denied voting privileges when voting booths were broken or were closed or locations moved.

In a lawsuit reviewed by the Florida Supreme Court, the Gore challenge was supported. When Governor Bush appealed the Florida Supreme Court's decision to the U.S. Supreme Court, the decision was reversed. The Supreme Court supported the final decision by the state of Florida to certify Bush as the winner. Although not cited in official papers, the Gore election staff and their lawyers frequently commented that Florida governor Jeb Bush, George Bush's brother, had contributed to problems throughout the election process.

One of the primary responsibilities that Gore had during his tenure was to head the

National Partnership for Reinventing Government. This Clinton administration initiative was directed at developing new ways to reduce the budget through cost savings in federal agencies. The project paid off, with savings of more than $137 billion, which included reducing the size of government and the costs of doing business.

As an avid environmentalist, Gore sought to include environmental issues at the forefront of the Clinton administration's agenda. Building on the goals he set in his best-selling 1992 book, *Earth in the Balance: Ecology and the Human Spirit*, Gore worked with Clinton to establish a White House office to oversee environmental issues. The National Environmental Council was created in the White House to complete the policy areas created by the National Economic Council and the Domestic Council. Two of Gore's Senate staff became senior members of the administration in environmental policy: KATHLEEN MCGINTY was named the White House director of the Office of Environmental Policy, and CAROL BROWNER was named the administrator of the Environmental Protection Agency.

Gore's efforts to use government to manage the environment included working with the major automakers to improve fuel efficiency, working with industries to combat global warming and depletion of the ozone layer, and new technologies that were environmentally friendly.

Among Gore's other areas of involvement in the administration were efforts to improve technology and telecommunications. He worked closely with congressional leaders to gain passage of the Telecommunications Act of 1996, which promoted competition in the telecommunications industry. He also launched a public-private partnership to ensure that every classroom and library in America had access to the Internet. He was passionate about the Internet, constantly seeking to improve the ways in which it could be used both publicly and privately.

As a member of the National Security Council, Gore often expressed positions on foreign policy issues. When Yugoslav president SLOBODAN MILOŠEVIĆ initiated hostile actions against Muslims in Kosovo, Gore supported military intervention. He took a similar position for military intervention in Haiti following the overthrow of President JEAN-BERTRAND ARISTIDE.

Gore is the son of former senator Albert Gore, Sr. (D-Tenn.) of Carthage, Tennessee. The senior Gore rose to national prominence as a champion of civil rights. Gore, who grew up in Washington, D.C., attended St. Albans School for boys. His father was considered a progressive southerner and often was at odds with other Democrats within the South. He died in 1998 at the age of 91.

Gore is married to MARY ELIZABETH (TIPPER) AITCHESON GORE (married May 19, 1970, in the Washington Cathedral in Washington, D.C.). He and Mrs. Gore have four children: Karenna, Kristin, Sarah, and Albert III, and live on a small farm near Carthage, Tennessee. Since the Gores had lived in the vice president's home at the former Naval Observatory in Washington, D.C., for the eight years he was vice president, they had no home to return to in Washington, D.C. After losing the 2000 election, the Gores returned to his family farm in Carthage, Tennessee.

Born on March 31, 1948, in Carthage, Gore received a B.A. in government, cum laude, from Harvard University (1969). While at Harvard, Gore was the roommate of Academy Award winner Tommy Lee Jones. After college, Gore volunteered for the U.S. Army and served in Vietnam as a reporter for *Stars and Stripes*. After returning to private life in Tennessee, Gore studied at Vanderbilt University Law School and worked on *The Tennessean*, a Nashville newspaper. He graduated from Vanderbilt Law School (1976) after attending night classes.

Gore, Mary Elizabeth (Tipper) Aitcheson
(1948–   ) *wife of Vice President Albert Gore*

Tipper Gore, as she is known, is the wife of Vice President Al Gore. During the eight years of the administration, she maintained an office in the Old Executive Office Building (renamed the Eisenhower Office Building in 2001), next to the White House.

During the Clinton administration, Mrs. Gore served as President Clinton's adviser on mental health policy. As mental health policy adviser to President Clinton, Mrs. Gore worked to educate the nation about the need for affordable mental health care. One of her goals was to have medical insurance plans deal with mental health as they did with other health benefits. Mrs. Gore worked with the health policy task force under Mrs. Clinton to ensure the inclusion of mental health benefits in the national health care program.

In addition to her advocacy for mental health, she became a spokesperson for a number of federal projects involving women and children. She served as cochair of "America Goes Back to School," an initiative launched by the Department of Education to work with students, parents, and teachers to promote a better environment for learning among the nation's children. And she became the national spokesperson for the Department of Health and Human Services' "Back to Sleep" campaign, which advocated putting infants on their backs to reduce the risk of Sudden Infant Death Syndrome.

Both Vice President and Mrs. Gore were avid sports enthusiasts, and during the Clinton administration Mrs. Gore served as chair of the National Youth Fitness Campaign of the President's Council on Physical Fitness and Sports. She worked with youth across the country, particularly young women, to increase fitness and physical activity.

Soon after Gore was elected to the House of Representatives in 1976, Mrs. Gore helped to found the Congressional Wives Task Force to focus on the issue of violence in children's television programming. She served as chair in 1978 and in 1979.

In 1985 she cofounded the Parents Music Resource Center (PMRC), along with Susan Baker, to help to give parents a greater ability to protect their children from inappropriate material in music. The PMRC was successful in gaining a voluntary agreement between the Recording Industry Association of America and the National Parent Teacher Association to place consumer labels on music which had violent or explicit lyrics. The music warning labels became the model for labeling in television and other media. In 1987, Mrs. Gore authored her first book, *Raising PG Kids in an X-Rated Society*, in which she detailed her work on behalf of parents and children.

In 1986, Mrs. Gore cofounded and chaired Families for the Homeless, a nonpartisan partnership of families that worked to raise public awareness of homeless issues. She worked with the National Mental Health Association (NMHA) to produce a photographic exhibit entitled "Homeless in America: A Photographic Project," which toured the nation.

In 1990, she founded the Tennessee Voices for Children, a coalition to promote the development of services for children and youth with serious behavioral, emotional, substance abuse, or other mental health problems. She also served as cochair of the Child Mental Health Interest Group, a nonpartisan group of congressional and administration spouses.

Born on August 19, 1948, Mrs. Gore was raised in Arlington, Virginia. She received a B.A. in psychology from Boston University

(1970) and an M.A. in psychology from George Peabody College at Vanderbilt University (1975). The Gores, who met at Al Gore's high school prom, were married on May 19, 1970, in the Washington Cathedral in Washington, D.C. After her husband was elected to Congress in 1976, Mrs. Gore began working as a photographer at *The Tennessean*, a Nashville newspaper, and remained there until Gore was elected vice president. Mrs. Gore remained an avid photographer and was regularly seen throughout her husband's tenure in office photographing pictures of events she and her husband were involved in.

They have four children: Karenna, Kristin, Sarah, and Albert III, and live on a small farm near Carthage, Tennessee. Since the Gores had moved to the vice president's home at the former Naval Observatory in Washington, D.C., for the eight years he was vice president, they had no home to return to in Washington, D.C. After losing the 2000 election, the Gores returned to his family farm in Carthage.

In 2002, Al and Tipper Gore wrote two books, *Joined at the Heart* and *The Spirit of Family*.

Graham, Lindsey O.
(1955–   ) *member of the Senate, member of the House of Representatives*

As a member of the Judiciary Committee in the House of Representatives, Lindsey Graham (R-S.C.) was one of 13 members of the majority party on the committee to serve as managers of the case against President Clinton during the 1999 Senate trial following his impeachment in the House of Representatives in December 1998.

Graham, in his January 16, 1999, statement at the Senate trial, argued that he didn't want to impeach President Clinton over a sexual affair with MONICA LEWINSKY because, he said, he understood "human failings." A consensual affair, Graham said, did not provide grounds for impeachment. He argued, however, that lying about the affair to a grand jury did qualify as grounds for impeachment.

During the House proceedings on impeachment, Graham had led questioning of witnesses in the Judiciary Committee hearings. On November 19, 1998, Graham questioned independent counsel KENNETH W. STARR. In Graham's questioning of Starr, he summed up his case against President Clinton. Graham stated of Clinton, "But what he did do is he lied through his teeth in a civil deposition."

Graham's strong rhetoric against Clinton had not been focused only on the president or on Democrats. Graham had been an outspoken member of the House within his own Republican Party throughout his tenure. In the fall of 1997, when President Clinton was in a battle with House Speaker Newt Gingrich over the budget, Graham sought a compromise with the president on the budget along with 10 other House Republicans, all of whom subsequently drew the wrath of Gingrich. Graham had consistently been at odds with Gingrich and took part in a failed attempt to oust Gingrich in 1996.

In his first run for office in 1992, Republican Lindsey Graham secured a seat in the South Carolina House of Representatives. During his tenure in the state House, Graham successfully pushed legislation barring gays from the state's National Guard. After only one term in the state House, Graham ran in 1994 for the U.S. House of Representatives when incumbent Democratic congressman Butler Derrick retired. Graham defeated the Democratic nominee, State Senator James Bryan, by supporting the "Contract with America," to represent the 3rd District of South Carolina. Graham became the first Republican to serve in the House from the 3rd District since 1877. In 1996, Graham won with 60 percent of the vote, and in 1998 ran without major party opposition to win 99.9 percent of the vote.

In 2002, Graham sought an open seat being vacated by incumbent senator Strom Thurmond. Thurmond, at 99 years old, had been continuously elected to the Senate from South Carolina since 1954. Graham, who ran on a promilitary and antiabortion platform, won the state with 68 percent of the vote. He was sworn into office on January 8, 2003. South Carolina had a second open seat in the Senate with the retirement of 80-year-old senator Ernest F. Hollings, who had served in the Senate since 1966. Hollings was succeeded by Elizabeth Dole in the 2002 election.

During the 2000 presidential election, Graham supported Senator John McCain. In 1998 McCain had sought Graham's help to win the 2000 South Carolina primary. McCain hoped to win Graham's district within the conservative northwest part of the state. Graham signed on to work for McCain before other candidates had declared their interest in the 2000 election.

At several points throughout his political career, Graham was accused of exaggerating his involvement in the Gulf War in 1991. Before and during the Gulf War, Graham was called to active duty in the South Carolina National Guard. He was sent to McEntire Air National Guard Station, where he was assigned to assist air force personnel in putting their legal affairs in order. After his assignment at McEntire, Graham often referred to himself as a veteran of Operation Desert Storm. His "Graham for Senate" Web site in 2002 referred to him as a "Gulf War Veteran."

As a congressman, Graham sat on three House committees: Judiciary, Education and the Workforce, and Armed Services.

Born on July 9, 1955, in central South Carolina, Graham received his B.A. (1977) and his M.A. (1978) from the University of South Carolina, and his J.D. from the University of South Carolina Law School (1981). Graham's life had been marked by tragedy at the age of 20. His parents both died (his mother from Hodgkin's disease, his father from a heart attack), and Graham became the legal guardian of his teenage sister.

After receiving his law degree, Graham worked for two years in the legal office of Shaw Air Force Base in Sumter, South Carolina, and then was chief prosecutor for the air force in Europe from 1984–88. When he left the air force, he returned to South Carolina and was assistant county attorney in Oconee County and had a private law practice (1988–92). In his private practice in 1992, he won a $5 million verdict in a medical malpractice case. He was one of four lawyers on the case who split the fee. Graham received over $200,000 for his work on the case.

Greenberg, Stanley Bernard
(1945–) *pollster and Democratic Party strategist*

Stanley Greenburg was part of the inner circle of President Clinton's 1992 campaign, overseeing the polling activities and developing campaign strategies. He did not take a position in the Clinton administration, but rather remained an outside consultant for the White House. He was later named general chairman of the Democratic National Committee.

Greenburg founded his company, Greenburg Research, in 1980. The company developed surveys and conducted focus groups for corporations and political candidates. He was the principal polling adviser to the Clinton-Gore campaign in 1992. After his success with the presidential campaign, he continued to manage polling for the Democratic National Committee, in addition to the campaigns of Prime Minister ANTHONY (TONY) CHARLES LYNTON BLAIR of England and President NELSON MANDELA of

South Africa. In 1999, Greenberg joined Democratic strategists JAMES CARVILLE, JR., and Robert Shrum on the campaign of EHUD BARAK for prime minister of Israel. Barak successfully challenged Prime Minister BENJAMIN NETANYAHU. Greenberg also joined with Carville in the Mexican election of 2000, when they worked for Francisco Labastida of the Institutional Revolutionary Party (PRI).

Greenberg also worked on the campaigns of Senator CHRISTOPHER JOHN DODD (D-Conn.), Senator Joseph Lieberman (D-Conn.), Governor Jim Florio (D-N.J.), and a number of candidates for the House of Representatives.

Although Greenberg had a number of political clients, he focused his company on corporate clients, specializing in research on globalization, international trade, corporate consolidation, and the Internet. Greenberg's corporate clients included Boeing Company, Monsanto, United Healthcare, the Business Roundtable, the National Basketball Association, and the Direct Marketing Association.

Born on May 10, 1945 in Philadelphia, Pennsylvania, Greenberg graduated with a B.A. from Miami University of Ohio (1967), and an M.A. (1968) and a Ph.D. (1972) from Harvard University.

Greenberg began his political career as a project assistant in the U.S. Office of Economic Opportunity in 1965. He then worked for Representative Lee Hamilton as a legislative assistant (1966), and in 1972 as director of field operations in New Haven, Connecticut, for Senator George McGovern's presidential campaign in 1992. Greenberg served as a project director with Barss, Reitzel & Associates (1967–70). He joined the faculty of Yale University in 1971 where he remained until 1980, when he founded his company, Greenburg Research.

He was the author of *Middle Class Dreams* (1995) and *The New Majority: Towards a Popular Progressive Politics* with Theda Skocpol (1997).

Greenspan, Alan
(1926–) *chairman, Board of Governors of the Federal Reserve System*

Alan Greenspan, chairman of the Board of Governors of the Federal Reserve System, was reappointed by President Clinton to four-year terms in 1996 and 2000. Greenspan had been appointed by President Reagan in 1987 and named as chairman in 1988. He was reappointed by President GEORGE HERBERT WALKER BUSH in 1992. Greenspan's current term expires in June 2004.

The Federal Reserve Board is composed of seven members, each appointed by the president, confirmed by the Senate, and serving a 14-year term. The Board has a chairman and a vice chairman, each appointed by the president for a four-year term, which can be renewed. As chairman of the Federal Reserve, Greenspan oversaw two committees: the Board of Governors, which handled regulation and administrative matters, and the Federal Open Market Committee, which established interest rates for government loans to banks.

Greenspan had been briefly involved in politics in 1968, when he served as director of domestic policy research for RICHARD MILHOUS NIXON's successful presidential campaign. Though he turned down a permanent position in the Nixon administration, he served on the presidential transition team and advised President Nixon informally from his Townsend-Greenspan Company. In 1974, President Nixon named Greenspan to the position of chairman of the Council of Economic Advisers. Greenspan accepted the position to deal with the rising inflation rate during the mid-1970s. He did not take office until September 1, 1974, nearly one month after President Nixon had resigned and President Ford had been sworn into office.

As chairman of the Council of Economic Advisers in a period of economic downturn,

Greenspan provided President Ford with economic advice on wage and price controls and the oil crisis. He also learned how to deal with members of Congress in frequent hearings on Capitol Hill at which he testified. When he served as chairman of the council, he had not yet received his Ph.D. He completed the degree in 1977.

With the election of Jimmy Carter in 1977, Greenspan returned to New York City to his consulting firm of Townsend-Greenspan. Following the 1981 election, President Reagan named Greenspan to serve as chairman of the National Commission on Social Security Reform (1981–83). During the Reagan administration, Greenspan was also appointed to the President's Economic Policy Advisory Board (1981–87) and the President's Foreign Intelligence Advisory Board (1983–85).

When Paul Volcker, the chairman of the Federal Reserve Board, unexpectedly announced his retirement in June 1987, President Reagan nominated Greenspan to the Board of Governors of the Federal Reserve Board. Greenspan accepted the nomination and was confirmed by the Senate on August 11, 1987. In 1988, Reagan named Greenspan chairman. After his appointment to the Federal Reserve Board, Greenspan

dissolved the Townsend-Greenspan firm when a suitable buyer could not be found.

Throughout his tenure at the Federal Reserve Board, Greenspan pursued a tight-money policy in order to combat inflation and encourage full employment. When the Dow Jones Industrial Average fell by 508 points on October 19, 1987, Greenspan reassured the financial markets that the Federal Reserve Board would provide rate changes to spur the economy.

Born on March 6, 1926, Greenspan received his B.S. in economics, summa cum laude (1948), his M.A. in economics (1950), and his Ph.D. (1977) from New York University. He began his Ph.D. studies at Columbia University but left Columbia when he ran out of money and worked as an economist for the National Industrial Conference Board. Although most of his career was spent in the public sector, Greenspan worked for 20 years as chief executive officer and president of Townsend-Greenspan and Co. in New York City (1954–74). Greenspan's company offered economic forecasts to large companies and financial institutions. Few corporations had their own professional staff economists at this time, making Greenspan's company very profitable.

Greenspan married NBC news reporter Andrea Mitchell in 1997 after a 12-year relationship.

Federal Reserve Board chairman Alan Greenspan (*Alex Wong/Getty Images*)

Griffin, Patrick
(1949–   ) *director, White House Office of Legislative Affairs*

Patrick Griffin served as assistant to the president and director of the Office of Legislative Affairs in the White House from December 1993 until February 1996. Griffin succeeded HOWARD PASTER, who resigned after internal White House conflicts on the management of the health care bill in Congress. IRA MAGAZINER and Hillary Clinton had taken control of the health care bill in Congress from Paster. By the time that Griffin took over the office of legislative affairs, the health care bill was no longer being actively considered in Congress.

The role of the congressional liaison (assistant to the president for legislative affairs) was to develop the strategy for advancing the president's agenda, in both domestic and foreign policy, in Congress. Griffin worked with the leaders in the House and Senate of both parties to create and pass legislation that met the president's legislative agenda. He also worked to stop legislation that the president opposed.

Among the bills that Griffin worked on during his tenure in the White House was the bill to create Most Favored Nation (MFN) status for China. Griffin had first worked with the foreign policy staff in the State Department and the National Security Council to develop the most appropriate language for the legislation. He then brought together the congressional liaison staffs from the State Department, U.S. Agency for International Development, the U.S. Information Agency, and the U.S. Trade Representative's Office to create the strategy for moving the Most Favored Nation status for China through Congress.

Another key agenda item that Griffin worked for on behalf of the president was the financial bailout by Congress for Mexico during its financial downturn. Griffin developed a strategy that incorporated the four congressional leaders—Senate Minority Leader Tom Daschle (D-S.D.), House Minority Leader Dick Gephardt (D-Kans.), House Speaker Newt Gingrich (R-Ga.), and Senate Majority Leader Robert Dole (R-Kans.). Although the congressional leadership supported the bailout, the bill failed to win support within Congress. President Clinton subsequently acted to provide financial help to Mexico through an executive order rather than through legislation.

Prior to his role as the congressional liaison for President Clinton, Griffin worked on the staffs of the Senate Budget Committee and of Senator Robert Byrd (D-W.V.). He had also been secretary to the Senate Democratic Conference. From 1985 to 1986, Griffin had worked at the public relations firm of Burson-Marsteller. He left in 1986 to form his own firm and became a founding member of the Washington, D.C., government relations firm of Griffin, Johnson, Dover & Stewart. Griffin remained with his firm until his appointment to the Clinton White House staff as director of legislative affairs in 1993.

He left the position with little discussion of why he was leaving or what his future plans were. In a statement released by the White House press secretary on January 4, 1996, Griffin said, "This is the most rewarding and challenging job of my life, and I will always be grateful to him [President Clinton] for giving me this opportunity. But two years in this job is like a career in most others. After a lot of thought, I have concluded that it is time for me to move on. At this time, I have made no decisions about future employment. I do look forward to assisting the president in other ways in the future."

Born in 1949 in Brooklyn, New York, Griffin graduated from St. Peter's College in New Jersey. He later received his M.A. in urban affairs and his Ph.D. in education from the University of Wisconsin.

Grunwald, Mandy

(1958–) *media strategist, 1992 Clinton-Gore campaign*

Mandy Grunwald, a media strategist for the 1992 Clinton-Gore presidential campaign, worked outside of the White House during the first year of the administration as a consultant on health care reform, which was managed by HILLARY DIANE RODHAM CLINTON. Grunwald chose not to join the administration in 1993 but to remain an outside political strategist. After a year, however, she withdrew from the White House and moved on to work on other political campaigns.

Clinton brought two partners from Greer, Margolis, Mitchell, Grunwald & Associates, Grunwald and Frank Greer, to work on his campaign designing media strategies. Grunwald became a key strategist for the campaign, urging Clinton to play the saxophone on the *Arsenio Hall* talk show and to appear on such popular television programs as *The Donahue Show* and *The Larry King Show*. She also urged him to appear on MTV. Grunwald's strategy was to have Clinton appear on a variety of non-mainstream media outlets, such as call-in shows, daytime talk shows, and town hall meetings.

After Clinton won the election, Grunwald formed a new media consulting firm, Grunwald, Eskew, and Donilon. One of their first clients was the White House. Grunwald directed the administration's effort to sell the health care plan, which Hillary Rodham Clinton and IRA MAGAZINER were developing, to the American public. She routinely set up press conferences for Magaziner to give detailed information on the health care plan.

Although not a member of the White House staff, Grunwald became a regular member of a group that met regularly in the White House to plan political strategy for President Clinton. The group included JAMES CARVILLE, JR., PAUL BEGALA, and STANLEY GREENBERG. During the presidential campaign, this team of political strategists had met in Little Rock, Arkansas, at the campaign headquarters in what became known as the War Room. Once the Clinton administration was in office, the group re-created their strategy sessions in Room 160 of the Old Executive Office Building and the room was referred to again as the War Room.

Throughout the four years of the first administration, Grunwald was often on television talk shows discussing issues. During the 1996 presidential campaign, she was regularly seen on television analyzing the strengths and weakness of both the Clinton campaign and the Dole campaign.

During the 2000 Senate campaign in New York, Grunwald was one of a core group of Democratic supporters who advised Mrs. Clinton on the campaign, along with HAROLD ICKES (President Clinton's former deputy chief of staff), and MARGARET ANN WILLIAMS (Mrs. Clinton's first-term chief of staff). Grunwald was brought into Mrs. Clinton's Senate campaign not only because of her friendship with the first lady, but because she had also worked on the three Senate campaigns of Senator Daniel Patrick Moynihan (D-N.Y.), whose seat Mrs. Clinton was vying for. Moynihan retired from the Senate in 2002. Mrs. Clinton captured the Democratic nomination in New York in 2000 for the open seat and subsequently defeated Republican Rick Lazio.

In addition to working for Mrs. Clinton's senatorial campaign, Grunwald was a media consultant for several gubernatorial candidates, including Oregon's Barbara Roberts, New Hampshire's Jeanne Shaheen and Colorado's Roy Romer, and the Senate campaign of Patrick J. Leahy of Vermont. Among Grunwald's international clients were FERNANDO HENRIQUE CARDOSO, who successfully sought the presidency of Brazil. Grunwald had been brought into the Cardoso campaign by James Carville, who was also a Cardoso adviser.

Grunwald received her B.A. from Harvard University (1979), and joined the New York City political consulting firm of D. H. Sawyer & Associates after graduation.

Guinier, Carol Lani

(1950–   ) *failed nominee for assistant attorney general and director of the Office of Civil Rights, Department of Justice*

On April 29, 1993, President Clinton nominated Lani Guinier as assistant attorney general and director of the Office of Civil Rights in the Department of Justice. Guinier, who had known President and Mrs. Clinton since they were students at Yale Law School, had built her career as an advocate for voting rights for minorities.

Guinier is an African-American woman, the daughter of a prominent African-American attorney and a Jewish mother. On June 3, 1993, just five weeks after submitting Guinier's name to the Senate, President Clinton withdrew her name due to a perception that she supported racial quotas in elected politics. Although she did not support such quotas, Clinton distanced himself from her nomination.

Her nomination was withdrawn primarily due to strong opposition within Democratic circles. Opposition included the leader of the Democratic Leadership Council, AL FROM, and Joseph Biden, the chairman of the Senate Judiciary Committee. One of the Senate's most vocal liberals, Senator EDWARD MOORE KENNEDY, also failed to support Guinier.

Guinier was barred by the White House from engaging in any discussions on her views prior to the Senate hearings and was unable to answer her critics. After her name was withdrawn by President Clinton, she stated that she believed she could have adequately explained her views and minimized, if not neutralized, the opposition had she been able to meet with the press and others as the criticisms were being leveled against her prior to the hearings.

Opposition to her nomination came from those who believed her positions were too liberal. Her writings had questioned whether there was tyranny by the majority if 51 percent of the vote received 100 percent of the power in an election. She noted that in many legislative districts the majority white population often controlled the elections, leaving minority populations with little representation. Although she was only debating the point in her writings, and not advocating a remedy, many believed that she was seeking to change the electoral system from the current winner-take-all structure to a structure which gave minorities a stronger chance at representation. She proposed "cumulative voting." Guinier expanded on these views in her 1994 book, *The Tyranny of the Majority: Fundamental Fairness in Representative Democracy*.

When President Reagan came into office in 1981, Guinier left the Justice Department and began to work for the National Association for the Advancement of Colored People (NAACP) Legal Defense and Educational Fund, where she won 31 of the 32 cases she argued in court (1981–88). In 1988 she left to join the faculty of the University of Pennsylvania Law School and after 10 years (1998) left the University of Pennsylvania Law School to join Harvard University Law School.

Born on April 19, 1950, Guinier received her A.B. from Radcliffe College (1971) and her J.D. from Yale University (1974). After clerking for Judge Damon J. Keith of the U.S. Court of Appeals, Sixth Circuit in Detroit, Michigan (1974–76), Guinier worked for four years under Assistant Attorney General Drew S. Days in the Civil Rights Division of the Department of Justice during the Carter administration (1977–81). She would be nominated in 1993 for the same position that Drew Days held.

H

Hackney, Sheldon

(1933–   ) *chairman, National Endowment of the Humanities*

President Clinton appointed Sheldon Hackney chairman of the National Endowment for the Humanities (NEH), a position he held for four years (1993–97). He was not reappointed by President Clinton for the second term of the administration.

Hackney was confirmed by the Senate on August 3, 1993, in a vote of 76-23 and was sworn into office on August 6, 1993, as the sixth NEH chairman. The 23 opposition votes included 22 Republicans and one Democrat, Senator Joseph Lieberman of Connecticut.

Lieberman's opposition stemmed from Hackney's tenure at the University of Pennsylvania. Hackney had punished a Jewish student who called a group of African-American students "water buffaloes," but had not punished a group of African-American students who trashed more than 14,000 copies of a student newspaper to protest the writings of a conservative columnist.

During his tenure at NEH, Hackney established a program to focus on pluralism in American society. In 1994, NEH set aside $1.6 million to fund grants for scholars to create projects for "exploring the question of plural-

ity in their own words, their own way." Hackney referred to this program as a "national conversation" on plurality. He sought to link scholars with the public to talk about common values and pluralism in the United States.

Hackney's leadership at NEH often received criticism within Congress. As a result, in 1995 Congress cut the NEH budget for fiscal 1996 by 36 percent, to $110 million from $172 million in fiscal 1995. In fiscal 1997, Congress kept the NEH appropriation at $110 million. A number of Republican members of Congress not only sought to reduce the budget for NEH during Hackney's tenure, but to eliminate the agency. Some conservative members of Congress, particularly the House, believed that many programs that were funded were unnecessary or should not be funded by a government agency.

Born on December 5, 1933, Hackney received his B.A. from Vanderbilt University (1955), and his M.A. (1963) and his Ph.D. (1966) from Yale University. From 1965–75, Hackney was on the faculty in the history department of Princeton University, including serving as provost from 1972–75. After leaving Princeton, Hackney served as president of Tulane University for five years (1975–80) and as president of the University of Pennsylvania (1980–93). Hackney returned to the University of Pennsylvania in 1997 as a history professor. He was widely known for his scholarship on the South, including his 1969 book, *Populism to Progressivism in Alabama*, which won the American Historical Association's Albert J. Beveridge prize for books in American history.

The National Endowment for the Humanities (NEH) is an independent federal agency created in 1965. It is the largest funder of humanities programs in the United States. The National Endowment for the Humanities provides grants for humanities projects in four funding areas: preserving and providing access to cultural resources, education, research, and public programs. The agency is run by a national council of 26 private citizens appointed by the president to serve staggered six-year terms.

Hale, Marcia L.

(1952–   ) *director of the Office of Intergovernmental Affairs, director of scheduling and advance*

Marcia Hale was appointed by President Clinton as assistant to the president and director of the Office of Intergovernmental Affairs in the White House in August 1993. She entered the White House in January 1993 as assistant to the president and director of scheduling and advance. Hale replaced Regina Montoya, who left the White House to return to Dallas to be with her family. During the 1992 presidential campaign, Hale was the director of the political operations of the Democratic Congressional Campaign Committee. She had previously worked as the field director for the Democratic Congressional Campaign Committee.

On October 14, 1993, Hale was appointed by President Clinton to the Advisory Commission on Intergovernmental Relations (ACIR). The ACIR was created to develop recommendations for intergovernmental cooperation. All 10 members are presidentially appointed. Hale's appointment to the ACIR signaled President Clinton's intention to bring the commission into the highest levels of presidential concern. During the 1980s, President Reagan had tried to dismantle many of the intergovernmental programs within the federal government. Clinton sought to prioritize intergovernmental cooperation by revitalizing ACIR, seeking increased funding from Congress and placing a White House staffer, Marcia Hale, on the commission. She remained director of the Office of Intergovernmental Affairs while serving on the ACIR.

Hale graduated with a B.A. in political science (1974) and a masters of public administration (1976) from the University of South Carolina. Her background included working as the legislative assistant for U.S. Representative Butler Derrick (D-S.C.) from 1979–81; as the director of the Office of the Governor of South Carolina (1982–83); director of scheduling for Hollings for President (1983–84); director of advance, Mondale-Ferraro campaign (1984); executive director, Voters for Choice Political Action Committee (1984–85); field director, Democratic Congressional Campaign Committee (1985–87); southern field director, convention manager, Dukakis for President, 1987–88); political consultant, Democratic Senatorial Campaign Committee (1989–91); political director, Democratic Congressional Campaign Committee (1991–93).

After leaving the White House in 1997, Hale joined Monsanto Corporation as director of international government affairs. MICHAEL (MICKEY) KANTOR, President Clinton's trade representative from 1992–96, was on the Monsanto Corporation board of directors when Hale was hired.

During the 2000 presidential campaign, Hale managed the Democratic National Convention in Los Angeles in August. She was asked to manage the convention by Vice President Gore's campaign manager, William Daley.

Hashimoto Ryutaro

(1937–) *prime minister of Japan*

On January 11, 1996, Hashimoto Ryutaro became prime minister of Japan following the resignation of Prime Minister Murayama. Hashimoto was reelected prime minister in November 1996 but resigned in 1998 when his political party, the Liberal Democratic Party (LDC), was defeated. Obuchi Keizo was his successor as prime minister.

Domestic policy was at the center of Hashimoto's two years in office. The primary goal of Hashimoto during his brief tenure as prime minister was to rebuild the nation's sagging economy, using private sector rather than government investment to stimulate the process. When Hashimoto was faced with a failing national economy, he began to make a number of changes in how the government encouraged private investment. Hashimoto ordered a panel of private sector experts to create a program that would encourage foreign competition in banking, telecommunications, construction, and other areas.

While he was prime minister, Hashimoto was a strong proponent of changing the United Nations charter to allow Japan to join the United States, Britain, France, China and Russia as permanent members on the United Nations Security Council. Many in the United States opposed this proposition, particularly World War II veterans. Hashimoto believed that Japan was not the aggressor in World War II and that its involvement was a battle against U.S. colonialism in Asia. The members of the United Nations Security Council did not support Japan's proposal, and it was subsequently dropped.

Tensions between the United States and Japan rose during Hashimoto's tenure, partly as a result of a September 1995 rape of a 12-year-old Okinawa girl by three U.S. soldiers stationed in Okinawa. Many in Japan urged Hashimoto to remove U.S. troops from Okinawa. Japanese authorities also demanded that the soldiers be tried for the offense in Japan. The United States refused to allow the soldiers to be tried outside of a United States military court, but did agree to some of the other Japanese demands. Hashimoto secured the return of some military facilities used by the United States military in Okinawa, which appeased some of the outraged Japanese citizens.

Although President Clinton did not travel to Japan during Hashimoto's tenure in office, he did meet with Hashimoto. Their meetings included the June 1996 meeting of the Group of Seven (G-7) in Lyon, France, and the May 1997 meeting of the Group of Eight (G-8), which now included Russia, in Denver, Colorado. During April 1997, Hashimoto visited the United States, New Zealand, and Australia.

In a foreign policy matter in which the United States was not directly involved, President Clinton supported Hashimoto in his decision not to give in to terrorists who had taken hostages in Peru. In December 1996, Peruvian Tupac Amaru terrorists held hundreds of party guests, many of them Japanese businessmen, at the home of the Japanese ambassador to Peru. Elite commandos from Peru attacked the ambassador's compound, and most hostages survived.

Born July 29, 1937, Hashimoto graduated from Keio University with a major in political science (1960). When his father died in 1963, Hashimoto ran for his father's former seat in Parliament as a member of the Liberal Democratic Party. Hashimoto held a number of government posts throughout the following three decades. In 1994, Hashimoto became minister of trade. He led trade talks between the United States and Japan in June 1995 and successfully kept the United States from levying tariffs on Japanese automobiles.

Following his success in the trade talks, Hashimoto was elected head of the Liberal

Democratic Party in 1995 and reelected head of the party in September 1997.

Hassan II, king of Morocco
(1929–1999) *Arab monarch*

King Hassan II of Morocco, who died on July 23, 1999, had been the longest-reigning monarch in the Arab world at the time. President Clinton joined world leaders for the funeral in Rabat, Morocco, becoming the first American president to visit Morocco since President Eisenhower's visit in 1959.

King Hassan II had ruled Morocco for 38 years, ascending to the throne in 1961 after the death of his father. He was crowned king on March 3, 1961, one week after his father's death on February 26.

King Hassan II, born July 9, 1929, was the son of King Mohammed V. Hassan was named Moulay Hassan, after King Hassan I, who ruled Morocco between 1873 and 1894. King Hassan II was educated at the Institute of Higher Juridical Studies in Rabat, which was part of the College of Law of Bordeaux, France. He received his B.A. in law in 1951 and his Ph.D. several years later.

Hassan had been a strong supporter of President Clinton's efforts to bring peace to the Middle East and had been an advocate of Arab-Israeli reconciliation. On March 15, 1995, King Hassan paid a state visit to the United States to discuss the peace process and economic trade issues. The relationship between the United States and Morocco during the Clinton administration was extremely strong.

During the 1990s, Hassan had been a quiet mediator in the Middle East peace process. His role in the peace process began in 1978, when he worked with President Carter to bring together Egypt and Israel in the Camp David peace accords. His role in the Middle East often angered some Arab leaders, however, as was evident when he sent troops to battle Iraq during the Persian Gulf War.

His reign was not always peaceful within his own country. He became known as the "great survivor," for surviving two serious coups. One coup involved an attack by renegade Moroccan fighter planes on his commercial flight. In the other coup, army officers tried to attack the royal palace but failed.

King Hassan's 35-year-old son, Crown Prince Sidi Mohammed, became the ruler of Morocco upon his father's death. He was crowned King Mohammed VI. King Mohammed VI made his first state visit to the United States on June 20, 2000, to build on the relationship with President Clinton that his father had begun. At that meeting, the king said that he was determined to work toward the peace that was initiated by his father, "and to promote dialogue and to defend legality so that all the peoples in the region may finally live together in dignity, stability, and concord."

Although King Hassan II began to promote trade between the United States and Morocco to combat the poverty and high unemployment in the country, King Mohammed VI was expected to move the process forward rapidly. King Mohammed was viewed by the Clinton administration as more liberal and more comfortable with the West and the United States than his father and many Arab leaders had been.

Hastert, J. Dennis (Denny)
(1942–   ) *Speaker of the House of Representatives, member of the House of Representatives*

In January 1999 Dennis Hastert (R-Ill.) was elected Speaker of the House of Representatives. Hastert was chosen by the Republican caucus in the House to replace Speaker-elect

ROBERT (BOB) LIVINGSTON. Livingston had been chosen by the House Republicans on November 18, 1998, for the Speakership (which was to be ratified in January by the full House) after NEWTON (NEWT) LEROY GINGRICH announced on November 6, 1998, that he would not seek reelection as Speaker. Livingston resigned as Speaker-elect on December 16, 1998, after *Hustler* magazine revealed an extramarital affair that Livingston had had. Hastert was then chosen by the Republican majority after Livingston resigned.

On January 6, 1999, the newly elected Speaker opened the session of the House by walking down from the podium and speaking on the floor of the House. "My legislative home is here on the floor with you," Hastert said, "and so is my heart." As Speaker, Hastert made a number of changes in the House organization. He supported the seniority system and was less interested in moving his own loyalists into committee chairmanships, which Gingrich had initiated soon after taking over as Speaker in 1996. Gingrich had also created task forces to manage legislation as an end run around committee chairs, a structure which Hastert chose not to continue.

Prior to his election to the speakership, Hastert had been chief deputy majority whip during 1995–96 and again in 1997–98. Hastert gained the respect of both Democrats and Republicans during his four years as deputy majority whip for his integrity and his ability to build bipartisan coalitions. When both Gingrich and Livingston resigned, the Republicans needed to ensure that the next Speaker was above reproach. Hastert, who had generally stayed out of the spotlight in the House, was known as a low-key, conservative, but easygoing colleague. When the Republicans needed a Speaker immediately, Hastert's name quickly surfaced.

Born on January 2, 1942, Hastert graduated from Wheaton College in Illinois (1964). He continued graduate studies at Northern Illinois University where he received his M.S. (1967). Before entering politics, Hastert was a history teacher and wrestling coach at Yorkville High School in Illinois. From 1975–76, he was president of the Illinois Wrestling Coaches Association. He left his teaching career in 1980 when he was appointed to complete a term in the Illinois House of Representatives. He was elected in 1982 and reelected in 1984. In 1986 he successfully ran for a seat in the U.S. House of Representatives from the 14th District of Illinois. He had been reelected in every House election since 1986.

Hastert has been a conservative member of the Republican Party, routinely voting against such measures as handgun control, including the five-day waiting period, and voted for each of the Contract with America votes. During his tenure in Congress, Hastert supported legislation to balance the federal budget, cut federal taxes, and reduce the size of the federal workforce. He was also an ardent supporter of deregulation in areas such as trucking and telecommunications.

Hastert was again elected Speaker of the House in 2001.

Hatch, Orrin Grant
(1934–   ) *member of the Senate*

Senator Orrin Hatch (R-Utah) was one of the strongest proponents for removing President Clinton from office during the impeachment trial of 1999. A conservative Republican, Hatch was a constant advocate of impeachment as the evidence mounted from independent counsel KENNETH W. STARR. The evidence indicated that President Clinton had an affair with MONICA LEWINSKY and had subsequently lied about the affair in depositions in civil cases.

Hatch had originally urged Clinton to apologize to the American people and to the Congress in order to avoid the impeachment proceedings. When Clinton ignored Hatch's suggestion and seemed to ridicule the suggestion, Hatch became determined to pursue President Clinton's impeachment and removal from office.

When the Senate did not have 67 votes to convict President Clinton, Hatch agreed on a strategy to end the proceedings. On January 22, 1999, Hatch supported a motion by ROBERT BYRD (D-W.V.), who said he would introduce a motion in the Senate to dismiss the charges. Hatch agreed, noting, "If we absolutely come to the conclusion that there are not 67 votes for conviction and that there never will be, then it seems to me we ought to find some way of bringing this to a close. I'd prefer an adjournment motion with an acknowledgment as part of it, with an acknowledgment that the House of Representatives' vote on impeachment is acknowledged, that we acknowledge that, if it's true, that we don't have 67 votes for a conviction and that we acknowledge that the House vote on impeachment is the highest form of censure possible under our system . . ."

In 2000, Hatch entered the presidential primaries. However, after his last-place showing in the Iowa caucuses in late January, Hatch abandoned his presidential nomination bid and endorsed front-runner GEORGE WALKER BUSH for the nomination. Hatch had received only 550 votes of the 24,000 cast in Iowa. As the only Mormon in the presidential race, Hatch believed that anti-Mormon bias hurt him in Iowa. He also noted that a Gallup Poll showed that 17 percent of the national population would not vote for a Mormon. He indicated that after the 1999 impeachment trial of President Clinton, he was determined to see a Republican in the White House. This prompted him to enter the race himself, and then once out of the race, to strongly support George W. Bush.

As chairman of the Senate Judiciary Committee during Republican control of the Senate,

and as ranking member of the committee during Democratic control in the Clinton administration, Hatch opposed many of the administration's nominees to the federal bench. When President Bush was elected in 2000, Hatch became one of the staunchest defenders of President Bush's nominees to the federal bench.

Among the bills that Hatch championed were the Freedom Restoration Act, the Omnibus Property Rights Act, the Antiterrorism and Effective Death Penalty Act, designation of the Mormon Trail, and the Children's Health Insurance Program (CHIP). His voting record in the Senate favored individual property rights, the death penalty, and a balanced budget amendment.

Hatch was first elected to the Senate from Utah in 1976, defeating the three-term incumbent, Frank Moss, with 54 percent of the vote. Hatch was reelected in 1982, 1988, 1994, and 2000.

Born on March 22, 1934, Hatch graduated from Brigham Young University majoring in history (1959) and earned his J.D. from the University of Pittsburgh (1962). In 1992, Hatch published a book, *Square Peg: Confessions of a Citizen Senator*, discussing his tenure in the Senate.

Helms, Jesse
(1921–   ) *member of the Senate*

First elected to the Senate in 1972, Jesse Helms (R-N.C.) was elected to five consecutive terms before leaving the Senate in 2003. He did not seek reelection in 2002. Helms was replaced in the Senate by ELIZABETH HANFORD DOLE, who defeated former White House chief of staff ERSKINE BOWLES.

Helms garnered only 53 percent of the vote in both the 1990 and 1996 elections in North Carolina, indicating solid but not overwhelming support in the state. The elections were always difficult to win for Helms, forcing him to spend an unprecedented $16 million in North Carolina in 1996. When first elected in 1972, his margin was 54 percent to 46 percent, which was similar to his electoral margins in 1996. He never gained more than 55 percent of the vote during his career. His Senate career was marked by his consistently conservative positions.

Helms's failure to gain a stronger plurality within North Carolina despite his longevity in the Senate stemmed from his reputation as anti-gay and bigoted against African Americans. The roots of his reputation for bias began early in his professional career. In 1960 Helms began a job as a television commentator. During his 12 years in television, he often complained about "civil rights agitators" including Martin Luther King, Jr., and about "sex perverts." Helms was also closely linked to the banking and tobacco industries, which led to strong opposition among both Democrats and Republicans. As a result, he was never able to build a strong political base in North Carolina.

Helms was originally a Democrat, but switched parties in 1972 to run for the Senate. When the Democratic Party's nominee, Senator B. Everett Jordan, a three-term incumbent, lost to Congressman Nick Galifianakis in the primary, based on the support of newly registered African-American voters, Helms switched parties to challenge Galifianakis. Helms became the first Republican to win a Senate race in North Carolina, largely due to the turnout of white voters who had previously voted Democratic.

Throughout his tenure in the Senate, Helms regularly backed legislation that was both business- and religion-oriented. He opposed legislation for minimum wage increases, food stamps, anti-pollution legislation, reparations for the internment of Japanese Americans during World War II, funding for the National Endowment for the Arts (NEA), and the establishment of Martin Luther King Day as a national holiday. He supported prayer in public schools, a constitu-

tional amendment to ban flag burning, and trade restrictions on Cuba. Throughout his career he also strongly opposed abortion rights, busing in public schools, and welfare programs. His opposition for funding for the National Endowment for the Arts included a speech on the floor of the Senate in which he said, "It is self-evident that many of the beneficiaries of NEA grants are contemptuous of traditional moral standards."

Helms was never a supporter of President Clinton. During the first term of the Clinton administration, Helms gave a television interview in which he stated that many members of the military believed President Clinton was unqualified to be commander in chief. This was based, Helms noted, on President Clinton's support for gays in the military and his opposition to the war in Vietnam. Helms noted that North Carolina had a large military population and that he believed they did not support Clinton. At one point in the interview, Helms said, "Mr. Clinton better watch out if he comes down here. He'd better have a bodyguard."

In 1994, following the Republican sweep of Congress, Helms became chairman of the Foreign Relations Committee. He became less confrontational with the Clinton administration and began to build bridges between Congress and the administration in some foreign policy areas. He supported the administration's enlargement of the NATO alliance and reform of the United Nations. However, Helms maintained strong opposition to many of President Clinton's policies. When President Clinton flew to Russia in June 2000 to meet with Russian president Vladimir Putin, Helms emphasized to Clinton that he would not support an arms control treaty that allowed the Antiballistic Missile Treaty to continue. He also led the Senate's opposition to the administration's nuclear test ban treaty in 1999.

Helms held the administration hostage on certain ambassadorial nominations. In 1997, when President Clinton nominated Massachusetts governor William F. Weld as ambassador to Mexico, Helms successfully blocked the nomination. Weld was viewed as "soft on drugs" and had hinted in his failed Senate campaign that he would not support Helms as chairman of the Foreign Relations Committee. Helms refused to hold hearings on the nomination in the Foreign Relations Committee, which effectively stopped further action.

In addition to the Foreign Relations Committee, Helms was a member of the Senate Committee on Agriculture, Nutrition and Forestry and a member of the Rules and Administration Committee. During his tenure on the Agriculture Committee, Helms avidly protected the tobacco industry.

Fred Barnes, editor of the conservative *Weekly Standard* described Helms in 1997. "Next to Ronald Reagan," Barnes said, "Helms is the most important conservative in the last twenty-five years."

By the time that the 80-year-old Helms retired from the Senate in January 2003, his health had begun to deteriorate. In April 2002 he underwent open-heart surgery to replace a heart valve. In recent years he had been diagnosed with prostate cancer and Paget's disease, a rare bone disease. In 1998 he had a knee replaced and often was seen in the Senate in a motorized wheelchair.

Born on October 18, 1921, Helms attended Wingate (North Carolina) Junior College and Wake Forest College. He served in the navy from 1942–45.

Herman, Alexis

(1947–   ) *secretary of labor, director, Office of Public Liaison*

Alexis Herman held two senior positions in the Clinton administration. During the first term she was assistant to the president and director of

Alexis Herman *(Department of Labor)*

the Office of Public Liaison (1993–97). During the second term she served as Secretary of Labor (1997–2001), becoming the first African-American woman to hold the position. After a three-month battle over her nomination as secretary of labor, Herman was confirmed by the Senate by an 85-13 vote on April 30, 1997. Vice President ALBERT (AL) GORE, JR., swore Herman into office on May 1, 1997. She succeeded ROBERT REICH in the position. During the second term, Herman also became the only African-American woman in the cabinet.

The delay in Herman's confirmation was primarily tied to a battle that Senator Don Nickles (R-Okla.) led against the Clinton administration, not against Herman. Nickles wanted President Clinton not to issue an executive order that was designed to encourage union labor on federal construction contracts.

Nickles said, "I don't have a problem with Alexis Herman being secretary of labor. My purpose was to make sure that the administration does not try to legislate by executive order."

Prior to working for the Clinton administration, Herman had been the deputy chairperson of the Democratic National Committee. RONALD H. BROWN, subsequently named secretary of commerce by President Clinton, was the chairman of the Democratic National Committee. Following President Clinton's election in November 1992, Herman was named deputy director of the Clinton-Gore Presidential Transition Office.

As director of the Office of Public Liaison in the White House, Herman's office served as an outreach office to various organizations that wanted to meet with the president or influence administration policymaking. She often decided which invitations for speaking engagements the president would accept, depending on which policies the administration wanted to support. In 1994, when President Clinton sought to build support for his crime bill, Herman accepted an invitation for Clinton to speak at the national convention of law enforcement personnel.

As an African American in the White House, Herman worked to build relations between the president and the Black Caucus in Congress and with African-American organizations throughout the country. One of the strongest political bases that President Clinton had during the 1992 election was among African-American voters, which Herman wanted to solidify again for the 1996 reelection campaign.

One of Herman's first official duties was to oversee the Senate confirmation hearings of Dr. JOYCELYN ELDERS as surgeon general in 1993. Elders, an African-American woman, faced stiff opposition over her pro-choice and other views. Following a long confirmation process, Elders won Senate confirmation.

After his reelection in 1996, President Clinton appointed Herman as secretary of labor. After her nomination, Clinton referred to Herman in a *Jet* magazine article as a "successful business woman and a leader in efforts to bring minorities into the economic mainstream. And for the past four years . . . has been my eyes and ears, working to connect the American people." Her confirmation hearings were rocky, however, with the opposition of labor unions and congressional Republicans. She quickly gained their support once in office for her handling of the United Parcel Service (UPS) strike in 1997.

Her tenure in the Department of Labor was marred in 1997 when Justice Department lawyers and FBI agents began an investigation into whether Herman had given a former business associate, Vanessa Weaver, undue access to the White House. Herman was charged with influence peddling by Laurent Yene, who had worked with Herman at her consulting firm, A.M. Herman and Associates, but the two had had a falling out. Yene accused Herman of funneling business to Weaver in exchange for contributions to Democratic organizations in 1996, and for taking 10 percent of consulting fees from business related to the White House.

After several months of internal investigations, Attorney General JANET RENO sought the appointment of an independent counsel to investigate the charges in May 1998. Independent Counsel RALPH LANCASTER conducted the investigation, including a September 1999 interview of President Clinton about Herman's conduct in the White House. The charges were dropped when no evidence was found against Herman.

Born on July 16, 1947, Herman graduated from Xavier University in New Orleans, Louisiana, (1969) after attending Spring Hill College in Mobile, Alabama. After graduation, she worked for Interfaith in Mobile as a community worker. She later worked for the

Recruitment and Training Program in Pascagoula, Mississippi, and the Minority Women Employment Program in Atlanta. In 1974, she became director of the Minority Women Employment Program.

Herman's first position in the federal government had been with the Carter administration as the director of the Women's Bureau in the Department of Labor. At 29 years old, Herman was one of the youngest senior members of the department and the highest-ranking African American in the department. With the defeat of President Carter in the 1980 elections, Herman left government but remained in Washington, D.C., where she founded A. M. Herman and Associates, a marketing and management company.

Her rise in the Democratic Party began in 1989 when Ronald Brown, the chair of the Democratic National Committee, chose Herman as chief of staff for the national committee. In 1991, she was promoted to deputy chairperson. In 1992 she was the chief executive officer for the Democratic Party's national convention at Madison Square Garden in New York City.

Heymann, Philip B.
(1932–) *deputy attorney general*

Heymann served as deputy attorney general, the second-ranking position in the Department of Justice, for just over one year. Appointed in January 1993, he resigned in March 1994 after what was described as a personality clash with Webster Hubbell, the third-ranking official in the Department of Justice. No details of what caused the clash were made public.

When the Carter administration took office, Heymann was asked to work in the Department of Justice where he served as assistant attorney general in the criminal division. With the election of Ronald Reagan, Heymann returned to Harvard Law School as director of the Harvard Law School Center for Criminal Justice. From 1985 to 1987 he accepted the position of associate dean of the Harvard Law School. After leaving the Clinton administration, Heymann became the James Barr Ames Professor of Law, and director of the Center for Criminal Justice at Harvard Law School.

Born on October 30, 1932, in Pittsburgh, Pennsylvania, Heymann received his B.A. in philosophy, summa cum laude, from Yale University (1954) and his J.D. from Harvard University Law School (1960). He also studied philosophy at the Sorbonne in Paris and was a Fulbright scholar. After graduating from law school, Heymann was a law clerk for Justice John Harlan of the U.S. Supreme Court (1960) and for four years worked in the Solicitor General's Office in the Department of Justice (1961–65). During the Johnson administration, Heymann was appointed the deputy administrator for the Bureau of Security and Consular Affairs in the Department of State (1966–67) and the executive assistant to the under secretary of state (1967–69). When President Nixon was elected, Heymann left the federal government to return to Harvard Law School, where he became a professor of law (1969–78). During the Watergate investigations, he served as associate special prosecutor during the summers of 1973–75.

In 1998 he published the book *Terrorism and America: A Commonsense Strategy for a Democratic Society*. After September 11, 2001, he donated the royalties from the book to the American Red Cross. During the 2000 presidential election, Heymann became a strong supporter of Vice President Al Gore.

Hilley, John L.
(1947–) *director of the Office of Legislative Affairs*

After serving on the staffs of two Democratic senators from 1991 to 1996, John Hilley was named assistant to the president and director of the Office of Legislative Affairs in 1996. In announcing the appointment of Hilley on January 5, 1996, President Clinton said, "There are few individuals with John's experience and understanding of the Congress. He has done excellent work on behalf of Senate Democrats, and I am very pleased that he will be coming to work at the White House." Hilley began his position at the White House on February 1, 1996.

One year after Hilley took office, President Clinton expanded his role. In an announcement on February 12, 1997, President Clinton stated that Hilley would add the role of senior adviser to the president, while continuing as director of legislative affairs.

During the spring of 1997, Hilley became a key member of the White House team that worked on a bipartisan budget agreement between the White House and the Congress. Hilley worked with Chief of Staff ERSKINE B. BOWLES, National Economic Council chair GENE SPERLING, and Director of the Office of Management and Budget FRANKLIN DELANO RAINES on the agreement. Hilley was the only member of the team who had worked in Congress and who had a direct working knowledge of the budget process.

Born on October 22, 1947, in Tampa, Florida, Hilley graduated with a B.A. (1970) and with a Ph.D. in economics (1978) from Princeton University. He joined the faculty of Lehigh University (1978–83), leaving to become the principal fiscal analyst, in the Congressional Research Office (CRO) in Washington, D.C. (1983–85). After two years at the CRO, Hilley joined the Senate Budget Committee staff as the senior economist and was named staff director of the committee in 1988 (1985–90).

In 1991, Hilley was named chief of staff to Senator GEORGE JOHN MITCHELL (D-Me.), where he stayed for four years (1991–95). In 1995 he was named chief counsel to Senate Minority Leader THOMAS ANDREW DASCHLE (D-S.D.). When Hilley left to take the position in the White House in 1996, Daschle said of Hilley, "Few people understand the issues and personalities of Capitol Hill as well as John Hilley. Republicans and Democrats alike respect John for his intelligence and his integrity. John's insights were extremely important to me this year, and I know Senate Democrats and I will continue to work closely with him as he advises the president."

Holbrooke, Richard C.
(1941–) *ambassador to the United Nations, assistant secretary of state for European and Canadian affairs, ambassador to Germany*

Richard Holbrooke was a key foreign policy adviser throughout the Clinton administration. He moved through a series of presidential appointments in foreign policy, from ambassador to Germany (1993), to assistant secretary of state for European and Canadian affairs (1994), and culminating in his role as U.S. ambassador to the United Nations (1999). He left government from 1996–99 to join an investment banking firm in New York City but returned when offered the United Nations position.

Holbrooke's first appointment in the Clinton administration was as ambassador to Germany. His tenure in Germany was relatively uneventful. After a little over a year in Germany, Holbrooke returned to the United States as assistant secretary of state for European affairs (October 1994). His first assignment in the Department of State was to deal with the expanding conflict in Bosnia where Serbian, Muslim, and Croatian political factions were jockeying for power. He had been to the region twice before in 1992, and his son worked with refugees in the region.

During the two years Holbrooke served as assistant secretary of state for European and

Canadian affairs, he focused primarily on reaching a diplomatic settlement in Bosnia. In 1995 Holbrooke was the chief negotiator for the Dayton peace accords. President Clinton brought the opposing factions in Bosnia together in Dayton, Ohio, to sign the accords. The accords ended the war in Bosnia.

Holbrooke left the administration in February 1996 for three years (1996–99) to return to Wall Street as an investment banker specializing in European affairs, as vice chairman of Credit Suisse First Boston (a New York City firm). While at Credit Suisse, Holbrooke served on a pro bono basis as the special pres-

idential envoy for Cyprus, where he lobbied the European Union to admit Turkey, and as special envoy in Bosnia and Kosovo. In the latter role, he negotiated the October 1998 agreement for peace between Serbia and Kosovo, and when that agreement failed to be kept, he delivered the final ultimatum to Belgrade on March 23, 1999, that the North Atlantic Treaty Organization (NATO) would begin bombing to stop the killing in Kosovo.

In 1999 he was called back into government by President Clinton and was named ambassador to the United Nations. As ambassador to the United Nations, he was accorded cabinet

Richard C. Holbrooke *(NATO Library)*

rank. After often contentious hearings, Holbrooke was confirmed by the Senate as ambassador to the United Nations on August 5, 1999, by vote of 81 to 16. Those opposed to Holbrooke's nomination, led by Senator Kay Bailey Hutchison (R-Tex.) argued that Holbrooke's decisions in the Balkans had failed. Hutchison stated, "I think he is tenacious in his beliefs, and I admire that in a person. I just believe that our foreign policy is going in the wrong direction in this country. I think we are going to pay a high price for it, and I think Richard Holbrooke is one of the architects of this policy that I believe is quite erroneous. So, for that reason, I will vote against Richard Holbrooke."

During his tenure as ambassador to the United Nations, Holbrooke brokered a deal with Jesse Helms (R-N.C.), who was chairman of the Senate Foreign Relations Committee, to pay part of the country's $1 billion debt to the United Nations if the United Nations revamped its organizational structure. Holbrooke also agreed to pressure the United Nations to reduce the U.S. budget share from 25 percent to 20 percent and its role in funding peacekeeping operations from 31 percent to 25 percent.

Although Holbrooke's professional career had focused on diplomacy, his intention after college was to be a journalist. When the *New York Times* rejected him for a job, Holbrooke took and passed the foreign service exam (1962). He emerged within the foreign service as a staff assistant to General Maxwell Taylor and went with Ambassador Henry Cabot Lodge and W. Averell Harriman to the Paris peace talks to end the Vietnam War. He continued in the State Department, moving up the political ladders for several years before his appointment as director of the Peace Corps in Morocco (1970–72). When he returned, he became managing editor of *Foreign Policy* (1972–76) and was a member of the Council on Foreign Relations and of the Trilateral Commission.

While on the Trilateral Commission, Holbrooke met Jimmy Carter, who was also a member of the Trilateral Commission. When Carter was elected president, Holbrooke was brought into the administration as assistant secretary of state for East Asian and Pacific affairs. At 35 years old, Holbrooke was one of the youngest assistant secretaries of state in recent times. Among his responsibilities for the region was building Sino-American relations, after the normalization of relations with China in 1978. Many in China had been hopeful that President Clinton would appoint Holbrooke to this position, rather than European affairs, given his background in working on Sino-American relations under President Carter.

After four years at the State Department, Holbrooke left government for the private sector when President Reagan was elected in 1980. Holbrooke became vice president of Public Strategies, a Washington-based consulting firm founded by James A. Johnson and Holbrooke (1981). Four years later he joined the investment banking firm of Lehman Brothers, at a reported annual salary of $900,000 (1985). While out of government, and divorced, Holbrooke began dating television reporter Diane Sawyer. He later married his second wife Kati Marton, the ex-wife of television news anchor Peter Jennings.

When another Democrat, President Clinton, regained the Oval Office, Holbrooke sought a political position within the administration. After serving in the State Department under President Carter, Holbrooke wanted an ambassadorial assignment. His preference was for Japan, but he accepted the appointment to Germany.

Had Vice President Al Gore won the 2000 election, it was widely believed that Holbrooke would have been selected as Gore's secretary of state.

Although he remained in the private sector following the election of GEORGE WALKER

BUSH in 2000, Holbrooke became a frequent guest on news programs and talk shows to discuss foreign policy. He was a counselor on the Council on Foreign Relations and was chairman of its Terrorism Task Force.

Holbrooke was coauthor of *Counsel to the President* (1991), the memoirs of Clark Clifford. His own book, *To End a War* (1998), was named one of the 10 best books of 1998 by the *New York Times*. He received his B.A. from Brown University (1962) and was a Fellow at the Woodrow Wilson School at Princeton University (1969).

Holcum, John D.
(1940–   ) *undersecretary of state for arms control; director, U.S. Arms Control and Disarmament Agency*

John D. Holcum, appointed by President Clinton as the director of the U.S. Arms Control and Disarmament Agency, was sworn into office on November 22, 1993. Holcum was subsequently appointed in 1998 as the undersecretary of state for arms control and international security as part of President Clinton's executive directive in 1997 that the Arms Control and Disarmament Agency be integrated into the Department of State. During 1998 Holcum oversaw that merger.

Among the issues that Holcum addressed while managing arms control in the Department of State was the Comprehensive Test Ban Treaty. When the Senate voted in October 1999 not to ratify the treaty, Holcum began to lobby to rebuild support for it. In a speech to the Foreign Policy Association in New York City on February 16, 2000, Holcum noted that, "President Clinton has made clear that the United States remains committed to the Comprehensive Test Ban Treaty. We will support the international monitoring system, and continue urging other countries to ratify." The Comprehensive Test Ban Treaty had been signed by 155 countries, including the United States, and ratified by 52 countries. Among the most successful treaties signed during his tenure was the Chemical Weapons Treaty, which had been negotiated under Presidents Reagan and Bush and finally passed under President Clinton. The treaty, signed by the United States in 1993, was finally ratified by the Senate and went into effect on April 29, 1997. As of January 31, 1997, 161 countries had signed the treaty and 68 countries had ratified it. During his eight years in the Clinton administration Holcum was also involved in confirming the nonnuclear status of the Ukraine, Belarus, and Kazakhstan, and the withdrawal from western Europe of almost all U.S. tactical nuclear weapons. Although he was deeply involved in strengthening the Biological Weapons Convention, the nonaligned states failed to move forward on many of the issues. Holcum was a strong supporter of maintaining the Anti-Ballistic Missile Treaty, which was later dismantled by President GEORGE WALKER BUSH.

Born on December 4, 1940, Holcum received his B.S. at Northern State Teachers College in mathematics and physical sciences, and his J.D., with honors, from the George Washington University School of Law (1970). From 1969–75 Holcom served as the legislative director for Senator George McGovern (D-S.D.) and managed the senator's work on the Foreign Relations Committee. When Senator McGovern ran for president in 1972, Holcum was his issues director in the primaries and his chief speechwriter in the general election campaign.

During the latter part of the Carter administration, Holcum was on the Policy and Planning Office staff in the Department of State, working on arms control issues (1979–81). From 1981 until 1992, Holcum practiced law in Washington, D.C., with the law firm of

O'Melveny and Myers, concentrating on regulatory and international issues.

After 20 years, Holcum returned to a presidential campaign as a defense and foreign policy adviser for Clinton in 1992. During the Democratic National Convention in New York City in 1992, Holcum served as executive director of the platform drafting committee.

After leaving the Clinton administration at the end of 2000, Holcum joined Atlas Air, Inc., as vice president, international and government affairs. Atlas Air operated air freighters to 100 cities and 46 countries.

Hubbell, Webster L.
(1948–) *associate attorney general, Department of Justice*

Webster Hubbell, a law partner of Hillary Rodham Clinton in Little Rock, Arkansas, at the Rose Law Firm, was appointed associate attorney general in January 1993. He resigned on March 14, 1994, after allegations arose of tax evasion and fraud in his law practice. Hubbell was a close friend of the Clintons and was at one time considered for the position of attorney general. When President Clinton decided to nominate a woman for attorney general, Hubbell was named to the senior Justice Department position of associate attorney general.

On August 5, 1994, KENNETH W. STARR was appointed as the independent counsel charged with investigating the involvement of President and Mrs. Clinton in illegal loans in their Whitewater land development project in Arkansas during the 1980s. When Starr examined the billing records of the Rose Law Firm, which handled the Whitewater project, he found numerous inaccuracies in Hubbell's billing records, which Starr alleged were criminal in intent.

Starr then began an investigation directly into Hubbell's billing records and determined that the inaccuracies were criminal. Most serious of the charges against Hubbell was that he billed personal expenses to his clients. Starr also charged Hubbell with tax evasion on unreported income at the law firm. Hubbell denied any wrongdoing and accused Starr of trying to coerce him into testifying falsely against Hillary Clinton with regard to the Whitewater land development project.

On December 6, 1994, Hubbell reached a plea agreement with Starr that he admitted to devising a "scheme to defraud" his clients and that he did "evade his income tax." Hubbell was sentenced to 19 months in federal prison by the sentencing judge. He served 16 months in federal prison.

After his release from prison, a number of people in the White House began to seek consulting work for Hubbell, including White House chief of staff THOMAS FRANKLIN MCLARTY III and others on the staff. They succeeded in finding a number of clients for Hubbell who paid large sums of money to him for his consulting services, amounting to $700,000 in the first year. Among his clients was Revlon, which paid Hubbell $60,000 for consulting work. Vernon Jordan, a close friend of President Clinton, arranged the fee for Hubbell. Since many of Hubbell's clients were prominent Democrats, or were connected to prominent Democrats, Starr charged that President Clinton and members of the White House staff had arranged to buy Hubbell's silence in the Starr investigation of Whitewater.

Starr then reindicted Hubbell for tax evasion. Although the U.S. District Court dismissed the charges brought by Starr, the U.S. Court of Appeals determined that the lower court had been wrong in dismissing the charges. The appeals court in February 1999 said that Starr had good cause to allege that friends of President Clinton had paid more than $700,000 to Hubbell in hush money, given the "timing, sources, and extent of the payments." But the appeals court asked the lower court to determine whether Starr had violated Hubbell's constitutional rights by using as evidence a number of tax documents that Hubbell had turned over as part of an immunity deal.

In July 1999, Hubbell pleaded guilty to one of 15 counts that Starr had brought against him, and the other charges were dropped. Starr dropped criminal tax charges against Hubbell, his wife, his lawyer, and his accountant. Hubbell remained bitter about the charges by Starr in both the 1994 and 1999 cases. He frequently stated that Starr had only used him to force testimony against President and Mrs. Clinton in the Whitewater land development project.

Born on January 18, 1948, in Little Rock, Arkansas, Hubbell received his B.S. from the University of Arkansas in Fayetteville (1970) and his J.D. from the University of Arkansas Law School (1973), where he was managing editor of the law review.

Hussein, king of Jordan
(1935–1999) *Arab monarch*

King Hussein ruled Jordan for 46 years before his death from cancer on February 7, 1999. He was officially the king of the Hashemite Kingdom of Jordan.

After his grandfather was assassinated in 1953, and his father, who suffered from schizophrenia, abdicated, Hussein was crowned king. Hussein's years in power were marked by changing relationships both within the Arab world and with the United States. In 1967, Jordan joined Egypt and Syria in the failed attack against Israel in the Six-Day War. Jordan lost substantial territory to Israel after the Six-Day War, including control of the West Bank and East Jerusalem.

When President Jimmy Carter initiated peace talks between Egypt and Israel, Jordan supported the efforts and the subsequent Camp David accords. In 1994, King Hussein and Israeli prime minister YITZHAK RABIN signed a peace treaty which formally ended 46 years of war between the two nations. When Rabin was assassinated in 1995, Hussein delivered a passionate tribute to his one-time foe.

Throughout his presidency, President Clinton worked to build on the Middle East peace efforts begun by President Carter. Clinton focused during the early part of his presidency on ending the conflict between Jordan and Israel as a further foundation to Middle East peace. As early as October 1993, Clinton created a working group at the White House, consisting of Crown Prince Hassan (King Hussein's brother), Foreign Minister SHIMON PERES of Israel, and President Clinton to explore ways in which the two countries could settle their conflicts. After nine months of discussions, an agreement was reached for cooperation between Jordan and Israel.

President Clinton brought King Hussein and Prime Minister Yitzhak Rabin together to sign the Washington Declaration and hosted a state dinner to celebrate the signing of the declaration on July 25, 1994, at the White House. The following day (July 26, 1994), King Hussein spoke to a joint session of Congress. The Washington Declaration was followed by the signing of the Treaty of Peace between Jordan and Israel on October 26, 1994. The treaty was signed on the Jordan-Israel border by King Hussein and Prime Minister Rabin. Secretary of State Warren Christopher represented the United States.

In spite of his support for Israel and his efforts to bring peace to the Middle East, Hussein refused to condemn Saddam Hussein for his invasion of Kuwait in 1990. After the Persian Gulf War and after Iraq retreated from Kuwait, King Hussein sought to be a peace broker in the region. He remained an ally of the United States throughout the war despite his failure to support American actions against Saddam Hussein.

In 1978 King Hussein married for the fourth time to an American, 26-year-old Lisa Halaby, who became Queen Noor after their marriage. After the death of King Hussein, his son by a former marriage ascended the throne. Abdullah II became king on February 7, 1999.

King Hussein was born in 1935.

Hussein, Saddam
(1937–   ) *president of Iraq*

Saddam Hussein, president of Iraq, maintained a tumultuous relationship with the United States following the Persian Gulf War. Throughout the Clinton administration, the United States maintained a policy of containment, supporting the economic embargo against Iraq and the subsequent United Nations resolutions. Hussein was removed from the presidency in April 2003 when President GEORGE WALKER BUSH sent U.S. forces to Iraq. The United States set up a transitional government in May 2003 until a new Iraqi government could be established.

The often shaky relationship between the United States and Iraq deteriorated in 1990 when Iraq invaded its neighboring Arab state of Kuwait. On August 28, 1990, Saddam Hussein declared that Kuwait was the 19th province of Iraq. In spite of United Nations efforts to expel Iraq, Saddam Hussein refused to remove his troops.

Six months later, the United States led a coalition of military forces into Kuwait to repel Iraqi troops. American-led troops began bombing Baghdad on January 16, 1991, and concluded in February. As a condition of Iraq's surrender, the United Nations sent weapons inspectors to insure that Iraq did not have weapons of mass destruction (chemical, biological, or nuclear weapons). In 1998 the United Nations weapons inspectors were refused entry and were not allowed to return.

Throughout the Clinton administration, an economic embargo remained in force on Iraq. However, in 1996 Saddam Hussein accepted an Oil for Food program, in which the economic embargo was lifted to allow Iraq to sell enough oil to purchase food and certain medical supplies.

In March 2003, during the administration of President George W. Bush, the United States led a coalition of forces into Iraq to remove Saddam Hussein from power. When American and British forces moved through Iraq to Baghdad, Hussein fled but was later captured. The United States took control of Baghdad and established a military government, with American and British troops, until a transitional government of Iraqi citizens could be set up.

As did many leaders in the Middle East, Saddam Hussein rose to power through a coup. In 1968 he led a bloodless coup against Iraq's president and overthrew the regime. He was elected vice chairman of the Revolution Command Council and subsequently nationalized all of the oil companies in the country. In 1977 he was elected assistant secretary-general of the Ba'ath Party, a position that propelled him in 1979 to the presidency. After solidifying his hold on power in Iraq, Saddam Hussein initiated the Iran-Iraq war in which 250,000 Iraqi soldiers were killed. A cease-fire was called by the two countries in 1988.

Saddam Hussein was born on April 28, 1937.

Hutchinson, Asa
(1950–   ) *member of the House of Representatives*

Asa Hutchinson was elected to Arkansas's 3rd Congressional District in 1996, taking over the seat vacated by his brother, Tim Hutchinson, who successfully ran for the Senate that year.

The 3rd District was one of Arkansas's strongest Republican areas, electing a Republican congressman continuously since 1967. Asa Hutchinson was elected in 1996 with 56 percent of the vote, and with 81 percent of the vote in 1998. In 2000 he ran unopposed for a third term.

When both Hutchinson brothers won their respective races in 1996, Arkansas became the second state with a brother-brother combination in the House and Senate. The other state was Michigan, with Senator Carl Levin and Representative Sander Levin.

During President Clinton's impeachment, Asa Hutchinson, as a member of the House Judiciary Committee, was one of 13 House managers prosecuting the case. The managers were HENRY JOHN HYDE (R-Ill.), James Sensenbrenner (D-Wisc.), Bill McCullum (R-Fla.), George Gekas (R-Pa.), Charles Canady (R-Fla.), Steve Buyer (R-Ind.), Ed Bryant (R-Tenn.), Steve Chabot (R-Ohio), ROBERT BARR (R-Ga.), Christopher Cannon (R-Utah), James Rogan (R-Calif.), LINDSEY O. GRAHAM (R-S.C.), and Asa Hutchinson (R-Ark.). While Asa Hutchinson prosecuted the case in the Senate, Tim Huchinson sat in the Senate as a judge.

Asa Hutchinson introduced the first article of impeachment in the House against President Clinton on December 18, 1998. He voted for all four articles of impeachment the following day. After the House had voted for impeachment, Hutchinson, as a manager, was tasked with presenting the articles of impeachment against President Clinton in the Senate.

Born on December 2, 1950, Hutchinson received his B.S. from Bob Jones University (1972) and his J.D. from the University of Arkansas (1975). His first elected position was in 1977, when he served as the Bentonville city attorney (1977–78). In 1982, he was appointed by President Reagan as U.S. attorney for the Western District of Arkansas and served during

Bill Clinton's tenure as governor of Arkansas (1982–85). At the age of 31, Hutchinson was the youngest U.S. attorney in the nation at the time. Among the cases he was involved in was the prosecution of ROGER CLINTON, JR., in 1984 on drug charges. Prior to successfully running for the U.S. House of Representatives, Hutchinson had unsuccessfully run for the U.S. Senate in 1986 and for Arkansas attorney general in 1990. He served as Arkansas Republican Party chairman from 1990–95.

While in the House, Hutchinson sat on the Judiciary Committee, the Veterans Committee, and the Transportation and Infrastructure Committee.

When President George W. Bush was elected in 2000, he asked Asa Hutchinson to serve as the director of the Drug Enforcement Administration (DEA). Hutchinson resigned from the House on August 3, 2001, to take over the DEA. He was the first member of Congress tapped by President Bush to move to the executive branch. Following the creation of the Department of Homeland Security, Hutchinson was tapped again by President Bush to be undersecretary for border and transportation security for the new department. He was appointed on January 29, 2003.

Hyde, Henry John
(1924–) *member of the House of Representatives*

Henry Hyde (R-Ill.), who represented the 6th District of Illinois in the House of Representatives, was first elected to the House in 1974. Hyde won with 53 percent of the vote, when Rep. Harold Collier retired. Hyde was reelected to the House in every subsequent election in which he ran.

Growing up in Chicago as an Irish-Catholic, Hyde was a Democrat in his early years. In 1952 he switched to the Republican Party and supported Dwight D. Eisenhower for president. He remained a Republican after the 1952 election.

Soon after taking office in 1975, Hyde was appointed to the Judiciary Committee and was chairman from 1995–2001. He also served on the International Relations Committee, including one term as chairman. As head of the Judiciary Committee, which was controlled by Republicans, he chaired the impeachment proceedings against President Clinton in 1998, initiating all of the committee's investigative actions. The most controversial of those was the series of questions Hyde sent to President Clinton which asked him to admit to or deny the information that independent counsel KENNETH W. STARR had assembled. On November 5, 1998, Hyde submitted the list of 81 questions about his relationship with MONICA LEWINSKY, all of which began "Do you admit or deny. . . ." Clinton did not reply. After the House voted to impeach President Clinton in December 1998, Hyde became one of 13 Republican members of the Judiciary Committee to act as managers in the Senate. The managers' role was to prosecute the president in the Senate trial. Despite Hyde's efforts as a manager, the Senate failed to convict the president.

Soon after the impeachment proceedings Hyde was the target of a story in Salon.com, an online magazine, in which his lengthy affair with a younger woman was described. Hyde admitted to the affair. He became the subject of numerous subsequent articles in the media for condemning President Clinton for his affair while conducting his own adulterous relationship.

Throughout his tenure in the House, Hyde had a conservative voting record. As a staunch Roman Catholic, Hyde opposed any government funding for abortions. In 1974 he was successful in attaching an amendment, known as the Hyde Amendment, to an appropriations bill that banned Medicaid funding for abortions.

Born on April 18, 1924, Hyde received a B.S. from Georgetown University (1947) and a J.D. from Loyola School of Law, Chicago (1949). In 1942 he enlisted in the navy and saw combat in the South Pacific and the Philippines. He was discharged in 1946 and remained in the U.S. Naval Reserve from 1946–68.

Ibarra, Mickey
(1951–) *director of the Office of Intergovernmental Affairs*

Mickey Ibarra served as director of the Office of Intergovernmental Affairs from 1997 to 2001, replacing MARCIA HALE. He was the primary liaison to state and local elected officials for the White House. Ibarra became one of the highest-ranking Hispanics for the second term of the Clinton administration.

During his tenure in the White House, Ibarra was named vice chair of the White House Task Force for the Salt Lake 2002 Winter Olympic Games. In addition, he cochaired the White House Task Force on Drug Use in Sports and cochaired the President's Interagency Group on Puerto Rico and Other Insular Areas.

Prior to his appointment in the administration, Ibarra was the political manager for the National Education Association, responsible for assisting with campaign strategy development, federal candidate support, political education, and state government affairs.

A longtime political activist, Ibarra had served as the chairman of the Democratic National Committee Hispanic Caucus and as an executive committee member of the Democratic National Committee. During the 1996 presidential campaign, Ibarra was named the director of special projects for the Clinton-Gore 1996 campaign. At the Democratic National Convention in Chicago in 1996, Ibarra was the director of VIP volunteers and worked as a senior adviser for the convention. In 1997 Ibarra was selected by *Hispanic* magazine as one of the "25 most powerful Hispanics in Washington, D.C."

Born on March 27, 1951, in Salt Lake City, Utah, Ibarra graduated with a B.A. from Brigham Young University (1976) and a master's degree in education from the University of Utah (1980). Ibarra taught for five years in Utah public high schools (1976–80) before joining the National Education Association, rising from a staff member to the international relations manager. From 1970–73 he served in the U.S. Army.

After leaving the administration, Ibarra formed Mickey Ibarra & Associates, Inc., a government and public affairs consulting firm in Washington, D.C.

Ickes, Harold M.
(1939–) *deputy chief of staff*

Harold Ickes had been deeply involved in Democratic politics for more than two decades before joining the Clinton presidential campaign in 1992 as director of the New York

Clinton for President campaign. Ickes had known Clinton but was not a close friend. His relationship with the Clintons was solidified, however, when he succeeded in keeping many Democrats in New York as supporters after the Gennifer Flowers story broke during the primaries. Ickes remained a key campaigner for Clinton during both the primaries and the general election.

When Clinton secured the Democratic nomination, Ickes moved to the Democratic National Committee as deputy chairman during the general election. He was also the convention manager for the Democratic National Convention in New York City that nominated Clinton as its presidential candidate. Following the 1992 election, President-elect Clinton named Ickes deputy director of the Clinton-Gore transition team.

Although it was widely speculated that Ickes would be offered a position in the White House at the start of the administration, he was never formally offered one because of problems in his background check. When federal investigators looked into his law firm, they found some clients who they believed were tied to organized crime. When his name was cleared, Ickes was offered the job of deputy chief of staff on December 22, 1993, working for Chief of Staff THOMAS FRANKLIN MCLARTY III. Ickes joined the White House staff on January 3, 1994.

Ickes's role as deputy chief of staff was primarily to design strategies for building political support for administration policies. Among his responsibilities was working with Hillary Clinton to move the health care bill through Congress and designing strategies for the 1994 mid-term congressional elections. When an independent counsel was appointed to investigate the Whitewater land development project, Ickes took on the additional role of managing the White House public relations strategy.

During the 1996 presidential election, Ickes was primarily involved in developing fund-raising strategies. His tactics, although successful at raising money, drew the attention of a congressional investigating committee. After the election, the committee began to hold hearings on allegations that Ickes had solicited funds for the campaign from his office in the White House. Federal law prohibited federal employees from engaging in political activity while at work. On June 26, 1997, Ickes gave his deposition to the Senate Governmental Affairs Committee, chaired by Fred D. Thompson (R-Tenn.), on his fund-raising activities for the 1996 Clinton-Gore campaign. He was eventually cleared of wrongdoing by the committee.

When Clinton won reelection in 1996, White House Chief of Staff LEON EDWARD PANETTA resigned, and a new chief of staff needed to be appointed. Although Ickes wanted the job, he was passed over by Clinton in favor of ERKSINE B. BOWLES who had served as deputy chief of staff from 1994–95. Ickes said in an interview that he read the announcement in the *Wall Street Journal* rather than being directly told by President Clinton. Ickes resigned as deputy chief of staff on January 20, 1997, rather than continue as a deputy. After leaving the White House, Ickes was appointed by the president to manage the logistics for the G-8 meeting which was to be held in Denver. After that assignment, he returned to New York City to practice law.

Born on September 4, 1939, in Baltimore, Maryland, Ickes received his B.A. from Stanford University (1964) and his J.D. from Columbia University Law School (1971). His professional career centered on Democratic politics. In 1968 he had been cochair of the New York presidential campaign for Eugene McCarthy. Two years later, Ickes became the campaign manager for the Democratic ticket of Arthur Goldberg for governor and Basil Patterson for lieutenant governor.

After McCarthy's failed presidential bid, Ickes went on to work for the 1972 presidential campaign of Edmund Muskie, and the 1976 presidential campaigns of Birch Bayh and Morris Udall. Four years later (1980) he joined the Democratic presidential campaign of Edward Kennedy and, in 1984, the campaign of Walter Mondale. In 1988, he shifted to a lesser-known Democratic contender, Rev. Jesse Jackson, who was seeking the Democratic presidential nomination. While working for Jackson, he met RONALD H. BROWN, chairman of the Democratic National Committee (DNC) and subsequently became special counsel to the DNC.

Throughout most of the 1970s he was counsel to the Boone Young management consulting firm in New York City. From 1978 to 1993, Ickes was a partner in Meyer, Suozzi, English, and Klein in New York City.

Harold Ickes was the son of Harold LeClair Ickes (1874–1952), secretary of interior under President Franklin Delano Roosevelt from 1933 to 1946. Harold LeClair Ickes had been an avid campaigner for Roosevelt, a role which his son would later play for Clinton.

Ikeda Yukihiko
(1937–   ) *Japan's minister for foreign affairs*

Ikeda Yukihiko was appointed the minister for foreign affairs for Japanese prime minister HASHIMOTO RYUTARO when Hashimoto entered office in 1996. When Hashimoto left office in 1998, Ikeda also did.

Ikeda was instrumental in establishing the framework for issues that would be discussed during President Clinton's April 6–7, 1996, visit to Japan. Working with National Security Adviser TONY LAKE, Ikeda sought to focus the meeting on continued security relations between the United States and Japan. Ikeda also designed a meeting between the two leaders in Santa Monica, California, on February 24 to discuss current security commitments and trade issues.

The key security issue was the insistence by the Clinton administration that the United States continue to have 47,000 troops in Okinawa. After the rape of a 12-year-old girl by U.S. soldiers in 1995, there was an outcry in Japan to reduce or end the American military presence in the country. President Clinton sought to reinforce the strong commitment that the United States had to Japan and to its security by selecting Japan as the first country for an official visit by the president.

In addition to security issues, Ikeda worked closely with CHARLENE BARSHEFSKY, the U.S. trade representative. Barshefsky and Ikeda developed a process that would reduce regulation in Japan and allow greater U.S. investment, particularly in the telecommunications sector. They also resolved issues on production of automobile parts.

On July 19, 2000, Barshefsky released the Third Joint State Report under the U.S.-Japan Initiative on Deregulation and Competition Policy. The report indicated a host of areas, from automobiles to energy, that were deregulated during the tenure of Ikeda Yukihiko.

As minister of foreign affairs, Ikeda was involved in the December 1996 hostage crisis in Peru. More than 500 hostages were taken at the ambassador's residence in Lima, Peru, by Tupac Amaru rebels. Ikeda was sent to Peru by the prime minister to win assurances that the government in Peru would not use violence to resolve the issue. After four days, he returned to Japan. When negotiators failed to resolve the crisis, sharpshooters stormed the residence and killed the kidnappers. Born May 13, 1937, Ikeda graduated from the Faculty of Law of the University of Tokyo (1961) and entered the Ministry of Finance the following month. He served in various senior government positions throughout his career, including the Ministry of Foreign Affairs, the

Ministry of Trade and Industry, and the Budget Bureau. He successfully ran for a seat in the House of Representatives in 1976 and subsequently served in a series of cabinet posts before being tapped in 1996 as minister for foreign affairs.

Inman, Bobby Ray

(1931–   ) *failed nominee for secretary of defense*

Admiral Bobby Ray Inman was nominated by President Clinton for secretary of defense in December 1993 following the announcement that secretary of defense LESLIE (LES) ASPIN, JR., would resign.

Inman had been deputy director of the Central Intelligence Agency (CIA) during the Reagan administration and had been director of the National Security Agency (NSA) in the Department of Defense during the Carter administration. He was well respected in the intelligence community and within Congress. When President Clinton needed to replace Aspin, who had had a series of clashes within the Department of Defense and with members of Congress, Clinton turned to Inman. Since Inman had successfully served under both Democratic and Republican administrations, he appeared to have broad bipartisan support.

However, soon after Inman's nomination, *New York Times* columnist William Safire wrote a derogatory column about him. In his column on December 23, 1993, Safire leveled a number of attacks against Inman, including that he had failed to pay taxes for household help. The column recalled a previous conversation they had had: "I asked him how a grown man could go through life calling himself 'Bobby'; he slammed down the phone."

Safire had been a critic of Inman's for a number of years, largely due to a decision that

Inman made in 1981 regarding Israel. As deputy director of the Central Intelligence Agency, Inman had limited the intelligence information that Israel received to a 250-mile radius. The radius did not include Libya and Iraq, which Safire and others believed was detrimental to Israel's ability to protect itself.

As a result of Safire's column, Inman withdrew his name from the nomination process on January 18, 1994. Following Inman's withdrawal, President Clinton nominated WILLIAM J. PERRY, deputy secretary of defense, for the position. Perry was confirmed on February 3, 1994, following a unanimous vote in the Senate.

Born on April 4, 1931, in Rhonesboro, Texas, Inman graduated from the University of Texas at Austin in 1950 and joined the navy in 1952. Inman rose through the ranks in naval intelligence, particularly after his work during the Yom Kippur War of 1973 in which he analyzed Arab and Soviet troop movements. In 1973 he was named director of U.S. Naval Intelligence, then was promoted to vice director of the U.S. Defense Intelligence Agency, and in 1977 was named director of the National Security Agency by President Jimmy Carter.

When President Reagan took office, he named Inman deputy director of the Central Intelligence Agency. Inman was also promoted by President Reagan to four-star admiral at the time of his CIA appointment. When Inman was confirmed by the Senate, Senator Barry Goldwater (R-Ariz.), chair of the Senate Intelligence Committee, told Inman, "If there's any such thing as the right man for the job at the right time, you're that man. I don't know of a man in the business better than you."

While at the Central Intelligence Agency, Inman began to clash with its director, William Casey, and with the national security staff in the Reagan White House, particularly with National Security Adviser Richard Allen.

Inman had become critical of a March 1981 executive order that allowed the Central Intelligence Agency a greater role in domestic activities such as wiretapping. According to Inman, "The CIA's role is abroad."

Inman resigned from the Central Intelligence Agency on April 21, 1982. He joined a computer technology firm, Microelectronics and Technology Corporation (MCC), and in 1983 was named its chief executive officer.

Jackson, Jesse
(1941–   ) *civil rights leader; founder, Rainbow Coalition; founder, Operation PUSH*

Jesse Jackson, a civil rights leader and activist, was a supporter of the 1992 Clinton-Gore campaign but never became a voice in the Clinton administration and never was close to the Clinton White House. He worked through his organization, the Rainbow Coalition, to increase minority voting participation and the number of jobs for minority workers.

In addition to his work with the Rainbow Coalition, Jackson became an international negotiator to secure the release of U.S. soldiers held as hostages. When three U.S. soldiers serving as part of the forces of the North Atlantic Treaty Organization (NATO) were captured by the Yugoslav army in March 1999, Jackson, along with an interfaith delegation, embarked on a diplomatic mission to negotiate their release. National Security Advisor SAMUEL BERGER warned Jackson that he did not have the authority to offer Yugoslav president SLOBODAN MILOŠEVIĆ concessions on behalf of the United States. He also warned that Jackson's safety could not be guaranteed. Jackson succeeded in his mission and returned to the United States with the three soldiers.

The Senate recognized Jackson's efforts with a commendation.

In May 1999, Jackson traveled to war-torn Sierra Leone where he negotiated a cease-fire agreement between Tejan Kabbah, the president of Sierra Leone, and rebel leader Foday Sankoh. In addition, Jackson negotiated the release of more than 2,000 prisoners.

In 2000, when teenager Raynard Johnson was found hanging by a belt from a tree in front of his home in Kokomo, Mississippi, Jackson drew national attention when he argued that it was a lynching, not a suicide. The issue was never resolved.

During the independent counsel's investigation of President Clinton's relationship with MONICA LEWINSKY, Jackson went to the White House to offer President Clinton both personal and ministerial support. Jackson never condemned President Clinton for the relationship and consistently offered both private and public support.

Jesse Jackson had been a voice for civil rights throughout his career. He became active in the Civil Rights movement first with the Council on Racial Equality (CORE) and then with the Rev. Martin Luther King, Jr. Jackson began working for King's Southern Christian Leadership Conference (SCLC) organizing black preachers in Chicago. He was part of the Selma, Alabama, march in 1965 and joined King in Memphis, Tennessee, in April 1968 to focus public attention on the plight of the city's striking sanitation workers. Jackson was with King hours before he was assassinated in Memphis.

Jackson remained with the Southern Christian Leadership Conference after King's death, but was suspended from the organization in 1970 in a conflict over Black Expo 70, which he staged in 1970. After leaving the Southern Christian Leadership Conference, Jackson founded his own organization, Operation PUSH (People United to Save Humanity) in 1971. He took much of the staff from the Southern Christian Leadership Conference and gained financial backing from organizations he had worked with at SCLC. The goal of Operation PUSH was to secure jobs for minorities and to encourage minority-owned businesses. He worked with Coca-Cola, Seven-Up and Burger King to hire more minorities and more minority businesses.

In September 1979 Jackson was criticized when he went to the Middle East and was photographed embracing YASSER ARAFAT, chairman of the Palestine Liberation Organization (PLO). The photograph contributed to increasing tension between the African-American community and the Jewish community at the time.

Jackson gained federal support for Operation PUSH in 1977 when the Department of Health, Education and Welfare awarded Operation PUSH contracts to develop programs to assist minority job training and minority businesses. The support of the Department of Health, Education and Welfare had been encouraged by former vice president Hubert Humphrey, who championed many of Jackson's programs.

When the Reagan administration came into office in 1981, support for Operation PUSH was dramatically reduced and was cut

Jesse Jackson *(Wong/Newsmakers)*

off entirely in February 1982. The Reagan administration explained the decision by pointing to poor record keeping by Operation PUSH and poor evaluations of their programs.

Jackson took a leave of absence from Operation PUSH to mount a presidential campaign, announcing his candidacy on November 3, 1983. He criticized the Reagan administration for its cutbacks in funding for programs that helped minorities and the poor. Jackson's campaign ended in early 1984. Although not related to the 1984 presidential campaign, Jackson received significant press coverage when he successfully negotiated the release of African-American navy pilot Robert Goodman, who had been shot down over Syria. In June 1984, however, he lost public goodwill when he visited Fidel Castro of Cuba and when he voiced opposition to the Reagan administration's invasion of Grenada.

During the 1984 presidential campaign, Jackson formed the National Rainbow Coalition for political action. He argued that it took a rainbow of people to win the nomination. Jackson resigned as president from the Rainbow Coalition/Operation PUSH in 2002. Born on October 8, 1941, in Greenville, South Carolina, Jackson graduated from North Carolina Agricultural and Technical College in Greensboro, South Carolina, (1964) and from the Chicago Theological Seminary (1966).

Jiang Zemin
(1926–) *president of China, general secretary of China*

Jiang Zemin succeeded Yang Shangkun on March 27, 1993, as president and general secretary of China. Power in the government of China was split among three senior party officials: Jiang as president and general secretary, Li Peng as premier, and Zhu Ronji as vice premier. Jiang was fluent in several languages, including Russian, English, and Romanian, and able to read French and Japanese. Jiang stepped down as general secretary in November 2002 and as president in March 2003.

He rose to power in 1989 when he succeeded DENG XIAOPING as chairman of the Central Military Commission, the organization that commands the national military. After being designated by Deng as the "core of the leadership of the third generation" (the third generation referred to the third generation of leaders after Mao and Deng), Jiang was elected president of China in March 1993. He had not been in power on June 3 and 4, 1989, when

Chinese troops shot at demonstrators in the prodemocracy rally in Beijing's Tiananmen Square and thus was not tainted by the actions of the troops.

President Jiang and President Clinton met regularly throughout the eight years of the Clinton administration, most often at meetings of the Asia-Pacific Economic Cooperation (APEC) group. In each of the eight years in which Clinton was in office, he met with Jiang to discuss Sino-American relations.

Jiang first met with President Clinton on November 19, 1993, when the Asia-Pacific Economic Cooperation meeting was held in Seattle. The two had a private conference. President Clinton agreed to support past agreements between China and the United States. The two leaders again met at an APEC meeting in Jakarta, Indonesia, on November 14, 1994. However, their only direct contact was an informal leadership meeting.

Nearly a year passed before Jiang and Clinton met again in New York at the 50th anniversary of the founding of the United Nations on October 24, 1995. Jiang met privately with Clinton briefly to discuss bilateral issues.

As was becoming a tradition by 1996, another year passed before Jiang and Clinton were to meet. On November 24, 1996, they again met at an APEC meeting, held in the Philippines.

In 1997 President Clinton invited Jiang to pay a state visit to the United States. Jiang flew to Washington, D.C., where he became the first Chinese president to pay a state visit to the president in 12 years.

The strong relationship that President Clinton built with China during the first term was jeopardized during the 1996 presidential election by Democratic fund-raiser JOHNNY CHUNG. Chung told federal investigators that he had funneled tens of thousands of dollars from a Chinese military officer to the Clinton campaign. The Clinton administration was tainted by the perception that China was trying to buy access to the administration. The Senate began a formal probe into the Clinton campaign on May 16, 1998. Senator Fred Thompson chaired the probe, which covered other allegations into campaign finance abuses in the 1996 election.

Again a year went by before the two leaders met, which was at the APEC meeting in Canada held on November 24, 1997. The following year, President Clinton paid a state visit to China. During a week from June 25–July 3, 1998, President Clinton met with President Jiang, and at the end of the visit they issued joint statements on South Asia, the protocol to the Biological Weapons Convention, and the issue of anti-personnel mines. In addition, President Clinton reaffirmed the one-China policy and stated that he did not support Taiwan's independence leading to a two-China policy. The issue of the fund-raising role of Johnny Chung was only briefly discussed, due to a meeting that Jiang had held with Secretary of State WARREN MINOR CHRISTOPHER in May. Christopher had defused the issue and assured Jiang that the administration never thought that China was trying to influence the United States elections with illegal contributions.

President Clinton would again meet Jiang on September 11, 1999, at the APEC meeting in Auckland, New Zealand, and at an APEC meeting on November 16, 2000, in Bandar Seri Begawan, Brunei. In addition to their regular meetings at APEC, the two met on September 8, 2000, in New York City to celebrate the United Nations Millennium Summit. Clinton again pledged to support the one-China policy.

Throughout his administration, President Clinton sought to build bridges to China and to Asia, evidenced by his regular attendance at the APEC meetings.

Jiang was born on August 17, 1926.

John Paul II
(1920–   ) *pope, Roman Catholic Church*

Pope John Paul II was elected the 263rd pope of the Roman Catholic Church in 1978, the first pope elected from Poland. Born Karol Wojtyla in Wadowice, Poland, he was named archbishop of Kraków, Poland, in 1964. He was named a cardinal on May 29, 1967, by Pope Paul VI.

President Clinton and Pope John Paul II met several times, including the 1999 Bilderberg conference, an annual meeting of international business leaders and politicians, which was held June 3–6, 1999, in Sintra, Portugal, and at the 1993 World Youth Day in Denver.

However, Pope John Paul never supported President Clinton publicly because of President Clinton's pro-choice position, which the Catholic Church rigorously opposed. Pope John Paul was never wary of putting political pressure from Catholics on the administration to alter its abortion position.

The pope convened an international youth conference, World Youth Day, in Denver in August 1993 to reinforce traditional church doctrine, which included opposition to abortion and to contraception. His strong statement against abortion at the Denver conference was viewed by many as a statement against the pro-choice position taken by President Clinton. At the Denver conference, Pope John Paul also expressed concern over any abuse of the innocent, which was in response to the pedophilia within the priesthood that had become worldwide news in the early 1990s.

In 1995, Pope John Paul released a second encyclical entitled *That They May Be One*, which acknowledged and apologized for past sins and errors committed in the name of the church. He accepted responsibility and asked for forgiveness in the hope that Christians could have "patient dialogue." Throughout the year he traveled to Australia and Bosnia and the United States, where he addressed the

United Nations during its 50th anniversary celebrations. He reaffirmed his opposition to abortion and his pro-life stand during his visit to the United Nations.

In March 1998 Pope John Paul issued *"We Remember: A Reflection on the Shoah* [Holocaust]," which was a papal apology for the Catholic Church's failure to act against Nazi atrocities during World War II. He made pilgrimages to Cuba in January 1998, and to the United States and Poland in 1999. He also went to Georgia, the former Soviet state, and to Iraq in 1999. He became the first modern pope to visit an Islamic country.

His travels took Pope John Paul to the Middle East in 2000, including Jordan, Israel, and the Palestinian territories, and to Portugal. The following year, Pope John Paul made a six-day pilgrimage to Greece, Syria, and Malta, retracing the footsteps of St. Paul. In Syria he became the first pope to enter a mosque. He met later in the year with Palestine Liberation Organization (PLO) chairman Yasser Arafat.

In 2001, as he turned 81, Pope John Paul's Parkinson's disease was becoming more evident. Although the Vatican denied that he suffered from the disease, one of his doctors publicly confirmed it.

Jones, Paula Corbin

(1966–   ) *accused President Clinton of sexual harassment in lawsuit*

Paula Corbin Jones alleged that Bill Clinton, then governor of Arkansas, propositioned her in a hotel room in 1991. Jones stated in her lawsuit that she was an employee of the state of Arkansas working at the Excelsior Hotel in Little Rock at the Governor's Quality Conference on May 8, 1991, when Clinton, who was speaking at the conference, asked her to meet him in his room. When she went, she alleged

that he propositioned her and made unwanted advances. Clinton denied the allegations.

The broader issue that arose from Jones's lawsuit was the allegation that he had been involved in a number of affairs, including one with a White House intern named MONICA LEWINSKY. It was the revelation about Lewinsky in this lawsuit that opened the door for KENNETH W. STARR's investigation into the Clinton-Lewinsky relationship.

Jones filed a lawsuit against Clinton in May 1994 after author David Brock wrote an article in a conservative magazine, *The American Spectator*, that accused Jones of being a willing participant in a series of extramarital affairs with Clinton. To ensure that no one believed Brock's version of her having an affair with Clinton, she sued Clinton in May 1994, alleging sexual harassment for the incident in 1991. She formally charged Clinton in the lawsuit with making unwanted sexual advances toward her. Her intention was, she stated, only to set the record straight that she was not having an affair with Clinton.

Jones claimed in her lawsuit that her rejection of Clinton cost her her job after she was denied promotions and was treated unfairly by her supervisors. She resigned in February 1993. Her lawsuit charged that President Clinton misused his position to discriminate against her and that as a result she was entitled to compensation.

President Clinton's lawyer, ROBERT BENNETT, stated that Jones offered to keep her allegations private in return for an out-of-court settlement. Bennett, at Clinton's behest, refused the offer.

On June 27, 1994, Clinton's attorneys filed motions in federal district court in Little Rock, to delay Jones's sexual harassment suit until Clinton was out of office. Bennett claimed in the filing that presidents should not have to defend themselves in civil suits while serving in office. During the process, pictures of Jones topless appeared in the January 1995 issue of *Penthouse*. She stated that a former boyfriend sold them to the magazine.

In December 1994 the federal district court ruled that Clinton was immune from civil lawsuits while in office, but in January 1996 the 8th U.S. Circuit Court of Appeals in St. Louis overturned the decision, allowing the Jones suit to proceed. On May 15, 1996, Clinton's lawyers filed a brief with the U.S. Supreme Court challenging the appeals court's ruling and seeking that the case be deferred while Clinton was in office. On June 24, 1996, the Supreme Court rejected the appeal, which allowed the case to go forward.

Judge SUSAN WEBBER WRIGHT of the U.S. District Court in Little Rock dismissed the Jones suit in May 1997 as having no merit. She agreed with the motion by the Clinton legal team for a summary judgment, which ended the case before it came to trial. Judge Wright agreed that there was no proof that Jones was emotionally afflicted or harmed in the workplace. When Jones filed an appeal with the 8th U.S. Circuit Court of Appeals, both sides began settlement talks. The first settlement proposal in 1997 failed but the second proposal in 1998 survived. In November 1997, Clinton offered a $700,000 settlement payment to charity, but Jones said she also wanted an apology. Clinton refused, and Jones's legal team subsequently quit when she refused the $700,000 settlement.

On January 11, 1998, another settlement proposal was made by Jones's new team of lawyers. They offered to settle for $2 million, which the Clinton legal team refused. Finally, in November 1998, Clinton reached an out-of-court settlement with Jones for $850,000. She received only a portion of the money, with her lawyers taking most of the settlement. The first team of attorneys in the case, Joseph Cammarata and Gilbert Davis, received $350,000. The Dallas law firm of Rader, Campbell,

Fisher, and Pyke received $283,000. The Rutherford Institute received $100,000 from Cammarata and Davis for financing the original case. The settlement did not provide any admission of guilt by President Clinton.

Two weeks after the settlement was reached, the circuit court dismissed the suit.

U.S. District Judge Susan Webber Wright fined President Clinton $25,000 and directed him to pay $90,000 in attorneys' fees for giving what Judge Wright said were "false, misleading and evasive answers" in the Jones case deposition.

Born on September 17, 1966, Jones graduated from high school in 1984 and attended secretarial courses.

Jordan, Vernon Eulion, Jr.
(1935–) *lawyer*

Vernon Jordan, a noted civil rights activist and Beltway power broker, worked with President Clinton on the 1992 presidential campaign and was a member of the president's kitchen cabinet throughout the eight years of the administration. Jordan became one of President Clinton's closest confidants. The two often played golf together, the Clintons vacationed at Jordan's Martha's Vineyard home, sailed on his yacht off the island's coast, and the two families shared Christmas dinner together. Jordan became known as a "Friend of Bill," or a FOB, which was a common term used to describe a small group of President Clinton's closest friends.

Jordan first worked with Clinton during the 1970s when Jordan was raising funds for the National Urban League in Little Rock, Arkansas. In 1991, Jordan invited Clinton to attend the Bilderberg Conference, an annual meeting of international business leaders and politicians. Here Clinton met a cadre of powerful and wealthy individuals who would later support him in his bid for the presidency.

Following the election, Jordan cochaired the Clinton-Gore transition team with Los Angeles lawyer WARREN MINOR CHRISTOPHER. During the transition, Jordan approached COLIN L. POWELL to accept the position of secretary of state, but Powell declined. Warren Christopher was subsequently named secretary of state. During the campaign, it was reported that Jordan would be high on the list for the cabinet, particularly attorney general. Although no public announcement was made, Jordan reportedly turned down the position because he did not want to disclose his finances.

Jordan was drawn into the MONICA LEWINSKY scandal by independent counsel KENNETH W. STARR, for helping Lewinsky find a job after her relationship with Clinton had become public. Starr alleged that Jordan was using his corporate influence to buy Lewinsky's silence by finding her a well-paying job in New York City. Jordan was brought into the impeachment process in 1998 and gave a deposition to members of the House Judiciary Committee investigating impeachment. His taped deposition was used in the 1999 impeachment trial against the president.

In the early part of Jordan's career, he worked as a lawyer with the National Association for the Advancement of Colored People (NAACP), to integrate schools. He later became director of the National Urban League. Jordan was shot in the back on May 29, 1980, by a white supremacist who said he was out to kill "race mixers."

Born on August 15, 1935, Jordan received his B.A. from DePauw University in Indiana (1957) and a J.D. from Howard University (1960). He was a fellow at the Institute of Politics at the John F. Kennedy School of Government, Harvard University, in 1969. Growing up in Atlanta, Jordan attended segregated schools. After leaving law school, he practiced law first in Atlanta (1960–61) and then in Pine Bluff, Arkansas (1964–65). In the interim, he was the Georgia field director for the NAACP (1961–63). For four years, he served as the director of the Voter Education Project for the Southern Regional Council (1964–68) and was briefly an attorney for the Office of Equal Opportunity in Atlanta (1969). As he had done for nearly a decade, Jordan continued to pursue equal opportunity for African Americans in 1970–71 as the executive director of the United Negro College Fund. In 1972 he left to become the president of the National Urban League, where he remained for nearly a decade.

After devoting most of his professional career to civil rights issues, Jordan reentered private practice in 1981 as a senior partner in the Washington, D.C., law firm of Akin, Gump, Strauss, Hauer & Feld. In 2000, Jordan left the law firm to become the senior managing director of an investment banking firm in New York City, Lazard Frères & Co. Jordan sat on the board of directors of 11 major companies. In 1998, the *Washington Post* reported that Jordan had an income of more than $800,000 from work on the directorships, in addition to the $1 million he earned from his law firm. Among his corporate directorships were America Online Latin America, Asbury Automotive Group, Callaway Golf Company, Clear Channel Communications, Jones & Company, Howard University (trustee), J.C. Penney Company, Revlon, Xerox Corporation, DaimlerChrysler, and Fuji Bank.

K

Kantor, Michael (Mickey)

(1939–   ) *secretary of commerce, U.S. trade representative*

President-elect Clinton named Mickey Kantor as the U.S. trade representative on December 24, 1992. He was sworn into office on January 22, 1993. As U.S. trade representative, Kantor had the title of ambassador.

Kantor remained in the trade position until 1996 when he replaced RONALD H. BROWN as secretary of commerce. Brown had been killed in a plane crash in Bosnia while on a trade mission. CHARLENE BARSHEFSKY was named U.S. trade representative to replace Kantor. President Clinton nominated Kantor on April 12, 1996, as secretary of commerce.

After serving for four years in the Clinton administration, Kantor left after the first term to return to private law practice at a firm in Washington, D.C. He was replaced as secretary of commerce by WILLIAM MICHAEL DALEY.

Among the issues that Kantor dealt with as the U.S. trade representative were developing access for U.S. companies to Japan's computer chip markets. In addition, he sought to solve disputes with European nations over steel exports, subsidies to the Airbus, and utilities contracts for U.S. companies. During his three years as trade representative, Kantor concluded more than 170 trade agreements, including an auto parts agreement with Japan.

Kantor, who was the 1992 Clinton-Gore campaign chairman and director of the transition team, had known President and Mrs. Clinton for a number of years before the presidential campaign. After the election, Kantor was named the chair of the December 1992 economic summit in Little Rock, Arkansas, that was held prior to the inauguration.

Kantor had been active in Democratic politics for a number of years, first working on a presidential campaign in 1972 when Sargent Shriver entered the race. Kantor served as the national campaign manager for Jerry Brown in 1976. During the Carter administration, Kantor worked with Mrs. Clinton on the board of directors of the Legal Services Corporation. In the early 1990s Kantor worked with WARREN MINOR CHRISTOPHER on the proposed reforms of the Los Angeles Police Department following the Rodney King trial. King, an African American, had been beaten by Los Angeles police when he was apprehended. Both Christopher and Kantor were Los Angeles lawyers.

Born on August 7, 1939, in Nashville, Tennessee, Kantor graduated with a B.A. from Vanderbilt University (1961) and with a J.D. from

Georgetown University Law Center (1968). After college, Kantor served in the navy for four years, 1961–65. After leaving the navy, he worked for the Small Business Administration as a management intern (1965–66) and was promoted to the associate administrator for investment at the Small Business Administration (1966–68). In 1968 he became a staff attorney for the South Florida Migrant Legal Services. He left in 1970 to become the deputy director and general counsel of the Migrant Research Project, where he worked for a year. From 1970 to 1971 he was the director of the Program Development and Training Division of the Office of Legal Services, in 1972 was named the associate director of the National Legal Aid and Defender Association, and executive director of Action for Legal Rights (1971–72).

Kantor joined the law firm of Manatt, Phelps, and Phillips in Los Angeles in 1975, where he remained until joining the Clinton administration in 1993. After leaving the Clinton administration, Kantor joined the law firm of Mayer, Brown, Rowe, and Maw in Washington, D.C., and served as one of Clinton's private attorneys during the impeachment process in Congress.

Kelley, Virginia Cassidy Clinton
(1923–1994) *mother of President Clinton*

Virginia Clinton Kelley, mother of President Clinton, died on January 6, 1994, of breast cancer. Kelley underwent a mastectomy in 1990 and had suffered a recurrence of the cancer in 1993. She was buried in the cemetery in Hope, Arkansas, near the grave of Clinton's father, William Blythe. The January 8, 1994, funeral, which was held at the Hot Springs, Arkansas, Convention Center Auditorium, was attended by nearly 3,000 mourners. Her death was unexpected. Her husband, Richard Kelley, called President Clinton to tell him of her death, at which time President Clinton flew directly to Arkansas.

Virginia Kelley had been married five times, twice to the same man. When she died, she was married to her fourth husband, Richard Kelley.

President Clinton's father, William Jefferson Blythe, was killed in a car accident in 1944, according to Virginia Kelley. However, there is conflicting material on this information. According to a biography by David Maraniss, *First in His Class*, Blythe was serving in Italy with the army for the nine months before Bill Clinton's birth. According to Maraniss, it was unlikely that Blythe was the father, although

Secretary of Commerce Mickey Kantor
(Department of Commerce)

Virginia Kelley firmly stated he was. President Clinton's name at birth, however, was William Jefferson Blythe, IV.

Born on June 6, 1923, in Hope, Arkansas, Virginia Cassidy left Hope after graduating from high school and moved to Shreveport, Louisiana, to study nursing at Tri-State Hospital. While there she met William Jefferson Blythe and they were married on September 3, 1943. Two months later, he was sent to Europe with the army and she returned to Hope, Arkansas, to live with her parents. He returned to Arkansas in December 1945 after being honorably discharged from the army. Blythe died in a car accident on May 17, 1946, after his car rolled twice before landing in a ditch on the side of the road. He survived the car accident but fell into a drainage ditch and drowned trying to get to the road for help.

Bill Clinton was born on August 19, 1946. After his birth, Virginia Cassidy Blythe went to live with her parents. She left soon after to attend school in New Orleans and left Bill with his grandparents. He remained with them for four years. On June 19, 1950, she married a car salesman, Roger Clinton, whom she had met in New Orleans. The three then moved to Hot Springs, Arkansas, where Roger Clinton ran the parts department of his brother's car dealership. Virginia and Roger Clinton had one child, Roger.

Roger Clinton, Sr., was an alcoholic and abusive to Virginia Clinton. Roger and Virginia divorced when Bill Clinton was 15 years old. They quickly reconciled and were remarried. Bill then legally changed his name to Clinton. Roger Clinton died of cancer in 1968.

Virginia Clinton then married Jeff Dwire, who ran a beauty shop in Hot Springs. Dwire died of diabetes in 1974, and she married Richard Kelley, a food broker.

She retired in 1981 from her job as a practicing nurse anesthetist. In 1994 her autobiography, *Leading with My Heart*, was published. She died soon after completing the book.

Kendall, David Evan

(1944–   ) *private attorney to President Clinton in Whitewater investigation, Monica Lewinsky investigation*

David Kendall, a member of the Washington, D.C., law firm of Williams and Connolly, served as President Clinton's private attorney from 1993 to 2001. Kendall represented President Clinton during the independent counsel's investigation of the Whitewater land project and in the MONICA LEWINSKY investigation.

Kendall was hired by President Clinton as his personal attorney in 1993 when independent counsel ROBERT FISKE began an investigation into the Whitewater land project in Arkansas. In January 1998, KENNETH W. STARR, who succeeded Fiske as the independent counsel on Whitewater, expanded the investigation into allegations that President Clinton lied under oath in the *Jones v. Clinton* lawsuit.

The perjury charge by Starr involved an alleged affair between President Clinton and Monica Lewinsky, a White House intern, that emerged in the *Jones v. Clinton* civil lawsuit. President Clinton denied to PAULA CORBIN JONES's lawyers that he had an affair with Lewinsky. Lewinsky's name had emerged in the lawsuit to corroborate information that President Clinton had had a number of affairs as governor of Arkansas.

Throughout 1998, Starr conducted a massive investigation of the Clinton-Lewinsky relationship. In February 1998, Kendall, who was representing President Clinton, publicly accused the independent counsel of "out of control leaks" on his investigation.

In September 1998 Starr released a report to the House of Representatives detailing President Clinton's involvement with Lewinsky. Lewinsky had cooperated with Starr and had provided detailed information on every encounter with President Clinton, which were recorded in Starr's report. The report led to the December 1998 impeachment of President Clinton.

Kendall, a criminal defense attorney, had recommended to President Clinton that he not provide Starr with any information except testimony that was "legally correct." Clinton did not admit to the relationship with Lewinsky in the deposition he gave to Starr, only that he had not had "sexual relations." Kendall believed that the language was legally correct.

Kendall's strategy for dealing with Starr was focused on the legal ramifications of the proceedings, not the political ramifications. The political ramifications, however, were as severe as the legal ones, for the Republicans in Congress believed that Kendall's phrases had been lies, not "legally correct" language. The House, as a result, impeached President Clinton in December 1998 but the Senate failed to convict in January 1999.

Born on May 2, 1944, in Sheridan, Indiana, Kendall received his B.A., summa cum laude and Phi Beta Kappa, from Wabash College (1966), his M.A. from Oxford University as a Rhodes scholar (1968), and his J.D. from Yale University School of Law (1971). Kendall became friends with President and Mrs. Clinton when they were all students at Yale Law School. After law school, Kendall was a law clerk for U.S. Supreme Court Justice Byron White (1971–72) and then enlisted in the army (1972–73).

His career began as an associate counsel for the National Association for the Advancement of Colored People (NAACP) in the Legal Defense and Educational Fund section (1973). He worked at the NAACP for five years, litigating civil rights cases and particularly death penalty cases. In 1977 he argued *Coker v. Georgia*, in which the Supreme Court declared the death penalty unconstitutional in cases of rape. Other Supreme Court cases he argued included the death penalty cases *Gilmore v. Utah* (1976) and *Chaney v. Heckler* (1985).

Kendall joined the law firm of Williams and Connolly in 1978 and became a partner in 1981 as a litigator in both civil and criminal cases. He also served as an adjunct professor at Georgetown University Law Center and sat on the board of directors of the NAACP Legal Defense and Educational Fund.

Kennedy, Edward Moore
(1932–   ) *member of the Senate*

Edward M. Kennedy, often referred to as Ted, was elected as a Democrat to the Senate from Massachusetts on November 6, 1962, to fill the unexpired term of his brother, President John F. Kennedy.

While in law school at the University of Virginia, Kennedy managed the successful Senate reelection campaign in Massachusetts of his brother John. After graduation from law school, Kennedy returned to Massachusetts and was appointed assistant district attorney in Suffolk County, Massachusetts. He was paid $1 per year for the job, at his request. The following year, 1962, he was elected to the Senate and was reelected in 1964, 1970, 1976, 1982, 1988, 1994, and 2000 for the term ending January 3, 2007.

Although Kennedy had been repeatedly elected to the Senate, he never succeeded in his aspirations to the presidency. He was an unsuccessful candidate for the Democratic Party nomination for president in 1980, when he challenged incumbent Jimmy Carter for the nomination. While in the Senate, he was elected the Democratic Party whip from 1969–71; chair of the Judiciary Committee (1979–81), chair of the Committee on Labor and Human Resources (1987–95), chair of the Committee on Health, Education, Labor and Pensions (January 3–20, 2001 and June 6,

2001–January 3, 2002). After the assassination of his brother, Senator Robert Kennedy (D-N.Y.), in 1968, Senator Edward Kennedy became the leader of the liberal wing of the Democratic Party. Senator Robert Kennedy was assassinated during his presidential campaign just after he had won the Democratic primary in California in June 1968.

However, Edward Kennedy's political future was marred in July 1969 in an accident on the island of Chappaquiddick off Martha's Vineyard. A passenger in his car, Mary Jo Kopechne, drowned when the car he was driving went off the road near the beach into a tidal pond. Although he had been considered a possible Democratic candidate for president in 1976, he withdrew his name from the race in 1974. His bid in 1980 for the presidency was ended, largely due to constant references to the Chappaquiddick incident.

Kennedy was a staunch supporter of President Clinton's health care reform and welfare reform proposals in 1993 and 1994. In 1997, Kennedy was also a staunch supporter of President Clinton's race initiative and his affirmative action position.

Following the impeachment of President Clinton in the House of Representatives in December 1998, Senator Kennedy became his staunch defender in the Senate trial. In a statement published in the *Congressional Record* on February 12, 1999, Kennedy said, "The impeachment process was never intended to become a weapon for a partisan majority in Congress to attack the President. To do so is a violation of the fundamental separation of powers doctrine at the heart of the Constitution. It is an invitation to future partisan majorities in future Congresses to use the impeachment power to undermine the President. It could weaken Republican and Democratic Presidents alike for years to come. This case is a constitutional travesty. We deplore the conduct of President Clinton that led to this year long distraction for the nation. But we should deplore even more the partisan attempt to abuse the Constitution by misusing the impeachment power."

Born on February 22, 1932, in Brookline, Massachusetts, Kennedy graduated from Milton Academy in 1950. After he left Milton Academy, he entered Harvard College, but was expelled after his freshman year for having another student take a Spanish final examination for him. Kennedy then enlisted in the army and remained for two years (1951–53). While in the army, he was stationed at the Paris headquarters of the Supreme Headquarters Allied Powers, Europe (SHAPE). After his discharge from the army he returned to the United States and received his A.B. from Harvard College (1956) and his J.D. from the University of Virginia Law School (1959). He also studied at the International Law School at the Hague in Holland (1958).

Kennedy was divorced from Joan Bennett Kennedy in 1984, with whom he had three children, and married Victoria Reggie in 1992.

Kessler, David

(1951–) *commissioner, Food and Drug Administration*

David Kessler was appointed by President GEORGE HERBERT WALKER BUSH in 1990 as commissioner of the Food and Drug Administration. He remained in the position until 1997, when he resigned to become dean of the Yale School of Medicine.

Kessler, a pediatrician by training, went to the Food and Drug Administration with an agenda to reorganize the agency and to improve its mandate to regulate potentially harmful consumer products. Among the products that he sought to regulate was tobacco.

In 1996, the Food and Drug Administration under Kessler's leadership defined nicotine as an addictive drug. President Clinton fully supported the decision and announced that the Food and Drug Administration would begin regulating cigarette and smokeless tobacco advertising and sales. Under the new regulations, tobacco purchasers would be required to be 18 years of age. Cigarette vending machines were to be banned from locations frequented by children, such as grocery stores. President Clinton had urged the Food and Drug Administration in 1995 to adopt the regulation that nicotine was an addictive drug. According to Kessler, one of the most important outcomes of the regulation was that it "would prevent kids from becoming addicted to nicotine."

In spite of Kessler's efforts to regulate the tobacco industry, Congress refused to approve the regulations. After Kessler left office, the tobacco industry did admit to the addictive qualities of tobacco as a result of a massive lawsuit filed by state attorneys general. The settlement resulted in billions of dollars being paid to the states by the tobacco companies.

Kessler also dealt with a wide variety of other issues during his tenure at the Food and Drug Administration, including improving packaging to reduce product tampering, more effective food labeling, and stopping the international traffic in contaminated body parts. One of the more controversial issues that Kessler tackled was his decision to ban silicone breast implants after evidence indicated they could rupture once implanted.

Born on May 31, 1951, in New York City, Kessler graduated with a B.A., magna cum laude, from Amherst College (1973), with a J.D. from the University of Chicago Law School (1977) and with an M.D. from Harvard Medical School (1979). He also earned an advanced professional certificate from New York University Graduate School of Business Administration in 1986.

Kessler had served as consultant to the health staff of the Senate Committee on Labor and Human Resources (1981–84). His experience on the Senate Committee provided insight into the federal bureaucracy and the problems of regulating consumer products that would serve him during his tenure at the Food and Drug Administration. From 1984 until his appointment by President Bush in 1990 to the Food and Drug Administration, Kessler was the medical director of the hospital of the Albert Einstein College of Medicine, teaching in the Department of Pediatrics and the Department of Epidemiology and Social Medicine. He also taught food and drug law at the Columbia University School of Law from 1986 to 1990.

After leaving the Clinton administration, he was named dean of the Yale Medical School, where he also taught internal medicine and pediatrics. Kessler published a book, *A Question of Intent*, about the Food and Drug Administration's battle with the tobacco industry. He continued to be an outspoken critic of the tobacco industry, stating, "Nicotine is an addictive drug. It is the number one preventable cause of death."

Klain, Ronald

(1961–   ) *chief of staff to the vice president, chief of staff to the attorney general, associate counsel to the president*

Ronald Klain was appointed associate counsel to the president in January 1993 and remained in the White House until February 1994. In 1994 he was named chief of staff to Attorney General JANET RENO, and in 1995 was named chief of staff to Vice President ALBERT (AL) GORE, JR. During the 1992 transition, Klain served as associate general counsel, in charge of reviewing candidates for cabinet positions.

In his role as White House associate counsel, Klain handled nominations for judicial appointments, including the president's nominees for the Supreme Court and for attorney general. Among his roles was to lead the confirmation teams for Supreme Court Justice RUTH BADER GINSBURG and for Attorney General Janet Reno. Klain worked under BERNARD NUSSBAUM, counsel to the president, in what was often a stormy relationship. Klain warned Nussbaum that LANI GUINIER's views on majoritarian politics might be difficult for the administration to defend in her Senate confirmation hearings, but Nussbaum went forward with the nomination. Guinier, nominated to head the Civil Rights Division in the Department of Justice, was soon forced to withdraw her nomination after substantial opposition arose. After a year of working on judicial nominations in the White House, and a failure to move into the inner circle of a White House staff often tied together by bonds to Arkansas, Klain met with Chief of Staff THOMAS FRANKLIN McLARTY III and sought another job in the administration. McLarty agreed and asked Klain to coordinate the administration's efforts to move the crime bill through Congress with Attorney General Janet Reno.

At the Department of Justice Klain led the successful effort by the administration to pass the Violent Crime Control Act of 1994, which included a ban on semiautomatic assault weapons and the "100,000 cops" program. After enactment of the legislation in October 1994, Klain became Reno's chief of staff but found the job difficult because, as he noted, Deputy Attorney General Jamie Gorelick "really ran the show." He remained in the Justice Department for just three more months. In February 1995 Klain left the Clinton administration to become staff director for the Senate Democratic Leadership Committee. He had been strongly supported for the position by the newly selected Senate Democratic leader, Senator Tom Daschle (D-S.D.).

The White House wanted Klain to return as deputy director of the domestic policy council, but he turned down the offer. Shortly thereafter, JOHN QUINN moved from Vice President Gore's office, where he was chief of staff, to the White House, as the counsel to the president. Quinn recommended to Vice President Gore that Klain take his position as chief of staff and Gore agreed, hiring Klain in November 1995. Klain oversaw all of the vice president's staff and the staff of Mrs. Gore. He was given the title assistant to the president and chief of staff to the vice president. He was replaced as Vice President Gore's chief of staff by Charles Burson in October 1999.

After leaving the White House, Klain joined the Los Angeles–based Washington, D.C., law firm of O'Melveny & Myers in October 1999. He remained involved in Democratic politics once in private practice, serving as an unpaid campaign strategist for the Gore-Lieberman presidential campaign in 2000. When Vice President Gore challenged the election results, Klain took on legal work for the campaign. On leave from O'Melveny & Myers in 2000, he served as general counsel of the Gore-Lieberman recount committee. He headed the legal team that challenged the Florida secretary of state's decision denying a recount of votes.

When he returned to O'Melveny & Myers, he became national chair of the firm's strategic counseling practice group. In 1994, Klain was named by *Time* magazine as one of the most promising 50 leaders in the country who were younger than 40. His wife, Monica Medina, served as general counsel for the National Oceanic and Atmospheric Administration (NOAA).

Born August 8, 1961, Klain received his B.A. from Georgetown University, summa cum laude (1983) and his J.D. from Harvard Law School, magna cum laude (1987). He was an editor of the *Harvard Law Review*. Before entering law school, Klain worked on the staff of Rep. Edward J. Markey (D-Mass.) as a legislative assistant for telecommunications issues and as Markey's campaign manager for his 1984 Senate campaign. From 1986–87 he worked on the minority staff of the Senate Judiciary Committee.

After graduation from law school, Klain served as a law clerk for Justice Byron R. White (1987–88). His clerkship led to a position as chief counsel of the Senate Judiciary Committee, where he remained until 1992. During 1988, he had also worked on the brief campaign of Senator Joseph Biden for president. Not surprisingly, Biden, who was chairman of the Senate Judiciary Committee, nominated Klain for the chief counsel's job on the committee (1989–92). He became the youngest chief counsel in the committee's history.

Klain left the Senate Judiciary Committee staff in 1992 to work for the Clinton campaign as the issues director in Washington and as part of the team that prepared Clinton for the presidential debates. After the election, Senator Biden recommended Klain for a White House position in the counsel's office, a recommendation that was supported by RICHARD WILSON RILEY, the personnel director for the transition team. In an interview with President-elect Clinton, Klain was immediately hired.

Koresh, David
(1959–1993) *cult leader*

David Koresh was the leader of the Branch Davidian cult in a compound outside of Waco, Texas. The cult was involved in a 51-day standoff with state, local, and federal officials, which ended when a building in the compound burned to the ground. The blaze, on April 19, 1993, resulted in the deaths of 80 people, including Koresh and 20 children.

Koresh was a ninth-grade dropout raised in Garland, Texas, a Dallas suburb. He was born Vernon Wayne Howell. He became enamored of the Bible at an early age, and formed his religious group, the Branch Davidians, as a renegade offshoot of the Seventh-Day Adventists.

Koresh became involved with the Branch Davidians in the mid-1970s. The cult believed that the world was coming to an end and that the righteous must fight their way to heaven. Members of the cult were taught to shoot guns as part of this requirement. The compound in Waco, Texas, had been owned by the sect since the 1950s and was used as a religious camp by Koresh and his followers.

Koresh had been the leader of the cult in Waco since 1987 when he won the leadership from George Roden in a cult test. Roden, then the leader of the cult, challenged Koresh to a test of divine powers to see who could resurrect an elderly woman who had been buried on the compound for two decades. For reasons that are unclear, Koresh shot at Roden 18 times and was later charged with attempted murder. The trial resulted in a hung jury, and the charges were dropped. Koresh became the leader of the cult when Roden then left.

Koresh demanded that his followers at the compound abide by strict rules: no meat, no alcohol, no caffeine. Men and women were segregated, with each having appropriate responsibilities on the farm. Bible study often lasted for 15 hours. Koresh had sexual relations with many of the women, fathering at least 20 children who were at the compound. The cult drew members from other countries, including Britain, Australia, New Zealand, Jamaica, and Israel. Of the 80 people in the compound, approximately 40 were black.

The crisis that led to the deaths of Koresh and the others began when reports surfaced of constant gunfire at the compound. The Bureau of Alcohol, Tobacco and Firearms (ATF) believed that weapons were being illegally brought into the compound. The ATF surrounded the compound for 51 days and demanded that Koresh and his followers surrender. The standoff ended in gunfire, which the ATF denied having started. In circumstances that remain unclear, the main building caught fire in the compound where Koresh stayed, and approximately 80 people in the building were killed.

The incident led to an inquiry in the Department of Justice to determine whether the ATF agents had acted appropriately. Attorney General JANET RENO eventually made changes in the ATF, which was a unit within the Department of Justice, but the ATF agents were not penalized. President Clinton was not involved in the decision making in the Waco incident nor in the Justice Department internal review.

In addition to the Department of Justice review of the deaths of the Branch Davidians in Waco, Reno appointed JOHN DANFORTH as special counsel to conduct an independent investigation. Danforth, a Republican, had served in the U.S. Senate for three terms (1977–95) representing Missouri. Reno appointed him on September 9, 1999, after he had left the Senate, to lead the Department of Justice investigation into the April 19, 1993, standoff in Waco. As special counsel, Danforth was charged with determining whether the government had made mistakes in the incident and whether any government employee had used incendiary devices or engaged in gunfire at the Mt. Carmel compound. He was also charged with determining if any federal employees, particularly the FBI agents, had committed perjury during the initial investigation or destroyed evidence.

Kuchma, Leonid
(1938–   ) *president of Ukraine*

Leonid Kuchma was elected president of Ukraine in June 1994 and reelected in November 1999 to a second term. Immediately after taking office, Kuchma created the Constitutional Commission, which led to the adoption of a constitution for Ukraine in 1996. Kuchma's career had been devoted to developing space technology rather than to politics. He had a Ph.D. in mechanical engineering and rose to become the director of the space engineering complex in the Ukraine (previously a Russian-led space complex before the breakup of the USSR).

At the heart of Kuchma's economic program for Ukraine was full integration into the European Union and membership in the North Atlantic Treaty Organization (NATO). His efforts to build stronger relations with the West included rapprochement with the United States. He succeeded in securing immediate financial assistance from President Clinton.

Kuchma visited the United States in 1993, seeking economic assistance for Ukraine's failing economy. In 1994 the inflation rate was a staggering 4,735 percent, which was brought down to 842 percent in 1994. The goal was to bring the rate down to 210 percent in 1995. President Clinton supported economic assistance for Ukraine and announced at Kuchma's visit to Washington, D.C., in 1994 that the United States would supply an emergency $100 million for food and energy with no strings attached. The World Bank also released a $500 million loan to help pay for energy bought from Russia. Russia and Turkemenistan, the main oil providers to Ukraine, deferred $350 million in energy payments.

Kuchma was elected chairman of the loose alliance of former Soviet republics, the Commonwealth of Independent States (CIS), on January 29, 2003. It was the first time that a non-Russian president had been chosen to head the group since its creation in 1991. Kuchma was unanimously elected chairman after Russian president VLADIMIR PUTIN nominated him at the CIS summit.

Born on August 9, 1938, Kuchma graduated from Dnepropetrovsk State University, Department of Physical Engineering (1960), and earned his Ph.D. in mechanical engineering from Dnepropetrovsk State University. From 1960 to 1982, Kuchma worked as a technical designer at the Pivdenne (Southern) Design Bureau of the Pivdennyi Machine (Building Works), which was the world's largest space industry complex. He later worked as a technical director at the Baykonur Space Launch Complex. In 1982 he was appointed the first deputy to the chief designer of Pivdenne, and from 1986–92 he worked as the director general of Pivdenne.

In 1990 and again in 1994 he was elected to the Ukrainian parliament (the Verkhovna Rada). In October 1992 Kuchma was appointed prime minister, where he remained until September 1993. At that time he was elected president of the Ukrainian Union of Industrialists and Entrepreneurs. In July 1994, after a nationwide election, running against six other candidates, Kuchma was elected president of Ukraine.

Since 1991 he has been a member of the Engineering Academy of Ukraine. In 1992, he joined the faculty of Dnepropetrovsk State University. He received the Lenin Prize and the State Prize of the Ukrainian SSR, for achievements in design and development of rocket and space technologies.

Kunin, Madeleine

(1933–) *ambassador to Switzerland, deputy secretary of education*

Madeleine Kunin served three terms as the governor of Vermont (1985–91). She was the state's first female governor. When President Clinton took office, Kunin was appointed deputy secretary of education in 1993 under Secretary of Education RICHARD RILEY.

She remained in the Department of Education until 1996, when she was named ambassador to Switzerland. While ambassador (1996–99), she was charged by President Clinton with facilitating the return of Swiss bank account funds to Holocaust survivors. The child of a Jewish family in Zurich, Kunin had fled Switzerland in her youth to escape a continent under attack by Nazi invasion. Her return to Switzerland as ambassador was a long road for the young woman who had escaped Hitler's brutal tyranny.

During her tenure as deputy secretary of education, Kunin was responsible for working with the White House on major initiatives such as national service, youth apprenticeship programs, and welfare reform. Among the most significant roles she played was overseeing the education bill the administration sought.

In 1995 she was a candidate for the New York State Education Commissioner. She withdrew her name from the list of six finalists, stating that she was going to remain at the Department of Education to deal with budget cuts. Since she had no experience as an educator, she was viewed as a long-shot candidate. Her withdrawal was viewed as a graceful exit from a job she would probably not have been offered.

After leaving her post as ambassador to Switzerland, Kunin became the Bicentennial Scholar in residence at Middlebury College in Vermont. She remained active in politics, working on Vice President ALBERT (AL) GORE JR.'s presidential campaign in 2000 as honorary cochair of the Vermont Democrats for Gore Committee.

Kunin was born on September 28, 1933, in Switzerland but fled with her brother and widowed mother to the United States in 1940 as Hitler advanced in Europe. The family settled in Queens, New York, with relatives and later moved to Pittsfield, Massachusetts. She became the first member of her family to graduate from college, securing a degree in history from the University of Massachusetts (1956). She later received a master's degree in journalism from Columbia University.

Since few newspapers would hire a woman, Kunin finally found a job as a reporter for the Burlington, Vermont, *Free Press*. She married and left work to raise her four children. In 1970 she returned to Switzerland with her family for the first time since she had fled 30 years earlier. The experience of seeing Switzerland again left her committed to social justice, leading to her entry into politics. She won a seat in the Vermont House of Representatives in 1972, was elected lieutenant governor in 1978, and won the governorship in 1984 after having lost the election for governor in 1982. She won three consecutive terms as governor, but did not seek a fourth two-year term in 1990.

After leaving the governor's office in 1990, Kunin accepted a fellowship at Radcliffe College for two years (1991–93).

Lader, Philip

(1946–) *ambassador to the United Kingdom; administrator, Small Business Administration; deputy chief of staff; deputy director, Office of Management and Budget*

Philip Lader, a South Carolina business executive, founded the Renaissance Institute weekends at Hilton Head Island, South Carolina, which President and Mrs. Clinton attended. The Clintons had attended the Renaissance weekends for nearly 10 years. Lader and his wife, Linda LeSourd, established the weekends in 1981. The Renaissance weekends were designed for leisure activities, but combined lectures and discussion groups for political leaders, business executives, retired military, and policymakers on Hilton Head Island.

Lader was brought into the administration as deputy director of the Office of Management and Budget (OMB) in January 1993 under LEON EDWARD PANETTA, director of the OMB. In a major shakeup of the White House staff, Lader was moved from OMB in November 1993 to his new role as deputy chief of staff under Chief of Staff THOMAS FRANKLIN McLARTY III. Lader replaced Deputy Chief of Staff ROY NEEL, who left the administration to enter the private sector.

Neel had been a Gore staffer in the Senate but was never given broad responsibility for managing White House operations. In contrast, Lader was given responsibility for overseeing all White House operations and staff, including the policy councils.

Nearly two years later, in October 1994, President Clinton appointed Lader to serve as the administrator of the Small Business Administration. He was confirmed unanimously by the Senate on October 11, 1994. When the Senate Small Business Committee reviewed his nomination, they endorsed it in a 22-0 vote. As head of the Small Business Administration, Lader was a member of the National Economic Council, one of the White House policy units, and sat on the president's cabinet.

Lader replaced ERSKINE B. BOWLES at the Small Business Administration. Bowles was a business executive from North Carolina, whom Clinton had also met at the Renaissance weekends. Bowles essentially swapped jobs with Lader, for Bowles was named deputy chief of staff in the White House replacing Lader. McLarty left in August 1994 and was replaced by Leon Panetta, director of the OMB, giving President Clinton a new team in the chief of staff's office with both Panetta and Bowles.

In 1997, Lader was nominated by President Clinton as the ambassador to the Court of St. James (Great Britain), where he remained until the end of the administration in 2001. He was confirmed unanimously as he had been at the Small Business Administration. Lader, who wanted to get to know the people of Great Britain, walked the length of England and Scotland in 1997 and 1998.

Born on March 17, 1946, Lader received his B.A., Phi Beta Kappa, from Duke University (1966), his M.A. from the University of Michigan in history (1967), studied law at Oxford University (1967–68), and received his J.D. at Harvard Law School (1972). Lader's professional career involved management in a variety of land development recreational projects, including the Sea Pines Company. He also served as president of Bond University (1991–93) in Australia and of South Carolina's Winthrop College (1986). In 2001 Lader became chairman of WPP Group, a worldwide advertising and communications services company which included J. Walter Thompson, Young & Rubicam, Ogilvy & Mather, Hill & Knowlton, and Burson-Marstellar. WPP Group had 51,000 employees in 106 countries.

Anthony Lake *(Courtesy of Anthony Lake)*

Lake, Anthony (Tony)

(1939–) *failed nominee for director of the Central Intelligence Agency (CIA), assistant to the president for national security*

Tony Lake served as the assistant to the president for national security and director of the National Security Council through the first term of the administration (1993–97). He was succeeded by SAMUEL BERGER as national security advisor in 1997.

At the beginning of the second term, Lake was nominated by President Clinton as director of the Central Intelligence Agency (CIA) to replace JOHN DEUTCH, who resigned. The Lake nomination was sent to the Senate in January 1997. But after the Senate confirmation hearings failed to produce substantial support for the nomination, Lake withdrew his name from consideration on March 17, 1997. President Clinton subsequently nominated GEORGE JOHN TENET as director of the Central Intelligence Agency, who was successfully confirmed by the Senate in July 1997.

It was evident that Lake's nomination was stalled and would not be favorably supported in the Senate. Senator Richard C. Shelby (R-Ala.), chairman of the Senate Intelligence

Committee, strongly opposed Lake and blocked the nomination. Lake left the administration after his failed confirmation hearings for a position at the Edmund A. Walsh School of Foreign Service at Georgetown University.

President Clinton nominated Tenet, the deputy director of the CIA, as director after Lake withdrew his name. Tenet was successfully confirmed.

Lake's failure to gain support for his nomination as CIA director stemmed from a combination of factors, including his political leanings, which many Republicans felt were too liberal, and his actions as national security advisor. Republicans were particularly concerned about Lake's support for a new policy toward Cuba which would have opened relations with the communist country. Republicans charged that Lake's Cuba policy was designed to court Cuban Americans in southern Florida who had traditionally voted Republican. They also charged that the Cuba policy contradicted efforts to deal with drug smuggling in Latin America, which Republicans believed was tied directly to Castro. Lake was also charged by Republicans with irregularities in the 1996 presidential campaign fund-raising, which he denied.

During his tenure as national security advisor, Lake negotiated peace agreements between Israel and the Palestine Liberation Organization (PLO). Lake developed the policy of "dual containment" of both Iraq and Iran, following the Iraq-Iran eight-year war in the 1980s. One of his key goals while in office was to strengthen the United Nations as a tool for solving international problems.

Although he did not know Clinton well, Lake worked for the Clinton campaign and became the senior foreign policy adviser for the 1992 presidential campaign. His relationship with Clinton during the campaign led to his appointment as the president's national security advisor. Lake's appointment as national security adviser was encouraged by Warren Christopher, who served as the codirector with Vernon Jordan of the transition team in 1992. Lake and Christopher had been friends for a number of years.

Born on April 2, 1939, Lake received his A.B., magna cum laude, from Harvard College (1961), studied international economics at Trinity College, Cambridge University for two years, and received his Ph.D. at the Woodrow Wilson School of Public and International Affairs, Princeton University (1974).

After graduating from college, Lake was selected as a foreign service officer with the Department of State (1962–70). He served as vice consul in Saigon, Vietnam (1963), as vice consul in Hue, Vietnam (1964–65), and as special assistant to the president for national security affairs, working under Henry Kissinger on the Nixon staff (1969–70). Lake resigned his position on the Nixon staff to protest the administration's extension of the Vietnam War into Cambodia.

From 1977–81, Lake was director of policy planning for President Carter in the Department of State. Lake reported directly to Secretary of State Cyrus Vance. In 1981, when the Carter administration left office, Lake left Washington, D.C., to accept a faculty position at Amherst College. In 1984 he left Amherst College to accept a position at Mt. Holyoke College, where he was named the Five College Professor for International Relations. He remained on the faculty of Mt. Holyoke until his appointment to the Clinton White House as national security advisor. Lake was also a member of the Council on Foreign Relations.

Lake served on the board of directors of the U.S. Fund for UNICEF, the International Committee of the Red Cross, the Carnegie Council on Ethics and International Affairs, and St. Mary's College of Maryland.

Lancaster, Ralph I., Jr.

(1930–) *independent counsel, investigation of Secretary of Labor Alexis Herman*

Ralph Lancaster was named the independent counsel, appointed by the U.S. Court of Appeals for the District of Columbia, in May 1998 to investigate allegations against Secretary of Labor ALEXIS HERMAN. The investigation ended in April 2000 with no charges filed against Herman.

The appointment of Lancaster in 1998 was the result of an investigation by Department of Justice lawyers and Federal Bureau of Investigation (FBI) agents into whether Herman had given a former business associate, Vanessa Weaver, undue access to the White House. The charges stemmed from Herman's tenure as director of public liaison in the White House during the first term.

Herman was charged with influence peddling by Laurent Yene, who had worked at Herman's consulting firm, A.M. Herman and Associates, but the two had had a falling out. Yene accused Herman of funneling business to Weaver in exchange for contributions to Democratic organizations in 1996 and for taking 10 percent of consulting fees from business related to the White House.

After several months of internal investigations, Attorney General JANET RENO sought the appointment of an independent counsel to investigate the charges in May 1998. Independent counsel Ralph Lancaster conducted the investigation, including a September 1999 interview of President Clinton about Herman's conduct in the White House. The charges were dropped when no evidence was found against Herman.

Born on May 19, 1930, in Bangor, Maine, Lancaster received his B.A. from the College of the Holy Cross (1952) and his LL.B. from Harvard Law School (1955). After law school, Lancaster served as a law clerk to Edward T. Gignoux, U.S. district judge for the District of Maine. Lancaster then joined the law firm of Pierce Atwood in Portland, Maine, in 1959. He rose to managing partner of the firm during his tenure there. When he was appointed the independent counsel to investigate Herman, he was with Pierce Atwood and he returned to Pierce Atwood after the investigation was completed.

In 1984 Lancaster was the counsel for the United States before the International Court of Justice at the Hague in the case concerning the delimitation of the maritime boundary in the Gulf of Maine. He also represented Chief Justice David Brock of New Hampshire in the investigation leading up to an impeachment trial.

Lee Teng-hui

(1923–) *president of Taiwan*

Lee Teng-hui was elected president by the National Assembly of the Republic of China, better known as Taiwan, on March 21, 1990. He became the first popularly elected president in the nation's history. Lee was reelected by a landslide in 1995. He left office in May 2000.

President Clinton supported a two-China policy, in which both China and Taiwan were recognized as sovereign nations. Clinton did not support any policy that allowed China to take over Taiwan militarily, which many in the Chinese political leadership supported. During 1995, China conducted missile tests designed to reinforce China's military power and its ability to overtake Taiwan at any time. China's constant efforts to minimize the role of Taiwan in the international community were evidenced in 2001 when Lee sought medical treatment in Japan. China protested when Japan granted Lee a visa for the medical treatment.

Since 1988 Lee had been president of the Kuomintang (KMT) party, which had provided the support for his presidential victory in 1990. During his 10 years as president of Taiwan, Lee oversaw the transformation of Taiwan into a multiparty democracy. With the rise of other political parties in Taiwan in the democratic tradition that Lee encouraged, the KMT party lost its dominance in the political structure. On April 1, 2000, after the presidential election, thousands of protesters demanded Lee's resignation for leading his KMT party to defeat. Ten thousand people demonstrated around the clock in front of the KMT party headquarters. They believed that had Lee not allowed the party to be divided, with James Soong Chu-yu leading a faction of the party in his own race for president, the party would have remained in power.

Lee was not a candidate for president in 2000, but quietly supported former Taipei mayor Chen Shui-bian of the Democratic Progressive Party (DPP). Members of the KMT party resented Lee's failure to support James Soong Chu-yu, an independent candidate and former KMT secretary-general. The KMT party splintered among the followers of Lee and those of Soong. Lee refused to support Soong.

In 1999, when the KMT was deciding whom to support for president and vice president, Lee refused to support Soong for either position. During the 2000 campaign, Lee rallied support against Soong and often appeared to support the other DPP candidate, Chen Shui-bian.

Born January 15, 1923, Lee graduated from Cornell University in 1968. Lee's support for western education was evidenced by the cabinet that he chose: the vice president of Taiwan had a degree from the University of Chicago and 18 of 32 cabinet members had doctorates from schools in the West.

Lee, Bill Lann

(1949–   ) *assistant attorney general for civil rights, Department of Justice*

Bill Lann Lee, a Chinese American, was nominated by President Clinton as assistant attorney general for civil rights in the Department of Justice in October 1997. Lee became the first person who was neither white nor African American to head the civil rights division. Lee replaced DEVAL PATRICK, who was African American, in the position.

Lee's confirmation was strongly opposed in the Republican-controlled Senate and was subsequently blocked. During his confirmation hearings, Lee made the mistake of noting that during his eight years at the National Association for the Advancement of Colored People (NAACP) Legal Defense and Education Fund (1989–97), he supported racial preferences, quotas, and forced busing. These positions angered most Republicans and quickly led to his defeat in the Senate Judiciary Committee.

Lee denied in the Senate hearings that he would use the Civil Rights Division to pursue affirmative action. He stated that the focus of the division would be on a variety of issues, including hate crimes. "I wanted to do more," Lee said of his role in the division, "in terms of litigation, and to take the legislative lead on hate crime, on housing discrimination, and particularly with respect to lending, and on Americans with Disabilities Act enforcement."

As a result of the Senate's failure to confirm, Lee was named assistant attorney general through a recess appointment in December 1997 (while the Senate was on Christmas recess). In March 1999 President Clinton renominated Lee in the Senate for the position of assistant attorney general, but committee chairman Orrin Hatch (R-Utah) said he "would support [Lee] for almost any other position in government but not for the head of the civil rights division." Recess appointments can be of two types. The first type is a recess appointment made by the president that lasts until the end of the upcoming session. The second type is a recess appointment that lasts until the end of the session after the one in which the appointment is made.

After Lee's recess appointment, Senator Orrin Hatch (R-Utah), chairman of the Senate Judiciary Committee and a strong opponent of Lee's confirmation, stated that "Lee would be among the most congressionally scrutinized bureaucrats in history." Hatch implied that his committee would conduct regular oversight hearings on Lee's division in the Justice Department and the decisions that it made. During the confirmation hearings, Hatch and other Republicans had noted that Lee was a strong supporter of affirmative action and could not be trusted to be unbiased about race relations.

On August 3, 2000, Lee was reappointed through a recess appointment (while the Senate was in summer recess for the Democratic and Republican national conventions). The recess appointment allowed Lee to remain in the position until the beginning of the next Congress. His confirmation had been strongly supported by the Asian-American community, which held rallies to support his 1997 Senate confirmation, and by the National Organization for Women (NOW).

Lee, the son of Chinese immigrant parents who operated a hand laundry in New York City's Harlem neighborhood, was born on February 5, 1949, and received his B.A., magna cum laude, Phi Beta Kappa, from Yale University (1971) and his J.D. from Columbia University Law School (1974). He was named the Stone scholar and won the prize for Best Moot Court Brief. After graduating from law school, Lee worked as an assistant counsel with the NAACP Legal Defense and Education Fund (1974–82). He left the NAACP in 1983 to work for the Center for Law in the Public Interest in Los Angeles, where he was the supervising attorney for civil rights litigation (1983–88). He returned to the NAACP in 1988 as the western regional counsel for the NAACP Legal Defense and Education Fund, which was headquartered in Los Angeles (1988–97). Lee was the first Asian American to work for the NAACP Legal Defense and Education Fund.

After leaving the Clinton administration, Lee worked for most of the year on an international human rights report as a visiting scholar at Columbia University Law School. The report was funded by the Ford Foundation. Later that year (1991), Lee became a partner in the law firm of Lieff, Cabraser, Heiman & Bernstein LLP, with offices in San Francisco and Washington, D.C.

Lee, Sheila Jackson
(1950–   ) *member of the House of Representatives*

Sheila Jackson Lee (D-Tex.), first elected to the House of Representatives from the 18th Congressional District in Texas in 1994, was a strong supporter of President Clinton in the House. She became one of his key supporters as a member of the House Judiciary Committee during the impeachment hearings in 1998.

Lee, an African American, won the House seat from incumbent Craig Washington (D-Tex.), also an African American, whom she defeated in the Democratic primary election. She won the general election in 1994 with 72 percent of the vote, the 1996 election with 77 percent of the vote, and was unopposed in the 1998 election. Before her election to the House, Lee had been a member of the Houston City Council since 1990.

Throughout her career, Jackson had been involved in breaking down racial barriers. Lee became one of the first group of women to integrate Yale University. She went on to become the first African-American woman to serve as an at-large city council member in Houston. Her goal, she stated, throughout her career "was to be a change maker, to make a difference, open doors that have been slammed shut, tread upon ground that has not been trod upon and reach beyond myself and help someone else."

As a member of the Judiciary Committee in the House, Lee opposed the Republican majority on the Judiciary Committee in their efforts to impeach President Clinton in 1998. She was a constant supporter of President Clinton throughout the impeachment process.

During her tenure in the House, she was elected vice chair of the Black Caucus, a group of African-American members of the House. After the 2000 presidential election, she used her position on the House Judiciary Committee to support election reform, calling for national standards for elections.

Twenty years earlier, Lee's seat in the House had been held by another prominent African American, Representative Barbara Jordan, who also represented Houston's 18th Congressional District. As had Jordan, Lee sat on the Judiciary Committee that held hearings on a president's impeachment. For Jordan it was President Nixon (1974) and for Lee it was President Clinton (1998).

Lee received her B.A. from Yale University and her J.D. from the University of Virginia. She served as a special counsel to the U.S. Select Committee on Assassinations for the 95th Congress and as a municipal judge in Houston prior to her election to the Houston City Council. While in the House of Representatives, she sat on the Judiciary and Science Committees.

Her husband, Dr. Elwyn Lee, was vice president of student affairs and special assistant to the president of the University of Houston.

Levitt, Arthur, Jr.
(1931–   ) *chairman, Securities and Exchange Commission*

Arthur Levitt, Jr., was sworn into office in July 1993 to a five-year term as chairman of the Securities and Exchange Commission (SEC) and was reappointed to a second five-year term in May 1998. He resigned in February 2001.

A long-time Democrat, Levitt resigned from the SEC on February 9, 2001, soon after the Bush administration took office, even though his term had not expired. However, by remaining for eight years as chair of the SEC, he became the longest-serving chairman in its history. The SEC, created in 1934 during the administration of Franklin Delano Roosevelt, was established to serve as the watchdog agency for investors in publicly traded companies and to ensure that they were independently audited.

Levitt was a major fund-raiser for the Democratic Party and for the Clinton presidential campaign in 1992. He was closely allied with a host of Democratic Party leaders, including Edward Rendell, who headed the Democratic National Committee.

As chair of the Securities and Exchange Commission, one of Levitt's goals was to have mutual fund companies issue prospectuses and disclosure forms that were easy for the average investor to read. The change in how these prospectuses and disclosures forms were written became one of the major legacies of Levitt's leadership. Another legacy was the improved ability of investors to understand the performance of the mutual funds they owned or wanted to invest in. Levitt's staff set up an Internet Web site for the SEC that allowed investors in mutual funds to evaluate their performance. Levitt constantly urged investors to be vigilant in their choice of investments and to be similarly vigilant in questioning their brokers. He was known during his tenure at the

SEC for holding town meetings on various financial topics.

One of the most popular innovations during Levitt's tenure was the creation of the Office of Investor Education and Assistance, which created the SEC's Web site to allow investors to see all corporate filings free of charge. He also held town meetings around the country to allow citizens to discuss any aspect of their problems with the investment process.

Levitt was known as a champion of investors for his oversight of mutual funds and for his town meetings. Among the causes he pursued as chairman of the SEC was to force the National Association of Securities Dealers (NASD) board to develop new rules for trading, after allegations of possible price fixing on its floor. One of his major goals was to encourage foreign companies to list on the U.S. exchanges.

As early as 1998, three years before the revelations in 2001 of corporate misconduct of companies such as Enron and WorldCom, Levitt urged companies to be forthright in their financial statements to investors. Levitt believed that too many outside auditors were joining corporate executives in "a game of winks and nods," as he described it. He argued that the auditors should not work as information technology consultants to their audit clients. The majority of the large accounting firms opposed him, and Levitt settled for a requirement that corporations disclose how much they pay accounting firms for auditing and for their other services.

Born on February 3, 1931, Levitt was a graduate, Phi Beta Kappa, of Williams College (1952), where he majored in English. After graduation, he began working in the marketing department of *Time* magazine in New York City. In 1959 he changed careers and accepted a position with Oppenheimer Industries in Kansas City, Missouri. He spent three years selling cattle tax shelters with Oppenheimer.

Finding that he preferred the financial world to the media world, Levitt returned to New York City in 1963 to join the Wall Street brokerage firm of Carter, Berlind & Weill. Levitt was later named a partner in the firm and rose to the position of president.

As president of Carter, Berlind & Weill, Levitt helped to guide the firm through several mergers before it was sold to American Express. Levitt left in 1978 to become chair and CEO of the American Stock Exchange (AMEX). Levitt modernized the operations at AMEX and kept it as an independent organization, rather than merging with the New York Stock Exchange.

When Levitt left the Clinton administration in January 2001, he joined M&T Bank in Buffalo, New York, as an advisory director. He also received a book contract to discuss his view of the nation's financial markets.

Lew, Jacob J. (Jack)

(1955–   ) *director, Office of Management and Budget; deputy director, Office of Management and Budget; associate director for legislative affairs and executive associate director, Office of Management and Budget*

Jacob Lew was nominated by President Clinton as director of the Office of Management and Budget (OMB) in 1998 and remained with the administration until 2001.

FRANKLIN D. RAINES, the director of the OMB at the time, resigned on May 20, 1998. When Lew was nominated by President Clinton at the White House on May 13, 1998, in a ceremony noting Raines's departure and Lew's appointment, Lew said, "It has been an honor to serve as deputy to ALICE RIVLIN and Frank Raines, on an economic team with ERSKINE B. BOWLES, ROBERT RUBIN, GENE SPERLING, JANET YELLIN, and LARRY SUMMERS; to work alongside ELI SEGAL to launch AmeriCorps, and with the First Lady on health care reform. I'm truly honored to be nominated today."

Prior to his appointment as director, Lew had held several positions in OMB during the Clinton administration, including deputy director (1995–98), executive associate director and associate director for legislative affairs (1994–95). Before moving to OMB, he had been in the White House as a special assistant to the president (1993–94).

Born August 29, 1955, Lew graduated with an A.B. from Harvard College (1978) and a J.D. from the Georgetown University Law Center (1983). He was executive director for the Center for Middle East Research (1992–93) and a partner with the firm of Van Ness, Feldman & Curtiss (1987–91). He was issues director for the Democratic National Committee's Campaign 88 and deputy director of the Office of Program Analysis in the City of Boston's Office of Management and Budget.

Lew began his political career in Washington, D.C., in 1973 as a legislative aide and became a principal domestic policy adviser to House Speaker Thomas P. "Tip" O'Neill, Jr., in 1979. He spent eight years at the House Democratic Steering and Policy Committee as assistant director and then executive director.

Lewinsky, Monica

(1973–) *involved in independent counsel's investigation of President Clinton*

Monica Lewinsky had an 18-month extramarital affair with President Clinton that became the subject of an investigation by an independent counsel, KENNETH W. STARR. The Starr investigation, with which Lewinsky cooperated, led to questions about President Clinton's truthful statements about the affair with Lewinsky to the independent counsel. Clinton denied the affair to Starr, leading to charges of perjury by Starr's office and leading eventually to impeachment. President Clinton was impeached in the House of Representatives in December 1998 but acquitted in the Senate in February 1999, based primarily on the perjury (denial of the affair) charges relating to the Lewinsky affair.

Lewinsky's relationship with President Clinton began while she was an intern in the White House. Lewinsky, who was 21, started in the White House as an unpaid intern in June 1995 and began a relationship with President Clinton in November 1995.

In December 1995, Lewinsky was given a paid position in the White House Office of Legislative Affairs, dealing with letters from members of Congress. Deputy Chief of Staff Evelyn Lieberman, who managed personnel in the White House, believed that Lewinsky had displayed "inappropriate and immature behavior" at the White House and transferred her to the Department of Defense to work in the press office. While working at the Department of Defense, Lewinsky met LINDA TRIPP, a career government employee, who tape-recorded her conversations with Lewinsky.

The impeachment proceedings were based on a report that Congress received from the independent counsel on the Lewinsky-Clinton affair. Kenneth Starr sent to Congress a graphic 453-page report, along with thousands of pages of supporting material, which detailed Lewinsky's affair with President Clinton. The material came directly from Monica Lewinsky's testimony to the grand jury after she had been granted immunity. The Starr Report, as it became known, was issued on September 11, 1998.

Monica Lewinsky provided direct testimony of the affair with President Clinton to the independent counsel, including times, dates, and details of their encounters. Lewinsky also gave prosecutors their strongest physical evidence— a stained dress she wore during an encounter with Clinton, which had his DNA on it.

The independent counsel was given substantial ammunition by Tripp, Lewinsky's friend and confidante, who on January 12, 1998, gave Kenneth Starr tapes that she had secretly made of telephone conversations in which Lewinsky, then a 21-year-old White House intern, spoke of an affair with Clinton. The next day, at Starr's request, the Federal Bureau of Investigation (FBI) gave Tripp a concealed recording device. The concealed microphone recorded the conversation between Tripp and Lewinsky when the two met at the Ritz-Carlton in Pentagon City for cocktails.

Lewinsky hired lawyers William Ginsburg and Nathaniel Speights after the recorded conversations from Linda Tripp were used as evidence against her. Ginsburg and Speights refused to allow Lewinsky to talk to Starr and his staff, leading to a series of legal maneuvers to force Lewinsky to testify. She subsequently fired Ginsburg and Speights and hired Plato Cacheris and Jacob Stein. Cacheris and Stein worked out an immunity deal with Starr on July 29, 1998, and Lewinsky began testifying on August 7, 1998, before a grand jury. The allegations from Lewinsky's grand jury testimony were incorporated into the Starr Report released to Congress in September 1998 and formed the basis of the perjury charges in the impeachment hearings in December 1998.

In March 2002 independent counsel ROBERT W. RAY, who replaced Kenneth Starr, issued his final report on the Lewinsky affair. The 237-page report detailing the affair between President Clinton and Monica Lewinsky stated that the independent counsel had enough evidence to prosecute President Clinton in court but chose not to, after Clinton admitted the affair. According to a statement by Ray, "The independent counsel concluded that sufficient evidence existed to prosecute [President Clinton] and that such evidence would probably be sufficient to obtain and sustain a conviction."

The independent counsel determined that prosecutors could prove that President Clinton obstructed justice by testifying falsely under oath that Lewinsky's affidavit denying a sexual relationship with him was "absolutely true," that he could not recall ever being alone with Lewinsky, and that he had not had sexual relations with her. Ray stated in his summary of the case that a criminal prosecution of President Clinton was not pursued by the office of the independent counsel, even though the evidence could have led to prosecution, because Clinton "had been punished in other ways." His reference was to the impeachment.

The denial of an affair with Lewinsky provided material for the lawsuit by PAULA CORBIN JONES, who charged sexual harassment by then-governor Clinton in an Arkansas hotel. Clinton's subsequent admission to the Lewinsky affair, after his denial, allowed the Jones lawyers to suggest that he was also lying about the Jones affair, which he also denied. President Clinton settled with Jones in an out-of-court settlement for $850,000, of which a significant part went to her lawyers. He was also fined $25,000 and ordered to pay $90,000 in lawyers' fees by U.S. District Judge SUSAN WEBBER WRIGHT, who oversaw the Jones lawsuit, for his "false, misleading, and evasive answers" with regard to Monica Lewinsky.

Monica Lewinsky was born on July 23, 1973, in San Francisco but raised in Beverly Hills. Her father was a well-known physician who owned a chain of cancer therapy clinics in suburban Los Angeles. She graduated (1991) from Bel Air Prep School in West Hollywood, California, and from Lewis and Clark College (1995) in Portland, Oregon. The summer after she finished college, Lewinsky went to Washington, D.C., as a White House intern. It was during that summer that the affair with President Clinton began.

She wrote a book in 1999 on her relationship with President Clinton and the subsequent Starr investigation entitled *Monica's Story*.

Lewis, Ann Frank
(1937–   ) *counselor to the president, director of communications, deputy director of communications*

Ann Lewis was named counselor to the president in 1999, having served as director of communications since 1996. She replaced THOMAS FRANKLIN MCLARTY III, who left the administration in 1998, although her role as counselor was considerably different.

Before being named assistant to the president and director of communications, she had spent two years as deputy director of communications. Much of her energy as director of communications was spent dealing with issues relating to the independent counsel's expanding investigation. As the MONICA LEWINSKY investigation became national news, Lewis became more involved in damage control. Lewis remained a staunch supporter of President Clinton throughout the entire investigation and the impeachment process. She was often seen on national television as the spokesperson for the administration.

She left the administration for a short period to serve as deputy campaign manager for the Clinton-Gore '96 presidential campaign. After the election, she returned to the White House.

Prior to joining the White House staff in 1995, Lewis had been vice president for public policy of the Planned Parenthood Federation of America (1994–95). However, most of her career had been spent in the political arena, beginning in 1978 as chief of staff to Representative Barbara Mikulski (D-Md.). In 1981 she was named political director of the Demo-

cratic National Committee (1981–85) and in 1985 became the national director for Americans for Democratic Action. She formed her own consulting firm, Ann F. Lewis, Inc., in 1993 and another consulting firm, Politics, Inc., in 1994.

Throughout her career, Lewis had been deeply involved in women's issues. In 1986 she cochaired an American delegation to a conference on current women's issues in Bonn, Germany. She was also involved with building democracies in the former Soviet republics. In 1991, Lewis went to Prague to attend a seminar for party officials for Eastern European nations and in the following years attended meetings for new Eastern European democracies.

Lewis was born on December 12, 1937, in Jersey City, New Jersey. She is the sister of Representative Barney Frank (D-Mass.).

Lindsey, Bruce R.
(1948–   ) *deputy counsel, senior adviser to the president, director of presidential personnel*

Bruce Lindsey was named senior adviser to the president and director of presidential personnel in January 1993. Lindsey's role was to ensure that the political appointments in the administration were managed through the White House rather than the departments. Lindsey moved in 1994 to the counsel's office as assistant to the president and deputy counsel to the president.

Lindsey had known President Clinton in Little Rock, Arkansas, for many years and was considered Clinton's closest friend and adviser in the White House. As former press secretary MICHAEL MCCURRY said of Lindsey, "He is supremely loyal to Bill Clinton."

Lindsey's role as deputy counsel was to protect the president from political fallout. It became Lindsey's job to deal with independent counsel KENNETH W. STARR, in the

Whitewater investigations. Later, Lindsey handled investigations into allegations that White House staff had asked for Federal Bureau of Investigation (FBI) files on former Republican White House staff (known as "Filegate") and the investigation into firings in the White House travel office (known as "Travelgate"). When the MONICA LEWINSKY case became public, Lindsey became the damage control coordinator in the White House. In 1998 Kenneth Starr subpoenaed Lindsey to tell prosecutors what he knew about the Clinton-Lewinsky relationship from conversations he had with President Clinton.

Although Lindsey was a central figure in all of the independent counsel's investigations into President and Mrs. Clinton's activities, he also was involved in a wide array of policy issues. Among those issues was the 1997 tobacco litigation settlement. Lindsey served as the White House liaison with Department of Health and Human Services secretary DONNA SHALALA on the final settlement between the federal government and the tobacco industry.

President Clinton's relationship to Lindsey began in 1968 when they both worked for Senator J. William Fulbright (D-Ark.). When Clinton failed to win reelection in 1980 as governor, he joined Lindsey's law firm. During the early part of the 1992 campaign, as Clinton was trying to win the Democratic primaries, Lindsey was regularly at his side. The two campaigned in the primary states, often for many days with few other staffers.

In 1996 independent counsel Kenneth Starr named Lindsey as an unindicted coconspirator for his role in financial transactions from the 1990 Clinton for Governor campaign. Starr charged Lindsey with trying to persuade two Arkansas bankers, Herby Branscum, Jr., and Robert M. Hill, with not filing the required federal forms when the campaign made large transactions in cash. Lindsey testified that he made no

such effort to persuade the bankers not to file the forms. The jury acquitted Branscum and Hill on some of the charges and deadlocked on the other charges. The case was dropped by Starr.

Lindsey's troubles with the independent counsel did not end in 1996. In 1997 Starr was investigating former Associate Attorney General WEBSTER HUBBELL, who received a large fee from Indonesian-based Lippo Group after he had left the Justice Department. Hubbell, the investigators believed, received the large fee as part of a political deal with the Clinton administration or with the national Democratic Party. Lindsey was queried by Starr but denied knowledge of Hubbell's financial arrangements. Hubbell had been a law partner of Mrs. Clinton at the Rose Law Firm in Little Rock, Arkansas, and was part of the Little Rock group of Clinton loyalists, which included Lindsey, that moved into the Clinton administration.

Starr again sought to bring Lindsey into an investigation of President Clinton in 1998 with regard to the Monica Lewinsky affair. Starr subpoenaed Lindsey to testify before a grand jury about President Clinton's relationship with Lewinsky. Lindsey testified four times before the grand jury. He did not answer all of the questions in the appearances and finally invoked executive privilege against having to answer further questions. As the president's deputy counsel, he argued, he was protected by executive privilege from answering questions about private conversations with the president. The Supreme Court rejected his claim of executive privilege on July 28, 1998.

Lindsey's role as a political troubleshooter in the White House was again examined in 2001 after President Clinton had left office. The House Government Reform Committee subpoenaed Lindsey in February 2001 to discuss the last-minute Clinton pardon of Marc Rich. The committee looked into connections between the pardon of Rich and donations he made or his former wife, Denise Rich, made to the Clinton library or to the Democratic National Committee.

Born on May 28, 1948, in Little Rock, Arkansas, Lindsey received his B.A. in history, with honors, from Rhodes College (1970) and his J.D. from Georgetown University Law Center (1975). After graduating from college, Lindsey went to work for Senator J. William Fulbright (D-Ark.) for two years (1970–71) and then worked for Congressman David Pryor (D-Ark.) for one year (1972). Lindsey was an Arkansas native who made his home in Little Rock.

He left Pryor's staff in Congress in 1972 to pursue his law degree at Georgetown University, but returned to Capitol Hill during 1973–74 to work as a legislative assistant to Senator Fulbright. After graduating from Georgetown University Law Center, Lindsey became the legal counsel for Governor David Pryor of Arkansas (1975–76). His career took a hiatus from politics for two years when he entered private practice in the law firm of Wright, Lindsey & Jennings (1976–78). When David Pryor was elected to the Senate, Lindsey returned to Capitol Hill as Pryor's legislative director (1978–81). After two years working for Pryor, Lindsey rejoined the law firm of Wright, Lindsey & Jennings, where he stayed for 10 years (1981–91). In 1990, Lindsey was the treasurer for the reelection campaign for Governor Bill Clinton. When Governor Clinton began a run for the presidency in 1992, Lindsey was the director of the Clinton for President campaign.

Livingston, Robert (Bob) L., Jr.
(1943–) *member of the House of Representatives*

Bob Livingston (R-La.) was elected to the House of Representatives in 1977 from the 1st Congressional District in Louisiana and was continuously elected for 22 years (1977–99). He served 11 terms but resigned from the House in 1999 following revelations of an extramarital affair.

As a member of the Appropriations Committee, and its chair from 1996–98, Livingston wielded substantial power in the House. A conservative Republican, Livingston gained power after the 1994 Republican victory in the House in which NEWTON (NEWT) LEROY GINGRICH, a conservative Republican from Georgia, was elected Speaker.

On November 6, 1998, after the midterm elections in which Republicans lost seats in the House, Gingrich announced that he would step down as Speaker. That announcement triggered a race for Speaker between Livingston and Representative Christopher Cox (R-Calif.). Cox soon dropped out of the race, and Livingston was unopposed in the end. He was elected by the members of the Republican caucus to replace Gingrich. He was to take over the office of Speaker from Gingrich in January 1999 at the beginning of the new Congress.

However, Livingston's plans to succeed Gingrich were derailed in late December 1998 during the impeachment proceedings against President Clinton. Amid published reports that Larry Flynt, publisher of *Hustler* magazine, was about to expose past extramarital affairs of Livingston and other members of Congress, Livingston resigned. "I concluded," said Livingston on December 21, 1998, "that I would not have been effectively leading 100 percent of Republicans. So it was a matter of cutting your losses." Livingston's wife and family stood by him throughout his ordeal.

After Livingston resigned from his position as Speaker-elect of the House in December, DENNIS HASTERT (R-Ill.) was elected by the House in January 1999.

Born on April 30, 1943, Livingston received his B.A. in economics from Tulane University (1967) and his J.D. from Tulane University

School of Law (1968). He did postgraduate work at the Loyola Institute of Politics (1973). He worked in the U.S. Attorney's Office, 1970–73, and in the Orleans Parish District Attorney's Office, 1974–75. As a result of his work in the U.S. Attorney's Office, he was named outstanding assistant U.S. attorney in 1973 by the Department of Justice. He left the U.S. Attorney's Office in 1975 to become the chief prosecutor of the organized crime unit in the Louisiana Attorney General's Office (1975–76).

After leaving Congress in 1999, Livingston formed the Livingston Group in Washington, D.C.

Lockhart, Joseph

(1960–   ) *White House press secretary, White House deputy press secretary*

Joe Lockhart was appointed by President Clinton as the assistant to the president and press secretary in October 1998, following the resignation of Press Secretary MICHAEL McCURRY. Lockhart joined the administration at the beginning of the second term after working for the Clinton campaign during the 1996 fall election. Having served as the press secretary for the 1996 Clinton-Gore campaign, Lockhart was named deputy press secretary in the White House.

During his tenure in the White House, Lockhart held a 1:00 P.M. press briefing every day, which was covered on C-SPAN. In particular, Lockhart dealt with questions from the media throughout the impeachment process in the House of Representatives in December 1998 and in the Senate trial in January 1999. Although he was never part of the inner circle in the White House, he was widely praised by White House staff and the president for his deft handling of media questions on the Monica Lewinsky scandal. He was regularly peppered with questions about the White House

strategy for dealing with the impeachment, as he had been with questions on the independent counsel's investigation.

Lockhart came under fire in January 2000 when he was questioned in a press briefing about Southern Baptist efforts to evangelize Hindus, Jews, and Muslims. Lockhart stated, "So I think he's [President Clinton] been very clear in his opposition to whatever organizations, including the Southern Baptists, that perpetuate ancient religious hatred." Southern Baptists responded that they did not hate other religions but felt they should attempt to convert non-Christians. Lockhart said he was trying to explain the president's support of religious tolerance.

Before joining the Clinton administration, Lockhart had been a television news producer, as was his wife, Laura Logan. Lockhart's parents had also been involved in television. His father, Raymond Lockhart, had been an NBC producer who covered national politics. His mother, Ann Lockhart, had worked at NBC before leaving her job to raise five children. Two of Lockhart's four sisters also worked in television news.

He began his career as a Public Broadcasting System (PBS) gofer at the 1972 Republican National Convention in Miami when he was only 12 years old. After high school, Lockhart applied to Georgetown University, but was turned down. He then wrote a letter to the dean of Georgetown University explaining why he should be reconsidered. The university did reconsider him, and he was admitted. But he left Georgetown in his junior year to work as a law firm messenger.

After encouragement from his father to merge his interests in politics and journalism, Lockhart volunteered as a press aide for President Jimmy Carter's reelection campaign. After the election, won by challenger Ronald Reagan, Lockhart returned to and graduated from Georgetown University. In 1984, Lockhart again went to work for a political campaign, but became a salaried worker rather than a volunteer. He joined the presidential bid of Democrat Walter Mondale.

His media career was well under way by then and he began to work for the fledgling newspaper, *USA Today*. He then went on to produce news for NBC, ABC, and CNN and in 1988 worked in the campaign of Democrat Michael Dukakis in his race against Vice President GEORGE HERBERT WALKER BUSH.

When his wife took a job with ABC News in London, Lockhart followed her and later worked for British SKY Broadcasting. He was in London during the 1992 presidential campaign. After living in London for several years, Lockhart and his wife returned to the United States. In 1996, Lockhart served in the reelection campaign as the Clinton-Gore campaign's press secretary.

Lott, Chester Trent

(1941–) *member of the Senate, member of the House of Representatives*

Elected Senate majority leader following the 1994 elections, Trent Lott (R-Miss.) became a stumbling block in the Senate for many of President Clinton's legislative proposals. President Clinton wanted to use the federal government to expand domestic programs, while Senator Lott sought to reduce the role of government and to cut the federal budget. One of the similarities between Senator Lott and President Clinton was that neither served in the military. When Republicans criticized President Clinton's handling of military issues and questioned his ability to serve as commander in chief because he had not served in the military, Lott remained silent.

Although Lott did not support many of the Clinton administration's proposals, President Clinton and Senator Lott never had the con-

tentious relationship that other members of Congress had with the president. They agreed on, among other issues, the ratification of the chemical weapons treaty. During the Starr investigation into Whitewater and into the Monica Lewinsky affair, Lott remained out of the limelight. The Republicans in the House of Representatives were the most vocal opponents of the president.

Lott's views, however, dramatically differed from President Clinton's on many issues. President Clinton had been a strong advocate for allowing homosexuals to serve in the military, a position that Senator Lott opposed. When President Clinton nominated James Hormel, who was gay, as ambassador to Luxembourg, Lott actively opposed the nomination. President Clinton was also an activist for improving race relations and civil rights, issues about which Lott often remained silent.

During his Senate career, Lott was a consistent conservative who supported tax reform, including abolishing the Internal Revenue Service (IRS), balancing the budget, and increased funding for Pascagoula, Mississippi's Ingalls shipyard. Lott remained a conservative southerner throughout his tenure in the House and Senate, regularly defending the flying of Confederate flags across the South and even promoting Confederate activities. He also supported building a presidential library for Jefferson Davis, president of the Confederacy during the Civil War. Throughout his career in both the House and the Senate, Lott opposed abortion rights and gun control, and advocated tax reduction, smaller government, deregulation of industry, and traditional family values. He supported a constitutional amendment for a balanced budget.

Lott resigned his position as majority leader in the spring of 2003 after pressure from the White House and from Republicans within the Senate. He remained in the Senate but not as majority leader. Lott's fall from power stemmed from remarks he made at a dinner event. Lott spoke at a celebration dinner for the 100th birthday of Senator Strom Thurmond (R-S.C.). In remarks to a large group gathered at the dinner, Lott stated that the country would have been "better off" had Thurmond won the presidential election in 1948. Both Democrats and Republicans accused Lott of implying that Thurmond, who was a staunch segregationist in 1948, would have allowed segregation to continue, thus making the country "better off." The outcry against Lott forced his resignation as majority leader.

Lott's career in Congress began as a member of the prestigious House Judiciary Committee. As a member of the Judiciary Committee in 1974, Lott did not believe that there was enough evidence against President Richard Nixon to impeach him during the Watergate investigation. He was one of 10 Republicans on the Judiciary Committee who rejected all of the charges against the president during the hearings. However, after the audio tapes were ordered released by the U.S. Supreme Court in *U.S. v. Nixon*, including recordings of President Nixon discussing key elements of a White House cover-up of the Watergate investigation, Lott and the other 10 Republicans reversed their position. They then supported the charges against Nixon drawn up by the majority Democrats on the House Judiciary Committee.

Born on October 9, 1941, Lott graduated with a B.P.A. (1963) and a J.D. (1967) from the University of Mississippi. He was a field representative for the University of Mississippi (1966–67) and then entered the practice of law in Pascagoula, Mississippi, with the law firm of Bryan & Gordon (1967). After practicing law for one year, he joined the staff of Congressman William M. Colmer (D-Miss.) as his administrative assistant.

Having worked for a conservative Democrat in the House, William Colmer, for five years, Lott had watched the political changes within his home state of Mississippi. During the 1970s Mississippi and most of the South was becoming more conservative and voting for Republicans. He successfully gauged the possibility of a Republican winning in the House and switched parties in 1972 to run for Colmer's seat when he retired. Lott had been a Democrat. He was elected in 1972 as a Republican to the 93rd Congress in the House of Representatives. The district included Oxford, Mississippi, the home of the University of Mississippi, and was the center of novelist William Faulkner's fictional Yoknapatawpha County. Lott was reelected seven times, serving in the House from 1973–89. In 1979, Lott was elected chairman of the House Republican Research Committee, the fifth-ranking House leadership position, and in 1980 was elected Republican whip in the House.

He was elected to the Senate in 1988. In 1994, he was elected Senate majority whip, defeating Alan Simpson (R-Wyo.). Senate majority leader Robert Dole (R-Kans.), a moderate, had supported Simpson, believing that Lott's positions were too conservative for the Republican Party, but Lott was able to win the election with the support of newer, more conservative members of the Senate elected in 1992 and 1994. He became the first person to be elected to the position of whip in both the House of Representatives and the Senate.

After two years as majority whip, Lott sought the highest party role as majority leader. With the resignation of Senator Dole as majority leader in 1996, when he began his presidential campaign, Lott decided to seek the party's highest office in the Senate. In 1996 he defeated fellow Mississippian Thad Cochran to become Senate majority leader. He was reelected majority leader in 1998 and in 2000. But in 2001, his power was abruptly overturned with the defection of Senator James Jeffords (R-Vt.). The Senate reverted to Democratic control in June 2001 when Senator Jeffords left the Republican Party to become an independent. This gave the Democratic Party a one-vote majority in the Senate and transferred leadership to the Democrats. Lott moved from majority leader to minority leader on June 5, 2001.

Following the 2002 elections, the Republicans regained control of the Senate and Lott was again elected majority leader. However, his tenure was short, for he resigned in the spring of 2003 following what were perceived as racist remarks.

His committee assignments in the Senate included Commerce, Science and Transportation, Finance, and the Rules Committee. He was elected to the Senate in 2000, for his third term, with 66 percent of the vote.

Magaziner, Ira

(1947–) *senior adviser to the president for policy development*

Ira Magaziner was named a senior adviser to the president for policy development in January 1993. His primary role in the White House was to work with HILLARY DIANE RODHAM CLINTON on developing the national health care plan. In this capacity, Magaziner coordinated the President's Task Force on National Health Care Reform, chaired by Mrs. Clinton. After the 1994 elections when Republicans took over the House of Representatives, the work on the national health care plan in the White House was essentially ended. Mrs. Clinton began to focus on other projects, and Magaziner moved to the Department of Commerce to manage federal regulation issues regarding the Internet.

Magaziner was one of the friends of President Clinton who came into office as a "Friend of Bill," or FOB. Magaziner and Clinton had known each other for 20 years from their days together as Rhodes scholars at Oxford University. The Clintons also spent time with Magaziner and his family at the Renaissance Weekends in Hilton Head Island, South Carolina, that PHILIP LADER had established.

Magaziner became the key player within the White House for the health care reform plan that had been the focus of the Clinton 1992 presidential campaign. He worked partly with the Domestic Policy Office in the White House and partly with the separate Health Care Reform Task Force that Mrs. Clinton chaired. When the health care reform plan still faced opposition in Congress, and ultimately died after the 1994 Republican takeover of the House, Magaziner refocused his efforts on Internet policy.

Magaziner was in charge of managing a host of Internet issues, such as domain name management, electronic commerce, tax and tariff issues regarding the Internet, and international electronic commerce and domain issues. At the center of his role was oversight of the presidential task force on Internet issues, which produced the report "A Framework for Global Electronic Commerce." Unlike the health care task force, which kept many of its policy discussions secret, the Internet task force was praised for its openness. Magaziner held public hearings and included numerous organizations in the discussions of the task force.

During his work for the Internet task force, Magaziner frequently traveled abroad to discuss international commerce issues related to the Internet, involving copyrights, value-added taxes, and the international organizations that should oversee the Internet. He proposed that the Organization for Economic Cooperation and Development (OECD) become the central player in international Internet oversight. He also supported ratification of copyright treaties that included the Internet, such as authorization of digital signatures.

In addition to commerce issues on the Internet, Magaziner worked on proposals to deal with children's use of the Internet. He favored the development of "blocking" technology, so that parents could block what they viewed as inappropriate material for their children, rather than regulating the material with sweeping legislation.

Born on November 8, 1947, Magaziner received his B.A. from Brown University (1969), where he was valedictorian, and studied at Balliol College, Oxford University, as a Rhodes scholar after graduation from Brown University. He was drawn to the financial world after college, where he became a successful corporate strategist for the Boston Consulting Group (1973–79). In 1979, he founded a corporate consulting firm, Telesis (1979–85). Six years later, he founded another successful consulting firm, SJS (1985–93), which he left to join the Clinton administration. As a corporate strategist he specialized in working with corporations in difficult situations. Among his clients were General Electric's consumer division and Wang Laboratories.

Magaziner's interest in developing turnaround strategies began while he was a student at Brown University, where he developed a 400-page report on reforming the curriculum. Magaziner led a campus campaign to revise the curriculum after he finished the report, finally leading to broad support on campus and creation of the New Curriculum. He moved next to developing a job creation program for Rhode Island, called the Greenhouse Compact. The plan emerged as a $250 million roadmap for rebuilding the state's economy, largely through venture capital supported by the state. The plan went to voters to approve but was rejected by a 4-1 margin.

In 1990 Magaziner was again drawn into policy issues when he was named to a workforce skills commission sponsored by the National Center on Education and the Economy. He and Mrs. Clinton both sat on the center's board. The report produced by the commission, "America's Choice: High Skills or Low Wages," encouraged national performance standards plus a comprehensive system of technical and professional certificates and associates' degrees. While the basics of the report were well received, many businesses objected to the recommendation that all companies, regardless of size, be required to spend 1 percent of their payrolls on skills training. President Clinton later adopted the plan during his campaign, but exempted small businesses from the requirement, stating that it would be too costly for many.

The *National Journal* described Magaziner in a 1992 article as a man who "has a flair for selling ideas." It was this flair that led to his successful private consulting firm, which made him a millionaire, and to his involvement in public policy issues.

Magaziner's expertise in the health care field emerged from a health care study group he created in Rhode Island in 1990, called Aging 2000. The Aging 2000 group was formed to study senior citizens' health-related issues. The program created advocacy groups that supported new health care proposals for Rhode Island's senior citizens. Magaziner also worked with the March of Dimes to reduce infant mortality within parts of Rhode Island, and was given their statewide award for his efforts.

Magaziner had been active in Democratic Party politics for more than a decade. He served as an informal adviser to Democratic presidential candidates Walter Mondale in 1984 and to Michael Dukakis in 1988.

Mandela, Nelson
(1918–   ) *president of South Africa*

Nelson Mandela was elected president of South Africa in April 1994 in the first all-race democratic elections in the nation's history. Mandela's African National Congress (ANC) party won 252 of the 400 seats in the National Assembly, the lower house of parliament. On May 9, 1994, at the first meeting of the National Assembly, Mandela was chosen as the head of state, replacing Frederik Willem de Klerk.

Mandela and de Klerk had worked since Mandela's release from prison in 1990 to dismantle apartheid and to create a government that would protect the rights of the minority

President Clinton and President Nelson Mandela of South Africa, July 4, 1993 *(AP Photo/Greg Gibson)*

white population. When Mandela was elected president, de Klerk was sworn in as one of two deputy presidents in a five-year Transitional Government of National Unity. As a result of their efforts to create a new democratic government in South Africa, Mandela and de Klerk shared the 1993 Nobel Peace Prize. Mandela was inaugurated as president of South Africa in May 1994 in a ceremony attended by dignitaries from around the world. The United States delegation was led by Vice President ALBERT (AL) GORE, JR., and MARY ELIZABETH (TIPPER) AITCHESON GORE, and included HILLARY DIANE RODHAM CLINTON, Secretary of Agriculture ALPHONSO MICHAEL (MIKE) ESPY, Secretary of Commerce RONALD H. BROWN, and members of Congress. Prior to the delegation's trip, the administration announced a three-year $600 million trade, aid, and investment package for South Africa.

Mandela, who was 80 years old, stepped down from the presidency of South Africa on June 16, 1999. He was replaced by President Thabo Mbeki, whom Mandela had strongly supported. In elections held on June 2, 1999, the African National Congress (ANC) party captured the majority of seats in parliament and subsequently chose Mbeki as president.

Before Mandela left office in June 1999, a rally was held in Johannesburg by the people of South Africa. Over 80,000 people packed the stadium on May 30, 1999, to wish Mandela well in the future and to thank him for his service to the nation.

In March 1998 President and Mrs. Clinton visited South Africa for a four-day trip. During the visit, President Clinton spoke before the South African Parliament, stating that he was "honored to address the South African Parliament, which was truly free at last." The audience included members of parliament, Mandela, and Mandela's heir apparent, Thabo Mbeki. In addition to the speech before parliament, President Clinton visited Robben Island,

where Mandela had been imprisoned for more than 20 years.

Six months later, in September 1998, President Clinton awarded Mandela the Congressional Gold Medal in Washington, D.C.

Born on July 18, 1918, in a village near Umbata in the Transkei, South Africa, Mandela grew up in a nation dominated by whites and ruled by the policies of apartheid. Mandela became one of the most visible leaders of the political movement to end apartheid, leading rallies against the government. In 1956, Mandela and 155 other black leaders were arrested by the government and charged with treason. All were acquitted after a trial that lasted into 1961. He was again jailed in 1963 and remained there for 27 years until his release in 1990 by President de Klerk.

Marshall, Thurgood, Jr.
(1956–   ) *director, Office of Cabinet Affairs; legislative affairs coordinator, Office of the Vice President*

Thurgood Marshall, Jr., served as assistant to the president and director of the Office of Cabinet Affairs in the White House for the second term of the Clinton administration, 1997–2001. Marshall was one of three senior staff in the White House at the time who were African American. The other two were BOB NASH, assistant to the president and director of presidential personnel, and MINYON MOORE, assistant to the president and director of political affairs.

As director of the Office of Cabinet Affairs, Marshall was responsible for managing cabinet meetings, apprising cabinet officers of issues on the agenda, and ensuring that issues addressed by the president in cabinet meetings had adequate follow-up.

Marshall first joined the administration in 1993 as a member of Vice President ALBERT (AL) GORE, JR.'s staff as deputy counsel and legislative affairs director for the vice president. Marshall had been a member of Gore's Senate staff between 1985 and 1988, and served as a counsel for the Senate Judiciary Committee from 1988 to 1992. When Gore was nominated for the vice presidency in 1992, Marshall began traveling with Gore's campaign staff. After the election, Marshall was a member of the presidential transition team. When the administration took office in January 1993, Marshall was named deputy counsel and legislative affairs director for the vice president. Marshall had worked earlier as deputy campaign manager for issues in the failed 1988 Gore for President campaign.

Marshall was also involved in a number of White House task forces and special projects after he was named cabinet secretary, including representing the administration in a series of town meetings on race issues in 1997, working on the 2000 and 2002 Olympic Games, and working with the president's Y2K Council, which managed the anticipated computer software issues related to the millennium date change. The name, "Y2K Council" was the shortened form of the longer name "Year 2000 Council."

His involvement in race relations included at least one town meeting that President Clinton initiated. During December 1997, the White House sought to reinvigorate its efforts on race relations through a series of town meetings around the country. The meetings were held with a number of administration officials, including President Clinton in Akron, Ohio; Mrs. Clinton in Boston, Massachusetts; Secretary of Education RICHARD RILEY in Baltimore, Maryland, and Thurgood Marshall, Jr., in Petersburg, Virginia. In addition to the town hall meetings, Secretary of Transportation RODNEY E. SLATER held a private meeting in Dallas with African-American business leaders.

Among his other roles in the White House, Marshall served as vice chair of the White House Olympic Task Force, which coordinated the preparation for the 2002 Winter Olympic Games in Salt Lake City, Utah. His role in 2002 was strengthened as a result of his membership in the official U.S. delegation to the 2000 Olympic Games.

Marshall also served on the presidential delegations to South Africa for the inauguration of Nelson Mandela, to Bosnia for the 1998 elections, and to Australia for the 2000 Olympic Summer Games.

Marshall, the son of civil rights activist and Supreme Court Justice Thurgood Marshall, received his B.A. (1978) from the University of Virginia and his J.D. (1981) from the University of Virginia School of Law. After graduation from law school, he clerked for U.S. District Judge Barrington D. Parker. He was born on August 12, 1956.

After leaving the Clinton administration, Marshall joined the Washington, D.C., law firm of Swidler, Berlin, Shereff, Friedman, in the government affairs division. He also was named to the board of directors of the National Fish and Wildlife Foundation and the United States Supreme Court Historical Society, and was a member of the American Bar Association's Standing Committee on Election Law. He served as vice chair of the Ethics Oversight Committee of the United States Olympic Committee. His wife, Colleen P. Mahoney, was a member of the law firm of Skadden, Arps, Slate, Meagher & Flom. She was a former deputy director of the enforcement division and acting general counsel of the Securities and Exchange Commission during the Clinton administration.

Matsch, Richard

(1930–) *federal judge, presided over the trial of Timothy McVeigh*

Judge Richard Matsch presided over the trial of Timothy McVeigh, accused of the bombing of the Murrah Federal Building in Oklahoma City, Oklahoma, on April 19, 1995. The bombing killed 168 men, women, and children. The children died in a day care center in the federal building.

Judge Matsch, on the U.S. Court of Appeals for the 10th Circuit, oversaw the case in Denver after McVeigh's defense attorneys succeeded in having the trial moved from Oklahoma City to Denver. The defense team believed that McVeigh could not receive a fair trial in Oklahoma City.

In the jury trial McVeigh was found guilty on June 2, 1997, of eight counts of first-degree murder and using a weapon of mass destruction. On June 13, 1997, he was sentenced to death by a unanimous vote of the jury. After a series of appeals on the death sentence, Judge Matsch ruled in June 2001 to allow the death sentence to go forward. In his ruling, Judge Matsch stated that as the presiding judge in McVeigh's trial, he became absolutely convinced of McVeigh's guilt.

McVeigh fired his attorney, Stephen Jones, and McVeigh's new lawyers appealed based on incompetence of his former lawyer. The appeal failed. At McVeigh's request, no further appeals were made. On January 11, 2001, McVeigh formally waived his right to appeal.

However, on May 31, 2001, McVeigh asked his lawyers to pursue an appeal after the Federal Bureau of Investigation (FBI) revealed that it failed to release thousands of documents to McVeigh's lawyers. On June 6, 2001, Judge Matsch denied the appeal and ruled that the execution could proceed. McVeigh was executed on June 11, 2001, by lethal injection at the federal prison in Terre Haute, Indiana.

On April 11, 2000, President Clinton opened the Oklahoma City memorial. It included 168 chairs bearing the names of the victims; the "survivor tree," an elm tree that lived through the bombing; a reflecting pool; and bronze gates that symbolically preserved the moment of the explosion.

Born on June 8, 1930, Judge Matsch was appointed to the U.S. District Court by President Nixon in 1974.

McAuliffe, Terence (Terry) R.
(1957–) *chairman of the Democratic National Committee; fund-raiser, Clinton-Gore campaigns*

Terry McAuliffe, a close friend of President and Mrs. Clinton, remained outside the administration throughout the Clinton presidency. A prodigious fund-raiser, McAuliffe raised significant amounts of money for the 1992 Clinton-Gore presidential campaign. In 1996 he was named national finance chairman for Clinton-Gore '96, and later national cochairman. In 1997, President Clinton appointed McAuliffe cochair of the 1997 presidential inaugural committee and in 2000, Vice President ALBERT (AL) GORE, JR., asked McAuliffe to chair the 2000 Democratic National Convention in Los Angeles.

McAuliffe was an early fund-raiser for Clinton's 1996 reelection campaign. Soon after the midterm elections, McAuliffe began to raise money to build a strong war chest to stave off Democratic challengers. After the Democratic Party's defeat in the 1994 midterm elections, in which Newt Gingrich and conservative Republicans gained control of the House of Representatives, Clinton believed he was vulnerable to a Democratic primary challenge. McAuliffe raised enough money to ensure that Clinton was well funded for any primary challenge.

Before leaving office, President Clinton recommended McAuliffe as chairman of the Democratic National Committee (DNC), which was approved by the members of the committee in February 2001.

In May 2000 McAuliffe told a media group that in the past six years (1994–2000), he had raised $300 million in donations for President Clinton and the Democratic Party, including the Clinton Presidential Library ($75 million), the president's legal defense fund ($8 million), the Gore 2000 Committee, Mrs. Clinton's race for the Senate from New York ($5 million), and other Democratic Party events.

When President Clinton left office and decided to purchase a house in New York's Westchester County town of Chappaqua, one of the most expensive communities in America to purchase a home, McAuliffe offered to guarantee the $1.35 million mortgage. The house was purchased for $1.7 million. McAuliffe offered to deposit $1.35 million with the mortgage lender, but the Clintons ultimately rejected the offer. After considerable opposition across the country, the Clintons chose not to accept the guarantee and pursued a conventional mortgage.

McAuliffe had been involved in Democratic Party politics for a number of years, including working for the 1976 campaign of President Jimmy Carter, the 1980 Carter-Mondale reelection campaign, and serving as the finance director for Representative RICHARD (DICK) A. GEPHARDT's (D-Mo.) 1988 presidential campaign. His relationship with Gephardt stemmed from his work as a lobbyist.

Born on February 9, 1957, McAuliffe received his B.A. from Catholic University, Washington, D.C., and his J.D. from the Georgetown University Law Center (1984).

McCaffrey, Barry

(1942–) *director, Office of National Drug Control Policy*

General (retired) Barry McCaffrey was nominated by President Clinton as director of the Office of National Drug Control Policy, more popularly referred to as the "drug czar." He was confirmed by the Senate on February 29, 1996, and resigned on January 7, 2001. The Office of National Drug Control Policy was part of the Executive Office of the President.

As director of the Office of National Drug Control Policy, McCaffrey was responsible for certifying the $19.2 billion federal drug control policy and for developing the U.S. national drug control strategy. McCaffrey oversaw a wide range of issues dealing with illegal drugs, including developing a media strategy to keep children from taking illegal drugs and other education programs, coordinating programs with all agencies in the federal government, and creating policies for stopping the influx of illegal drugs into the United States.

In his Senate confirmation hearings in February 1996, McCaffrey focused his attention on the health problems created by drug abuse. "Dealing with the problem of illegal drugs abuse," he said, "is more akin to dealing with skin cancer. Wars are relatively straightforward. You identify the enemy, select a general, assign him a mission and resources, and leave him get the job done. In this struggle against drug abuse, there is no silver bullet, no quick way to reduce drug use or the damage it causes."

During McCaffrey's tenure as drug czar, he sought to end illegal drug use by changing the habits of repeat drug users through treatment programs and by keeping illegal drugs out of the hands of children. He supported children's education programs as a foundation for a national drug strategy.

One of McCaffrey's roles was to focus on the use of performance-enhancing drugs used by athletes. He urged the International Olympic Committee to increase its oversight of performance-enhancing drugs among athletes. For American athletes, he stated that there would be no statute of limitation on Olympic drug offenses. "If we've found out that you've won by cheating [using performance-enhancing drugs], we'll strip you of your honors," he said.

In his efforts to stop drugs from entering U.S. cities from international drug dealers, McCaffrey focused much of his energies on the Colombian drug trade. In July 1999, McCaffrey went to Colombia to reinforce the United States efforts to eradicate coca and poppies and to substitute other crops for farming in Colombia. He also emphasized U.S. military efforts to stop drug smugglers.

Prior to retiring from the U.S. Army, McCaffrey had been commander in chief of the U.S. Armed Forces Southern Command, coordinating national security operations in Latin America. His expertise in drug control issues stemmed from his role at the Southern Command, which involved military interdiction in drug-trafficking activities. The Southern Command, or SOUTHCOM, is the branch of the military responsible for coordinating the counterdrug operations in Central and South American countries. The command was established by a Joint Chiefs of Staff strategy for Defense Department antidrug activities called for in 1989 legislation.

He was approached by members of the Clinton administration to take over the Office of National Drug Control Policy as a result of his extensive work with interdiction and issues related to illegal drugs while running the Southern Command.

During Operation Desert Storm in 1991 during the Persian Gulf War, McCaffrey commanded the 24th Infantry Division and led the 200-kilometer "left hook" attack in the Euphrates River valley of Iraq. He also served in combat in Vietnam and the Dominican Republic. He has been awarded two Distinguished Service Crosses, a Bronze Star, and three Purple Hearts. McCaffrey was the youngest officer in the army to attain the rank of four star general.

After leaving the Clinton administration, McCaffrey was named the Olin Distinguished

Professor at the United States Military Academy. He was also president of his own consulting firm based in Alexandria, Virginia, and was a military analyst for NBC News.

Born on November 17, 1942, McCaffrey graduated from Phillips Academy in Andover, Massachusetts, and the U.S. Military Academy at West Point, New York. He received a master's degree in civil government from American University.

McCaffrey was replaced by John P. Walters when President GEORGE WALKER BUSH entered office in 2001.

McCurdy, David Keith
(1950–) *member of the House of Representatives*

Representative Dave McCurdy (D-Okla.) represented the 4th District of Oklahoma from 1981–95. He left the House of Representatives to form a business consulting and investment firm, the McCurdy Group.

During his career in the House of Representatives, McCurdy was involved in a number of key pieces of legislation, including the 1988 National Superconductivity Competitiveness Act; the 1985 Goldwater-Nickles Act, which reorganized the Department of Defense; the Nunn-McCurdy Amendment of 1982, requiring congressional notification of Department of Defense overruns of 15 percent or more; and the 1993 National Service Trust Act.

McCurdy, who sat on the House Intelligence Committee, also advocated integrating homosexuals into the Central Intelligence Agency (CIA). Because of his knowledge of intelligence matters, McCurdy sought the position of secretary of defense in the Clinton administration but failed to be offered it. The position went to a colleague of McCurdy's, Representative LESLIE (LES) ASPIN, JR. (D-Wisc.).

As a member of the House of Representatives during the first term of the Clinton administration, McCurdy was best known for his sponsorship of the national service legislation, introduced in May 1993 in the House. The bill that emerged, the National and Community Service Trust Act of 1993, created AmeriCorps and the Corporation for National Service. McCurdy was not only one of the original sponsors of the bill, but also a strong supporter as it moved through Congress. President Clinton signed the bill after acknowledging the support that McCurdy had consistently provided in the House.

Born on March 30, 1950, McCurdy received his B.A. from the University of Oklahoma (1972) and his J.D. from the University of Oklahoma Law School (1975). He served in the U.S. Air Force Reserve as a Judge Advocate General. McCurdy's wife, Dr. Pam McCurdy, was a physician specializing in child psychiatry.

In 1998 McCurdy was elected president of Electronic Industries Alliance, which was the national trade organization representing U.S. manufacturers in the electronics industry. The Electronic Industries Alliance had a staff of 260 and a budget of $50 million.

McCurry, Michael Demaree
(1954–   ) *White House press secretary*

Michael McCurry served as assistant to the president and press secretary from January 1995 to September 1998. He had first worked in the Clinton administration for Secretary of State WARREN MINOR CHRISTOPHER, for whom he was press secretary from March 1993 until he went to the White House. He was named White House press secretary on January 5, 1995, following the December 1994 departure of Press Secretary DEE DEE MYERS.

During McCurry's tenure on the White House staff, he regularly answered questions on the independent counsel's investigation of Whitewater and related matters. When the impeachment hearings began in 1998, McCurry was not included in many of the president's strategy sessions. As a result, he was unable to give the press any more information than they were receiving from the president's White House counsel, CHARLES RUFF, or from the president's private counsel, DAVID KENDALL. McCurry subsequently resigned in September, in the midst of the hearings in the House of Representatives.

McCurry had not been part of the original campaign team in 1992 nor had he been brought into the White House in 1993. The first press secretary for the president, Dee Dee Myers, had been the press secretary on the 1992 presidential campaign. When LEON EDWARD PANETTA became chief of staff in August 1994, he sought to reorganize the White House staff, including bringing in a new press secretary. McCurry, who had a long history in Democratic Party politics and was currently the press secretary in the Department of State, was urged to take the position by Secretary of State Warren Christopher.

McCurry, however, never melded into the senior staff of the White House, who remained largely friends of the Clintons from Arkansas or staff members from the 1992 presidential campaign. Although he received the elevated title, assistant to the president, rather than deputy assistant, which Dee Dee Myers had had, he was never part of the president's inner circle.

When the Monica Lewinsky scandal broke, McCurry asked to kept out of any strategy sessions that would force him to mislead the press. He insisted that at all times he be honest in his answers to the press. By not knowing certain facts, he believed, he could honestly deny knowing whether or not President Clinton had been involved with MONICA LEWINSKY.

By July 1998, however, McCurry indicated he was unable to remain as the president's press secretary due to personal concerns about the degree of President Clinton's involvement with

Monica Lewinsky. He resigned effective September 30, 1998. His deputy, JOSEPH LOCKHART, was then promoted to press secretary.

Prior to joining the administration, McCurry served as director of communications for the Democratic National Committee (1988–90); national press secretary in the vice presidential campaign of Senator LLOYD MILLARD BENTSEN, JR. (D-Tex.), in 1988; political strategist in the Democratic presidential campaigns of Senator John Glenn (D-Ohio) in 1984, Governor BRUCE EDWARD BABBITT of Arizona (1988), and Senator Bob Kerrey (D-Nebr.) in 1992. He also ran the press office at the 1988 Democratic National Convention and served as a communications adviser to the Clinton-Gore campaign in 1992.

McCurry's political career started in the U.S. Senate as press secretary for the Senate Committee on Labor and Human Resources from 1976–81 and for the committee's chair, Senator Harrison A. Williams, Jr. (D-N.J.). He left the committee to work as press secretary for Senator Daniel Patrick Moynihan (D-N.Y.) from 1981–83. He was later a senior vice president in the consulting firm of Robinson, Sawyer, Lake, Lehrer & Montgomery in Washington, D.C.

Born on October 27, 1954, McCurry received his B.A., magna cum laude, from the Woodrow Wilson School of Public and International Affairs at Princeton University (1976) and his M.A. from Georgetown University (1985).

McDougal, James (Jim)
(1941–1998) and
McDougal, Susan
(1954–   ) *defendants in Whitewater land development investigation*

Susan McDougal and her ex-husband, Jim McDougal, were the target of the independent counsel's investigation into the Whitewater land development project in which President and Mrs. Clinton were partners. The McDougals and JIM GUY TUCKER had been business partners of President and Mrs. Clinton in the project. They had purchased land in northern Arkansas to develop as a vacation community dominated by time-share homes. The investigation centered on the financing of the project.

In 1978, attorney general Bill Clinton and his wife joined in a partnership with Jim and Susan McDougal and Tucker to purchase 200 acres of riverfront property in Arkansas to sell as vacation homes. The Whitewater Development Corporation, which they formed, later received a $300,000 loan from banker David Hale. Starr's investigation focused on whether Clinton had, as attorney general, pressured Hale.

Susan McDougal was tried in April 1996 with Jim McDougal and with the current Arkansas governor, Jim Guy Tucker, on four counts of fraud and conspiracy in the Whitewater land project financing. Federal prosecutors accused the three defendants of defrauding the Small Business Administration and improperly using funds from the Madison Guaranty Savings and Loan, which they owned. One prosecutor noted that the McDougals had used the savings and loan "as their own private piggy bank."

During the nine-week trial, the government's star witness was David Hale, who made the claim that Bill Clinton, then governor, had discussed an illegal $300,000 loan with him and Susan McDougal. Though not a defendant in the case, President Clinton denied the charges in a videotaped interview taken at the White House on April 28, 1996. All three (Susan McDougal, Jim McDougal, and Tucker) were convicted on May 28, 1996, on Whitewater-related fraud charges.

Susan McDougal was convicted of all the charges and sentenced in September 1996 to three 24-month prison terms to run concurrently, plus three years' probation on the fourth felony charge. She was also given an additional 18 months in prison on civil contempt charges when she refused to answer further questions from the independent counsel's staff. After Hale testified that Governor Clinton had pressured him for a loan, Starr called Susan McDougal back to testify. She refused, leading to a civil and later criminal contempt charge against her.

She was released from prison in July 1998 due to a medical problem, after serving the entire contempt sentence and four months of the Whitewater sentence. Her sentence was reduced to time served.

Jim Guy Tucker was convicted on two of the seven fraud charges against him and in August 1996 received four years' probation, after the judge took into account the former governor's chronic liver disease and the need for a liver transplant. Tucker resigned from office hours after the verdict. Jim McDougal was convicted of 18 of the 19 charges against him. Facing up to 84 years in prison and $4.5 million in fines, McDougal agreed to cooperate with Starr's office. His cooperation included a reduced prison sentence and in April 1997 he was sentenced to three years in prison and a year of house arrest, three years of probation, and a $10,000 fine. McDougal, who had a history of heart problems, died of a heart attack in jail in March 1998. In addition to her legal problems from the Whitewater land development project, Susan McDougal faced unrelated charges of embezzlement from a former job. Conductor Zubin Mehta and his wife, Nancy, accused McDougal of embezzlement while she was working as their bookkeeper and personal assistant between 1989 and 1992. In a 1998 lawsuit, they charged that she embezzled $50,000 from them. During the trial, the judge barred any mention of the Whitewater case or independent counsel Kenneth Starr. McDougal was acquitted of all charges against her brought by Mehta on November 24, 1998.

On April 23, 1998, Susan McDougal was again called before the Little Rock, Arkansas, grand jury. As she had before, McDougal refused to answer certain questions posed by prosecutors. The grand jury indicted her in May 1998 for obstruction of justice and dual criminal contempt charges for her refusal to testify before the panel in September 1976 and in April 1998. She finally agreed to testify, asserting that President Clinton testified truthfully in 1996 about the Whitewater land deal. She also said that she never spoke with Clinton about a $300,000 Small Business Administration loan taken out by the McDougals. She also accused her former husband of lying to Whitewater prosecutors after he agreed to cooperate with the investigation.

The jury found McDougal not guilty of obstruction of justice but was deadlocked on two counts of criminal contempt. U.S. District Judge George Howard declared a mistrial and the independent counsel's office did not retry the case. Susan McDougal was pardoned by President Clinton in January 2001.

McGinty, Kathleen (Katie) Alana

(1963–   ) *chair, Council on Environmental Quality; director, National Economic Council*

Kathleen (Katie) McGinty was named by President Clinton as the deputy assistant to the president and director of the White House Office on Environmental Policy on February 8, 1993. McGinty had been the senior environmental adviser to Vice President ALBERT (AL) GORE, JR., while he was in the Senate.

When he appointed McGinty, President Clinton also created the White House Office on Environmental Policy, which replaced the Council on Environmental Quality (CEQ). The CEQ had been created in 1969 by President

Nixon as the focal point for environmental issues in the White House decision structure. However, the council had been largely ignored during the Reagan and Bush administrations, when most environmental policymaking was handled by the Environmental Protection Agency or the cabinet departments.

President Clinton said in his announcement on the creation of the Office of Environmental Policy on February 8, 1993, that it would "be responsible for coordinating environmental policy within the federal government. The director of the White House Office on Environmental Policy will participate in each of the major policy councils: the National Security Council, the National Economic Council, and the Domestic Policy Council, and work closely with relevant federal agencies."

The restructuring, according to President Clinton, would allow for a slimmed-down office that would be deeply involved in White House policymaking rather than having only a limited advisory role. According to the president's announcement, "The Office on Environmental Policy replaced the Council on Environmental Quality, expanding the influence of the council with a more efficient and effectively focused mandate to coordinate and influence environmental policy. The office will retain some of the responsibilities of the CEQ, while others will be returned more appropriately and effectively to the relevant federal agencies, creating at the White House a more effective means of focusing on policymaking and development." President Clinton also pledged to elevate the Environmental Protection Agency to cabinet status. He submitted a proposal to Congress in 1993 but Congress failed to approve it. The commitment to a stronger environmental office in the White House fulfilled a campaign promise by President Clinton in 1992 to raise the profile of environmental issues.

After two years, President Clinton restructured his environmental advisory system and reestablished the Council on Environmental Quality. The White House Office on Environmental Policy was merged with the Council on Environmental Quality on September 23, 1994. The White House made the decision to merge the two units "in order to give continued strength to environmental policymaking in the administration."

When President Clinton announced that the Council on Environmental Quality would be reconstituted, he announced that McGinty would be nominated as its chair. He submitted her name to the Senate for confirmation, but the Senate did not act on the nomination during the fall term. On January 4, 1995, President Clinton announced that he had made a recess appointment for McGinty to chair the Council on Environmental Quality. She was not confirmed by the Senate until December 22, 1995.

As chair of the Council on Environmental Quality, McGinty administered the National Environmental Policy Act of 1969. Among the projects she was involved with were the Clean Water Acton Plan aimed at runoff pollution, the Superfund toxic waste program, restoration of the Florida Everglades, and forest management in the Pacific Northwest.

Before joining the Clinton administration, McGinty had served as Senator Al Gore's (D-Tenn.) senior legislative assistant for energy and environmental policy. In that role, she had also been the congressional staff coordinator for the Senate delegation to the United Nations Conference on the Environment and Development, held in June 1992 in Rio de Janeiro, and had been the official member of the U.S. Delegation to Negotiations on the Framework Convention on Climate Change and the Antarctic Protocol.

Born May 11, 1963, McGinty was the ninth of 10 children. She graduated from St. Joseph's University in Philadelphia with a B.S.

in chemistry (1985) and from Columbia University Law School with a J.D (1988). After law school she was a law clerk to U.S. Circuit Judge H. Robert Mayer, Court of Appeals for the Federal Circuit, in Washington, D.C.

She was awarded a Congressional Fellowship by the American Chemical Society (1990), based on her research during college, while she worked for the Atlantic Richfield Chemical Company. As a Fellow, she worked in Senator Gore's office on science education issues and initiatives to strengthen patent protections for process inventions. McGinty was then named to Gore's staff, where she remained until her appointment as director of the White House Office on Environmental Policy in the Clinton administration.

McGinty left the Clinton administration in November 1998 to become a senior visiting fellow for Tata Energy Resource Institute in New Delhi, India (1998–99). In March 2000 she joined Troutman Sanders, LLC, as a senior policy analyst. As the 2000 presidential election geared up, she joined the staff of the Democratic National Committee as an environmental policy adviser, where she remained until April 2001. In June 2001 she was named vice president of asset management for the Washington, D.C., firm of Natsource.

When Edward Rendell was elected governor of Pennsylvania in 2002, he named McGinty his secretary of environmental protection.

McLarty, Thomas Franklin, III
(1946–   ) *special envoy to the Americas, counselor to the president, chief of staff*

Thomas "Mack" McLarty, the first appointment made by President-elect Clinton to his White House staff, was named White House chief of staff soon after the November election. McLarty, who had known President Clinton since they were in kindergarten together in

Hope, Arkansas, became an integral part of the transition planning after the election. McLarty worked closely with President-elect Clinton in choosing cabinet nominees. "I was part of a small group in Little Rock," McLarty said, "that spent countless hours going over list after list of critically important cabinet selections." McLarty remained one of President Clinton's closest friends and most trusted advisers throughout the administration.

During his tenure as chief of staff, McLarty was deeply involved in shepherding legislation through Congress for the 1993 deficit reduction package, the Family Medical Leave Act, and the North American Free Tree Agreement (NAFTA). He was only slightly involved in the health care reform legislation, which HILLARY DIANE RODHAM CLINTON and IRA MAGAZINER oversaw.

On June 17, 1994, President Clinton announced a change in the chief of staff's office, moving McLarty to the position of counselor to the president, and bringing in LEON EDWARD PANETTA, director of the Office of Management and Budget, as White House chief of staff. When McLarty sensed that changes needed to be made in the White House staff, he suggested that Panetta, who had been an ally throughout the first year of the administration, replace him. McLarty had also built strong bridges to DAVID GERGEN and Vice President ALBERT (AL) GORE, JR., both of whom supported his choice of Panetta for the chief of staff position.

McLarty had been criticized for giving President Clinton too much latitude in the number of people he saw and the meetings he participated in. McLarty tried to bring the approach of an "honest broker" to the White House, which allowed many voices to be heard in the decision process. He tried to be a facilitator, ensuring that President Clinton hear multiple views on policy issues.

However, the result was often chaotic decision making in the White House and too many people with easy access to the president offering conflicting opinions. A story in the *National Journal* referred to "a presidency that's adrift" to describe the policy-making structure in the White House. Panetta restructured the chief of staff's office to ensure that the president's time was more carefully managed and that White House staff did not move in and out of the Oval Office at will. Policy matters were more often presented in memoranda before they were discussed with the president in the Oval Office.

McLarty served as counselor to the president for a year and a half, with several roles. In announcing his appointment as counselor, President Clinton said of McLarty, "His new role will permit him to spend much more time as my personal representative to the people who are so important to the success of this administration's efforts—Democrats and Republicans in Congress, constituent groups of all kinds, friends who helped to bring me to the White House." While this appeared to be the central role that McLarty would play, President Clinton in the same announcement described another role that McLarty would play as counselor to the president. "In addition, I am asking him to assume greater responsibility in shepherding our legislative package through Congress . . . and help to lay the groundwork for summits this year with the Latin and Asian leaders."

McLarty began as counselor to the president working on the first assignment, primarily dealing with Democratic moderates and business leaders, but soon focused his time on the second assignment, building bridges to Latin American and Asian commerce. He managed the 1994 Summit of the Americas and became deeply involved in working on commerce issues in Latin American countries.

His expertise in Latin American issues led to his third assignment in the White House, as the special envoy to the Americas. As special envoy to the Americas, McLarty made over 50 trips to various countries in Latin America, including as the U.S. representative to the 50th anniversary observance of the Organization of American States in Colombia. He also helped to organize the Summit of the Americas in Chile. McLarty remained as the Special Envoy to the Americas until June 1998 when he left the administration.

As White House chief of staff, McLarty became embroiled in the independent counsel's investigation of Travelgate as part of the broad Whitewater investigation. In addition, the Republican-controlled House Governmental Affairs Committee criticized McLarty's role in the travel office firings, suggesting that he approved the dismissals and then, inappropriately, was put in charge of an internal review of the firings.

In April 1997, McLarty was again the subject of the independent counsel's Whitewater investigation when he was called before a grand jury in Little Rock, Arkansas. He was questioned about his efforts to help former Justice Department official WEBSTER HUBBELL find employment. KENNETH W. STARR, the independent counsel, charged that McLarty had been part of a scheme to buy Hubbell's silence in the Whitewater land development investigation in return for finding him employment. McLarty testified that the charges "were absolutely not true."

McLarty resigned from the White House staff in June 1998. In announcing McLarty's departure in April 1998, President Clinton said, "Mack represents to me everything that is good and decent in public service. Honesty and civility, fidelity and kindness aren't just words to him, they're a way of life."

McLarty received his B.A. in business administration, summa cum laude, from the University of Arkansas at Fayetteville (1969), where he was student government president. After graduating from college, he returned to

Hope, Arkansas, to work with his father's automobile dealership. He was the founder and president of McLarty Leasing Company in 1969 in Little Rock, Arkansas, (1969–79) and in 1979 became president of McLarty Companies (1979–83).

In 1974 he was elected to the board of directors of Arkansas Louisiana Gas Company (Arkla) and in 1983 he was named chief operating officer of Arkla Gas in Shreveport, Louisiana, and was named chief executive officer, president, and chairman of the board of Arkla in 1985. Arkla was one of the largest corporations in the nation, listed on the Fortune 500 list.

McLarty had had a substantial career in politics in addition to his business career. At the age of 23, McLarty was elected to the Arkansas House of Representatives (1970–72). He then was elected chairman of the Arkansas State Democratic Party (1974–76), and was the treasurer for the gubernatorial campaigns of David Pryor (1974) and of Bill Clinton (1978).

Prior to joining the Clinton administration, McLarty had built strong bipartisan relationships. In 1989 he was named to the St. Louis Federal Reserve Board (1989–92) by President GEORGE HERBERT WALKER BUSH and was also named by President Bush to the National Petroleum Council. In 1999, McLarty joined with former secretary of state and national security advisor Henry Kissinger to form Kissinger McLarty Associates, a Washington, D.C., consulting firm. In addition to his consulting work, he became a member of the board of directors of the Asbury Automotive Group, Inc., one of the nation's largest automotive retailers with 132 franchises at 91 dealership locations throughout the country. McLarty was chairman of the North Point platform which owned five dealerships in Arkansas for Asbury Automotive.

He served on the board of directors of Hendrix College, the board of visitors of the University of Arkansas, Little Rock, and was the former chairman of the board of the United Negro College Fund Campaign.

Michel, Robert (Bob) Henry
(1923–   ) *member of the House of Representatives*

Bob Michel (R-Ill.) represented the 18th Congressional District surrounding Peoria, Illinois, in the House of Representatives for 19 consecutive terms. Michel was first elected to Congress in 1956, for a term that began January 3, 1957, and his last term ended on January 3, 1995.

He was elected minority leader in the House by the Republican minority in 1981 and remained minority leader until 1995. His tenure as minority leader included the first two years of the Clinton administration, 1993–95.

He did not seek reelection in the 1994 elections. Michel announced his decision not to seek reelection, stating that he had intended to retire in 1992. However, he decided not to retire when he believed that Republicans could win the House in 1992 and he would be elected the first Republican Speaker since 1955. When the Democrats continued their hold on the House in the 1992 election, and Michel did not become majority leader, he decided not to seek reelection in 1994.

Whether he would have been challenged for his job as party leader by NEWTON (NEWT) LEROY GINGRICH (R-Ga.) in 1995 is unknown, but it was likely that the challenge would have been mounted and that Gingrich would have won. Newt Gingrich ushered in the 1994 House election of conservatives with his Contract for America and was then elected Speaker in 1995. Michel, a political moderate, never built bridges to the conservative factions in the House who had suddenly moved into power in the 1994 elections.

Michel was generally a conciliator in the House and consistently worked with Speaker Thomas S. Foley (D-Wash.) to create bipartisan support for legislation. When Michel announced he would not seek reelection, Foley praised Michel, saying that Michel possessed "a shared esteem for the institution of Congress" despite political differences. Newt Gingrich, who succeeded Michel, became more confrontational in his relationship with Democrats in the House than Michel had been, leading to increased tensions between Democrats and Republicans in the House and with the Clinton White House.

Michel, although known as a conciliator, never supported the major Clinton initiative of 1993 and 1994: the health care reform initiative. As had many Republicans in the House, Michel opposed the concept of universal health care that was proposed by the Health Care Task Force in the White House. Michel also removed himself from the major debate over the National Service bill in 1993, which was supported by many Republicans.

Born on March 2, 1923, Michel served during World War II in the 39th Infantry Regiment as a combat infantryman in England, France, Belgium, and Germany from February 19, 1943, to January 26, 1946. He received two Bronze Stars, the Purple Heart, and four battle stars. When he returned from the war, he attended college and received his B.S. from Bradley University (1948). His first political job was as the administrative assistant to Representative Harold Velde (1949–56). After leaving the House of Representatives in 1995, Michel joined the Washington, D.C., firm of Hogan & Hartson as a senior adviser for corporate and governmental affairs. Michel's papers and memorabilia were donated to the Dirksen Congressional Center in Oklahoma.

Mikva, Abner Joseph
(1926–) *White House counsel*

Abner Mikva was named by President Clinton as White House counsel on August 11, 1994,

replacing LLOYD CUTLER, who had accepted the position for only 130 days. Cutler had been brought into the White House as counsel after the abrupt resignation of BERNARD NUSSBAUM. Mikva joined the White House staff on October 1, 1994. He remained as White House counsel until November 1, 1995, when he returned to Chicago. Mikva was replaced by JACK QUINN.

Among the issues that Mikva dealt with as White House counsel was the Department of Justice investigation into the Waco, Texas, deaths of DAVID KORESH and his followers. Mikva also became entangled in various Whitewater inquiries by the independent counsel, KENNETH W. STARR. Mikva became a staunch defender of President Clinton, repeatedly stating that the Whitewater investigation into President and Mrs. Clinton's partnership in the Whitewater Land Development Corporation had no merit.

Judge Mikva relinquished a lifetime position as a federal judge to serve as White House counsel. Mikva had been on the federal bench since 1979, when he was nominated by President Clinton for the federal appeals court, but his nomination was fiercely opposed by the National Rifle Association. Mikva was finally confirmed by the Senate after a protracted six-month lobbying campaign against him and was sworn in as a circuit judge on the United States Court of Appeals for the District of Columbia Circuit on September 17, 1979. He became chief judge on January 19, 1991.

Prior to his appointment to the federal court, Mikva, a Democrat, had served for more than two decades both in the Illinois legislature and in the U.S. Congress. He had been elected to the Illinois legislature in 1956, where he served five consecutive terms (1956–66). In 1968, he was elected to the U.S. House of Representatives, representing Chicago and Cook County. He ran and won against the Democratic political machine in Chicago and was consistently at odds with Mayor Richard J. Daley. During his tenure in the House of Representatives, Mikva served on both the Judiciary and the Ways and Means committees and was chairman of the Democratic Study Group, which was comprised of more than 250 House Democrats.

Mikva was out of Congress for one term, from 1972 to 1974, when the Republican Party redistricted and he lost the election. He ran again in 1974, was reelected, and remained in the House until he was appointed to the U.S. Court of Appeals in 1979.

In World War II, Mikva was a navigator in the Army Air Corps. He graduated with a B.A., Phi Beta Kappa, from the University of Wisconsin–Madison and with a J.D., cum laude, from the University of Chicago Law School (1951), where he was editor-in-chief of the law review and a member of the Order of the Coif, the national legal honor society. Following graduation from law school, Mikva was law clerk to U.S. Supreme Court Justice Sherman Minton.

After his clerkship with Justice Minton, Mikva returned to Chicago to practice law, becoming a partner of Justice Arthur Goldberg.

Milošević, Slobodan
(1941–   ) *president of the Federal Republic of Yugoslavia, president of Serbia*

Slobodan Milošević resigned the presidency of the Federal Republic of Yugoslavia in October 2000 after losing the September 24, 2000, elections. His popularity had plummeted after the United States–led bombing of Kosovo. He was replaced by Vojislav Kostunica. Milošević refused to concede the election until protesters filled the streets of Belgrade. On October 5, 2000, Milošević finally conceded.

Milošević remained in Belgrade, trying to regain his power. However, in April 2001

Slobodan Milošević *(Getty Images)*

President Kostunica ordered that Milošević be held accountable for war crimes and ordered him imprisoned in Belgrade. Troops were sent to Milošević's Belgrade home to arrest him but he refused. After a 26-hour standoff with police at his home, he surrendered after being promised a fair trial and that he would not immediately be turned over to the United Nations war crimes tribunal. On June 28, 2001, Milošević was handed over to the International Court at The Hague, where he was tried for war crimes in Croatia, Bosnia, and Kosovo.

He was accused of expelling non-Serbs from Croatia and Bosnia, which had declared independence in 1991 and 1992 from Yugoslavia, and for war crimes in Kosovo. Milošević refused to recognize the International Court at The Hague as legitimate and refused any legal defense. He defended himself against a list of charges that ran 125 pages and had over 1 million documents in evidence. Throughout the trial, which began in February 2002, Milošević suffered various medical problems, including high blood pressure, which often set back the proceedings. The trial may continue for years.

Milošević was born on August 20, 1941, in Požarevac, Yugoslavia. After joining the Communist Party when he was 18, he began his education in Belgrade. He graduated from the Faculty of Law at Belgrade University in 1964, becoming a successful businessman in Belgrade. From 1978 to 1983 he was president of the United Bank of Belgrade. In 1984 he was elected head of Belgrade's Communist Party organization.

In 1990 he was elected president of the Republic of Serbia, ousting President Ivan Stambolić, who had been his mentor in politics and in the Communist Party. As president, he resisted political reform, and as tensions increased, Croatia and Slovenia declared their independence in 1991, and Bosnia-Herzegovina was formed in 1992. He backed Serbian rebels as they attempted to regain Bosnia, leading to massive killings in Bosnia by Serb forces.

In 1995, Milošević signed a peace agreement with Bosnia, allowing Bosnian independence. In 1997 Serbia and Montenegro combined and Milošević was elected president of the newly created Federal Republic of Yugoslavia. His apparent goal when elected president in 1997 was to create a Serb-dominated Yugoslavia.

Soon after the creation of the Federal Republic of Yugoslavia, which included the province of Kosovo, nonviolent civil disobedience began in Kosovo as Albanian Muslims protested Serbian rule and sought independence.

In 1998, the Kosovars pushed for independence from the Federal Republic of Yugoslavia. Milošević then began a period of "ethnic cleansing" in Kosovo, in which at least 2,000 Muslims, who were ethnic Albanians, were killed and more than 400,000 driven from their homes in an effort to make Kosovo a Serbian province.

In March 1999, after Milošević refused both United States and NATO demands for a settlement with Kosovo, the United States led a bombing campaign against Serb forces in Kosovo. In June 1999, Milošević agreed to withdraw from Kosovo, and NATO peacekeepers entered the region.

Mitchell, George John
(1933–) *member of the Senate*

Senator George Mitchell (D-Me.) was elected to the Senate in 1982 and 1988 but did not seek reelection in 1994. He left the Senate to return to private law practice, accepting a position with the Washington, D.C., law firm of Verner, Liipfert, Bernhard, McPherson, and Hand in 1995.

Mitchell had been appointed in 1980 by Maine's governor to complete the unexpired term of Senator Edmund Muskie (D-Me.), who resigned to become secretary of state. Muskie replaced CYRUS VANCE, who left the Carter administration over the decision to use the military to rescue the American hostages held in Tehran, Iran.

Mitchell rose to Senate majority leader, a position he held from 1989 until 1995 when he retired. As Senate majority leader, Mitchell championed many of the Clinton administration's legislative initiatives. He was the leading advocate in the Senate for health care reform. His 1,400-page health care bill called for a new subsidy plan for health care for those that could not afford it and a health care program for low-income pregnant women and children. Mitchell hoped that the health care bill would become a landmark program completely reforming the federal health care delivery system. Republicans fought the legislation and ultimately succeeded in killing all but a few parts of Mitchell's legislation.

Soon after Mitchell announced in 1994 that he would retire from the Senate, Supreme Court Justice Harry A. Blackmun announced he would also retire. President Clinton suggested that he would name Mitchell to replace Blackmun, but Mitchell declined. Mitchell preferred to remain in the private sector after leaving the Senate. Part of the reason for Mitchell's decision may have been to devote more time to his new wife from his second marriage in December 1994.

But President Clinton continued to urge that Mitchell reengage in the public sector. Mitchell finally agreed in 1995 to serve as the head of a commission negotiating a cease-fire in Northern Ireland. Mitchell's commission produced a report recommending that both the Irish and the British dispose of terrorist weapons and begin talks. Prime Minister John Major wanted all weapons disposed of before talks could begin. The recommendations of the commission fell apart soon after when the Irish Republican Army (IRA) blew up an area in London, killing two people.

During the 1996 presidential election, President Clinton turned to Mitchell to help with the debates with the Republican candidate, Senator ROBERT (BOB) JOSEPH DOLE. Mitchell represented Dole in the mock debates, mastering Dole's mannerisms and likely answers. Mitchell's relationship with Clinton became so strong that, after the election, he considered Mitchell for secretary of state at WARREN MINOR CHRISTOPHER's suggestion. MADELEINE KORBEL ALBRIGHT was ultimately chosen, which fulfilled President Clinton's goal of naming the first woman to the position.

Born on August 20, 1933, in Waterville, Maine, Mitchell graduated from Bowdoin College (1954) and from the Georgetown University Law Center (1960). After graduating from law school, Mitchell became a lawyer in the Antitrust Division of the Department of Justice. In 1962, Mitchell was named the executive assistant to Senator Muskie, which provided him with his first involvement in Congress and in electoral politics. After entering private law practice in 1970, Mitchell tried his hand at electoral politics with a run for governor of Maine in 1974. He lost the election to an independent in a three-way race.

With Muskie's support, Mitchell was appointed the U.S. attorney for Maine by President Carter in 1977. In 1979, again with Muskie's backing, Mitchell was appointed to the U.S. District Court for northern Maine. He remained on the bench only one year, when he was appointed to the Senate to fill Muskie's unexpired term.

Mitterrand, François
(1916–1996) *president of France*

François Mitterrand served as president of France from his election in 1981 until 1995, becoming the first socialist president of the Fifth Republic of France. After leaving office in 1995, he retired to a relatively private life in Champ de Mars and died there of cancer on January 8, 1996. Mitterrand was replaced by JACQUES CHIRAC and his conservative party.

After his election as president in 1981, Mitterrand began to move toward socialist goals, such as a shortened work week, longer holidays, a stronger social security system, and the nationalization of the nation's banks. The result of Mitterrand's programs was an increase in government debt and greater government regulation. By 1986, the franc had been devalued and the right had gained control of Parliament. When Mitterrand stepped down in 1995, the elections that followed were largely a repudiation of his socialist programs.

Mitterrand championed a strong European Union, which, he believed, was the best way to blunt a unified Germany after the fall of the Berlin Wall.

Soon after President Clinton took office, he invited Mitterrand to the White House. They met in Washington, D.C., on March 9, 1993, where they discussed events in the former Yugoslavia and issues surrounding President SLOBODAN MILOŠEVIĆ and Bosnia and other matters related to trade between France and the United States.

Mitterrand was born on October 26, 1916, the son of a rural stationmaster near Bordeaux, France. When Germany invaded France in World War II, Mitterrand joined the resistance. He was wounded in the war and became a German prisoner of war. After three attempts, he escaped from prison and returned to France. For a brief period, he worked with Marshal Pétain's pro-Nazi Vichy government, but he later downplayed his role with the Pétain regime and emphasized his role with the French resistance during the war.

Moore, Minyon
(1958–   ) *director of the Office of Political Affairs, deputy director of the Office of Political Affairs*

Minyon Moore was named assistant to the president and director of the Office of Political Affairs by President Clinton in 1999, becoming one of the highest-ranking female African Americans in the administration. She remained in the position until 2000 when she left to return to the staff of the Democratic National Committee.

Prior to being promoted to director of the Office of Political Affairs, Moore had served as its deputy director, appointed in March 1997. Moore joined a number of White House staff and cabinet officers who had moved from the Democratic National Committee to the administration. She had been the national political director for the Democratic National Commit-

tee before her appointment to the White House staff. ALEXIS HERMAN, assistant to the president, director of the office of public liaison, and secretary of labor, and RONALD H. BROWN, secretary of commerce, had also been with the Democratic National Committee.

Moore was one of three African Americans appointed to the senior staff of the White House in March 1997. THURGOOD MARSHALL, JR., was named assistant to the president and cabinet secretary, and Robert Johnson was named deputy assistant to the president and deputy director for public liaison. President Clinton actively sought to include African Americans in his cabinet and his White House staff as part of his 1992 campaign promise to have an "administration that looks like one America."

At the Democratic National Committee, Moore had been deputy chief of staff, assistant to the chairman, director of public liaison, and national political director. In addition, she had been the project director (1992) of the Democratic National Committee's Voter Project. Her involvement in national politics included serving as the deputy national political director of the National Rainbow Coalition (1988–93) founded by the Rev. JESSE JACKSON, as the national deputy field director for the Dukakis-Bentsen 1988 campaign, and as the executive assistant to the president of Operation PUSH, Inc., (1988), of which Jackson was director. From 1982–85 she worked as the promotional services director for the Encyclopaedia Britannica Educational Corp.

After Moore left the Clinton administration in 2001, TERENCE (TERRY) R. MCAULIFFE, chairman of the Democratic National Committee, appointed her as the chief operating officer of the Democratic National Committee. She was responsible for the day-to-day management and oversight of the party's activities, including political operations, communications, research strategy, and fund-raising.

The Democratic National Committee had a budget of $60 million at the time.

She left in August 2002 to join the Dewey Square Group, a political consulting firm, to head their state and local government section.

Morris, Richard (Dick)

(1948–   ) *political strategist for Clinton-Gore 1992 presidential campaign, political adviser to President Clinton*

Dick Morris had been a long-standing political adviser to President Clinton, having first worked for Clinton in his 1979 gubernatorial campaign in Arkansas. He became a key adviser during the 1992 presidential campaign, working closely with campaign strategists JAMES CARVILLE, JR., PAUL BEGALA, and STANLEY GREENBERG.

After the election, Morris chose not to join the administration but to remain an outside political adviser. Neither Carville nor Begala joined the administration at the time, but GEORGE ROBERT STEPHANOPOULOS was named director of communications. Begala joined the administration in the second term.

Morris had been the architect of Clinton's massive polling strategy during the 1992 campaign and during the early part of the administration. But Morris soon lost his influence in the White House, as many disapproved of his extensive polling. He was also viewed by many in the White House as arrogant and difficult to work with. By 1994, he was rarely involved in polling decisions and had lost his role as a key political strategist.

After the 1994 midterm elections, in which conservative Republicans gained control of the House of Representatives, President Clinton again began talking to Morris about political strategy. But the discussions were held in private, often in late-night phone calls. Morris was rarely invited to the White House. Even-

tually, President Clinton began bringing Morris back into political discussions in the White House and by 1995 Morris was again active in political strategy sessions for the president.

In mid-1995 Morris designed a television campaign for President Clinton, for which he was paid a 15 percent commission on every ad. He earned $2 million from the campaign. Morris began to poll daily, determining what the ad campaign should focus on. He then began to work on the 1996 reelection campaign, devising themes and strategies.

Morris's political loyalties, it turned out, were not to Clinton but to money. Morris began secretly working for Senator CHESTER TRENT LOTT (R-Miss.) in 1996.

Morris fell out of favor with the White House in August 1996 after revelations in a tabloid newspaper that Morris, who was married but had no children, had been involved with a $200-an-hour escort, Sherry Rowlands, for over a year. She revealed to the tabloid some of his sexual habits, including a foot fetish and other details. As reporters began to cover Morris's relationship with the escort, they also found that he had had a 10-year relationship with a Texas woman. The relationship had given him a daughter.

While Morris's wife, Eileen McGann, remained by his side throughout the fallout from the tabloid stories, she divorced him the following year. He wrote a book about his role in the Clinton presidency, *Behind the Oval Office*, in 1997, which detailed his relationship with President Clinton and his role in the 1992 campaign and during the first term of the administration. The book was often not flattering to the president or many of his advisers, which again brought distance to the relationship between Morris and the White House. His publisher, Random House, paid Morris $2.5 million for the book.

Morris had several earlier problems with his finances, including being a partner in a consulting firm that went bankrupt in 1983. He spent enormous sums of money on travel and fine restaurants and enjoyed the trappings of financial success.

Morris, born in 1948 in New York City, attended Columbia University. By the late 1970s, Morris was working as a political consultant to various Democratic Party candidates in New York City. When he was hired by candidate Bill Clinton in 1979 for the Arkansas gubernatorial race, it was Morris's first out-of-state political race.

Moynihan, Daniel Patrick
(1927–2003) *member of the Senate*

Daniel Patrick Moynihan (D-N.Y.), first elected to the Senate in 1976, retired from the Senate after four terms. He did not seek reelection in 2000 and died in 2003. HILLARY DIANE RODHAM CLINTON succeeded Moynihan in the Senate.

Writing in *U.S. News and World Report* in March 2003 soon after Moynihan's death, editor-at-large DAVID GERGEN wrote that Moynihan "was a luminous beacon, ever pointing us toward deeper truths." Gergen quoted political analyst Michael Barone, who said that Moynihan was "the nation's best thinker among politicians since Lincoln and its best politician among thinkers since Jefferson."

Throughout the Clinton administration, Moynihan served as both an ally and a foe as chairman of the Senate Finance Committee, particularly with the national service bill, the health care reform bill, and the welfare reform bill.

When the national service bill was being considered, President Clinton sought Moynihan's support but did not seek his advice. ELI SEGAL in the White House managed the development of the legislation. In both the health care and welfare reform cases, Moynihan was more aggressive and sought changes in the administration's proposals. There was a particularly difficult relationship between the administration's health care task force, managed by Mrs. Clinton, and Moynihan. Having worked on health care and authored a universal health care proposal himself in both the Nixon and Ford administrations, Moynihan felt that he had not been fully consulted as the health care proposal was being developed in the White House. He also felt that welfare reform should be tackled by the administration before health care reform. Moynihan argued that the nation had universal health care, and no one was deprived. For Moynihan, restructuring welfare would improve the plight of the urban poor by building a job structure that worked.

Moynihan not only was critical of the Clinton administration's priorities in Congress, but also of President Clinton's personal matters. When issues of financial improprieties arose regarding President and Mrs. Clinton's loans for the Whitewater land development project, Moynihan became the highest-ranking Democrat to call for an independent counsel.

His first foray into politics came with the 1960 John F. Kennedy–Richard Nixon presidential election. He knew members of the Kennedy campaign staff, and after the election he was named assistant to Secretary of Labor Arthur Goldberg. In 1963, Moynihan was named assistant secretary of labor. After President Kennedy's assassination in 1963, Moynihan remained with the administration of President Lyndon Johnson. In 1965, Moynihan wrote a report called *The Negro Family: The Case for National Action*, which argued that illegitimacy rates and a "tangle of pathology" put African-American families at risk of falling income and a greater dependency on welfare. He was attacked for his report by civil rights leaders who mistakenly believed that Moynihan was blaming African Americans for their plight. He was not.

After leaving the Johnson administration and joining the faculty of Harvard University-

Massachusetts Institute of Technology (MIT) Joint Center for Urban Studies, Moynihan wrote *Beyond the Melting Pot* in collaboration with sociologist Nathan Glazer.

In 1969 the newly elected president, Richard Nixon, brought Moynihan into his administration as a senior staff member focused on urban affairs and as the director of the Urban Affairs Council. Nixon created the Urban Affairs Council to deal with inner-city poverty, which Nixon believed had largely contributed to the riots during the summer of 1968. Moynihan never fit into the Nixon White House structure and was soon promoted to a "counselor" with few specific responsibilities. In 1975, President Ford appointed Moynihan as ambassador to India.

After serving for one year as ambassador to India, Moynihan launched a successful campaign in 1976 to win the Senate seat from New York. Moynihan was reelected in 1982 and 1988, but did not seek reelection in 2000.

Born on March 6, 1927, in Tulsa, Oklahoma, Moynihan started City College in New York City in 1943 but after a year of college he joined the Naval Reserve and trained at Middlebury College. The navy finally sent Moynihan to finish his education at Tufts University from which he graduated with his B.S.N., cum laude (1946), his B.A. (1948), and M.A. (1949). He then began studying for his Ph.D. at the Fletcher School of Law and Diplomacy at Tufts University and completed his work in 1961. During his work at Tufts, he won a Fulbright scholarship and attended the London School of Economics.

Mubarak, Hosni
(1928–   ) president of Egypt

On July 23, 1952, the monarchy of Egypt was overthrown in a bloodless military coup led by Colonel Gamal Abdel Nasser, and the country was declared a republic one year later. In June 1956 Nasser was elected president. After his death in 1970, Vice President Anwar Sadat became president. When Sadat was assassinated in 1981 by a group of Egyptians who opposed his peace efforts with Israel, Vice President Hosni Mubarak succeeded him as president.

Sadat and Israeli prime minister Menachem Begin had participated in the 1978 peace agreement known as the Camp David accords, which were negotiated by President Jimmy Carter. When Mubarak was elected president in 1981, he reaffirmed his commitment to the Camp David accords and to Middle East peace.

The peace agreement that President Carter negotiated in 1978 remained the framework for Middle East peace negotiations for future American presidents, including President Clinton. During his administration, President Clinton focused on negotiating a peace agreement between Israel and the Palestine Liberation Organization (PLO). President Clinton secured some compromises on the relationship between the Israelis and the PLO with his sponsorship of the Oslo Accords in 1993 between Israel and the PLO. Another agreement between Israel and the PLO was negotiated in Egypt in 1995 with Mubarak's assistance.

But relations became strained between Israel and Egypt during the tenure of BENJAMIN NETANYAHU (1996–99), a period when Israel began to increase its building program of housing settlements outside of Jerusalem. Egypt objected to any settlements which would cut off Arab neighborhoods from Palestinian territory. Little progress was made in peace negotiations with the PLO during this period.

After Netanyahu left office and EHUD BARAK (1999) and ARIEL SHARON (2001) had been elected in Israel, Mubarak became more engaged in the peace process and tried to address broader issues of Middle East peace.

Mubarak was born on May 4, 1928, in the village of Kafr-el-Meselha in the Nile River Delta province of Menoufiya. He enrolled at the National Military Academy, graduating in 1949, and then pursued a two-year course at the Air Force Academy and from 1951–59 he was a flight instructor at the academy.

He rose through the ranks of the air force, becoming commander of the Air Force Academy (1967), air force chief of staff (1969), and commander in chief of the air force and deputy minister of war (1972).

During the October 1973 Arab-Israeli War, Mubarak became widely known for his successful offensive against the Israelis on the first day of the war. When a cease-fire was arranged by the United Nations in late October 1973, President Sadat sent Mubarak to every Arab country to explain the Egyptian government's position on reaching a peaceful settlement to the war. Sadat subsequently named Mubarak as his vice president on April 15, 1975.

Mubarak was elected in 1980 to the vice chairmanship of the National Democratic Party (NDP), which was the second most important political position in the country. When Sadat was assassinated on October 6, 1981, by Islamic fundamentalists, Mubarak was nominated by the NDP as its presidential candidate. The Egyptian parliament approved his immediate succession to the presidency, which was confirmed on October 13 by a national referendum. The president of Egypt serves for six-year terms, and Mubarak was reelected in 1987, 1993, and 1999.

Myers, Dee Dee
(1961–   ) *press secretary*

Dee Dee Myers became the first female press secretary when appointed by President Clinton in January 1993. She was named press secretary on January 14, 1993, during a press briefing that included appointments of several members of the White House staff. Myers remained in the position until December 1994 when MICHAEL MCCURRY, the State Department press secretary, replaced her.

Myers joined the Clinton campaign in 1991, working for the Clinton for President campaign. She continued to work for the campaign through the election in 1992, serving as the Clinton-Gore 1992 press secretary and later as the presidential transition press secretary.

When named to the White House staff, her title was press secretary and deputy assistant to the president within the Office of Communications. GEORGE ROBERT STEPHANOPOULOS was the director of the Office of Communications. As a deputy assistant to the president, rather than assistant to the president, as Stephanopoulos was, Myers did not have direct access to President Clinton. Her primary role was in the daily press briefings in the White House.

Myers became part of a major staff shakeup in the White House in June 1994 and was asked to resign. At the heart of the shake-up was an attempt to bring greater order and discipline to the White House staff, which had become known for its chaotic handling of issues. Chief of Staff THOMAS FRANKLIN MCLARTY III was replaced by LEON EDWARD PANETTA, the director of the Office of Management and Budget. Panetta made numerous staff changes within the White House, including within his own office. One of the changes he sought was Myers's departure, but she refused to leave. She appealed to President Clinton for an additional six months on the job to allow her time to find a position and to give the appearance that she had not been pushed out.

Myers often lacked full information on issues on which she was briefing the press and was frequently criticized for her inability to discuss issues in depth. The problem in her press briefings was that she was not part of the White House senior staff, which was limited to those with the title assistant to the president, and often was not part of policy discussions in the White House. She was asked to brief the press without full knowledge of how decisions were reached. One of her most difficult briefings was on the firings in the White House travel office. She stated to the press that she had known nothing about the firings, but President Clinton stated that the senior staff had been discussing it for weeks. Her credibility as a White House insider plummeted. When

Michael McCurry replaced Myers in December 1994, he insisted on the title assistant to the president and insisted on being fully informed on issues that he needed to discuss with the press.

Myers was also inexperienced in dealing with the White House press corps. At 31, Myers was among the youngest White House staff members and had little experience dealing with the national press except during the campaign.

At Myers's last White House press briefing on December 22, 1994, President Clinton walked into the press room to wish her well

Dee Dee Myers *(AP Photo/Greg Gibson)*

and talk to reporters about her excellent job as press secretary.

In spite of her departure from the White House staff, she remained intensely loyal to President Clinton. When the president was under investigation by the independent counsel, KENNETH W. STARR, Myers became his staunch defender. She was frequently on television defending the president and criticizing the politicization of the independent counsel's investigation.

Born on September 1, 1961, Myers graduated from Santa Clara University in 1983 and began her career working in California politics. Prior to her work on the Clinton campaign, she had been the press secretary for Dianne Feinstein in her 1990 bid for governor of California. Myers had also worked on the presidential campaigns of Massachusetts governor Michael Dukakis in 1988 and former vice president Walter Mondale in 1984. From 1985–88 she was the press secretary for Los Angeles mayor Tom Bradley and in 1989 served on the campaign to reelect Bradley. For a short time after working for Bradley, she formed a communications and political consulting firm before joining the Clinton campaign in 1991. Her clients included San Francisco mayor Frank Jordan, California state senator Art Torres, the League of Conservation Voters, and the Los Angeles Educational Partnership.

After leaving the White House, Myers became the cohost of the CNBC television program *Equal Time*, where she remained from 1995 to 1997. She then opened her own consulting firm, Dee Dee Myers & Associates, and became a regular commentator on political talk shows on television and a lecturer on politics through the Harry Walker Agency. She was also a contributing editor to *Vanity Fair* magazine.

N

Nadler, Jerrold Lewis

(1947–) *member of the House of Representatives*

Jerrold Nadler (D-N.Y.) represented New York's 8th Congressional District, which included Brooklyn and parts of Manhattan. He was first elected to the House of Representatives in a special election in 1992 after serving for 16 years in the New York State Assembly (1977–92). In 2002, Nadler was reelected to his sixth term with 75 percent of the vote.

Nadler was one of the earliest supporters of President Clinton during the investigation by independent counsel KENNETH W. STARR. As a member of the House Judiciary Committee, Nadler was an outspoken opponent of impeachment in 1998. In subcommittee hearings in November 1998, Nadler referred to Starr's perjury and obstruction-of-justice investigation as a "jihad," or holy war. Nadler was among a group of Democrats who believed that the Starr investigation was politically motivated by conservative Republicans seeking to oust President Clinton from office for political reasons.

In September 1998 Nadler opposed the Republican majority on the Judiciary Committee, led by Representative HENRY JOHN HYDE (R-Ill.), who wanted to release the final report sent to Congress by Starr on the MONICA LEWINSKY investigation. The material, which included graphic descriptions by Lewinsky about the relationship with President Clinton, was released by the House.

After the president's impeachment in December 1998, Nadler accused Republican members of the House of engaging in "sexual McCarthyism." He used the phrase to describe both the investigation of President Clinton and the resignation of Speaker-elect ROBERT (BOB) L. LIVINGSTON, JR. (R-La.), over sexual affairs. "Bob Livingston's resignation . . . is a surrender to a developing sexual McCarthyism," said Nadler. "We are losing sight of the distinction between sins, which ought to be between a person and his family and his God, and crimes, which are the concern of the state and of society as a whole."

Nadler's voting record in the House included support for legislation that banned assault weapons and that outlawed bias crimes. In 1996 Nadler voted against the Communications Decency Act that banned certain material from being placed on the Internet. It was targeted at indecent material that children might view. Nadler argued that technologies were available on computers to screen out inappropriate material for children without censoring free speech for adults. The U.S. Supreme Court overturned the law in 1997.

Born on June 13, 1947, Nadler graduated from Columbia University and Columbia Law School. He roomed with DICK MORRIS at Columbia University. Morris used his skills as a political strategist to help Nadler to get elected student body president.

Nadler was a member of the National Governing Council of the American Jewish Congress and was a member of the United States Holocaust Memorial Council. He also served as a member of the New York State board of directors of NARAL (the National Abortion Rights Action League) and the ADA (Americans for Democratic Action). He had been a past president of District 7-A of the Zionist Organization of America and served as a member of the board of the Women's Inter-Arts Center.

He was a delegate to the Democratic National Convention from New York in 2000.

Nash, Robert (Bobby) J.

(1947–   ) director, Office of Presidential Personnel; undersecretary for small community and rural development, Department of Agriculture; associate director, Office of Presidential Personnel

Bobby Nash was appointed assistant to the president and director of the Office of Presidential Personnel in 1995, after serving briefly as the associate director of the Office of Presidential Personnel in 1993. Soon after joining the White House staff, Nash was appointed undersecretary for small community and rural development in the Department of Agriculture. He remained there from 1993 to 1995, when he returned to the White House staff.

After the 1992 election, Nash was named to the presidential transition team to work on personnel issues and was named to the White House Personnel Office when President Clinton took office.

Born on September 26, 1947, in Texarkana, Arkansas, Nash received his B.A. from the University of Arkansas at Pine Bluff (1969) and an M.A. in urban studies from Howard University (1972). After graduating from college, Nash served as an employment counselor at the Arkansas State Employment Security Department (1969–70). In 1970 he moved to Washington, D.C., to become a management analyst with the Office of the Deputy Mayor (1970–71). He remained in city government after leaving the deputy mayor's office in 1971, moving to Fairfax, Virginia, as the assistant to the city manager of Fairfax (1971–72). He returned to Washington, D.C., in 1972 as the administrative officer for the National Training and Development Service (1972–74).

In 1974 he was named the director of community and regional planning for the Arkansas State Department of Planning (1974–75) and in 1975 was named vice president of the Winthrop Rockefeller Foundation, in Little Rock, Arkansas. He remained until 1982, when he was named the senior executive assistant to the governor of Arkansas for economic development (1982–89). In 1989, he was the president and secretary of the board of the Arkansas Development Finance Authority (1989–92). Nash joined the Clinton White House staff in 1993.

Nash, William L.

(1943–   ) commanding general, peacekeeping forces in Bosnia

Major General William L. Nash served as commanding general of the U.S. Army peacekeeping forces in Bosnia. He commanded the 1st Armored Division from June 1995 to May 1997. From December 1995 to November 1996 he also served as the commander of Task Force Eagle, a multinational division with more than 25,000 soldiers from 12 nations, which oversaw the enforcement of the military provisions of the Dayton Peace Accord in Bosnia and Herzegovina. General Nash became the first American officer since the end of World War II to exercise tactical control of Russian and Polish forces during the peace-keeping efforts in Bosnia in 1996.

General Nash left military service in 1998 after 34 years in the military, but was brought back into government service as a civilian as the regional administrator for the United Nations in northern Kosovo, with headquarters in Mitrovica. He became the senior United Nations official in Mitrovica, charged with overseeing the civil administration of Kosovo after the air campaign by the North Atlantic Treaty Organization (NATO).

In January 1999, after a year in Bosnia, General Nash joined a Washington, D.C., think tank, the National Democratic Institute for Global Affairs, as the director of the Global Civil-Military Relations Program. The National Democratic Institute (NDI) fostered programs that created democratic, civilian control of the military by improving the capacity of civilian institutions in emerging democracies. Nash traveled for NDI to Europe, Asia, Africa, and Latin America promoting civilian control of the military.

In April 2002 United Nations secretary-general KOFI ANNAN again brought Nash back into public service by naming him to the United Nations fact-finding team to develop accurate information on the Jenin refugee camp.

Prior to joining the National Democratic Institute, Nash was a fellow and visiting lecturer at the John F. Kennedy School of Government at Harvard University. In addition, he was a senior fellow and director of the Center for Preventive Action at the Council on Foreign Relations.

Born August 10, 1943, he graduated from the U.S. Military Academy at West Point, New York.

Neel, Roy M.

(1945–) *deputy chief of staff, chief of staff to the vice president*

Roy M. Neel served as White House deputy chief of staff under THOMAS FRANKLIN MCLARTY III for six months during the first year of the administration, from June until December 1993. Neel replaced MARK GEARAN, who was named director of communications in a senior staff reorganization by McLarty. Neel's role in the White House as deputy chief of staff was to manage day-to-day activities in the White House, including personnel issues.

Neel began his tenure in the administration as chief of staff to Vice President ALBERT (AL) GORE, JR., in January 1993, where he remained until moving to the White House as deputy chief of staff. Neel had been a long-time aide to Gore during his tenure in both the House and the Senate, first joining the Gore staff in 1977. He had been legislative director and then chief of staff while Gore was in the Senate. As a Senate staffer, Neel became one of Gore's principal advisers in telecommunications policy. After the 1992 presidential election, Neel was named chief of staff to Gore.

Neel left the White House at the same time that HOWARD PASTER, the congressional liaison, left. The White House underwent another major reorganization of staff at the end of 1993 with the loss of Neel and Paster. BRUCE LINDSEY moved from his job as White House personnel director to senior adviser to the president, a job that was called "the president's political eyes and ears." PHILIP LADER, deputy director for management at the Office of Management and Budget, became the deputy chief of staff.

Neel left the White House at the end of 1993 to assume a new position as president and chief executive officer of the United States Telephone Association, a position he formally began on March 1, 1994. He announced his departure in November 1993, to be effective at the end of the year. The United States Telephone Association lobbied in Washington, D.C., on behalf of the telephone industry.

Neel remained at the United States Telephone Association throughout the remainder of the Clinton administration. However, when Gore lost the 2000 election, Neel left the association when his political connections in the new administration of President-elect George W. Bush were not as strong. Neel had taken a leave of absence in July 2000 to work for the Gore presidential campaign and resigned on March 31, 2001.

Netanyahu, Benjamin
(1949–) *prime minister of Israel*

Benjamin Netanyahu, widely known as "Bibi," served as prime minister of Israel from the Likud Party from 1996 to 1999, defeating Israeli prime minister SHIMON PERES (Labor Party) in the May 1996 elections. Netanyahu won the election as a hard-liner, persuading the country that they should oppose relinquishing Israeli control of the city of Jerusalem and should not allow land to be taken away in peace negotiations. He also opposed Israel's 1993 land-for-peace agreement with the Palestine Liberation Organization (PLO) in the Oslo Accord, which granted self-rule to Palestinians living in the West Bank and the Gaza Strip. The Oslo Accord was negotiated by Peres and by Palestine Liberation Organization (PLO) chairman YASSER ARAFAT and signed in Washington, D.C., in a ceremony hosted by President Clinton.

Netanyahu lost the election in 1999 to EHUD BARAK, who favored stronger relations with the Palestinians.

President Clinton worked during his administration to encourage a peaceful resolution to the territorial issues between Israel and the Palestinians. On October 23, 1998, Prime Minister Netanyahu and Chairman Arafat signed the Wye River Memorandum at a retreat on the Wye River on the eastern shore of Maryland organized by President Clinton.

The Wye River negotiations were overseen by ARIEL SHARON, who was appointed by Netanyahu as the foreign minister and chief negotiator for Israel. At President Clinton's invitation, King HUSSEIN of Jordan flew to the signing. Hussein had been undergoing treatment for cancer at the Mayo Clinic (Rochester, Minnesota), but had been instrumental in bringing peace to the Middle East.

The Wye River memorandum was a land-for-security agreement between Israel and the PLO. However, in December 1998, Netanyahu suspended the agreement after increasing violence in the Palestinian-held territories and increased suicide bombings.

Born on October 21, 1949, Netanyahu received his B. Sc. in architecture from the Massachusetts Institute of Technology (MIT) in 1974 and his M.Sc. in management studies from MIT in 1976. After leaving MIT, he accepted a job with the Boston Consulting Group, an international business consulting firm. However, he had been on the job only a few months when his brother, Jonathan, was killed in the commando raid in Entebbe, Uganda, to release a hijacked jetliner. After his brother's death, Netanyahu returned to Israel and was named director of the Jonathan Institute, in honor of his brother, in Jerusalem. From 1980–82 he was director of marketing for Rim Industries in Jerusalem.

Netanyahu began his career in government in 1982 when he was named deputy chief mission officer at the Israeli embassy in Washington, D.C. From 1984 to 1988 Netanyahu served as the ambassador to the United Nations from Israel. He was a member of the U.S.-Israel Strategic Talks in 1984. He had served in the Israeli army from 1967–72 in the antiterrorism unit. While a commando in the Israeli army, Netanyahu had participated in several high-profile missions, including a rescue of a hijacked jetliner outside Tel Aviv in 1971.

Benjamin Netanyahu's political career began when he was elected to the Knesset in 1988. He served as deputy foreign minister from 1988–92, as deputy minister, Office of the Prime Minister, from 1991–92, and as leader of the right-wing Likud Party in 1993. He was elected prime minister in 1996 in the first direct election of a prime minister in Israel, serving in this position until July 1999. In November 2002 Netanyahu was named foreign minister by Prime Minister Ariel Sharon.

He remained deeply opposed to Yasser Arafat, the leader of the PLO, even after his tenure as prime minister. He was, as were many in the Israeli leadership, outraged at the Palestinian suicide bombings that had escalated in 2001 and 2002. Speaking before the U.S. Senate on April 10, 2002, Netanyahu said "Yasser Arafat brazenly pursues an ideology of policide—the destruction of a state—and meticulously promotes a cult of suicide."

Nickles, Donald Lee
(1948–) *member of the Senate*

Don Nickles (R-Okla.) was elected to the U.S. Senate in 1980 and sworn in on January 3, 1981. He was reelected to the Senate in 1986, 1992, and in 1998, winning his last election in 1998 with 66 percent of the vote. In 1996 he was elected Republican whip and in 2001 was elected the assistant majority leader.

During the Clinton administration, Nickles opposed a variety of administration-sponsored bills, including the Btu and gasoline taxes in 1993. In 1998 he held up the nomination of Jane Henney as director of the Food and Drug Administration (FDA) until Secretary of Health and Human Services DONNA SHALALA agreed not to seek a manufacturer for RU-486 (the "day after" pill for aborting pregnancies) or to support abortions under Medicaid. In 1999 he opposed the confirmation of RICHARD C. HOLBROOKE as ambassador to the United Nations. He also opposed the administration's national service program, calling AmeriCorps "a boondoggle."

Nickles represented a conservative base in Oklahoma and remained conservative in his voting record in the Senate. *Congress Daily* described Nickles as "the keeper of the conservative flame." His voting record included votes against allowing abortions on military bases, for restricting rules on personal bankruptcy, supporting a balanced budget constitutional amendment, increasing penalties for drug offenses, opposing the Comprehensive Nuclear Test Ban Treaty, supporting deployment of a missile defense system, and opposing federal mandatory sentences for crimes involving firearms. He also opposed expanding job discrimination to include sexual orientation and opposed federal set-asides for minority contracts.

Born on December 6, 1948, Nickles received his B.A. from Oklahoma State University in 1971 and spent six years (1970–76) in the Army Reserve National Guard. He later entered private business as the vice president and general manager of Nickles Machine Corporation in Ponca City, Oklahoma. In 1978 he successfully ran for the Oklahoma State Senate, where he remained until his successful run for the U.S. Senate in 1980. At the age of 31, Nickles became the youngest Republican elected to the U.S. Senate. In 1992, after winning election to his third term, he became the first Oklahoma Republican elected to a third term in the U.S. Senate.

Nickles served on the Senate Finance Committee, the Energy and Natural Resources Committee, Budget Committee, and Rules and Administration Committee. He was also the ranking member of the Social Security Subcommittee of the Finance Committee and the ranking member of the Subcommittee on Energy Research, Development, Production, and Regulation. Nickles referred to himself as "one of the few members of Congress with a background in small business."

Nixon, Richard Milhous
(1913–1994) *president of the United States*

President Richard Nixon, 37th president of the United States, died on April 22, 1994, during the first term of the Clinton administration.

The funeral was held on April 27, 1994, in Yorba Linda, California, at the Richard M. Nixon Library and Birthplace. President Clinton joined the four living past presidents, Gerald R. Ford, Jimmy Carter, Ronald Reagan, and GEORGE HERBERT WALKER BUSH, and their wives. They sat together in the first row of seats. This marked the first funeral for an American president since Lyndon B. Johnson's funeral in 1973.

President Nixon's coffin was covered with an American flag and rested on a catafalque during the funeral. Many of President Nixon's staff and cabinet officers attended the funeral, including former vice president Spiro T. Agnew, who resigned in 1973 after pleading no contest to a charge of tax evasion. Forty-seven senators, 64 representatives, and 11 former members of Congress joined President Clinton on Air Force One and five other Air Force planes in the flight from Washington, D.C., to California for the funeral.

In his eulogy, President Clinton quoted from President Nixon's 1968 speech accepting the Republican nomination. He also spoke of "the force of a driving dream" that had carried President Nixon from his humble beginnings to the presidency of the United States. Clinton included in his eulogy, "He made mistakes; and, they, like his accomplishments, are part of his life and record. But the enduring lesson of Richard Nixon is that he never gave up being part of the action and passion of the times." Other speakers included Senator Bob Dole (R-Kans.), whose voice cracked as he quoted President Nixon saying, "In the end what matters is that you have always lived life to the hilt."

In the front row on one side were the former presidents and President and Mrs. Clinton. On the other side of the front row sat the Nixon family, including Julie Nixon Eisenhower and Tricia Nixon Cox and their families.

Born on January 9, 1913, Nixon received his A.B. from Whittier College (1934) and his LL.B. with honors from Duke University Law School (1937). He practiced law in Whittier, California, for five years (1937–42), and in Washington, D.C., as an attorney with the Office of Emergency Management Administration for six months in 1942. He successfully ran for office from the 12th Congressional District in California and served two terms (1947–51). In 1950, he won a seat in the U.S. Senate, where he remained until 1953 when he was tapped as vice president by Dwight D. Eisenhower.

Nixon served two terms as vice president, 1953–61. In 1960 he secured the Republican nomination for president but lost in an exceedingly close race to Senator John F. Kennedy (D-Mass.). Kennedy received 34,226,731 popular votes, and 303 electoral votes, and Nixon received 34,108,157 popular votes, and 219 electoral votes.

After his failed run for the presidency in 1960, Nixon joined the Los Angeles law firm of Adams, Duque & Hazeltine (1961–63). He then moved to New York City with the law firm of Mudge, Stern, Baldwin & Todd and in 1964 formed the firm Nixon, Mudge, Rose, Guthrie & Alexander in New York City.

In 1968 Nixon again won the Republican nomination for president but, unlike in 1960, was successful in capturing the election. Nixon received 31,785,480 popular votes, and 301 electoral votes, the Democratic challenger Hubert Humphrey (D-Minn.) received 31,275,166 popular votes, and 191 electoral votes, and Governor George C. Wallace of Alabama received 9,906,473 popular votes, and 46 electoral votes.

Nixon served for one full term (1969–73) and part of a second term before he resigned from office in August 1974. After he was forced by the U.S. Supreme Court to release audio tapes from conversations in the Oval Office in *U.S. v. Nixon*, Nixon resigned. The tapes proved his involvement in the White House cover-up of the break-in at the Democratic National Committee's headquarters in the Watergate apartment complex during the 1972 presidential campaign.

Nunn, Samuel (Sam) Augustus
(1938–   ) *member of the Senate*

Sam Nunn (D-Ga.) represented Georgia in the U.S. Senate for 24 years from 1973–97. He retired from the Senate to join the Atlanta law firm of King and Spalding. After leaving the Senate, Nunn became cochairman and chief executive officer of the Nuclear Threat Initiative (NIT), a foundation committed to reducing the global threat of nuclear and other weapons of mass destruction. He also was named a distinguished professor in the Sam Nunn School of International Affairs at Georgia Tech University.

During his tenure in the Senate, Nunn served as chairman of the Senate Armed Services Committee and the Permanent Subcom-

mittee on Investigations. He also served on the Intelligence Committee and the Small Business Committee. He was considered a conservative Democrat in the Senate, representative of the changing political nature of the South, which often elected Republicans in the 1970s and 1980s. Nunn was never closely aligned with President Clinton nor with the moderate and centrist Democrats who were involved in the Democratic Leadership Council.

Nunn's expertise in the Senate was in defense issues and matters relating to the Department of Defense. He authored the landmark Department of Defense Reorganization Act with Senator Barry Goldwater (R-Ariz.) and the Nunn-Lugar Cooperative Threat Reduction Program with Senator Richard Lugar (R-Ind.). The program provided assistance to Russia and the former Soviet republics for securing and destroying their excess nuclear, biological, and chemical weapons.

During the first year of the Clinton administration, Senator Nunn became embroiled in a priority issue of the administration to change the manner in which gays were dealt with by the military. Rather than have the military expel anyone who was homosexual, the Clinton administration wanted to change the policy for sexual orientation not to be a factor in military service. The military establishment objected, seeking Senator Nunn's intervention in the administration's change of policy. Rather than suspend the ban on military service by homosexuals, Senator Nunn and military leaders agreed with the Clinton administration that the military would stop asking new recruits about their sexual orientation and would not actively seek to discharge homosexuals in the military. The issue was resolved on January 29, 1993.

Even after leaving the Senate, Sam Nunn was a widely respected expert on national security issues. On July 23, 2001, Senator Nunn was invited to the House Government Reform Committee, Subcommittee on National Security, Veterans Affairs, and International Affairs to address the possible use of smallpox as a biological weapon by terrorists.

Born on September 8, 1938, Nunn attended Georgia Tech and Emory University and graduated from Emory University Law School with honors (1962). He served one term in the U.S. House of Representatives (1963) and then joined the law firm of Nunn, Geiger & Rampey, in Perry, Georgia (1964–73). He was elected to the Georgia House of Representatives in 1968 and served until 1972. In a special election in November 1972 he was elected to the U.S. Senate and was thereafter reelected four times. He retired in 1997.

After leaving office, Nunn was named to the board of directors of the Coca-Cola Company, Dell Computer, General Electric, Internet Security Systems, Scientific-Atlanta, Texaco, and Total System Services.

Nussbaum, Bernard J.
(1931–   ) *White House counsel*

Bernard Nussbaum was named White House counsel in January 1993 but resigned on March 5, 1994, effective April 5, 1994. During his tenure in the White House, Nussbaum became embroiled in a number of high-profile issues, including the failed nominations of ZOE BAIRD and KIMBA WOOD and later with the Whitewater investigation. After a little over a year on the job, Nussbaum abruptly resigned.

Nussbaum's relationship to President and Mrs. Clinton spanned nearly two decades. He had been friends with Hillary Clinton since 1974 when he was special counsel for the House Judiciary Committee's impeachment hearings of President Richard Nixon, and he hired Hillary Clinton as a staff member for the committee. Nussbaum kept in touch with the Clintons over the years. He was, for example, invited but did not attend Bill Clinton's first

inauguration as governor of Arkansas in 1979. When Clinton announced his intention to run for president in 1991, Nussbaum became an early supporter and fund-raiser, and remained active in the 1992 presidential campaign. Following the election, Nussbaum was among the first appointments to the White House staff. One description of Nussbaum at the time was that "He is a very skilled lawyer, very loyal, and very close to the Clintons."

Nussbaum, who moved into the inner circle of the president's advisory team in the White House, oversaw every legal document that the president was involved with. Among the legal issues that Nussbaum reviewed for the president were the three appointments for attorney general, all judicial nominations, the problems in Bosnia, and gays in the military. When President and Mrs. Clinton were charged by the independent counsel with financial improprieties in the loans from Madison Guaranty Savings and Loan in the Whitewater land development project, Nussbaum became the intermediary with the independent counsel. One of the prime reasons for his resignation was the criticism he had received for arranging White House briefings on bank regulators' actions in the Whitewater project.

During the first month of the administration, Nussbaum dealt with the failed appointments of two nominees for attorney general, Zoe Baird and Kimba Wood. His office was responsible for ensuring that the nominees for attorney general had been adequately scrutinized before Senate confirmation hearings. Nussbaum's office failed in its first two attempts to move nominees forward for attorney general. Both Baird and Wood removed their names after the Senate Judiciary Committee charged that they had failed to pay adequate social security taxes for household help and for nannies for their children. After two failures, Nussbaum suggested JANET RENO, who was successfully confirmed. Soon after, Nussbaum began dealing with the independent counsel on the Whitewater investigation and on the investigation into Deputy White House Counsel VINCENT W. FOSTER, JR.'s death. All of the Whitewater records belonging to President and Mrs. Clinton that the independent counsel sought had been reviewed by Nussbaum and Foster before they were given to the investigators.

Nussbaum refused to allow Federal Bureau of Investigation (FBI) agents into Foster's office immediately after Foster was found dead from a gunshot wound in a park off the George Washington Parkway outside of Washington, D.C. In a formal report on Foster's death prepared by the U.S. Park Service, which had jurisdiction to investigate the death, Nussbaum was criticized for impeding the investigation by removing the files related to Whitewater and insisting that administration attorneys sit in on interviews with witnesses.

His problems with the independent counsel over documents related to the Whitewater investigation and with the investigation into Foster's death led to his resignation in March 1994 as White House counsel.

After leaving the White House and returning to private law practice, he continued to be brought into investigations by the independent counsel. In November 1996, Nussbaum faced questioning by KENNETH W. STARR, the independent counsel, on his role in the hiring of Craig Livingstone. Livingstone, a White House staff member, was accused by Starr of having obtained reports from the FBI on former staff in the Bush administration. At a congressional hearing on Livingstone's use of FBI files, Nussbaum denied having talked with Mrs. Clinton about hiring Livingstone. The FBI uncovered a document in which Nussbaum wrote that Mrs. Clinton "highly recommended" hiring Livingstone. The investigation was later closed.

Born March 11, 1931, Nussbaum graduated from Columbia University in 1958 and from Harvard University Law School in 1961 where he was an editor of the *Harvard Law Review*. After law school, Nussbaum became an assistant U.S. attorney in the Southern District of New York, working for Robert M. Morgenthau (1961–66). After five years with the U.S. Attorney's Office, Nussbaum joined the law firm of Wachtell, Lipton, Rosen & Katz in New York City. He remained with Wachtell until he was tapped as White House counsel and returned to the firm after leaving the White House. He also served as a trustee of Mt. Sinai Hospital and the Jewish Theological Seminary.

O'Leary, Hazel Reid
(1937–   ) *secretary of energy*

Hazel O'Leary was appointed secretary of energy by President Clinton and sworn into office on January 22,1993. She resigned in January 1997 at the end of the first term, having announced her decision to resign on November 14, 1996. O'Leary was among four African Americans appointed to the cabinet in 1993. The four African Americans were O'Leary, RONALD H. BROWN (secretary of commerce), ALPHONSO MICHAEL (MIKE) ESPY (secretary of agriculture), and JESSE BROWN (secretary of veterans affairs). She became the first woman and the first African American to head the Department of Energy. Her successor at the Department of Energy in 1997 was FEDERICO PEÑA, who had moved from the position of secretary of transportation.

Among her more controversial acts as secretary of energy was "the openness initiative" in December 1996. She supported the Department of Energy's releasing the records which detailed inventories and locations of 111.4 metric tons of plutonium produced, used, and stored in the United States from World War II until 1996. O'Leary argued that the commitment to openness strengthened national security by inviting citizens to help the government make the right decisions. She received strong criticism for the action from the Department of Defense, the Department of State, and from Republicans. Her efforts to declassify the plutonium records were part of what she called the "veil of secrecy" that shrouded the Department of Energy. She promised when she took office to reduce the amount of classified information in the Department of Energy. In 1994 she signed an agreement with Russia to exchange technical information in the field of nuclear warhead safety and security, which included open warhead design information.

Another controversial decision by O'Leary was her announcement on May 4, 1995, that she would cut the department's workforce by 3,788 employees, or 27 percent, over the next five years, saving an estimated $1.7 billion. The cuts were an attempt to save the Department of Energy, which many Republicans in Congress had targeted for elimination. The Department of Energy, created in the Carter administration, was often considered an unneeded bureaucracy by Republicans in both houses of Congress. The proposal was reinvigorated after the 1994 elections when conservative Republicans gained control of the House of Representatives. O'Leary's proposal to shrink the Department of Energy responded to hearings that were scheduled in the House on June 8, 1995, for legislation abolishing the department.

O'Leary began a major campaign in 1995 to keep her department from being abolished by the Congress. She assembled a coalition of supporters, including environmental activists who want to see the department continue funding for solar, wind, and energy conservation programs. Other supporters included community activists who did not want the abolition of the department's efforts to clean up 130 former nuclear weapons sites across the country. The cleanup involved nearly 60 percent of the department's budget. Research organizations and universities joined the lobbying effort for fear of losing research dollars that the department provided. The Department of Energy managed 28 national laboratories among its research activities. The department was ultimately saved when members of Congress focused on other issues.

During her tenure as secretary of energy, O'Leary was often the subject of intense media scrutiny. She took what were called lavish trips around the world on trade issues. In October 1996 the Department of Energy Inspector General issued a report on the spending and travel practices of O'Leary, focusing on four trade missions to Hong Kong and India. She also hired a private consulting firm to rank the reporters covering her. Although the report was critical of her spending on the trade missions, it did not accuse her of impropriety.

After leaving office, O'Leary became involved in ethical questions following the 1996 presidential elections. JOHNNY CHUNG accused her of asking him for $25,000 for a charity called Africare in return for meeting with Chinese energy executives, including the president of China Petrochemical Corp., Huaren Sheng. According to Johnny Chung in a televised interview with NBC reporter Tom Brokaw, O'Leary told him, "It will be nice if you make your donation to Africare," if a meeting is held. The Department of Justice investigated and determined that O'Leary had sold "face time."

Secretary of Energy Hazel R. O'Leary *(Department of Energy)*

As a result, the Department of Justice staff sought an independent counsel. On December 2, 1997, Attorney General JANET RENO rejected appointing an independent counsel.

Born on May 17, 1937, as Hazel Reid, O'Leary received her B.A. from Fisk University in Nashville, Tennessee (1959) and her J.D. from Rutgers University Law School (1966). Her career included serving as executive vice president and general counsel for O'Leary and Associates, Inc., in Washington, D.C. (1981–89), a company she founded with her late husband, John O'Leary. The company helped with the development of power plants and lobbied state and federal legislatures on energy issues.

She later became executive vice president of Northern States Power Company in Minneapolis (1989–93) and president of Northern

States Power Company (1993). After she left the Clinton administration in 1997, O'Leary became president of O'Leary & Associates in Chevy Chase, Maryland. In 2000, she joined the investment firm of Blaylock & Partners in New York City.

Onassis, Jacqueline Bouvier Kennedy
(1929–1994) *wife of President John F. Kennedy*

Jacqueline Kennedy Onassis died on May 19, 1994, from cancer. The widow of President John F. Kennedy and of Greek shipping magnate Aristotle S. Onassis, she had removed herself from politics and become a successful book editor for Doubleday and Co. in New York City.

Soon after Mrs. Onassis died, President Clinton proposed renaming Lafayette Park, across Pennsylvania Avenue from the White House, the "Jacqueline Kennedy Onassis Park." Although proposed, the park was never renamed. President Clinton was an admirer of both President and Mrs. Kennedy, and in his eulogy to her stated that she had "a gift of grace and style and dignity and heroism."

As first lady, Jacqueline Kennedy had been involved in supervising the redecoration of the White House and encouraged preservation of nearby buildings. She helped plan the final phases of the Kennedy Center for Performing Arts in Washington, D.C., which was built at the end of the Eisenhower administration but renamed for President Kennedy. Among her many projects at the White House was planning the Rose Garden. She worked with her friend Mrs. Paul Mellon, an avid gardener who had planted rose gardens at her Georgetown home, to design the White House Rose Garden.

When President Kennedy was assassinated on November 22, 1963, in Dallas, Texas, Mrs. Kennedy was seated next to her husband in the car. She accompanied his casket to Washington, D.C., on Air Force One and walked in the funeral procession to Arlington National Cemetery. Following her death, she was buried in Arlington National Cemetery next to President Kennedy. Her youngest child was also buried at Arlington National Cemetery.

Five years after President Kennedy's assassination, on October 28, 1968, she married Aristotle S. Onassis, who was 23 years older than she. Although the marriage often had difficult periods and they lived apart, the couple never divorced. Onassis died in March 1975. After his death, Mrs. Onassis began a publishing career in New York City, working first for Viking Press and later for Doubleday and Co.

Born on July 28, 1929, in Southhampton, New York, she grew up in a wealthy, cultured family and became skilled in horsemanship. Her parents divorced and her mother, Janet, married Hugh D. Auchincloss in 1942. After the divorce, she lived with her mother and Auchincloss in his home, called Merrywood, in Washington, D.C., and at his summer estate in Newport, Rhode Island.

Two years after her graduation from college, she married John F. Kennedy on September 12, 1953, and they had three children: Caroline (1957–), John (1960–99) and Patrick, who died two days after his birth in 1963. She attended Vassar College in 1948–49 but graduated with a B.A. from George Washington University in 1951. During 1949 she studied at the Sorbonne in Paris. Before being promoted at Doubleday in 1982, Onassis had been an associate editor at Doubleday from 1978–82, and an editor at Viking Press from 1975–77.

Packwood, Robert William
(1932–) *member of the Senate*

Senator Robert Packwood (R-Ore.) resigned from the Senate on October 1, 1995, after the Senate Ethics Committee censured him on a unanimous vote. He was censured for sexual misconduct with 17 women, attempting to obstruct the committee's investigation, and using his position to solicit employment for his wife from individuals with interests in legislation that he could influence. He resigned rather than face an almost certain expulsion from the Senate upon the committee's recommendation.

Packwood, who had been investigated in the Senate for nearly two years, was accused by several women of improper sexual advances. Women who had worked with him over a span of 20 years supported the allegations of sexual harassment. The Senate voted 9-6 in November 1993 to seek a federal court order compelling Packwood to turn over his diaries. Packwood was also accused of improperly soliciting a job for his wife, Georgie. When she filed for divorce in 1993, her divorce papers provided the Ethics Committee with more information for its investigation.

During the first two years of the Clinton administration, Packwood often opposed administration-sponsored legislation. As the ranking Republican in 1993 and 1994 on the Senate Finance Committee, he worked with Finance Committee chair Senator DANIEL PATRICK MOYNIHAN (D-N.Y.) to refocus the health care plan. When the Republicans gained control of the Senate after the 1994 elections, Packwood essentially ended the deliberations in the Finance Committee on the Clinton administration's health care bill. In January 1995, Packwood became chair of the Senate Finance Committee and refocused the committee's work from health care reform to restructuring the tax code.

While in the Senate, he had served as chairman of the Republican Senatorial Campaign Committee (1977–79, 1981–83), and as chairman of the Republican Conference (1981–85). His committee assignments included chair of the Committee on Commerce, Science and Transportation (1981–85), Committee on Finance, (1985–87 and January 3, 1995–September 8, 1995), when he resigned his chairmanship, having announced his intention to resign from the Senate.

Born on September 11, 1932, in Portland, Oregon, Packwood graduated from Willamette University in Salem, Oregon, (1954) and from the New York University School of Law (1957). He practiced law in Portland, Oregon, until he was elected to the Oregon state legislature in

1963 (1963–68). In 1968 he was elected to the Senate and reelected in 1974, 1980, 1986, and 1992.

After leaving the Senate in 1995, Packwood formed a Washington-based consulting firm. In July 1996, the Justice Department sent Packwood's lawyers a one-line letter stating it would not prosecute him for issues raised by the Senate Ethics Committee. The letter said, "This will inform you that the Public Integrity Section has declined prosecution and closed its investigation of allegations that your client, Robert Packwood, obstructed justice."

Panetta, Leon Edward

(1938–   ) *White House chief of staff, director of the Office of Management and Budget, member of the House of Representatives*

Leon Panetta began his tenure in the Clinton administration as director of the Office of Management and Budget (OMB), where he served from January 21, 1993, to July 16, 1994. However, after a year and a half at OMB, President Clinton moved Panetta to the White House where he remained until the end of the first term in 1997.

In a major shake-up of the White House staff in the summer of 1994, Panetta was moved to the White House in July 1994 as the president's chief of staff to replace THOMAS FRANKLIN McLARTY III. Named as chief of staff on June 27, 1994, Panetta officially began his new position on July 17, 1994.

Panetta was replaced at the Office of Management and Budget by his deputy, ALICE RIVLIN. When Panetta replaced McLarty, McLarty was named counselor to the president. As White House chief of staff, Panetta was charged by President Clinton with bringing order to the management structure of the White House. Former chief of staff Mack McLarty had allowed too many people to see

President Clinton, which had been Clinton's intention. The result was that decisions were being made at the last minute and with little adequate White House review. As soon as he took office, Panetta mandated that all decision memoranda sent to the president and all meetings with the president were to be approved by him first. In addition, he insisted that meetings be held on time and that they have fixed agendas. In general, Panetta tried to bring order to a White House management structure that was often called chaotic. Instead of a decision process in the White House that included "kicking the idea around," Panetta wanted formal decision structures that brought clear memoranda to the president's desk in fixed periods of time.

One of Panetta's major roles for President Clinton came in the fall of 1995 when the Republican-controlled House of Representatives refused to support the administration's budget proposals. Panetta led a White House team, including economic adviser GENE SPERLING, to negotiate a budget with the House that favored the White House proposed budget. Panetta understood the House Budget Committee's negotiating tactics, since he had been chairman of the committee during his tenure in the House.

In addition to changes in the management structure of the White House, Panetta made changes in White House personnel. The most visible personnel change was that of the press secretary. Panetta wanted a more seasoned press secretary and brought in MICHAEL McCURRY from the State Department. The current press secretary, DEE DEE MYERS, was asked to resign in December 1994. In addition, Panetta made a number of changes within the chief of staff's office.

Panetta's expertise in both the budget and Congress stemmed from his 16 years in the House of Representatives. In 1976 Panetta won a seat in the House from California's 16th

Leon Panetta (right), accompanying President Clinton *(AP Photo/Dennis Cook)*

(now 17th) Congressional District and remained in office from 1977 until 1993. He served eight full terms and was in his ninth term when he was nominated by President Clinton for the position of director of the Office of Management and Budget.

While in the House of Representatives, Panetta was a member of and chair of the

House Budget Committee and was a member of the House Agriculture Committee and the House Administration Committee. He was named chairman of the Budget Committee in 1979 and as such served the maximum six years allowed by the Democratic caucus (1979–85). He regained the chairmanship of the committee in 1989 until he left to join the Clinton administration. As chairman of the House Budget Committee, Panetta had immersed himself in the technical details of the budget and the budget process.

Known as a deficit hawk, Panetta's appointment as director of the Office of Management and Budget signaled the administration's commitment to deficit reduction. As Panetta's deputy at the Office of Management and Budget, President Clinton named Alice Rivlin, a Brookings Institution scholar who was the first director of the Congressional Budget Office and also a deficit hawk. When Panetta went to the White House as chief of staff, Rivlin was named director of the Office of Management and Budget.

Panetta was born in Monterey, California, on June 28, 1938, the son of Italian immigrants. He received his B.A., magna cum laude, from the University of Santa Clara (1960), and his J.D. from the University of Santa Clara Law School (1963), where he was an editor of the law review. From 1964 to 1966 he served as a first lieutenant in the army, and received the Army Commendation Medal.

After graduating from law school, Panetta became a legislative assistant in the California Senate to Senate Minority Whip Thomas H. Kuchel (1966–69). When President Nixon brought former California lieutenant governor Robert H. Finch to Washington, D.C., as secretary of health, education and welfare (HEW) in 1969, Finch brought Leon Panetta as director of the Office of Civil Rights in HEW. Panetta was a Republican when he joined the

Nixon administration. Panetta remained at HEW only one year before resigning over a dispute with the Nixon White House (1969–70). Panetta wanted desegregation in southern states to be tied to the release of federal education funds in those states. The Nixon White House and Attorney General John Mitchell did not want to deal with the issue until after the 1972 election in order to preserve their electoral support in the South. As a result of his experience in the Department of Health, Education and Welfare in the Nixon administration, Panetta switched parties and registered as a Democrat.

When Panetta resigned from the Department of Health, Education and Welfare he accepted a position in New York City in the mayor's office (1970–71). He remained in New York City only a year before he returned to California and began to practice law in Monterey with the firm of Panetta, Thompson & Panetta (1971–76).

After leaving the Clinton administration in 1997, Panetta returned to Monterey, where he became director of the Panetta Institute, a bipartisan study center on public policy.

Paster, Howard
(1944–   ) *director of the Office of Legislative Affairs*

Howard Paster was appointed assistant to the president and director of the Office of Legislative Affairs in the White House in January 1993. His role was to oversee the congressional lobbying of all administration-sponsored legislation and to track all legislation in Congress. The Office of Legislative Affairs was divided into staff who lobbied in the House of Representatives and staff who lobbied in the Senate.

Paster was hired at the White House based on his depth of expertise in congressional affairs, which no one on the 1992 campaign staff possessed. He was one of the few White House senior staff who had not been part of the 1992 presidential campaign. Most senior White House staff had worked in Arkansas with President Clinton or had been key advisers or full-time staff on the campaign. Paster had been brought to the attention of the Clinton transition staff by Michael Berman, a longtime Paster friend and a top member of the Clinton campaign. Speaker of the House THOMAS FOLEY and House Majority Leader RICHARD (DICK) A. GEPHARDT, as well as Senate Majority Leader GEORGE JOHN MITCHELL, all endorsed Paster for the job.

Although Paster was the president's legislative director, he was marginalized during the White House lobbying efforts for the health care reform bill. First Lady HILLARY DIANE RODHAM CLINTON and IRA MAGAZINER, director of the health care task force, handled not only the policy development for the bill but the congressional lobbying. Both Chief of Staff THOMAS FRANKLIN MCLARTY III and Paster were left out of the decision making on the health care bill. Paster's biggest success came in 1993 with passage of the tax reform package.

Paster left the administration after two years (1993–94), completing one full session of Congress, adhering to the unwritten rule within the office of legislative affairs that staff, particularly the director, remain through a full session of Congress. His decision to leave drew a great deal of attention outside of the White House. Two of the top White House staff, Paster and ROY NEEL, resigned at the end of 1994 to take lucrative positions in the private sector. Paster went to Hill and Knowlton, and Neel went to the United States Telephone Association. They were able to leave the administration to lobby within the federal government because President Clinton had changed the internal ethics rules in 1993 for

White House staff. The previous rules had prevented the staff from lobbying for five years, but the change in 1993 allowed lobbying one year after leaving the White House.

Paster remained close to many White House staff. In 1998 he was recruited into the lobbying campaign to stop the impeachment proceedings over the MONICA LEWINSKY affair.

Born December 23, 1944, in Brooklyn, New York, Paster graduated with a B.A., with honors, from Alfred University (1966) and an M.S. in journalism from Columbia University (1967).

Paster left the White House in 1994 to accept a position as chairman and chief executive of Hill and Knowlton, a Washington, D.C., public relations and lobbying firm. Paster had been director of Hill & Knowlton's Washington, D.C., office prior to moving into the White House as director of legislative affairs. In 2002, Paster negotiated a lucrative contract for Hill and Knowlton in Saudi Arabia with the Saudi Basic Industries Corp. Part of Hill and Knowlton's responsibilities were to ensure that the United States did not dramatically shift policy toward Saudi Arabia after the terrorist attacks of September 11, 2001.

In 2001, Paster was elected to the board of trustees of the Woodrow Wilson National Fellowship Foundation for a three-year term.

Patrick, Deval Laurdine
(1956–) *assistant attorney general and director of the Office of Civil Rights, Department of Justice*

Deval Patrick was assistant attorney general and director of the Office of Civil Rights in the Department of Justice. He was nominated by President Clinton on February 1, 1994, following the failed nomination of LANI GUINIER. After Guinier's nomination failed, President

Clinton nominated John Payton, the District of Columbia corporation counsel, but he withdrew his name after questions arose about Payton's voting record. Patrick was nominated after Payton.

During his Senate confirmation hearings, Patrick said that he would move "firmly, fearlessly, and unambiguously to enforce antidiscrimination laws." His nomination was confirmed by the Senate on March 17, 1994. The nomination of Patrick, an African American, continued the administration's efforts toward racial and gender diversity in the senior levels of the federal government.

Born on July 31, 1956, in Chicago, Illinois, Patrick graduated from Milton Academy (1974). Patrick received his A.B. from Harvard College (1978) and his J.D. from Harvard Law School with honors (1982). After graduating from law school, he received a federal clerkship with Judge Stephen Reinhardt of the U.S. Court of Appeals, 9th Circuit, in California and in 1983 joined the National Association for the Advancement of Colored People (NAACP) Legal Defense and Educational Fund in New York City as a staff attorney. He specialized in capital punishment and voting rights cases. One of the cases he tried was *McCleskey v. Kemp*, the 1987 Supreme Court death-penalty appeal of Warren McCleskey. McCleskey was an African American accused of murdering a white man. Patrick argued that juries are more likely to use capital punishment against African Americans, but the Supreme Court disagreed. After four years at the NAACP, he joined a law firm in Boston, Hill and Barlow, but continued to handle cases for the NAACP Legal Defense and Educational Fund.

He left the administration after the first term, having served four years as the director of the Office of Civil Rights. He joined the Coca-Cola Company in Atlanta, Georgia, as general counsel.

Pearson, Daniel S.

(1930–) *independent counsel investigating Ronald Brown, secretary of commerce*

Daniel Pearson was appointed by a special panel of the U.S. Court of Appeals, District of Columbia, as the independent counsel to investigate improper financial dealings by Secretary of Commerce RONALD H. BROWN. The investigation began in 1995 but ended in 1996 following the death of Brown in a plane crash on April 4, 1996, in the mountains of Croatia. The plane carrying Brown and 32 other people crashed into a hillside while trying to land in bad weather near the Croatian port city of Dubrovnik.

On July 6, 1995, Pearson was appointed independent counsel and charged with the investigation of Brown's financial dealings. Allegations against Brown involved questions of whether Brown had accepted gifts from Nolanda Hill, a Dallas businesswoman. Hill's gifts to Brown were said to total $500,000 in 1993, which were related to a business venture that Brown and Hill owned, called First International, Inc. Brown was also accused of omitting financial information on his financial disclosure forms to the administration. In addition, Pearson was looking into allegations that Brown's son, Michael, had been hired by an Oklahoma natural gas company seeking to gain favor with the Department of Commerce.

After Brown was killed in the 1996 plane crash, the investigation was ended. Pearson said in the final report of the independent counsel's office, "My office's investigation of Secretary Brown ended with his death. The unfinished state of the investigation and considerations of fairness preclude our office from drawing conclusions about the allegations regarding possible criminal conduct by the secretary." Parts of the investigation were transferred to the Office of Public Integrity in the Department of Justice for further work.

The cost of the Pearson investigation was $3.3 million.

Born on October 9, 1930, in New York City, Pearson received his B.A. from Amherst College (1955) and his J.D. from Yale University School of Law (1958). Soon after law school, Pearson served as assistant U.S. attorney, Southern District of Florida. After entering private practice, he was named as a special counsel for the Dade County grand jury and special assistant state attorney, 11th Judicial Circuit of Florida. In 1979 he began teaching trial advocacy as an adjunct professor at the University of Miami School of Law. Pearson was appointed in 1980 by Governor Bob Graham to the Third District Court of Appeal, Florida's intermediate appeals court for Dade and Monroe Counties.

He left the Third District Court of Appeal in 1989 to join the law firm of Holland & Knight in Miami, Florida. His law practice included dispute resolution, including mediation for disputes over housing discrimination, civil rights, employment discrimination, sexual harassment, and other issues.

Peña, Federico F.
(1947–   ) *secretary of energy, secretary of transportation*

Federico Peña was appointed secretary of transportation by President Clinton and sworn into office on January 21, 1993. At the end of the first term Peña was moved to the Energy Department to replace outgoing Secretary of Energy HAZEL O'LEARY. The appointment of Peña, who was a Hispanic American, fulfilled a campaign pledge by President Clinton to build a cabinet that "looked like America" and that included both gender and racial diversity. President Clinton appointed four African Americans and one Hispanic, Peña, to the cabinet as part of his campaign pledge for cabinet diversity.

Peña served four years as secretary of transportation and a year and half as secretary of energy, resigning from the Department of Energy on June 30, 1998. He was succeeded as secretary of energy by WILLIAM (BILL) BLAINE RICHARDSON, who served through the remainder of the second term.

Peña, the former two-term mayor of Denver, was originally slated for a deputy secretary position. It was widely believed that Chicago banker WILLIAM MICHAEL DALEY, brother of Chicago Mayor RICHARD MICHAEL DALEY, would be chosen for secretary of transportation, but in a surprise move, President Clinton chose Peña. One explanation for the choice of Peña as a cabinet secretary rather than as a deputy secretary was that President Clinton originally sought to appoint a Hispanic, Representative Bill Richardson, as secretary of interior. But when Richardson met resistance from environmentalists, President Clinton chose not to appoint him. Instead, as part of his commitment to build a diverse cabinet, President Clinton chose another Hispanic-American, Peña.

Peña was selected for the transition team to oversee transportation issues. His selection as secretary of transportation was reportedly based on his successful promotion of the new Denver International Airport. During his second term as mayor, Peña had led a drive to build a new airport to make Denver the regional center of trade. Peña succeeded, over substantial opposition, in building the new airport 20 miles outside of Denver at a cost of $1.7 billion.

The Department of Transportation was among the key departments promoted by President Clinton in the 1992 election that would be part of the economic recovery process. President Clinton pledged to boost the national economy by pumping billions of federal dollars into highways, mass transit, railways, high-speed rail lines, and airports. Peña sought to build on President Clinton's pledge by refocusing the department away from a focus on highway issues. Soon after his appointment, Peña said of his new role, "My responsibility as the new secretary of transportation is a very simple one: to bring a new perspective to transportation that says that transportation investments are more than simply building bridges and viaducts and building highways—it's trying to bring in the concerns of the environment as we balance our transportation programs. It is also investing in high technology like high-speed rail, as other nations are doing."

Peña proved to run an activist cabinet office, tackling a broad range of issues in his first year in office. Among the issues were support for United Air Lines, which had filed a complaint against Japan for rejecting United's plans to fly between Tokyo and Sydney, Australia, and support for US Airways to form an alliance with British Airways if British Airways invested $300 million in US Air. He also ordered General Motors in 1993 to recall 4.7 million pickup trucks with side-mounted gasoline tanks. Although General Motors actively fought the decision for the recall, they eventually reached a settlement that ended the recall but provided for General Motors to pay $53 million, matched by $27 million from the National Highway Traffic Safety Administration, for a program of research on automotive safety issues. Peña also revamped the Federal Aviation Administration, securing congressional approval for the agency to develop its own hiring and purchasing rules, and downsized the Department of Transportation by 11,000 employees.

One of the low points of his tenure as secretary of transportation came on May 11, 1996, when a ValuJet airliner crashed in the Florida Everglades, killing all 110 people on board. He defended the safety record of ValuJet, even though it was later determined that ValuJet had allowed oxygen-filled tanks on board. The tanks were believed to have exploded, causing the airliner to crash. In June 1996 Peña finally shut down ValuJet.

In 1995 the Justice Department began an investigation into whether Peña had violated federal law when Los Angeles awarded a transit contract to his former management company, Peña Investment Advisors. Attorney General JANET RENO announced on March 16, 1995, that the Department of Justice had found no evidence against Peña and that the investigation was closed.

After four years as secretary of transportation, Peña was moved to the position of secretary of energy when Hazel O'Leary resigned from that post at the end of the first term. Peña was moved after President Clinton learned that he had decided to leave the cabinet and return to Denver. Concerned that the administration would have no Hispanic representation, President Clinton offered Peña the position in the Energy Department.

As secretary of energy, Peña continued the focus on building new sources of energy, including solar and wind, and developing new science and technology for energy sources. Peña was sworn into office on March 12, 1997, following his Senate confirmation. Peña remained in the Department of Energy for a year and a half. He announced his resignation on April 6, 1998, to be effective on June 30, 1998, citing a desire to return to Denver with his young children.

Born on March 15, 1947, in Laredo, Texas, and raised in Brownsville, Texas, he attended St. Joseph's Academy, a Catholic high school. He received his B.A. from the University of Texas at Austin (1969) and his J.D. from the University of Texas School of Law (1972). Following law school, Peña moved to Denver, where he joined his brother Alfredo in his private law practice. Peña also worked as a staff lawyer for the Mexican-American Legal Defense and Educational Fund (1972–74), where he litigated police brutality and voting rights cases. He later moved to the Chicano Education Project, where he worked for four years supporting bilingual education in the public schools.

Peña's political career began in 1978 when he successfully ran for a seat in the Colorado General Assembly. He served two terms in the General Assembly before running for mayor of Denver in 1993. Peña won the election by a narrow margin, defeating 14-year incumbent mayor William McNichols. Hispanics made up only 18 percent of the population at the time. Peña's first term as mayor was often turbulent, including a 1988 recall campaign by his opponents when the city failed to adequately deal with a paralyzing snowstorm in December 1987. The recall petition fell short by 2,000 signatures of forcing a new election. When Peña left the Clinton administration in 2001, he returned to the financial management firm of Peña Investment Advisors, which he founded after he left office as mayor in 1992. Peña had served two terms as mayor but declined to run for a third term.

Peres, Shimon

(1923–) *winner of 1994 Nobel Peace Prize, prime minister of Israel, foreign minister of Israel*

Shimon Peres was appointed acting prime minister following the assassination of Prime Minister YITZHAK RABIN on November 5, 1995. After being approved by the Knesset, Peres was sworn in as prime minister and as defense minister. He served in both positions until the May 1996 elections. In May 1996 Peres lost the election for prime minister to BENJAMIN NETANYAHU from the Likud Party.

Unlike Yitzhak Rabin, EHUD BARAK, or Benjamin Netanyahu, Peres did not have an illustrious record to display during the elections. Peres was perceived by many in Israel as part of the old Israeli elite who had emigrated from Europe. In spite of his weak military record in comparison to other national leaders, he was able to use his noncombat record as a strength to promote peace. His record allowed him to build relations with the Palestine Liberation Organization (PLO) and led to the eventual signing in 1993 of the Oslo Accords with the PLO. Peres's tenure as prime minister in 1995–96 was his second term in the office. He had served for two years as prime minister nearly 10 years earlier. Peres was named prime minister in 1984 in a deal brokered between the Likud Party and his Labor Party, after the indecisive elections in 1984 forced a coalition government called the National Unity Government. Peres served as prime minister for the first half of the term of the coalition government between the Likud Party and the Labor Party. Two years later (1986), he handed over the reins of government to Yitzhak Shamir for the second half of the term. Peres became deputy prime minister and foreign minister when Shamir became prime minister.

Peres was born in August 1923 in Vishneva, Poland. His family moved to Israel in 1934. Peres was conscripted into the armed forces in Israel in 1947 and managed arms purchases as one of his assignments. Later, Peres was appointed head of Israel's navy and then director of the Defense Ministry's procurement delegation in the United States. From 1953 to 1959, Peres served as director general of the Defense Ministry, a post to which he was appointed by Prime Minister David Ben-Gurion.

Peres's political career began in 1959 when he was elected to Israel's parliament, the

Knesset. From 1959 to 1965 he served as deputy defense minister. He held a series of positions in government over the next several years, including an appointment as defense minister from 1974 to 1977. In 1977 he was elected chairman of the Labor Party, a position he held until 1992. He lost the 1992 elections for Labor Party chair to Yitzhak Rabin. In 1997, Ehud Barak took over as head of the Labor Party.

Peres was appointed foreign minister in 1992, and on December 10, 1994, was awarded the Nobel Peace Prize along with Prime Minister Yitzhak Rabin and PLO chairman YASSER ARAFAT. Peres had participated in secret peace negotiations in Norway when he was foreign minister, signing the Oslo Agreement in 1993 in Washington, D.C., on September 13, 1993.

From 1996 to 1999, Peres served as a member of the Knesset and from July 1999 through March 2001 was minister of regional cooperation. He lost a bid for president in July 2000 in a secret ballot in parliament, but in March 2001 was appointed minister of foreign affairs and deputy prime minister.

Perot, Henry Ross

(1930–   ) *independent presidential candidate, Reform Party presidential candidate*

Ross Perot began a presidential campaign early in 1992 as an unaffiliated candidate who pledged to remain independent and to personally finance his campaign. Reportedly, Perot disliked Vice President GEORGE HERBERT WALKER BUSH, who was the Republican nominee for president, because he had not done enough as vice president to support efforts to find POWs in Vietnam. He also believed that Bush was actually a resident of Washington, D.C., and only claimed he was a resident of Texas because he rented a hotel suite in Houston.

Perot had been unhappy that Bush had won the 1988 presidential election and decided in 1992 to challenge him in the general election. Perot went on a nationally televised program, *Larry King Live*, and asked that volunteers around the country get signatures to put his name on the ballot. He eventually was placed on enough ballots to run for president and poured $37 million of his own money into the race, receiving 19 percent of the vote in the November election.

Perot might have had a stronger showing in the November election, but he left the race in July 1992 believing that he could not win. He also claimed that the Democratic Party had been revitalized and could win the election. Perot reentered the race in October 1992 after polls showed that voters liked Perot's status as an "outsider." Clinton chose not to mount an active campaign against Perot, instead stressing his own status as an "outsider" but noting that his Democratic Party could achieve its goals in Congress.

After Bush's loss to Clinton in the 1992 election, Republicans derided Perot for his candidacy. Republicans accused Perot of taking the election from George Bush since many Perot voters were conservative Republicans who liked his message of fiscal austerity. But once Clinton took office, Perot redirected his attacks from Bush to Clinton. The following year, 1993, Perot established a watchdog organization called United We Stand, to monitor the federal government and the Democratic and Republican Parties.

Perot remained highly visible during the first term of the Clinton administration, seeking to maintain a national image for a run for president in 1996. He regularly attacked President Clinton during the first term, including leading an effort to stop the passage of the North America Free Trade Agreement (NAFTA).

In 1995 Perot founded a new political party, the Reform Party, to serve as a springboard for his 1996 presidential election campaign. In 1996, at the Reform Party's national convention, Perot was nominated as the party's candidate for president and won 8 percent of the vote in the November 1996 election.

During the 1992 campaign, Perot had directed his campaign against Vice President Bush, assuming Bush to be the front-runner and based on his own dislike. During the 1996 campaign, Perot directed his campaign against President Clinton. Perot often made unpleasant comments about President Clinton, suggesting that he was too corrupt to serve as president and that he couldn't be trusted to babysit one's children. Perot often commented about President Clinton's personal life, including references to the PAULA CORBIN JONES allegations of sexual harassment.

After two failed tries to capture the Oval Office, it was unclear whether Perot would again try in the 2000 elections. Perot's Reform Party had been splintered in the past few years with a number of popular politicians seeking to keep Perot out of the national limelight. Minnesota governor Jesse Ventura, a member of the Independent Party/Reform Party, became a leader in the anti-Perot wing of the party. After significant internal fighting, the party nominated former Republican activist and Nixon speechwriter Patrick Buchanan as its candidate in 2000. Perot distanced himself from the party at that point. He did not run on another platform in 2000 and simply dropped out of the public limelight for the election cycle.

Born on June 27, 1930, in Texarkana, Texas, Perot was raised in Texarkana and attended Texarkana Junior College. In 1949 he entered the U.S. Naval Academy and graduated in 1953. After graduation, Perot served at sea for four years on a destroyer and an aircraft carrier.

In 1962 Perot founded a data processing company, Electronic Data Processing, using a $1,000 loan from his wife. He had been a salesman for IBM (1957–62) when he founded it, but Electronic Data Systems (EDS) became a multibillion-dollar company employing 70,000 people. Perot sold EDS to General Motors in 1984 for $2.5 billion. The ownership that he retained in the company made him the largest individual stockholder in General Motors and gave him a seat on the board of directors. Perot resigned from the board in 1986 in a dispute and General Motors bought out Perot's stock for $700 million. In 1988, Perot founded another computer service company, Perot Systems.

Perot became involved with the Department of Defense in 1969, when he joined a project to secure the release of prisoners of war in Vietnam. Perot received the Medal for Distinguished Public Service from the Department of Defense for his efforts. Ten years later Perot again became involved in a military issue, but this time he financed a private rescue mission for two EDS employees taken hostage by the Iranian government in 1979. The mission was led by retired Green Beret colonel Arthur "Bull" Simons. Perot went into Iran with the rescue mission and removed the two EDS employees from prison. The rescue was later chronicled in a book, *On Wings of Eagles*, by Ken Follett.

Perry, William J.

(1927–   ) *secretary of defense, deputy secretary of defense*

William Perry was nominated as secretary of defense in 1994 after the resignation of LESLIE (LES) ASPIN, JR., and was sworn into office on February 3, 1994, following a unanimous vote in the Senate. Perry had served as deputy secretary of defense from March 5, 1993, until his confirmation as secretary. Perry served the remainder of President Clinton's first term but was replaced by WILLIAM SEBASTIAN COHEN for the second term of the administration.

President Bill Clinton (left) and Secretary of Defense William J. Perry (right) are escorted by Col. David H. Huntoon as they inspect the troops at Fort Myer, Virginia, January 14, 1997. *(Department of Defense)*

When President Clinton nominated Perry as secretary of defense, he stated that Perry had been "at the cutting edge on defense issues" and that in "every aspect of his work, Bill Perry has earned high respect from members of both parties in Congress, in the military among those who study military strategy, and in the business community."

During the Carter administration, Perry had been undersecretary of defense for research engineering. He was responsible for all weapons systems procurement and all research and development. He was the secretary of defense's principal adviser on technology, communications, intelligence, and atomic energy. When the Reagan administration came into office, Perry was asked in 1983 to serve on the President's Commission on Strategic Forces.

Perry's tenure as secretary of defense was marked by difficult budget decisions. He opposed a $150 million Senate effort to preserve an option to buy more B-2 bombers. Perry, who championed the stealth bomber, believed the cost of $10 billion or more for 20 additional B-2 bombers was not justified.

He also sought pay increases for the military after finding that many were using food stamps. Perry argued that the failure to provide adequate salaries contributed to morale problems. He championed more on-base housing for service personnel. For Perry, dealing with pay and housing issues was part of President Clinton's plan for improving the readiness of the military.

President Clinton chose to replace Perry after two years on the job with William Cohen, the former Maine senator who had not run for reelection in 1996. Cohen, who was a Republican, was considered a stronger advocate in Congress for increasing defense spending and more knowledgeable about the bureaucracy in the Department of Defense. Cohen had served on the Senate Armed Services Committee and the Senate Select Committee on Intelligence.

Born on October 11, 1927, in Vandergrift, Pennsylvania, Perry received his B.S. (1949) and his M.S. (1950) from Stanford University, and his Ph.D. from Pennsylvania State University (1957), all in mathematics. He was a noncommissioned officer in the Army Corps of Engineers, serving in Japan and Okinawa. He joined the Reserve Officer Training Corps (ROTC) in 1948 and was commissioned a second lieutenant in the Army Reserves in 1950. He remained in the Army Reserves until 1955.

Perry had been the laboratory director for General Telephone and Electronic (1954–64). He founded and served as president of the electronics firm ESL (1964–77). He also served as executive vice president of Hambrecht and Quist Inc., an investment banking firm in San Francisco specializing in high technology companies (1981–85).

After leaving government in 1997, Perry joined the Stanford faculty as a professor in the School of Engineering and the Institute for International Studies, and was a senior fellow at the Hoover Institution. From 1989–93 he had been the codirector of the Center for International Security and Arms Control at Stanford University. He cochaired the Aspen Strategy Group of the Aspen Institute for Humanistic Studies, was a trustee of the Carnegie Endowment for International Peace, and was a Fellow of the American Academy of Arts and Sciences. President Clinton appointed Perry to the President's Foreign Intelligence Advisory Board.

Podesta, John David
(1949–   ) *White House chief of staff, White House deputy chief of staff, White House staff secretary*

John Podesta was appointed White House chief of staff in October 1998. He became the fourth White House chief of staff in the Clinton administration, following THOMAS FRANKLIN MCLARTY III, LEON EDWARD PANETTA, and ERSKINE B. BOWLES. Podesta replaced Bowles, who resigned to consider running for political office from North Carolina.

Podesta had held a number of positions in the White House before being promoted to chief of staff, including deputy chief of staff (1997–98) and staff secretary (1993–95). During a two-year break at the end of the first term, Podesta taught at Georgetown University Law Center as a visiting professor of law (January 1995 to January 1997). During this absence from the White House, Podesta also served as an adviser in the Senate to THOMAS ANDREW DASCHLE (D-S.D.).

Podesta's primary role as staff secretary, which was his first appointment in the White House, was to manage the paper flow to and from President Clinton. In this position, he served as an adviser to President Clinton on government information, privacy telecommunications security, and regulatory policy. He was a leading expert in Washington, D.C., in technology policy. He left the White House in January 1995 to teach law at Georgetown University Law Center and then returned in 1997 as deputy chief of staff to Erskine Bowles. Bowles's appointment as chief of staff in 1997, replacing Leon Panetta, precipitated a staff shake-up in the White House. Bowles wanted to appoint his own people, which led to the appointment of Podesta.

During his tenure as deputy chief of staff, Podesta served as the White House spokesman on the Whitewater investigation. He also headed up the White House damage control team on the MONICA LEWINSKY scandal. He was one of several White House staff who were called before the grand jury convened by independent counsel KENNETH W. STARR.

After serving for two years as deputy chief of staff, Podesta was promoted to chief of staff in 1998. As the impeachment hearings began in December 1998, and the Senate trial was conducted in January 1999, Podesta became the principal spokesperson for the White House. Podesta was a constant advocate for President Clinton both during and after the impeachment process.

Born on January 8, 1949, in Chicago, Podesta graduated with a B.A. from Knox College in Illinois (1971) and a J.D. from Georgetown University Law Center (1976). After graduating from law school, Podesta became a trial attorney in the U.S. Department of Justice (1976–77) and then served as special assistant to the director of ACTION (1978–79). As a Democrat, he then was able to move into a position in 1979 as counsel to the Senate Judiciary Committee (1979–81) and continued in the Senate as chief minority counsel to the Senate Judiciary Subcommittee (1981–86). He was then named chief counsel of the Senate Agriculture Committee (1987–88). Having worked in the federal government for 12 years, Podesta branched out on his own and formed Podesta Associates with his brother Tony. John Podesta became president and general counsel for the next five years (1988–93). He was named to the White House staff in 1993 and remained in the administration until 2001.

After leaving the administration, Podesta returned to Georgetown University School of Law as a visiting professor. In 2001, Podesta was elected to the board of directors of the League of Conservation Voters, an organization dedicated to protecting the environment through political action.

Powell, Colin L.
(1937–) *chairman, Joint Chiefs of Staff*

General Colin Powell was named chairman of the Joint Chiefs of Staff on October 1, 1989, and retired on September 30, 1993.

During his four years as chairman of the Joint Chiefs of Staff, Powell oversaw military incursions during the Bush administration into Panama (1989) to capture General Manuel Noriega, and into the Persian Gulf (1990–91) to free Kuwait from an Iraqi invasion. Powell had been appointed by President GEORGE HERBERT WALKER BUSH on October 1, 1989, to a four-year term as chairman of the Joint Chiefs of Staff. Traditionally, the chairman is appointed by the president and steps down when there is a change in the White House.

After leaving military service when he retired on September 30, 1993, Powell began to lecture across the country on various issues. He also wrote a memoir, *My American Journey*, and embarked on a nationwide tour in 1995 to promote the book.

In 1996, historian Stephen Ambrose began a campaign to have Powell run for the Republican nomination for president. Ambrose wrote two powerful articles in *Newsweek* magazine designed to build support for Powell's candidacy. At the heart of Ambrose's argument was that Powell was another Dwight David Eisenhower who would provide both national and international leadership. Powell declined the efforts of Ambrose, stating that his wife, Alma, did not want him to run. She was apparently concerned that as an African American he would be assassinated during the campaign.

Powell's commitment to public service throughout his life led President Clinton to seek his help in building a major initiative on behalf of children. Powell was asked by President Clinton to chair the Presidents' Summit for America's Future which was held in Philadelphia on April 27–29, 1997. After chairing the summit, Powell began to work full time on behalf of children as chairman of *America's Promise—The Alliance for Youth*, which was a national organization dedicated to the advancement of children in the United States.

In Powell's military career, he had worked directly with three presidents, Ronald Reagan, George Bush, and Bill Clinton. In addition to his selection as a White House Fellow in 1972, Powell was named in December 1987 as the National Security Advisor to President Ronald Reagan, a position he held until January 1989. His tenure in the White House included the ongoing investigation into the Iran-contra scandal, which included the former national security advisor, Admiral John Poindexter, and a member of his staff, Oliver North. Powell worked closely with chief of staff Howard Baker to defuse the congressional investigation into the affair. Prior to his White House appointment as national security advisor, Powell had been the military assistant to Secretary of Defense Caspar Weinberger (1983–86).

After he left the White House at the outset of the Bush administration, Powell returned to active military duty as commander in chief, Forces Command, headquartered at Fort McPherson, Georgia.

Born on April 5, 1947, in New York City and raised in the South Bronx by immigrant parents from Jamaica, Powell graduated with a B.A. in geology from City College of New York (1958). While in college, Powell joined the Reserve Officer Training Corps (ROTC) and was commissioned as a second lieutenant

in the army in June 1958. During his military career he was awarded the Decorated Legion of Merit, the Bronze Star, Air Medal, and Purple Heart. In 1993, Queen Elizabeth II of England named Powell an honorary knight commander of the Most Honorable Order of the Bath. Powell's civilian awards included two Presidential Medals of Freedom, the President's Citizens Medal, the Congressional Gold Medal, the Secretary of State Distinguished Service Medal, and the Secretary of Energy Distinguished Service Medal.

In January 2001, Powell became the first African American nominated and confirmed as secretary of state.

Primakov, Yevgeny Maksimovich
(1929–   ) *foreign minister of Russia, premier of Russia*

As Russian foreign minister during the first two years of the Clinton administration, Yevgeny Primakov played a key role in dealing with the Balkans crisis but became an adversary rather than an ally in the process. When President Clinton supported North Atlantic Treaty Organization (NATO) air strikes against Kosovo, Primakov bitterly opposed them. He ignored the arms embargo by NATO countries against Yugoslavia and supported President SLOBODAN MILOŠEVIĆ.

Primakov had never been strongly aligned with the United States. During the Persian Gulf War, Primakov was named Mikhail Gorbachev's special envoy to the region. He tried to persuade Iraqi leader SADDAM HUSSEIN to withdraw from Kuwait. Fluent in English and Arabic, Primakov never condemned Hussein, but rather urged him to withdraw before coalition forces attacked.

When a group of hard-liners attempted a coup against Gorbachev on August 24, 1991, Primakov remained loyal to Gorbachev and declared the coup illegal. But the coup forced Gorbachev to remain under house arrest, as the coup leaders told the nation that Gorbachev was too ill to rule. The coup failed and Gorbachev returned to power. But the Soviet Union was beginning to fall, and with the fall, the power of Gorbachev ebbed away.

On September 2, 1991, President GEORGE HERBERT WALKER BUSH recognized the breakaway republics of Lithuania, Latvia, and Estonia as independent nations. The Soviet Union continued to fall apart, and on December 24, 1991, President Bush acknowledged the breakup of the Soviet Union by recognizing the Russian Republic as an independent nation. The following day, Gorbachev resigned and the Commonwealth of Independent States, comprising 11 former Soviet republics, was established.

Despite his ties to Gorbachev, Primakov helped to usher in the administration of BORIS YELTSIN as president of the new Russian Republic. Under Yeltsin, Primakov was first named director of the foreign intelligence service, then in 1996 was appointed foreign minister, and named Russia's premier in September 1998. But his relationship with Yeltsin soured as Primakov began to court members of the communist-controlled Duma, and on May 12, 1999, he was fired by President Yeltsin. In 1999 Primakov declared his intention to run for president of Russia in the June 2000 elections. His campaign for the presidency failed, and he subsequently became president of the Russian Chamber of Trade and Industry.

Primakov's expertise in Middle East affairs, and his ability to speak Arabic, brought a new role for Russia as an intermediary in the Middle East when he was foreign minister.

Primakov was born on October 29, 1929, in Kiev, Ukraine, but was raised in Tbilisi, Georgia. He was educated at the Moscow Institute of Oriental Studies and worked for the state broadcasting and television services

from 1953–62. In 1959 he joined the Communist Party. From 1970 to 1977 he was the deputy director of world economics and international relations at the Soviet Academy of Sciences and was promoted to director in 1985. In the interim, 1977 to 1985, he headed the Moscow Institute of Oriental Studies and analyzed international affairs as a member of a group of foreign policy advisers to Leonid Brezhnev. He was elected to the Congress of People's Deputies in 1989 and was a member of the Politburo during 1989–90.

Putin, Vladimir
(1952–   ) president of Russia, prime minister of Russia

Vladimir Putin was named acting president of Russia on January 1, 2000, when President BORIS YELTSIN resigned on New Year's Eve. He was elected to a full term in general elections on March 26, 2000. Putin had been prime minister for the previous two years (1999–2000).

On June 3, 2000, President Clinton visited Moscow for a two-day summit with the newly elected Putin. He met again with Putin in New York on September 6–8, 2000, at the United Nations Millennium Summit.

During the year that Putin served, the last year of the Clinton administration, the issue of Chechen independence remained a major point of contention between the two nations. Putin sent thousands of Russian soldiers to put down the insurrection in Chechnya for independence. President Clinton opposed the massive use of force against the insurgents.

Putin, born on October 7, 1952, in Leningrad, graduated from the Leningrad State University where he studied law and German (1975). His early career was centered in the secret police, the KGB, where he worked from 1975–90. He worked in counterintelligence, then moved to foreign intelligence. In 1985 the KGB sent him to Dresden, East Germany, to work in political intelligence. He was in East Germany in 1989 when the Berlin Wall fell.

After the fall of the Berlin Wall, Putin returned to Leningrad, which soon reverted to its original name of St. Petersburg. He began working at his alma mater, Leningrad State University, teaching international affairs and monitoring international visitors. His mentor at the university, Anatoly Sobchak, convinced him to leave the KGB and enter politics. When Sobchak successfully ran for mayor of St. Petersburg, he brought Putin in as the deputy mayor. When Sobchak lost his reelection campaign in 1996, Putin resigned.

Putin, who had become known for his reforms in city government operations in St. Petersburg, was named by President Boris Yeltsin as an aide to the director of property administration in Moscow. He was later named in 1998 by President Yeltsin as head of the new Federal Security Bureau, which was created to replace the KGB. In August 1999, President Yeltsin abruptly fired Prime Minister Sergei Stepashin and named Putin as prime minister. Only six months later, on New Year's Eve, Yeltsin resigned and installed Putin as acting president.

Q

Quinn, John (Jack) M.

(1949–   ) *White House counsel, chief of staff to the vice president*

Jack Quinn was named chief of staff to Vice President ALBERT (AL) GORE, JR., following the 1992 election. He remained with the vice president until 1995, when he moved to the White House as counsel to the president. Quinn was named White House counsel on September 25, 1995, to be effective November 1, 1995. At the announcement of Quinn's appointment as White House counsel, Vice President Gore said, "Jack Quinn will make an excellent White House counsel. As both my friend and close adviser for many years, he has consistently provided me with counsel that is steady, wise, and greatly appreciated." Quinn replaced ABNER MIKVA in the position of White House counsel.

When Quinn was named chief of staff to Vice President Gore, he was also given the title "assistant to the president." The addition of a vice presidential staffer to the president's senior staff, which had not been done in previous administrations, was designed to ensure that Quinn was included in the White House senior staff meetings and to foster greater communication between the president's and the vice president's staffs. Gore had sought these lines of communication between the two

offices when he accepted President Clinton's offer to be the vice presidential candidate. After serving for two years as the vice president's chief of staff, and having regularly worked with the White House senior staff, Quinn was tapped for the position of White House counsel.

Quinn had known Vice President Gore since 1988, when Quinn worked on Gore's unsuccessful presidential campaign. During the 1992 presidential campaign, Quinn helped Gore to prepare for the vice presidential debate. Quinn also served as general counsel for the Clinton-Gore 1992 campaign and for the presidential transition.

Quinn's experience in presidential campaigns included not only Gore's 1988 campaign but also Gary Hart's 1984 presidential campaign, where Quinn served as general counsel.

Soon after taking office, Quinn became embroiled with the Whitewater investigation. It was Quinn's responsibility to coordinate the president's response to the congressional hearings and to the independent counsel's investigation. Quinn left the White House in 1997 to return to private law practice. He was replaced by CHARLES RUFF.

However, days before the Clinton administration was to leave office in January 2001, Quinn lobbied President Clinton to support a pardon for his client, fugitive financier Marc Rich. President Clinton granted the pardon, but received significant criticism for granting it. Attorneys in the Department of Justice who had prosecuted Rich believed that the pardon was unjustified.

Born on August 16, 1949, Quinn received his B.A. from Georgetown University (1971) and his J.D. from Georgetown University Law Center (1975), where he was an editor of the *Georgetown Law Journal*. During and after col-

lege, Quinn worked on the staff of the Senate Select Committee on Nutrition and Human Needs (1969–73). From 1973 to 1975 he was a legislative assistant and then chief legislative assistant to Senator Floyd K. Haskell (D-Colo.). When Morris Udall ran for president in 1975–76, Quinn served as the campaign director for Udall for President. After the failed Udall campaign, Quinn joined the Washington, D.C., law firm of Arnold and Porter (1979–93).

R

Rabin, Yitzhak
(1922–1995) *winner of 1994 Nobel Peace Prize,
prime minister of Israel*

Prime Minister Yitzhak Rabin was assassinated
on November 4, 1995, at a peace rally in Tel
Aviv by an Israeli extremist opposed to the
peace process that Rabin had initiated. The
assassin, Yigal Amir, 25, said at his arraignment
that he killed Rabin because Rabin wanted "to
give our country to the Arabs."

In an effort to bridge the growing divisions between Israel and the Palestinians,
Prime Minister Rabin and Palestine Liberation Organization (PLO) chairman YASSER
ARAFAT began a series of secret peace negotiations in Norway in January 1993. The talks
were kept ultrasecret, with only a few people
within each group familiar with the talks or
the material being discussed. On September
9, 1993, Rabin and Arafat exchanged letters
in which the PLO recognized Israel's right
to exist as a nation, and in turn, Rabin recognized the PLO as the representative of the
Palestinian people. On September 13, 1993,
a "Declaration of Principles" (better known
as the Oslo Accords) between Israel, signed
by Israeli foreign minister SHIMON PERES,
and the PLO, signed by PLO executive
council member Abou Abbas, was held in a
ceremony hosted by President Clinton in
Washington, D.C.

President and Mrs. Clinton joined heads of
state from around the world at the funeral for
Rabin. President Clinton was accompanied on
Air Force One to Israel by former presidents
Jimmy Carter and George Bush, and former
secretary of state George Schultz who represented President Ronald Reagan. In addition to
the former presidents and former secretary of
state Schultz, the United States delegation
included Clinton administration officials and
members of Congress. Both President Gerald
Ford and former first lady Nancy Reagan were
invited, but neither was able to attend.

President Clinton signed a proclamation
that ordered all flags to fly at half staff at U.S.
government, military, and ambassadorial buildings as a sign of respect for Rabin and for the
peace process. The flags remained at half staff
until after the burial.

Security for the funeral was immense, to
protect both the U.S. delegation and delegations from Arab nations. Israel placed 10,000
police and soldiers at the funeral to protect the
world leaders.

Before leaving for the funeral, President
and Mrs. Clinton signed a book of condolences at the Israeli embassy in Washington.
President Clinton wrote, "Prime Minister

Rabin gave his life to Israel, first as a soldier for its freedom, then finally as a martyr for its lasting peace. For his example, his friendship to the United States, and his friendship to me, I am eternally grateful." Mrs. Clinton wrote, "God bless Prime Minister Rabin, the people of Israel, and all who take risks for peace."

Prior to the funeral, President and Mrs. Clinton paid their respects at the Knesset where Rabin's body lay in state. He then met with Rabin's widow, Leah. After the funeral, President Clinton made brief remarks at Jerusalem's Mount Herzl Cemetery, calling Rabin a "martyr for peace" and "a man completely without pretense." An estimated 1 million people out of a nation of 5 million people filed past the coffin as it lay in state outside the Knesset.

The funeral was attended by Egyptian president HOSNI MUBARAK and Jordan's king HUSSEIN, among other Arab leaders. Syrian president Hafez Assad did not attend but did condemn the assassination as a "tragic event."

Rabin became chief of staff for the Israeli military in 1964 and directed the armed forces during the Six-Day War in 1967. He succeeded Golda Meir as prime minister in 1974 but resigned in 1977. He was elected prime minister the final time in 1992. Rabin shared in the 1994 Nobel Peace Prize with Shimon Peres and with Yasser Arafat.

Rabin was born in Jerusalem in 1922. His education was at the Kadoorie Agricultural College, where he graduated with distinction (1936–40). He graduated from the Staff College (1953) and received his Ph.D. from Hebrew University in Jerusalem (1967). He joined the Israeli military in 1940 and by 1948 was the commander of the Harel Brigade during the War of Independence (1948–49). For the next 20 years, he remained in the military in a variety of positions, including as the head of the Northern Command (1956–59), as chief of operations and deputy chief of staff (1959–64); and as

chief of staff (1964–68) overseeing the Six-Day War.

He retired from the military on January 1, 1968, and was shortly afterward appointed ambassador to the United States. In 1973, Rabin returned to Israel and was elected to the Knesset as a member of the Labor Party. Rabin was appointed minister of labor by Golda Meir in 1974. When Meir's government fell on June 2, 1974, Rabin was elected prime minister by the Knesset. Rabin became the first native-born prime minister of Israel.

During his tenure as prime minister from 1974 to 1975, Rabin signed the Memorandum of Understanding between the United States and Israel in 1975. After losing the 1977 elections, Rabin returned to the Knesset as a member of the Labor Party.

He returned to power as minister of defense during the coalition government between 1984 and 1990 when the National Unity Government was formed. When the election process changed and national elections were held in 1992, Rabin's Labor Party won the majority in the Knesset and he again became prime minister. In July 1992 when the new government was formed, Rabin became prime minister and simultaneously the minister of defense and acting minister of religious affairs and labor and social affairs.

Rabin's autobiographical *Service Notebook* was published in 1979. His book on Lebanon, *Peace of Galilee*, was published in 1983.

Raines, Franklin Delano

(1949–) *director, Office of Management and Budget*

Franklin Raines served for two years (1996–98), as director of the Office of Management and Budget (OMB). Raines, who replaced ALICE RIVLIN as OMB director, was a member of the president's cabinet in that position and the first

African American to head OMB. He was replaced by JACOB LEW as director of OMB.

During his tenure as budget director for the Clinton administration, Raines was the president's key negotiator in the talks that led to the bipartisan Balanced Budget Act of 1997.

Raines left the administration on May 20, 1998, to head Fannie Mae, which provided home ownership financing. He became chairman and chief executive officer of Fannie Mae on January 1, 1999 and also the first African American to head the Federal National Mortgage Association (Fannie Mae). Fannie Mae was a federally chartered corporation to provide housing loans to low-income families. Its charter provided that it would buy mortgages issued by banks and other lenders and sell them to investors as mortgage-backed securities.

Prior to joining the Clinton administration in 1996, Raines had been vice chairman of Fannie Mae, in charge of the company's legal, credit policy, finance, and other corporate functions. From 1979 to 1991 he had been a partner with Lazard Frères & Company, an investment banking firm in New York City.

Born in Seattle, Washington, on January 14, 1949, Raines received his A.B., cum laude, from Harvard College and his J.D. from Harvard Law School (1976). He also attended Magdalen College, Oxford University, as a Rhodes scholar. After returning from Oxford University, Raines spent two years in the Carter administration at the OMB. From 1977 to 1979, Raines was associate director for economics and government in OMB and was the assistant director of the White House Domestic Policy Staff.

After leaving the Clinton administration, Raines was elected to the board of directors of Fannie Mae, Pfizer, AOL Time Warner, PepsiCo, and was an overseer for TIAA-CREF. He also served on the board of the National Urban League. He had previously served as chairman of the visiting committee of the John F. Kennedy School of Government at Harvard University, and as president of the board of overseers of Harvard University.

Rangel, Charles Bernard
(1930–) *member of the House of Representatives*

Charles Rangel (D-N.Y.) represented the 15th Congressional District of New York, which included Harlem, the Upper West Side, and Washington Heights in New York City. He was first elected in 1970.

Rangel was closely aligned with President Clinton and with the Clinton administration's policies. One of the few policies that they disagreed on was trade with Cuba. President Clinton sought to keep the trade embargo in place while Rangel sought to remove it.

During the impeachment hearings in 1998, Rangel remained a staunch ally of President Clinton. Rangel was frequently on television voicing his support for the president and his distaste for KENNETH W. STARR and the independent counsel's investigation.

When President Clinton left office, he established his post-presidency office in Manhattan. The high cost of the Manhattan office space led to significant criticism and forced President Clinton to seek office space elsewhere. Congressman Rangel immediately offered Clinton office space in Harlem. Rangel argued that Clinton would be making a powerful statement to the African-American community, which had always supported him, that Harlem could be revitalized. President Clinton accepted Rangel's offer and moved his official offices to Harlem in 2001. President Clinton wanted his offices to be in New York City after his wife, HILLARY DIANE RODHAM CLINTON, won a Senate seat from New York in the 2000 elections. They purchased a home in suburban New York in Westchester County.

Rangel was a member of the powerful House Ways and Means Committee, including its subcommittee on trade. The Trade Subcommittee had jurisdiction over all international trade agreements. He was involved in international trade conferences and negotiating sessions on trade issues. In addition, President Clinton appointed him to the President's Export Council, which sought to build consensus on international trade issues among its membership of business, labor, congressional, and administration officials.

Rangel's involvement in trade issues led to his role as the primary author of the Federal Empowerment demonstration project to revitalize urban neighborhoods throughout the country. He also was the primary sponsor of the Community Renewal and New Markets Act of 2000, which expanded empowerment zones. Rangel had been coauthor of the 1992 Empowerment Zone legislation with Representative Jack Kemp (R-N.Y.).

Rangel was one of the founding members of the Congressional Black Caucus and used the caucus as a tool to build broad coalitions for legislation affecting minorities.

Born in New York City's Harlem on June 11, 1930, Rangel graduated from New York University (1957) and St. John's University School of Law (1960). Following law school, he was an assistant U.S. attorney for the Southern District of New York. He was elected to the New York State Assembly (1966–70) and in 1970 was elected to the U.S. House of Representatives. Rangel defeated fellow Democrat Adam Clayton Powell, Jr. He was reelected to every succeeding Congress.

Rasco, Carol Hampton
(1948–   ) *senior adviser to the secretary of education, chair of the Domestic Policy Council*

Carol Rasco served as assistant to the president for domestic policy and chair of the Domestic Policy Council in the White House throughout the first term of the administration. During the second term of the administration she joined the Department of Education as the senior adviser to Secretary RICHARD RILEY and director of the America Reads Challenge. The America Reads Challenge was an initiative created by the administration to ensure that all children could read well by the third grade.

BRUCE REED, who had been Rasco's deputy, replaced Rasco as the domestic policy adviser in the White House. The change in domestic policy advisers at the beginning of the second term was part of a larger shake-up in both the White House and the cabinet in 1997.

President Clinton announced Rasco's move to the Department of Education on December 17, 1996, stating, "Carol has served my administrations for over 14 years, most recently as my Domestic Policy Advisor. In the second term, she asked to move into a position more focused on issues related to children and families. Her work for the past 28 years as a teacher, middle school counselor, volunteer, parent, disability advocate, and policy counselor at the state and national level qualify her for this new challenge."

Rasco first worked with Governor Bill Clinton when she lobbied his office in Arkansas on behalf of children with disabilities. Her son was disabled and wheelchair-bound. She was subsequently offered a job in the administration in Little Rock dealing with disability issues.

She remained committed to disability issues when she moved to the White House. One of her goals as a presidential adviser was to support legislation that assisted the disabled, from programs dealing with technology to housing. She supported legislation, for example, that ensured that buildings, public places, and schools were accessible for wheelchairs.

As President Clinton's domestic policy adviser, Rasco had a staff of 33 in the Domestic

Policy Council. The Domestic Policy Council and the National Economic Council had a combined budget of $4,032,000 for fiscal 2001. The Domestic Policy Council, which was formally established by President Clinton seven months into the first term, was chaired by the president in its meetings but its staff was managed by Rasco.

Rasco met regularly with President Clinton and was a member of the president's senior staff. She sent weekly reports to the president on issues being developed by the staff and on meetings held by the staff. The report was also sent to HILLARY DIANE RODHAM CLINTON. Both President and Mrs. Clinton responded to Rasco's reports with comments.

Rasco's tenure in the White House was often overshadowed by ROBERT RUBIN, the director of the National Economic Council. Rubin was charged by the president with developing programs to stimulate the economy, which was the key campaign pledge of 1992. Rubin was viewed as more dynamic than Rasco and more closely aligned with President Clinton on developing new economic programs. She was rarely seen on television programs to discuss administration policy and rarely gave interviews to the media.

Rasco, although a senior member of the White House staff, was never considered a major power in the White House. During the first two years of the administration, the key administration focus in domestic policy was the health care reform bill. However, the Health Care Task Force was managed by IRA MAGAZINER and by Mrs. Clinton, rather than by Rasco's Domestic Policy Council. As a consequence, Rasco had little interaction on the health care reform issue, and policies that she was working on were often considered second-tier by the president. Both Robert Rubin and Hillary Clinton dominated the policymaking apparatus of the White House during 1993 and 1994. When the Republicans took control of the House of Representatives in 1995, the administration pulled back from many new legislative initiatives, again reducing the power of Rasco.

Born on January 13, 1948, in Columbia, South Carolina, Rasco attended Hendrix College (1965–66) and received her B.S.E. from the University of Arkansas (1969) and her M.S. from the University of Central Arkansas (1972). She began her career as an elementary teacher in Fayetteville, Arkansas, in 1969. After several positions in teaching, Rasco was named as the liaison to human services by Governor Bill Clinton in Little Rock (1983–85). In 1985 she was appointed executive assistant for governmental operations to Governor Clinton (1985–91) and became senior executive assistant to Governor Clinton in 1991–92.

When she left the Clinton administration in November 2000, she was named CEO of the nonprofit organization, Reading Is Fundamental (RIF).

Ray, Robert W.

(1960–) *independent counsel for the Whitewater investigation; deputy independent counsel, Whitewater investigation; deputy independent counsel, investigation of Mike Espy, secretary of agriculture; staff, independent counsel, investigation of Mike Espy, secretary of agriculture*

Robert W. Ray took over the Whitewater investigation and various other investigations from KENNETH W. STARR on October 18, 1999. Ray became the third independent counsel for Whitewater. ROBERT FISKE began the investigation in January 1994 but was replaced by Starr in August 1994. Starr returned to his law practice at the Washington, D.C., law firm of Kirkland & Ellis after resigning on March 12, 2002, and turning the investigation over to his deputy, Julie Thomas.

Fiske had been named by Attorney General JANET RENO to investigate President and Mrs. Clinton after allegations of financial improprieties in the loans that they and their partners secured in Little Rock, Arkansas, for the Whitewater land development project. The independent counsel act had lapsed, allowing Reno to appoint the independent counsel directly in January 1994. When Congress reauthorized the law in mid-1994, a special three-judge panel of the U.S. Court of Appeals for the District of Columbia was required to name the independent counsel. The panel named Kenneth Starr in August 1994.

By the time Ray took over from Starr, the investigation had led to the convictions of the Clintons' Whitewater business partners, JAMES (JIM) AND SUSAN McDOUGAL. President and Mrs. Clinton were never implicated in any wrongdoing with Whitewater. The investigation had spanned a series of other investigations, including the death of VINCENT W. FOSTER, JR., financial dealings of WEBSTER HUBBELL, "Travelgate," "Filegate," and MONICA LEWINSKY.

Ray joined Starr's staff in April 1999, moving from the staff of independent counsel DONALD SMALTZ in the investigation of Secretary of Agriculture ALPHONSO MICHAEL (MIKE) ESPY. He had started with Smaltz in 1995 and been appointed deputy independent counsel on November 5, 1998.

When he took over the Whitewater investigation from Starr, Ray was charged by the three-judge panel with finishing the investigation into any attempts by the White House to influence the testimony of a former White House volunteer, Kathleen Willey, and the investigation into HILLARY DIANE RODHAM CLINTON's role in the firing of the White House travel office staff ("Travelgate"). In addition, Ray was responsible for preparing the final report on the independent counsel investigations on all other matters.

Ray cleared President and Mrs. Clinton in the financial dealings of the Whitewater land development project on September 20, 2000. In his statement Ray said, "This office has determined that the evidence was insufficient to prove to a jury beyond a reasonable doubt that either President or Mrs. Clinton knowingly participated in any criminal activity." Ray's report went to the three-judge federal panel. One month before the final report was issued, Ray closed his office in Little Rock, which handled most of the investigative work. At its peak, the Little Rock office had more than three dozen lawyers, Federal Bureau of Investigation (FBI) agents, and others.

Ray then began to increase the size of his staff to prepare for pursuing a perjury case against President Clinton in relation to Monica Lewinsky's testimony. Ray had earlier cleared the Clintons in the 1993 firing of the White House travel office staff and the White House acquisition of FBI file summaries on Republicans.

On his last day in office, President Clinton acknowledged that he testified falsely about his affair with Monica Lewinsky and struck a deal with Ray that allowed him to avoid criminal prosecution. President Clinton had testified before a federal grand jury in August 1998, stating he did not have a sexual affair with Lewinsky.

President Clinton signed a consent order on January 19, 2001, with Ray. The consent order called for Ray not to prosecute President Clinton after he left office. In return, President Clinton agreed to accept a five-year suspension of his law license in Arkansas and to pay a $25,000 fine. He also agreed not to seek any legal fees incurred from the Lewinsky investigation to which he might be entitled under the independent counsel act.

In a statement released by President Clinton on January 19, 2001, he said, "I tried to walk a fine line between acting lawfully and testifying falsely, but I now recognized that I did not fully accomplish this goal and that certain of my responses to questions about Ms. Lewinsky were false." The statement was the first time that President Clinton admitted giving false testimony in the PAULA CORBIN JONES sexual harassment case, when he denied having an affair with Lewinsky.

President Clinton also said in a statement issued on January 19, 2001, "Today I signed a consent order in the lawsuit brought by the Arkansas Committee on Professional Conduct, which brings to an end that proceeding. I've accepted a five-year suspension of my law license, agreed to pay a $25,000 fine to cover counsel fees and acknowledge a violation of one of the Arkansas model rules of professional conduct because of testimony in my Paula Jones case deposition. The disbarment suit will not be dismissed."

Ray resigned on March 12, 2002, and handed the office over to his deputy, Julie Thomas. Thomas was sworn in as the independent counsel at the U.S. District Courthouse in Washington, D.C.

Ray received his B.A., magna cum laude, from Princeton University (1982) and his J.D. from Washington and Lee School of Law (1985). After law school, he served as an assistant U.S. attorney in the Southern District of New York working for U.S. Attorney Rudolph Giuliani. He continued with the U.S. Attorney's Office under U.S. Attorney Mary Jo White.

In September 1995, White detailed Ray to the independent counsel's office, working for Donald Smaltz, from his job in the Organized and Violent Crime Unit. Smaltz led the independent counsel investigation into improprieties by Secretary of Agriculture Mike Espy. On November 5, 1998, Ray was promoted to deputy independent counsel to Smaltz.

Following his resignation as independent counsel in 2002, Ray joined the law firm of Pit-ney, Hardin, Kipp and Szuch, LLP in Morristown, New Jersey.

Reed, Bruce
(1960–) *director, Domestic Policy Council; deputy director, Domestic Policy Council*

Bruce Reed was named assistant to the president and director of the Domestic Policy Council at the start of the second term in 1997 when CAROL RASCO moved to the Department of Education. Reed had been Rasco's deputy in the White House during the first term of the administration.

Reed began his career as chief speechwriter to Senator ALBERT (AL) GORE, JR., where he worked from 1985 to 1989. His first speechwriting assignment was to discuss the future of the Democratic Party after Ronald Reagan's landslide victory in the 1984 election. During Gore's unsuccessful presidential bid in 1988, Reed worked on the campaign. Reed was one of several staff from Vice President Gore's Senate office who moved into the White House in January 1993.

Reed left the Gore staff in 1989 for the Democratic Leadership Council (DLC), where he served as policy director, and where he first met Governor Bill Clinton of Arkansas. His work at the DLC included serving as editor for the organization's magazine, *The New Democrat*.

Governor Clinton and Senator Gore had been deeply involved with creating and building the Democratic Leadership Council as a think tank for centrist Democrats. In 1991 Governor Clinton asked Reed to help draft his announcement of his presidential candidacy, and in 1992 Reed was named deputy campaign manager for Policy for the Clinton-Gore campaign.

During his tenure in the White House, Reed helped to write the 1996 welfare reform law. He also developed the administration's agenda on crime, education, tobacco, and other domestic policy issues. The second term of the Clinton administration had fewer domestic initiatives than it had planned, due to the takeover of the House of Representatives in the 1994 elections by conservative Republicans, the investigations of KENNETH W. STARR, and the impeachment proceedings.

Reed was born in Boise, Idaho, on March 16, 1960. He received his B.A. from Princeton University (1982) and his M.A. in English literature from Oxford University, where he was a Rhodes scholar (1984).

When Reed left the Clinton administration, he returned to the Democratic Leadership Council as president.

Reich, Robert Bernard
(1946–) *secretary of labor*

Robert Reich was appointed secretary of labor by President Clinton and served throughout the first term. Reich was confirmed on January 22, 1993, and resigned on January 10, 1997. He was succeeded by ALEXIS HERMAN as secretary of labor in the second term.

Reich had known President Clinton since both were together at Oxford University as Rhodes scholars. In spite of their past friendship, Reich was never a part of President Clinton's inner circle and often felt that decisions on issues were made without his input. He was never comfortable in the administration and left it believing that he had been held back by the White House in programs that he wanted to move forward.

Throughout the first two years of the administration, Reich had a particularly difficult relationship with ROBERT RUBIN and other senior staff at the National Economic Council. Reich often did not agree with policies being developed by the Rubin team. Surprisingly, Reich had been a potential candidate to head the National Economic Council but asked President Clinton for a cabinet job instead, where he believed he would have greater opportunities to be a policy advocate.

During the impeachment hearings in 1998, Reich offered tepid support for Clinton. At one point he publicly stated that he believed the president had an "inappropriate" relationship with MONICA LEWINSKY and that Clinton's behavior was "reckless." In one newspaper article written in 1998, Reich stated, "Without trust, Mr. Clinton has only the public's approval of how he is doing his job, which rests largely on the continued strength of the economy—a perilous foundation."

Born on June 24, 1946, in Scranton, Pennsylvania, Reich received his B.A. from Dartmouth College (1968), his M.A. from Oxford

Secretary of Labor Robert B. Reich *(Department of Labor)*

University as a Rhodes scholar, and his J.D. from Yale University Law School (1973). His first job following law school was as an assistant solicitor general during the Ford administration. He later moved to the Federal Trade Commission (FTC) as a staff attorney. (1976–81). When he left the commission, he was named professor of business and public policy at the John F. Kennedy School of Government at Harvard University (1981–93). He left the Kennedy School of Government in 1993 to join the Clinton administration as secretary of labor.

When he left the administration at the end of the first term, he accepted a position as the Maurice B. Hexter Professor of Social and Economic Policy at Brandeis University in Waltham, Massachusetts.

Reich had been involved in politics since 1968, when he was an intern for Senator Robert Kennedy (D-N.Y.). After Senator Kennedy's assassination in June 1968, Reich joined the 1968 presidential campaign of Eugene McCarthy. He later worked on the campaigns of Walter Mondale in 1984 and Michael Dukakis in 1988.

Reich was a member of the governing board of the political reform group Common Cause (1981–85) and a trustee for Dartmouth College (1989–93). He was the founder of the periodical *American Prospect*.

A year after leaving office, Reich published his memoir, *Locked in the Cabinet* (1997), detailing his four years in the Clinton administration. In 2002, Reich mounted a campaign for governor of Massachusetts, but was defeated in the primary election. Reich's unflattering look at the Clinton administration in *Locked in the Cabinet* may be one of the reasons that President Clinton failed to endorse Reich in his bid for the governor's office in 2002. Clinton endorsed Reich's Democratic rival, Steven Grossman. The gubernatorial election was won by the Republican candidate, Mitt Romney.

Reich's wife, Professor Clare Dalton, was an associate dean at Northeastern University Law School.

Reid, Harry
(1939–   ) *member of the Senate, member of the House of Representatives*

Harry Reid (D-Utah) was first elected to the Senate in 1986, having served two terms in the House of Representatives. In 1998 Reid was elected Democratic whip in the Senate, making him the most senior Democrat after Senate minority leader THOMAS ANDREW DASCHLE (D-S.D.)

Reid was a supporter of the Clinton administration, including supporting its positions on abortion and the environment. In one of Reid's rare disagreements with President Clinton on abortion, he voted to ban partial birth abortions in spite of President Clinton's opposition to the ban. Both Reid and Clinton opposed legislation to speed development of nuclear waste burial at Yucca Mountain, 100 miles northwest of Las Vegas.

In September 1999, Reid hosted a fund-raiser with President Clinton, one of many Democratic National Campaign Committee held across the country. The luncheon, at a Las Vegas hotel, involved a $10,000-per-person contribution to the committee.

Both President Clinton and Senator Reid shared strong backing from organized labor. Reid consistently received support from the culinary and construction unions in Las Vegas. According to Reid's staff, "Labor is our strongest weapon."

During the impeachment hearings, Reid was one of President Clinton's staunchest defenders. Not until the end of the administration did Reid publicly criticize the president for pardons given out late in the term. Reid claimed that President Clinton "made a terrible mistake" in pardoning Marc Rich.

Born on December 2, 1939, in Searchlight, Nevada, Reid received his B.S. from Utah State University (1961) and his J.D. from George Washington University Law School (1964). While he was a law student, Reid worked during the night as a police officer on Capitol Hill.

After completing law school Reid served as the attorney for the city of Henderson, Nevada. In 1968 he was elected to the Nevada State Assembly and in 1970 was elected lieutenant governor. At 30, he was the youngest lieutenant governor in the state's history. In 1977 he was appointed chairman of the Nevada Gaming Commission. After returning to private practice, Reid won the first of two terms in the House of Representatives in 1982. In the House, he introduced the Taxpayer Bill of Rights and legislation to protect Nevada's wilderness.

After his election to the Senate in 1986, Reid became an advocate for Native Americans as a member of the Senate Indian Affairs Committee. He also championed broader distribution of public water throughout Nevada. Reid served on the Environment and Public Works Committee, including as chair, and served on the Appropriations Committee, the Select Committee on Aging, the Indian Affairs Committee, and the Select Committee on Ethics.

Reno, Janet
(1938–) *attorney general*

Janet Reno was nominated for attorney general by President Clinton on February 11, 1993. When she was sworn into office on March 12, 1993, she became the first female attorney general in the nation's history. Reno served throughout both terms of the administration, leaving office in January 2001.

Reno was the third nominee for the position of attorney general, following the failed nominations of ZOE BAIRD and Judge KIMBA WOOD. Both women were derailed in their Senate confirmation hearings. President Clinton sought to name a woman as attorney general as part of his pledge to build a cabinet "that looked like America."

After reviewing a list of possible candidates for the position that included Reno, President Clinton called Senator Bob Graham (D-Fla.) who championed her. Reno was at the time the elected state attorney general in Dade County, Florida, who had built a substantial record for curbing illegal drugs in the Miami area and for children's advocacy work.

Although the attorney general traditionally had been part of the president's inner circle, Reno was not. Because she had neither been part of the presidential campaign in 1992 nor served with President Clinton in Arkansas, she had little personal rapport with him and hardly knew him. She was one of the few members of the senior levels of the administration who had relatively no interaction with President Clinton prior to joining the administration. Their only interaction had been the one meeting in which she went to the White House to discuss her nomination for the position in February 1993.

As attorney general, Reno was praised for her role in investigating the 1995 Oklahoma City bombing and for her investigation of the Unabomber, both of which ended in successful prosecutions. However, she was criticized for her handling of the Ruby Ridge incident and the Branch Davidian compound in Waco, Texas. Reno submitted her resignation after the deaths of the Branch Davidians at Waco, but her resignation was rejected by President Clinton.

Among the cases that she authorized as attorney general was the landmark antitrust suit brought against Microsoft Corp. She also secured massive fines against a host of companies for antitrust violations and scrutinized corporate mergers for antitrust violations. The largest criminal fine in the history of the Justice

U.S. Attorney General Janet Reno *(U.S. Department of Justice)*

NETH W. STARR to widen the investigation into other areas, including the MONICA LEWINSKY affair. She also authorized independent counsels to investigate Secretary of Labor ALEXIS HERMAN, Secretary of Interior BRUCE EDWARD BABBIT, Secretary of Housing and Urban Affairs HENRY G. CISNEROS, Secretary of Agriculture ALPHONSO MICHAEL (MIKE) ESPY, Secretary of Commerce RONALD H. BROWN, and White House staff member ELI SEGAL.

Born on July 21, 1938, in Miami, Florida, Reno graduated from Cornell University in chemistry (1960) and with her LL.B. from Harvard University Law School (1963). Reno's father had been an immigrant to the United States from Denmark.

After law school, she joined the law firm of Brigham & Brigham (1963–67) before forming her own law firm, Lewis & Reno (1967–71). She left private practice in 1971 to work as the staff director of the Judiciary Committee for the Florida House of Representatives in Tallahassee and helped revise the Florida court system. In 1973 she accepted a position with the Dade County state's attorney's office where she worked for three years before leaving in 1976 to join a private practice, Hector and Davis.

In 1978 Reno was appointed state attorney general for Dade County, Florida, and was elected to the office in November 1978. She was elected four more times, leaving in 1993 when she was named U.S. attorney general. During her terms as state attorney general for Dade County, she helped reform the juvenile justice system, pursued delinquent fathers for child support payments, and established the Miami Drug Court.

After leaving the Clinton administration, Reno embarked on a campaign for the governorship of Florida in 2002. She lost in a heated primary to Tampa attorney Bill McBride. McBride lost in the general election to Governor Jeb Bush.

Department, $500 million, was levied against Swiss pharmaceuticals maker Hoffmann–La Roche for its part in a vitamin price-fixing scheme.

As attorney general, Reno was tasked with investigating ethics violations and criminal allegations against senior members of the Clinton administration. She also made recommendations for the appointment of an independent counsel under the Ethics in Government Act if the Department of Justice determined that one was appropriate. Reno authorized the appointment of an independent counsel against President Clinton in the Whitewater investigation and then allowed independent counsel KEN-

Richardson, William (Bill) Blaine

(1947–   ) *secretary of energy; U.S. ambassador to the United Nations; member, House of Representatives*

William (Bill) Blaine Richardson joined the Clinton administration in the second term as the U.S. ambassador to the United Nations (1997–98), having been nominated as ambassador on December 13, 1996, and sworn into office on February 13, 1997.

Richardson was named by President Clinton as secretary of energy in 1998. He was confirmed by the Senate on July 31, 1998, and sworn into office on August 18, 1998, replacing FEDERICO F. PEÑA, who returned to Denver. One of Richardson's strengths as the president's nominee for secretary of energy was that he had built a strong foundation of bipartisan support during his 14 years in the House of Representatives. Although a staunch Democrat, Richardson had collaborated frequently with Senator Pete Domenici (R-N.M.). Domenici chaired the appropriations panel in the Senate Budget Committee that controlled funding for the Energy Department.

Prior to joining the administration, Richardson served seven terms in the House from New Mexico (1983–97). President Clinton had worked with Richardson in the House, and Richardson had been a strong supporter of the Clinton-Gore campaign in 1992. Richardson was an activist secretary of energy, focusing on issues relating to the proliferation of uranium both for nuclear energy and for nuclear weapons. As secretary of energy, Richardson began a program to remove 10 million tons of radioactive uranium mill tailings that threatened the Colorado River. Among the international agreements that Richardson signed were a series of nonproliferation agreements, including one in which Russia would convert uranium from its nuclear weapons into fuel for U.S. nuclear reactors.

Although Richardson had built strong relations in Congress, he was unable to stop the creation of the National Nuclear Security Administration within the Department of Energy. Richardson strongly opposed the new agency, arguing that it would be insulated from the Energy Department's staff and the department would lose oversight control of nuclear security issues. Although the new unit was headed by an undersecretary for nuclear security, Richardson was concerned that the agency would be too independent of other departmental programs.

Richardson, a Hispanic American, was serving as the administration's ambassador to the United Nations when he was tapped for secretary of energy. He had been considered by President Clinton in 1997 for secretary of energy, but the position went to another Hispanic American, Federico Peña.

Richardson's tenure as the U.S. ambassador to the United Nations was somewhat rocky as a result of his relationship with Secretary of State MADELEINE KORBEL ALBRIGHT, who had also been appointed in 1997. Albright often tried to curb Richardson's independence as ambassador,

Secretary of Energy Bill Richardson *(Department of Energy)*

a position which fell under the secretary of state. At one point in a debate in the United Nations over Iraq, Albright chose Thomas Pickering, a veteran State Department diplomat, to make the case rather than Richardson.

Born on November 15, 1947, in Pasadena, California, Richardson was the child of a Mexican mother and a non-Hispanic father who was a banker from Boston working in Mexico. The family lived in Mexico City until Richardson was 13, when they moved to Concord, Massachusetts. He moved to New Mexico in 1978 and was elected to Congress there in 1982.

Richardson received his B.A. from Tufts University (1970) and his M.A. from the Fletcher School of Law and Diplomacy at Tufts University (1971). Elected from New Mexico's 3rd Congressional District in 1982, one of the country's most ethnically diverse districts, Richardson served seven terms in the House (1983 to 1997). While in the House of Representatives, Richardson was a member of the Resources Committee, the Permanent Select Committee on Intelligence, the Commerce Committee, and the Helsinki Commission on Human Rights. In addition, he chaired the Subcommittee on Native American Affairs during the 103rd Congress.

During his tenure in Congress, President Clinton sent Richardson on a number of diplomatic missions in which he successfully won the release of hostages, American servicemen, and prisoners in North Korea, Iraq, and Cuba. He also secured the release of an Albuquerque resident who was kept hostage in Sudan. In 1996, a group of 75 bipartisan members of the House nominated Richardson for the Nobel Peace Prize for his diplomatic efforts for hostage releases.

In November 2002, Richardson was elected governor of New Mexico, defeating state representative John Sanchez with nearly 60 percent of the vote.

Riley, Richard Wilson
(1933–) *secretary of education*

Richard Riley, who had championed education as governor of South Carolina, was named secretary of education by President Clinton and sworn into office on January 22, 1993. Riley became the first secretary of education to stay for two terms since the department's creation by Congress in 1979.

President Clinton's relationship with Riley began when both were Democratic governors of southern states. They worked together on a host of issues through the National Governor's Conference, particularly the education reform agenda. Riley was an active supporter of the Clinton-Gore campaign in 1992 and was named to the transition team after the election.

Throughout his tenure as secretary of education, Riley was a steadfast supporter of improving the quality of education across the nation. In a 1994 interview Riley described his goals for the department, stating, "I want more than anything in the world to impact . . . the education for all children in America." In addition, he said, "education is far and above any other issue in terms of preparing [the nation] for the future—and for the present."

Riley was a respected advocate for education among professional education organizations, both at the time he took office and after he took office. His priority in the department quickly became ensuring the development and implementation of the administration's plan to encourage nationwide standards-based education. The plan, called Goals 2000, sought to raise national education standards by the year 2000.

The main focus of the Department of Education under Riley was elementary and secondary education, but he also worked for a number of college-related programs. Early in his term the department helped to develop

Secretary of Education Richard W. Riley
(Department of Education)

the Student Loan Reform Act, which allowed the federal government to make direct loans to students.

When Republicans took control of the House of Representatives in 1995, Riley had to fend off Republican-sponsored attempts to cut funding with the Department of Education and proposals to abolish his department. President Clinton remained firmly committed to the Department of Education and strongly endorsed the department in his 1997 State of the Union Address.

Riley was born in Greenville County, South Carolina, on January 2, 1933. He received his B.A., cum laude, from Furman University (1954) and served as an officer on a Navy minesweeper after college. He received his LL.B. from the University of South Carolina Law School (1959). After four years of practicing law at his family's law firm in

Greenville, South Carolina, Riley ran for and was elected to the South Carolina House of Representatives (1963–67), and then to the South Carolina Senate (1967–77). In 1978 he was elected governor of South Carolina, a position he held for two terms (1979–87). Riley had been so popular as governor that the state constitution was amended to enable him to run for a second term.

Furman University named a building in honor of Riley: the Richard W. Riley Computer Science and Mathematics Building.

Rivlin, Alice Mitchell

(1931–   ) *vice chairman, Board of Governors of the Federal Reserve System; director, Office of Management and Budget; deputy director, Office of Management and Budget*

Alice Rivlin was named director of the Office of Management and Budget (OMB) in 1994 when LEON EDWARD PANETTA, the former director, was named White House chief of staff. She was confirmed by the Senate on January 21, 1993, as deputy director of OMB and confirmed by the Senate on October 7, 1994, as director of OMB.

Rivlin, who served as the first director of the Congressional Budget Office (1975–83) had been a contender for the top job at OMB. Panetta eventually won the job and Rivlin was chosen as his deputy.

During her three years at the Office of Management and Budget as both deputy director and director, Rivlin was known as a deficit hawk. Her recommendations to President Clinton consistently urged reducing federal expenditures and increasing taxes in order to balance the federal budget. Among the techniques to balance the budget that she supported were cuts in Social Security benefits for those within higher income brackets and cuts in certain discretionary programs.

Rivlin was appointed vice chair of the Board of Governors of the Federal Reserve System in 1996. She left the position in July 1999 to return to the Brookings Institution and devote more time to her role as chairman of the Financial Assistance Authority in Washington, D.C.

The Financial Assistance Authority was created by Congress in 1995 to run the finances of Washington, D.C., after it nearly went bankrupt. Rivlin was appointed by President Clinton to the authority on May 29, 1998, and she became chair on September 1, 1998. Her interest in the financial affairs of Washington, D.C., stemmed from her work as chair of the 1990 Commission on Budget and Financial Priorities of the District of Columbia, which was known as the Rivlin Commission.

The report prepared by the Rivlin Commission recommended cutting 6,000 jobs from the municipal bureaucracy and proposed cutting 10,000 jobs from the Police Department over an eight-year span. While she was at the Office of Management and Budget, she remained involved in the financial affairs of Washington, D.C., as President Clinton's point person for the District of Columbia. When she was nominated by President Clinton to the Financial Assistance Authority, she was able to continue to implement the recommendations from the 1990 report prepared by her commission. She remained chair of the commission until 2001.

Rivlin's career in government began in 1968 at the end of the Johnson administration, when she spent two years as assistant secretary for planning and evaluation in the Department of Health, Education and Welfare (1968–69). She returned to the federal government during the Carter administration, serving not in the executive branch but in the legislative branch, as the first director of the Congressional Budget Office (1975–83). In 1983 she left the Congressional Budget Office to become director of the Economic Studies Program at the John F. Kennedy School of Government at Harvard University.

Born on March 4, 1931, in Philadelphia, Pennsylvania, Rivlin was raised in Bloomington, Indiana. Rivlin received her B.A. from Bryn Mawr College (1952), her M.A. from Radcliffe College (1955), and her Ph.D. in economics from Harvard University (1958). She was married to economist Sidney G. Winter.

Rivlin was the winner in 1983 of the prestigious MacArthur Fellowship. She served on the boards of directors of Union Carbide Corporation, Unisys Corporation, and was chair of the Governing Council of the Wilderness Society. In 2003 she rejoined the Brookings Institution as a senior fellow in economic studies.

Robinson, Mary Bourke

(1944–) *United Nations high commissioner for human rights, president of Ireland*

Mary Robinson was sworn in as Ireland's first woman president in December of 1990. Her ability to bridge the schism between Roman Catholics and Protestants in Ireland was largely due to circumstances of her own life, for although she was a Roman Catholic, she married a Protestant, Nicholas Robinson.

The continuing war between the Roman Catholics and the Protestants in Northern Ireland led to a series of peace talks in Belfast, sponsored by the British and Irish governments. At the request of Britain and Ireland, President Clinton sent former senator GEORGE MITCHELL (D-Me.) to chair the talks in 1995.

On June 13, 1996, President Robinson made her second state visit to Washington, D.C., and mistakenly called President Clinton, "President Kennedy." During the visit she urged the United States to become involved in the plight of Rwanda and Burundi. President Robinson had been the first head of state to visit Rwanda in the aftermath of the 1994 genocide there. She was also the first head of state to visit Somalia following the 1992 crisis there. Although President Robinson met with President Clinton in the Oval Office for a time, the official welcoming activities were held at Fort Myer, an army base across the Potomac River from the White House.

Robinson supported the legalization of birth control and divorce in Ireland's Senate where she served from 1969 to 1989 as a member of the Labor Party. She had left politics in 1990 and was a full-time faculty member at Trinity College, but she was coaxed out of retirement to run for the presidency on the Labor Party ticket.

After she won the presidency, Robinson said, "My role as president will be to take on a different role—being guardian of the constitution as the people decide it. My role will be to enhance self-development of women and to carry through my own concept and sense of feminism."

Robinson's support of limited abortions came to a head during her presidency when a 14-year-old girl was raped, and her parents took her to England for the abortion. Although Robinson supported an abortion for the child, she could not allow it to happen in Ireland where the procedure was illegal. She used the case to advocate laws that allowed abortion, if only in certain cases. Her approval ratings rose as high as 87 percent during her presidency.

Born on May 21, 1944, in Ballina, Ireland, Robinson received her master of arts degree in 1970 from Trinity College, Ireland, and her barrister-at-law degree from the King's Inns, Dublin, and a master of laws degree at Harvard University Law School. She served as a member of the Irish parliament, 1969–89, and a member of the Dublin City Council from 1979–83. From 1975 to 1990 she also was a lecturer in European Community law at Trinity College in Dublin.

When Robinson left her position as president of Ireland in 1997, she was named the high commissioner for human rights by the United Nations for a four-year term. Her appointment to the United Nations post had strong support from President Clinton, who pledged the administration's full cooperation with her new role.

Rostenkowski, Daniel David
(1928–   ) *member, House of Representatives*

Daniel Rostenkowski was elected to the House of Representatives from the 8th (now 5th) Congressional District of Illinois in 1958 and remained in the House for 36 years, until 1995. He lost his seat in the 1994 election after federal charges were brought against him. The federal investigation began in 1993 and ended in 1994.

In June 1994 Rostenkowski was indicted by a federal grand jury on 17 counts, including embezzlement from the public purse. The primary charge was that Rostenkowski had cashed in $21,300 of postage stamps that had been bought for his office with taxpayer money. He was also charged with putting ghost employees on his payroll and with using taxpayer money to reward supporters with gifts such as crystal Capitol domes and congressional chairs inscribed with Rostenkowski's name. He denied the charges but was found guilty and sentenced to jail. He served 17 months in federal prison and paid a $100,000 fine after pleading guilty to two counts of mail fraud.

As the senior Democrat and chair of the House Ways and Means Committee when President Clinton came into office in 1993, Rostenkowski was a key player in moving the administration's budget proposals through Congress. He piloted the president's first budget to a one-vote victory in 1993, and during the debate on the North American Free Trade

Agreement (NAFTA) in November 1993, Rostenkowski helped to win the House of Representatives with a 234-200 vote.

Born on January 2, 1928, in Chicago, Rostenkowski attended Loyola University (1948–51). He was elected to the House of Representatives in the Illinois General Assembly in 1952 and to the Illinois Senate in 1954 and in 1956. He was in the U.S. House of Representatives from 1959 to 1995 and a delegate to the Democratic National Convention every four years from 1960 to 1992.

Rubin, Robert
(1938–) *secretary of the Treasury, chair of the National Economic Council*

Robert Rubin was named by President Clinton as assistant to the president and chair of the National Economic Council on January 20, 1993. Rubin's top two deputies at the National Economic Council, W. BOWMAN CUTTER and GENE SPERLING, were also appointed in January 1993.

Created by President Clinton through executive order in 1993 to coordinate economic policy recommendations from the cabinet officers and to advise the president on policy options, the National Economic Council was part of the Office of Policy Development in the White House. The Office of Policy Development included three units: the Domestic Council, headed by CAROL RASCO; the Environmental Policy Council, headed by KATHLEEN McGINTY; and the National Economic Council, headed by Rubin.

He served at the National Economic Council in the White House for two years before being nominated by President Clinton in 1995 as the secretary of the Treasury. He replaced LLOYD MILLARD BENTSEN, JR., as secretary of the Treasury on January 10, 1995, after easily winning Senate confirmation in a 99-0 vote.

Rubin's unanimous confirmation as secretary of the Treasury reflected strong congressional support for policies that he had favored as chair of the National Economic Council. Rubin built his record at the National Economic Council as an advocate for deficit reduction, noting in his confirmation hearings that "This [economic] recovery would not have happened without the deficit reduction program" that Congress passed in 1993.

During his tenure both in the White House and as secretary of the treasury, Rubin was widely credited by Wall Street and business leaders for developing policies that provided a major expansion in the U.S. economy. The country had little inflation and the lowest unemployment rate in 24 years. In an article in *Business Week* magazine in March 1997, the lead story began "The Treasury Secretary has emerged as the most powerful player in the Clinton cabinet."

Rubin resigned as secretary of the Treasury on May 12, 1999, effective July 2, 1999, to return to the private sector as chairman of the Executive Committee of Citigroup, Inc. Citigroup gave Rubin a salary, bonus, and stock options valued at $40 million the year he joined the firm.

Rubin had not been part of President Clinton's inner circle from either Arkansas or the 1992 presidential campaign but had long been a fund-raiser for Democrats and active in Democratic Party circles. He had been a major fund-raiser in 1988 for Michael Dukakis's failed presidential campaign and was closely aligned to New York City's Democratic mayor, David Dinkins. Rubin first met Clinton in 1991, as he began his run for the presidency and he subsequently became one of the campaign's economic advisers. Rubin and other Goldman, Sachs & Co. partners contributed nearly $100,000 to the Clinton campaign and raised more than $1 million more. However, during his tenure in the White House as chair of the National Economic Council and as secretary of the Treasury, Rubin had moved into President Clinton's inner circle and was considered one of his closest advisers.

Rubin had little experience in Washington, D.C., having spent his career on Wall Street in New York City. Rubin became the second member of President Clinton's economic team who did not have strong roots in the nation's capital. The chair of the Council of Economic Advisers, LAURA D'ANDREA TYSON, was an academic from the University of California at Berkeley who also lacked Washington experience. The director of the Office of Management and Budget (OMB), LEON EDWARD PANETTA, his deputy director, ALICE RIVLIN, and Secretary of the Treasury Lloyd Bentsen all had considerable Washington experience.

Rubin, however, was not without political skills. When President GEORGE HERBERT WALKER BUSH and his treasury secretary, Nicholas Brady, had supported a transaction tax on securities, Rubin formed a coalition of Wall Street investment bankers and others to lobby against the tax.

As chair of the National Economic Council, Rubin led the White House's lobbying effort for passage of the North American Free Trade Agreement (NAFTA) in Congress. He also persuaded President Clinton that if deficit reduction was made a priority of the administration, interest rates and inflation would fall. Rubin worked in tandem with deficit hawks Leon Panetta and Alice Rivlin in the Office of Management and Budget to refocus and cut federal spending. Tyson, who was not a deficit hawk and was quoted as saying "the deficit is not the most important thing," remained out of the troika of Rubin, Panetta, and Rivlin that formed economic policy for the administration. One of the most difficult decisions by Rubin involved the loans that the United States made to Mexico as it was facing bankruptcy. Rubin convinced President Clinton that Mexico was a central player in the world economy and that American markets would suffer were Mexico to default on its current loans. The United States led an international $50 billion bailout of Mexico and provided $20 billion of that amount in December 1994. Mexico successfully repaid the loans ahead of schedule.

But the administration was split over some of Rubin's policies. ROBERT REICH, secretary of labor, was one of Rubin's strongest critics. Reich suggested that corporations that were downsizing, such as AT&T, should be given tax breaks to reduce the downsizing and protect workers' jobs. Rubin did not support the plan, which became a public embarrassment for President Clinton when Reich began writing op-ed pieces to the *New York Times* on his tax relief proposal. President Clinton had to demand that Reich stop his attacks on Rubin's economic plans. Reich eventually left the cabinet at the end of the first term.

During his six years in the administration (1993–99), the media referred to Rubin's economic programs as "Rubinomics." His policies contributed to the increase in the Dow Jones Industrial Average from 3242 in 1993 to 10193 in 1999, the drop in interest rates from 7.32 in 1993 to 5.19 in 1999, and reduction of the unemployment rate from 7.3 percent in 1993 to 4.3 percent in 1999.

Rubin entered the administration after a career of 26 years at Goldman, Sachs & Co., the investment banking firm. He joined Goldman, Sachs & Co. in 1966 as an associate, became a general partner in 1971, and joined the management committee in 1980. Rubin was named vice chairman and co-chief operating officer from 1987 to 1990 and served as co-senior partner and cochairman from 1990 to 1992. Before joining Goldman, Sachs & Co., Rubin was an attorney at the firm of Cleary, Gottlieb, Steen & Hamilton in New York City (1964–66) immediately after law school.

Rubin's wealth from his years at Goldman, Sachs & Co. was estimated at over $125 million.

In 1992, his last year at the investment banking firm, he earned $26 million.

Born on August 29, 1938, in New York City, Rubin graduated summa cum laude in economics from Harvard College in 1960 and from Yale Law School in 1964. He then attended the London School of Economics.

Ruff, Charles Frederick Carson
(1939–2000) *White House counsel*

Charles Ruff, who was wheelchair-bound, was named White House counsel by President Clinton in February 1997 in the midst of the investigation into the president's relationship with MONICA LEWINSKY. Ruff served as the counsel to President Clinton during the House of Representatives impeachment and during the Senate trial. When asked why he accepted the position in the middle of the Lewinsky scandal, Ruff replied, "When the President of the United States asks you to do something, you don't say, 'Let me think about it,' you say, 'How can I help you, Mr. President?'"

Ruff became President Clinton's chief defender during the Senate trial. When he began his opening remarks on January 19, 1999, at the Senate trial, Ruff described the House indictment as "a witches' brew of charges" resting on "shifting sand castles of speculation." Ruff was never theatrical in his presentation of the president's case in the Senate trial, but remained calm, focused, and straightforward. Although the House managers often became theatrical in their arguments against President Clinton, Ruff simply rebutted the evidence that they had presented. After Ruff's presentation, the Senate did not vote to convict the president.

Ruff's staff in the counsel's office included BRUCE LINDSEY, Lanna A. Breuer, and Cheryl D. Mills, all of whom were closely involved in the impeachment process. Ruff also worked closely with President Clinton's private attorneys, DAVID E. KENDALL, ROBERT S. BENNETT, and MICHAEL (MICKEY) KANTOR.

Ruff maintained a strategy of providing little information to anyone outside of the small circle of lawyers working on the impeachment case. No one in the White House, except for a very small group in the counsel's office, knew the details of the president's defense. MICHAEL McCURRY, the White House press secretary, was particularly dissatisfied with Ruff's failure to inform him of details on the case and eventually resigned over the conflict.

Ironically, Ruff had been part of President Nixon's impeachment process more than 20 years earlier as an assistant special prosecutor in the Watergate investigation. He was among the staff that successfully prosecuted Attorney General John Mitchell for his role in the Watergate burglary and cover-up. He had been a member of the Watergate special prosecutor's office from 1973–77 and became the fourth and final special prosecutor in the Watergate investigation, following Archibald Cox, Leon Jaworski, and Henry S. Ruth.

Ruff had been one of President Clinton's top choices for attorney general in 1993, but he never was formally offered the job. In its background investigation of Ruff, the Federal Bureau of Investigation (FBI) determined that Ruff had failed to pay Social Security taxes for his once-weekly, 71-year-old cleaning woman. Ruff argued that he did not believe he was required to pay the Social Security taxes since the woman was beyond retirement age. President Clinton decided not to nominate him for attorney general, as a result of problems that his first nominee, ZOE BAIRD, had in the confirmation process. When Baird withdrew her name as a candidate for attorney general, President Clinton had narrowed his choice for his next nomination to Ruff, former Virginia governor Gerald L. Baliles, and Judge KIMBA WOOD. He chose Wood. She, too, had difficulties in the confirmation process. President Clinton's third choice, JANET RENO, was confirmed.

Born on August 1, 1939, in Cleveland, Ohio, Ruff graduated from Swarthmore College (1960) and from Columbia University Law School (1963). After law school, Ruff received a Ford Foundation grant to move to Liberia with his wife and two daughters to teach law. After he returned from Africa, Ruff joined the staff of the Department of Justice in the Organized Crime Section (1967–73). In 1973 he joined the faculty of Georgetown University Law Center.

In 1982, Ruff joined the Washington, D.C., law firm of Covington & Burling. His clients included Senator John Glenn (D-Ohio) who was one of the "Keating Five" accused of taking bribes from Charles Keating in a savings and loan scandal. Glenn was cleared of wrongdoing in 1990. Ruff also defended Senator Charles Robb (D-Va.) in 1990, when he was charged with illegally taping the phone conversation of a political rival, Virginia lieutenant governor Douglas Wilder.

Ruff left Covington & Burley in 1995, leaving his $475,000-a-year job to become the chief counsel for the District of Columbia at $80,000. In response to why he left Covington & Burley, Ruff said, "because it offered an opportunity to work in areas that I cared a lot about, including juvenile delinquency and abuse."

Ruff died on November 19, 2000, at the age of 61 at D.C. General Hospital from a heart attack. He had been wheelchair-bound for many years as a result of Guillain-Barré syndrome that he had contracted while teaching in Liberia.

Rugova, Ibrahim
(1945–   ) *president of Kosovo*

The crisis in Yugoslavia during the administration of President Clinton was complicated by the efforts of Kosovar Albanians to declare Kosovo "an autonomous province of Serbia." As early as 1981, Kosovars (Kosovo Albanians) had tried to have their part of Serbia recognized as the seventh republic of the Yugoslav Federation. Throughout the 1980s, the government of Yugoslavia refused to accede to the Kosovar demands, leading to bloody confrontations.

On December 23, 1989, the Lidhja Demokratike te Kosovos (Democratic League of Kosovo; LDK) was founded, with numbers reaching as high as 800,000 members. On September 7, 1990, the Kosovars established their own parliament and created a secret independent republic. On October 19, 1991, a government was formally formed with Ibrahim Rugova as president.

After the dissolution of Yugoslavia and the fall of its president, SLOBODAN MILOŠEVIĆ, Kosovo succeeded in gaining a degree of independence. On March 4, 2002, Rugova was elected Kosovo's first president in an unusual compromise developed by the United Nations. Kosovo remained a province of Serbia, Yugoslavia's dominant republic, but it was administered by the United Nations and NATO from 1999, after NATO's 78-day bombing campaign forced an end to Milošević's oppression of the ethnic Albanian majority. The United Nations and NATO supported the election in which Rugova was elected president.

S

Satcher, David

(1941–) *U.S. surgeon general, director of the Centers for Disease Control and Prevention*

David Satcher was nominated to the position of assistant secretary of health and surgeon general on September 12, 1997, but did not take office until February 1998, after he was confirmed by the Senate. In accepting President Clinton's nomination, Satcher said that his goal would be "to take the best science in the world and place it firmly within the grasp of all Americans." As surgeon general, Satcher oversaw the Public Health Service within the Department of Health and Human Services.

The five-month-long confirmation process was strained by conservative Republicans who opposed his position on late-term abortion. Although he had been approved by the Senate Labor and Human Resources Committee with a 12 to 5 vote, a number of Republicans threatened to filibuster the Senate vote to block his confirmation. Satcher replaced Dr. Philip Lee, who resigned. Satcher became one of the highest-ranking African Americans in the administration.

Although the confirmation process had been marred by political disputes, the medical community strongly supported Satcher. The American Medical Association (AMA) lobbied forcefully for his confirmation.

Satcher, an expert on sickle-cell anemia, first joined the Clinton administration in 1993 when he was named the director of the Centers for Disease Control and Prevention (CDC) and administrator of the Agency for Toxic Substances and Disease Registry in Atlanta. He became the first African American to head the agency. Among the programs that he pursued at the CDC were immunization for children and breast cancer screening. His first wife had died in 1976 from breast cancer.

During his tenure as surgeon general, Satcher dealt with the controversy over needle exchange programs to reduce the spread of HIV. His office, using research from the American Medical Association, the National Institutes of Health, and the Institute of Medicine, concluded that needle exchange programs decrease transmission of HIV and do not increase drug use. Although Satcher supported needle exchange programs, legislation was passed by Congress banning federal funds for the programs.

Born on March 2, 1941, in Anniston, Alabama, Satcher received his B.S. from Morehouse College in Atlanta, Phi Beta Kappa (1963), and his M.D. and Ph.D. from Case Western Reserve University (1970). After medical school, Satcher worked in a hospital in a predominantly African-American part of south central Los Angeles. After the Watts riots in Los Angeles, he established a free clinic in Watts (1974–79). While in Los Angeles, he was on the faculty of the University of California, Los Angeles, School of Medicine and Public Health, and the King-Drew Medical Center in Los Angeles, where he developed and chaired the King-Drew Department of Family Medicine. From 1977–79, Satcher served as the interim dean of the Charles R. Drew Postgraduate Medical School. He also directed the King-Drew Sickle Cell Research Center for six years. Satcher left Los Angeles in 1979 to return to Atlanta as the director of the community medicine department at Morehouse School of Medicine (1979–82).

In 1982 Satcher was named president of Meharry Medical College in Nashville, Tennessee, which trained 40 percent of the nation's African-American doctors and dentists. Satcher combined the Medical School with Hubbard Hospital and together the two institutions received a federal grant of $55 million to build the medical school.

After leaving the Clinton administration, Satcher was named a Fellow at the Kaiser Family Foundation. In the fall of 2002, he became the director of the National Center for Primary Care at the Morehouse School of Medicine.

Schröder, Gerhard Fritz Kurt
(1944–   ) *chancellor of Germany*

When Gerhard Schröder, a member of the Social Democratic Party, unseated Helmut Kohl, a member of the Christian Democratic Union, he ended Kohl's 16-year reign as chancellor of Germany.

Schröder came to power in 1998 as part of a changing political party, the Social Democrats, in Germany that was moving to the "new center." Although Schröder was identified with a liberal political base, during the 1998 campaign he moved the party to a more moderate or centrist position. He adopted the slogan, "We won't change everything—we'll just do things better," and modeled himself after Prime Minister ANTHONY (TONY) CHARLES LYNTON BLAIR of Britain and President Clinton. Both Blair and Clinton believed that they had moved their traditionally liberal parties to a more centrist position.

According to *Time* magazine, which covered the German election in 1998, if elected, Schröder would join "the left-of-center politicians who are scrapping traditional big-spending and big-government socialist ideologies and adopting free-market solutions. Following fast on Bill Clinton's second-term budget balancing and Tony Blair's welfare-to-work New Labor in Britain, in addition to equally pragmatic policies of social democrats in Europe's northern tier from Sweden to the Netherlands—another such leader in the heart of Europe in Germany would implant the Third Way as the dominant Western political model."

Schröder modeled his 1998 campaign after President Clinton's 1996 reelection themes of jobs and the economy. He also felt a kinship with President Clinton due to their backgrounds. Schröder's father was killed in World War II and his mother then raised the family on meager wages from her job as a cleaning woman.

As chancellor, Schröder supported a strong commitment to the North Atlantic Treaty Organization (NATO) and to the European Union, and built a strong relationship with President Clinton.

After President Clinton left office, the relationship that Schröder had with the United States began to deteriorate over the Middle East. Schröder led German opposition to the 2003 war in Iraq, in which the United States and Britain led a coalition of forces against

SADDAM HUSSEIN. Both Germany and France led European opposition to the war in Iraq.

Born in Mossenberg, Lower Saxony, Germany on April 7, 1944, Schröder received his undergraduate degree from Göttingen University in 1971 and his law degree in 1976. He then practiced law in Hanover, Germany (1976–80) and during this period was elected chairman of the Young Social Democrats (1978–80). In 1980 he was elected to the Bundestag representing Hanover. After six years in the Bundestag, Schröder returned to Lower Saxony where he was elected leader of the opposition in the state parliament of Lower Saxony (1986–90) and in 1990 was elected premier of Lower Saxony (1990–98). After eight years as premier of Lower Saxony, Schröder was elected prime minister of Germany in 1998.

Segal, Eli J.

(1945–   ) *chief executive officer, Corporation for National Service; assistant to the president for national service*

Eli Segal was tapped for the White House by President Clinton in January 1993 to serve as the assistant to the president for national service, a position he held until February 1996. In October 1993 Segal was confirmed by the Senate in the additional position as the first chief executive officer of the Corporation for National Service. He remained at the helm of the Corporation for National Service until the fall of 1995, when HARRIS WOFFORD replaced him. Segal was named at that time to the board of directors of the corporation.

Segal had worked on the 1992 presidential campaign as the chief of staff, coordinating all day-to-day activities of the campaign, and was named chief financial officer of the transition following the election.

Segal's role in the White House was to shepherd legislation that would create a pro-gram for national service. The heart of the national service was the AmeriCorps program which was designed to be the domestic equivalent of the Peace Corps. AmeriCorps, which was formally created by the Corporation for National Service in 1994, was a volunteer pro-gram to provide services in low-income areas around the nation. When the legislation was passed in October 1993, Segal moved from the White House staff to the legislatively created Corporation for National Service, which included AmeriCorps.

The AmeriCorps program grew, by the end of the Clinton administration, to 50,000 people, mostly recent college graduates, in national service roles. President Clinton said that the AmeriCorps program was based on President Kennedy's inaugural address in 1961 in which he said, "Ask not what your country can do for you, ask what you can do for your country."

The legislation that created the National Service Corporation in 1993 provided funding for AmeriCorps that allowed high school and college students to have their educations supported in part, if they would then volunteer for service projects. Service projects included projects in the environment, health and human service, education, and public safety in communities around the country.

Prior to working for the Clinton campaign, Segal had been involved in a number of political campaigns. He had served in 1987 as the national finance chair of the short-lived campaign for president of Senator Gary Hart (D-Colo.), and in 1972 as assistant campaign manager for McGovern for president, where he first worked with President Clinton. Segal and Clinton renewed their friendship in 1969 at a reunion on Martha's Vineyard of alumni from Senator Eugene McCarthy's (D-Minn.) 1968 presidential campaign.

Segal left the White House in 1997 to head the Welfare to Work Partnership as its chief executive officer and president.

Born in Brooklyn, New York, on April 18, 1945, Segal attended Brandeis University (1962–65) and graduated with his B.A. from the University of Michigan (1966) and with his J.D. from Georgetown University Law Center (1973). After graduating from law school he joined the New York City law firm of Weil, Gotshal, and Mangel (1973–77), leaving in 1977 to become legal director of the National Organization for Women (NOW) Legal Defense and Education Fund. He served as legal director from 1977 to 1982 and as general counsel from 1981 to 1986.

Segal owned and was the chief executive officer of several consumer product companies, including a Boston-based direct marketer of puzzles and games called Bits & Pieces, Inc. He was also the publisher of *GAMES* magazine.

Seidman, Ricki

(1955–   ) *deputy associate attorney general, Department of Justice; assistant to the president and director of scheduling and advance; assistant to the president and counselor to the chief of staff; deputy director of the Office of Communications*

Ricki Seidman was named director of the Office of Scheduling and Advance in September 1993, after holding two less senior jobs in the White House during the first nine months of the administration. She was first appointed as deputy director of communications in the White House in January 1993, which was similar to the position she had held throughout the transition. Six months later, in July 1993, she was asked to join Chief of Staff THOMAS FRANKLIN MCLARTY III's staff as the counselor to the chief of staff. After three months with the chief of staff, Seidman was named the director of scheduling and advance in September 1993.

The decision to move Seidman from the office of communications to the chief of staff's office was made by McLarty. McLarty made three major staff changes, which were announced by the White House on June 25, 1993. Those staff changes included moving Seidman to the chief of staff's office, promoting JOAN BAGGETT to assistant to the president and political director, and promoting RAHM EMANUEL as assistant to the president and deputy communications director.

When McLarty promoted Seidman to counselor to the chief of staff, he said, "Ricki Seidman is a person of varied and substantial talents who has taken on a wide range of responsibilities both inside and outside of the Communications Department. Her talent for analyzing complex situations and her tireless efforts had made her an essential part of the president's team. In her new capacity, she will be an even more valued adviser and aide both to the president and to myself."

Seidman remained in the White House for two years. She left the administration during the 1996 presidential election to serve as executive director of Rock the Vote, a nonprofit organization to encourage young people to participate in the political process. Their goal was to register 1 million new voters for the 1996 election. The Rock the Vote effort was supported in part by MTV, the music channel on television.

She returned to the administration in 1997 when she was named the deputy associate attorney general. Her role was to advise the attorney general on a wide range of policy issues, including youth issues and issues relating to youth civil rights.

Seidman had been the director of the Rapid Response Team for the 1992 Clinton-Gore campaign, which was at the center of the "war room" in Little Rock during the campaign. After the election, she was named the deputy director of communications for the transition team.

Seidman's involvement in presidential campaigns began in 1984, when she worked as a campaign organizer for former vice president Walter Mondale's 1984 presidential campaign. She was the manager for Nancy Dick's senatorial campaign in 1988, and the deputy campaign director of the 1988 Dukakis-Bentsen California campaign. She had also been a staff attorney with the U.S. Commission on Civil Rights and legal director for People for the American Way.

People for the American Way was a public interest group that opposed several of the judicial nominees during the Reagan and Bush administrations. It was one of the more active interest groups that opposed the nomination of Robert Bork for the U.S. Supreme Court. When the Senate was considering the appointment of Clarence Thomas for the Court, Senator EDWARD MOORE KENNEDY hired Seidman for his staff. Kennedy opposed the nomination of Thomas.

Seidman received her B.A. from Miami University and her J.D. from the University of Georgia Law School.

Sessions, William Steele

(1930–) *director, Federal Bureau of Investigation*

William Sessions was fired by President Clinton on July 19, 1993, as director of the Federal Bureau of Investigation (FBI) for extending FBI resources for personal use. He was replaced by LOUIS FREEH.

President Clinton called a news conference on July 19, 1993, to announce the firing of Sessions. He stated that Attorney General JANET RENO, who was present at the news conference, had reviewed the performance of Sessions and recommended to the president that his tenure be terminated.

The decision to fire Sessions stemmed from a performance evaluation given to Sessions on January 20, 1993, the last day of the administration of President GEORGE HERBERT WALKER BUSH. Attorney General William Barr issued a strong reprimand to Sessions in his performance evaluation, stating that Sessions had regularly abused FBI resources. He stated that the evidence against Sessions was "overwhelming" and "inexcusable."

The reprimand by Attorney General Barr on January 20th was pursued by the Clinton administration. The reprimand included evidence gathered by the Office of Financial Responsibility in the Department of Justice. The report stated that Sessions grossly misused FBI resources for his wife, Alice Johnson. Among the charges was that he bumped his FBI security detail from an FBI plane so that his wife could accompany him on a trip at taxpayers' expense. The security detail then took a commercial plane. The report also stated that FBI aircraft were diverted to pick up Mrs. Sessions in other cities and that FBI agents were required to take Mrs. Sessions to have her nails done and to shop. In addition, the FBI reluctantly put up a $10,000 security fence at Sessions's home at his request.

Sessions had been a U.S. district court judge. He was appointed in 1974 to the Western District of Texas and in 1980 became the chief judge of that court. On November 1, 1987, Sessions resigned his commission as a district court judge to become director of the FBI and was sworn into office on November 2, 1987.

Born on May 27, 1930, in Fort Smith, Arkansas, Sessions received his B.A. from Baylor University (1956) and his J.D. from Baylor University School of Law (1958). From 1958 until 1969, Sessions practiced law with the law firm of Haley, Fulbright, Winniford, Sessions, and Bice. In 1969 he left the law firm to join the Department of Justice in Washington, D.C., as the chief of the Government Operations Section, Criminal Division. In 1971 he was appointed U.S. attorney for the Western District of Texas.

Shalala, Donna Edna
(1941–) *secretary of health and human services*

Donna Shalala was named secretary of health and human services (HHS) in January 1993. She was nominated by President Clinton on January 20, 1993, the first day of the administration, and confirmed on January 22, 1993. She remained in the post throughout the entire eight years of the administration.

Although she was easily confirmed in the Senate, Senator Trent Lott (R-Miss.) questioned her on her efforts while she was chancellor of the University of Wisconsin at Madison to double the number of minority undergraduate students and hire more minority faculty. He was concerned that she supported quotas, which he did not support.

The Department of Health and Human Services, the federal government's largest department, had a fiscal-year 2000 budget of $387 billion and over 61,000 employees. HHS administered a wide variety of programs, including Medicare, Medicaid, and federal welfare and children's health programs. Among the agencies that were incorporated into HHS were the Social Security Administration, the Food and Drug Administration (FDA), the National Institutes of Health (NIH), and the Centers for Disease Control and Prevention (CDC).

During her tenure at HHS, Shalala actively worked with President Clinton and the Domestic Policy Council in the White House to create a welfare reform initiative. Among the projects fostered while she was at the helm of HHS were programs to make health insurance available to children in low-income families, to reduce teen pregnancy, to raise child immunization rates, and to end the use of drugs and alcohol by children. She also worked with the surgeon general, who worked through HHS, to improve efforts to combat infectious diseases and to create national programs to combat breast cancer.

One of the continuing issues that she dealt with in HHS was ensuring that the Medicare Trust Fund, administered by HHS, would be solvent through the year 2023. In 1996, Shalala proposed to members of Congress to cut $100 billion from the growth of Medicare over the following six years. She proposed to reduce fees to hospitals, doctors, and other health care providers, which would increase the number of years Medicare would remain solvent. Most of her proposals were later enacted by Congress.

Her more difficult task during her eight years in office was devising plans to protect parts of the welfare program and Medicaid, which Congress wanted to cut. Many congressional Republicans supported deep cuts to both welfare

Secretary of Health and Human Services Donna E. Shalala *(Department of Health and Human Services)*

and Medicaid, particularly after the 1994 elections that ushered in a wave of conservative Republicans and led to the election of NEWTON (NEWT) LEROY GINGRICH (R-Ga.) as Speaker of the House.

Born on February 14, 1941 in Cleveland, Ohio, Shalala received her A.B. from Western College (1962), and her Ph.D. in urban affairs from the Maxwell School of Citizenship and Public Affairs at Syracuse University (1970). After college she joined the Peace Corps where she worked in Iran (1962–64).

Most of her early career was spent in academia, including the City University of New York (CUNY) (1970–72) and Columbia University (1972–79).

Her career ventured out of academia in 1975 when she became director and treasurer of the Municipal Assistance Corporation, which dealt with New York City's fiscal crisis. When the Carter administration came into office, Shalala was named assistant secretary for policy development and research in the Department of Housing and Urban Development (HUD) (1977–80). When Ronald Reagan was elected in 1980, Shalala left the federal government and was named president of Hunter College at CUNY (1980–87). After seven years as president of Hunter College, Shalala was named chancellor of the University of Wisconsin–Madison. She remained there from 1993 to 1997, when she joined the Clinton administration as secretary of health and human services.

After leaving the Clinton administration, Shalala was named president of the University of Miami on June 1, 2001.

Shalikashvili, John Malchase David
(1936–) *chairman, Joint Chiefs of Staff*

President Clinton named Army General John Shalikashvili chairman of the Joint Chiefs of Staff on August 11, 1993, to replace General COLIN L. POWELL, after his retirement on September 30, 1993. Shalikashvili assumed his duties as chairman of the Joint Chiefs of Staff on October 25, 1993.

The chairman of the Joint Chiefs of Staff serves as the principal military adviser to the president, the secretary of defense, and the National Security Council.

In announcing General Shalikashvili's appointment, President Clinton called him a "soldier's soldier, a proven warrior, a creative and flexible visionary." Shalikashvili was chosen over Marine Corps general Joseph P. Hoar, who was on a short list of two candidates prepared by Secretary of Defense LESLIE (LES) ASPIN, JR.

Born on June 27, 1936, in Warsaw, Poland, Shalikashvili fled with his parents from Poland to the United States in 1944 ahead of the advancing Russian forces. His father had been a Georgian army officer. The family first went to Germany and then to the United States, settling in Peoria, Illinois. Shalikashvili, then 16 years old, learned to speak English from American films.

He was drafted into the U.S. Army, attended officer candidate school at Fort Sill, Oklahoma, and was commissioned a second lieutenant in 1959. From 1961 to 1963 he taught at the Army Air Defense School. From 1965 to 1968 he was assigned to the 32nd Artillery Defense Command in Europe and was promoted to major in 1967. He served in Vietnam from 1968 to 1969, where he was decorated for his combat role as an adviser to South Vietnamese units.

He received a master's degree in international affairs from George Washington University in 1970 before tours of duty in Korea in 1971 and 1972. He later became the commanding general of the Ninth Infantry Division at Fort Lewis, Washington (1989), and the deputy commander in chief of the U.S. Army in Europe (1990). In 1991, he became the assistant to the chairman of the Joint Chiefs of Staff. He was promoted to the position of Supreme Allied Commander in Europe, overseeing the military forces in the North Atlantic Treaty Organization (NATO) in 1992. He remained at NATO until his nomination as chairman of the Joint Chiefs of Staff.

After General Shalikashvili left his post as chairman of the Joint Chiefs in 1997, he was asked by President Clinton to remain in the administration as a special adviser to the president and the secretary of state for the Comprehensive Nuclear Test Ban Treaty. Shalikashvili headed a task force that developed a set of recommendations on the treaty, addressing concerns raised in the Senate ratification process. In October 1999 the Senate rejected the treaty by a vote of 51-48.

Speaking at the Non-Proliferation Conference 2000 sponsored by the Carnegie Endowment for International Peace, Shalikashvili said, "I believe this treaty is too important to our national security, to our international security, and to American leadership to be left on the shelf."

On January 15, 2001, only five days before leaving office, President Clinton issued a statement that recommended to the incoming Bush administration that they support ratifying the Comprehensive Nuclear Test Ban Treaty. President Clinton asked President-elect Bush to review the recommendations made by Shalikashvili on the test ban treaty, which strongly supported its ratification. GEORGE WALKER BUSH opposed the treaty, calling it "unenforceable." Bush's senior advisers were divided on the treaty in 2001, with Secretary of State Colin Powell favoring the treaty, but Secretary of Defense Donald Rumsfeld opposing it.

General Shalikashvili retired from the army after his four years as chairman of the Joint Chiefs of Staff. He was named a visiting professor at the Institute for International Studies at Stanford University after leaving the Clinton administration.

Simpson, Alan Kooi
(1931–   ) *member of the Senate*

Alan Simpson (R-Wyo.) served for 18 years in the Senate, including 10 years as the Republican Party whip (1985–95). Simpson, a conservative Republican, scored 88/100 points on the ratings by the American Conservative Union in 1994.

Simpson, a frequent opponent of government regulation, was a member of the Senate Judiciary Committee and the Senate Finance Committee. He also served for one term as chairman of the Committee on Veterans' Affairs.

During his tenure in the Senate, Simpson was aligned with conservative factions and with the more conservative members of the Senate. In 1994, for example, Simpson introduced legislation to reduce legal immigration into the United States annually from 675,000 to 500,000. He also tried to limit the number of political refugees that the United States accepted from 80,000 per year to 12,000 per year.

After leaving the Senate, Simpson was named director of the Institute of Politics at the John F. Kennedy School of Government at Harvard University and remained there from 1998 to 2000. He left Harvard in 2000 to practice law with his two sons in Cody, Wyoming.

In 2000 the University of Wyoming created the Alan K. Simpson Institute for Western Politics and Leadership, where Simpson devoted much of his time. The Simpson Institute was funded in part by a gift from Julienne Michel who contributed $500,000 as seed money and pledged a $1 million estate gift to the institute. Simpson gave the institute his papers from his career as governor of

Wyoming and from his Senate career, in addition to other family papers. Simpson had received both his undergraduate degree and his law degree from the University of Wyoming.

Born on September 2, 1931, Simpson received his B.S. (1954) and his J.D. (1958) from the University of Wyoming. After college he joined the Reserve Officer Training Corps (ROTC), was commissioned a second lieutenant, and was soon sent to Germany in the last months of the U.S. occupation. He returned to Wyoming to complete law school.

After practicing law in his father's Cody law office, Simpson was named assistant attorney general of Wyoming (1958–59) and was elected Park County's state representative to the Wyoming legislature (1964–77). In his 13 years in the Wyoming House, he was majority whip, majority floor leader, and Speaker Pro-tem.

Simpson was elected to the U.S. Senate on November 7, 1978, for the six-year term commencing January 3, 1979. He was appointed by the governor on January 1, 1979, to fill the two-day vacancy caused by the resignation of Clifford P. Hansen for the term ending January 3, 1979. Simpson was reelected in 1984 and 1990.

Slater, Rodney E.
(1955–) *secretary of transportation; administrator, Federal Highway Administration*

Rodney Slater was sworn in as secretary of transportation on February 14, 1997, succeeding FEDERICO F. PEÑA who was named secretary of energy. Slater, an African American, was one of two African Americans appointed to the cabinet in the second term. ALEXIS HERMAN, also African American, was named secretary of labor in the second term. President Clinton had made a campaign pledge in 1992 to bring racial and gender diversity to the cabinet.

When President Clinton nominated Slater, he said that Slater had proven himself capable of building bridges "both of steel and of goodwill to bring people closer together," and added that "Slater is the right person to help us meet the many transportation needs and challenges we face as we enter the 21st century."

Slater's appointment as secretary of transportation had bipartisan support in Congress in addition to broad support from trucking and airline executives. Consumer advocate Ralph Nader was among the few who criticized Slater's appointment, arguing that Slater lacked a commitment to both airline and automobile safety.

During Slater's tenure in the Department of Transportation, its budget was increased from $40 billion in 1997 to $60 billion in 2001, the largest increase in the department's history.

Slater's first role in the administration was as the administrator for the Federal Highway Administration (1993–97). The Federal Highway Administration (FHA) oversaw the 160,000-mile federal highway system. His appointment to the highway administration stemmed from his experience as the chairman of the Arkansas Highway Commission during the administration of then governor Bill Clinton. During his four years at the FHA, he became a popular administrator and was widely praised for moving quickly to repair the damage from an earthquake in Northbridge, California, in 1984, which destroyed major highways and bridges.

Born on February 23, 1955, in Marianna, Arkansas, Slater graduated from Eastern Michigan University (1977) and from the University of Arkansas Law School (1980). After graduation from law school, Slater served as an assistant attorney general in Arkansas. While working in the attorney general's office in Little Rock, Slater became close to Governor Bill Clinton.

In 1983, Slater was named executive assistant to the governor for economic and community programs and was later named special assistant for community and minority affairs. In 1987, Clinton appointed Slater as a member of the Arkansas Highway Commission. In 1992, Slater was promoted to the chairmanship of the commission. He was also the director of governmental relations for Arkansas State University from 1987–93, since the Arkansas Highway Commission was not a full-time position.

After leaving the Clinton administration in January 2001, Slater joined the lobbying firm of Patton Boggs as a partner in Washington, D.C. He was named head of the transportation practice group at Patton Boggs.

Smaltz, Donald C.
(1937–) *independent counsel investigating Mike Espy, secretary of agriculture*

Los Angeles lawyer Donald C. Smaltz was named by the Special Division of the United States Court of Appeals for the District of Columbia on September 9, 1994, to investigate charges against Secretary of Agriculture ALPHONSO MICHAEL (MIKE) ESPY, involving allegations that Espy accepted gifts from corporations doing business with the Department of Agriculture. The court charged Smaltz with investigating "to the maximum extent authorized by [law]" whether Secretary Espy "committed a violation of any federal criminal law . . . relating in any way to the acceptance of gifts by him from organizations or individuals with business pending before the Department of Agriculture."

Smaltz placed over the door to his office a poster-size version of the mandate given him by the court to investigate charges against Espy. Above the poster, Smaltz placed an inscription from Plato which read, "The servants of the nation are to render their services without any taking of presents . . . The disobedient shall, if convicted, die without ceremony."

Smaltz was originally appointed in 1994 to investigate whether Espy broke the law by accepting tickets to a Dallas Cowboys playoff game and $1,009 in airfare for himself and his girlfriend, Patricia Dempsey, from Tyson Foods Inc. The investigation broadened into other allegations that Epsy accepted gifts, leading to charges that Espy accepted $35,458 in illegal gifts.

In a 38-count indictment on August 27, 1997, a federal grand jury said Espy violated the Meat Inspection Act of 1907, which prohibits Agriculture Department employees from taking anything of value from companies they are supposed to regulate, and for lying to the FBI and the department's inspector general.

In November 1998, U.S. District Judge Ricard M. Urbina dismissed eight of the most serious charges against Espy. Urbina ruled that Smaltz and his team of federal prosecutors had failed to show criminal conduct in Espy's acceptance of Super Bowl tickets and a Waterford crystal bowl from two corporations doing business with the Department of Agriculture. In a trial on the remaining counts in December 1998, Espy was acquitted of 30 corruption charges brought against him by Smaltz. The jury was composed of 12 jurors, 11 of whom were white and one of whom was African American. The cost of the investigation when it closed in April 1999, was $21 million.

Smaltz graduated from Penn State University (1958) and the Dickinson School of Law (1961). After receiving his law degree, Smaltz served as a trial attorney for the U.S. Army's Judge Advocate General Corps. He then worked as the assistant U.S. attorney general in Los Angeles, where he specialized in white-collar crime. He entered private practice in 1975. In 1994, when he was asked to run the Espy investigation, he was a senior partner in Smaltz and Anderson, a 10-member law firm in Los Angeles that handled only litigation.

Soderberg, Nancy E.

(1958–   ) *alternate U.S. representative for special political affairs to the United Nations, alternate U.S. representative to the United Nations General Assembly, deputy assistant to the president for national security affairs, special assistant to the president for national security affairs and staff director of the National Security Council*

President Clinton named Nancy E. Soderberg as a recess appointment on December 16, 1997, to be the alternate U.S. representative for special political affairs at the United Nations and as alternate U.S. representative to the sessions of the United Nations General Assembly. Soderberg was nominated for both positions on the same day. She held the rank of ambassador while at the United Nations.

In her capacity as alternate U.S. representative for special political affairs at the United Nations, Soderberg represented the United States in the Security Council and assisted with the formulation of the U.S. position on certain Security Council issues. She had primary responsibility in the United Nations for the various peacekeeping operations. She spoke fluent French and Spanish. Prior to being named to the United Nations positions, Soderberg served as the deputy assistant to the president for national security affairs at the National Security Council from September 1995 to 1997. Prior to this, she served as the special assistant to the president and staff director of the National Security Council, responsible for day-to-day crisis management, briefing the president, and developing national security policies. She was the youngest deputy and the highest-ranking woman in the National Security Council staff.

During the 1992 transition, Soderberg was the deputy director of the transition team for national security. During the presidential campaign, she had been the foreign policy director for the Clinton-Gore campaign.

Before joining the Clinton administration, Soderberg worked as the senior foreign policy adviser to Senator Edward M. Kennedy.

Born on March 13, 1958, in Puerto Rico, she received her B.A. from Vanderbilt University (1980) and her M.S. in foreign service from Georgetown University (1984). From 1982–84 she worked as a budget analyst at the Bank of New England in Boston, where she prepared the bank's budget. Soderberg was a member of the Council on Foreign Relations.

After leaving the Clinton administration in 2001, Soderberg joined the International Crisis Group (ICG) as vice president and director of the New York office. ICG was an international nonprofit organization, based in Brussels, which advocated policies to prevent and contain conflict.

Sperling, Gene

(1959–   ) *director of the National Economic Council, deputy director of the National Economic Council*

In December 1996 President Clinton named Gene Sperling as assistant to president and director of the National Economic Council. Before being named director, Sperling had served as deputy director of the National Economic Council for three years under ROBERT RUBIN (1993–95) and then under LAURA D'ANDREA TYSON (1995–96). When he was named in December 1996, Sperling became the third director of the National Economic Council.

Created by President Clinton through executive order in 1993 to coordinate economic policy recommendations from the cabinet officers and to advise the president on policy options, the National Economic Council was part of the Office of Policy Development in the White House. The Office of Policy Development included three units at the outset of the administration: the Domestic Council, headed by CAROL RASCO; the Environmental Policy Council, headed by KATHLEEN McGINTY; and the National Economic Council, headed by Rubin.

The National Economic Council was originally chaired by Rubin, who served as assistant to the president for economic policy and as director of the National Economic Council. Rubin had two deputies: W. Bowman Cutter, and Sperling. Sperling was responsible for domestic issues and coordination of policy and "message," and Cutter was responsible for the international economic policies of the National Economic Council.

Rubin, Sperling, and Cutter worked closely together throughout the first two years of the administration to develop a variety of economic stimulus packages. One of the strengths of their collegial working relationship was that all three understood the political realities of moving their programs through Congress.

In April 2000, Sperling led the U.S. delegation to the World Education Forum in Dakar, Senegal. At the forum, organized under auspices of the United Nations, representatives from around the world adopted a "Framework for action" to ensure that all children had access to a basic education. Sperling was one of the keynote speakers and read a statement of support from President Clinton.

Prior to joining the Clinton administration, Sperling had been the economic policy adviser for the 1992 Clinton presidential campaign. During the transition, Sperling was the deputy director of economic policy. Before joining the Clinton campaign, he had been an economic adviser to Governor Mario Cuomo of New York from 1990 to 1992. Sperling joined the Clinton campaign after GEORGE ROBERT STEPHANOPOULOS lobbied him to move from the Cuomo staff to the Clinton campaign staff.

Born in 1959 in Ann Arbor, Michigan, Sperling received his B.A. from the University of Minnesota (1982), attended the Wharton Business School (1987), and received his J.D. from the Yale Law School, where he was senior editor of the *Yale Law Journal* (1985).

After leaving the administration, Sperling was named a Senior Fellow with the Council on Foreign Relations, and director for the Center for Universal Education at the Council on Foreign Relations. He was also a contributing writer and a consultant on the NBC television series *The West Wing*, which chronicled a fictional White House staff.

Starr, Kenneth W.
(1946–   ) *independent counsel, Whitewater investigation*

Kenneth Starr was named by a three-judge panel of the U.S. District Court for the District of Columbia, in August 1994, as the independent counsel for the Whitewater investigation of President and Mrs. Clinton.

Starr followed ROBERT B. FISKE, JR., as the independent counsel. Fiske had been appointed by Attorney General JANET RENO in January 1994, during the period in which the Ethics in Government Act had lapsed. When the Ethics in Government Act was reauthorized by Congress several months later, the independent counsel was required to be chosen by the panel rather than by the attorney general. The panel determined that Fiske had not been aggressive enough in his investigation of President and Mrs. Clinton and replaced him with Starr.

Starr was originally charged with examining possible financial irregularities in the loans that President and Mrs. Clinton secured with their business partners from the Madison Guaranty Savings and Loan for the Whitewater land development project in Arkansas. Starr eventually did find financial irregularities with the loans, but charged others. President and Mrs. Clinton were never charged in the Whitewater case. Starr secured convictions in May 1996 of three Whitewater defendants: former Arkansas governor JIM GUY TUCKER, and JAMES (JIM) McDOUGAL and SUSAN McDOUGAL.

The Whitewater investigation opened the door for Starr to pursue a number of other investigations concerning President and Mrs. Clinton. In 1994 Starr subpoenaed records regarding the Whitewater land development project from the Rose Law Firm in Little Rock, where Mrs. Clinton had been a partner. The subpoena was for billing records of the firm relating to Madison Guaranty Savings and Loan. The files could not be found and were not found until January 1996, when Mrs. Clinton said she found them in the White House residence. Starr expanded his probe into whether President and Mrs. Clinton had obstructed justice by hiding the records. They denied the charges and said they had been packed in boxes they had not known about. The charges were later dropped.

During the course of the Whitewater investigation, Starr again expanded the investigation in March 1996 to include Mrs. Clinton's role in the firing of the staff in the White House travel office in 1993. The investigation became known as "Travelgate." He also investigated Mrs. Clinton and other White House staff for obtaining Federal Bureau of Investigation files on former White House staff under President GEORGE HERBERT WALKER BUSH in what became known as "Filegate." No charges were brought against Mrs. Clinton in either case after the investigation was completed.

The largest part of the Whitewater investigation that Starr pursued was the MONICA LEWINSKY case. Starr became involved in the Lewinsky case when a friend of Lewinsky, LINDA TRIPP, brought Starr tape recordings of her conversations with Lewinsky. He sought permission from Attorney General Reno to expand his investigation into allegations of perjury and obstruction of justice by President Clinton and VERNON EULION JORDAN, JR.

Reno then submitted a petition to the three-judge federal panel which oversaw the independent counsel. Her petition stated, "The Department of Justice has received information from Independent Counsel Kenneth Starr that Monica Lewinsky, a former White House employee and witness in the civil case of *Jones v. Clinton*, may have submitted a false affidavit and suborned perjury from another witness in the case." The petition further stated, "It would be appropriate for Independent Counsel Kenneth Starr to handle this matter because he is currently investigating similar allegations involving possible efforts to influence witnesses in his own investigation."

The panel approved Reno's request. They said, "The Independent Counsel shall have jurisdiction and authority to investigate to the maximum extent authorized by the Independent Counsel Reauthorization Act of 1994 whether Monica Lewinsky or others suborned perjury, obstructed justice, intimidated witnesses, or otherwise violated federal law . . . in dealing with witnesses, attorneys, or others concerning the civil case of *Jones v. Clinton*."

Starr and his staff then began to focus their energies on the Lewinsky case. In return for not prosecuting Lewinsky for perjury, Starr received Lewinsky's cooperation in the investigation. She provided detailed information of her affair with President Clinton while she was an intern at the White House. He had denied the affair in depositions in the PAULA CORBIN JONES lawsuit, *Jones v. Clinton*.

Starr released his final report (3,183 pages) in the fall of 1998 to the House Judiciary Committee, which then released it to the public. The report, which included graphic information that Lewinsky had provided on her affair with President Clinton, concluded that President Clinton had lied under oath in the

Jones v. Clinton depositions about the affair and had lied to Starr's investigators. After reading the report, Republican members of the House of Representatives on the Judiciary Committee initiated impeachment proceedings.

The 36-member House Judiciary Committee voted along party lines (21 Republicans) to impeach the President. President Clinton was impeached by the House in December 1998 but was not convicted in the trial in the Senate in January 1999.

Throughout his tenure as the independent counsel investigating President and Mrs. Clinton, Starr remained a partner in the law firm of Kirkland & Ellis, earning up to $1 million per year from his private practice at the law firm. He argued for the Brown and Williamson Tobacco Co. in an appeals case involving class-action lawsuits and represented the state of Wisconsin on the use of school vouchers.

Many Democrats, including Clinton political strategist JAMES CARVILLE, JR. viewed Starr's investigation as politically motivated. They denounced Starr for taking private clients during the investigation and for speaking at a law school founded by evangelist and religious broadcaster Pat Robertson. Carville frequently noted that Starr was an active Republican tied to conservative religious groups and to conservatives in the Reagan and Bush administrations who sought to destroy President Clinton. Carville pointed out, for example, that Starr had also reopened the investigation into the death of White House deputy counsel VINCENT W. FOSTER, JR., in 1993 after Fiske had closed the investigation.

Criticism by Democrats mounted in February 1997 against Starr when he announced that he was resigning as independent counsel effective August 1, 1997, to accept a position as dean of the law school at conservative Pepperdine University in Malibu, California. Democrats, who had often portrayed Starr as a politically motivated prosecutor, pointed out that Pepperdine University Law School was very conservative and had been funded primarily by conservative donors. Starr reversed the decision and continued as independent counsel.

Born on July 21, 1946, in Vernon, Texas, Starr spent two years at Harding College, a Church of Christ school in Searcy, Arkansas, before transferring to George Washington University. He received his M.A. from Brown University and his law degree from Duke University. He then served as a law clerk for Chief Justice Warren Burger of the U.S. Supreme Court (1975–77). Starr joined the law firm of Gibson, Dunn & Crutcher (1977–81) after his clerkship with Chief Justice Burger.

When Ronald Reagan was elected in 1981, Starr began working at the Justice Department under Attorney General William French Smith (1981–83). Reagan then appointed Starr as a judge for the U.S. Circuit Court of Appeals for the District of Columbia (1983–89). When George H. W. Bush took over the Oval Office in 1989, he named Starr the solicitor general in the Department of Justice. Starr remained as solicitor general throughout the four years of the Bush administration (1989–93).

After leaving his job as solicitor general in 1993, Starr joined Kirkland & Ellis in Washington, D.C. He was soon after asked by Congress to evaluate the diaries of Senator ROBERT PACKWOOD (R-Ore.), who was the subject of an ethics evaluation for sexual harassment.

Stein, Lawrence (Larry)
(1954–   ) *director of the Office of Legislative Affairs*

Larry Stein was named by President Clinton as assistant to the president and director of the Office of Legislative Affairs in January 1998.

Prior to joining the White House staff, Stein had been senior vice president for strategic and international development for the NASDAQ stock market. Stein developed the strategies for the NASDAQ stock exchange's global expansion and other international exchanges, including the Deutsche Bourse, the Osaka Stock Exchange, and the London Stock Exchange. He also worked on the repeal of the Sarbanes-Oxley corporate accountability act.

As the president's chief lobbyist in Congress, Stein was charged by President Clinton with improving the White House's strained relationship with Democrats in the House of Representatives, created largely by JOHN L. HILLEY. Stein succeeded Hilley as director of the White House Office of Legislative Affairs. President Clinton decided to replace Hilley before the 1998 midterm election cycle.

Hilley had burned bridges for the White House with House Democrats during his negotiation of the balanced budget deal with Republicans in 1997. House Democrats believed that Hilley had made deals with House Republicans without discussing it with them first. He was accused by the House Democrats of making deals "behind their backs" and soon became a liability for the White House.

Stein was named by President Clinton to the White House staff based on the recommendation of JOHN DAVID PODESTA, deputy chief of staff to President Clinton. Podesta had worked for several Senate committees as a Democratic staffer during the 1980s and briefly for Senator THOMAS ANDREW DASCHLE (D-S.D.) during the mid-1990s, and knew Stein. Stein, who had been the policy director for the Senate Democratic Caucus, had also served as the staff director for the Senate Budget Committee.

After leaving the administration in 2001, Stein was named president of the Harbour Group, managing the firm's government relations service.

Stein received his B.A. from Allegheny College and his M.A. from Vanderbilt University.

Stephanopoulos, George Robert

(1961–   ) *senior adviser to the president for policy and strategy, director of communications*

George Stephanopoulos joined the Clinton-Gore presidential campaign in 1992 and was named director of communications and deputy campaign manager. He quickly became a key member of the political strategy team and the "rapid response team" that worked from campaign headquarters in Little Rock, Arkansas, in what became known as the war room. Stephanopoulos, also charged with overseeing the speechwriting team, developed the phrases that would be used in speeches on the campaign's economic policy statements.

By the time the 1992 campaign was over, Stephanopoulos had built a reputation as a major political strategist. Writing in December 1992, *Newsweek* magazine referred to Stephanopoulos as "one of America's great political operatives" as a result of his campaign work for the Clinton campaign. *Time* magazine, in an article in late November 1992, referred to Stephanopoulos as "one of the savviest communicators in the business."

Stephanopoulos joined the Clinton campaign after actively pursuing work on a presidential campaign in 1992. When Representative RICHARD (DICK) A. GEPHARDT (D-Mo.) decided against running for president in 1991, Stephanopoulos began looking for a presidential campaign to support. Stephanopoulos first looked at the campaign being put together by Senator Bob Kerrey (D-Neb.), but did not have a favorable interview with the campaign manager, Sue Casey. A friend of Stephanopoulos's arranged an interview with Governor Bill Clinton, who was putting together a campaign staff for his run for the presidency. Clinton and

Stephanopoulos met at the Washington, D.C., office of Clinton's pollster, STANLEY BERNARD GREENBERG. Clinton hired him.

After the election, Stephanopoulos was named by President Clinton to a post similar to the one he held in the campaign: director of communications. But he also remained a close political adviser to the president, particularly in the early months of the administration.

During his first months in the White House, Stephanopoulos became the political strategist for the issues on gays in the military. President Clinton tried to change the strict no-gays policy that had long been the rule within the military services. The administration was opposed both within Congress and from the military over its proposal to change the no-gays policy. After considerable maneuvering led by Stephanopoulos, the administration compromised with a "don't ask, don't tell" policy, which decreed that the military could no longer question recruits or active military about sexual orientation.

Stephanopoulos was given a new job in mid–1993 with the title senior adviser to the president. Five months into the administration, Chief of Staff THOMAS FRANKLIN McLARTY III made a series of changes among the senior White House staff, moving staff from one position to another. MARK D. GEARAN was shifted from deputy chief of staff to assistant to the president and communications director. Stephanopoulos, who had been communications director, was moved to the position of senior adviser to the president for policy and strategy.

The change in job titles and job responsibilities coincided with the addition of DAVID GERGEN to the White House staff. Gergen, a Republican, had worked in the communications offices of Presidents Nixon, Ford, and Reagan and was given the title counselor to the president. After four years as a senior member of the White House staff, and having worked on President Clinton's presidential campaigns in

George R. Stephanopoulos, with President Clinton behind him (AP Photo/J. Scott Applewhite)

both 1992 and 1996, Stephanopoulos left the administration. He wrote in his memoirs of his four years in the administration that he left because he was exhausted, noting that he had seen his doctor for problems of stress related to overwork.

Stephanopoulos left the Clinton administration after the 1996 campaign and joined the faculty of Columbia University as a visiting professor. In 1999 he wrote a book entitled *All Too Human: A Political Education*. The book detailed the 1992 and 1996 presidential campaigns and his tenure in the White House. Some of the book was unflattering to President Clinton and to members of the campaign and White House staffs. As a result of the book, his relationship with President Clinton and the White House deteriorated.

Stephanopoulos portrayed himself as nonpartisan after leaving the White House and was hired by ABC News in 1997 as a news analyst. In June 2002 he was named the anchor of ABC's Sunday morning program, *This Week*.

Stephanopoulos had worked in politics throughout his career. His first job was as an administrative assistant to Representative Edward Feighan (D-Ohio) (1982–84, 1986–88). In 1988 he was named the deputy communications director of the Dukakis-Bentsen presidential campaign. After Dukakis failed to win the election, Stephanopoulos joined the staff of House Majority Leader Dick Gephardt as his executive floor manager (1989–91).

Stephanopoulos was born on February 10, 1961, in Fall River, Massachusetts, and raised in Cleveland, Ohio. He received his B.A. in political science, summa cum laude, from Columbia University (1982) and, as a Rhodes scholar, attended Balliol College at Oxford University, where he received his master's degree in theology (1986).

Stiglitz, Joseph E.

(1943–   ) *chairman of the Council of Economic Advisers, member of the Council of Economic Advisers*

Joseph Stiglitz was nominated in January 1993 by President Clinton to be a member of the Council of Economic Advisers. Following the departure of LAURA D'ANDREA TYSON, Stiglitz was named chair of the Council of Economic Advisers in 1995 and sworn into office on June 28, 1995. He remained at the helm of the Council of Economic Advisers for two years, leaving on February 10, 1997, to become the chief economist and executive vice president of the World Bank. Stiglitz was replaced as chair of the Council of Economic Advisers by JANET YELLEN.

His expertise was in macroeconomics, particularly in the area of the "economics of information," which recognized that information was often imperfect. His research analyzed the consequences of this fact on the performance of market economics.

Stiglitz's tenure in the Clinton administration was often marred by difficult relations with both the White House and the Treasury Department. He was regularly at odds with LAWRENCE SUMMERS, deputy secretary of the Department of the Treasury, over Summers's support for reducing the deficit. After Stiglitz left the administration to join the World Bank, he and Summers had public disagreements over economic policy.

Stiglitz became known as an antagonist among the administration's economic policymakers, often disagreeing with policies emerging from the National Economic Council under ROBERT RUBIN and the Treasury Department. He also opposed LEON EDWARD PANETTA, director of the Office of Management and Budget, and his efforts toward deficit reduction. Stiglitz was also criticized for his "stereotypical, absentminded professor" image. As an article in the *American Prospect* described Stiglitz, he was "crooked of tie and unkempt of hair, never showing much concern for hierarchy or order."

Stiglitz graduated with a B.A. in economics from Amherst College and a Ph.D. in economics from the Massachusetts Institute of Technology. From 1969 to 1979 he was on the economics faculty of Yale University, from 1979 to 1988 on the faculty of economics of Princeton University, and from 1988 to 1993 on the faculty of economics of Stanford University.

In 2001, Stiglitz shared the Nobel Prize in economics.

Summers, Lawrence

(1954–   ) *secretary of the Treasury; deputy secretary of the Treasury; undersecretary for international affairs, Department of the Treasury*

Lawrence Summers was nominated by President Clinton on May 12, 1999, to replace ROBERT RUBIN as secretary of the Treasury. Summers was confirmed by the Senate on July 2, 1999, and sworn into office the same day.

Before moving to the top position as secretary of the Treasury, Summers had served in the administration as undersecretary of international affairs. He joined the administration on April 5, 1993, and remained in the position of undersecretary until August 10, 1995. He was responsible for the formulation and execution of international economic policies and was elected chairman of the Organization for Economic Cooperation in May 1994. Summers served with Secretary of the Treasury LLOYD MILLARD BENTSEN, JR., who resigned at the end of 1994.

In 1995 he was promoted to deputy secretary of the Treasury, which was the second-highest ranking position in the department, six months after Rubin was named secretary of the Treasury (January 1995). In his new position as deputy secretary, Summers focused on international policy issues, tax policy issues, and issues relating to the financial system. He worked closely with President Clinton and the White House staff on international cooperation issues raised at the G-7 meetings.

Summers joined others in the administration, including Rubin and Office of Management and Budget director LEON EDWARD PANETTA, as a deficit hawk. Summers was committed to reducing the federal deficit and moving the economy into an era of budget surpluses.

Born in 1954 in New Haven, Connecticut, Summers graduated from the Massachusetts Institute of Technology (MIT) in 1975 and from Harvard University with a Ph.D. in 1982. Most of his professional career had been spent in academia. He was a professor of economics at Harvard University (1983–93) and in 1987 was given the added appointment as the Nathaniel Ropes Professor of Political Economy at Harvard University (1987–93). At the age of 28, Summers was Harvard University's youngest tenured faculty member.

Summers took a leave of absence from the faculty of Harvard University when he was named the vice president of development economics and the chief economist at the World Bank (1991–93). Prior to his tenure at Harvard, he had been a domestic policy economist on the staff of the president's Council of Economic Advisers (CEA) (1982–83). From 1979 to 1982 he had been a faculty member of the economics faculty at the Massachusetts Institute of Technology (MIT).

After leaving the Clinton administration in 2001, Summers served as the Arthur Okin Distinguished Fellow in Economics, Globalization, and Governance at the Brookings Institution in Washington, D.C. He was named president of Harvard University soon after.

Sweeney, John Joseph

(1934–   ) *president of the American Federation of Labor–Congress of Industrial Organizations*

John Sweeney, who had been president of the Service Employees International Union, challenged Lane Kirkland for the presidency of the American Federation of Labor–Congress of Industrial Organizations (AFL-CIO) in 1995. During the campaign for the presidency of the AFL-CIO between Sweeney and Kirkland, Kirkland was forced to resign. Sweeney then defeated Thomas Donohue, who had been appointed interim president, for the presidency of the AFL-CIO in the first such contested election in the organization's history.

Sweeney was generally a supporter of the Clinton administration, but often clashed on key issues. Organized labor had traditionally supported Democratic candidates for president and had supported President Clinton in both the 1992 and 1996 presidential campaigns. When the Clinton administration supported ergonomics standards, the AFL-CIO was a strong supporter. The ergonomics standards were supported by organized labor but opposed by such business community members as the National Association of Manufacturers and the Chamber of Commerce.

One of the key issues that Sweeney opposed President Clinton on was U.S. trade policy, which Sweeney believed favored business. On November 30, 1999, Sweeney led the AFL-CIO to protest the World Trade Organization summit that was being held in Seattle. Sweeney and other labor leaders were opposed to the position that the World Trade Organization had taken to pursue globalization and an expansion of the World Trade Organization's powers.

Sweeney took the position that the World Trade Organization was dominated by business and ignored problems of exploited labor and human rights violations in countries in which U.S. companies did business. Sweeney argued that "the World Trade Organization enforces copyrights, but not worker's rights."

The position that Sweeney took in Seattle at the World Trade Organization was similar to one he had taken at the World Economic Forum in Davos, Switzerland, in 1998. He argued at the World Economic Forum that nations need to pay more attention to "workers worldwide. This includes human rights as well as labor standards and environmental protection."

After the September 11, 2001, terrorist attacks, President Bush created a new process to screen baggage and passengers at airports using federal screeners. The system for screening had previously involved private screeners. Under the new system, 60,000 federal screeners would be hired but would not have collective bargaining rights. Sweeney strongly opposed President Bush's decision to deny collective bargaining rights to the newly hired federal screeners, calling it "another assault on the established rights of workers to union representation."

Born on May 4, 1934, in the Bronx, New York, Sweeney graduated from Iona College. He rose within organized labor from president of the Service Employees International Union to president of the AFL-CIO, the nation's largest labor organization.

Talbott, Nelson Strobridge (Strobe), III
(1946–   ) *deputy secretary of state; ambassador at large, Department of State*

Strobe Talbott joined the administration in April 1993, when he was named by President Clinton as ambassador at large in the Department of State responsible for U.S. policy toward Russia and the former Soviet republics. After a year as ambassador at large, Talbott was named deputy secretary of state. He was confirmed by the Senate on February 22, 1994, as deputy secretary of state and sworn into office by Secretary of State WARREN MINOR CHRISTOPHER on February 23, 1994. During the first months of the administration, before his nomination as ambassador at large, Talbott had been rumored to be in line to be the ambassador to Russia. In 1996, he was also rumored to be in line for the director of the Central Intelligence Agency (CIA). When JOHN DEUTCH resigned as director of the (CIA) in December 1996, National Security Advisor Anthony Lake was nominated by President Clinton for the position. When Lake failed to win the support of the Senate Intelligence Committee, he withdrew his name. Talbott was among the names on a list of four candidates considered by President Clinton for

the position when Lake withdrew. GEORGE JOHN TENET, the deputy director of the CIA, was eventually chosen by President Clinton.

Talbott was one of a number of Rhodes scholars that President Clinton brought into the administration. Clinton had roomed with Talbott at Oxford University when both were Rhodes scholars. Talbott, who did not work on the campaign, was referred to as a "FOB," or Friend of Bill. The Friends of Bill were a small group of old friends, rather than campaign staff, who became part of President Clinton's inner circle.

In his job as ambassador at large, Talbott built a strong relationship with Secretary of State Warren Christopher. Although Talbott could talk directly with President Clinton about issues relating to the former Soviet republics, he worked through Christopher and the appropriate State Department channels. When President Clinton called Talbott directly, Talbott reported the call to Christopher and discussed the issues raised in the call.

When Deputy Secretary of State Clifton Wharton, Jr., resigned in December 1993, Christopher asked Talbott to take on the new role as deputy secretary of state. Talbott continued to oversee policy toward both Russia and the former Soviet republics, roles he handled as

Deputy Secretary of State Strobe Talbott *(NATO Library)*

ambassador at large. One of the major issues he dealt with as deputy secretary of state were the 1999 negotiations with President SLOBODAN MILOŠEVIĆ of Yugoslavia relating to Kosovo. In June 1999, Talbott oversaw the negotiations for the withdrawal of Milošević's forces from Kosovo. The negotiations included both members of the North Atlantic Treaty Organization (NATO) and Russia.

Talbott, a 22-year veteran of *Time* magazine, had no previous experience in the federal government, and many were skeptical whether Talbott could maneuver through the career bureaucracy at the State Department. His tenure at *Time* magazine included serving as the Washington bureau chief from 1984–89 and a high-profile role as a commentator on television news programs.

Talbott's qualifications for the position as ambassador at large stemmed from his familiarity with Soviet issues. He had become fluent in Russian by the time he was 16 when he began learning Russian at Hotchkiss prep school in Connecticut. While at Yale University, Talbott became a Russian language and Russian literature major, studying under the 19th-century Russian lyric poet Fyodor I. Tyuchev. He continued his study of Russian

literature as a Rhodes scholar at Oxford University. In a speech at Amherst College dedicating its Russian culture center, Talbott explained that he had been fascinated by Russia since he was 11 and watched the Soviet Union launch the *Sputnik 1* satellite.

While at Oxford, Talbott became a stringer for *Time* magazine and was asked to substitute for the magazine's Moscow bureau chief temporarily. The following year, *Time* asked the 24-year-old Talbott to translate and edit tapes of reminiscences that they had acquired of former Soviet premier Nikita Khrushchev. The tapes that Talbott translated were published in 1970 as *Khrushchev Remembers.*

Talbott became a full-time correspondent for *Time* in 1971. He was the Eastern European correspondent from 1971–73, the State Department correspondent from 1973–75, the White House correspondent from 1976–77, the diplomatic correspondent from 1977–84, and was named the Washington bureau chief in 1985. His assignments included the coverage of the Iranian revolution, visits by Henry Kissinger and James Schlesinger to the People's Republic of China, and the presidential mission to Hanoi. In 1979 *Time* asked him to reconstruct the two and a half years of the Strategic Arms Limitation Treaty (SALT) talks, which ran as a cover story for the magazine on May 21, 1979. He expanded the article into a book entitled *Endgame: The Inside Story of SALT II* (1979). He later wrote another book, *Deadly Gambits: The Reagan Administration and the Stalemate of Arms Control* (1984), which discussed the politics of arms control. His interest in arms control was followed by another book, *The Master of the Game: Paul Nitze and the Nuclear Peace* (1988), on Paul Nitze's arms control efforts through his work in the State Department.

Born on April 25, 1946, in Dayton, Ohio, Talbott received his B.A., summa cum laude and Phi Beta Kappa, from Yale University

(1968) and his B.Litt. from Oxford University (1971). He was a member of the Council on Foreign Relations. Other books by Talbott include *Reagan and Gorbachev* (1987), written with Michael Mandelbaum, and *At the Highest Levels: The Inside Story of the End of the Cold War* (1993) written with Michael R. Beschloss.

Tenet, George John
(1953–) *director, Central Intelligence Agency; acting director, Central Intelligence Agency; deputy director, Central Intelligence Agency*

George Tenet was nominated by President Clinton on March 19, 1997, to be director of the Central Intelligence Agency (CIA) and sworn into office on July 11, 1997. He had served for two years as the deputy director of the CIA.

When JOHN DEUTCH resigned in December 1996 as director of the CIA, President Clinton nominated his national security advisor, ANTHONY LAKE, for the position. But Senate Intelligence Committee chairman Richard C. Shelby (R-Ala.) blocked Lake's nomination. Tenet was nominated by President Clinton when Lake withdrew his name on March 17, 1997, from the confirmation process. Shelby and other Republicans on the committee viewed Lake as too liberal, and they had not supported many of the decisions Lake had made as national security advisor.

Tenet was chosen from among several names that emerged when Deutch resigned. The other candidates were Deputy Attorney General Jamie Gorelick; Morton Abramowitz, the outgoing head of the Carnegie Endowment for International Peace; and NELSON STROBRIDGE (STROBE) TALBOTT III, the deputy secretary of state.

President Clinton's choice of Tenet was due to a combination of his working knowledge of the CIA after serving as deputy director for two years, and his strong working

relations in Congress. After the four-month hearings into the nomination of Lake, President Clinton needed to bring closure to the vacant position of the director of the CIA. Tenet appeared to be the perfect choice, having already built bridges to Congress. As Shelby noted after learning that Tenet had been nominated, "I have known George Tenet for several years and believe him to be a man of integrity and professionalism."

Tenet was quickly confirmed by the Senate, although he encountered a small problem when the Justice Department reported to the Senate Intelligence Committee a discrepancy in his background check. Tenet had not reported on his financial disclosure sheet property he had inherited from his father in 1983. The Senate Intelligence Committee determined that it was not serious enough to stop his confirmation. The committee voted unanimously to recommend the nomination, which was approved by a voice vote in the full Senate on July 10, 1997.

Tenet was widely praised during his tenure in the Clinton administration for improving the morale in the CIA and securing increased funding for the agency. In 1998, Congress supported increases of more than $1.5 billion for intelligence activities, including covert operations in Iraq.

Born on January 5, 1953, in Flushing, New York, Tenet received his B.S.F.S. from Georgetown University School of Foreign Service (1976) and his M.I.A. from the School of International Affairs at Columbia University (1978). He was named in 1978 as research director of the American Hellenic Institute, a nonprofit organization that worked to foster trade and commerce between Cyprus, Greece, and the United States. He left the American Hellenic Institute in 1979 to become the international programs director for the Solar Energy Industries Association (1970–82). He entered government service in 1982 as a legislative assistant for Senator John Heinz (R-Pa.), where he worked for three years (1982–85). He moved to a Senate committee in 1985, as a member and then staff director of the Senate Intelligence Committee under the chairmanship of Senator David Boren (D-Okla.). As staff director, he was responsible for coordinating all of the committee's oversight and legislative activities, including the strengthening of covert action–reporting requirements.

Following the 1992 presidential election, Tenet served on the national security transition team. When President Clinton entered office, Tenet joined the National Security Council staff as a special assistant to the president for national security affairs and senior director for intelligence programs (1993–95). Tenet was named deputy director of the CIA in 1995.

President GEORGE WALKER BUSH asked Tenet to remain at the helm of the CIA, making him the first CIA director in 28 years to remain in office in a new presidential administration.

Thomason, Harry

(1940–   ) *friend of President Clinton; campaign adviser, 1992 and 1996 presidential campaigns*

Harry Thomason, and his wife, Linda Bloodworth Thomason, were television producers and friends of President and Mrs. Clinton from Little Rock, Arkansas. Linda Bloodworth Thomason was the primary writer for their television programs and Harry Thomason was the producer. They had produced a series of hit television programs, including *Designing Women*, *Hearts Afire*, and *Evening Shade* when they became active in the 1992 presidential election.

Thomason had met Clinton when Thomason was a high school football coach in Arkansas. They remained friends as Thomason branched off into film production. The television show *Evening Shade* was produced in

Arkansas as a result of Thomason's strong roots there.

Thomason and his wife were active in the 1992 and 1996 campaigns as media advisers and political strategists, and produced the 1992 inauguration events in Washington, D.C. Linda Thomason produced a documentary about Bill Clinton which was shown at the 1992 Democratic convention.

Although many involved in the inner circle of the 1992 campaign took jobs in the administration, Thomason and his wife continued in television and films. Thomason, however, was a regular visitor to see the president in the early months of the administration, serving as an unpaid adviser. He had a temporary office in the East Wing and a White House pass, and joined a group of other Arkansans who met once a week for dinner and made recommendations to President Clinton on managing the White House.

Thomason became concerned that the White House travel office was not running efficiently and recommended in May 1993 that a new staff be hired. The staff, many of whom had been in the White House through several administrations, were asked to leave. Thomason subsequently urged that travel business be handled by a consulting firm in which he had a partial interest. The result was an investigation by the Federal Bureau of Investigation (FBI) and later by independent counsel KENNETH W. STARR.

After spending the first few months of the administration as a regular visitor to the White House, Thomason soon returned to his work as a television producer. But when Starr began a more intense investigation of the White House, particularly the MONICA LEWINSKY scandal, Thomason returned to Washington, D.C., to help President Clinton. He worked closely with a group of Clinton friends, including HAROLD ICKES, to develop a public response to Starr's investigation throughout 1998.

Thurman, Sandra (Sandy) L.
(1953–) *director, Office of AIDS Policy*

Sandy Thurman, former executive director for AID Atlanta, was appointed assistant to the president and director of the Office of AIDS Policy by President Clinton on April 7, 1997. She replaced PATRICIA FLEMING. The name of the office had changed slightly since Fleming was nominated, when the position was called the National AIDS Policy Coordinator. However, the authority of the position had significantly changed. Neither KRISTINE GEBBIE, the first AIDS coordinator, nor Fleming had the title assistant to the president that Thurman was given. The elevated title reflected the importance that the administration placed in 1997 on finding a cure for AIDS.

In a ceremony held in the Roosevelt Room of the White House to announce her appointment, President Clinton said, "My door is open to her. . . . I've worked with her, and I can attest she tells it like it is. She speaks the truth unvarnished. She won't hold back in this office." She succeeded Patsy Fleming, who was often criticized for not pursuing an aggressive enough agenda.

In a brief statement after her appointment, Thurman pledged to improve Medicaid, housing, and welfare services for people with AIDS and to fight "the devastating effects that homophobia and racism continue to have on this epidemic."

Thurman became a constant advocate for finding an AIDS vaccine. Partly due to her activism, President Clinton announced on May 19, 1998, that he had proclaimed a national goal of finding a vaccine for AIDS by the year 2007. President Clinton announced the creation of a dedicated AIDS vaccine research unit at the National Institutes of Health (NIH). Between 40 and 50 scientists would be brought together from other programs to staff the center, with the federal government contributing

$17 million on AIDS research in 1998. In one speech on AIDS in 1997, President Clinton compared the race to the moon in the 1960s to the race to cure AIDS in the 2000 decade.

Thurman had been the director of Citizen Exchange of the United States Information Agency (1997) prior to being named director of the Office of AIDS Policy. She also had served on the Presidential Advisory Council on HIV/AIDS. She had been a longtime AIDS activist, including serving as director of Advocacy Programs at the Task Force for Child Survival at the Carter Presidential Center in Atlanta (1993–96). Her position at the center included global health concerns of children, such as immunization programs and the eradication of polio.

From 1988–93, Thurman was the executive director of AID Atlanta. In 1992, she was named director of the Clinton for President campaign for the Georgia Democratic primary.

Born in Atlanta, Georgia, she received a B.A. in human resources management from Mercer University.

Torricelli, Robert
(1951–) *member of the Senate*

Senator Robert Torricelli (D-N.J.) was one of President Clinton's staunchest supporters during the impeachment proceedings of 1998 and the Senate trial in 1999. However, Torricelli was often a thorn in the side of the administration. He sharply criticized President Clinton's Kosovo policy in 1999 and said that President Clinton lacked a clear policy in the Balkans. Torricelli was considered a maverick in the Senate and was not considered closely aligned with the Clinton administration.

He took a consistent hard line against Fidel Castro's presidency in Cuba and opposed any efforts to end the trade embargo on Cuba that the Clinton administration proposed. In

September 2000, Torricelli joined Senator Fred Thompson (R-Tenn.) in sponsoring legislation that penalized Chinese companies that sold nuclear, chemical, or biological weapons. The White House opposed the legislation.

Torricelli was a prodigious fund-raiser and was able to build a huge war chest for his 2002 reelection campaign. But he was not well-liked among his colleagues, in part due to his failure to stay in tune with either Democrats or Republicans, or any particular coalition. One columnist called Torricelli "the most disliked member of the Senate."

Torricelli faced mounting legal problems during his one term in office and was forced out of office by his own party in mid-2002. Democrats in both New Jersey and in the Senate feared that Torricelli's legal problems would lead to his defeat in New Jersey and give the Republicans a seat in the Senate. Torricelli had become involved with a South Korean businessman in 1995 who alleged later that he had rewarded Torricelli for his political help with gifts, contributions, and other favors. The issue was constantly on the front pages of New Jersey newspapers, with accusations that Torricelli had used his Senate office for personal gain.

The issue of protecting New Jersey's Senate seat was critical to Senate Democrats in 2002. Democrats had gained a one-vote majority in 2001 with the defection of Senator James Jeffords (R-Vt.), which they did not want to lose should Torricelli lose in New Jersey. Under pressure from Senate Democrats, Torricelli resigned his seat and the New Jersey Democratic Party chose former senator Frank Lautenberg to run in his place in the November elections. Lautenberg won in November 2002 and protected the New Jersey Senate seat for the Democrats. In spite of the New Jersey election, the Democrats lost control of the Senate in the 2002 midterm elections.

Before his election to the Senate, Torricelli had won a seat in 1982 in the House of Representatives from the 9th Congressional District. During his tenure in the House, he had been a supporter of the Gulf War resolution in 1991.

Born on August 26, 1951, in Paterson, New Jersey, Torricelli received his B.A. (1974) and his J.D. (1974) from Rutgers University. In 1977, he received his M.P.A. from the John F. Kennedy School of Government at Harvard University.

Tripp, Linda
(1949–   ) *witness against President Clinton for independent counsel Kenneth Starr*

Linda Tripp provided evidence to independent counsel KENNETH W. STARR in his investigation of President Clinton's relationship with MONICA LEWINSKY. Tripp's testimony was critical to Starr in order to force Lewinsky to provide information on her relationship with President Clinton.

Tripp befriended Lewinsky while both worked at the Department of Defense. Lewinsky had first worked in the White House before being transferred to the Department of Defense.

Lewinsky's relationship with President Clinton began while she was an intern in the White House. Lewinsky, who was 21, started in the White House as an unpaid intern in June 1995 and began a relationship with President Clinton in November 1995.

In December 1995, Lewinsky was given a paid position in the White House Office of Legislative Affairs, dealing with letters from members of Congress. Deputy Chief of Staff Evelyn Lieberman, who managed personnel in the White House, believed that Lewinsky had "inappropriate and immature behavior" at the White House and transferred Lewinsky to the Department of Defense to work in the press office. While working at the Department of

Defense, Lewinsky met Tripp, a career government employee.

Tripp, more than 20 years older than Lewinsky, began talking to Lewinsky in the summer of 1996, and the two became friends. According to Tripp's testimony given to Starr, at one point in their conversations she mentioned to Lewinsky that she had heard rumors from friends in the White House about a relationship that Lewinsky had with President Clinton. Lewinsky confirmed the information and eventually Tripp gave the information to Starr.

Tripp had secretly tape-recorded her conversations with Lewinsky in December 1997, and provided the tapes to Starr. Tripp not only gave testimony to Starr about her conversations with Lewinsky about the relationship with President Clinton, she agreed to be wired by federal prosecutors for taping more conversations with Lewinsky. On January 13, 1998, Tripp met for lunch with Lewinsky at the Pentagon City Ritz Carlton Hotel wearing a hidden microphone which was monitored by Federal Bureau of Investigation (FBI) agents.

Tripp continued in later meetings with Lewinsky to tape-record their conversations. Tripp provided Starr with 20 hours of taped conversations with Lewinsky. While wearing microphones for Starr, she questioned Lewinsky on the details of the relationship with President Clinton, which Lewinsky answered in detail, and sought information on other people who might have known about the relationship.

During one taped conversation, Tripp attempted to have Lewinsky implicate VERNON JORDAN in a cover-up of the relationship. According to transcripts of the conversation, Tripp said, "Vernon Jordan is behind you. He's a very powerful man." But Lewinsky repeatedly denied Jordan's involvement.

Starr released his final report (3,183 pages) in the fall of 1998 to the House Judiciary Committee, which then released it to the public. The report, which included graphic informa-

tion on Lewinsky's affair with President Clinton, concluded that President Clinton had lied under oath in the *Jones v. Clinton* depositions about the affair and had lied to Starr's investigators. After reading the report, Republican members of the House of Representatives on the Judiciary Committee initiated impeachment proceedings.

President Clinton was impeached by the House in December 1998 but was not convicted in the trial in the Senate in January 1999.

After her testimony became public, the state of Maryland initiated a criminal prosecution against Tripp for violating a law that prohibited "one-party-consent taping." Maryland requires that both parties must be informed if their conversation is tape-recorded. Tripp argued that she had immunity from prosecution from Starr. The state of Maryland argued that they were basing their case on public information from press accounts, her testimony was not required, and her Fifth Amendment rights had not been violated. After hearings in Maryland state court, the case was dismissed.

Linda Tripp was born on November 11, 1949, in Jersey City, New Jersey. There is no public record of Tripp's educational background.

Tsongas, Paul
(1941–1997) *sought Democratic nomination for president, 1992 primaries (lost to Bill Clinton)*

Former Massachusetts senator Paul Tsongas (D-Mass.) sought the Democratic Party's nomination for president in the 1992 primaries. During the first Democratic Party primary in New Hampshire in February 1992, Tsongas joined a group of four other Democrats who were actively vying for the party's nomination. The other Democrats in the New Hampshire primary were Governor Bill Clinton, Senator

Tom Harkin (D-Iowa), Senator Bob Kerrey (D-Neb.), and former governor Jerry Brown of California. The Democrats were trying to unseat incumbent president GEORGE HERBERT WALKER BUSH in the November 1992 election. President Bush was challenged only by former Nixon speechwriter Patrick Buchanan in the Republican primary in New Hampshire.

Bill Clinton won the February 18 New Hampshire primary, with Tsongas coming in second. Clinton then won the Georgia primary on March 3 and the South Carolina primary on March 7. Senator Kerry dropped out of the race on March 5 and Senator Harkin dropped out on March 9. Clinton then swept the five southern states on "Super Tuesday," March 10.

With Harkin and Kerry out of the race, only three candidates remained in the Democratic primaries: Clinton, Tsongas, and Brown. When Clinton won the Michigan and Illinois primaries on March 17, Tsongas dropped out.

Tsongas suspended his candidacy on March 19, 1992, believing he could not win the Democratic Party's nomination. Governor Clinton had amassed the majority of primary delegates through that point and was clearly on his way to winning the remaining delegates. Although Jerry Brown had won Connecticut, Tsongas believed that the next major primary states, New York and Pennsylvania, would be easily won by Clinton. Tsongas said in withdrawing that he "refused to be a spoiler."

Clinton clinched the nomination after winning the June 2 primaries, which included New Jersey, Ohio, and California. With Brown's loss in his home state of California, he was effectively out of the race.

Tsongas left the Senate in 1984 after being diagnosed with lymphoma, a cancer of the lymph nodes. By 1992, he believed that he had successfully beat the cancer and was healthy enough to run for president.

However, his cancer recurred and in 1996 he began cancer treatments. He died on January 18, 1997, at the age of 55 from pneumonia, brought on by complications from the cancer treatment.

Tsongas was a moderate Republican until his opposition to the Vietnam War led him to switch parties. He ran for the House of Representatives in 1974 and was elected as a Democrat. After two terms in the House, he was elected to the Senate in 1978. He was a popular member of the Senate but in 1983 cancer struck him. He left the Senate in 1984, choosing not to run for reelection to deal with the cancer. He underwent a series of treatments, including bone-marrow transplants.

Born on February 14, 1941, in Lowell, Massachusetts, Tsongas earned his B.A. from Columbia University and his J.D. from Harvard University.

Tucker, Jim Guy, Jr.
(1943–) *governor of Arkansas*

Governor Jim Guy Tucker, Jr. of Arkansas, who succeeded Bill Clinton as governor on December 12, 1992, was convicted in May 1996 of fraud and conspiracy by a federal jury in Little Rock, Arkansas. The case against Tucker was prosecuted by the staff of independent counsel KENNETH W. STARR as part of the Whitewater land project investigation. After the conviction, Tucker announced he would resign by July 15, 1996. Tucker paid a fine but did not serve prison time. He was sentenced to 18 months home detention because of poor health.

Tucker was convicted with JAMES (JIM) and SUSAN McDOUGAL, who were business partners of President and Mrs. Clinton in the Whitewater land project. In 1978, then attorney general Bill Clinton and his wife joined in a partnership with Jim and Susan McDougal to purchase 200 acres of riverfront property in Arkansas to sell as vacation homes. The Whitewater Development Corporation, which they formed, received a $300,000 loan from banker David Hale. Starr's investigation focused on whether Clinton had, as attorney general, pressured Hale.

Starr's investigation never proved that President Clinton had in any way pressured Hale and Clinton was exonerated in that matter. However, Starr's investigation led to charges against Jim and Susan McDougal of other illegal activities in the Madison Guaranty Savings and Loan, which they owned. The charges against them concerned a series of real estate deals allegedly involving bogus land appraisals, fraudulent loan applications, and misapplied federal funds. The 48-page, 21-count indictment never mentioned the Clintons or the Whitewater land development project.

Tucker was indicted at the same time for fraudulent loans he secured, which were related to both David Hale and the McDougals' savings and loan.

Tucker was specifically charged with fraud from a company he owned called Castle Sewer and Water (CSW). Tucker formed CSW on the last day of 1985 to buy the utility system at a real estate development called Castle Grande. Madison Financial, a subsidiary of Jim and Susan McDougal's Madison Guaranty Savings and Loan, had just bought the Castle Grande property. Tucker used a $150,000 loan from David Hale's company, Capital Management Services, which was a federally funded small business investment company that was only supposed to make loans to disadvantaged businesses. The indictment by Kenneth Starr, for which Tucker was convicted, argued that the Hale loan to him was illegal.

In 1998 Tucker pleaded guilty in another case brought by Starr, one alleging the misapplication of profits earned in a cable television deal. He promised to cooperate in exchange for avoiding a jail sentence. Starr hoped that

Tucker would provide evidence against President and Mrs. Clinton in one form or another, but Tucker did not have anything to offer Starr.

Born on June 13, 1943, in Oklahoma City, Oklahoma, Jim Guy Tucker, Jr. graduated with a B.A. from Harvard College (1964) and a J.D. from the University of Arkansas (1968). He joined the law firm of Rose, Barron, Nash, Williamson, Carroll, and Clay in Little Rock after law school, where he worked for two years (1968–70). In 1971 he became a prosecuting attorney for the 6th Judicial District in Arkansas (1971–72) and was elected attorney general of Arkansas for two terms, 1973–75 and 1975–77. After his second term as attorney general ended, Tucker formed the law firm of Tucker and Stafford (1979–82). He then formed the law firm of Mitchell, Williams, Selig and Tucker in 1982. In 1990, Tucker was elected lieutenant governor of Arkansas when Bill Clinton was elected governor. When Bill Clinton was elected president in 1992, Tucker moved into the governor's office.

Tyson, Laura D'Andrea
(1947–   ) *director, National Economic Council; chair, Council of Economic Advisers*

Laura D'Andrea Tyson was nominated by President Clinton as chair of the Council of Economic Advisers (CEA) in January 1993. She became the first woman named to head the three-person Council of Economic Advisers since it was legislatively created in 1946. When Tyson left in 1995, she was replaced by JOSEPH STIGLITZ.

As chair of the Council of Economic Advisers, Tyson was responsible for providing the president and the National Economic Council with advice and analysis on all economic policy matters, for preparing the administration's economic forecasts, and for the annual *Economic Report of the President.*

After two years as chairman of the Council of Economic Advisers, President Clinton tapped Tyson to replace ROBERT RUBIN (who was named secretary of the Treasury) as head of the National Economic Council. When she was tapped as the director of the National Economic Council on February 21, 1995, she became the highest ranking member of President Clinton's White House staff.

She remained at the helm of the National Economic Council for the remaining two years of the first term of the administration, leaving at the end of 1996 to return to the faculty of the University of California at Berkeley.

Tyson, an economics professor at the University of California, was only slightly involved in the 1992 presidential campaign, offering advice when she was asked. But after the election, she became an integral part of the economic policy transition team. It was due to her role on the transition team, rather than her role in the campaign, that led to her appointment as chair of the Council of Economic Advisers.

When asked by an interviewer for the Public Broadcasting System (PBS) how she became involved in the campaign, she responded, "I had been active in the 1980's with various groups that worked on the issue of changing global competitiveness. Through that set of commissions I met a number of people like Bob Rubin and Bob [ROBERT] REICH, who ended up being involved in the campaign for President Clinton. . . . They asked me if I wanted to join . . . so I agreed to sign on. But I didn't do a whole lot during the campaign; I stayed out here in California. But then I got a call to work on the transition team, and from there I was asked by the president to head the Council of Economic Advisers."

Born on June 28, 1947, in Bayonne, New Jersey, Tyson received her B.A. from Smith College, summa cum laude, (1969) and her Ph.D. in economics (1974) from the Massachusetts Institute of Technology (MIT). Her surname, Tyson, is from her first marriage which ended in the mid-1970s. She later married Erik Tarloff, a television and film screenwriter.

Before joining the faculty of the University of California at Berkeley, she had worked for a short time at the World Bank in Washington, D.C., then accepted a three-year position on the economics faculty at Princeton University (1974–77). She left Princeton to join the faculty of the University of California at Berkeley (1978–93). In the 1989–90 academic year, Tyson taught at the Harvard Business School.

Tyson left the Clinton administration in December 1996 after four years in the administration to return to the University of California at Berkeley, where she held the Class of 1939 Chair in Economics and Business Administration. On July 1, 1998, she was named dean of the Haas School of Business at the University of California at Berkeley. In January 2002 she was named dean of the London Business School in London, England. At both the Haas School of Business and the London Business School, Tyson was the first woman named as dean.

Tyson was also a contributing writer for *Business Week* magazine.

She was a principal of the Law & Economics Consulting Group and a member of the boards of directors of Ameritech Corporation; Eastman Kodak Company; Morgan Stanley, Dean Witter, Discover & Co,; and the Council on Foreign Relations and the John D. and Catherine T. MacArthur Foundation.

Vance, Cyrus Roberts

(1917–2002) *special envoy of the United Nations secretary-general on Greece-FYROM negotiations; secretary of state, Carter administration*

Cyrus Vance had built a record of international negotiation throughout his professional career, as an international lawyer in his early career, as secretary of the army during the Kennedy administration, as a peace negotiator during the Johnson administration, as secretary of state during the Carter administration, and as a peace negotiator for the United Nations in 1991 and 1992 in the Balkans.

With the support of the Clinton administration, the secretary-general of the United Nations asked Vance to serve as his special envoy for the negotiations between Greece and the Former Yugoslav Republic of Macedonia (FYROM). Vance served in this capacity from 1993 until his death in 2002.

Born on March 27, 1917, in Clarksburg, West Virginia, Vance graduated from the Kent School (high school), received his B.A. from Yale University (1939), and his LL.D. from the University of West Virginia Law School (1942). After practicing law in several New York City law firms throughout the 1940s and 1950s and becoming a well-known international lawyer, he changed careers from a private attorney to a government attorney. He became general counsel to the Senate Space and Aeronautics Committee in 1956, where he drafted the legislation establishing the National Aeronautics and Space Administration (NASA). When the Kennedy administration entered office, Vance was named general counsel at the Department of Defense (1961–62). In 1962 he was named secretary of the army, a position he held throughout the remainder of the Kennedy administration (1962–63). In 1964 he was named by President Johnson as the deputy secretary of defense, where he remained until 1967.

He then returned to his New York City law firm of Simpson, Thacher & Bartlett and undertook a number of special assignments for President Johnson. In 1967 President Johnson named Vance special representative of the president of the United States in Cyprus, and in 1968 he was named to the same position in Korea. In 1969, Vance was named by President Johnson as the U.S. negotiator to the Paris Peace Conference on Vietnam (1968–69).

When President RICHARD MILHOUS NIXON entered office in 1969, Vance resumed his practice of law with his New York City firm. Eight years later, when the Democrats recaptured the

White House, President Jimmy Carter asked Vance to again enter the world of international diplomacy as the secretary of state. Vance served as secretary from January 21, 1977, to April 28, 1980, when he resigned over decisions that were made by President Carter to rescue hostages in Tehran, Iran, held in the American embassy. Vance had never been strongly aligned with Zbigniew Brzezinski, the president's national security advisor, who largely controlled major foreign policy decisions.

Vance's skills in international negotiation were sought in 1992 by the United Nations. The secretary-general of the United Nations sent Vance as his personal emissary to South Africa and Nagorno-Karabakh. In 1991–92, Vance served as the cochairman of the United Nations–European Community International Conference on the Former Yugoslavia. In this capacity, Vance was head of the United Nations' efforts to negotiate an end to the violence following the dissolution of Yugoslavia. Vance worked closely with Lord David Owen of the European Community to pursue peace initiatives in Bosnia and Herzegovina. Vance had helped to force a cease-fire in Croatia in 1991, but he had a more difficult time with Bosnia and Herzegovina.

Vance continued to work with the United Nations throughout the tenure of the Clinton administration. From 1993 to 2002, Vance was the special envoy of the United Nations secretary-general on the Greece-FYROM negotiations.

In 1983 Vance published his memoirs, *Hard Choices.*

Varmus, Harold E.
(1939–) *director of the National Institutes of Health*

Dr. Harold Varmus, a Nobel laureate, was named by President Clinton in August 1993 as director of the National Institutes of Health (NIH). Varmus became the first Nobel laureate to hold the position. He replaced Dr. Bernadine Healy, who had been appointed by President GEORGE HERBERT WALKER BUSH.

The National Institutes of Health, an agency within the Department of Health and Human Services, was the principal biomedical research agency for the federal government. The agency, with a budget of $11 billion in 1993, conducted its own research, trained researchers, and supported research by universities and other organizations on a 300-acre facility in Bethesda, Maryland. NIH had 14,700 employees, including four Nobel laureates.

The nomination of Varmus was delayed for several months after the start of the administration as various coalitions sought to influence the president's decision on the nominee. Healy had been criticized for poor relations with Congress and within the National Institutes of Health. She was also actively criticized by gay and lesbian groups, who believed she had done little to promote AIDS research.

Two candidates emerged as the top contenders for director of NIH: Dr. Harold Varmus, a physician, and Judith Rodin, Ph.D. Rodin was a psychologist and the provost at Yale who received the backing of behavioral scientists. Rodin was also a woman, which was important to the Clinton agenda of the inclusion of women in senior administration positions. The American Psychological Society mounted a campaign for Rodin, including seeking the support of AIDS activists.

However, Varmus had the support of the scientific community and many within NIH. As a basic researcher, as were most of the scientists in NIH, Varmus was viewed as more compatible with the scientific and research mission of the agency. After six months of debate in the White House, Varmus was finally selected for the position and successfully confirmed by the Senate.

Born on December 18, 1939, in Oceanside, New York, Varmus received his B.A., magna cum laude, from Amherst College (1961), his M.A. in literature from Harvard University (1962), and his M.D. from Columbia University Medical School (1966). After graduation from medical school, Varmus was an intern and resident at Presbyterian Hospital in New York City (1966–68).

After completing his medical training at Presbyterian Hospital, Varmus became a clinical associate at NIH in Bethesda, Maryland (1968–70), and in 1970 joined the faculty in microbiology of the University of California in San Francisco. He moved through the ranks at the University of California from lecturer to professor, where he remained until 1993 when President Clinton named him NIH director (1970–93).

Varmus resigned at the end of 1999 to become the president and chief executive officer of Memorial Sloan-Kettering Cancer Center in New York City in 2000.

Varmus was the recipient of the Nobel Prize in physiology or medicine in 1989, an award he shared with his colleague Michael Bishop. They discovered through their research that normal cells contain genes that malfunction to produce cancer.

Varney, Christine A.

(1955–) *federal trade commissioner, secretary to the cabinet*

Christine Varney was named by President Clinton as deputy assistant to the president and secretary to the cabinet in January 1993. The position of secretary to the cabinet had been at the rank of assistant to the president in the George H. W. Bush administration (1989–93), but was downgraded at the beginning of the Clinton administration. Her position as secretary to the cabinet was the primary point of contact between the president and the members of the cabinet. She was responsible for the overall coordination of several major issues between the White House and the cabinet. Varney also coordinated the governmentwide response to natural disasters.

She remained in the position of secretary to the cabinet for two years. In 1994 Varney was nominated by President Clinton to the Federal Trade Commission. While at the Federal Trade Commission, Varney became the commission's expert on Internet issues.

Varney had been active in Democratic Party politics since 1989, when she was named the general counsel of the Democratic National Committee (1989–91). She left the Democratic National Committee in 1991 and joined the Washington, D.C., law firm of Hogan and Hartson, where she remained until she joined the Clinton administration in 1993.

An election law specialist, Varney was named chief counsel of the Clinton-Gore campaign in 1992 and after the election she was named general counsel of the 1993 Presidential Inaugural Committee.

Born on December 17, 1955, in Washington, D.C., Varney received her B.A., magna cum laude, from the State University of New York at Albany (1977), and an M.P.A., magna cum laude, from the Maxwell School at Syracuse University (1979). She received her J.D. from Georgetown University Law Center (1986).

After leaving the Federal Trade Commission in 1997, Varney returned to Hogan and Hartson as head of the Internet practice group at the firm. When she left the Federal Trade Commission, she explained her reasons for leaving government. "I'm leaving," she said, "because I've been in government at this level for five years. It's important to keep in touch with the private sector. I want to overcome and eliminate the barriers in electronic commerce for U.S. businesses." She added, "and the money's not bad."

Waldman, Michael

(1955–　) *director, office of speechwriting; policy coordination*

Michael Waldman was named by President Clinton as assistant to the president and director, office of speechwriting, in 1995 after serving for two years as a special assistant to the president for policy coordination, where he was the principal policy adviser on campaign reform and political reform. He was named to the White House staff in January 1993.

During the 1992 presidential campaign, Waldman served as the deputy communications director. He also served in the same capacity throughout the transition following the election.

From 1989 to 1992, when he joined the Clinton-Gore campaign, Waldman was the director of Public Citizens's Congress Watch. Prior to his work with Congress Watch, he had been a public interest lawyer.

During his tenure in the White House, Waldman wrote or edited approximately 2,000 speeches, including four State of the Union addresses and two inaugural addresses. He also helped to write President Clinton's acceptance speech at the 1996 Democratic convention.

Waldman graduated from Columbia College and New York University School of Law.

After leaving the White House, Waldman joined the faculty as a lecturer in public policy at the John F. Kennedy School of Government at Harvard University. In 2000 he published a book on his experiences as President Clinton's chief speechwriter entitled, *POTUS Speaks: Finding the Words That Defined the Clinton Presidency.* The term POTUS referred to the *P*resident *o*f *t*he *U*nited *S*tates. The term was often used by the Secret Service to refer to the president.

Watkins, W. David

(1941–　) *director of the Office of Management and Administration*

David Watkins was named by President Clinton in January 1993 as assistant to the president and director of the Office of Management and Administration within the White House. He was fired by President Clinton in May 1994 for using a government-owned helicopter for a golf trip. Watkins and a colleague (Alphonso Maldon, Jr., director of the White House military office) took the presidential helicopter, Marine One, from Washington to a private country club near Camp David, Maryland, for an afternoon golf game.

Watkins had been involved in another negative high-profile issue earlier in the administration with regard to the 1993 firing of the White House travel office staff. A contract for the travel office business, which primarily coordinated air travel for the media accompanying President Clinton on trips, was given to a private company. The company was selected by Watkins after being recommended by HARRY THOMASON. Thomason was a media adviser, also from Arkansas, who had worked on the 1992 Clinton-Gore campaign. Thomason had a part interest in the private travel company.

The independent counsel, KENNETH W. STARR, investigated the travel office firings (which became known as "Travelgate") to determine whether Mrs. Clinton had pressured Watkins for political reasons. Mrs. Clinton was cleared by Starr of any wrongful actions. In her testimony to Starr, she denied any involvement in the firings. When Starr's investigators asked Mrs. Clinton directly, "Did you have any role in it," she replied, "No, I did not." Watkins apparently made the decision to fire the travel office after determining that a private company could handle the work at less expense. The controversy arose when he chose a private company affiliated with Thomason and the firings were considered by the investigators as potentially illegal.

Watkins had been embroiled in another issue that the independent counsel investigated as part of the larger Whitewater investigation. Watkins, as director of the office of management and administration, prepared a memo for White House staff in 1996 which directed that a computer system, nicknamed "Big Brother," within the White House, could not be used for fund-raising. The database, which was used to coordinate President Clinton's contacts with top political supporters, was ruled by Watkins to be government property. "The White House database," Watkins wrote, "will be government property and cannot be given to or used by a campaign entity." Watkins was not

accused of any wrongdoing, but his memo became part of a larger investigation by Starr.

The relationship between Clinton and Watkins stemmed from their Arkansas background. Both Watkins and President Clinton had been born in Hope, Arkansas. But President Clinton's family moved when he was three years old. Although Clinton had not known Watkins in Hope, Watkins was a friend of THOMAS FRANKLIN MCLARTY III, who also grew up in Hope, Arkansas. Although Clinton and Watkins had been born in the same community, they did not become friends until Clinton was running for governor in 1982. Watkins began handling media work for the gubernatorial campaign. After his initial work in 1982, Watkins continued to work in each of President Clinton's primary and general election gubernatorial campaigns from 1982 to 1990, Watkins as a media consultant.

When President Clinton began considering a run for the presidency in 1991, Watkins was one of a small group that began to pull together a presidential campaign structure in Little Rock. During the 1992 presidential campaign, Watkins served as the chief operating officer for the Clinton-Gore campaign. He had been the chief operating officer and campaign manger for the 1991–92 Clinton for President campaign.

Born on July 30, 1941, in Hope, Arkansas, he received his B.A. from the University of Arkansas (1963). Watkins was founder and chairman of an advertising firm, Watkins & Associates in Little Rock, Arkansas (1975–91). By 1980, it was the second-largest advertising firm in Arkansas.

He was also the founder and chief executive officer of Faded Blue Music Company in Nashville, Tennessee (1977–80), and the founder and chief executive officer of a long-distance phone company, TMC of Arkansas (1982–88). He was founder and president of Arkansas Cellular Communications in Little Rock (1982–88).

Weld, William Floyd

(1945–) *failed nominee as ambassador to Mexico, governor of Massachusetts*

Governor William Weld, a popular two-term governor of Massachusetts, was nominated by President Clinton as ambassador to Mexico in 1997, but was not confirmed by the Senate. Weld withdrew his name from consideration in the Senate after Senator Jesse Helms (R-N.C.), chairman of the Senate Foreign Relations Committee, refused to allow the name to be considered. Weld resigned the governorship on July 29, 1997, to lobby in Washington, D.C., for confirmation.

Weld, a moderate Republican, was nominated by President Clinton in part to build bipartisanship in the administration. President Clinton had successfully nominated another Republican in 1996, Senator WILLIAM SEBASTIAN COHEN (R-Me.), as his secretary of defense. Weld's nomination was in part for political reasons, for it gave possible Democratic candidate Joseph P. Kennedy II a stronger chance at winning the governor's race if Weld were no longer in office.

When the Clinton administration originally decided to choose Weld for a diplomatic position, several countries, including India, were considered. But Weld preferred Mexico since he spoke Spanish and had studied Mexico. Weld's problems in moving through the appointment process were only beginning in the spring of 1997 during the early skirmishes with the Clinton administration over the country of assignment. During the summer of 1997, as the Senate confirmation process began, Senator Jesse Helms vowed to block the nomination in his Foreign Relations Committee. Helms believed that Weld, who was pro-choice, was too liberal on many issues. Helms refused to hold a hearing on Weld, effectively ending the nomination process. Weld withdrew his name on September 26, 1997.

Weld had not built a strong reservoir of support among Republicans in Washington, D.C., over the years. In 1988 Weld had quit as assistant attorney general in the Reagan administration, accusing Attorney General Edwin Meese of corruption. Conservatives, such as Helms, were furious.

After failing to win Senate confirmation, Weld returned to the private sector. After practicing law for McDermott, Will and Emery in New York City, he formed Leeds Weld & Co. in New York City. Leeds Weld was a private equity fund focused on investing in the education and training industry.

West, Togo Dennis, Jr.

(1942–) *secretary of veterans affairs, secretary of the army*

Togo West was nominated as secretary of veterans affairs in December 1997, after Deputy Secretary HERSHEL W. GOBER withdrew his nomination in July 1997. West became acting secretary of veterans affairs on January 2, 1998, and was confirmed by the Senate in April. He was sworn into office on May 5, 1998. President Clinton's nomination of West, an African American, contributed to the administration's efforts to create a cabinet with ethnic and gender diversity.

Gober withdrew his nomination on October 24, 1997, following allegations that he had made unwanted sexual advances toward two women. Gober had been nominated to replace JESSE BROWN, who resigned in July 1997 due to health problems. Brown died in 2002 of amyotrophic lateral sclerosis, commonly known as Lou Gehrig's disease.

During his tenure as secretary of veterans affairs, West dealt with building the financial base for the agency's 170 hospitals and improving veterans benefits. He was well received in Congress and often secured more funding for programs than he lobbied for. He continued the programs of former secretary of veterans affairs Jesse Brown to deal with veterans who were exposed to Agent Orange in the Vietnam War and with veterans who had unexplained illnesses from their tour of duty in the Persian Gulf War.

His most difficult period came when allegations arose that he had given preferred locations in Arlington National Cemetery to certain Democratic Party donors, a charge that he adamantly refuted. The allegations appeared to have been politically oriented and the issue died down after no facts could be found to support the allegations.

Prior to serving as secretary of veterans affairs, West had been the secretary of the army, formally taking office in November 1993. During that period West became embroiled in a number of controversial issues. He became an advocate for women in the army, demanding equity and an end to sexual harassment of female soldiers. In November 1996 West ordered an investigation into the sexual harassment scandal at Maryland's Aberdeen Proving Ground. West also appointed a task force to consider changes in the army's sexual harassment policies and training. The *Boston Globe* commented in its review of the army's efforts in dealing with sexual harassment, "West has been a calm and consistent voice," prodding the department to further investigate sexual harassment charges and to develop policies that ended sexual harassment. West also sought to deal with issues of racial discrimination through new training programs on overt and covert racial discrimination.

Born June 21, 1942, in Winston-Salem, North Carolina, West received his B.A. (1965) and his J.D., cum laude (1968), from Howard University. Following graduation from law school, West was commissioned as a second lieutenant in the army artillery corps (1965–68) and then served in the army judge advocate general's corps (JAG) (1969–73). He joined the

Washington, D.C., law firm of Covington and Burling in 1973, where he practiced for two years (1973–75). He served briefly at the Department of Justice in 1975 and 1976, and then returned to Covington and Burling in 1976 until he joined the Carter administration in 1977.

He then began a series of positions within the federal government, beginning as an associate attorney general in the Department of Justice (1975–76), as general counsel for the Department of the Navy (1977–79), as special assistant to the secretary and deputy secretary of the Department of Defense (1979–80), and as general counsel of Department of Defense (1980). As a Democrat, most of his advancement had taken place during the Carter administration, so when the Reagan administration came into office, and a new secretary of defense

Togo West, Jr. *(Department of Veterans Affairs)*

was named by President Reagan, West left the federal government and was later named the managing partner of Patterson, Belknap, Webb, and Tyler (1984–90). In 1990 West left to join Northrop Corporation as senior vice president for government relations (1993–97).

Wilhelm, David C.
(1956–   ) *chair of the Democratic National Committee*

President Clinton named David Wilhelm as chairman of the Democratic National Committee in January 1993, and he remained in the post through 1994. Wilhelm succeeded RONALD H. BROWN, who was named by President Clinton as secretary of commerce.

Wilhelm first met President Clinton in 1991 in Chicago at a political event and was soon after asked to join the campaign. Wilhelm became the national campaign manager of the Clinton-Gore campaign in 1992. His role as the campaign manager included directing the political operations of the campaign, overseeing the strategy to win the electoral college, and approving details of the post-convention bus tour for Bill Clinton and Al Gore.

Wilhelm described his role on the campaign, "I did everything that [JAMES] CARVILLE [JR.] and [GEORGE] STEPHANOPOULOS didn't do." While Carville and Stephanopoulos handled the day-to-day operation of the War Room in Little Rock, Wilhelm managed the state campaigns, focusing on each precinct. Wilhelm became the member of the campaign team focused on the nuts and bolts of winning a state, while Carville and Stephanopoulos focused on the campaign message.

As chairman of the Democratic National Committee, Wilhelm was responsible for fundraising for candidates in the midterm congressional elections, as well as for the presidential election. When the Democrats lost the House

of Representatives in 1994, Wilhelm began to increase the role and the visibility of the Democratic National Committee.

Wilhelm had been involved in politics since he was in college. During his sophomore year at Ohio University in 1976, Wilhelm began working for the presidential campaign of Jimmy Carter. In 1979, Wilhelm went to Washington, D.C., as an intern for Senator Howard Metzenbaum (D-Ohio), but left to work for the Citizens for Tax Justice, which was affiliated with the American Federation of Labor–Congress of Industrial Organizations (AFL-CIO).

In 1984 Wilhelm left Citizens for Tax Justice in Washington, D.C., and joined the Senate campaign of Paul Simon (D-Ill.). When Simon won, Wilhelm returned to Washington, D.C., as director of Citizens for Tax Justice. In 1987, Wilhelm signed on for another political campaign, running the presidential campaign in Iowa of Senator Joseph Biden (D-Del.). Biden's campaign floundered quickly, and he withdrew from the race. In 1990, Wilhelm managed the winning campaign of Richard Daley for mayor of Chicago.

Born on October 10, 1956, Willhelm received his B.A., magna cum laude, from Ohio University (where his father taught geography) in 1978 and a master's in public policy from the John F. Kennedy School of Government at Harvard University in 1979.

When tapped to head the Clinton campaign in 1991, Wilhelm was the president of Woodland Venture Management Company.

Williams, Margaret (Maggie) Ann
(1954–   ) *chief of staff to First Lady Hillary Rodham Clinton*

Margaret (Maggie) Ann Williams was named chief of staff to First Lady Hillary Rodham Clinton in January 1993.

Although her work was primarily in the first lady's office, Williams became involved in two issues that had ongoing investigations.

The first issue involved the 1996 reelection campaign. Williams was charged with accepting a $50,000 gift from JOHNNY CHUNG for the Democratic National Committee in the White House. The federal Hatch Act barred political contributions from being solicited or received on federal property.

In 1997 the Department of Justice began to look into several irregularities in the campaign finances of the Clinton-Gore 1996 campaign, which included the $50,000 Williams had taken on behalf of the Democratic National Committee. Several Republicans in Congress asked Attorney General JANET RENO to appoint an independent counsel for the investigation, but she refused, stating that the Justice Department had not found enough evidence to lead to such an appointment.

Williams also became involved in the independent counsel's investigation of Deputy White House Counsel VINCENT W. FOSTER, JR.'s death. The independent counsel examined whether Mrs. Clinton and Williams had taken folders related to the Whitewater investigation from Foster's office after his death. Both she and Mrs. Clinton denied that they took the folders. The Senate convened a special panel to further investigate whether Mrs. Clinton and Williams had taken folders after Foster's death. Republicans on the Senate Whitewater Committee, chaired by ALFONSE (AL) MARCELLO D'AMATO (R-N.Y.), believed that Mrs. Clinton and Williams had taken the folders and obstructed justice by tampering with the independent counsel's investigation. In the hearings, Williams again denied that she had taken folders from Foster's office. Williams took two lie-detector tests but Secret Service agent Henry O'Neill testified that he saw Williams remove a box. In June 1996 the committee concluded its work without commenting on whether Williams took files, but did comment that she was evasive and uncooperative.

With legal costs totaling $300,000 from the investigations, Williams left the administration at the end of the first term. She married and moved to Paris. After she left the administration, Governor Roy Romer of Colorado, general chairman of the Democratic National Committee, said it had been "wrong" and "ill advised" for Williams to accept the $50,000 check from Chung in 1996. She did not publicly comment on Romer's remarks.

Williams joined the campaign staff of Mrs. Clinton in 2000 during her campaign for the Senate from New York.

Born on December 25, 1954, in Kansas City, Missouri, Williams graduated with a B.A. from Trinity College and an M.A. from the University of Pennsylvania Annenberg School of Communications.

Witt, James Lee

(1944–) *director, Federal Emergency Management Agency*

James Lee Witt was nominated by President Clinton as the director of the Federal Emergency Management Agency (FEMA) in January 1993 and was sworn into office on April 5, 1993, after being confirmed by the Senate. Witt had been the director of the Office of Emergency Services for Arkansas prior to his new position at FEMA. In February 1996, President Clinton elevated Witt to cabinet status, the first time that FEMA had ever been represented in the president's cabinet.

During his tenure at FEMA, Witt handled 348 presidentially declared disasters in 6,521 counties in all 50 states and territories, which included earthquakes, floods, and hurricanes.

From 1966–78, Witt had served as president of Witt Construction. In 1978 he was elected judge for Yell County, serving as the chief elected officer for the county, with judicial responsibilities for county and juvenile court. He became the youngest elected official in Arkansas. He was reelected six times to the position before being tapped by Governor Bill Clinton to run the Arkansas Office of Emergency Services.

Born in 1944 in Dardanelle, Arkansas, Witt remained in Arkansas in various roles in both the private and the public sectors before being tapped by President Clinton as head of FEMA.

After leaving office in 2001, Witt founded James Lee Witt Associates, which provided disaster mitigation planning and preparation services.

Wofford, Harris

(1926–   ) *chief executive officer, Corporation for National Service; member of the Senate*

President Clinton nominated Harris Wofford as chief executive officer for the Corporation for National Service on July 18, 1995, and he was confirmed by the Senate in September 1995. Wofford replaced ELI J. SEGAL. The Corporation for National Service was the umbrella organization for all federally funded volunteer and service programs.

Wofford had been appointed to the U.S. Senate in 1991 by Democratic governor Robert Casey to fill the vacancy caused by the death in a plane crash of Senator John Heinz, III (R-Pa.). Wofford served the remainder of Heinz's term, but was defeated in the 1994 election by Congressman Rick Santorum.

President Clinton had a 10-year professional relationship with Wofford prior to his appointment to the Corporation for National Service. Both Wofford and President Clinton had been deeply involved in securing legislation for a national service program for a number of years. When Wofford was Governor Casey's secretary of labor, he had worked with then-governor Clinton as part of the National Governors Association to develop the National and Community Service Act of 1990. As secretary of labor, Wofford established the Office of Citizen Service in Pennsylvania, which promoted school-based service learning. In 1991, as a newly elected senator, Wofford worked for passage of another service program, the National Civilian Community Corps.

When the Clinton administration came into office, the White House staff began working with Wofford to create the National and Community Service Trust Act, which created AmeriCorps and the Corporation for National and Community Service. Wofford worked closely with Eli Segal, the president's expert on the national service program in the White House.

In 2000, Wofford convened and chaired the Working Group on Human Needs and Faith-Based Community Initiatives, which issued the report *Finding Common Ground*. He also served on the National Commission on Service Learning and helped draft its report *Learning in Deed*.

Born April 9, 1926, Wofford received his B.A. from the University of Chicago (1948) and his LL.B. from Yale University Law School (1954) and a J.D. from Howard University Law School (1954). Before returning to Washington, D.C., after his appointment to the Senate in 1991, Wofford had served in a number of positions in the federal government. He served as an assistant to U.S. ambassador Chester Bowles from 1953–54. After graduation from law school, Wofford joined the Washington, D.C., law firm of Covington & Burling, where he stayed for four years (1954–58). In 1958, he was a legal assistant at the Commission on Civil Rights (1958–59) and a special assistant to President John F. Kennedy and chair of the subcabinet group on civil rights (1961–62). Wofford was one of the framers, with Sargent Shriver, of the Peace

Corps during the Kennedy administration and served as the associate director from 1964–66 during the Johnson administration. During its first year of operation in 1962, Wofford was named the Peace Corps's Special Representative to Africa and director of its Ethiopia program. He entered Pennsylvania state politics in 1986 when he was named secretary of labor by Democratic governor Robert Casey.

Most of Wofford's career had been spent in academia and in private law practice. From 1970 to 1978 Wofford was president of Bryn Mawr College and in 1978 became a partner in the Philadelphia law firm of Schader, Harrison, Segal & Lewis where he remained until 1986 when he was tapped for Governor Casey's cabinet.

In March 2001, Wofford was elected to the board of directors of America's Promise and as chairman of the board of directors in 2002. Wofford also served on the boards of Youth Service America and the Points of Light Foundation.

He was the author of a number of publications, including *Of Kennedys and Kings: Making Sense of the Sixties* (1980).

Wood, Kimba Maureen

(1944–   ) *failed nominee for attorney general*

President Clinton nominated Judge Kimba Wood as attorney general in February 1993 but withdrew her name. Wood was the second of three nominees that President Clinton made for attorney general. Both ZOE BAIRD, the first nominee, and Wood withdrew their names from Senate consideration. The third candidate, JANET RENO, was successfully confirmed by the Senate as attorney general on March 12, 1993.

All three candidates for attorney general were women. During his presidential campaign, President Clinton had pledged to include more women and minorities in his cab-

inet. He had promised to build a cabinet that "looked like America" and not to have an all white, male cabinet as most presidents did. Although he did not specifically mention the Department of Justice, many believed that he would be the first president to name a woman as attorney general.

The first nominee, Zoe Baird, had difficulty in the confirmation process when her background check by the Federal Bureau of Investigation (FBI) revealed that she had hired illegal aliens, a Peruvian couple, for child care and household help. When the Senate began to hold hearings on her confirmation, a number of Republicans objected to her failure to follow the legal requirement of paying the appropriate taxes. The allegation was made that if she was to be the nation's chief law enforcement officer, she had to be above reproach. She withdrew her name from consideration.

After Baird withdrew her name, President Clinton nominated another woman, Kimba Wood. Wood was a federal judge, appointed by President Reagan to the U.S. District Court in New York in 1988. The other candidates were CHARLES F. C. RUFF, a Washington, D.C. criminal attorney and former Virginia governor Gerald L. Baliles, a friend of President Clinton when both were governors.

Wood's nomination never went forward after White House staff questioned her on the nanny she employed. Wood had hired a babysitter from Trinidad in March 1986 before hiring illegal aliens was outlawed. Wood explained to the White House staff that she paid all social security taxes on the worker, who eventually became a legal U.S. resident. However, the White House senior staff determined that her situation was too close to Zoe Baird's situation and decided not to pursue her nomination. Wood withdrew her name from the nomination process.

During her tenure on the U.S. District Court, Wood had made national headlines in

1990 when she sentenced Wall Street junk-bond broker Michael Milken to 10 years in prison rather than a lighter sentence. She later reduced the sentence to two years.

Born on January 2, 1944, in Port Townsend, Washington, Wood received her B.A. from Connecticut College, cum laude, and her master's degree from the London School of Economics. She received her J.D. from Harvard Law School (1969). After law school she worked in the legal services program in the Office of Economic Opportunity. In 1971, she joined the law firm of LaBoeuf, Lamb, Leiby & MacRae, where she became a litigation and antitrust specialist.

Wood's name, Kimba, was the result of her mother searching through an atlas for suggestions and choosing the name of a small town in southern Australia.

Woolsey, R. James
(1941–) *director, Central Intelligence Agency*

James Woolsey was appointed in January 1993 as director of the Central Intelligence Agency, replacing Robert Gates. Woolsey was confirmed by the Senate in February 1993. The choice of Woolsey was made because he was an outsider who was tasked with reinvigorating the sagging morale within the agency. The White House chose not to promote from within the Central Intelligence Agency and purposely sought a candidate from outside its ranks.

Shortly after being confirmed, Woolsey issued a statement describing the mission of the Central Intelligence Agency as a result of the changing structure of international relations after the fall of the Soviet Union. He said, "We have slain a large dragon [the Soviet Union], but we now live in a jungle filled with a bewildering variety of poisonous snakes." Woolsey convinced President Clinton, who had originally sought to cut the budget of the

Central Intelligence Agency, that more not less money was needed to deal with the "poisonous snakes."

Woolsey had served in a variety of roles in the federal government throughout his career. During his military service in 1969–70, he served on the U.S. delegation to the Strategic Arms Limitation Talks (SALT I) held in Helsinki and Vienna. He was appointed by President Reagan as a delegate at large to the U.S.-Soviet Strategic Arms Reduction Talks (START I) and Nuclear and Space Arms Talks (NST) from 1983–86. During the Carter administration he was appointed undersecretary of the navy (1977–79) and during the Bush administration was named ambassador to the Negotiation on Conventional Armed Forces in Europe (1989–91). His history of working in both Democratic and Republican administrations contributed to his bipartisan support during his confirmation hearings. Woolsey was easily confirmed.

Woolsey began his career as program analyst in the Department of Defense, and in 1973 he was named general counsel of the Senate Armed Services Committee (1917–73). He left the Senate in 1973 to join the law firm of Shea & Gardner in Washington, D.C., where he stayed from 1973 to 1989. He left the firm to serve at the Negotiation on Conventional Armed Forces in Europe for two years. In 1991 he rejoined the law firm for another two years (1991–93). After two years as director of the Central Intelligence Agency, 1993–95, he again rejoined the law firm. His specialty was representing U.S. arms companies.

Born on September 21, 1941, in Tulsa, Oklahoma, Woolsey received his B.A., with great distinction and Phi Beta Kappa, from Stanford University (1963), his M.A. from Oxford University while a Rhodes scholar (1965), and his LL.B. from Yale University, where he was managing editor of the *Yale Law Journal* (1968).

Wright, Susan Webber

(1948–   ) *judge, U.S. District Court, Eastern District of Arkansas*

Judge Susan Webber Wright oversaw the federal lawsuit filed in Little Rock, Arkansas, by PAULA CORBIN JONES against President Clinton in *Jones v. Clinton*. Jones accused President Clinton of sexual harassment while he was governor of Arkansas.

Wright was nominated by President GEORGE HERBERT WALKER BUSH on September 21, 1989, to a seat on the U.S. District Court for the Eastern District of Arkansas. She was confirmed by the Senate on January 23, 1990, and was named chief judge of the court in 1998.

In May 1994 Paula Corbin Jones filed a civil suit against President Clinton seeking $700,000 in damages for "willful, outrageous and malicious conduct" at the Excelsior Hotel in Little Rock on May 8, 1991. She accused Clinton of "sexually harassing and assaulting her," and then defaming her with denials. Judge Wright oversaw the lawsuit.

President Clinton filed a motion in August 1994 to dismiss Jones's suit on the grounds of presidential immunity and in December 1994 Wright ruled that the trial could not take place until Clinton completed his term and was out of office. Her decision was reversed by the Eighth U.S. Court of Appeals in St. Louis in January 1996. After the appeals court decision to allow the trial to progress without delay, President Clinton appealed in May 1996 to the U.S. Supreme Court. In May 1997 the Supreme Court upheld the appeals court decision and allowed the Jones lawsuit to proceed. Wright set a May 17, 1998, trial date.

In April 2000, Wright dismissed the Jones lawsuit against President Clinton, saying that her lawyers had failed to provide enough evidence in their case. "The Plaintiff's allegations," she said in her ruling, "fall far short of the rigorous standards for establishing a claim of outrage." She further said in her ruling, "While the court will certainly agree that plaintiff's allegations describe offensive conduct, the court . . . has found that the governor's [Clinton] alleged conduct does not constitute sexual assault." The case was appealed, but Jones agreed to a settlement of $850,000 on November 13, 1998. The federal appeals court then dismissed Jones's appeal.

In December 2000 Wright ordered President Clinton to pay more than $90,000 in fines for giving false testimony under oath in the Jones lawsuit about his affair with MONICA LEWINSKY. President Clinton's private attorney, ROBERT BENNETT, responded to Webber's decision to levy fines by saying, "We accept the judgment of the court and will comply with it." The fines were used to reimburse the court and Jones's legal teams for work that stemmed from President Clinton's January 1998 deposition, in which he denied having had sexual relations with Lewinsky, testimony that Wright called "intentionally false." Wright ordered President Clinton to pay the Rutherford Institute and the law firm of Rader, Campbell, Fisher (which both represented Jones) $89,484. The district court received $1,202.

It was the *Jones v. Clinton* lawsuit that uncovered the allegations of a relationship between President Clinton and Lewinsky. Kenneth Starr learned of the relationship from the lawsuit and broadened his Whitewater investigation into the Clinton-Lewinsky relationship.

Webber had first known President Clinton during law school, where she had taken a course from Clinton when he was a professor at the University of Arkansas Law School. In 1974 she worked for his Republican opponent in his race for attorney general of Arkansas.

Webber received a B.A. from Randolph-Macon Women's College (1970), an M.P.A. from the University of Arkansas at Fayetteville

(1973), and a J.D. from the University of Arkansas at Fayetteville Law School (1975).

After graduating from law school, Webber served as a law clerk for Judge J. Smith Henley, U.S. Court of Appeals for the Eighth Circuit (1975–76), and in 1976 joined the faculty of the University of Arkansas at Little Rock Law School (1976–90). In 1990, she was confirmed for the District Court for the Eastern District of Arkansas.

Y

Yellen, Janet Louise

(1946–   ) chair of the Council of Economic Advisers; member of the Board of Governors, Federal Reserve System

Janet Yellen was appointed by President Clinton as the chair of the Council of Economic Advisers and was confirmed by the Senate on February 13, 1997. Prior to her appointment to the Council of Economic Advisers, Yellen had served as a member of the board of governors of the Federal Reserve System, to which she had been appointed by President Clinton in February 1994. As the council's chair, she replaced JOSEPH E. STIGLITZ, who left to become the World Bank's chief economist. Yellen left as chair of the Council of Economic Advisers on August 3, 1999.

Yellen was sought for the position at the Council of Economic Advisers by both White House staff and Treasury Secretary ROBERT RUBIN because of her strong performance at the Federal Reserve. She had often been called in to brief members of the council on such topics as the labor markets and welfare reform. She was viewed by the Clinton economic team as not only a strong economist but also someone who could work with members of

Congress to explain administration economic policies.

Yellen, born on August 13, 1946, in Brooklyn, New York, graduated summa cum laude from Brown University (1967) and received her Ph.D. from Yale University (1971). After receiving her doctorate from Yale, Yellen was named to the faculty as an assistant professor at Harvard University (1971–76). She served as an economist with the Federal Reserve's board of governors from 1977–78, specializing in issues of international trade and finance, including stabilization of international currency exchange rates. She joined the faculty of the Haas School of Business at the University of California at Berkeley, where she taught from 1980 until her appointment in 1994 to the board of governors. She returned to the University of California at Berkeley after leaving the Council of Economic Advisers in 1999.

Yellen was married to George A. Akerlof, also an economics professor at the University of California at Berkeley. Yellen and Akerlof were coauthors of numerous academic articles. They wrote extensively about welfare reform, including research on how slashing welfare benefits deterred poor single women from

President Clinton (left) shakes hands with President Boris Yeltsin at the end of a joint press conference in Helsinki, Finland, March 21, 1997. *(AP Photo/Alexander Zemlianichenko)*

having children. Her research broadly focused on issues of unemployment.

Yeltsin, Boris Nikolayevich
(1931–) *president of Russia*

Boris Yeltsin was elected on June 12, 1991, as president of the Russian Federation and resigned on New Year's Eve, 1999. VLADIMIR PUTIN replaced Yeltsin as president of Russia in March 2000. Yeltsin resigned on New Year's Eve 1999, and Putin became acting president until national elections were held in March 2000.

President Clinton met with Yeltsin in March 1997 in Helsinki, Finland, regarding decisions of the North Atlantic Treaty Organization (NATO) on its own enlargement, and regarding Russian membership in the Group of 7 (G-7) economic meetings. Russia wanted full membership in the group, making it the Group of 8, but President Clinton failed to offer Russia full membership in G-7 at the time. By 1999, Yeltsin had succeeded in including Russia in the economic meetings.

In November 1999 relations between the United States and Russia deteriorated over the demand by the United States that Russia stop bombing in Chechnya, which was seeking independence from Russia. Yeltsin insisted to President Clinton at a summit in Istanbul, Turkey, that "You have no right to criticize Russia for Chechnya. There will be no negotiations with bandits and murderers." Yeltsin accused NATO and the United States of carrying out bombing in Kosovo but denouncing Russia for bombing in Chechnya.

The Chechen bombing issue may have been a response to Yeltsin's anger at being marginalized during the NATO activities in the Balkans in dealing with SLOBODAN MILOŠEVIĆ. Russia was given a limited role in dealing with Bosnia and with Kosovo.

Born on February 1, 1931, in Sverdlovsk (now Yekaterinburg), Yeltsin graduated from Ural Polytechnic Institute (1955) majoring in construction. He was an engineer and builder by profession. Yeltsin worked on various construction projects from 1955–68 and became chief engineer for a large housing construction plant. He joined the Communist Party in 1961 during former premier Nikita Khrushchev's anti-Stalinist reforms. In 1976, Yeltsin became first chairman of the Sverdlovsk party committee.

While chairman of the committee, Yeltsin met Gorbachev who held the same position in Stavropol. When Gorbachev took power in 1985, he brought Yeltsin to Moscow to reform the corrupt Moscow party hierarchy. Yeltsin became dissatisfied with Gorbachev's slow-moving reforms and resigned from the party leadership in 1987 and from the Politburo in 1988. Yeltsin was demoted to a deputy construction minister.

When Gorbachev began free elections in 1989, Yeltsin won a landslide victory for a seat in the Congress of People's Deputies and was later elected speaker in May 1990. In July 1990 Yeltsin left the Communist Party as tensions increased between Gorbachev, president of the USSR, and Yeltsin, who was president of one member state, Russia.

In the nation's first democratic elections, held on June 12, 1991, Yeltsin was elected president of Russia. When a coup sought to remove Gorbachev from power on August 18, 1991, and he was confined to house arrest at his summer residence in the Crimea, Yeltsin delivered a speech from atop an armored vehicle in Moscow denouncing the coup. The coup failed, its leaders fled, and Gorbachev returned briefly to power. A week later, the presidents of Russia, Ukraine, and Belarus signed a treaty creating the Commonwealth of Independent States. On December 24, 1991, Russia took over the Soviet Union's seat in the United Nations. The next day Gorbachev resigned.

Yeltsin ran into problems over his leadership when the Congress of People's Deputies voted to impeach him on March 26, 1993. In a national referendum held on April 25, 1993, he won 58 percent of the vote and avoided losing his job. He succeeded on December 12, 1993, in having a referendum pass on a new constitution, which increased his presidential powers.

A year later Yeltsin began his attempt to crush the three-year-old Chechen rebellion by sending Russian troops to Chechnya. By spring 1995 Russian troops controlled the capital, Grozny. Months of bombing of Grozny led to thousands of deaths of Chechen civilians and hundreds of thousands became refugees.

In 1995 Yeltsin suffered two heart attacks and his health continued to deteriorate over the next four years. At times, he was absent from his job for weeks without any public bulletins on where he was or the state of his health.

In 1996 Yeltsin ran for reelection, facing stiff opposition from Gennady Zyuganov. Yeltsin won the election in July. However, in November 1996 Yeltsin underwent quadruple heart bypass surgery and remained in the hospital for months. His health continued to deteriorate for the next three years, leading to his abrupt resignation on New Year's Eve 1999.

Zedillo, Ernesto Ponce de León
(1951–) *president of Mexico*

Ernesto Zedillo, a member of the Institutional Revolutionary Party (PRI), was elected president of Mexico on August 21, 1994, and inaugurated on December 1, 1994. The inauguration was attended by Vice President Gore.

Zedillo left office in 2000 when VICENTE FOX was elected president. Fox's National Action Party took control of the presidency after a 70-year domination of the Mexican government by the PRI.

In October 1995, Zedillo made his first official trip to the United States to meet with Secretary of the Treasury ROBERT RUBIN and with President Clinton. In private meetings, President Clinton and Zedillo focused on the problems with the Mexican economy, drug trafficking, and illegal aliens. They also attended a state dinner held at the White House on October 11.

Improvements to the Mexican economy were a key part of the discussions in the October 1995 meeting, focusing on the international $50 billion bailout that the United States had engineered for Mexico in December 1994. The United States provided $20 billion of that amount. In welcoming Zedillo to the White House, President Clinton praised Mexico for

implementing "hard measures to stabilize the economy while holding to the road of reform." Clinton further added that a prosperous Mexico "will be an even greater partner in trade."

One of the most frequent issues that Zedillo and President Clinton dealt with was the drug trafficking from Mexico to the United States. In May 1997 President Clinton traveled to Mexico City to discuss details of steps that were being taken by Mexico and by the United States to fight drug trafficking. In a garden ceremony at the presidential palace, President Clinton and Zedillo signed a declaration committing their nations to devise a joint strategy for combating drugs.

Clinton met a total of 11 times with Zedillo, including the March 2000 signing of the Mexico boundary line agreement. In a Roosevelt Room ceremony in the White House, Secretary of State MADELEINE KORBEL ALBRIGHT and Mexican foreign minister Rosario Green with Zedillo and President Clinton watching, signed the agreement establishing U.S. and Mexican boundary lines in the oil-rich area of the Gulf of Mexico.

Zedillo, born on December 17, 1951, in Mexico City, majored in economics and graduated in 1973 from the University of Bradford (England). The next year, he obtained a Mexican fellowship to study at Yale University, where he received his M.A. and Ph.D. (1978) in economics.

In 1987 Zedillo was appointed under secretary of planning and budget for the national government. When President Salinas took office in December 1988, he appointed Zedillo, who had worked in his campaign, as secretary for programming and budget. Zedillo made radical changes in Mexico's economy, including plans for a free market economy. In 1992 Salinas appointed Zedillo secretary of education, where he decentralized the Mexican education system.

In 1993, Luis Donaldo Colosio was chosen as the PRI presidential candidate for the 1994 elections. Colosio selected Zedillo as his campaign manager. However, Colosio was assassinated in Tijuana on March 23, 1994, while campaigning. Six days later the PRI named Zedillo as its candidate for president. He was elected on August 21, 1994.

Zhu Rongji

(1928–   ) *prime minister of China*

In March 1998 Zhu Rongji was elected by China's parliament as prime minister for a five-year term. President JIANG ZEMIN was reelected for another five year term at the same time. When Zhu was elected, his supporters argued that at the age of 69 he had no other political ambitions beyond his five-year term, and would therefore be able to make tough economic decisions to rebuild China's sagging economy. His most difficult job in rebuilding the economy was to reduce China's large government bureaucracy and to create new jobs to deal with rising unemployment.

In April 1999 President Clinton met in Washington, D.C., with Zhu to discuss China's status in the World Trade Organization (WTO) but the issue was not resolved. China had attempted for 13 years to gain entrance into the WTO. The United States had blocked China's admission due to U.S. charges of human rights abuses in China. Zhu described the charges as "unfair" and an intrusion into the internal affairs of China.

At the April 1999 meeting, Zhu and President Clinton pledged to continue working on the WTO issue and to develop a comprehensive trade package by the end of the year. Zhu also agreed to cooperate with U.S. investigations into alleged Chinese espionage of nuclear weapons secrets from American laboratories during the 1980s and 1990s and into allegations that China's chief of military intelligence secretly funneled money to subsidize contributions to President Clinton's 1996 reelection campaign. At the end of the meeting, both President Clinton and Zhu met with reporters for a 90-minute news conference.

Zhu was born in 1928 in Changsha, Hunan province. He graduated from Qinghua, China's engineering university, in 1951 where he studied electrical engineering. He began work as the deputy head of the production planning office of the planning division of the Department of Industry of Northwest China. By 1957 he was deputy division head of the General Office of the Director in the State Planning Commission.

In 1970, during the cultural revolution, Zhu was purged and underwent "reeducation" at a May Seventh Cadre school until 1975. From 1975 to 1979 Zhu served as deputy director and deputy chief engineer of the Power and Communication Engineering Company, under the Bureau of Pipeline Construction of the Ministry of the Petroleum Industry. From 1979 to 1982 he worked for the State Economic Commission as the division chief and was appointed a member of the State Economic Commission in 1982 and vice minister in charge of the commission from 1983 to 1987. In 1987 he was appointed mayor of Shanghai. In 1991 Zhu became vice premier of the State Council Production Office where he launched a series of new economic policies. He also was named governor of the central bank. Zhu served as a member of the Standing Committee of the Political Bureau of the Central Committee of the Communist Party from 1993 to 1995. In 1995 he became vice premier of the People's Republic of China and in 1997 was reelected a member of the Standing Committee of the Political Bureau of the Central Committee.

APPENDICES

CHRONOLOGY

1993

January 20—President Clinton delivers first inaugural address.

January 22—President Clinton withdraws nomination of Zoe Baird for attorney general after allegations that she hired illegal aliens for domestic work.

January 25—President Clinton announces formation of Health Care Reform Task Force.
—Two Central Intelligence Agency (CIA) officials shot to death outside CIA headquarters in Langley, Virginia.

February 5—President Clinton signs first major legislation, Family Medical Leave Act.
—Federal Trade Commission (FTC) takes no action against Microsoft after 2-2 split between commissioners.
—President Clinton meets with Canadian prime minister Brian Mulroney in White House on trade issues and NAFTA.

February 6—President Clinton gives first radio address.

February 26—Attack on the World Trade Center, as a minibus loaded with more than 1,000 pounds of explosives explodes in an underground garage. Six people die, approximately 1,000 are injured.

February 28—Bureau of Alcohol, Tobacco and Firearms (ATF) agents attempt to arrest David Koresh at the Branch Davidian compound in Waco, Texas. After an exchange of gunfire, 4 ATF agents are killed, 16 are wounded, and an undetermined number of Branch Davidians are killed and wounded, following a two-month standoff.

March 9—President Clinton meets with President François Mitterrand of France in White House.

March 12—North Korea announces it will withdraw from the Nuclear Non-Proliferation Treaty.

March 15—President Clinton meets with Israeli prime minister Yitzhak Rabin in White House.

March 16—President Clinton and exiled president Jean-Bertrand Aristide of Haiti meet in White House to discuss U.S. actions to restore democracy in Haiti.

April 1—The International Atomic Energy Agency's (IAEA) board of governors rules that North Korea was in noncompliance with its safeguards agreement with the agency by refusing to permit special inspections at two suspected nuclear waste sites in North Korea and referred the issue to the UN Security Council for action.

April 4—President Clinton meets with Russian president Boris Yeltsin at the Vancouver Summit to promote access to each other's markets and cooperation in defense conversion.

April 7—Hugh Rodham, father of First Lady Hillary Rodham Clinton, dies.

April 19—Federal Bureau of Investigation (FBI) attempts to storm the Branch Davidian compound in Waco, Texas, after a lengthy stall in negotiations. A fire breaks out and David Koresh and 95 of his followers die in the inferno.

May 19—Clinton administration fires several longtime employees of the White House travel office—results in Travelgate scandal.

June 11—After reaching an agreement with the United States, North Korea withdraws its decision to withdraw from the Nuclear Non-Proliferation Treaty.

June 14—President Clinton nominates Ruth Bader Ginsberg for the Supreme Court.

June 22–23—After a six-year hiatus, the Unabomber resumes his postal bomb attacks, striking two scientists, both of whom survive with injuries.

June 26—United States attacks Iraqi Intelligence Service complex in Baghdad in response to Iraqi assassination attempt against former president George H. W. Bush during a visit to Kuwait on April 14, 1993.

July 3—President Clinton announces the United States will extend its moratorium on nuclear testing.

July 7—President Clinton attends G-7 Summit in Tokyo, Japan.

July 10—President Clinton attends state dinner in Seoul, South Korea.

July 11—President Clinton delivers brief remarks on North Korean nuclear proliferation at the Demilitarized Zone (DMZ) between North and South Korea.

July 19—William Sessions is fired as director of the Federal Bureau of Investigation.
—President Clinton overturns military ban on homosexuals serving in the armed forces, initiating his "don't ask, don't tell" policy.

July 20—White House Counsel Vincent Foster commits suicide.
—New director, District Court Judge Louis J. Freeh, is nominated for Federal Bureau of Investigation.

July 29—Trial of Lyle and Erik Menendez for 1989 murder of their parents begins in Los Angeles.

August 3—Ruth Bader Ginsburg confirmed by Senate for Supreme Court.

August 10—President Clinton signs Budget Reconciliation Bill.

August 12—President meets with Pope John Paul II in Denver during four-day Christian youth conference where pope was speaking.

August 21—Justice Department takes over Microsoft investigation.

September 13—The Oslo Accords are signed by Israeli foreign minister Shimon Peres and Palestine Liberation Organization (PLO) executive council member Abou Abbas in Washington, D.C., as Israeli prime minister Yitzhak Rabin, PLO chairman Yasser Arafat, President Clinton, and other dignitaries look on.

September 14—President Clinton signs side agreements to North American Free Trade Agreement.

September 21—President Clinton holds signing ceremony in White House Rose Garden for National Service Act.

September 22—President Clinton announces health care reform proposals to joint session of Congress.

September 27—President Clinton addresses United Nations General Assembly.

September 30—President Clinton speaks at Fort Myer, Virginia, at a full military retirement ceremony for General Colin Powell, chairman of the Joint Chiefs of Staff.

October 3—Eighteen U.S. Rangers are killed in a firefight in Mogadishu, Somalia.

October 5—China conducts a nuclear test.

October 6—President Clinton orders 5,300 new combat troops and an aircraft carrier to Somalia "to protect our troops and to complete our mission," and announces that he will bring all American combat forces home by March 31.

October 22—President and Mrs. Clinton meet with members of Congress at Statuary Hall in the Capitol to discuss the health care reform proposal.

November 1—The Maastricht Treaty, creating the European Union, goes into effect.

November 2–3—Secretary of Defense Les Aspin travels to Tokyo and Seoul to discuss North Korean nuclear proliferation.

November 4—President Clinton sends North American Free Trade Agreement legislation to Congress.

November 17—House of Representatives approves North American Free Trade Agreement.

November 20—Senate approves North American Free Trade Agreement.

November 30—President Clinton signs Brady Handgun Violence Prevention Act, known as the Brady Bill.

December—U.S. Air Force destroys missile silo, the first of 500 agreed to under START I.

December 4—President Clinton meets in Canoga Park, California, with California Economic Roundtable.

December 5—Ukraine accedes to the Non-Proliferation Treaty as a nonnuclear state.

December 8—President Clinton signs North American Free Trade Agreement.

December 20—President Clinton announces he and Mrs. Clinton will release all records pertaining to Whitewater Land Development, the land development project in Arkansas.

1994

January 1—Implementation of the North American Free Trade Agreement begins.

January 6—President Clinton's mother, Virginia Kelley, dies of cancer.

January 10—President Clinton attends NATO summit, Brussels, Belgium.

January 13—Jury in the trial of Lyle and Erik Menendez announces that it is deadlocked, resulting in a mistrial.

January 14—President Clinton and Russian president Boris Yeltsin issue declaration that, as of the end of May, nuclear missiles of the United States or Russia will target no country, at NATO summit in Belgium.

January 17—An earthquake strikes in the area of Los Angeles, California, killing 51 people.

January 20—President Clinton requests an independent counsel for Whitewater investigation.
—Attorney General Janet Reno names New York attorney Robert B. Fiske, Jr., as independent counsel for the Whitewater investigation.

January 25—President Clinton gives State of the Union address to Congress.

February 3—President Clinton ends trade embargo against Vietnam.

February 9—North Atlantic Treaty Organization issues ultimatum giving Bosnian Serbs 10 days to withdraw heavy guns from around Sarajevo.

February 14—Kazakhstan accedes to the Nuclear Non-Proliferation Treaty as a non-nuclear state.

February 20—Four hundred Russian peacekeepers arrive in the vicinity of Sarajevo. United Nations declares it is satisfied that Serbia is withdrawing guns.

February 21—Central Intelligence Agency veteran Aldrich Ames and his wife, Rosario, arrested by the FBI on espionage charges.

February 28—U.S. fighters, operating under North Atlantic Treaty Organization command, shoot down four Bosnian Serb warplanes for violating a "no-fly" zone over Bosnia.
—Interim provisions of the Brady Bill take effect.

March 4—Independent Counsel Robert Fiske begins questioning senior White House aides in Whitewater investigation.

March 14—President Clinton extends nuclear testing moratorium through September 1995.

March 17—Central Intelligence Agency director James Woolsey confirms existence of North Korean intermediate-range ballistic missiles.

March 21—United States orders deployment of Patriot missiles to South Korea to defend against North Korean missiles.

March 24—North Korea denounces U.S. decision to deploy Patriot missiles to South Korea, calling it "virtual" declaration of war.
—Representative Jim Leach (R-Iowa) gives floor speech stating he has evidence of a cover-up by the Resolution Trust Corporation related to the Whitewater investigation.
—President Clinton defends Whitewater land development project in Arkansas in nationally televised speech.

March 25—Last U.S. troops leave Somalia.

April 6—President of Rwanda is killed when his airplane is hit by a missile. The prime minister is killed in retaliation, setting off a war that will kill at least 250,000 and create many more refugees.
—Justice Blackmun announces his intention to retire from the Supreme Court.

April 10—NATO conducts air strikes in Bosnia.

April 20—President Clinton talks to media in White House about U.S. air strikes in Bosnia.

April 22—Former president Richard Nixon dies at the age of 81.

April 27—President and Mrs. Clinton attend funeral of President Richard Nixon in Yorba Linda, California, with former presidents and their wives.

April 28—Former CIA case worker Aldrich Ames and his wife plead guilty to espionage charges.

May 6—Paula Corbin Jones files formal complaint accusing President Clinton of sexual harassment and defamation of character stemming from a May 9, 1991, incident while he was governor of Arkansas.
—Chunnel under the English Channel opens, connecting France and Great Britain with an underground tunnel used by high-speed train.

May 10—Nelson Mandela is inaugurated as the first black president of South Africa.
—German officials discover weapons-grade plutonium in a garage in Stuttgart.

May 13—State dinner honors Emperor Akihito of Japan.
—International mediators announce new Bosnian peace plan.

May 17—President Clinton nominates Stephen Breyer to the Supreme Court.

May 19—Former first lady, Jacqueline Kennedy Onassis, dies at age 64.

May 31—Representative Dan Rostenkowski (D-Ill.), chairman of the House Ways and Means Committee, receives a 17-count indictment from a federal grand jury.

—North Korea tests new anti-ship missile in Sea of Japan.

June 2—North Korea test-fires another anti-ship missile in the Sea of Japan.

June 3—India test-fires ballistic missiles.

June 12—Nicole Brown Simpson, ex-wife of football star O. J. Simpson, and her friend, Ronald Goldman, are murdered in Los Angeles, California.

June 17—Arrest warrant issued for O. J. Simpson, who is apprehended after a nationally televised pursuit.

June 20—President and Mrs. Clinton are questioned under oath by independent counsel Robert Fiske in Whitewater investigation.

June 27—President Clinton announces White House chief of staff Thomas McLarty to become counselor to the president; Leon Panetta to become White House chief of staff.

June 30—Whitewater independent counsel Robert Fiske issues a preliminary finding concluding that Vincent Foster's death was a suicide and that contacts between the White House and the Treasury Department had not broken any laws.

July 8—Kim Il Sung, leader of North Korea, dies at the age of 82 and is succeeded by his son, Kim Jong Il.

July 9—President Clinton attends G-7 conference in Naples, Italy.

July 15—Microsoft and the Justice Department sign a consent degree related to software bundling.

July 20—Serbs reject international peace plan for Bosnia.

July 21—Gunfire at United Nations plane at Sarajevo airport wounds a U.S. civilian and forces Defense Secretary William Perry to cancel visit.

July 26—The House Banking Committee begins Whitewater hearings.
—President Clinton hosts state dinner for King Hussein of Jordan and Prime Minister Rabin of Israel.

July 29—Senate Banking Committee begins Whitewater hearings.

August 5—Robert B. Fiske, Jr., is replaced by Kenneth Starr as independent counsel investigating Whitewater.

August 10—Nuclear reactor fuel is seized at Munich Airport.

August 29—Roger Altman resigns as deputy secretary of the Treasury under Whitewater cloud.

September 12—President Clinton inducts the first 20,000 volunteers into AmeriCorps.

September 14—President Clinton makes nationally televised speech announcing that the United States will lead UN-authorized mission to restore Jean-Bertrand Aristide to power in Haiti.

September 19—U.S.-led forces restore Jean-Bertrand Aristide to power in Haiti.

September 26—In a press conference on Capitol Hill, Senator George Mitchell (D-Me.) announces that President Clinton's Health Care Reform package will not pass.

September 27—More than 300 Republican candidates sign the "Contract with America"

authored by Representative Newt Gingrich (R-Ga.).
—President Boris Yeltsin of Russia visits White House.

October 4—President Clinton hosts Nelson Mandela at White House state dinner.

October 25—Susan Smith rolls her car with her two young boys into a lake, initially claiming they were abducted. The nation is shocked when the truth is discovered.

October 26—President Clinton is in Jordan to witness Israeli-Jordanian peace treaty.

October 31—Hanspeter Kleiner of Switzerland officially opens the Conference on Security and Cooperation in Europe mission in Sarajevo.

November 8—Republicans win control of House of Representatives and Senate in midterm elections.

November 21—Largest military action in North Atlantic Treaty Organization history fails to take out Serb jets at Croatian Serb air base.

November 25—Serbs detain 55 Canadian peacekeepers to use as human shields.

December 6—President Clinton's friend and former associate attorney general, Webster Hubbell, pleads guilty to mail fraud and tax evasion.

December 8—President Clinton signs GATT–Uruguay Round agreement.

December 9—President Clinton fires Surgeon General Jocelyn Elders.

December 10—Advertising executive Thomas J. Moser is killed by a package bomb from the Unabomber.

December 11—Russian troops invade Chechnya.

December 14—Police in Czechoslovakia seize six pounds of weapons-grade uranium in Prague, believed to have been smuggled out of Russia.

December 20—Former president Jimmy Carter announces nationwide cease-fire in Bosnia after two-day mediation.

1995

January 4—Newt Gingrich is elected Speaker of the House of Representatives.

January 17—Earthquake in Japan kills more than 5,000 people.

January 23—O. J. Simpson goes on trial for the murder of ex-wife Nicole Brown Simpson and Ronald Goldman.

January 24—President Clinton delivers State of the Union address to Congress.

January 25—Russia initially mistakes launching of a Norwegian/U.S. research rocket for a nuclear attack and briefly considers launching retaliatory attack on the United States.

January 30—Smithsonian Institution cancels planned exhibit of *Enola Gay* in response to pressure from veterans groups. The *Enola Gay* was the U.S. airplane that dropped the atomic bomb on Hiroshima, Japan, on August 6, 1945.
—President Clinton meets with National Governors Association.
—President Clinton authorizes a $20 billion loan to Mexico as part of an international bailout in response to a peso devaluation crisis in December.

February 2—President Clinton nominates Dr. Henry Foster to be surgeon general, but his nomination is blocked by the Senate.

February 3—President Clinton announces proposal to increase minimum wage by $.90 per hour to $5.15 per hour over a two-year period.

February 6—Space Shuttle *Discovery* and Russian space station *Mir* rendezvous in space.

February 13—International tribunal indicts 21 Serbs on war crimes charges in Bosnia.

February 14—U.S. District Judge Stanley Sporkin throws out consent decree reached between Microsoft and the Justice Department.

February 23—Address by President Clinton to Canadian parliament.

March 11—President Clinton nominates John Deutch to be director of the Central Intelligence Agency.

March 15—President Clinton meets with King Hassan of Morocco at White House.

March 20—First successful use of chemical weapon in a terrorist attack as Aum Shinrikyo cult spread vaporized sarin in the Tokyo subway.

March 23—Bosnian army launches offensive near Tuzla.
—President Clinton meets with President Jean-Bertrand Aristide of Haiti.

April 8—U.S. aid plane hit by gunfire in Bosnia, forcing suspension of all United Nations aid flights to Sarajevo.

April 19—Bomb explodes at the Alfred P. Murrah Federal Building in Oklahoma City, Oklahoma.

April 21—Timothy McVeigh is arrested in connection with the Oklahoma City bombing hours before he is expected to make bail on a firearms charge. Terry Nichols surrenders to authorities in Kansas.

April 24—California Forestry Association president Gilbert Murray is killed by a package bomb from the Unabomber.

April 30—President Clinton widens the U.S. trade embargo against Iran.

May 2—A U.S. F-16 is downed on United Nations patrol in Bosnia.

May 8—President Clinton attends V-E Day 50th anniversary ceremony.

May 11—Nuclear Non-Proliferation Treaty is extended by the United States.

May 12—Pilot of downed F-16 plane is rescued in Bosnia.

May 15—China conducts underground nuclear test.

May 21—Former secretary of defense Les Aspin dies.

May 24—United Nations commander in Bosnia issues ultimatum to Serbs to withdraw heavy weapons from around Sarajevo.

May 25—North Atlantic Treaty Organization attacks Bosnian Serb ammunition depot, and Serbs shell United Nations–protected towns.

May 27—Serbs seize weapons and United Nations peacekeepers in attack on United Nations weapons-collection sites around Sarajevo.

May 28—Serbs capture British peacekeepers in Goradze, bringing total number of United Nations peacekeepers held to more than 350. France, Britain, and the United States ready more forces for Bosnia.

June 13—French president Jacques Chirac announces France will resume nuclear testing.

June 14—One hundred Chechen terrorists storm Russian town of Budennovsk, killing scores and taking over 100 hostages. Russian commando raid fails. After negotiations, Chechens evacuate town, eventually releasing hostages.

June 15—President Clinton attends G-7 meetings in Halifax, Nova Scotia, Canada.

June 16—Appellate Court throws out Judge Sporkin's ruling against the Microsoft/Justice Department consent decree. The matter is sent to another district court judge.

June 24—Jonas Salk, who invented the polio vaccine in the 1950s, died at the age of 80.

July 10—Russian president Boris Yeltsin suffers a heart attack.

July 18—Senator Alfonse D'Amato (R-N.Y.) opens 13 days of Senate Whitewater hearings.

July 25—Bomb explodes in the Paris metro, the first of a series of eight.

August 7—Representative Jim Leach (R-Iowa) opens House Banking Committee hearings into Whitewater.

August 11—Timothy McVeigh and Terry Nichols are indicted for murder and conspiracy in connection with the Oklahoma City bombing.

August 17—Jim and Susan McDougal and Jim Guy Tucker are indicted by a grand jury for fraud and conspiracy.
—China conducts another underground nuclear test.

August 21—U.S. District Judge Thomas Penfield Jackson approves the consent decree between Microsoft and the Justice Department.

August 30—North Atlantic Treaty Organization launches first air strikes in "Operation Deliberate Force" in Bosnia.

September 2—President Clinton attends 50th anniversary ceremony of V-J Day.

September 5—France conducts an underground nuclear test in the South Pacific, provoking rioting in Tahiti.

September 6—The Senate Select Committee on Ethics votes 6-0, recommending the expulsion of Senator Robert Packwood (R-Ore.) for sexual misconduct, influence peddling, and obstruction of justice.

September 7—Senator Robert Packwood (R-Ore.) announces his resignation from the U.S. Senate.

September 19—After consulting with law enforcement, the *Washington Post*, with financial assistance from the *New York Times*, publishes the Unabomber's *Manifesto*.

September 28—Middle East Peace accords signed between prime minister Yitzhak Rabin and Palestine Liberation Organization chairman Yasser Arafat.

October 1—France conducts second nuclear test in South Pacific. French commandos seize *Greenpeace* ship in international waters.

October 2—Jury begins deliberations in O. J. Simpson murder trial.

October 3—Jury acquits O. J. Simpson in the murders of Nicole Brown Simpson and Ronald Goldman.

October 4—Pope Paul John II meets with President Clinton.

October 5—Bosnia cease-fire announced to begin on October 10.

October 11—Opening statements in the retrial of Lyle and Erik Menendez for the 1989 murder of their parents.

October 17—The eighth in a series of bombings on the Paris metro injuries at least 29 people.

October 20—President Clinton attends Mideast Economic Summit at Ohio State University. —Attorney General Janet Reno authorizes federal prosecutors to seek the death penalty against Timothy McVeigh and Terry Nichols in connection with the Oklahoma City bombing.

October 22—United Nations opens three-day session to commemorate its 50th anniversary.

October 23—President Clinton meets with Russian president Boris Yeltsin in New York City.

October 24—President Clinton meets with Chinese president Jiang Zemin in New York City.

October 27—France conducts third nuclear test.

November 1—Bosnian peace talks begin in Dayton, Ohio.

November 4—Israeli prime minister Yitzhak Rabin is assassinated at a peace rally in Tel Aviv, Israel.

November 6—U.S. government is partially shut down due to federal budget impasse between the president and Congress.

November 10—Nigeria executes Ken Saro-Wiwa, winner of the Nobel Peace Prize.

November 13—The first attack against U.S. military forces in Saudi Arabia occurs when a car bomb explodes outside a training facility in Riyadh, killing six and injuring about 60 people.

November 21—The presidents of Serbia, Croatia, and Bosnia-Herzegovina sign a peace treaty in Dayton, Ohio, known as the Dayton Accords.
—France conducts fourth nuclear test in South Pacific.

December 4—Chief U.S. District Judge Richard Matsch of Denver is appointed to preside over the trial of Timothy McVeigh and Terry Nichols in connection with the Oklahoma City bombing.

December 6—President Clinton vetoes budget reconciliation bill.
—White House AIDS Conference is held.

December 9—Belarus agrees to transfer remaining Soviet missiles to Russia.

December 14—President Clinton travels to France to sign the Paris Agreement on Peace in Bosnia-Herzegovina at a ceremony in the Elysée Palace in Paris.

December 15—The Association of Southeast Asian Nations agrees to a nuclear-free zone extending from Myanmar (Burma) to the Philippines, and from Laos and Vietnam to Indonesia, at their meeting in Bangkok.
—North Korea reaches $4.5 billion deal whereby U.S. provides two nuclear reactors in exchange for a nuclear freeze.

December 18—U.S. government "shutdown" begins due to budget dispute between the White House and Congress.

December 21—The White House turns over Whitewater notes to independent counsel.

December 27—France conducts fifth nuclear test in South Pacific.

December 28—James Woolsey resigns as director of the Central Intelligence Agency under a cloud from the Aldrich Ames spy scandal.

December 31—United States and North Korea agree to begin talks on North Korean exports of Scud missiles.

1996

January 4—First Lady Hillary Rodham Clinton's missing Whitewater billing records from the Rose Law firm are found.

January 6—U.S. government shutdown ends with budget approved by Congress.

January 9—President Clinton vetoes H. R. 4, "Personal Responsibility and Work Opportunity Act of 1995," promising to work with Congress to craft a bipartisan welfare reform bill.

January 23—President delivers State of the Union address.

January 26—U.S. Senate ratifies START II.

January 27—France conducts sixth nuclear test in South Pacific.
—First Lady Hillary Clinton testifies before a federal grand jury regarding her billing records at the Rose Law Firm.

January 29—French president Jacques Chirac announces French nuclear tests are completed.

January 31–February 3—French president Jacques Chirac makes state visit to the United States.

February 5—President Clinton is subpoenaed to testify at the trial of Jim and Susan McDougal and Jim Guy Tucker.

February 20—Judge Matsch moves Oklahoma City bombing trial to Denver.

February 24—Cuba shoots down two small planes in or near its airspace, piloted by members of Miami-based expatriate group "Brothers to the Rescue."

March 4—Jim and Susan McDougal and Governor Jim Guy Tucker go on trial in Little Rock, Arkansas, for their part in Whitewater.

March 12—President Clinton signs the Helms-Burton Act, tightening the U.S. embargo on Cuba in response to the downing of two private planes in February.

March 20—Jury convicts Lyle and Erik Menendez of the 1989 murder of their parents.

March 21—Secretary of State Warren Christopher visits Prague before traveling to Moscow.

March 23—President Lee Teng-hui becomes the first freely elected president of Taiwan. The elections precipitated a crisis with China over the status of Taiwan and were held despite naval and other military pressure from China.

March 25—France, Britain and the United States sign the South Pacific Nuclear Free Zone Treaty.

April 4—Secretary of Commerce Ronald Brown is killed in a plane crash over mountains in Croatia.

April 11—Forty-three African nations sign Treaty of Pelindaba at Cairo establishing African nuclear-free zone.

April 13—Theodore John Kaczynski, known as the Unabomber, is arrested by a task force in

Montana on information provided by his brother, David Kaczynski.

April 16–18—President Clinton makes state visit to Japan. Among other events, meets with Japanese prime minister Hashimoto and discusses security in the Korean peninsula.

April 21—U.S. and North Korean officials discuss missile proliferation at a meeting in Berlin, Germany.

April 24—Palestinian Council meets for the first time in Gaza.

April 30—U.S. Court of Appeals turns down request by Senators Bennett Johnston (D-La.) and Harry Reid (D-Nev.) to have Kenneth Starr removed from Whitewater investigation.

May 9—President Clinton's videotaped testimony is played for the jury at the Whitewater trial of Jim and Susan McDougal and Jim Guy Tucker.

May 24—United States imposes sanctions, effective immediately, on North Korea and Iran for violating the U.S. Arms Export Control Act.

May 28—Jury finds Jim and Susan McDougal and Jim Guy Tucker guilty of 24 of the 30 counts in the Whitewater trial.

May 29—Benjamin Netanyahu is elected prime minister of Israel.

May 30—White House surrenders Travelgate documents to independent counsel.

June 1—Ukraine delivers last Soviet-era nuclear warhead to Russia for destruction.

June 4—President Clinton proposes Hope Scholarship during commencement address given at Princeton University.

—United States announces it will lift sanctions against North Korea in exchange for terminating its missile program and exports.

June 17—First Lady Hillary Rodham Clinton provides written responses to Senate Whitewater investigators.

June 18—Senate concludes Whitewater investigation. Senate Republicans issue report accusing First Lady Hillary Rodham Clinton and White House aides of obstruction while Senate Democrats issue a report concluding that neither the president, the first lady, nor their associates are guilty of any wrongdoing.

June 19—House of Representatives begins hearings investigating whether or not the White House improperly collected Federal Bureau of Investigation (FBI) background files.

June 20—Attorney General Janet Reno requests independent counsel Kenneth Starr to look into allegations of improper use of FBI background files by the White House.

June 25—White House turns over 2,000 Travelgate documents to independent counsel.
—Truck bombing of the Khobar Towers apartment complex near the King Abdul Aziz Air Base in Saudi Arabia kills 19 Americans and injures approximately 250.

June 27–29—President Clinton travels to France for the G-7 Economic Summit.

July 4—Boris Yeltsin is reelected as president of Russia.

July 9—Senator Strom Thurmond (R-S.C.) convenes hearings on Khobar Towers bombing in Saudi Arabia.

July 17—TWA flight 800, en route from New York to Paris, crashes into the Atlantic Ocean shortly after takeoff, killing all on board.

July 23—At a conference in Jakarta, Indonesia, Secretary of State Warren Christopher and Russian foreign minister Yevgeny Primakov declare support for the draft Treaty on the Comprehensive Ban of Nuclear Tests.

July 25—President Clinton announces formation of the White House Commission on Aviation Safety & Security, headed by Vice President Al Gore.

July 30—House of Representatives passes welfare reform bill.
—Secretary of Defense William Cohen issues annual report that includes U.S. nuclear policy for the post–cold war world, concluding that the United States will retain strategic nuclear weapons for deterrence purposes.

August 13—Secretary of State Warren Christopher visits North Atlantic Treaty Organization headquarters in Brussels, Belgium.

August 19—Jim Guy Tucker is sentenced to four years' probation for role in Whitewater.

August 20—Susan McDougal is sentenced to two years in prison for her role in Whitewater. Sentencing for Jim McDougal is delayed pending his cooperation with Whitewater prosecutors.
—President Clinton authorizes increase in the minimum wage.

August 22—President Clinton signs welfare reform legislation.

August 29—President Clinton and Vice President Gore are renominated at the Democratic National Convention.

August 31—Russia and Chechnya agree to cease-fire.

September 5—Secretary of State Warren Christopher travels to France to meet with President Jacques Chirac.

September 9—The White House Commission on Aviation Safety and Security, also known as the Gore Commission, issues its initial report.

September 10—United Nations General Assembly adopts the Comprehensive Nuclear Test Ban Treaty.

September 19—Secretary of State Warren Christopher and Secretary of Defense William Perry meet with Japanese minister of foreign affairs Ikeda Yukihiko and minister of state and director-general of defense agency Usui Hideo in Washington, D.C.

September 20—House Government Reform and Oversight Committee approves Travelgate report divided along party lines: ". . . the committee concluded that the Clintons, on the urging of Hollywood producer Harry Thomason, ordered the travel workers fired in 1993 to turn the profitable contract over to Clinton associates."

September 24—President Clinton is the first to sign the Comprehensive Nuclear Test Ban Treaty. Seventy nations, including the United States, sign the treaty on the first day.

October 6–7—Secretary of State Warren Christopher visits Israel and meets with Israeli prime minister Benjamin Netanyahu and Palestine Liberation Organization chairman Yasser Arafat.

October 23—Civil liability trial begins for O. J. Simpson in the deaths of Nicole Brown Simpson and Ronald Goldman.

November 5—President Clinton and Vice President Gore win reelection.

November 6—Warren Christopher informs President Clinton that he will not serve as secretary of state during Clinton's second term.

November 12–14—Secretary of State Warren Christopher travels to France to attend a meeting of the steering board of the Bosnian Peace Implementation Council.

November 20—Secretary of State Warren Christopher issues a statement in China summarizing U.S.-Chinese talks on nuclear proliferation, chemical weapons, Taiwan, and Korea.

December 5—President Clinton nominates Madeleine Albright to be secretary of state. She becomes the first woman in U.S. history in that post.

December 6—The Connecticut Yankee nuclear reactor, the second oldest in the United States, is shut down.

December 13—President Clinton nominates William Daley as secretary of commerce. Mickey Kantor had been acting secretary of commerce following Ron Brown's death in plane crash in Bosnia.

December 18—Terrorists invade the residence of the Japanese ambassador to Peru, taking approximately 200 hostages.

December 25—Jon Benet Ramsey is murdered in her Boulder, Colorado, home.

1997

January 1—Kofi Annan begins term as secretary-general of the United Nations.

January 11—President Clinton's attorneys argue before the Supreme Court that the Paula Jones lawsuit should be suspended while he is in office because it will undermine the office of the president.

January 20—President Clinton delivers second Inaugural Address.

January 30—Kenneth Starr subpoenas White House for documents connected to Riady family and the Lippo Group.

February 4—President Clinton delivers State of the Union address.
—Jury finds in favor of the plaintiffs in civil trial of O. J. Simpson, who is ordered to pay $25 million to the family of Ronald Goldman, with an award for the family of Nicole Brown Simpson a few days later.

February 17—Gore Commission issues its final report. Among its recommendations, "In the area of security, the Commission believes that the threat against civil aviation is changing and growing, and that the federal government must lead the fight against it. The Commission recommends that the federal government commit greater resources to improving aviation security, and work more cooperatively with the private sector and local authorities in carrying out security responsibilities."

February 17–18—Secretary of State Madeleine Albright travels to France to meet with French president Jacques Chirac.

February 19—Chinese leader Deng Xiaoping dies at the age of 92.

March 11—White House acknowledges that President Clinton was aware that some of his friends had hired Webster Hubbell prior to his trial.

March 19—President Clinton nominates George Tenet as director of the Central Intelligence Agency. He is currently serving as acting director.

March 20–21—President Clinton attends two-day summit with Russian president Boris Yeltsin at Helsinki. The presidents discuss North Atlantic Treaty Organization expansion, among other topics, issuing a joint statement at the end.

March 26—Thirty-nine members of Heaven's Gate cult, including their leader, Marshall Applewhite, are found dead near San Diego, California.

March 31—Jury selection begins in Oklahoma City bombing trial of Timothy McVeigh.

April 5—White House Chief of Staff Erskine Bowles testifies before the Whitewater grand jury regarding his efforts to find work for Webster Hubbell in 1994.

April 7—President Clinton appoints Sandy Thurman director of Office of National AIDS Policy.

April 14—Jim McDougal is sentenced to three years in prison and one year of house arrest, and fined $10,000 for his part in Whitewater.

April 23—Peruvian Special Forces storm the residence of the Japanese ambassador, freeing the hostages after a four-month standoff. Two soldiers and one hostage die in the operation.

April 25—Senate ratifies Chemical Weapons Convention.

April 29—Chemical Weapons Convention takes effect.

April 30—President Clinton nominee Alexis Herman is confirmed as secretary of labor, ending three-month confirmation battle.

May 1—Tony Blair becomes prime minister of Great Britain.

May 6—Documents released in Little Rock, Arkansas, indicate that independent counsel Kenneth Starr considers First Lady Hillary Clinton a "central figure" in the Whitewater investigation.

May 27—Supreme Court rules that the Paula Corbin Jones lawsuit against President Clinton should be allowed to proceed.

June 2—Timothy McVeigh is convicted of murder in connection with the Oklahoma City federal building bombing.

June 11–13—United States and North Korea engage in talks concerning North Korea's role in nuclear proliferation. No agreement is reached.

June 20–22—Group of 7/Group of 8 (G-7/G-8) Summit takes place in Denver, Colorado.

June 25—*Washington Post* reports that independent counsel Kenneth Starr is interviewing state troopers to find women President Clinton may have been romantically involved with while he was governor of Arkansas in an attempt to determine if Clinton had confided Whitewater matters to anyone.

June 30—Midnight. Territory of Hong Kong reverts to Chinese sovereignty.

July 2—United States conducts sub-critical nuclear test at Nevada test site, which United States insists does not violate the Comprehensive Test Ban Treaty.

July 8—At the Madrid Summit, NATO invites Poland, Hungary, and the Czech Republic to begin negotiations on becoming NATO members.

August 5—President Clinton signs balanced budget plan.

August 31—Princess Diana of Great Britain is killed in an auto accident.

September 3—Attorney General Janet Reno launches a probe into allegations of fraud connected with phone calls made by Vice President Gore in connection with the 1996 presidential campaign.

September 8—Alexander Lebed, former Russian national security adviser, claims that Russia is missing 100 "suitcase nukes."

September 14—Attorney General Janet Reno launches a probe to investigate allegations of campaign fraud against President Clinton in relation to phone calls made from the White House for the 1996 Presidential campaign.

September 26—U.S. and Russia agree to modification of Anti-Ballistic Missile Treaty and to extend completion date of START II.

October 12—President Clinton departs on a seven-day trip to South America, with visits to Venezuela, Brazil, and Argentina.

October 21—The U.S. Justice Department files a complaint against Microsoft for violating a 1995 antitrust agreement.

October 31—Russian Duma ratifies the Chemical Weapons Convention.

December 1–10—Meeting of the United Nations Framework Convention on Climate Change produces Kyoto Protocol for the reduction of greenhouse gasses.

December 3—Attorney General Janet Reno concludes that it is not necessary to appoint independent counsel in the fund-raising probes of Clinton and Gore phone calls.

December 5–8—Secretary of State Madeleine Albright travels to France to meet with French president Jacques Chirac and Israeli prime minister Benjamin Netanyahu.

December 11—Former secretary of housing and urban development Henry Cisneros is indicted by a federal grand jury for lying during his confirmation hearing.

December 12—U.S. District Judge Thomas Jackson issues a preliminary injunction against Microsoft, forcing it to stop requiring manufacturers to install Internet Explorer on PCs equipped with Windows 96.

December 15—President Clinton nominates Bill Lann Lee acting assistant attorney general for human rights.

December 22—President Clinton visits Sarajevo.

December 23—Terry Nichols is convicted of involuntary manslaughter and conspiracy in the Oklahoma City bombing.

1998

January 10—Commonwealth Edison announces it will close two of its 12 nuclear generators.

January 16—President Clinton signs "Charter of Friendship" with Latvia, Estonia, and Lithuania, obligating the United States to seek early membership for these states in NATO.

—Special Division approves petition by Attorney General Janet Reno to authorize independent counsel Kenneth W. Starr to investigate allegations of perjury by former White House intern Monica Lewinsky.

January 17—President Clinton gives videotaped deposition in Paula Corbin Jones case.

January 21—President Clinton publicly denies having had an affair with Monica Lewinsky.

January 22—The Unabomber, Theodore Kaczynski, reaches an agreement with prosecutors and pleads guilty to killing three people and injuring two.

January 26—On national television, President Clinton denies having had sexual relations with former White House intern Monica Lewinsky. The president states, "I did not have sexual relations with that woman, Miss Lewinsky."

January 27—President Clinton delivers State of the Union address; his approval ratings soar to the highest of his presidency.

January 29–30—Secretary of State Madeleine Albright travels to France to meet with French president Jacques Chirac and Israeli prime minister Benjamin Netanyahu.

February 2—President Clinton signs the first balanced budget since 1969.

March 3—President Clinton's longtime friend and adviser Vernon Jordan begins testimony before the grand jury investigating the Monica Lewinsky scandal.

March 8—Secretary of State Madeleine Albright travels to France to discuss the Kosovo crisis.

March 16—Democratic fund-raiser Johnny Chung pleads guilty to funneling illegal donations to the 1996 Clinton-Gore campaign.

March 23—President Clinton and First Lady Hillary Rodham Clinton begin 11-day trip to Africa.

April 1—Judge Susan Webber Wright throws out Paula Corbin Jones's lawsuit against President Clinton, ruling the suit "without merit."

April 6—Pakistan announces it has successfully tested a medium-range missile.

April 10—Former senator George Mitchell (D-Me.) brokers a peace agreement in Northern Ireland. Known as the "Good Friday Agreement," it is accepted by a plebiscite in an all-Ireland poll on May 22.

April 30—Senate ratifies North Atlantic Treaty Organization expansion, including Poland, Hungary, and the Czech Republic.

May 6—United States places sanctions on North Korean company for aiding Pakistan in its nuclear missile program.

May 11—India announces it conducted three nuclear tests.

May 13—India announces that it conducted two more nuclear tests.

May 15—Former Democratic fund-raiser Johnny Chung tells federal investigators that he funneled money from the Chinese government into the Clinton-Gore 1996 campaign fund.

May 18—Justice Department and 20 states file a lawsuit against Microsoft, accusing the com-

pany of using its dominance in PC software to drive competitors out of business.

May 28—Pakistan announces that it has conducted five nuclear test explosions.

June 16—North Korea announces it will continue its nuclear missile program, both for development and for export.

June 17—President Clinton meets Chinese president Jiang Zemin in Beijing, China.

June 19—Treaty establishing the International Criminal Court is agreed to in Rome. The United States is among the seven countries refusing to sign the agreement.

June 22—Iran test-fires a medium-range missile.

June 25—United States, Japan, and South Korea agree to cooperate to put pressure on North Korea to end its nuclear and missile programs.

July 10—Senator Robert Torricelli (D-N.J.) travels to North Korea to discuss possible missile launch.

July 27—Secret Service agent testifies before a federal grand jury about Monica Lewinsky's visits to the White House.

August 7—Bombs explode at the U.S. embassy buildings in Nairobi, Kenya, and Dar es Salaam, Tanzania, resulting in numerous injuries and in severe damage to both installations and surrounding buildings.

August 17—Russia devalues the ruble after failing to get necessary IMF austerity measures passed by the Duma. The ruble falls to about a quarter of its value by the end of the year.
—President Clinton testifies on videotape to a federal grand jury about his relationship with

Monica Lewinsky. Later, in a televised address, President Clinton admits he and Lewinsky had a relationship and apologizes for having "misled" the nation and his wife.

August 20—President Clinton orders cruise missile attack on al Shifa Pharmaceutical plant in Khartoum, Sudan, alleging production of VX nerve gas. Al-Qaeda camps in Afghanistan are also targeted. The strikes are in retaliation for attacks on U.S. embassies in Kenya and Tanzania on August 7, 1998.

August 31—North Korea conducts the first test flight of its new Intermediate Range Ballistic Missile. It flew across the Sea of Japan and over the Japanese island of Honshu.

September 1—President Clinton meets with Russian president Boris Yeltsin for summit in Moscow.

September 2—President Clinton and President Boris Yeltsin sign an agreement designed to prevent nuclear accidents.

September 3—Senator Joseph Lieberman (D-Conn.) condemns the Clinton-Lewinsky affair on the Senate floor.

September 4—North Korea denies that it launched an IRBM, instead claiming it launched a satellite.

September 9—Kenneth Starr delivers report to Congress.

September 11—House of Representatives releases the Starr Report (from independent counsel Kenneth Starr) to the public, revealing in graphic detail the alleged sexual encounters between President Clinton and Monica Lewinsky. Report also lists possible grounds for impeachment, including allegations of perjury, witness tampering, obstruction of justice, and abuse of power.

September 16—United States and North Korea agree to resume missile talks on October 1, 1998.

September 21—Congress funds the "nuclear cities" program, designed to address nuclear proliferation by preventing nuclear scientists from moving to states such as Iraq and Iran.

September 27—Gerhard Schröder elected chancellor of Germany.

September 30—President Clinton announces first budget surplus (1998 fiscal year) in nearly 30 years.

October 1—United States and North Korea begin missile talks.

October 2—State Department warns North Korea it could face "very negative consequences" if it conducts further missile tests or exports any more missiles.

October 8—House of Representatives votes to begin an impeachment investigation by the judiciary committee of President Clinton's conduct in the Lewinsky affair.

October 15—White House Conference on School Safety is held.

October 23—Israeli prime minister Benjamin Netanyahu and Palestine Liberation Organization chairman Yasser Arafat sign the Wye River Memorandum at a retreat on the Wye River on the eastern shore of Maryland.

October 26–November 4—Hurricane Mitch hits Central America, claiming more than 11,000 lives.

November 3—Democrats make gains in the House of Representatives in midterm elections.

November 4—Osama bin Laden and Muhammad Atef are indicted November 4 in Manhattan federal court for the August 7 bombings of the U.S. embassies in Nairobi, Kenya, and Dar es Salaam, Tanzania, and for conspiring to kill Americans outside the United States.

November 13—Webster Hubbell, former Justice Department official and friend of President Clinton, is indicted on 15 counts of fraud and perjury related to the Whitewater investigation. —President Clinton agrees to pay $850,000 to settle out-of-court the Paula Corbin Jones sexual harassment lawsuit.

December 15—Chairman Richard Butler of the United Nations Special Commission issues a report to United Nations Secretary-General Kofi Annan concluding that Iraq is not cooperating with United Nations weapons inspectors.

December 16–19—Joint U.S.-British air strikes on Iraq target Iraq's weapons-of-mass-destruction systems.

December 19—House of Representatives votes to impeach President Clinton on charges of perjury and obstruction of justice. Two of four articles of impeachment are approved by House.

December 23—Defense Secretary William Cohen announces partial troop withdrawal from the Persian Gulf, reducing Persian Gulf forces to about 22,000. —Iraqi government bans United Nations flights into Iraq in response to U.S.-British air strikes.

December 25—North Korea informs United States that it is ready to launch another medium-range missile.

1999

January 7—President Clinton's impeachment trial begins in the Senate. Senate President Pro Tempore Strom Thurmond (R-S.C.) swears in Chief Justice of the United States William Rehnquist as presiding officer.

January 19—President Clinton delivers State of the Union address.

January 22—Japan demands that North Korea end its ballistic missile tests.

February 7—King Hussein of Jordan dies. He is succeeded by his son Abdullah.

February 12—Senate acquits President Clinton of the impeachment charges.

February 13–14—Secretary of State Madeleine Albright travels to France to meet with delegates to the Kosovo Peace Conference.

February 17—Japan's Defense Agency says North Korea has technology to build a missile that could hit the United States.

February 20–23—Secretary of State Madeleine Albright represents United States at Kosovo Peace Conference in Rambouillet, France.

February 21—India and Pakistan issue the Lahore Declaration, resolving the crisis stemming from the 1998 nuclear tests.

March 6–7—Japan and North Korea hold informal talks in Singapore on North Korea's missile program.

March 24—The North Atlantic Treaty Organization launches air strikes against Serbia for failing to make peace in Kosovo, beginning "Operation Allied Force."

March 31—United States announces that North Korea has offered to suspend missile program in exchange for cash compensation. United States counteroffers to release sanctions in stages.

April 11—India test-fires an intermediate-range ballistic missile.

April 12—Judge Susan Webber Wright finds President Clinton in contempt for false testimony in the Paula Corbin Jones lawsuit.

April 14—Pakistan test-fires a medium-range ballistic missile in response to India's test on April 11.

April 15—Pakistan test-fires a short-range ballistic missile.

April 19—Navy kills a security guard and injures four others in a training accident at their Vieques, Puerto Rico, firing range, setting off protests.

April 20—Shooting rampage by two students at Columbine High School resulting in 15 deaths, including the suicides of the two shooters.

April 23–25—French president Jacques Chirac meets with President Clinton while in United States for NATO summit.

May 10—White House Summit on Youth and Violence is held.

May 17—Ehud Barak is elected prime minister of Israel.

May 25—Special Envoy William Perry arrives in North Korea for talks aimed at persuading North Korea to abandon its suspected nuclear armaments program. Perry brings with him a letter from President Clinton to North Korean leader Kim Jong Il.

June 4—First Lady Hillary Rodham Clinton says she will consider running for the U.S. Senate from New York.

June 10—President Clinton appoints a panel to study the relationship between the U.S. Navy and the island of Vieques, Puerto Rico.
—U.S. tests theater missile defense system.

June 16—Vice President Al Gore announces he will run for the presidency.

June 16–17—President Clinton travels to France to discuss peacekeeping in Kosovo with French president Jacques Chirac.

June 25—India seizes North Korean vessel carrying nuclear components to Pakistan.

July 16—John F. Kennedy, Jr., dies in a plane crash along with his wife and her sister.

August 2—China test-fires an intercontinental ballistic missile.

August 30—East Timor votes for independence from Indonesia in a referendum backed by the United Nations, resulting in conflict with the pro-Indonesian military.

September 21—Earthquake in Taiwan kills more than 2,100 people.

September 22—United States and Russia establish Joint Center for Y2K Strategic Stability to detect false missile attack alarms due to Y2K computer problems.

September 30—India test-fires surface-to-air missile.

October 5—India test-fires medium-range missile.

October 13—Senate rejects the Comprehensive Nuclear Test Ban Treaty.
—President Clinton visits Kosovo.

October 18—Special Panel on Military Operations on Vieques recommends that the U.S. Navy phase out operations on Vieques.

October 19—Senate begins hearings on the navy's use of the Vieques firing range.

November 5—District Court finds that Microsoft holds monopoly power in the market for PC operating systems and that the company's actions harmed consumers.

November 10—Russia threatens to end nuclear arms reduction talks with the United States unless Washington upholds the Anti-Ballistic Missile Treaty.

December 3—President Clinton announces decision on future of Vieques, including a 50 percent reduction in use, and a five-year phase-out. Plan is rejected by the government of Puerto Rico.

December 31—In a surprise move, Russian president Boris Yeltsin resigns.

2000

January 3–10—Israeli prime minister Ehud Barak comes to Shepherdstown, West Virginia, to hold talks with Syrian foreign minister Farouk Sharaa, hosted by President Clinton.

January 11—President Clinton announces increased aid for Colombia.

January 12—President Clinton creates three new national monuments: the Grand Canyon-Parashant National Monument and the Agua Fria National Monument in Arizona, and the California Coastal National Monument. The president also signed a proclamation expanding Pinnacles National Monument in California.
—President Clinton announces $21 billion plan to expand Earned Income Credit.

January 13—President Clinton announces "First Accounts" initiative.
—President Clinton announces increased funding to study environmental causes of disease.

January 18—During visit to Boston, President Clinton announces new federal funding for firearms enforcement.
—White House announces largest to-date funding increase for HIV and AIDS.

January 19—President Clinton releases new health care initiative.
—President Clinton announces New Markets agenda during visit to New York.

January 20—President Clinton proposes College Opportunity Tax Cut.

January 23—Canadian prime minister Jean Chrétien has private meeting with President Clinton.

January 24—President Clinton announces new Equal Pay Initiative.

January 24–26—President Andrés Pastrana of Colombia visits the United States, has private meeting with President Clinton.

January 26—White House announces "Responsible Fatherhood Initiative."

January 27—President Clinton announces FY 2001 budget will pay down national debt by 2013.
—President Clinton delivers his final State of the Union address.

January 31—President Clinton issues a directive ordering the navy to abide by a referendum in Puerto Rico on the continued use of the naval firing range at Vieques.
—Illinois governor George Ryan announces an effective stay of all executions in Illinois until further investigation.

February 1—President Clinton, in a televised speech on Puerto Rican Television, outlines directive on Vieques to the people of Puerto Rico.

February 2—Senator Russell Feingold delivers open letter to President Clinton requesting that he suspend all federal executions pending an investigation into the death penalty.

February 3–4—President René Préval of Haiti visits the United States and has private meeting with President Clinton.

February 7—President Clinton releases White House FY 2001 budget.

February 8—President Clinton signs an executive order banning discrimination in federal hiring on the basis of genetic testing.

February 12–21—President Heydar Aliyev of Azerbaijan tours the United States, has private meeting with President Clinton.

February 14—President Clinton gives first presidential online interview.

February 22–24—Juan Carlos I of Spain makes a state visit to the United States.

March 15–18—Prime Minister Bertie Ahern of Ireland visits United States, has private meeting with President Clinton.

March 22—President Clinton addresses Indian parliament.

March 24–30—President Hosni Mubarak of Egypt pays working visit to United States.

March 25—President Clinton visits Pakistan.

March 26—Vladimir Putin wins election to the Russian presidency.

April 1—Mediator Judge Richard Posner announces end of negotiations between the government and Microsoft after no agreement was reached.

April 2–4—President Ali Abdallah Salih of Yemen makes a working visit to United States.

April 3—U.S. District Judge Thomas Jackson rules that Microsoft violated the nation's antitrust laws by using its monopoly power to stifle competition.

April 25—President Clinton vetoes a bill that would have allowed the shipment of thousands of tons of nuclear waste to Yucca Mountain in Nevada.

April 26–28—King Harald V of Norway visits President Clinton during private trip to United States.

April 28—President Ólafur Grimsson of Iceland pays private visit to United States.
—President Tarja Halonen of Finland pays private visit to United States.
—Justice Department and a group of state attorneys general ask U.S. District Judge Thomas Penfield Jackson to split Microsoft into two separate companies.

May 1—President Clinton announces United States will pay off $216 billion of the national debt that year.

May 3—President Clinton announces school accountability program during visit to school in Kentucky.

May 4–5—Japanese prime minister Mori Yoshiro pays working visit to United States.

May 6–10—President Miguel Angel Rodríguez of Costa Rica pays working visit to United States.

May 14—President Clinton and First Lady Hillary Clinton address Million Mom March.

May 22–25—President Thabo Mbeki of South Africa comes to United States on state visit, including stop at Austin, Texas.

June 3—President Clinton arrives in Moscow for a two-day summit with Russian president Vladimir Putin.

June 5—The U.S. Supreme Court dismisses tax charges against Clinton friend and former Justice Department official Webster Hubbell, which arose out of the Whitewater investigation.

June 5–8—King Abdullah II of Jordan visits United States, where he discusses the Middle East peace process with President Clinton.

June 8–9—President Ernesto Zedillo of Mexico meets with President Clinton.

June 12—President Abdurrahman Wahid of Indonesia meets with President Clinton.

June 12–14—President Fernando de la Rúa of Argentina meets with President Clinton.

June 19–22—King Mohammed VI of Morocco meets with President Clinton.

June 24–29—President Robert Kocharian of Armenia meets with President Clinton.

June 26—At the White House with British prime minister Tony Blair, President Clinton announces that the first complete mapping of the human genome is completed.

July 11–25—President Clinton hosts peace summit at Camp David with Israeli prime minister Ehud Barak and Palestinian Authority chairman Yasser Arafat. No peace agreement is reached, but a trilateral statement is issued.

July 21—Former senator and special counsel John Danforth issues a preliminary report exonerating the FBI in the deaths of the Branch Davidians at their compound in Waco, Texas.

July 26–28—President Joseph Estrada of the Philippines visits the United States.

August 3—George W. Bush receives the Republican nomination for president.

August 7–10—President Stjepan Mesić and Prime Minister Ivica Račan of Croatia visit United States.

August 23–25—President-elect Vicente Fox of Mexico meets with President Clinton, also visits Dallas, Texas.

August 26–28—President Clinton visits Nigeria.

August 28—President Clinton visits Tanzania.

August 29—President Clinton visits Egypt.

September 1—President Clinton decides to delay deployment of a limited National Missile Defense system, citing limited information.

September 1–20—Prime Minister Giuliano Amato of Italy visits United States

September 6–8—United Nations Millennium Summit meets in New York. President Clinton meets with various foreign leaders.

September 7—President Clinton addresses the UN Security Council during the United Nations Millennium summit.

September 13—Wen Ho Lee, the nuclear scientist fired from Los Alamos National Laboratory after being accused of stealing classified information, is released from jail after agreeing to plead guilty and to provide federal investigators with information.

September 26—U.S. Supreme Court refuses to consider government's bid to break up Microsoft, sending the case back to lower court.

September 27–28—Prime Minister Willem Kok of the Netherlands visits United States.

October 7—President Clinton vetoes a water and energy spending bill on environmental grounds.

October 12—U.S. Navy destroyer USS *Cole* is attacked by terrorists in the Yemeni harbor of Aden, killing four U.S. sailors and wounding others.

October 15–16—President Clinton attends emergency Mideast Summit in Egypt on Israeli-Palestinian violence.

October 16–19—Prime Minister Sheikh Hasina of Bangladesh visits United States.

October 24—King Abdullah II of Jordan visits United States.

November 19—President Clinton vetoes Intelligence Authorization Act.

November 12—Prime Minister Ehud Barak of Israel meets with President Clinton.

December 18—Prime Minister Jacques Chirac of France attends U.S.–European Union summit.

December 19–23—President Clinton hosts talks between Palestinians and Israeli negotiators in Washington.

2001

January 19—On the last night of his presidency, President Clinton issues more than 100 pardons, with those pardoned including Henry Cisneros, Marc Rich, Patty Hearst, Susan McDougal, and brother Roger Clinton.

January 20—President Clinton leaves office, George W. Bush is sworn in as president.

Principal U.S. Government Officials of the Clinton Years

Supreme Court

William Hubbs Rehnquist, Chief Justice, 1972–
John Paul Stevens, 1975–
Sandra Day O'Connor, 1981–
Antonin Scalia, 1986–

Anthony M. Kennedy, 1988–
David Hackett Souter, 1990–
Clarence Thomas, 1991–
Ruth Bader Ginsburg, 1993–
Stephen G. Breyer, 1994–

Executive Departments

Department of Agriculture
Secretary of Agriculture
  Mike Espy, 1993–94
  Daniel Robert Glickman, 1995–2001

Department of Commerce
Secretary of Commerce
  Ronald H. Brown, 1993–96
  Mickey Kantor, 1996–97
  William M. Daley, 1997–2000
  Norman A. Mineta, 2000–01

Department of Defense
Secretary of Defense
  Les Aspin, 1993–94
  William J. Perry, 1994–97
  William S. Cohen, 1997–2001

Department of Education
Secretary of Education
  Richard W. Riley, 1993–2001

Department of Energy
Secretary of Energy
  Hazel R. O'Leary, 1993–97
  Federico F. Peña, 1997–98
  Bill Richardson, 1998–2001

Department of Health and Human Services
Secretary of Health and Human Services
  Donna E. Shalala, 1993–2001

Department of Housing and Urban Development
Secretary of Housing and Urban Development
  Henry G. Cisneros, 1993–97
  Andrew M. Cuomo, 1997–2001

Department of the Interior
Secretary of the Interior
   Bruce Babbitt, 1993–2001

Department of Justice
Attorney General
   Janet Reno, 1993–2001

Department of Labor
Secretary of Labor
   Robert B. Reich, 1993–97
   Alexis M. Herman, 1997–2001

Department of State
Secretary of State
   Warren M. Christopher, 1993–97
   Madeleine R. Albright, 1997–2001

Department of Transportation
Secretary of Transportation
   Frederico F. Peña, 1993–97
   Rodney E. Slater, 1997–2001

Department of the Treasury
Secretary of the Treasury
   Lloyd M. Bentsen, 1993–94
   Robert E. Rubin, 1995–99
   Lawrence H. Summers, 1999–2001

Department of Veterans Affairs
Secretary of Veterans Affairs
   Jesse Brown, 1993–97
   Togo D. West, Jr., 1998–2001

REGULATORY COMMISSION AND INDEPENDENT AGENCIES

Central Intelligence Agency
Director of Central Intelligence
   R. James Woolsey, 1993–95
   John M. Deutch, 1995–96
   George J. Tenet, 1997–2004

Environmental Protection Agency
Administrator
   Carol M. Browner, 1993–2001

Federal Emergency Management Agency (FEMA)
Director
   James Lee Witt, 1993–2001

Federal Reserve System
Chair
   Alan Greenspan, 1987–

National Endowment of the Arts
Chair
   Jane Q. Alexander, 1993–97
   William Ivey, 1998–2001

National Aeronautics and Space Administration (NASA)
Administrator
   Daniel S. Goldin, 1992–2001

Securities and Exchange Commission
Chair
   Arthur Levitt (D), 1993–2001

UNITED STATES HOUSE OF REPRESENTATIVES

103rd Congress (1993–95)

Speaker of the House
Thomas S. Foley (D-Washington)

Majority Leader
Richard A. Gephardt (D-Missouri)

Minority Leader
Robert J. Michel (R-Illinois)

Majority Whip
David E. Bonior (D-Michigan)

Minority Whip
Newt Gingrich (R-Georgia)

104th Congress (1995–97)

Speaker of the House
Newt Gingrich (R-Georgia)

Majority Leader
Richard K. Armey (R-Texas)

Minority Leader
Richard A. Gephardt (D-Missouri)

Majority Whip
Tom DeLay (R-Texas)

Minority Whip
David E. Bonior (D-Michigan)

105th Congress (1997–99)

Speaker of the House
Newt Gingrich (R-Georgia)

Majority Leader
Richard K. Armey (R-Texas)

Minority Leader
Richard A. Gephardt (D-Missouri)

Majority Whip
Tom DeLay (R-Texas)

Minority Whip
David E. Bonior (D-Michigan)

106th Congress (1999–2001)

Speaker of the House
J. Dennis Hastert (R-Illinois)

Majority Leader
Richard K. Armey (R-Texas)

Minority Leader
Richard A. Gephardt (D-Missouri)

Majority Whip
Tom DeLay (R-Texas)

Minority Whip
David E. Bonior (D-Michigan)

UNITED STATES SENATE

103rd Senate (1993–95)

President
Al Gore (D)

President Pro Tempore
Robert C. Byrd (D-West Virginia)

Majority Leader
George C. Mitchell (D-Maine)

Minority Leader
Robert Dole (R-Kansas)

Majority Whip
Wendell H. Ford (D-Kentucky)

Minority Whip
Alan K. Simpson (R-Wyoming)

104th Senate (1995–97)
President
Al Gore (D)

President Pro Tempore
Strom Thurmond (R-South Carolina)

Majority Leader
Robert Dole (R-Kansas)

Minority Leader
Thomas A. Daschle (D-South Dakota)

Majority Whip
Trent Lott (R-Mississippi), 1995–96
Don Nickles (R-Oklahoma), 1996–97

Minority Whip
Wendell H. Ford (D-Kentucky)

105th Senate (1997–99)
President
Al Gore (D)

President Pro Tempore
Strom Thurmond (R-South Carolina)

Majority Leader
Trent Lott (R-Mississippi)

Minority Leader
Thomas A. Daschle (D-South Dakota)

Majority Whip
Don Nickles (R-Oklahoma)

Minority Whip
Wendell H. Ford (D-Kentucky)

106th Senate (1999–2001)
President
Al Gore (D)

President Pro Tempore
Strom Thurmond (R-South Carolina)

Majority Leader
Trent Lott (R-Mississippi)

Minority Leader
Thomas A. Daschle (D-South Dakota)

Majority Whip
Don Nickles (R-Oklahoma)

Minority Whip
Harry M. Reid (D-Nevada)

SELECTED PRIMARY DOCUMENTS

1. Inaugural Address
January 21, 1993

From: *Facts On File World News Digest*, January 21, 1993

My fellow citizens, today we celebrate the mystery of American renewal. This ceremony is held in the depth of winter, but by the words we speak and the faces we show the world, we force the spring. A spring reborn in the world's oldest democracy that brings forth the vision and courage to reinvent America.

When our founders boldly declared America's independence to the world and our purposes to the Almighty, they knew that America, to endure, would have to change. Not change for change's sake but change to preserve America's ideas—life, liberty, the pursuit of happiness. Though we march to the music of our time, our mission is timeless. Each generation of Americans must define what it means to be an American.

On behalf of our nation, I salute my predecessor, President Bush, for his half-century of service to America.

And I thank the millions of men and women whose steadfastness and sacrifice triumphed over depression, fascism and communism. Today, a generation raised in the shadows of the Cold War assumes new responsibilities in a world warmed by the sunshine of freedom but threatened still by ancient hatreds and new plagues.

Raised in unrivaled prosperity, we inherit an economy that is still the world's strongest but is weakened by business failures, stagnant wages, increasing inequality and deep divisions among our own people.

When George Washington first took the oath I have just sworn to uphold, news traveled slowly across the land by horseback and across the ocean by boat. Now the sights and sounds of this ceremony are broadcast instantaneously to billions around the world. Communications and commerce are global, investment is mobile, technology is almost magical, and ambition for a better life is now universal.

We earn our livelihood in America today in peaceful competition with people all across the Earth. Profound and powerful forces are shaking and remaking our world. And the urgent question of our time is whether we can make change our friend and not our enemy.

This new world has already enriched the lives of millions of Americans who are able to complete and win in it. But when most people are working harder for less, when others cannot work at all, when the cost of health care devastates families and threatens to bankrupt our enterprises great and small, when the fear of crime robs law-abiding citizens of their freedom, and when millions of poor children cannot even imagine the lives we are calling them to lead, we have not made change our friend.

We know we have to face hard truths and take strong steps, but we have not done so. Instead, we have drifted, and that drifting has eroded our resources, fractured our economy and shaken our confidence.

Though our challenges are fearsome, so are our strengths. Americans have ever been a restless, questing, hopeful people, and we must bring to our task today the vision and will of those who came before us. From our Revolution to the Civil War, to the Great Depression, to the civil rights movement, our people have always mustered the determination to construct from these crises the pillars of our history.

Thomas Jefferson believed that to preserve the very foundations of our nation we would need dramatic change from time to time. Well my fellow Americans, this is our time. Let us embrace it.

Our democracy must be not only the envy of the world but the engine of our own renewal. There is nothing wrong with America that cannot be cured by what is right with America. And so today we pledge an end to the era of deadlock and drift, and a new season of American renewal has begun.

To renew America we must be bold. We must do what no generation has had to do before. We must invest more in our own people—in their jobs and in their future—and at the same time cut our massive debt. And we must do so in a world in which we must compete for every opportunity.

It will not be easy. It will require sacrifice. But it can be done and done fairly. Not choosing sacrifice for its own sake, but for our own sake.

We must provide for our nation the way a family provides for its children. Our founders saw themselves in the light of posterity. We can do no less. Anyone who has ever watched a child's eyes wander into sleep knows what posterity is. Posterity is the world to come. The world for whom we hold our ideals, from whom we have borrowed our planet and to whom we bear sacred responsibility.

We must do what America does best: offer more opportunity to all and demand more responsibility from all.

It is time to break the bad habit of expecting something for nothing from our government or from each other. Let us all take more responsibility not only for ourselves and our families but for our communities and our country.

To renew America we must revitalize our democracy. This beautiful capital, like every capital since the dawn of civilizations, is often a place of intrigue and calculation. Powerful people maneuver for position and worry endlessly about who is in and who is out, who is up and who is down, forgetting those people whose toil and sweat send us here and pay our way.

Americans deserve better, and in this city today there are people who want to do better. And so I say to all of you here, let us resolve to reform our politics so that power and privilege no longer shout down the voice of the people.

Let us put aside personal advantage so that we can feel the pain and see the promise of America.

Let us resolve to make our government a place for what Franklin Roosevelt called bold, persistent experimentation, a government for our tomorrows, not our yesterdays.

Let us give this capital back to the people to whom it belongs.

To renew America, we must meet challenges abroad as well as at home. There is no longer a clear division between what is foreign and what is domestic. The world economy, the world environment, the world AIDS crisis, the world arms race—they affect us all.

Today, as an old order passes, the new world is more free but less stable. Communism's collapse has called forth old animosities and new damages. Clearly, America must continue to lead the world we did so much to make.

While America rebuilds, at home, we will not shrink from the challenges nor fail to seize the opportunities of this new world. Together with our friends and allies we will work to shape change lest it engulf us. When our vital interests are challenged or the will and conscience of the international community is defied, we will act, with peaceful diplomacy whenever possible, with force when necessary.

The brave Americans, serving our nation today in the Persian Gulf and Somalia, and wherever else they stand, are testament to our resolve.

But our greatest strength is the power of our ideas, which are still new in many lands. Across the world we see them embraced and we rejoice. Our hopes, our hearts, our hands are with those on every continent who are building democracy and freedom. Their cause is America's cause.

The American people have summoned the change we celebrate today. You have raised your voices in an unmistakable chorus, you have cast your votes in historic numbers, and you have changed the face of Congress, the presidency and the political process itself. Yes, you, my fellow Americans, have forced the spring.

Now we must do the work the season demands. To that work I now turn with all the authority of my office. I ask the Congress to join with me. But no president, no Congress, no government can undertake this mission alone. My fellow Americans, you, too, must play your part in our renewal.

I challenge a new generation of young Americans to a season of service; to act on your idealism by helping troubled children, keeping company with those in need, reconnecting our torn communities. There is so much to be done. Enough, indeed, for millions of others who are still young in spirit to give of themselves in service, too.

In serving, we recognize a simple but powerful truth: We need each other and we must care for one another.

Today we do more than celebrate America, we rededicate ourselves to the very idea of America: An idea born in revolution and renewed through two centuries of challenge; an idea tempered by the knowledge that but for fate we, the fortunate and the unfortunate, might have been each other; an idea ennobled by the faith that our nation can summon from its myriad diversity the deepest measure of unity; an idea infused with the conviction that America's long, heroic journey must go forever upward.

And so, my fellow Americans, as we stand at the edge of the 21st century, let us begin anew with energy and hope, with faith and discipline. And let us work until our work is done. The scripture says. "And let us not be weary in well-doing, for in due season we shall reap if we faint not."

From this joyful mountaintop of celebration we hear a call to service in the valley. We have heard the trumpets, we have changed the guard. And now each in our own way, and with God's help, we must answer the call.

Thank you, and God bless you all.

2. Remarks to the 48th Session of the United Nations General Assembly in New York City
September 27, 1993

Public Papers of the Presidents of the United States: William J. Clinton, 1993. Vol. 2. Washington, D.C.: U.S. Government Printing Office, pages 1,612–1,618

Thank you very much. Mr. President, let me first congratulate you on your election as President of this General Assembly. Mr. Secretary-General, distinguished delegates and guests, it is a great honor for me to address you and to stand in this great chamber which symbolizes so much of the 20th century: Its darkest crises and its brightest aspirations.

I come before you as the first American President born after the founding of the United Nations. Like most of the people in the world today, I was not even alive during the convulsive World War that convinced humankind of the need for this organization, nor during the San Francisco Conference that led to its birth. Yet I have followed the work of the United Nations throughout my life, with admiration for its accomplishments, with sadness for its failures, and conviction that through common effort our generation can take the bold steps needed to redeem the mission entrusted to the U.N. 48 years ago.

I pledge to you that my Nation remains committed to helping make the U.N.'s vision a reality. The start of this General Assembly offers us an opportunity to take stock of where we are, as common shareholders in the progress of humankind and in the preservation of our planet.

It is clear that we live at a turning point in human history. Immense and promising changes seem to wash over us every day. The cold war is over. The world is no longer divided into two armed and angry camps. Dozens of new democracies have been born. It is a moment of miracles. We see Nelson Mandela stand side by side with President de Klerk, proclaiming a date for South Africa's first nonracial election. We see Russia's first popularly elected President, Boris Yeltsin, leading his nation on its bold democratic journey. We have seen decades of deadlock shattered in the Middle East, as the Prime Minister of Israel and the Chairman of the Palestine Liberation Organization reached past enmity and suspicion to shake each other's hands and exhilarate the entire world with the hope of peace.

We have begun to see the doomsday welcome of nuclear annihilation dismantled and destroyed. Thirty-two years ago, President Kennedy warned this chamber that humanity lived under a nuclear sword of Damocles that hung by the slenderest of threads. Now the United States is working with Russia, Ukraine, Belarus, and others to take that sword down, to lock it away in a secure vault where we hope and pray it will remain forever.

It is a new era in this hall as well. The superpower standoff that for so long stymied the United Nations work almost from its first day has now yielded to a new promise of practical cooperation. Yet today we must all admit that there are two powerful tendencies working from opposite directions to challenge the authority of nation states everywhere and to undermine the authority of nation states to work together.

From beyond nations, economic and technological forces all over the globe are compelling the world towards integration. These forces are fueling a welcome explosion of entrepreneurship and political liberalization. But they also threaten to destroy the insularity and independence of national economies, quickening the pace of change and making many of our people feel more insecure. At the same time, from within nations, the resurgent aspirations of ethnic and religious groups challenge governments on terms that traditional nation states cannot easily accommodate.

These twin forces lie at the heart of the challenges not only to our National Government but also to all our international institutions. They require all of us in this room to find new ways to work together more effectively in pursuit of our national interests and to think anew about whether our institutions of international cooperation are adequate to this moment.

Thus, as we marvel at this era's promise of new peace, we must also recognize that serious threats remain. Bloody ethnic, religious, and civil wars rage from Angola to the Caucasus to Kashmir. As weapons of mass destruction fall into more hands, even small conflicts can threaten to take on murderous proportions. Hunger and disease continue to take a tragic toll, especially among the world's children. The malignant neglect of our global environment threatens our children's health and their very security.

The repression of conscience continues in too many nations. And terrorism, which has taken so many innocent lives, assumes a horrifying immediacy for us here when militant fanatics bombed the World Trade Center and planned to attack even this very hall of peace. Let me assure you, whether the fathers of those crimes or the mass murderers who bombed Pan Am Flight 103, my Government is determined to see that such terrorists are brought to justice.

At this moment of panoramic change, of vast opportunities and troubling threats, we must all ask ourselves what we can do and what we should do as a community of nations. We must once again dare to dream of what might be, for our dreams may be within our reach. For that to happen, we must all be willing to honestly confront the challenges of the broader world. That has never been easy.

When this organization was founded 48 years ago, the world's nations stood devastated by war or exhausted by its expense. There was little appetite for cooperative efforts among nations. Most people simply wanted to get on with their lives. But a farsighted generation of leaders from the United States and elsewhere rallied the world. Their efforts built the institutions of postwar security and prosperity.

We are at a similar moment today. The momentum of the cold war no longer propels us in our daily actions. And with daunting economic and political pressures upon almost every nation represented in this room, many of us are turning to focus greater attention and energy on our domestic needs and problems, and we must. But putting each of our economic houses in order cannot mean that we shut our windows to the world. The pursuit of self-renewal, in many of the world's largest and most powerful economies, in Europe, in Japan, in North America, is absolutely crucial because unless the great industrial nations can recapture their robust economic growth, the global economy will languish.

Yet, the industrial nations also need growth elsewhere in order to lift their own. Indeed, prosperity in each of our nations and regions also depends upon active and responsible engagement in a host of shared concerns. For example, a thriving and democratic Russia not only makes the world safer, it also can help to expand the world's economy. A strong GATT agreement will create millions of jobs worldwide. Peace in the Middle East, buttressed as it should be by the repeal of outdated U.N. resolutions, can help to unleash that region's great economic potential and calm a perpetual source of tension in global affairs. And the growing economic power of China, coupled with greater political openness, could bring enormous benefits to all of Asia and to the rest of the world.

We must help our publics to understand this distinction: Domestic renewal is an overdue tonic, but isolationism and protectionism are still poison. We must inspire our people to look beyond their immediate fears toward a broader horizon.

Let me start by being clear about where the United States stands. The United States occupies a unique position in world affairs today. We recognize that, and we welcome it. Yet, with the cold war over, I know many people ask whether the United States plans to retreat or remain active in the world and, if active, to what end. Many people are asking that in our own country as well. Let me answer that question as clearly and plainly as I can. The United States intends to remain engaged and to lead. We cannot solve every problem, but we must and will serve as a fulcrum for change and a pivot point for peace.

In a new era of peril and opportunity, our overriding purpose must be to expand and strengthen the world's community of market-based democracies. During the cold war we sought to contain a threat to the survival of free institutions. Now we seek to enlarge the circle of nations that live under those free institutions. For our dream is of a day when the opinions and energies of every person in the world will be given full expression, in a world of thriving democracies that cooperate with each other and live in peace.

With this statement, I do not mean to announce some crusade to force our way of life and doing things on others or to replicate our institutions, but we now know clearly that throughout the world, from Poland to Eritrea, from Guatemala to South Korea, there is an enormous yearning among people who wish to be the masters of their own economic and political lives. Where it matters most and where we can make the greatest difference, we will, therefore, patiently and firmly align ourselves with that yearning.

Today, there are still those who claim that democracy is simply not applicable to many cultures, and that its recent expansion is an aberration, an accident in history that will soon fade away. But I agree with President Roosevelt, who once said, "The democratic aspiration is no mere recent phase of human history. It is human history."

We will work to strengthen the free market democracies by revitalizing our economy here at home, by opening world trade through the GATT, the North American Free Trade Agreement and other accords, and by updating our shared institutions, asking with you and answering the hard questions about whether they are adequate to the present challenges.

We will support the consolidation of market democracy where it is taking new root, as in the states of the former Soviet Union and all over Latin America. And we seek to foster the practices of good government that distribute the benefits of democracy and economic growth fairly to all people.

We will work to reduce the threat from regimes that are hostile to democracies and to support liberalization of nondemocratic states when they are willing to live in peace with the rest of us.

As a country that has over 150 different racial, ethnic and religious groups within our borders, our policy is and must be rooted in a profound respect for all the world's religions and cultures. But we must oppose everywhere extremism that produces terrorism and hate. And we must pursue our humanitarian goal of reducing suffering, fostering sustainable development, and improving the health and living conditions, particularly for our world's children.

On efforts from export control to trade agreements to peacekeeping, we will often work in partnership with others and through multilateral institutions such as the United Nations. It is in our national interest to do so. But we must not hesitate to act unilaterally when there is a threat to our core interests or to those of our allies.

The United States believes that an expanded community of market democracies not only serves our own security interests, it also advances the goals enshrined in this body's Charter and its Universal Declaration of Human Rights. For broadly based prosperity is clearly the strongest form of preventive diplomacy. And the habits of democracy are the habits of peace.

Democracy is rooted in compromise, not conquest. It rewards tolerance, not hatred. Democracies rarely wage war on one another. They make more reliable partners in trade, in diplomacy, and in the stewardship of our global environment. In democracies with the rule of law and respect for political, religious, and cultural minorities are more responsive to their own people and to the protection of human rights.

But as we work toward this vision we must confront the storm clouds that may overwhelm our work and darken the march toward freedom. If we do not stem the proliferation of the world's deadliest weapons, no democracy can feel secure. If we do not strengthen the capacity to resolve conflict among and within nations, those conflicts will smother the birth of free institutions, threaten the development of entire regions, and continue to take innocent lives. If we do not nurture our people and our planet through sustainable development, we will deepen conflict and waste the very wonders that make our efforts worth doing.

Let me talk more about what I believe we must do in each of these three categories: nonproliferation, conflict resolution, and sustainable development.

One of our most urgent priorities must be attacking the proliferation of weapons of mass destruction, whether they are nuclear, chemical, or biological, and the ballistic missiles that can rain them down on populations hundreds of miles away. We know this is not an idle problem. All of us are still haunted by the pictures of Kurdish women and children cut down by poison gas. We saw Scud missiles dropped during the Gulf war that would have been far graver in their consequence if they had carried nuclear weapons. And we know that many nations still believe it is in their interest to develop weapons of mass destruction or to sell them or the necessary technologies to others for financial gain.

More than a score of nations likely possess such weapons, and their number threatens to grow. These weapons destabilize entire regions. They could turn a local conflict into a global human and environmental catastrophe. We simply have got to find ways to control these weapons and to reduce the number of states that possess them by supporting and strengthening the IAEA and by taking other necessary measures.

I have made nonproliferation one of our Nation's highest priorities. We intend to weave it more deeply into the fabric of all of our relationships with the world's nations and institutions. We seek to build a world of increasing pressures for nonproliferation but increasingly open trade and technology for those states that live by accepted international rules.

Today, let me describe several new policies that our Government will pursue to stem proliferation. We will pursue new steps to control the materials for nuclear weapons. Growing global stockpiles of plutonium and highly enriched uranium are raising the danger of nuclear terrorism for all nations. We will press for an international agreement that would ban production of these materials for weapons forever.

As we reduce our nuclear stockpiles, the United States has also begun negotiations toward a comprehensive ban on nuclear testing. This summer I declared that to facilitate these negotiations, our Nation would suspend our testing if all other nuclear states would do the same. Today, in the face of disturbing signs, I renew my call on the nuclear states to abide by that moratorium as we negotiate to stop nuclear testing for all time.

I am also proposing new efforts to fight the proliferation of biological and chemical weapons. Today, only a handful of nations has ratified the Chemical Weapons Convention. I call on all nations, including my own, to ratify this accord quickly so that it may enter into force by January 13th, 1995. We will also seek to strengthen the biological weapons convention by making every nation's biological activities and facilities open to more international students.

I am proposing as well new steps to thwart the proliferation of ballistic missiles. Recently, working with Russia, Argentina, Hungary, and South Africa, we have made significant progress toward that goal. Now, we will seek to strengthen the principles of the missile technology control regime by transforming it from an agreement on technology transfer among just 23 nations to a set of rules that can command universal adherence.

We will also reform our own system of export controls in the United States to reflect the realities of the post-cold-war world, where we seek to enlist the support of our former adversaries in the battle against proliferation.

At the same time that we stop deadly technologies from falling into the wrong hands, we will work with our partners to remove outdated controls that unfairly burden legitimate commerce and unduly restrain growth and opportunity all over the world.

As we work to keep the world's most destructive weapons out of conflict, we must also strengthen the international community's ability to address those conflicts themselves. For as we all now know so painfully, the end of the cold war did not bring us to the millennium of peace. And indeed, it simply removed the lid from many cauldrons of ethnic, religious, and territorial animosity.

The philosopher, Isaiah Berlin, has said that a wounded nationalism is like a bent twig forced down so severely that when released, it lashes back with fury. The world today is thick with both bent and recoiling twigs of wounded communal identities.

This scourge of bitter conflict has placed high demands on United Nations peacekeeping forces. Frequently the blue helmets have worked wonders. In Namibia, El Salvador, the Golan Heights, and elsewhere, U.N. peacekeepers have helped to stop the fighting, restore civil authority, and enable free elections.

In Bosnia, U.N. peacekeepers, against the danger and frustration of that continuing tragedy, have maintained a valiant humanitarian effort. And if the parties of that conflict take the hard steps needed to make a real peace, the international community including the United States must be ready to help in its effective implementation.

In Somalia, the United States and the United Nations have worked together to achieve a stunning humanitarian rescue, saving literally hundreds of thousands of lives and restoring the conditions of security for almost the entire country. U.N. peacekeepers from over two dozen nations remain in Somalia today. And some, including brave Americans, have lost their lives to ensure that we complete our mission and to ensure that anarchy and starvation do not return just as quickly as they were abolished.

Many still criticize U.N. peacekeeping, but those who do should talk to the people of Cambodia, where the U.N.'s operations have helped to turn the killing fields into fertile soil through reconciliation. Last May's elections in Cambodia marked a proud accomplishment for that war-weary nation and for the United Nations. And I am pleased to announce that the United States has recognized Cambodia's new government.

U.N. peacekeeping holds the promise to resolve many of this era's conflicts. The reason we have supported such missions is not, as some critics in the United States have charged, to subcontract American foreign policy but to strengthen our security, protect our interests, and to share among nations the costs and effort of pursuing peace. Peacekeeping cannot be a substitute for our own national defense efforts, but it can strongly supplement them.

Today, there is wide recognition that the U.N. peacekeeping ability has not kept pace with the rising responsibilities and challenges. Just 6 years ago, about 10,000 U.N. peacekeepers were stationed around the world. Today, the U.N. has some 80,000 deployed in 17 operations on 4 continents. Yet until recently, if a peacekeeping commander called in from across the globe when it was nighttime here in New York, there was no one in the peacekeeping office even to answer the call. When lives are on the line, you cannot let the reach of the U.N. exceed its grasp.

As the Secretary-General and others have argued, if U.N. peacekeeping is to be a sound security investment for our nation and for other U.N. members, it must adapt to new times. Together we must prepare U.N. peacekeeping for the 21st century. We need to begin by bringing the rigors of military and political analysis to every U.N. peace mission.

In recent weeks in the Security Council, our Nation has begun asking harder questions about proposals for new peacekeeping missions: Is there a real threat to international peace? Does the proposed mission have clear objectives? Can an end point be identified for those who will be asked to participate? How much will the mission cost? From now on, the United Nations should address these and other hard questions for every proposed mission before we vote and before the mission begins.

The United Nations simply cannot become engaged in every one of the world's conflicts. If the American people are to say yes to U.N. peacekeeping, the United Nations must know when to say no. The United Nations must also have the technical means to run a modern world-class peacekeeping operation. We support the creation of a genuine U.N. peacekeeping headquarters with a planning staff, with access to timely intelligence, with a logistics unit that can be deployed on a moment's notice, and a modern operations center with global communications.

And the U.N.'s operations must not only be adequately funded but also fairly funded. Within the next few weeks, the United States will be current in our peacekeeping bills. I have worked hard with the Congress to get this done. I believe the United States should lead the way in being timely in its payments, and I will work to continue to see that we pay our bills in full. But I am also committed to work with the United Nations to reduce our Nation's assessment for these missions.

The assessment system has not been changed since 1973. And everyone in our country knows that our percentage of the world's economic pie is not as great as it was then. Therefore, I believe our rates should be reduced to reflect the rise of other nations that can now bear more of the financial burden. That will make it easier for me as President to make sure we pay in a timely and full fashion.

Changes in the U.N.'s peacekeeping operations must be part of an even broader program of United Nations reform. I say that again not to criticize the United Nations but to help to improve it. As our Ambassador Madeleine Albright has suggested, the United States has always played a twin role to the U.N., first friend and first critic.

Today corporations all around the world are finding ways to move from the Industrial Age to the Information Age, improving service, reducing bureaucracy, and cutting costs. Here in the United States, our Vice President Al Gore and I have launched an effort to literally reinvent how our Government operates. We see this going on in other governments around the world. Now the time has come to reinvent the way the United Nations operates as well.

I applaud the initial steps the Secretary-General has taken to reduce and to reform the United Nations bureaucracy. Now, we must all do even more to root out waste. Before this General Assembly is over, let us establish a strong mandate for an Office of Inspector General so that it can attain a reputation for toughness, for integrity, for effectiveness. Let us build new confidence among our people that the United Nations is changing with the needs of our times.

Ultimately, the key for reforming the United Nations, as in reforming our own Government, is to remember why we are here and whom we serve. It is wise to recall that the first words of the U.N. Charter are not "We, the government," but, "We, the people of the United Nations." That means in every country the teachers, the workers, the farmers, the professionals, the fathers, the mothers, the children, from the most remote village in the world to the largest metropolis, they are why we gather in this great hall. It is their futures that are at risk when we act or fail to act, and it is they who ultimately pay our bills.

As we dream new dreams in this age when miracles now seem possible, let us focus on the lives of those people, and especially on the children who will inherit this world. Let us work with a new urgency, and imagine what kind of world we could create for them over the coming generations.

Let us work with new energy to protect the world's people from torture and repression. As Secretary of State Christopher stressed at the recent Vienna conference, human rights are not something conditional, founded by culture, but rather something universal granted by God. This General Assembly should create, at long last, a high commissioner for human rights. I hope you will do it soon and with vigor and energy and conviction.

Let us also work far more ambitiously to fulfill our obligations as custodians of this planet, not only to improve the quality of life for our citizens and the quality of our air and water and the Earth itself but also because the roots of conflict are so often entangled with the roots of environmental neglect and the calamity of famine and disease.

During the course of our campaign in the United States last year, Vice President Gore and I promised the American people major changes in our Nation's policy toward the global environment. Those were promises to keep, and today the United States is doing so. Today we are working with other nations to build on the promising work of the U.N.'s Commission on Sustainable Development. We are working to make sure that all nations meet their commitments under the Global Climate Convention. We are seeking to complete negotiations on an accord to prevent the world's deserts from further expansion. And we seek to strengthen the World Health Organization's efforts to combat the plague of AIDS, which is not only killing millions but also exhausting the resources of nations that can least afford it.

Let us make a new commitment to the world's children. It is tragic enough that 1.5 million children died as a result of wars over the past decade. But it is far more unforgivable that during that same period, 40 million children died from diseases completely preventable with simply vaccines or medicine. Every day, this day, as we meet here, over 30,000 of the world's children will die of malnutrition and disease.

Our UNICEF Director, Jim Grant, has reminded me that each of those children had a name and a nationality, a family, a personality, and a potential. We are compelled to do better by the world's children. Just as our own Nation has launched new reforms to ensure that every child has adequate health care, we must do more to get basic vaccines and other treatment for curable diseases to children all over the world. It's the best investment we'll ever make.

We can find new ways to ensure that every child grows up with clean drinkable water, that most precious commodity of life itself. And the U.N. can work even harder to ensure that each child has at least a full primary education, and I mean that opportunity for girls as well as boys.

And to ensure a healthier and more abundant world, we simply must slow the world's explosive growth in population. We cannot afford to see the human race doubled by the middle of the next century. Our Nation has, at last, renewed its commitment to work with the United Nations to expand the availability of the world's family planning education and services. We must ensure that there is a place at the table for every one of our world's children. And we can do it.

At the birth of this organization 48 years ago, another time of both victory and danger, a generation of gifted leaders from many nations stepped forward to organize the world's efforts on behalf of security and prosperity. One American leader during that period said this: It is time we steered by the stars rather than by the light of each passing ship. His generation picked peace, human dignity, and freedom. Those are good stars; they should remain the highest in our own firmament.

Now history has granted to us a moment of even greater opportunity, when old dangers are ebbing and old walls are crumbling, future generations will judge us, every one of us, above all, by what we make of this magic moment. Let us resolve that we will dream larger, that we will work harder so that they can conclude that we did not merely turn walls to rubble but instead laid the foundation for great things to come.

Let us ensure that the tide of freedom and democracy is not pushed back by the fierce winds of ethnic hatred. Let us ensure that the world's most dangerous weapons are safely reduced and denied to dangerous hands. Let us ensure that the world we pass to our children is healthier, safer, and more abundant than the one we inhabit today.

I believe—I know that together we can extend this moment of miracles into an age of great work and new wonders.

Thank you very much.

3. State of the Union Address January 25, 1994

Public Papers of the Presidents of the United States: William J. Clinton, 1994. Vol. 1. Washington, D.C.: U.S. Government Printing Office, pages 126–135

Thank you very much. Mr. Speaker, Mr. President, Members of the 103d Congress, my fellow Americans:

I'm not at all sure what speech is in the TelePrompTer tonight—[laughter]—but I hope we can talk about the state of the Union.

I ask you to begin by recalling the memory of the giant who presided over this Chamber with such force and grace. Tip O'Neill liked to call himself "a man of the House." And he surely was that. But even more, he was a man of the people, a bricklayer's son who helped to build the great American middle class. Tip O'Neill never forgot who he was, where he came from, or who sent him here. Tonight he's smiling down on us for the first time from the Lord's gallery. But in his honor, may we, too, always remember who we are, where we come from, and who sent us here. If we do that we will return over and over again to the principle that if we simply give ordinary people equal opportunity, quality education, and a fair shot at the American dream, they will do extraordinary things.

We gather tonight in a world of changes so profound and rapid that all nations are tested. Our American heritage has always been to mas-

ter such change, to use it to expand opportunity at home and our leadership abroad. But for too long and in too many ways, that heritage was abandoned, and our country drifted.

For 30 years, family life in America has been breaking down. For 20 years, the wages of working people have been stagnant or declining. For the 12 years of trickle-down economics, we built a false prosperity on a hollow base as our national debt quadrupled. From 1989 to 1992, we experienced the slowest growth in a half century. For too many families, even when both parents were working, the American dream has been slipping away.

In 1992, the American people demanded that we change. A year ago I asked all of you to join me in accepting responsibility for the future of our country. Well, we did. We replaced drift and deadlock with renewal and reform. And I want to thank every one of you here who heard the American people, who broke gridlock, who gave them the most successful teamwork between a President and a Congress in 30 years.

This Congress produced a budget that cut the deficit by half a trillion dollars, cut spending, and raised income taxes on only the wealthiest Americans. This Congress produced tax relief for millions of low-income workers to reward work over welfare. It produced NAFTA. It produced the Brady bill, now the Brady law. And thank you, Jim Brady, for being here, and God bless you, sir.

This Congress produced tax cuts to reduce the taxes of 9 out of 10 small businesses who use the money to invest more and create more jobs. It produced more research and treatment for AIDS, more childhood immunizations, more support for women's health research, more affordable college loans for the middle class, a new national service program for those who want to give something back to their country and their communities for higher education, a dramatic increase in high-tech investments to move us from a defense to a domestic high-tech economy. This Congress produced a new law, the motor voter bill, to help millions of people register to vote. It produced family and medical leave. All passed; all signed into law with not one single veto.

These accomplishments were all commitments I made when I sought this office. And in fairness, they all had to be passed by you in this Congress. But I am persuaded that the real credit belongs to the people who sent us here, who pay our salaries, who hold our feet to the fire.

But what we do here is really beginning to change lives. Let me just give you one example. I will never forget what the family and medical leave law meant to just one father I met early one Sunday morning in the White House. It was unusual to see a family there touring early Sunday morning, but he had his wife and his three children there, one of them in a wheelchair. I came up, and after we had our picture taken and had a little visit, I was walking off and that man grabbed me by the arm and he said, "Mr. President, let me tell you something. My little girl here is desperately ill. She's probably not going to make it. But because of the family leave law, I was able to take time off to spend with her, the most important time I ever spent in my life, without losing my job and hurting the rest of my family. It means more to me than I will ever be able to say. Don't you people up here ever think what you do doesn't make a difference. It does."

Though we are making a difference, our work has just begun. Many Americans still haven't felt the impact of what we've done. The recovery still hasn't touched every community or created enough jobs. Incomes are still stagnant. There's still too much violence and not enough hope in too many places. Abroad, the young democracies we are strongly supporting still face very difficult times and look to us for leadership. And so tonight, let us resolve to continue the journey of renewal, to create more and better jobs, to guarantee health security for all, to reward work over welfare, to promote democracy abroad, and to begin to reclaim our streets from violent crime and drugs and gangs, to renew our own American community.

Last year we began to put our house in order by tackling the budget deficit that was driving us toward bankruptcy. We cut $255 billion in spending, including entitlements, and over 340 separate budget items. We froze domestic spending and used honest budget numbers.

Led by the Vice President, we launched a campaign to reinvent Government. We cut staff, cut perks, even trimmed the fleet of Federal limousines. After years of leaders whose rhetoric attacked bureaucracy but whose action expanded it, we will actually reduce it by 252,000 people over the next 5 years. By the time we have finished, the Federal bureaucracy will be at its lowest point in 30 years.

Because the deficit was so large and because they benefited from tax cuts in the 1980s, we did ask the wealthiest Americans to pay more to reduce the deficit. So on April 15th, the American people will discover the truth about what we did last year on taxes. Only the top 1— [applause]—yes, listen, the top 1.2 percent of Americans, as I said all along, will pay higher income tax rates. Let me repeat: Only the wealthiest 1.2 percent of Americans will face higher income tax rates, and no one else will. And that is the truth.

Of course, there were, as there always are in politics, naysayers who said this plan wouldn't work. But they were wrong. When I became President, the experts predicted that next year's deficit would be $300 billion. But because we acted, those same people now say the deficit is going to be under $180 billion, 40 percent lower than was previously predicted.

Our economic program has helped to produce the lowest core inflation rate and the lowest interest rates in 20 years. And because those interest rates are down, business investment and equipment is growing at 7 times the rate of the previous 4 years. Auto sales are way up. Home sales are at a record high. Millions of Americans have refinanced their homes. And our economy has produced 1.6 million private sector jobs in 1993, more than were created in the previous 4 years combined.

The people who supported this economic plan should be proud of its early results, proud. But everyone in this Chamber should know and acknowledge that there is more to do.

Next month I will send you one of the toughest budgets ever presented to Congress. It will cut spending in more than 300 programs, eliminate 100 domestic programs, and reform the ways in which governments buy goods and services. This year we must again make the hard choices to live within the hard spending ceilings we have set. We must do it. We have proved we can bring the deficit down without choking off recovery, without punishing seniors or the middle class, and without putting our national security at risk. If you will stick with this plan, we will post 3 consecutive years of declining deficits for the first time since Harry Truman lived in the White House. And once again, the buck stops here.

Our economic plan also bolsters our strength and our credibility around the world. Once we reduced the deficit and put the steel back into our competitive edge, the world echoed with the sound of falling trade barriers. In one year, with NAFTA, with GATT, with our efforts in Asia and the national export strategy, we did more to open world markets to American products than at any time in the last two generations. That means more jobs and rising living standards for the American people, low deficits, low inflation, low interest rates, low trade barriers, and high investments. These are the building blocks of our recovery. But if we want to take full advantage of the opportunities before us in the global economy, you all know we must do more.

As we reduce defense spending, I ask Congress to invest more in the technologies of tomorrow. Defense conversion will keep us strong militarily and create jobs for our people here at home. As we protect our environment, we must invest in the environmental technologies of the future which will create jobs. This year we will fight for a revitalized Clean Water Act and a Safe Drinking Water Act and a reformed Superfund program. And the Vice President is right, we must also work with the private sector to connect every classroom, every clinic, every library, every hospital in America into a national information superhighway by the year 2000. Think of it: Instant access to information will increase productivity, will help to educate our children. It will provide better medical care. It will create jobs. And I call on the Congress to pass legislation to establish that information superhighway this year.

As we expand opportunity and create jobs, no one can be left out. We must continue to enforce fair lending and fair housing and all civil rights laws, because America will never be complete in its renewal until everyone shares in its bounty.

But we all know, too, we can do all these things—put our economic house in order, expand world trade, target the jobs of the future, guarantee equal opportunity—but if we're honest we'll all admit that this strategy still cannot work unless we also give our people the education, training, and skills they need to seize the opportunities of tomorrow.

We must set tough, world-class academic and occupational standards for all our children and give our teachers and students the tools they need to meet them. Our Goals 2000 proposal will empower individual school districts to experiment with ideas like chartering their schools to be run by private corporations or having more public school choice, to do whatever they wish to do as long as we measure every school by one high standard: Are our children learning what they need to know to compete and win in the global economy? Goals 2000 links world-class standards to grassroots reforms. And I hope Congress will pass it without delay.

Our school-to-work initiative will for the first time link school to the world of work, providing at least one year of apprenticeship beyond high school. After all, most of the people we're counting on to build our economic future won't graduate from college. It's time to stop ignoring them and start empowering them.

We must literally transform our outdated unemployment system into a new reemployment system. The old unemployment system just sort of kept you going while you waited for your old job to come back. We've got to have a new system to move people into new and better jobs, because most of those old jobs just don't come back. And we know that the only way to have real job security in the future, to get a good job with a growing income, is to have real skills and the ability to learn new ones. So we've got to streamline today's patchwork of training programs and make them a source of new skills for our people who lose their jobs. Reemployment, not unemployment, must become the centerpiece of our economic renewal. I urge you to pass it in this session of Congress.

And just as we must transform our unemployment system, so must we also revolutionize our welfare system. It doesn't work. It defies our values as a nation. If we value work, we can't justify a system that makes welfare more attractive than work if people are worried about losing their health care. If we value responsibility, we can't ignore the $34 billion in child support absent parents ought to be paying to millions of parents who are taking care of their children. If we value strong families, we can't perpetuate a system that actually penalizes those who stay together. Can you believe that a child who has a child gets more money from the Government for leaving home than for staying home with a parent or a grandparent? That's not just bad policy, it's wrong. And we ought to change it.

I worked on this problem for years before I became President, with other Governors and with Members of Congress of both parties and with the previous administration of another party. I worked on it with people who were on welfare, lots of them. And I want to say something to everybody here who cares about this issue. The people who most want to change this system are the people who are dependent on it. They want to get off welfare. They want to go back to work. They want to do right by their kids.

I once had a hearing when I was a Governor, and I brought in people on welfare from all over America who had found their way to work. The woman from my State who testified was asked this question: What's the best thing about being off welfare and in a job? And without blinking an eye, she looked at 40 Governors, and she said, "When my boy goes to school and they say, 'What does your mother do for a living?' he can give an answer." These people want a better system, and we ought to give it to them.

Last year we began this. We gave the States more power to innovate because we know that a lot of great ideas come from outside Washington, and many States are already using it. Then this Congress took a dramatic step. Instead of taxing people with modest incomes into poverty, we helped them to work their way out of poverty by dramatically increasing the earned-income tax credit. It will lift 15 million working families out of poverty, rewarding work over welfare, making it possible for people to be successful workers and successful parents. Now that's real welfare reform.

But there is more to be done. This spring I will send you a comprehensive welfare reform bill that builds on the Family Support Act of 1988 and restores the basic values of work and responsibility. We'll say to teenagers, "If you have a child out of wedlock, we will no longer give you a check to set up a separate household. We want families to stay together"; say to absent parents who aren't paying their child support, "If you're not providing for your children, we'll garnish your wages, suspend your license, track you across State lines, and if necessary, make some of you work off what you owe." People who bring children into this world cannot and must not walk away from them. But to all those who depend on welfare, we should offer ultimately a simple compact. We'll provide the support, the job training, the child care you need for up to 2 years. But after that, anyone who can work, must, in the private sector wherever possible, in community service if necessary. That's the only way we'll ever make welfare what it ought to be, a second chance, not a way of life.

I know it will be difficult to tackle welfare reform in 1994 at the same time we tackle health care. But let me point out, I think it is inevitable and imperative. It is estimated that one million people are on welfare today because it's the only way they can get health care coverage for their children. Those who choose to leave welfare for jobs without health benefits, and many entry-level jobs don't have health benefits, find themselves in the incredible position of paying taxes that help to pay for health care coverage for those who made the other choice, to stay on welfare. No wonder people leave work and go back to welfare to get health care coverage. We've got to solve the health care problem to have real welfare reform.

So this year, we will make history by reforming the health care system. And I would say to you, all of you, my fellow public servants, this is another issue where the people are way ahead of the politicians. That may not be popular with either party, but it happens to be the truth.

You know, the First Lady has received now almost a million letters from people all across America and from all walks of life. I'd like to share just one of them with you. Richard Anderson of Reno, Nevada, lost his job and with it, his health insurance. Two weeks later his wife, Judy, suffered a cerebral aneurysm. He rushed her to the hospital, where she stayed in intensive care for 21 days. The Andersons' bills were over $120,000. Although Judy recovered and Richard went back to work at $8 an hour, the bills were too much for them, and they were literally forced into bankruptcy. "Mrs. Clinton," he wrote to Hillary, "no one in the United States of America should have to lose everything they've worked for all their lives because they were unfortunate enough to become ill." It was to help the Richard and Judy Andersons of America that the First Lady and so many others have worked so hard and so long on this health care reform issue. We owe them our thanks and our action.

I know there are people here who say there's no health care crisis. Tell it to Richard and Judy Anderson. Tell it to the 58 million Americans who have no coverage at all for some time each year. Tell it to the 81 million Americans with those preexisting conditions. Those folks are paying more, or they can't get insurance at all, or they can't ever change their jobs because they or someone in their family has one of those preexisting conditions. Tell it to the small businesses burdened by the skyrocketing cost of insurance. Most small businesses cover their employees, and they pay on average 35 percent more in premiums than big businesses or Government. Or tell it to the 76 percent of insured Americans, three out of four, whose policies have lifetime limits, and that means they can find themselves without any coverage at all just when they need it the most. So if any of you believe there's no crisis, you tell it to those people, because I can't.

There are some people who literally do not understand the impact of this problem on people's lives. And all you have to do is go out and listen to them. Just go talk to them anywhere in any congressional district in this country. They're Republicans and Democrats and independents; it doesn't have a lick to do with party. They think we don't get it. And it's time we show them that we do get it.

From the day we began, our health care initiative has been designed to strengthen what is good about our health care system: the world's best health care professionals, cutting-edge research and wonderful research institutions, Medicare for older Americans. None of this, none of it should be put at risk.

But we're paying more and more money for less and less care. Every year fewer and fewer Americans even get to choose their doctors. Every year doctors and nurses spend more time on paperwork and less time with patients because of the absolute bureaucratic nightmare the present system has become. This system is riddled with inefficiency, with abuse, with fraud, and everybody knows it. In today's health care system, insurance companies call the shots. They pick whom they cover and how they cover them. They can cut off your benefits when you need your coverage the most. They are in charge.

What does it mean? It means every night millions of well-insured Americans go to bed just an illness, an accident, or a pink slip away from having no coverage or financial ruin. It means every morning millions of Americans go to work without any health insurance at all, something the workers in no other advanced country in the world do. It means that every year more and more hard-working people are told to pick a new doctor because their boss has had to pick a new plan. And countless others turn down better jobs because they know if they take the better job, they will lose their health insurance. If we just let the health care system continue to drift, our country will have people with less care, fewer choices, and higher bills.

Now, our approach protects the quality of care and people's choices. It builds on what works today in the private sector, to expand employer-based coverage, to guarantee private insurance for every American. And I might say, employer-based private insurance for every American was proposed 20 years ago by President Richard Nixon to the United States Congress. It was a good idea then, and it's a better idea today.

Why do we want guaranteed private insurance? Because right now 9 out of 10 people who have insurance get it through their employers. And that should continue. And if your employer is providing good benefits at reasonable prices, that should continue, too. That ought to make the Congress and the President feel better.

Our goal is health insurance everybody can depend on: comprehensive benefits that cover preventive care and prescription drugs; health premiums that don't just explode when you get sick or you get older; the power, no matter how small your business is, to choose dependable insurance at the same competitive rates governments and big business get today; one simple form for people who are sick; and most of all, the freedom to choose a plan and the right to choose your own doctor.

Our approach protects older Americans. Every plan before the Congress proposes to slow the growth of Medicare. The difference is this: We believe those savings should be used to improve health care for senior citizens. Medicare must be protected, and it should cover prescription drugs, and we should take the first steps in covering long-term care. To those who would cut Medicare without protecting seniors, I say the solution to today's squeeze on middle class working people's health care is not to put the squeeze on middle class retired people's health care. We can do better than that.

When it's all said and done, it's pretty simple to me. Insurance ought to mean what it used to mean: You pay a fair price for security, and when you get sick, health care's always there, no matter what.

Along with the guarantee of health security, we all have to admit, too, there must be more responsibility on the part of all of us in how we use this system. People have to take their kids to get immunized. We should all take advantage of preventive care. We must all work together to stop the violence that explodes our emergency rooms. We have to practice better health habits, and we can't abuse the system. And those who don't have insurance under our approach will get coverage, but they'll have to pay something for it, too. The minority of businesses that provide no insurance at all, and in so doing shift the cost of the care of their employees to others, should contribute something. People who smoke should pay more for a pack of cigarettes. Everybody can contribute something if we want to solve the health care crisis. There can't be any more something for nothing. It will not be easy but it can be done.

Now, in the coming months I hope very much to work with both Democrats and Republicans to reform a health care system by using the market to bring down costs and to achieve lasting health security. But if you look at history we see that for 60 years this country has tried to reform health care. President Roosevelt tried. President Truman tried. President Nixon tried. President Carter tried. Every time the special interests were powerful enough to defeat them. But not this time.

I know that facing up to these interests will require courage. It will raise critical questions about the way we finance our campaigns and how lobbyists yield their influence. The work of change, frankly, will never get any easier until we limit the influence of well-financed interests who profit from this current system. So I also must now call on you to finish the job both Houses began last year by passing tough

and meaningful campaign finance reform and lobby reform legislation this year.

You know, my fellow Americans, this is really a test for all of us. The American people provide those of us in Government service with terrific health care benefits at reasonable costs. We have health care that's always there. I think we need to give every hard-working, tax-paying American the same health care security they have already given to us.

I want to make this very clear. I am open, as I have said repeatedly, to the best ideas of concerned Members of both parties. I have no special brief for any specific approach, even in our own bill, except this: If you send me legislation that does not guarantee every American private health insurance that can never be taken away, you will force me to take this pen, veto the legislation, and we'll come right back here and start all over again.

But I don't think that's going to happen. I think we're ready to act now. I believe that you're ready to act now. And if you're ready to guarantee every American the same health care that you have, health care that can never be taken away, now—not next year or the year after—now is the time to stand with the people who sent us here, now.

As we take these steps together to renew our strength at home, we cannot turn away from our obligation to renew our leadership abroad. This is a promising moment. Because of the agreements we have reached this year, last year, Russia's strategic nuclear missiles soon will no longer be pointed at the United States, nor will we point ours at them. Instead of building weapons in space, Russian scientists will help us to build the international space station.

Of course, there are still dangers in the world: rampant arms proliferation, bitter regional conflicts, ethnic and nationalist tensions in many new democracies, severe environmental degradation the world over, and fanatics who seek to cripple the world's cities with terror. As the world's greatest power, we must, therefore, maintain our defenses and our responsibilities.

This year, we secured indictments against terrorists and sanctions against those who harbor them. We worked to promote environmentally sustainable economic growth. We achieved agreements with Ukraine, with Belarus, with Kazakhstan to eliminate completely their nuclear arsenal. We are working to achieve a Korean Peninsula free of nuclear weapons. We will seek early ratification of a treaty to ban chemical weapons worldwide. And earlier today, we joined with over 30 nations to begin negotiations on a comprehensive ban to stop all nuclear testing.

But nothing, nothing is more important to our security than our Nation's Armed Forces. We honor their contributions, including those who are carrying out the longest humanitarian air lift in history in Bosnia, those who will complete their mission in Somalia this year and their brave comrades who gave their lives there. Our forces are the finest military our Nation has ever had. And I have pledged that as long as I am President, they will remain the best equipped, the best trained, and the best prepared fighting force on the face of the Earth.

Last year I proposed a defense plan that maintains our post-cold-war security at a lower cost. This year many people urged me to cut our defense spending further to pay for other Government programs. I said no. The budget I send to Congress draws the line against further defense cuts. It protects the readiness and quality of our forces. Ultimately, the best strategy is to do that. We must not cut defense further. I hope the Congress, without regard to party, will support that position.

Ultimately, the best strategy to ensure our security and to build a durable peace is to support the advance of democracy elsewhere. Democracies don't attack each other. They make better trading partners and partners in diplomacy. That is why we have supported, you

and I, the democratic reformers in Russia and in the other states of the former Soviet bloc. I applaud the bipartisan support this Congress provided last year for our initiatives to help Russia, Ukraine, and the other states through their epic transformations.

Our support of reform must combine patience for the enormity of the task and vigilance for our fundamental interest and values. We will continue to urge Russia and the other states to press ahead with economic reforms. And we will seek to cooperate with Russia to solve regional problems, while insisting that if Russian troops operate in neighboring states, they do so only when those states agree to their presence and in strict accord with international standards.

But we must also remember as these nations chart their own futures—and they must chart their own futures—how much more secure and more prosperous our own people will be if democratic and market reforms succeed all across the former Communist bloc. Our policy has been to support that move, and that has been the policy of the Congress. We should continue it.

That is why I went to Europe earlier this month, to work with our European partners, to help to integrate all the former Communist countries into a Europe that has a possibility of becoming unified for the first time in its entire history, its entire history, based on the simple commitments of all nations in Europe to democracy, to free markets, and to respect for existing borders.

With our allies we have created a Partnership For Peace that invites states from the former Soviet bloc and other non-NATO members to work with NATO in military cooperation. When I met with Central Europe's leaders, including Lech Walesa and Vaclav Havel, men who put their lives on the line for freedom, I told them that the security of their region is important to our country's security.

This year we must also do more to support democratic renewal and human rights and sustainable development all around the world. We will ask Congress to ratify the new GATT accord. We will continue standing by South Africa as it works its way through its bold and hopeful and difficult transition to democracy. We will convene a summit of the Western Hemisphere's democratic leaders from Canada to the tip of South America. And we will continue to press for the restoration of true democracy in Haiti. And as we build a more constructive relationship with China, we must continue to insist on clear signs of improvement in that nation's human rights record.

We will also work for new progress toward the Middle East peace. Last year the world watched Yitzhak Rabin and Yasser Arafat at the White House when they had their historic handshake of reconciliation. But there is a long, hard road ahead. And on that road I am determined that I and our administration will do all we can to achieve a comprehensive and lasting peace for all the peoples of the region.

Now, there are some in our country who argue that with the cold war, America should turn its back on the rest of the world. Many around the world were afraid we would do just that. But I took this office on a pledge that had no partisan tinge, to keep our Nation secure by remaining engaged in the rest of the world. And this year, because of our work together, enacting NAFTA, keeping our military strong and prepared, supporting democracy abroad, we have reaffirmed America's leadership, America's engagement. And as a result, the American people are more secure than they were before.

But while Americans are more secure from threats abroad, I think we all know that in many ways we are less secure from threats here at home. Every day the national peace is shattered by crime. In Petaluma, California, an innocent slumber party gives way to agonizing tragedy for the family of Polly Klaas. An ordi-

nary train ride on Long Island ends in a hail of 9-millimeter rounds. A tourist in Florida is nearly burned alive by bigots simply because he is black. Right here in our Nation's Capital, a brave young man named Jason White, a policeman, the son and grandson of policemen, is ruthlessly gunned down. Violent crime and the fear it provokes are crippling our society, limiting personal freedom, and fraying the ties that bind us.

The crime bill before Congress gives you a chance to do something about it, a chance to be tough and smart. What does that mean? Let me begin by saying I care a lot about this issue. Many years ago, when I started out in public life, I was the attorney general of my State. I served as a Governor for a dozen years. I know what it's like to sign laws increasing penalties, to build more prison cells, to carry out the death penalty. I understand this issue. And it is not a simple thing.

First, we must recognize that most violent crimes are committed by a small percentage of criminals who too often break the laws even when they are on parole. Now those who commit crimes should be punished. And those who commit repeated violent crimes should be told, "When you commit a third violent crime, you will be put away, and put away for good; three strikes and you are out."

Second, we must take serious steps to reduce violence and prevent crime, beginning with more police officers and more community policing. We know right now that police who work the streets, know the folks, have the respect of the neighborhood kids, focus on high crime areas, we know that they are more likely to prevent crime as well as catch criminals. Look at the experience of Houston, where the crime rate dropped 17 percent in one year when that approach was taken.

Here tonight is one of those community policemen, a brave, young detective, Kevin Jett, whose beat is eight square blocks in one of the toughest neighborhoods in New York. Every day he restores some sanity and safety and a sense of values and connections to the people whose lives he protects. I'd like to ask him to stand up and be recognized tonight. Thank you, sir. [Applause]

You will be given a chance to give the children of this country, the law-abiding working people of this country—and don't forget, in the toughest neighborhoods in this country, in the highest crime neighborhoods in this country, the vast majority of people get up every day and obey the law, pay their taxes, do their best to raise their kids. They deserve people like Kevin Jett. And you're going to be given a chance to give the American people another 100,000 of them, well trained. And I urge you to do it.

You have before you crime legislation which also establishes a police corps to encourage young people to get an education and pay it off by serving as police officers; which encourages retiring military personnel to move into police forces, an inordinate resource for our country; one which has a safe schools provision which will give our young people the chance to walk to school in safety and to be in school in safety instead of dodging bullets. These are important things.

The third thing we have to do is to build on the Brady bill, the Brady law, to take further steps to keep guns out of the hands of criminals. I want to say something about this issue. Hunters must always be free to hunt. Law-abiding adults should always be free to own guns and protect their homes. I respect that part of our culture; I grew up in it. But I want to ask the sportsmen and others who lawfully own guns to join us in this campaign to reduce gun violence. I say to you, I know you didn't create this problem, but we need your help to solve it. There is no sporting purpose on Earth that should stop the United States Congress from banishing assault weapons that out-gun police and cut down children.

Fourth, we must remember that drugs are a factor in an enormous percentage of crimes. Recent studies indicate, sadly, that drug use is on the rise again among our young people. The crime bill contains—all the crime bills contain—more money for drug treatment for criminal addicts and boot camps for youthful offenders that include incentives to get off drugs and to stay off drugs. Our administration's budget, with all its cuts, contains a large increase in funding for drug treatment and drug education. You must pass them both. We need them desperately.

My fellow Americans, the problem of violence is an American problem. It has no partisan or philosophical element. Therefore, I urge you to find ways as quickly as possible to set aside partisan differences and pass a strong, smart, tough crime bill. But further, I urge you to consider this: As you demand tougher penalties for those who choose violence, let us also remember how we came to this sad point. In our toughest neighborhoods, on our meanest streets, in our poorest rural areas, we have seen a stunning and simultaneous breakdown of community, family, and work, the heart and soul of civilized society. This has created a vast vacuum which has been filled by violence and drugs and gangs. So I ask you to remember that even as we say no to crime, we must give people, especially our young people, something to say yes to.

Many of our initiatives, from job training to welfare reform to health care to national service, will help to rebuild distressed communities, to strengthen families, to provide work. But more needs to be done. That's what our community empowerment agenda is all about, challenging businesses to provide more investment through empowerment zones, ensuring banks will make loans in the same communities their deposits come from, passing legislation to unleash the power of capital through community development banks to create jobs, opportunity, and hope where they're needed most.

I think you know that to really solve this problem, we'll all have to put our heads together, leave our ideological armor aside, and find some new ideas to do even more. And let's be honest, we all know something else too: Our problems go way beyond the reach of Government. They're rooted in the loss of values, in the disappearance of work, and the breakdown of our families and our communities.

My fellow Americans, we can cut the deficit, create jobs, promote democracy around the world, pass welfare reform and health care, pass the toughest crime bill in history, but still leave too many of our people behind. The American people have got to want to change from within if we're going to bring back work and family and community. We cannot renew our country when within a decade more than half of the children will be born into families where there has been no marriage. We cannot renew this country when 13-year-old boys get semiautomatic weapons to shoot 9-year-olds for kicks. We can't renew our country when children are having children and the fathers walk away as if the kids don't amount to anything. We can't renew the country when our businesses eagerly look for new investments and new customers abroad but ignore those people right here at home who would give anything to have their jobs and would gladly buy their products if they had the money to do it. We can't renew our country unless more of us—I mean, all of us—are willing to join the churches and the other good citizens, people like all the—like ministers I've worked with over the years or the priests and the nuns I met at Our Lady of Help in east Los Angeles or my good friend Tony Campollo in Philadelphia, unless we're willing to work with people like that, people who are saving kids, adopting schools, making streets safer. All of us can do that. We can't renew our country until we realize that governments don't raise children, parents do.

Parents who know their children's teachers and turn off the television and help with the homework and teach their kids right from wrong, those kinds of parents can make all the difference. I know; I had one. I'm telling you, we have got to stop pointing our fingers at these kids who have no future and reach our hands out to them. Our country needs it, we need it, and they deserve it.

So I say to you tonight, let's give our children a future. Let us take away their guns and give them books. Let us overcome their despair and replace it with hope. Let us, by our example, teach them to obey the law, respect our neighbors, and cherish our values. Let us weave these sturdy threads into a new American community that can once more stand strong against the forces of despair and evil because everybody has a chance to walk into a better tomorrow.

Oh, there will be naysayers who fear that we won't be equal to the challenges of this time. But they misread our history, our heritage. Even today's headlines, all those things tell us we can and we will overcome any challenge.

When the earth shook and fires raged in California, when I saw the Mississippi deluge the farmlands of the Midwest in a 500-year flood, when the century's bitterest cold swept from North Dakota to Newport News, it seemed as though the world itself was coming apart at the seams. But the American people, they just came together. They rose to the occasion, neighbor helping neighbor, strangers risking life and limb to save total strangers, showing the better angels of our nature.

Let us not reserve the better angels only for natural disasters, leaving our deepest and most profound problems to petty political fighting. Let us instead be true to our spirit, facing facts, coming together, bringing hope, and moving forward.

Tonight, my fellow Americans, we are summoned to answer a question as old as the Republic itself: What is the state of our Union?

It is growing stronger, but it must be stronger still. With your help and God's help, it will be.

Thank you, and God bless America.

4. The President's News Conference on Whitewater (excerpt) March 24, 1994

Public Papers of the Presidents of the United States: William J. Clinton, 1994. Vol. 1. Washington, D.C.: U.S. Government Printing Office, pages 543–552

The President. Good evening, ladies and gentlemen. Yesterday we were reminded that protecting our democracy and expanding its promise around the world can be costly and dangerous. Here at home we mourn the loss of the servicemen in the tragic aircraft accident at Pope Air Force Base, and we pray for a speedy recovery for those who were injured. This tragedy reminds us that the men and women who serve in the military put their lives at risk in the service of our Nation.

In Mexico, an assassin killed Luis Donaldo Colosio, the Presidential candidate of the Institutional Revolutionary Party. We send our condolences and our prayers to his family. And I urge the Mexican people at this difficult time to continue their strides toward economic and political reform and progress.

With the Congress beginning its Easter recess tomorrow, this is a good time to assess the real work we are getting done on behalf of the American people. We're moving forward on our economic plan. The budget now moving through Congress, when passed, will give us 3 consecutive years of deficit reduction for the first time since Harry Truman was President. In 1995, we'll have the lowest budget deficit as a percentage of our annual income of any of the major industrialized countries. A recovering economy produced 2

million jobs last year, and we're on track to create 2 million more in '94.

Around the world, America's efforts have helped to bring much needed calm to Sarajevo and led to an important political accord between the Bosnian Muslims and Croats. Our call for restraint has helped to start talks again in the Middle East. We will continue our efforts to stop North Korea's nuclear program and to seek progress on human rights in China, working to build a more positive relationship with that very important nation. This Friday, a week ahead of schedule, our troops will return home from Somalia. Because of their courageous efforts, Somalia can now build its own future, a step it made in the right direction today with the accord between the leaders of the two largest factions in that country.

Since we came here, our country has been moving in the right direction. Just today, the House of Representatives passed our legislation to limit the influence of lobbyists. Our administration is completing work on a comprehensive welfare reform proposal. We have presented to the Congress our very important reemployment proposal, to change the unemployment system to provide immediate retraining to those who lose their jobs. In a few days, with bipartisan support, the country will have an education reform law that sets national standards for our public schools. In a few weeks, Congress will pass a crime bill and put more police on the street, tougher gun laws on the books, and make "three strikes and you're out" the law of the land. Speaker Foley assured me last night that the crime bill will be item number one on the agenda of the House when it returns to work.

And in a few months we will succeed in passing health care reform. Just yesterday the House Subcommittee on Health passed legislation to provide health security for every American. And while there will be lots of twists and turns in the legislative process, this year Congress will pass and I will sign a health reform which guarantees health care security to every American that can never be taken away, with the right to choose a doctor, with a plan that outlaws insurance abuses: no more dropping coverage or cutting benefits, no more lifetime limits, no more raising rates just because someone in your family has been sick or some are older than others. We want to preserve and strengthen Medicare. And we believe in this administration that those health benefits should be guaranteed through the workplace, building on what works today.

I know that many people around America must believe that Washington is overwhelmingly preoccupied with the Whitewater matter. But our administration is preoccupied with the business we were sent here to do for the American people. The investigation of Whitewater is being handled by an independent Special Counsel whose appointment I supported. Our cooperation with that counsel has been total. We have supplied over 14,000 documents, my tax returns dating back to 1978, and made available every administration witness he has sought.

I support the actions of the House and the Senate clearing the way for hearings at an appropriate time that does not interfere with Mr. Fiske's responsibilities. And I will fully cooperate with their work as well. Tomorrow I will make available my tax returns dating back to 1977 when I first held public office. Cooperation, disclosure, and doing the people's business are the order of the day.

This is the best moment we have had in decades to do the hard work on so many issues that affect not only our own progress and prosperity but the very way we think about ourselves as a nation. The American people should know that I and my administration will not be distracted. We are com-

mitted to taking advantage of this rare moment and achieving these important goals.

Terry [Terence Hunt, Associated Press].

Whitewater

Q. Mr. President, you just said that you would release your tax returns back to 1977. Questions also have been raised about whether you made money or lost money in your Whitewater investment. Do you still believe that you lost about $70,000? And do you have any reason to believe that you owe any back taxes?

The President. I am certain that we lost money. I do not believe we owe any back taxes. If it is determined that we do, of course, we will pay. I am now sure that we lost something less than $70,000, based on an interview I heard on television, or I heard about on television, with Jim McDougal with one of the networks, where he said that he felt that one of the loans I had taken from a bank where we also borrowed money for the land development corporation, he said he thought one of those was a personal loan.

And so I started racking my brain to try to remember what that might have been, and by coincidence, I was also rereading the galleys of my mother's autobiography, just fact checking it, and I noticed that she mentioned there something that I had genuinely forgotten, which is that I helped her to purchase the property and what was then a cabin on the place that she and her husband, Dick Kelley, lived back in 1981, and that I was a co-owner of that property with her for just a few months. After they married, he bought my interest out.

So that's where that—I borrowed the money to go into that investment. I paid the money back with interest. That was unrelated to Whitewater. All the other losses that we have documented to date we believe clearly are tied to the investment Hillary and I made in Whitewater. So we, in fact, lost some $20,700 less than the Lyons report indicated because that loan came from a different place or came for different purposes. And there was another $1,500 payment I made on it. So whatever the total in the Lyons report was, you should subtract from that $20,700 and another $1,500. And we believe we can document that clearly.

Tomorrow, my counsel, David Kendall, will brief the press on the evidence that we have, what's in the tax returns. You will see when you see the tax returns that those losses were clearly there. And he will be glad to support it with other information as well.

Helen [Helen Thomas, United Press International].

Q. Mr. President, do you know of any funds, any money—Whitewater seems to be about money—having gone into any of your gubernatorial campaigns or into Whitewater, particularly federally insured money? Do you know of any money that could have gone in?

The President. No. I have no knowledge of that. I have absolutely no knowledge of that.

Rita [Rita Braver, CBS News].

Q. President Clinton, you just mentioned James McDougal, your former business partner. A lot of questions have been raised about his business practices. Can you tell us what drew you to him to begin with and whether or not you still have faith now that he was—that he is an honest businessman?

The President. Well, I can tell you that when I entered my relationship with him—let's go back to then and not now—I knew Mr. McDougal and had known him for many years. I met him in the late sixties when he was running Senator Fulbright's office in Arkansas. I knew that sometime around that time, perhaps later, he got into the real estate business. When I entered into this investment, it was with a person I had known many years who was in the real estate business who had never been in the S&L business or the banking business. That all happened at a later time. He had done quite well.

The reason we lost money on Whitewater is not surprising; a lot of people did at that time. Interest rates, as you'll remember, went through the roof in the early eighties. People stopped immigrating to my State to retire, at least in the numbers they had all during the seventies, and the market simply changed. So we didn't sell as many lots, and the venture was not successful. So we lost the money. Principally, the money I lost was on the interest payments I had to make on the loans, which were never reimbursed because the venture never turned a profit.

Q. Do you still believe in his honesty now and do you think that he———

The President. All I can tell you, to the best of my knowledge, he was honest in his dealings with me. And that's all I can comment on. As I said, when I heard about his comments on television, since he had—he's always told you that I had nothing to do with the management of Whitewater, that Hillary had nothing to do with it; we didn't keep the books or the records; that this investment was made, as you know, back in 1978 and that we were essentially passive investors; that none of our money was borrowed from savings and loans and we had nothing to do with the savings and loan. So that's what he has always said. So when he said he didn't think this note, where I borrowed money from a bank, not an S&L, in 1981 had anything to do with Whitewater, I started thinking about it. We talked about it. We couldn't remember what else it could have been until

I literally just happened to cross that in reading my mother's autobiography.

Andrea [Andrea Mitchell, NBC News].

Q. Mr. President, Congressman Leach made some very dramatic charges today. He said that Whitewater is really about the arrogance of power, and he didn't just mean back in Arkansas. He said that Federal regulators tried to stop investigators for the Resolution Trust Corporation in Kansas City from putting Whitewater into their criminal referrals. That would amount to a coverup and possibly obstruction of justice. Do you have any knowledge of that?

The President. Absolutely not. And it is my understanding———

Q. And are you looking into it?

The President. Let me just say this, it's my understanding that Mr. Leach was rather careful in the words that he used, and apparently he didn't even charge that any political appointee of our administration had any knowledge of this. So he may be talking about an internal dispute within the RTC from career Republican appointees, for all I know. Keep in mind, until I came here, all the appointees of the RTC were hired under previous Republican administrations. There has never been a Democratic President since there's been an RTC. And I can tell you categorically I had no knowledge of this and was not involved in it in any way, shape, or form.

Q. Well, in light of all that's happened so far, Mr. President, do you think you made any mistakes in the initial investment and in the way the White House has handled this?

The President. I certainly don't think I made a mistake in the initial investment. It was a perfectly honorable thing to do, and it was a perfectly legal thing to do. And I didn't make any money, I lost money. I paid my debts. And then later on, as you know, Hillary and I tried to make sure that the corporation was closed down in an appropriate way and paid any obligations that it owed after we were asked to get involved at a very late stage and after Mr. McDougal had left the S&L. So I don't think that we did anything wrong in that at all. And I think we handled it in an appropriate way. We were like a lot of people; we invested money, and we lost.

I'd be the last person in the world to be able to defend everything we've done here in the sense that whatever we did or didn't do has sparked an inordinate amount of interest in a 16-year-old business venture that lost money. But to suggest—let me just say again, I have had absolutely nothing to do, and would have nothing to do, with any attempt to influence an RTC regulatory matter. And I think if you look at the actions of the RTC just since I've been President and you examine the facts that everybody that works there was appointed by a previous Republican administration, the evidence is clear that I have not done that.

Yes.

Q. Mr. President, you've been kind of tough at times on people you felt made out during the eighties and didn't pay their fair share. Can you tell us, sir, tonight that you have abided by the very high ethical standards———

The President. Absolutely.

Q.———to which you've sought to hold others? And also, sir, if it turns out that you do owe something in back taxes, will you be prepared perhaps to revise some of those judgments you've made about others?

The President. No, not at all. I ask you to tell the American people what percentage of my income I paid in taxes in every year where I reported my tax returns. And let me tell you what my wife and I spent the eighties doing:

I was the lowest paid Governor of any State in the country. I don't complain about it. I was proud of that. I didn't do it for the money. I worked on creating jobs and improving education for the children of my State. Every year I was Governor, my wife worked in a law firm that had always done business with the State. She never took any money for any work she did for the State. And indeed, she gave up her portion of partnership income that otherwise came to the firm, and instead every year gave an enormous percentage of her time to public service work, helping children and helping education and doing a lot of other things, giving up a lot of income.

Now, we did that because we wanted to. The fact that we made investments, some of which we lost money on, some of which we made money on, has nothing to do whatever with the indictment that I made about the excesses of the eighties. And we always made every effort to pay our taxes. I would remind you that we, like most middle class folks, we turned our records over to an accountant. I always told the accountant to resolve all doubts in favor of the Government. I never wanted any question raised about our taxes.

When it turned out in our own investigation of this Whitewater business that one year we had inadvertently taken a tax deduction for interest payments when, in fact, it was principal payment, even though the statute of limitations had run, we went back and voluntarily paid what we owed to the Federal Government. And if it turns out we've made some mistake inadvertently, we will do that again. But I have always tried to pay my taxes. And you will see when you look at all the returns that we've always paid quite a considerable percentage of our income in taxes.

Yes.

White House Staff

Q. Mr. President, during the campaign you said your administration would set a higher standard. Yet in the travel office case last year, your own Chief of Staff found some of your aides used their official position to advance their personal interests, while recently we've seen a senior White House official delinquent in Social Security taxes that disqualified others from serving in your administration, and others in the White House neglecting until recently to undergo a security clearance required of other Government officials handling classified information. Why, sir, do you think it's so difficult for members of your staff to live up to your campaign promise?

The President. First of all, let's deal with those things, each in turn. Now, the finding was not that anybody who worked for me sought to advance themselves personally, financially in the travel office issue. That was not the finding. We found that the issue had not been well handled. And I might say, unlike other White Houses that stonewalled, denied, or delayed, we did our own internal investigation and admitted what mistakes we made and made some changes there. I'm proud of that.

Secondly, no one was barred from serving in our administration because they hadn't paid Social Security taxes, but people were barred from serving in Presidential-appointed positions that required Senate confirmation unless they complied with administration policy. Mr. Kennedy did not do that entirely, and he has been reassigned. He has had a difficult time, and I am convinced that he has done a lot of work that's been very valuable for us. But I think that he should not have done what he did, and I think he should fully pay. He has done that. I think that's what he should have done.

Now, on the White House passes thing, let's just talk about what the facts are. About 90 percent of the people who work here have been through all the clearances. The others are going through the clearances. I learned when I read about this that apparently previous administrations had had some of the same problems, that is, they'd been lax because of the cumbersome nature of the process. So we've now basically put in rules that say that anybody who comes to work here now has to get all this done in 30 days or is immediately on leave without pay. They can't get paid unless they do it. I asked Mr. McLarty and Mr. Cutler to fix this and make sure it never happens again. So I feel confident that we have.

But since you raised the issue, let me also ask you to report to the American people that we have and we have enforced higher standards against ethical conflicts than any previous administration. When people leave the White House, they can't lobby the White House. If they're in certain positions, they can't lobby the White House for a long time. If they're in certain positions now, they can never lobby on behalf of a foreign government.

I have supported a campaign finance reform bill that I am hoping the Congress will pass, and I believe they will, which will change the nature of financing political campaigns. I have supported a very tough lobby reform bill which will require more disclosure and more restraint on the part of lobbyists and public officials than ever before. And we will comply with those laws.

So I think our record, on balance, is quite good here. And when we make mistakes, we try to admit them, something that has not been the order of the day in the past.

Peter [Peter Maer, NBC Mutual Radio].

Whitewater

Q. Thank you, Mr. President. So many things have happened since this Whitewater story broke or resurfaced, depending on your point of view: Your Counsel has resigned; a number of your top aides have been subpoenaed because of their contacts with Treasury officials in on the investigation. I'm curious, who do you blame more than anything else for the Whitewater mess that the administration in is now?

The President. Well, I don't think it's useful to get into blame. I think what's important is that I answer the questions that you have that are legitimate questions, that I fully cooperate with the Special Counsel, which was requested widely by the press and by the members of the Republican Party—and who is himself a Republican—that we fully cooperate. And we've done that. Senator Inouye from Hawaii pointed out today, he said, "I've been experienced in these investigations." He said, "You folks have claimed no executive privilege. You've fully cooperated. No one can quarrel with that." And then I get back to the work of getting unemployment down, jobs up, passing a health care bill, passing the crime bill, moving this country forward. I think the worst thing that can happen is for me to sort of labor over who should be blamed for this. There will probably be enough blame to go around. I'm just not concerned about it.

Q. To follow up, sir, do you feel ill served in any way by your staff?

The President. I think on the—I've told you what I think about these meetings. Now, let's go back to the facts of the meetings. We now know that Mr. Altman's counsel checked with the ethics officer in Treasury before he came over and gave the briefings to the White House. But I have said—so it appears at least that the counsel thought that Mr. Altman had an ethical clearance to come and do this briefing. We certainly know that no one in the White House, at least to the best of my knowledge, has tried to use any information to in any way improperly influence the RTC or any Federal agency.

Would it have been better if those had not occurred? Yes, I think it would have been. Do we have people here who wouldn't do anything wrong but perhaps weren't sensitive enough to how something could look in retrospect by people who are used to having problems in a Presidency or used to having people not telling the truth? I think that we weren't as sensitive as we should have been. And I've said before, it would have been better if that hadn't occurred.

But I think the one thing you have to say is, you learn things as you go along in this business. None of this, in the light of history, will be as remotely important as the fact that by common consensus we had the most productive first year of a Presidency last year of anyone in a generation. That's what matters, that we're changing people's lives. That's what counts. And I'm just going to keep working on it.

Yes.

Q. Mr. President, you and your wife have both used the phrase, "bewildered, confused about why all the interest in Whitewater." Yet, in the Arkansas savings and loan business, your wife represented Madison Savings and Loan before the Arkansas Savings and Loan Board, whose head was a former lawyer who had done work for Madison Savings and Loan. Do you not see any conflicts of interest in your action, or your wife's actions, which would appear to contradict what you just said about her not doing any work before the State, that would cause people to question your actions?

The President. No, that's not what I said. I did not say—I said that when my wife did business, when her law firm represented some State agency itself—State agencies all over America use private lawyers—if she did any work for the State, she never took any pay for it. And when the firm got income from State work, she didn't take her partnership share of that income. She gave that up because she wanted to bend over backwards to avoid the appearance of conflict.

Was there anything wrong with her representing a client before a State agency? And if you go back and look at the facts, basically the firm wrote the securities commissioner a letter saying, is it permissible under Arkansas law to raise money for this S&L in this way? And it showed that she was one of the contacts on it, and the securities commissioner wrote her back and said it's not against the law. That was basically the extent of her representation.

Now, all I can do is tell you that she believed there was nothing unethical about it. And today, in an interview, Professor Steven Geller of New York University, who is a widely respected national expert on legal ethics, once again said there was nothing at all unethical in doing this. These kinds of things happen when you have married couples who have professions. And the most important thing there is disclosure. There was no sneaking around about this. This was full disclosure. Professor Geller—I brought the quote here—said, "I think this is a bum rap on Mrs. Clinton, and I'm amazed that it keeps getting recirculated." Now, there's a person who doesn't work for us whose job it is to know what the code of professional responsibility requires.

Yes.

Q. Mr. President, one thing that puzzled a lot of people is why, if you did nothing wrong, did you act for so long as if you had something to hide. And now that you're about to release these documents to the public, your tax records and other things, do you think it would have helped if you had released these documents to the public earlier? Would it have stopped this issue from reaching the proportions that it has?

The President. I don't have any idea. But I don't think I acted as if I had anything to hide. After all, I did volunteer—I had already given out my tax returns going back to 1980. And then keep in mind, when the furor arose at the request for the Special Counsel—even though everybody at the time said, "Well, we don't think he's done anything wrong; there's no evidence that either he or the First Lady have done anything wrong; we still think there ought to be a special counsel"—I said we would give all this over to the Special Counsel. It was only after the Special Counsel had all the information that the people who first wanted the Special Counsel then decided they wanted the documents as well. So we're making them available.

Perhaps I should have done it earlier, but you will see essentially what I've told you and things that you basically already know.

Yes, Gwen [Gwen Ifill, New York Times].

Q. Mr. President, you said a few minutes ago that the people in the RTC who are involved in Congressman Leach's allegations are all career Republican officials. But aren't they members of your administration? And do you plan to take any action in speaking to either Mr. Bentsen or Mr. Altman about taking action and investigation of Mr. Leach's charges?

The President. I think the last thing in the world I should do is talk to the Treasury Department about the RTC. [Laughter] You all have told me that that creates the appearance of impropriety. I don't think we can have a—it's not just a one-way street; it's a two-way street. Mr. Leach will see that

whatever should be done is done. But I can tell you, I have had no contact with the RTC. I've made no attempt to influence them. And you can see by some of the decisions that they have made that that is the furthest thing, it seems to me, that ought to be on your mind.

Q. Do you abandon all responsibility for a department, a Cabinet department in your Government?

The President. I haven't abandoned all responsibility. You can't have it both ways. Either we can talk to them or we can't. I just think this is a matter of public record now. And Mr. Leach will certainly see to it that it's looked into. He's already said that that's his job, and I'm sure he will see that it is.

Yes.

Q. With so many questions swirling around Whitewater and the Rose law firm, there's some concern that the moral authority of the First Lady is eroding as well. Are you reconsidering her role as the point person for health care reform?

The President. Absolutely not. Absolutely not. People should not be able to raise questions and erode people's moral authority in this country. There ought to have to be evidence and proof. We live in a time when there is a great deal of question-raising. It seems to be the order of the day. But I know what the facts are, and I'm giving you the facts on this.

Here we just had—all these questions were raised about whether she was properly or improperly representing a client before a State agency—to do something, I might add, that the Federal Government had asked savings and loans to do, that is, go out and raise more capital to become more solvent. So that's what she was doing in the full light of day, in full disclosure.

Now we have, even in retrospect, an eminent national expert saying that she is getting a bum rap. When people ask questions that don't have any basis—I think you should ask whatever questions you want to ask, and I think that we should do our best to answer them. But I think that the 20-year record she made as a lawyer, never before having her ethics questioned, never before having her ability questioned, when everybody who knew her knew that every year she was giving up a whole lot of income to do public business, to advance the cause of children and to advance the cause of our State—no, I don't think so. I think in the end when all these questions get asked and answered, her moral authority will be stronger than it has ever been, because we will have gone through this process and been very forthcoming, as we are, to the Special Counsel. And then in the end, people will compare how we did this with how previous administrations under fire handled their business. And I think it will come out quite well.

5. Address to the Nation on Haiti
September 15, 1994

Public Papers of the Presidents of the United States: William J. Clinton, 1994. Vol. 2. Washington, D.C.: U.S. Government Printing Office, pages 1,558–1,561

My fellow Americans, tonight I want to speak with you about why the United States is leading the international effort to restore democratic government in Haiti.

Haiti's dictators, led by General Raoul Cedras, control the most violent regime in our hemisphere. For 3 years, they have rejected every peaceful solution that the international community has proposed. They have broken an agreement that they made to give up power. They have brutalized their people and destroyed their economy. And for 3 years, we and other nations have worked exhaustively to find a diplomatic solution, only to have the dictators reject each one.

Now the United States must protect our interests, to stop the brutal atrocities that threaten tens of thousands of Haitians, to secure our borders, and to preserve stability and promote democracy in our hemisphere and to uphold the reliability of the commitments we make and the commitments others make to us.

Earlier today, I ordered Secretary of Defense Perry to call up the military reserve personnel necessary to support United States troops in any action we might undertake in Haiti. I have also ordered two aircraft carriers, the U.S.S. *Eisenhower* and the U.S.S. *America*, into the region. I issued these orders after giving full consideration to what is at stake. The message of the United States to the Haitian dictators is clear: Your time is up. Leave now, or we will force you from power.

I want the American people to understand the background of the situation in Haiti, how what has happened there affects our national security interests and why I believe we must act now. Nearly 200 years ago, the Haitian people rose up out of slavery and declared their independence. Unfortunately, the promise of liberty was quickly snuffed out, and ever since, Haiti has known more suffering and repression than freedom. In our time, as democracy has spread throughout our hemisphere, Haiti has been left behind.

Then, just 4 years ago, the Haitian people held the first free and fair elections since their independence. They elected a parliament and a new President, Father Jean-Bertrand Aristide, a Catholic priest who received almost 70 percent of the vote. But 8 months later, Haitian dreams of democracy became a nightmare of bloodshed. General Raoul Cedras led a military coup that overthrew President Aristide, the man who had appointed Cedras to lead the army. Resisters were beaten and murdered. The dictators launched a horrible intimidation campaign of rape, torture, and mutilation. People starved; children died; thousands of Haitians fled their country, heading to the United States across dangerous seas. At that time, President Bush declared the situation posed, and I quote, "an unusual and extraordinary threat to the national security, foreign policy, and economy of the United States."

Cedras and his armed thugs have conducted a reign of terror, executing children, raping women, killing priests. As the dictators have grown more desperate, the atrocities have grown ever more brutal. Recent news reports have documented the slaying of Haitian orphans by the nation's deadly police thugs. The dictators are said to suspect the children of harboring sympathy toward President Aristide for no other reason than he ran an orphanage in his days as a parish priest. The children fled the orphanages for the streets. Now they can't even sleep there because they're so afraid. As one young boy told a visitor, "I do not care if the police kill me because it only brings an end to my suffering."

International observers uncovered a terrifying pattern of soldiers and policemen raping the wives and daughters of suspected political dissidents, young girls, 13, 16 years old; people slain and mutilated, with body parts left as warnings to terrify others; children forced to watch as their mothers' faces are slashed with machetes. A year ago, the dictators assassinated the Minister of Justice. Just last month, they gunned down Father Jean-Marie Vincent, a peasant leader and close friend of Father Aristide. Vincent was executed on the doorstep of his home, a monastery. He refused to give up his ministry, and for that, he was murdered.

Let me be clear: General Cedras and his accomplices alone are responsible for this suffering and terrible human tragedy. It is their actions that have isolated Haiti.

Neither the international community nor the United States has sought a confrontation. For nearly 3 years, we've worked hard on diplomatic efforts. The United Nations, the Organization of American States, the Caribbean community, the six Central American Presidents all have sought a peaceful end to this crisis. We have tried everything: persuasion and negotiation, mediation and condemnation. Emissaries were dispatched to Port-au-Prince and were turned away. The United Nations labored for months to reach an agreement acceptable to all parties.

Then last year, General Cedras himself came here to the United States and signed an agreement on Governors Island in New York in which he pledged to give up power, along with the other dictators. But when the day came for the plan to take effect, the dictators refused to leave and instead increased the brutality they are using to cling to power.

Even then, the nations of the world continued to seek a peaceful solution while strengthening the embargo we had imposed. We sent massive amounts of humanitarian aid, food for a million Haitians and medicine to try to help the ordinary Haitian people, as the dictators continued to loot the economy. Then this summer, they threw out the international observers who had blown the whistle on the regime's human rights atrocities.

In response to that action, in July the United Nations Security Council approved a resolution that authorizes the use of all necessary means, including force, to remove the Haitian dictators from power and restore democratic government. Still, we continued to seek a peaceful solution, but the dictators would not even meet with the United Nations Special Envoy. In the face of this continued defiance and with atrocities rising, the United States has agreed to lead a multinational force to carry out the will of the United Nations.

More than 20 countries from around the globe, including almost all the Caribbean community and nations from as far away as Poland, which has so recently won its own freedom, Israel and Jordan, which have been struggling for decades to preserve their own security, and Bangladesh, a country working on its own economic problems, have joined nations like Belgium and Great Britain. They have all agreed to join us because they think this problem in our neighborhood is important to their future interests and their security.

I know that the United States cannot, indeed we should not, be the world's policeman. And I know that this is a time with the cold war over that so many Americans are reluctant to commit military resources and our personnel beyond our borders. But when brutality occurs close to our shores, it affects our national interests. And we have a responsibility to act.

Thousands of Haitians have already fled toward the United States, risking their lives to escape the reign of terror. As long as Cedras rules, Haitians will continue to seek sanctuary in our Nation. This year, in less than 2 months, more than 21,000 Haitians were rescued at sea by our Coast Guard and Navy. Today, more than 14,000 refugees are living at our naval base in Guantanamo. The American people have already expended almost $200 million to support them, to maintain the economic embargo. And the prospect of millions and millions more being spent every month for an indefinite period of time loom ahead unless we act.

Three hundred thousand more Haitians, 5 percent of their entire population, are in hiding in their own country. If we don't act, they could be the next wave of refugees at our door. We will continue to face the threat of a mass exodus of refugees and its constant threat to stability in our region and control of our borders.

No American should be surprised that the recent tide of migrants seeking refuge on our shores comes from Haiti and from Cuba. After all, they're the only nations left in the Western Hemisphere where democratic government is denied, the only countries where dictators have managed to hold back the wave of democracy and progress that has swept over our entire region and that our own Government has so actively promoted and supported for years.

Today, 33 of the 35 countries in the Americas have democratically elected leaders. And Haiti is the only nation in our hemisphere where the people actually elected their own government and chose democracy, only to have tyrants steal it away.

There's no question that the Haitian people want to embrace democracy; we know it because they went to the ballot box and told the world. History has taught us that preserving democracy in our own hemisphere strengthens America's security and prosperity. Democracies here are more likely to keep the peace and to stabilize our region. They're more likely to create free markets and economic opportunity, and to become strong, reliable trading partners. And they're more likely to provide their own people with the opportunities that will encourage them to stay in their nation and to build their own futures. Restoring Haiti's democratic government will help lead to more stability and prosperity in our region, just as our actions in Panama and Grenada did.

Beyond the human rights violations, the immigration problems, the importance of democracy, the United States also has strong interests in not letting dictators, especially in our own region, break their word to the United States and the United Nations. In the post-cold-war world, we will assure the security and prosperity of the United States with our military strength, our economic power, our constant efforts to promote peace and growth. But when our national security interests are threatened, we will use diplomacy when possible and force when necessary.

In Haiti, we have a case in which the right is clear, in which the country in question is nearby, in which our own interests are plain, in which the mission is achievable and limited, and in which the nations of the world stand with us. We must act.

Our mission in Haiti, as it was in Panama and Grenada, will be limited and specific. Our plan to remove the dictators will follow two phases. First, it will remove dictators from power and restore Haiti's legitimate, democratically elected government. We will train a civilian-controlled Haitian security force that will protect the people rather than repress them. During this period, police monitors from all around the world will work with the authorities to maximize basic security and civil order and minimize retribution.

The Haitian people should know that we come in peace. And you, the American people, should know that our soldiers will not be involved in rebuilding Haiti or its economy. The international community, working together, must provide that economic, humanitarian, and technical assistance necessary to help the Haitians rebuild.

When this first phase is completed, the vast majority of our troops will come home, in months, not years. I want our troops and their families to know that we'll bring them home just as soon as we possibly can.

Then, in the second phase, a much smaller U.S. force will join forces from other members of the United Nations. And their mission will leave Haiti after elections are held next year and a new Haitian government takes office in early 1996.

Tonight I can announce that President Aristide has pledged to step down when his term ends, in accordance with the constitution he has sworn to uphold. He has committed himself to promote reconciliation among all Haitians and to set an historic example by peacefully transferring power to a duly elected successor. He knows, as we know, that when you start a democracy, the most important election is the second election. President Aristide has told me that he will consider his mission fulfilled not when he regains office but when he leaves office to the next democratically elected President of Haiti. He has pledged to honor the Haitian voters who put their faith in the ballot box.

In closing, let me say that I know the American people are rightfully concerned whenever our soldiers are put at risk. Our volunteer military is the world's finest, and its leaders have worked hard to minimize risks to all our forces. But the risks are there, and we must be prepared for that.

I assure you that no President makes decisions like this one without deep thought and prayer. But it's my job as President and Commander in Chief to take those actions that I believe will best protect our national security interests.

Let me say again, the nations of the world have tried every possible way to restore Haiti's democratic government peacefully. The dictators have rejected every possible solution. The terror, the desperation, and the instability will not end until they leave. Once again, I urge them to do so. They can still move now and reduce the chaos and disorder, increase the security, the stability, and the safety in which this transfer back to democracy can occur.

But if they do not leave now, the international community will act to honor our commitments; to give democracy a chance, not to guarantee it; to remove stubborn and cruel dictators, not to impose a future.

I know many people believe that we shouldn't help the Haitian people recover their democracy and find their hard-won freedoms, that the Haitians should accept the violence and repression as their fate. But remember, the same was said of a people who more than 200 years ago took up arms against a tyrant whose forces occupied their land. But they were a stubborn bunch, a people who fought for their freedoms and appealed to all those who believed in democracy to help their cause. And their cries were answered, and a new nation was born, a nation that ever since has believed that the rights of life, liberty, and the pursuit of happiness should be denied to none.

May God bless the people of the United States and the cause of freedom. Good night.

6. State of the Union Address January 24, 1995

Public Papers of the Presidents of the United States: William J. Clinton, 1995. Vol. 1. Washington, D.C.: U.S. Government Printing Office, pages 75–86

Mr. President, Mr. Speaker, Members of the 104th Congress, my fellow Americans: Again we are here in the sanctuary of democracy, and once again our democracy has spoken. So let me begin by congratulating all of you here in the 104th Congress and congratulating you, Mr. Speaker.

If we agree on nothing else tonight, we must agree that the American people certainly voted for change in 1992 and in 1994. And as I look out at you, I know how some of you must have felt in 1992. [Laughter]

I must say that in both years we didn't hear America singing, we heard America shouting. And now all of us, Republicans and Democrats alike, must say, "We hear you. We will work together to earn the jobs you have given us." For we are the keepers of a sacred trust, and we must be faithful to it in this new and very demanding era.

Over 200 years ago, our Founders changed the entire course of human history by joining together to create a new country based on a single powerful idea: "We hold these truths to be self-evident, that all men are created equal, . . . endowed by their Creator with certain unalienable Rights, and among these are Life, Liberty and the pursuit of Happiness."

It has fallen to every generation since then to preserve that idea, the American idea, and to deepen and expand its meaning in new and different times: to Lincoln and to his Congress to preserve the Union and to end slavery; to Theodore Roosevelt and Woodrow Wilson to restrain the abuses and excesses of the industrial revolution and to assert our leadership in the world; to Franklin Roosevelt to fight the failure and pain of the Great Depression and to win our country's great struggle against fascism; and to all our Presidents since to fight the cold war. Especially, I recall two who struggled to fight that cold war in partnership with Congresses where the majority was of a different party: to Harry Truman, who summoned us to unparalleled prosperity at home and who built the architecture of the cold war; and to Ronald Reagan, whom we wish well tonight and who exhorted us to carry on until the twilight struggle against communism was won.

In another time of change and challenge, I had the honor to be the first President to be elected in the post-cold-war era, an era marked by the global economy, the information revolution, unparalleled change and opportunity and insecurity for the American people. I came to this hallowed Chamber 2 years ago on a mission, to restore the American dream for all our people and to make sure that we move into the 21st century still the strongest force for freedom and democracy in the entire world. I was determined then to tackle the tough problems too long ignored. In this effort I am frank to say that I have made my mistakes, and I have learned again the importance of humility in all human endeavor. But I am also proud to say tonight that our country is stronger than it was 2 years ago. [Applause] Thank you.

Record numbers of Americans are succeeding in the new global economy. We are at peace, and we are a force for peace and freedom throughout the world. We have almost 6 million new jobs since I became President, and we have the lowest combined rate of unemployment and inflation in 25 years. Our businesses are more productive. And here we have worked to bring the deficit down, to expand trade, to put more police on our streets, to give our citizens more of the tools they need to get an education and to rebuild their own communities.

But the rising tide is not lifting all boats. While our Nation is enjoying peace and prosperity, too many of our people are still working harder and harder, for less and less. While our businesses are restructuring and growing more productive and competitive, too many of our people still can't be sure of having a job next year or even next month. And far more than our material riches are threatened, things far more precious to us, our children, our families, our values.

Our civil life is suffering in America today. Citizens are working together less and shouting at each other more. The common bonds of community which have been the great strength of our country from its very beginning are badly frayed. What are we to do about it?

More than 60 years ago, at the dawn of another new era, President Roosevelt told our Nation, "New conditions impose new requirements on Government and those who conduct Government." And from that simple proposition, he shaped the New Deal, which helped to restore our Nation to prosperity and define the relationship between our people and their Government for half a century.

That approach worked in its time. But we today, we face a very different time and very different conditions. We are moving from an industrial age built on gears and sweat to an information age demanding skills and learning and flexibility. Our Government, once a champion of national purpose, is now seen by many as simply a captive of narrow interests, putting more burdens on our citizens rather than equipping them to get ahead. The values that used to hold us all together seem to be coming apart.

So tonight we must forge a new social compact to meet the challenges of this time. As we enter a new era, we need a new set of understandings, not just with Government but, even more important, with one another as Americans.

That's what I want to talk with you about tonight. I call it the New Covenant. But it's grounded in a very, very old idea, that all Americans have not just a right but a solemn responsibility to rise as far as their God-given talents and determination can take them and to give something back to their communities and their country in return. Opportunity and responsibility: They go hand in hand. We can't have one without the other. And our national community can't hold together without both.

Our New Covenant is a new set of understandings for how we can equip our people to meet the challenges of a new economy, how we can change the way our Government works to fit a different time, and, above all, how we can repair the damaged bonds in our society and come together behind our common purpose. We must have dramatic change in our economy, our Government, and ourselves.

My fellow Americans, without regard to party, let us rise to the occasion. Let us put aside partisanship and pettiness and pride. As we embark on this new course, let us put our country first, remembering that regardless of party label, we are all Americans. And let the final test of everything we do be a simple one: Is it good for the American people?

Let me begin by saying that we cannot ask Americans to be better citizens if we are not better servants. You made a good start by passing that law which applies to Congress all the laws you put on the private sector, and I was proud to sign it yesterday. But we have a lot more to do before people really trust the way things work around here. Three times as many lobbyists are in the streets and corridors of Washington as were here 20 years ago. The American people look at their Capital, and they see a city where the well-connected and the well-protected can work the system, but the interests of ordinary citizens are often left out.

As the new Congress opened its doors, lobbyists were still doing business as usual; the gifts, the trips, all the things that people are concerned about haven't stopped. Twice this month you missed opportunities to stop these practices. I know there were other considerations in those votes, but I want to use something that I've heard my Republican friends say from time to time, "There doesn't have to be a law for everything." So tonight I ask you to just stop taking the lobbyists' perks. Just stop. We don't have to wait for legislation to pass to send a strong signal to the American people that things are really changing. But I also hope you will send me the strongest possible lobby reform bill, and I'll sign that, too.

We should require lobbyists to tell the people for whom they work what they're spending, what they want. We should also curb the role of big money in elections by capping the cost of campaigns and limiting the influence of PAC's. And as I have said for 3 years, we should work to open the airwaves so that they can be an instrument of democracy, not a weapon of destruction, by giving free TV time to candidates for public office.

When the last Congress killed political reform last year, it was reported in the press that the lobbyists actually stood in the Halls of this sacred building and cheered. This year, let's give the folks at home something to cheer about.

More important, I think we all agree that we have to change the way the Government works. Let's make it smaller, less costly, and smarter; leaner, not meaner. [Applause]

I just told the Speaker the equal time doctrine is alive and well. [Laughter]

The New Covenant approach to governing is as different from the old bureaucratic way as the computer is from the manual typewriter. The old way of governing around here pro-

tected organized interests. We should look out for the interests of ordinary people. The old way divided us by interest, constituency, or class. The New Covenant way should unite us behind a common vision of what's best for our country. The old way dispensed services through large, top-down, inflexible bureaucracies. The New Covenant way should shift these resources and decisionmaking from bureaucrats to citizens, injecting choice and competition and individual responsibility into national policy. The old way of governing around here actually seemed to reward failure. The New Covenant way should have built-in incentives to reward success. The old way was centralized here in Washington. The New Covenant way must take hold in the communities all across America. And we should help them to do that.

Our job here is to expand opportunity, not bureaucracy, to empower people to make the most of their own lives, and to enhance our security here at home and abroad. We must not ask Government to do what we should do for ourselves. We should rely on Government as a partner to help us to do more for ourselves and for each other.

I hope very much that as we debate these specific and exciting matters, we can go beyond the sterile discussion between the illusion that there is somehow a program for every problem, on the one hand, and the other illusion that the Government is a source of every problem we have. Our job is to get rid of yesterday's Government so that our own people can meet today's and tomorrow's needs. And we ought to do it together.

You know, for years before I became President, I heard others say they would cut Government and how bad it was, but not much happened. We actually did it. We cut over a quarter of a trillion dollars in spending, more than 300 domestic programs, more than 100,000 positions from the Federal bureaucracy in the last 2 years alone. Based on decisions already made, we will have cut a total of more than a quarter of a million positions from the Federal Government, making it the smallest it has been since John Kennedy was President, by the time I come here again next year.

Under the leadership of Vice President Gore, our initiatives have already saved taxpayers $63 billion. The age of the $500 hammer and the ashtray you can break on "David Letterman" is gone. Deadwood programs, like mohair subsidies, are gone. We've streamlined the Agriculture Department by reducing it by more than 1,200 offices. We've slashed the small business loan form from an inch thick to a single page. We've thrown away the Government's 10,000-page personnel manual.

And the Government is working better in important ways: FEMA, the Federal Emergency Management Agency, has gone from being a disaster to helping people in disasters. You can ask the farmers in the Middle West who fought the flood there or the people in California who have dealt with floods and earthquakes and fires, and they'll tell you that. Government workers, working hand in hand with private business, rebuilt southern California's fractured freeways in record time and under budget. And because the Federal Government moved fast, all but one of the 5,600 schools damaged in the earthquake are back in business.

Now, there are a lot of other things that I could talk about. I want to just mention one because it will be discussed here in the next few weeks. University administrators all over the country have told me that they are saving weeks and weeks of bureaucratic time now because of our direct college loan program, which makes college loans cheaper and more affordable with better repayment terms for students, costs the Government less, and cuts out paperwork and bureaucracy for the Government and for the universities. We shouldn't cap that program. We should give every college in America the opportunity to be a part of it.

Previous Government programs gathered dust. The reinventing Government report is getting results. And we're not through. There's going to be a second round of reinventing Government. We propose to cut $130 billion in spending by shrinking departments, extending our freeze on domestic spending, cutting 60 public housing programs down to 3, getting rid of over 100 programs we do not need, like the Interstate Commerce Commission and the Helium Reserve Program. And we're working on getting rid of unnecessary regulations and making them more sensible. The programs and regulations that have outlived their usefulness should go. We have to cut yesterday's Government to help solve tomorrow's problems.

And we need to get Government closer to the people it's meant to serve. We need to help move programs down to the point where States and communities and private citizens in the private sector can do a better job. If they can do it, we ought to let them do it. We should get out of the way and let them do what they can do better. Taking power away from Federal bureaucracies and giving it back to communities and individuals is something everyone should be able to be for.

It's time for Congress to stop passing on to the States the cost of decisions we make here in Washington. I know there are still serious differences over the details of the unfunded mandates legislation, but I want to work with you to make sure we pass a reasonable bill which will protect the national interests and give justified relief where we need to give it.

For years, Congress concealed in the budget scores of pet spending projects. Last year was no different. There was a $1 million to study stress in plants and $12 million for a tick removal program that didn't work. It's hard to remove ticks. Those of us who have had them know. [Laughter] But I'll tell you something, if you'll give me line-item veto, I'll remove some of that unnecessary spending.

But I think we should all remember, and almost all of us would agree, that Government still has important responsibilities. Our young people—we should think of this when we cut—our young people hold our future in their hands. We still owe a debt to our veterans. And our senior citizens have made us what we are. Now, my budget cuts a lot. But it protects education, veterans, Social Security, and Medicare, and I hope you will do the same thing. You should, and I hope you will.

And when we give more flexibility to the States, let us remember that there are certain fundamental national needs that should be addressed in every State, North and South, East and West: Immunization against childhood disease, school lunches in all our schools, Head Start, medical care and nutrition for pregnant women and infants, all these things, all these things are in the national interest.

I applaud your desire to get rid of costly and unnecessary regulations. But when we deregulate, let's remember what national action in the national interest has given us: safer food for our families, safer toys for our children, safer nursing homes for our parents, safer cars and highways, and safer workplaces, cleaner air, and cleaner water. Do we need common sense and fairness in our regulations? You bet we do. But we can have common sense and still provide for safe drinking water. We can have fairness and still clean up toxic dumps, and we ought to do it.

Should we cut the deficit more? Well, of course we should. Of course we should. But we can bring it down in a way that still protects our economic recovery and does not unduly punish people who should not be punished but instead should be helped.

I know many of you in this Chamber support the balanced budget amendment. I certainly want to balance the budget. Our administration has done more to bring the budget down and to save money than any in a very, very long time. If you believe passing this amendment is the right thing to do, then you have to be straight with the American people. They have a right to know what you're going to cut, what taxes you're going to raise, and how it's going to affect them. We should be doing things in the open around here. For example, everybody ought to know if this proposal is going to endanger Social Security. I would oppose that, and I think most Americans would.

Nothing has done more to undermine our sense of common responsibility than our failed welfare system. This is one of the problems we have to face here in Washington in our New Covenant. It rewards welfare over work. It undermines family values. It lets millions of parents get away without paying their child support. It keeps a minority but a significant minority of the people on welfare trapped on it for a very long time.

I've worked on this problem for a long time, nearly 15 years now. As a Governor, I had the honor of working with the Reagan administration to write the last welfare reform bill back in 1988. In the last 2 years, we made a good start at continuing the work of welfare reform. Our administration gave two dozen States the right to slash through Federal rules and regulations to reform their own welfare systems and to try to promote work and responsibility over welfare and dependency.

Last year I introduced the most sweeping welfare reform plan ever presented by an administration. We have to make welfare what it was meant to be, a second chance, not a way of life. We have to help those on welfare move to work as quickly as possible, to provide child care and teach them skills, if that's what they need, for up to 2 years. And after that, there ought to be a simple, hard rule: Anyone who can work must go to work. If a parent isn't paying child support, they should be forced to pay. We should suspend drivers' licenses, track them across State lines, make them work off what they owe. That is what we should do.

Governments do not raise children, people do. And the parents must take responsibility for the children they bring into this world.

I want to work with you, with all of you, to pass welfare reform. But our goal must be to liberate people and lift them up from dependence to independence, from welfare to work, from mere childbearing to responsible parenting. Our goal should not be to punish them because they happen to be poor.

We should, we should require work and mutual responsibility. But we shouldn't cut people off just because they're poor, they're young, or even because they're unmarried. We should promote responsibility by requiring young mothers to live at home with their parents or in other supervised settings, by requiring them to finish school. But we shouldn't put them and their children out on the street. And I know all the arguments, pro and con, and I have read and thought about this for a long time. I still don't think we can in good conscience punish poor children for the mistakes of their parents.

My fellow Americans, every single survey shows that all the American people care about this without regard to party or race or region. So let this be the year we end welfare as we know it. But also let this be the year that we are all able to stop using this issue to divide America. No one is more eager to end welfare—[applause]—I may be the only President who has actually had the opportunity to sit in a welfare office, who's actually spent hours and hours talking to people on welfare. And I am telling you, the people who are trapped on it know it doesn't work; they also want to get off. So we can promote, together, education and work and good parenting. I have no problem with punishing bad behavior or the refusal to be a worker or a student or a responsible parent. I just don't want to punish poverty and past mistakes. All of us have made our mistakes, and none of us can change our yesterdays. But

every one of us can change our tomorrows. And America's best example of that may be Lynn Woolsey, who worked her way off welfare to become a Congresswoman from the State of California.

I know the Members of this Congress are concerned about crime, as are all the citizens of our country. And I remind you that last year we passed a very tough crime bill: longer sentences, "three strikes and you're out," almost 60 new capital punishment offenses, more prisons, more prevention, 100,000 more police. And we paid for it all by reducing the size of the Federal bureaucracy and giving the money back to local communities to lower the crime rate.

There may be other things we can do to be tougher on crime, to be smarter with crime, to help to lower that rate first. Well, if there are, let's talk about them, and let's do them. But let's not go back on the things that we did last year that we know work, that we know work because the local law enforcement officers tell us that we did the right thing, because local community leaders who have worked for years and years to lower the crime rate tell us that they work. Let's look at the experience of our cities and our rural areas where the crime rate has gone down and ask the people who did it how they did it. And if what we did last year supports the decline in the crime rate—and I am convinced that it does—let us not go back on it. Let's stick with it, implement it. We've got 4 more hard years of work to do that.

I don't want to destroy the good atmosphere in the room or in the country tonight, but I have to mention one issue that divided this body greatly last year. The last Congress also passed the Brady bill and, in the crime bill, the ban on 19 assault weapons. I don't think it's a secret to anybody in this room that several Members of the last Congress who voted for that aren't here tonight because they voted for it. And I know, therefore, that some of you who are here because they voted for it are under enormous pressure to repeal it. I just have to tell you how I feel about it.

The Members of Congress who voted for that bill and I would never do anything to infringe on the right to keep and bear arms to hunt and to engage in other appropriate sporting activities. I've done it since I was a boy, and I'm going to keep right on doing it until I can't do it anymore. But a lot of people laid down their seats in Congress so that police officers and kids wouldn't have to lay down their lives under a hail of assault weapon attack, and I will not let that be repealed. I will not let it be repealed.

I'd like to talk about a couple of other issues we have to deal with. I want us to cut more spending, but I hope we won't cut Government programs that help to prepare us for the new economy, promote responsibility, and are organized from the grass roots up, not by Federal bureaucracy. The very best example of this is the national service corps, AmeriCorps. It passed with strong bipartisan support. And now there are 20,000 Americans, more than ever served in one year in the Peace Corps, working all over this country, helping people person-to-person in local grassroots volunteer groups, solving problems, and in the process earning some money for their education. This is citizenship at its best. It's good for the AmeriCorps members, but it's good for the rest of us, too. It's the essence of the New Covenant, and we shouldn't stop it.

All Americans, not only in the States most heavily affected but in every place in this country, are rightly disturbed by the large numbers of illegal aliens entering our country. The jobs they hold might otherwise be held by citizens or legal immigrants. The public service they use impose burdens on our taxpayers. That's why our administration has moved aggressively to secure our borders more by hiring a record number of new border guards, by deporting twice as many criminal aliens as ever before, by

cracking down on illegal hiring, by barring welfare benefits to illegal aliens. In the budget I will present to you, we will try to do more to speed the deportation of illegal aliens who are arrested for crimes, to better identify illegal aliens in the workplace as recommended by the commission headed by former Congresswoman Barbara Jordan. We are a nation of immigrants. But we are also a nation of laws. It is wrong and ultimately self-defeating for a nation of immigrants to permit the kind of abuse of our immigration laws we have seen in recent years, and we must do more to stop it.

The most important job of our Government in this new era is to empower the American people to succeed in the global economy. America has always been a land of opportunity, a land where, if you work hard, you can get ahead. We've become a great middle class country. Middle class values sustain us. We must expand that middle class and shrink the under class, even as we do everything we can to support the millions of Americans who are already successful in the new economy.

America is once again the world's strongest economic power: almost 6 million new jobs in the last 2 years, exports booming, inflation down. High-wage jobs are coming back. A record number of American entrepreneurs are living the American dream. If we want it to stay that way, those who work and lift our Nation must have more of its benefits.

Today, too many of those people are being left out. They're working harder for less. They have less security, less income, less certainty that they can even afford a vacation, much less college for their kids or retirement for themselves. We cannot let this continue. If we don't act, our economy will probably keep doing what it's been doing since about 1978, when the income growth began to go to those at the very top of our economic scale and the people in the vast middle got very little growth, and people who worked like crazy but were on the bottom then fell even further and further behind in the years afterward, no matter how hard they worked.

We've got to have a Government that can be a real partner in making this new economy work for all of our people, a Government that helps each and every one of us to get an education and to have the opportunity to renew our skills. That's why we worked so hard to increase educational opportunities in the last 2 years, from Head Start to public schools, to apprenticeships for young people who don't go to college, to making college loans more available and more affordable. That's the first thing we have to do. We've got to do something to empower people to improve their skills.

The second thing we ought to do is to help people raise their incomes immediately by lowering their taxes. We took the first step in 1993 with a working family tax cut for 15 million families with incomes under $27,000, a tax cut that this year will average about $1,000 a family. And we also gave tax reductions to most small and new businesses. Before we could do more than that, we first had to bring down the deficit we inherited, and we had to get economic growth up. Now we've done both. And now we can cut taxes in a more comprehensive way. But tax cuts should reinforce and promote our first obligation: to empower our citizens through education and training to make the most of their own lives. The spotlight should shine on those who make the right choices for themselves, their families, and their communities.

I have proposed the middle class bill of rights, which should properly be called the bill of rights and responsibilities because its provisions only benefit those who are working to educate and raise their children and to educate themselves. It will, therefore, give needed tax relief and raise incomes in both the short run and the long run in a way that benefits all of us.

There are four provisions. First, a tax deduction for all education and training after high school. If you think about it, we permit businesses to deduct their investment, we permit individuals to deduct interest on their home mortgages, but today an education is even more important to the economic well-being of our whole country than even those things are. We should do everything we can to encourage it. And I hope you will support it. Second, we ought to cut taxes $500 for families with children under 13. Third, we ought to foster more savings and personal responsibility by permitting people to establish an individual retirement account and withdraw from it, tax-free, for the cost of education, health care, first-time homebuying, or the care of a parent. And fourth, we should pass a "GI bill" for America's workers. We propose to collapse nearly 70 Federal programs and not give the money to the States but give the money directly to the American people, offer vouchers to them so that they, if they're laid off or if they're working for a very low wage, can get a voucher worth $2,600 a year for up to 2 years to go to their local community colleges or wherever else they want to get the skills they need to improve their lives. Let's empower people in this way, move it from the Government directly to the workers of America.

Now, any one of us can call for a tax cut, but I won't accept one that explodes the deficit or puts our recovery at risk. We ought to pay for our tax cuts fully and honestly.

Just 2 years ago, it was an open question whether we would find the strength to cut the deficit. Thanks to the courage of the people who were here then, many of whom didn't return, we did cut the deficit. We began to do what others said would not be done. We cut the deficit by over $600 billion, about $10,000 for every family in this country. It's coming down 3 years in a row for the first time since Mr. Truman was President, and I don't think anybody in America wants us to let it explode again.

In the budget I will send you, the middle class bill of rights is fully paid for by budget cuts in bureaucracy, cuts in programs, cuts in special interest subsidies. And the spending cuts will more than double the tax cuts. My budget pays for the middle class bill of rights without any cuts in Medicare. And I will oppose any attempts to pay for tax cuts with Medicare cuts. That's not the right thing to do.

I know that a lot of you have your own ideas about tax relief, and some of them I find quite interesting. I really want to work with all of you. My test for our proposals will be: Will it create jobs and raise incomes; will it strengthen our families and support our children; is it paid for; will it build the middle class and shrink the under class? If it does, I'll support it. But if it doesn't, I won't.

The goal of building the middle class and shrinking the under class is also why I believe that you should raise the minimum wage. It rewards work. Two and a half million Americans, two and a half million Americans, often women with children, are working out there today for $4.25 an hour. In terms of real buying power, by next year that minimum wage will be at a 40-year low. That's not my idea of how the new economy ought to work.

Now, I've studied the arguments and the evidence for and against a minimum wage increase. I believe the weight of the evidence is that a modest increase does not cost jobs and may even lure people back into the job market. But the most important thing is, you can't make a living on $4.25 an hour, especially if you have children, even with the working families tax cut we passed last year. In the past, the minimum wage has been a bipartisan issue, and I think it should be again. So I want to challenge you to have honest hearings on this, to get together, to find a way to make the minimum wage a living wage.

Members of Congress have been here less than a month, but by the end of the week, 28 days into the new year, every Member of Congress will have earned as much in congressional salary as a minimum wage worker makes all year long.

Everybody else here, including the President, has something else that too many Americans do without, and that's health care. Now, last year we almost came to blows over health care, but we didn't do anything. And the cold, hard fact is that, since last year, since I was here, another 1.1 million Americans in working families have lost their health care. And the cold, hard fact is that many millions more, most of them farmers and small business people and self-employed people, have seen their premiums skyrocket, their copays and deductibles go up. There's a whole bunch of people in this country that in the statistics have health insurance but really what they've got is a piece of paper that says they won't lose their home if they get sick.

Now, I still believe our country has got to move toward providing health security for every American family. But I know that last year, as the evidence indicates, we bit off more than we could chew. So I'm asking you that we work together. Let's do it step by step. Let's do whatever we have to do to get something done. Let's at least pass meaningful insurance reform so that no American risks losing coverage for facing skyrocketing prices, that nobody loses their coverage because they face high prices or unavailable insurance when they change jobs or lose a job or a family member gets sick.

I want to work together with all of you who have an interest in this, with the Democrats who worked on it last time, with the Republican leaders like Senator Dole, who has a long-time commitment to health care reform and made some constructive proposals in this area last year. We ought to make sure that self-employed people in small businesses can buy insurance at more affordable rates through voluntary purchasing pools. We ought to help families provide long-term care for a sick parent or a disabled child. We can work to help workers who lose their jobs at least keep their health insurance coverage for a year while they look for work. And we can find a way—it may take some time, but we can find a way—to make sure that our children have health care.

You know, I think everybody in this room, without regard to party, can be proud of the fact that our country was rated as having the world's most productive economy for the first time in nearly a decade. But we can't be proud of the fact that we're the only wealthy country in the world that has a smaller percentage of the work force and their children with health insurance today than we did 10 years ago, the last time we were the most productive economy in the world. So let's work together on this. It is too important for politics as usual.

Much of what the American people are thinking about tonight is what we've already talked about. A lot of people think that the security concerns of America today are entirely internal to our borders. They relate to the security of our jobs and our homes and our incomes and our children, our streets, our health, and protecting those borders. Now that the cold war has passed, it's tempting to believe that all the security issues, with the possible exception of trade, reside here at home. But it's not so. Our security still depends upon our continued world leadership for peace and freedom and democracy. We still can't be strong at home unless we're strong abroad.

The financial crisis in Mexico is a case in point. I know it's not popular to say it tonight, but we have to act, not for the Mexican people but for the sake of the millions of Americans whose livelihoods are tied to Mexico's well-being. If we want to secure American jobs, preserve American exports, safeguard America's borders, then we must pass the stabilization program and help to put Mexico back on track.

Now let me repeat: It's not a loan. It's not foreign aid. It's not a bailout. We will be given a guarantee like cosigning a note, with good collateral that will cover our risks. This legislation is the right thing for America. That's why the bipartisan leadership has supported it. And I hope you in Congress will pass it quickly. It is in our interest, and we can explain it to the American people because we're going to do it in the right way.

You know, tonight, this is the first State of the Union Address ever delivered since the beginning of the cold war when not a single Russian missile is pointed at the children of America. And along with the Russians, we're on our way to destroying the missiles and the bombers that carry 9,000 nuclear warheads. We've come so far so fast in this post-cold-war world that it's easy to take the decline of the nuclear threat for granted. But it's still there, and we aren't finished yet.

This year I'll ask the Senate to approve START II to eliminate weapons that carry 5,000 more warheads. The United States will lead the charge to extend indefinitely the Nuclear Non-Proliferation Treaty, to enact a comprehensive nuclear test ban, and to eliminate chemical weapons. To stop and roll back North Korea's potentially deadly nuclear program, we'll continue to implement the agreement we have reached with that nation. It's smart. It's tough. It's a deal based on continuing inspection with safeguards for our allies and ourselves.

This year I'll submit to Congress comprehensive legislation to strengthen our hand in combating terrorists, whether they strike at home or abroad. As the cowards who bombed the World Trade Center found out, this country will hunt down terrorists and bring them to justice.

Just this week, another horrendous terrorist act in Israel killed 19 and injured scores more. On behalf of the American people and all of you, I send our deepest sympathy to the families of the victims. I know that in the face of such evil, it is hard for the people in the Middle East to go forward. But the terrorists represent the past, not the future. We must and we will pursue a comprehensive peace between Israel and all her neighbors in the Middle East.

Accordingly, last night I signed an Executive order that will block the assets in the United States of terrorist organizations that threaten to disrupt the peace process. It prohibits financial transactions with these groups. And tonight I call on all our allies and peace-loving nations throughout the world to join us with renewed fervor in a global effort to combat terrorism. We cannot permit the future to be marred by terror and fear and paralysis.

From the day I took the oath of office, I pledged that our Nation would maintain the best equipped, best trained, and best prepared military on Earth. We have, and they are. They have managed the dramatic downsizing of our forces after the cold war with remarkable skill and spirit. But to make sure our military is ready for action and to provide the pay and the quality of life the military and their families deserve, I'm asking the Congress to add $25 billion in defense spending over the next 6 years.

I have visited many bases at home and around the world since I became President. Tonight I repeat that request with renewed conviction. We ask a very great deal of our Armed Forces. Now that they are smaller in number, we ask more of them. They go out more often to more different places and stay longer. They are called to service in many, many ways. And we must give them and their families what the times demand and what they have earned.

Just think about what our troops have done in the last year, showing America at its best, helping to save hundreds of thousands of people in Rwanda, moving with lightning speed to head off another threat to Kuwait, giving freedom and democracy back to the people of Haiti. We have proudly supported peace and prosperity and freedom from South Africa to Northern Ireland, from Central and Eastern Europe to Asia, from Latin America to the Middle East. All these endeavors are good in those places, but they make our future more confident and more secure.

Well, my fellow Americans, that's my agenda for America's future: expanding opportunity, not bureaucracy; enhancing security at home and abroad; empowering our people to make the most of their own lives. It's ambitious and achievable, but it's not enough. We even need more than new ideas for changing the world or equipping Americans to compete in the new economy, more than a Government that's smaller, smarter, and wiser, more than all of the changes we can make in Government and in the private sector from the outside in.

Our fortunes and our posterity also depend upon our ability to answer some questions from within, from the values and voices that speak to our hearts as well as our heads; voices that tell us we have to do more to accept responsibility for ourselves and our families, for our communities, and yes, for our fellow citizens. We see our families and our communities all over this country coming apart, and we feel the common ground shifting from under us. The PTA, the town hall meeting, the ball park, it's hard for a lot of overworked parents to find the time and space for those things that strengthen the bonds of trust and cooperation. Too many of our children don't even have parents and grandparents who can give them those experiences that they need to build their own character and their sense of identity.

We all know that while we here in this Chamber can make a difference on those things, that the real differences will be made by our fellow citizens, where they work and where they live and that it will be made almost without regard to party. When I used to go to the softball park in Little Rock to watch my daughter's league and people would come up to me, fathers and mothers, and talk to me, I can honestly say I had no idea whether 90 percent of them were Republicans or Democrats. When I visited the relief centers after the floods in California, northern California, last week, a woman came up to me and did something that very few of you would do. She hugged me and said, "Mr. President, I'm a Republican, but I'm glad you're here." [Laughter]

Now, why? We can't wait for disasters to act the way we used to act every day, because as we move into this next century, everybody matters. We don't have a person to waste. And a lot of people are losing a lot of chances to do better. That means that we need a New Covenant for everybody.

For our corporate and business leaders, we're going to work here to keep bringing the deficit down, to expand markets, to support their success in every possible way. But they have an obligation when they're doing well to keep jobs in our communities and give their workers a fair share of the prosperity they generate.

For people in the entertainment industry in this country, we applaud your creativity and your worldwide success, and we support your freedom of expression. But you do have a responsibility to assess the impact of your work and to understand the damage that comes from the incessant, repetitive, mindless violence and irresponsible conduct that permeates our media all the time.

We've got to ask our community leaders and all kinds of organizations to help us stop our most serious social problem, the epidemic of teen pregnancies and births where there is no marriage. I have sent to Congress a plan to target schools all over this country with antipregnancy programs that work. But Government can only do so much. Tonight I call on parents and leaders all across this country to join together in a national campaign against teen pregnancy to make a difference. We can do this, and we must.

And I would like to say a special word to our religious leaders. You know, I'm proud of the fact the United States has more houses of worship per capita than any country in the world. These people who lead our houses of worship can ignite their congregations to carry their faith into action, can reach out to all of our children, to all of the people in distress, to those who have been savaged by the breakdown of all we hold dear. Because so much of what must be done must come from the inside out and our religious leaders and their congregations can make all the difference, they have a role in the New Covenant as well.

There must be more responsibility for all of our citizens. You know, it takes a lot of people to help all the kids in trouble stay off the streets and in school. It takes a lot of people to build the Habitat for Humanity houses that the Speaker celebrates on his lapel pin. It takes a lot of people to provide the people power for all of the civic organizations in this country that made our communities mean so much to most of us when we were kids. It takes every parent to teach the children the difference between right and wrong and to encourage them to learn and grow and to say no to the wrong things but also to believe that they can be whatever they want to be.

I know it's hard when you're working harder for less, when you're under great stress, to do these things. A lot of our people don't have the time or the emotional stress, they think, to do the work of citizenship.

Most of us in politics haven't helped very much. For years, we've mostly treated citizens like they were consumers or spectators, sort of political couch potatoes who were supposed to watch the TV ads either promise them something for nothing or play on their fears and frustrations. And more and more of our citizens now get most of their information in very negative and aggressive ways that are hardly conducive to honest and open conversations. But the truth is, we have got to stop seeing each other as enemies just because we have different views.

If you go back to the beginning of this country, the great strength of America, as de Tocqueville pointed out when he came here a long time ago, has always been our ability to associate with people who were different from ourselves and to work together to find common ground. And in this day, everybody has a responsibility to do more of that. We simply cannot wait for a tornado, a fire, or a flood to behave like Americans ought to behave in dealing with one another.

I want to finish up here by pointing out some folks that are up with the First Lady that represent what I'm trying to talk about—citizens. I have no idea what their party affiliation is or who they voted for in the last election. But they represent what we ought to be doing.

Cindy Perry teaches second graders to read in AmeriCorps in rural Kentucky. She gains when she gives. She's a mother of four. She says that her service inspired her to get her high school equivalency last year. She was married when she was a teenager—stand up, Cindy. She was married when she was a teenager. She had four children. But she had time to serve other people, to get her high school equivalency, and she's going to use her AmeriCorps money to go back to college.

Chief Stephen Bishop is the police chief of Kansas City. He's been a national leader—stand up, Steve. He's been a national leader in using more police in community policing, and he's worked with AmeriCorps to do it. And the crime rate in Kansas City has gone down as a result of what he did.

Corporal Gregory Depestre went to Haiti as part of his adopted country's force to help secure democracy in his native land. And I might add, we must be the only country in the world that could have gone to Haiti and taken Haitian-Americans there who could speak the language and talk to the people. And he was one of them, and we're proud of him.

The next two folks I've had the honor of meeting and getting to know a little bit, the Reverend John and the Reverend Diana Cherry of the A.M.E. Zion Church in Temple Hills, Maryland. I'd like to ask them to stand. I want to tell you about them. In the early eighties, they left Government service and formed a church in a small living room in a small house, in the early eighties. Today that church has 17,000 members. It is one of the three or four biggest churches in the entire United States. It grows by 200 a month. They do it together. And the special focus of their ministry is keeping families together.

Two things they did make a big impression on me. I visited their church once, and I learned they were building a new sanctuary closer to the Washington, D.C., line in a higher crime, higher drug rate area because they thought it was part of their ministry to change the lives of the people who needed them. The second thing I want to say is that once Reverend Cherry was at a meeting at the White House with some other religious leaders, and he left early to go back to this church to minister to 150 couples that he had brought back to his church from all over America to convince them to come back together, to save their marriages, and to raise their kids. This is the kind of work that citizens are doing in America. We need more of it, and it ought to be lifted up and supported.

The last person I want to introduce is Jack Lucas from Hattiesburg, Mississippi. Jack, would you stand up? Fifty years ago, in the sands of Iwo Jima, Jack Lucas taught and learned the lessons of citizenship. On February 20th, 1945, he and three of his buddies encountered the enemy and two grenades at their feet. Jack Lucas threw himself on both of them. In that moment, he saved the lives of his companions, and miraculously in the next instant, a medic saved his life. He gained a foothold for freedom, and at the age of 17, just a year older than his grandson who is up there with him today—and his son, who is a West Point graduate and a veteran—at 17, Jack Lucas became the youngest Marine in history and the youngest soldier in this century to win the Congressional Medal of Honor. All these years later, yesterday, here's what he said about that day: "It didn't matter where you were from or who you were, you relied on one another. You did it for your country."

We all gain when we give, and we reap what we sow. That's at the heart of this New Covenant. Responsibility, opportunity, and citizenship, more than stale chapters in some remote civic book, they're still the virtue by which we can fulfill ourselves and reach our God-given potential and be like them and also to fulfill the eternal promise of this country, the enduring dream from that first and most sacred covenant. I believe every person in this country still believes that we are created equal and given by our Creator the right to life, liberty and the pursuit of happiness. This is a very, very great country. And our best days are still to come.

Thank you, and God bless you all.

7. Address to the Nation on Implementation of the Peace Agreement in Bosnia-Herzegovina November 27, 1995

Public Papers of the Presidents of the United States: William J. Clinton, 1995. Vol. 2. Washington, D.C.: U.S. Government Printing Office, pages 1,784–1,787

Good evening. Last week, the warring factions in Bosnia reached a peace agreement as a result of our efforts in Dayton, Ohio, and the support of our European and Russian partners. Tonight I want to speak with you about implementing the Bosnian peace agreement and why our values and interests as Americans require that we participate.

Let me say at the outset, America's role will not be about fighting a war. It will be about helping the people of Bosnia to secure their own peace agreement. Our mission will be limited, focused, and under the command of an American general. In fulfilling this mission, we will have the chance to help stop the killing of innocent civilians, especially children, and at the same time, to bring stability to Central Europe, a region of the world that is vital to our national interests. It is the right thing to do.

From our birth, America has always been more than just a place. America has embodied an idea that has become the ideal for billions of people throughout the world. Our Founders said it best: America is about life, liberty, and the pursuit of happiness. In this century especially, America has done more than simply stand for these ideals. We have acted on them and sacrificed for them. Our people fought two World Wars so that freedom could triumph over tyranny. After World War I, we pulled back from the world, leaving a vacuum that was filled by the forces of hatred. After World War II, we continued to lead the world. We made the commitments that kept the peace, that helped to spread democracy, that created unparalleled prosperity, and that brought victory in the cold war.

Today, because of our dedication, America's ideals—liberty, democracy, and peace—are more and more the aspirations of people everywhere in the world. It is the power of our ideas, even more than our size, our wealth, and our military might, that makes America a uniquely trusted nation.

With the cold war over, some people now question the need for our continued active leadership in the world. They believe that, much like after World War I, America can now step back from the responsibilities of leadership. They argue that to be secure we need only to keep our own borders safe and that the time has come now to leave to others the hard work of leadership beyond our borders. I strongly disagree.

As the cold war gives way to the global village, our leadership is needed more than ever because problems that start beyond our borders can quickly become problems within them. We're all vulnerable to the organized forces of intolerance and destruction; terrorism; ethnic, religious, and regional rivalries; the spread of organized crime and weapons of mass destruction and drug trafficking. Just as surely as fascism and communism, these forces also threaten freedom and democracy, peace and prosperity. And they, too, demand American leadership.

But nowhere has the argument for our leadership been more clearly justified than in the struggle to stop or prevent war and civil violence. From Iraq to Haiti, from South Africa to Korea, from the Middle East to Northern Ireland, we have stood up for peace and freedom because it's in our interest to do so and because it is the right thing to do.

Now, that doesn't mean we can solve every problem. My duty as President is to match the demands for American leadership to our strategic interest and to our ability to make a difference. America cannot and must not be the world's policeman. We cannot stop all war for all time, but we can stop some wars. We cannot save all women and all children, but we can save many of them. We can't do everything, but we must do what we can.

There are times and places where our leadership can mean the difference between peace and war, and where we can defend our fundamental values as a people and serve our most basic, strategic interests. My fellow Americans, in this new era there are still times when America and America alone can and should make the difference for peace.

The terrible war in Bosnia is such a case. Nowhere today is the need for American leadership more stark or more immediate than in Bosnia. For nearly 4 years a terrible war has torn Bosnia apart. Horrors we prayed had been banished from Europe forever have been seared into our minds again: skeletal prisoners caged behind barbed-wire fences; women and girls raped as a tool of war; defenseless men and boys shot down into mass graves, evoking visions of World War II concentration camps; and endless lines of refugees marching toward a future of despair.

When I took office, some were urging immediate intervention in the conflict. I decided that American ground troops should not fight a war in Bosnia because the United States could not force peace on Bosnia's warring ethnic groups, the Serbs, Croats, and Muslims. Instead, America has worked with our European allies in searching for peace, stopping the war from spreading, and easing the suffering of the Bosnian people.

We imposed tough economic sanctions on Serbia. We used our airpower to conduct the longest humanitarian airlift in history and to enforce a no-fly zone that took the war out of the skies. We helped to make peace between two of the three warring parties, the Muslims and the Croats. But as the months of war turned into years, it became clear that Europe alone could not end the conflict.

This summer, Bosnian Serb shelling once again turned Bosnia's playgrounds and marketplaces into killing fields. In response, the United States led NATO's heavy and continuous air strikes, many of them flown by skilled and brave American pilots. Those air strikes, together with the renewed determination of our European partners and the Bosnian and Croat gains on the battlefield, convinced the Serbs, finally, to start thinking about making peace.

At the same time, the United States initiated an intensive diplomatic effort that forged a Bosnia-wide cease-fire and got the parties to agree to the basic principles of peace. Three dedicated American diplomats, Bob Frasure,

Joe Kruzel, and Nelson Drew, lost their lives in that effort. Tonight we remember their sacrifice and that of their families. And we will never forget their exceptional service to our Nation.

Finally, just 3 weeks ago, the Muslims, Croats, and Serbs came to Dayton, Ohio, in America's heartland, to negotiate a settlement. There, exhausted by war, they made a commitment to peace. They agreed to put down their guns, to preserve Bosnia as a single state, to investigate and prosecute war criminals, to protect the human rights of all citizens, to try to build a peaceful, democratic future. And they asked for America's help as they implement this peace agreement.

America has a responsibility to answer that request, to help to turn this moment of hope into an enduring reality. To do that, troops from our country and around the world would go into Bosnia to give them the confidence and support they need to implement their peace plan. I refuse to send American troops to fight a war in Bosnia, but I believe we must help to secure the Bosnian peace.

I want you to know tonight what is at stake, exactly what our troops will be asked to accomplish, and why we must carry out our responsibility to help implement the peace agreement. Implementing the agreement in Bosnia can end the terrible suffering of the people, the warfare, the mass executions, the ethnic cleansing, the campaigns of rape and terror. Let us never forget a quarter of a million men, women, and children have been shelled, shot, and tortured to death. Two million people, half of the population, were forced from their homes and into a miserable life as refugees. And these faceless numbers hide millions of real personal tragedies, for each of the war's victims was a mother or daughter, a father or son, a brother or sister.

Now the war is over. American leadership created the chance to build a peace and stop the suffering. Securing peace in Bosnia will also help to build a free and stable Europe. Bosnia lies at the very heart of Europe, next-door to many of its fragile new democracies and some of our closest allies. Generations of Americans have understood that Europe's freedom and Europe's stability is vital to our own national security. That's why we fought two wars in Europe. That's why we launched the Marshall plan to restore Europe. That's why we created NATO and waged the cold war. And that's why we must help the nations of Europe to end their worst nightmare since World War II, now.

The only force capable of getting this job done is NATO, the powerful military alliance of democracies that has guaranteed our security for half a century now. And as NATO's leader and the primary broker of the peace agreement, the United States must be an essential part of the mission. If we're not there, NATO will not be there; the peace will collapse; the war will reignite; the slaughter of innocents will begin again. A conflict that already has claimed so many victims could spread like poison throughout the region, eat away at Europe's stability, and erode our partnership with our European allies.

And America's commitment to leadership will be questioned if we refuse to participate in implementing a peace agreement we brokered right here in the United States, especially since the Presidents of Bosnia, Croatia, and Serbia all asked us to participate and all pledged their best efforts to the security of our troops.

When America's partnerships are weak and our leadership is in doubt, it undermines our ability to secure our interests and to convince others to work with us. If we do maintain our partnerships and our leadership, we need not act alone. As we saw in the Gulf war and in Haiti, many other nations who share our goals will also share our burdens. But when America does not lead, the consequences can be very grave, not only for others but eventually for us as well.

As I speak to you, NATO is completing its planning for IFOR, an international force for peace in Bosnia of about 60,000 troops. Already more than 25 other nations, including our major NATO allies, have pledged to take part. They will contribute about two-thirds of the total implementation force, some 40,000 troops. The United States would contribute the rest, about 20,000 soldiers.

Later this week, the final NATO plan will be submitted to me for review and approval. Let me make clear what I expect it to include and what it must include for me to give final approval to the participation of our Armed Forces.

First, the mission will be precisely defined with clear, realistic goals that can be achieved in a definite period of time. Our troops will make sure that each side withdraws its forces behind the frontlines and keeps them there. They will maintain the cease-fire to prevent the war from accidentally starting again. These efforts, in turn, will help to create a secure environment so that the people of Bosnia can return to their homes, vote in free elections, and begin to rebuild their lives. Our Joint Chiefs of Staff have concluded that this mission should and will take about one year.

Second, the risks to our troops will be minimized. American troops will take their orders from the American general who commands NATO. They will be heavily armed and thoroughly trained. By making an overwhelming show of force, they will lessen the need to use force. But unlike the U.N. forces, they will have the authority to respond immediately and the training and the equipment to respond with overwhelming force to any threat to their own safety or any violations of the military provisions of the peace agreement.

If the NATO plan meets with my approval, I will immediately send it to Congress and request its support. I will also authorize the participation of a small number of American troops in a NATO advance mission that will lay the groundwork for IFOR, starting sometime next week. They will establish headquarters and set up the sophisticated communication systems that must be in place before NATO can send in its troops, tanks, and trucks to Bosnia.

The Implementation Force itself would begin deploying in Bosnia in the days following the formal signature of the peace agreement in mid-December. The international community will help to implement arms control provisions of the agreement so that future hostilities are less likely and armaments are limited, while the world community, the United States and others, will also make sure that the Bosnian Federation has the means to defend itself once IFOR withdraws. IFOR will not be a part of this effort.

Civilian agencies from around the world will begin a separate program of humanitarian relief and reconstruction, principally paid for by our European allies and other interested countries. This effort is also absolutely essential to making the peace endure. It will bring the people of Bosnia the food, shelter, clothing, and medicine so many have been denied for so long. It will help them to rebuild, to rebuild their roads and schools, their power plants and hospitals, their factories and shops. It will reunite children with their parents and families with their homes. It will allow the Bosnians freely to choose their own leaders. It will give all the people of Bosnia a much greater stake in peace than war, so that peace takes on a life and a logic of its own.

In Bosnia we can and will succeed because our mission is clear and limited and our troops are strong and very well-prepared. But my fellow Americans, no deployment of American troops is risk-free, and this one may well involve casualties. There may be accidents in the field or incidents with people who have not given up their hatred. I will take every measure possible to minimize these risks, but we must be prepared for that possibility.

As President, my most difficult duty is to put the men and women who volunteer to serve our Nation in harm's way when our interests and values demand it. I assume full responsibility for any harm that may come to them. But anyone contemplating any action that would endanger our troops should know this: America protects its own. Anyone, anyone, who takes on our troops will suffer the consequences. We will fight fire with fire and then some.

After so much bloodshed and loss, after so many outrageous acts of inhuman brutality, it will take an extraordinary effort of will for the people of Bosnia to pull themselves from their past and start building a future of peace. But with our leadership and the commitment of our allies, the people of Bosnia can have the chance to decide their future in peace. They have a chance to remind the world that just a few short years ago the mosques and churches of Sarajevo were a shining symbol of multiethnic tolerance, that Bosnia once found unity in its diversity. Indeed, the cemetery in the center of the city was just a few short years ago a magnificent stadium which hosted the Olympics, our universal symbol of peace and harmony. Bosnia can be that kind of place again. We must not turn our backs on Bosnia now.

And so I ask all Americans and I ask every Member of Congress, Democrat and Republican alike, to make the choice for peace. In the choice between peace and war, America must choose peace.

My fellow Americans, I ask you to think just for a moment about this century that is drawing to close and the new one that will soon begin. Because previous generations of Americans stood up for freedom and because we continue to do so, the American people are more secure and more prosperous. And all around the world, more people than ever before live in freedom. More people than ever before are treated with dignity. More people

than ever before can hope to build a better life. That is what America's leadership is all about.

We know that these are the blessings of freedom. And America has always been freedom's greatest champion. If we continue to do everything we can to share these blessings with people around the world, if we continue to be leaders for peace, then the next century can be the greatest time our Nation has ever known.

A few weeks ago, I was privileged to spend some time with His Holiness Pope John Paul II, when he came to America. At the very end of our meeting, the Pope looked at me and said, "I have lived through most of this century. I remember that it began with a war in Sarajevo. Mr. President, you must not let it end with a war in Sarajevo."

In Bosnia, this terrible war has challenged our interests and troubled our souls. Thankfully, we can do something about it. I say again, our mission will be clear, limited, and achievable. The people of Bosnia, our NATO allies, and people all around the world are now looking to America for leadership. So let us lead. That is our responsibility as Americans.

Good night, and God bless America.

8. State of the Union Address January 23, 1996

Public Papers of the Presidents of the United States: William J. Clinton, 1994. Vol. 1. Washington, D.C.: U.S. Government Printing Office, pages 79–87

Thank you very much. Mr. Speaker, Mr. Vice President, Members of the 104th Congress, distinguished guests, my fellow Americans all across our land: Let me begin tonight by saying to our men and women in uniform around the world and especially those helping peace take root in Bosnia and to their families, I thank you. America is very, very proud of you.

My duty tonight is to report on the state of the Union, not the state of our Government but of our American community, and to set forth our responsibilities, in the words of our Founders, to form a more perfect Union.

The state of the Union is strong. Our economy is the healthiest it has been in three decades. We have the lowest combined rates of unemployment and inflation in 27 years. We have completed—created nearly 8 million new jobs, over a million of them in basic industries like construction and automobiles. America is selling more cars than Japan for the first time since the 1970's. And for 3 years in a row, we have had a record number of new businesses started in our country.

Our leadership in the world is also strong, bringing hope for new peace. And perhaps most important, we are gaining ground in restoring our fundamental values. The crime rate, the welfare and food stamp rolls, the poverty rate, and the teen pregnancy rate are all down. And as they go down, prospects for America's future go up.

We live in an age of possibility. A hundred years ago we moved from farm to factory. Now we move to an age of technology, information, and global competition. These changes have opened vast new opportunities for our people, but they have also presented them with stiff challenges. While more Americans are living better, too many of our fellow citizens are working harder just to keep up, and they are rightly concerned about the security of their families.

We must answer here three fundamental questions: First, how do we make the American dream of opportunity for all a reality for all Americans who are willing to work for it? Second, how do we preserve our old and enduring values as we move into the future? And third, how do we meet these challenges together, as one America?

We know big Government does not have all the answers. We know there's not a program for every problem. We know, and we have worked to give the American people a smaller, less bureaucratic Government in Washington. And we have to give the American people one that lives within its means. The era of big Government is over. But we cannot go back to the time when our citizens were left to fend for themselves.

Instead, we must go forward as one America, one nation working together to meet the challenges we face together. Self-reliance and teamwork are not opposing virtues; we must have both. I believe our new, smaller Government must work in an old-fashioned American way, together with all of our citizens through State and local governments, in the workplace, in religious, charitable, and civic associations. Our goal must be to enable all our people to make the most of their own lives, with stronger families, more educational opportunity, economic security, safer streets, a cleaner environment in a safer world.

To improve the state of our Union, we must ask more of ourselves, we must expect more of each other, and we must face our challenges together.

Here, in this place, our responsibility begins with balancing the budget in a way that is fair to all Americans. There is now broad bipartisan agreement that permanent deficit spending must come to an end. I compliment the Republican leadership and the membership for the energy and determination you have brought to this task of balancing the budget. And I thank the Democrats for passing the largest deficit reduction plan in history in 1993, which has already cut the deficit nearly in half in 3 years.

Since 1993, we have all begun to see the benefits of deficit reduction. Lower interest rates have made it easier for businesses to borrow and to invest and to create new jobs. Lower interest rates have brought down the cost of home mortgages, car payments, and credit card rates to ordinary citizens. Now it is time to finish the job and balance the budget.

Though differences remain among us which are significant, the combined total of the proposed savings that are common to both plans is more than enough, using the numbers from your Congressional Budget Office, to balance the budget in 7 years and to provide a modest tax cut.

These cuts are real. They will require sacrifice from everyone. But these cuts do not undermine our fundamental obligations to our parents, our children, and our future by endangering Medicare or Medicaid or education or the environment or by raising taxes on working families.

I have said before, and let me say again, many good ideas have come out of our negotiations. I have learned a lot about the way both Republicans and Democrats view the debate before us. I have learned a lot about the good ideas that each side has that we could all embrace.

We ought to resolve our remaining differences. I am willing to work to resolve them. I am ready to meet tomorrow. But I ask you to consider that we should at least enact these savings that both plans have in common and give the American people their balanced budget, a tax cut, lower interest rates, and a brighter future. We should do that now and make permanent deficits yesterday's legacy.

Now it is time for us to look also to the challenges of today and tomorrow, beyond the burdens of yesterday. The challenges are significant. But our Nation was built on challenges. America was built on challenges, not promises. And when we work together to meet them, we never fail. That is the key to a more perfect Union. Our individual dreams must be realized by our common efforts.

Tonight I want to speak to you about the challenges we all face as a people. Our first challenge is to cherish our children and strengthen America's families. Family is the foundation of American life. If we have stronger families, we will have a stronger America.

Before I go on, I'd like to take just a moment to thank my own family and to thank the person who has taught me more than anyone else over 25 years about the importance of families and children, a wonderful wife, a magnificent mother, and a great First Lady. Thank you, Hillary.

All strong families begin with taking more responsibility for our children. I've heard Mrs. Gore say that it's hard to be a parent today, but it's even harder to be a child. So all of us, not just as parents but all of us in our other roles—our media, our schools, our teachers, our communities, our churches and synagogues, our businesses, our governments—all of us have a responsibility to help our children to make it and to make the most of their lives and their God-given capacities.

To the media, I say you should create movies and CD's and television shows you'd want your own children and grandchildren to enjoy.

I call on Congress to pass the requirement for a V-chip in TV sets so that parents can screen out programs they believe are inappropriate for their children. When parents control what their young children see, that is not censorship; that is enabling parents to assume more personal responsibility for their children's upbringing. And I urge them to do it. The V-chip requirement is part of the important telecommunications bill now pending in this Congress. It has bipartisan support, and I urge you to pass it now.

To make the V-chip work, I challenge the broadcast industry to do what movies have done, to identify your program in ways that help parents to protect their children. And I invite the leaders of major media corporations in the entertainment industry to come to the White House next month to work with us in a positive way on concrete ways to improve what our children see on television. I am ready to work with you.

I say to those who make and market cigarettes, every year a million children take up smoking, even though it's against the law. Three hundred thousand of them will have their lives shortened as a result. Our administration has taken steps to stop the massive marketing campaigns that appeal to our children. We are simply saying: Market your products to adults, if you wish, but draw the line on children.

I say to those who are on welfare, and especially to those who have been trapped on welfare for a long time: For too long our welfare system has undermined the values of family and work instead of supporting them. The Congress and I are near agreement on sweeping welfare reform. We agree on time limits, tough work requirements, and the toughest possible child support enforcement. But I believe we must also provide child care so that mothers who are required to go to work can do so without worrying about what is happening to their children.

I challenge this Congress to send me a bipartisan welfare reform bill that will really move people from welfare to work and do the right thing by our children. I will sign it immediately.

Let us be candid about this difficult problem. Passing a law, even the best possible law, is only a first step. The next step is to make it work. I challenge people on welfare to make the most of this opportunity for independence. I challenge American businesses to give people on welfare the chance to move into the work force. I applaud the work of religious groups and others who care for the poor. More than anyone else in our society, they know the true difficulty of the task before us, and they are in a position to help. Every one of us should join them. That is the only way we can make real welfare reform a reality in the lives of the American people.

To strengthen the family we must do everything we can to keep the teen pregnancy rate going down. I am gratified, as I'm sure all Americans are, that it has dropped for 2 years in a row. But we all know it is still far too high. Tonight I am pleased to announce that a group of prominent Americans is responding to that challenge by forming an organization that will support grassroots community efforts all across our country in a national campaign against teen pregnancy. And I challenge all of us and every American to join their efforts.

I call on American men and women in families to give greater respect to one another. We must end the deadly scourge of domestic violence in our country. And I challenge America's families to work harder to stay together. For families who stay together not only do better economically, their children do better as well.

In particular, I challenge the fathers of this country to love and care for their children. If your family has separated, you must pay your child support. We're doing more than ever to make sure you do, and we're going to do more. But let's all admit something about that, too: A check will never substitute for a parent's love and guidance. And only you—only you can make the decision to help raise your children. No matter who you are, how low or high your station in life, it is the most basic human duty of every American to do that job to the best of his or her ability.

Our second challenge is to provide Americans with the educational opportunities we'll all need for this new century. In our schools, every classroom in America must be connected to the information superhighway, with computers and good software and well-trained teachers. We are working with the telecommunications industry, educators, and parents to connect 20 percent of California's classrooms by this spring, and every classroom and every library in the entire United States by the year 2000. I ask Congress to support this education technology initiative so that we can make sure this national partnership succeeds.

Every diploma ought to mean something. I challenge every community, every school, and every State to adopt national standards of excellence, to measure whether schools are meeting those standards, to cut bureaucratic red tape so that schools and teachers have more flexibility for grassroots reform, and to hold them accountable for results. That's what our Goals 2000 initiative is all about. I challenge every State to give all parents the right to choose which public school their children will attend and to let teachers form new schools with a charter they can keep only if they do a good job.

I challenge all our schools to teach character education, to teach good values and good citizenship. And if it means that teenagers will stop killing each other over designer jackets, then our public schools should be able to require their students to wear school uniforms.

I challenge our parents to become their children's first teachers. Turn off the TV. See that the homework is done. And visit your children's classroom. No program, no teacher, no one else can do that for you.

My fellow Americans, higher education is more important today than ever before. We've created a new student loan program that's made it easier to borrow and repay those loans, and we have dramatically cut the student loan default rate. That's something we should all be proud of because it was unconscionably high just a few years ago.

Through AmeriCorps, our national service program, this year 25,000 young people will earn college money by serving their local communities to improve the lives of their friends and neighbors.

These initiatives are right for America, and we should keep them going. And we should also work hard to open the doors of college even wider. I challenge Congress to expand work-study and help one million young Americans work their way through college by the year 2000, to provide a $1,000 merit scholarship for the top 5 percent of graduates in every

high school in the United States, to expand Pell grant scholarships for deserving and needy students, and to make up to $10,000 a year of college tuition tax deductible. It's a good idea for America.

Our third challenge is to help every American who is willing to work for it achieve economic security in this new age. People who work hard still need support to get ahead in the new economy. They need education and training for a lifetime. They need more support for families raising children. They need retirement security. They need access to health care. More and more Americans are finding that the education of their childhood simply doesn't last a lifetime.

So I challenge Congress to consolidate 70 overlapping, antiquated job training programs into a simple voucher worth $2,600 for unemployed or underemployed workers to use as they please for community college tuition or other training. This is a "GI bill" for America's workers we should all be able to agree on.

More and more Americans are working hard without a raise. Congress sets the minimum wage. Within a year, the minimum wage will fall to a 40-year low in purchasing power. Four dollars and 25 cents an hour is no longer a minimum wage, but millions of Americans and their children are trying to live on it. I challenge you to raise their minimum wage.

In 1993, Congress cut the taxes of 15 million hard-pressed working families to make sure that no parents who work full time would have to raise their children in poverty and to encourage people to move from welfare to work. This expanded earned-income tax credit is now worth about $1,800 a year to a family of four living on $20,000. The budget bill I vetoed would have reversed this achievement and raised taxes on nearly 8 million of these people. We should not do that. We should not do that.

But I also agree that the people who are helped under this initiative are not all those in our country who are working hard to do a good job raising their children and at work. I agree that we need a tax credit for working families with children. That's one of the things most of us in this Chamber, I hope, can agree on. I know it is strongly supported by the Republican majority. And it should be part of any final budget agreement.

I want to challenge every business that can possibly afford it to provide pensions for your employees. And I challenge Congress to pass a proposal recommended by the White House Conference on Small Business that would make it easier for small businesses and farmers to establish their own pension plans. That is something we should all agree on.

We should also protect existing pension plans. Two years ago, with bipartisan support that was almost unanimous on both sides of the aisle, we moved to protect the pensions of 8 million working people and to stabilize the pensions of 32 million more. Congress should not now let companies endanger those workers' pension funds. I know the proposal to liberalize the ability of employers to take money out of pension funds for other purposes would raise money for the Treasury, but I believe it is false economy. I vetoed that proposal last year, and I would have to do so again.

Finally, if our working families are going to succeed in the new economy, they must be able to buy health insurance policies that they do not lose when they change jobs or when someone in their family gets sick. Over the past 2 years, over one million Americans in working families have lost their health insurance. We have to do more to make health care available to every American. And Congress should start by passing the bipartisan bill sponsored by Senator Kennedy and Senator Kassebaum that would require insurance companies to stop dropping people when they switch jobs and stop denying coverage for preexisting conditions. Let's all do that.

And even as we enact savings in these programs, we must have a common commitment to preserve the basic protections of Medicare and Medicaid, not just to the poor but to people in working families, including children, people with disabilities, people with AIDS, senior citizens in nursing homes. In the past 3 years, we've saved $15 billion just by fighting health care fraud and abuse. We have all agreed to save much more. We have all agreed to stabilize the Medicare Trust Fund. But we must not abandon our fundamental obligations to the people who need Medicare and Medicaid. America cannot become stronger if they become weaker.

The "GI bill" for workers, tax relief for education and childrearing, pension availability and protection, access to health care, preservation of Medicare and Medicaid, these things, along with the Family and Medical Leave Act passed in 1993, these things will help responsible, hard-working American families to make the most of their own lives.

But employers and employees must do their part as well, as they are doing in so many of our finest companies, working together, putting the long-term prosperity ahead of the short-term gain. As workers increase their hours and their productivity, employers should make sure they get the skills they need and share the benefits of the good years as well as the burdens of the bad ones. When companies and workers work as a team they do better, and so does America.

Our fourth great challenge is to take our streets back from crime and gangs and drugs. At last we have begun to find a way to reduce crime, forming community partnerships with local police forces to catch criminals and prevent crime. This strategy, called community policing, is clearly working. Violent crime is coming down all across America. In New York City, murders are down 25 percent; in St. Louis, 18 percent; in Seattle, 32 percent. But we still have a long way to go before our streets are safe and our people are free from fear.

The crime bill of 1994 is critical to the success of community policing. It provides funds for 100,000 new police in communities of all sizes. We're already a third of the way there. And I challenge the Congress to finish the job. Let us stick with a strategy that's working and keep the crime rate coming down.

Community policing also requires bonds of trust between citizens and police. I ask all Americans to respect and support our law enforcement officers. And to our police, I say, our children need you as role models and heroes. Don't let them down.

The Brady bill has already stopped 44,000 people with criminal records from buying guns. The assault weapons ban is keeping 19 kinds of assault weapons out of the hands of violent gangs. I challenge the Congress to keep those laws on the books.

Our next step in the fight against crime is to take on gangs the way we once took on the mob. I'm directing the FBI and other investigative agencies to target gangs that involve juveniles in violent crime, and to seek authority to prosecute as adults teenagers who maim and kill like adults.

And I challenge local housing authorities and tenant associations: Criminal gang members and drug dealers are destroying the lives of decent tenants. From now on, the rule for residents who commit crime and peddle drugs should be "one strike and you're out."

I challenge every State to match Federal policy to assure that serious violent criminals serve at least 85 percent of their sentence.

More police and punishment are important, but they're not enough. We have got to keep more of our young people out of trouble, with prevention strategies not dictated by Washington but developed in communities. I challenge all of our communities, all of our adults, to give our children futures to say yes to. And I challenge Congress not to abandon the crime bill's support of these grassroots prevention efforts.

Finally, to reduce crime and violence we have to reduce the drug problem. The challenge begins in our homes, with parents talking to their children openly and firmly. It embraces our churches and synagogues, our youth groups and our schools. I challenge Congress not to cut our support for drug-free schools. People like the D.A.R.E. officers are making a real impression on grade-school children that will give them the strength to say no when the time comes.

Meanwhile, we continue our efforts to cut the flow of drugs into America. For the last 2 years, one man in particular has been on the front lines of that effort. Tonight I am nominating him, a hero of the Persian Gulf war and the commander in chief of the United States Military Southern Command, General Barry McCaffrey, as America's new drug czar. General McCaffrey has earned three Purple Hearts and two Silver Stars fighting for this country. Tonight I ask that he lead our Nation's battle against drugs at home and abroad. To succeed, he needs a force far larger than he has ever commanded before. He needs all of us. Every one of us has a role to play on this team.

Thank you, General McCaffrey, for agreeing to serve your country one more time.

Our fifth challenge: to leave our environment safe and clean for the next generation. Because of a generation of bipartisan effort we do have cleaner water and air, lead levels in children's blood has been cut by 70 percent, toxic emissions from factories cut in half. Lake Erie was dead, and now it's a thriving resource. But 10 million children under 12 still live within 4 miles of a toxic waste dump. A third of us breathe air that endangers our health. And in too many communities the water is not safe to drink. We still have much to do.

Yet Congress has voted to cut environmental enforcement by 25 percent. That means more toxic chemicals in our water, more smog in our air, more pesticides in our food. Lobbyists for polluters have been allowed to write their own loopholes into bills to weaken laws that protect the health and safety of our children. Some say that the taxpayer should pick up the tab for toxic waste and let polluters who can afford to fix it off the hook. I challenge Congress to reexamine those policies and to reverse them.

This issue has not been a partisan issue. The most significant environmental gains in the last 30 years were made under a Democratic Congress and President Richard Nixon. We can work together. We have to believe some basic things. Do you believe we can expand the economy without hurting the environment? I do. Do you believe we can create more jobs over the long run by cleaning the environment up? I know we can. That should be our commitment.

We must challenge businesses and communities to take more initiative in protecting the environment, and we have to make it easier for them to do it. To businesses this administration is saying, if you can find a cheaper, more efficient way than Government regulations require to meet tough pollution standards, do it, as long as you do it right. To communities we say, we must strengthen community right-to-know laws requiring polluters to disclose their emissions, but you have to use the information to work with business to cut pollution. People do have a right to know that their air and their water are safe.

Our sixth challenge is to maintain America's leadership in the fight for freedom and peace throughout the world. Because of American leadership, more people than ever before live free and at peace. And Americans have known 50 years of prosperity and security.

We owe thanks especially to our veterans of World War II. I would like to say to Senator Bob Dole and to all others in this Chamber who fought in World War II, and to all others on both sides of the aisle who have fought bravely in all our conflicts since: I salute your service, and so do the American people.

All over the world, even after the cold war, people still look to us and trust us to help them seek the blessings of peace and freedom. But as the cold war fades into memory, voices of isolation say America should retreat from its responsibilities. I say they are wrong.

The threats we face today as Americans respect no nation's borders. Think of them: terrorism, the spread of weapons of mass destruction, organized crime, drug trafficking, ethnic and religious hatred, aggression by rogue states, environmental degradation. If we fail to address these threats today, we will suffer the consequences in all our tomorrows.

Of course, we can't be everywhere. Of course, we can't do everything. But where our interests and our values are at stake, and where we can make a difference, America must lead. We must not be isolationist. We must not be the world's policeman. But we can and should be the world's very best peacemaker.

By keeping our military strong, by using diplomacy where we can and force where we must, by working with others to share the risk and the cost of our efforts, America is making a difference for people here and around the world. For the first time since the dawn of the nuclear age—for the first time since the dawn of the nuclear age—there is not a single Russian missile pointed at America's children.

North Korea has now frozen its dangerous nuclear weapons program. In Haiti, the dictators are gone, democracy has a new day, the flow of desperate refugees to our shores has subsided. Through tougher trade deals for America, over 80 of them, we have opened markets abroad, and now exports are at an all-time high, growing faster than imports and creating good American jobs.

We stood with those taking risks for peace: in Northern Ireland, where Catholic and Protestant children now tell their parents violence must never return; in the Middle East, where Arabs and Jews who once seemed destined to fight forever now share knowledge and resources and even dreams.

And we stood up for peace in Bosnia. Remember the skeletal prisoners, the mass graves, the campaign to rape and torture, the endless lines of refugees, the threat of a spreading war. All these threats, all these horrors have now begun to give way to the promise of peace. Now our troops and a strong NATO, together with our new partners from central Europe and elsewhere, are helping that peace to take hold.

As all of you know, I was just there with a bipartisan congressional group, and I was so proud not only of what our troops were doing but of the pride they evidenced in what they were doing. They knew what America's mission in this world is, and they were proud to be carrying it out.

Through these efforts, we have enhanced the security of the American people, but make no mistake about it: Important challenges remain.

The START II treaty with Russia will cut our nuclear stockpiles by another 25 percent. I urge the Senate to ratify it now. We must end the race to create new nuclear weapons by signing a truly comprehensive nuclear test ban treaty this year.

As we remember what happened in the Japanese subway, we can outlaw poison gas forever if the Senate ratifies the Chemical Weapons Convention this year. We can intensify the fight against terrorists and organized criminals at home and abroad if Congress passes the anti-terrorism legislation I proposed after the Oklahoma City bombing, now. We can help more people move from hatred to hope all across the world in our own interest if Congress gives us the means to remain the world's leader for peace.

My fellow Americans, the six challenges I have just discussed are for all of us. Our seventh challenge is really America's challenge to those of us in this hallowed Hall tonight: to reinvent our Government and make our democracy work for them.

Last year this Congress applied to itself the laws it applies to everyone else. This Congress banned gifts and meals from lobbyists. This Congress forced lobbyists to disclose who pays them and what legislation they are trying to pass or kill. This Congress did that, and I applaud you for it.

Now I challenge Congress to go further, to curb special interest influence in politics by passing the first truly bipartisan campaign finance reform bill in a generation. You, Republicans and Democrats alike, can show the American people that we can limit spending and we can open the airwaves to all candidates.

I also appeal to Congress to pass the line item veto you promised the American people.

Our administration is working hard to give the American people a Government that works better and costs less. Thanks to the work of Vice President Gore, we are eliminating 16,000 pages of unnecessary rules and regulations, shifting more decisionmaking out of Washington, back to States and local communities.

As we move into the era of balanced budgets and smaller Government, we must work in new ways to enable people to make the most of their own lives. We are helping America's communities, not with more bureaucracy but with more opportunities. Through our successful empowerment zones and community development banks, we're helping people to find jobs, to start businesses. And with tax incentives for companies that clean up abandoned industrial property, we can bring jobs back to places that desperately, desperately need them.

But there are some areas that the Federal Government should not leave and should address and address strongly. One of these areas is the problem of illegal immigration. After years of neglect, this administration has taken a strong stand to stiffen the protection of our borders. We are increasing border controls by 50 percent. We are increasing inspections to prevent the hiring of illegal immigrants. And tonight I announce I will sign an Executive order to deny Federal contracts to businesses that hire illegal immigrants.

Let me be very clear about this: We are still a nation of immigrants; we should be proud of it. We should honor every legal immigrant here, working hard to be a good citizen, working hard to become a new citizen. But we are also a nation of laws.

I want to say a special word now to those who work for our Federal Government. Today the Federal work force is 200,000 employees smaller than it was the day I took office as President. Our Federal Government today is the smallest it has been in 30 years, and it's getting smaller every day. Most of our fellow Americans probably don't know that. And there's a good reason—a good reason: The remaining Federal work force is composed of hard-working Americans who are now working harder and working smarter than ever before to make sure the quality of our services does not decline.

I'd like to give you one example. His name is Richard Dean. He's a 49-year-old Vietnam veteran who's worked for the Social Security Administration for 22 years now. Last year he was hard at work in the Federal Building in Oklahoma City when the blast killed 169 people and brought the rubble down all around him. He reentered that building four times. He saved the lives of three women. He's here with us this evening, and I want to recognize Richard and applaud both his public service and his extraordinary personal heroism. But Richard Dean's story doesn't end there. This last November, he was forced out of his office when the Government shut down. And the second time the Government shut down he continued helping Social Security recipients, but he was working without pay.

On behalf of Richard Dean and his family, and all the other people who are out there working every day doing a good job for the American people, I challenge all of you in this Chamber: Let's never, ever shut the Federal Government down again.

On behalf of all Americans, especially those who need their Social Security payments at the beginning of March, I also challenge the Congress to preserve the full faith and credit of the United States, to honor the obligations of this great Nation as we have for 220 years, to rise above partisanship and pass a straightforward extension of the debt limit and show people America keeps its word.

I know that this evening I have asked a lot of Congress and even more from America. But I am confident: When Americans work together in their homes, their schools, their churches, their synagogues, their civic groups, their workplace, they can meet any challenge.

I say again, the era of big Government is over. But we can't go back to the era of fending for yourself. We have to go forward to the era of working together as a community, as a team, as one America, with all of us reaching across these lines that divide us—the division, the discrimination, the rancor—we have to reach across it to find common ground. We have got to work together if we want America to work.

I want you to meet two more people tonight who do just that. Lucius Wright is a teacher in the Jackson, Mississippi, public school system. A Vietnam veteran, he has created groups to help inner-city children turn away from gangs and build futures they can believe in. Sergeant Jennifer Rodgers is a police officer in Oklahoma City. Like Richard Dean, she helped to pull her fellow citizens out of the rubble and deal with that awful tragedy. She reminds us that in their response to that atrocity the people of Oklahoma City lifted all of us with their basic sense of decency and community.

Lucius Wright and Jennifer Rodgers are special Americans. And I have the honor to announce tonight that they are the very first of several thousand Americans who will be chosen to carry the Olympic torch on its long journey from Los Angeles to the centennial of the modern Olympics in Atlanta this summer, not because they are star athletes but because they are star citizens, community heroes meeting America's challenges. They are our real champions. Please stand up. [Applause]

Now each of us must hold high the torch of citizenship in our own lives. None of us can finish the race alone. We can only achieve our destiny together, one hand, one generation, one American connecting to another.

There have always been things we could do together, dreams we could make real which we could never have done on our own. We Americans have forged our identity, our very Union, from the very point of view that we can accommodate every point on the planet, every different opinion. But we must be bound together by a faith more powerful than any doctrine that divides us, by our belief in progress, our love of liberty, and our relentless search for common ground.

America has always sought and always risen to every challenge. Who would say that having come so far together, we will not go forward from here? Who would say that this age of possibility is not for all Americans?

Our country is and always has been a great and good nation. But the best is yet to come if we all do our parts.

Thank you. God bless you, and God bless the United States of America. Thank you.

9. Remarks Accepting the Presidential Nomination at the Democratic National Convention in Chicago
August 29, 1996

Public Papers of the Presidents of the United States: William J. Clinton, 1996. Vol. 2. Washington, D.C.: U.S. Government Printing Office, pages 1,409–1,417.

The President. Thank you. Thank you very much. Mr. Chairman, Mr. Vice President, my fellow Democrats, and my fellow Americans, thank you for your nomination. I don't know if I can find a fancy way to say this, but I accept. [Applause] Thank you.

So many have contributed to the record we have made for the American people, but one above all, my partner, my friend, and the best Vice President in our history, Al Gore.

Tonight I thank the city of Chicago, its great mayor, and its wonderful people for this magnificent convention. I love Chicago for many reasons, for your powerful spirit, your sports teams, your lively politics, but most of all for the love and light of my life, Chicago's daughter, Hillary.

Four years ago, you and I set forth on a journey to bring our vision to our country, to keep the American dream alive for all who were willing to work for it, to make our American community stronger, to keep America the world's strongest force for peace and freedom and prosperity.

Four years ago, with high unemployment, stagnant wages, crime, welfare, and the deficit on the rise, with a host of unmet challenges and a rising tide of cynicism, I told you about a place I was born, and I told you that I still believed in a place called Hope.

Well, for 4 years now, to realize our vision we have pursued a simple but profound strategy: opportunity for all, responsibility from all, a strong united American community.

Four days ago, as you were making your way here, I began a train ride to make my way to Chicago through America's heartland. I wanted to see the faces, I wanted to hear the voices of the people for whom I have worked and fought these last 4 years. And did I ever see them.

I met an ingenious business woman who was once on welfare in West Virginia; a brave police officer, shot and paralyzed, now a civic leader in Kentucky; an autoworker in Ohio, once unemployed, now proud to be working in the oldest auto plant in America to help make

America number one in auto production again for the first time in 20 years. I met a grandmother fighting for her grandson's environment in Michigan. And I stood with two wonderful little children proudly reading from their favorite book, "The Little Engine That Could."

At every stop, large and exuberant crowds greeted me. And maybe more important, when we just rolled through little towns, there were always schoolchildren there waving their American flags, all of them believing in America and its future. I would not have missed that trip for all the world, for that trip showed me that hope is back in America. We are on the right track to the 21st century. [Applause] Thank you.

Look at the facts. Just look at the facts: 4.4 million Americans now living in a home of their own for the first time; hundreds of thousands of women have started their own new businesses; more minorities own businesses than ever before; record numbers of new small businesses and exports.

Look at what's happened. We have the lowest combined rates of unemployment, inflation, and home mortgages in 28 years. Look at what happened: 10 million new jobs, over half of them high-wage jobs; 10 million workers getting the raise they deserve with the minimum wage law; 25 million people now having protection in their health insurance because the Kennedy-Kassebaum bill says you can't lose your insurance anymore when you change jobs, even if somebody in your family has been sick; 40 million Americans with more pension security; a tax cut for 15 million of our hardest working, hardest pressed Americans, and all small businesses; 12 million Americans—12 million of them—taking advantage of the family and medical leave law so they can be good parents and good workers. Ten million students have saved money on their college loans. We are making our democracy work.

We have also passed political reform, the line item veto, the motor voter bill, tougher registration laws for lobbyists, making Congress live under the laws they impose on the private sector, stopping unfunded mandates to State and local government. We've come a long way; we've got one more thing to do. Will you help me get campaign finance reform in the next 4 years? [Applause] Thank you.

We have increased our investments in research and technology. We have increased investments in breast cancer research dramatically. We are developing a supercomputer—a supercomputer that will do more calculating in a second than a person with a hand-held calculator can do in 30,000 years. More rapid development of drugs to deal with HIV and AIDS and moving them to the market quicker have almost doubled life expectancy in only 4 years. And we are looking at no limit in sight to that. We'll keep going until normal life is returned to people who deal with this.

Our country is still the strongest force for peace and freedom on Earth. On issues that once before tore us apart, we have changed the old politics of Washington. For too long, leaders in Washington asked who's to blame. But we asked, what are we going to do?

On crime, we're putting 100,000 police on the streets. We made "three strikes and you're out" the law of the land. We stopped 60,000 felons, fugitives, and stalkers from getting handguns under the Brady bill. We banned assault rifles. We supported tougher punishment and prevention programs to keep our children from drugs and gangs and violence. Four years now—for four years now—the crime rate in America has gone down.

On welfare, we worked with States to launch a quiet revolution. Today there are 1.8 million fewer people on welfare than there were the day I took the oath of office. We are moving people from welfare to work.

We have increased child support collections by 40 percent. The Federal work force is the smallest it has been since John Kennedy. And the deficit has come down for 4 years in a row for the first time since before the Civil War, down 60 percent on the way to zero. We will do it.

We are on the right track to the 21st century. We are on the right track, but our work is not finished. What should we do? First, let us consider how to proceed. Again I say, the question is no longer who's to blame but what to do.

I believe that Bob Dole and Jack Kemp and Ross Perot love our country, and they have worked hard to serve it. It is legitimate, even necessary, to compare our record with theirs, our proposals for the future with theirs. And I expect them to make a vigorous effort to do the same. But I will not attack. I will not attack them personally or permit others to do it in this party if I can prevent it. [Applause] Thank you. My fellow Americans, this must be—this must be—a campaign of ideas, not a campaign of insults. The American people deserve it.

Now, here's the main idea. I love and revere the rich and proud history of America, and I am determined to take our best traditions into the future. But with all respect, we do not need to build a bridge to the past; we need to build a bridge to the future. And that is what I commit to you to do.

So tonight, tonight let us resolve to build that bridge to the 21st century, to meet our challenges and protect our values. Let us build a bridge to help our parents raise their children, to help young people and adults to get the education and training they need, to make our streets safer, to help Americans succeed at home and at work, to break the cycle of poverty and dependence, to protect our environment for generations to come, and to maintain our world leadership for peace and freedom. Let us resolve to build that bridge.

Tonight, my fellow Americans, I ask all of our fellow citizens to join me and to join you in building that bridge to the 21st century. Four years from now, just 4 years from now—think of it—we begin a new century, full of enormous possibilities. We have to give the American people the tools they need to make the most of their God-given potential. We must make the basic bargain of opportunity and responsibility available to all Americans, not just a few. That is the promise of the Democratic Party. That is the promise of America.

I want to build a bridge to the 21st century in which we expand opportunity through education, where computers are as much a part of the classroom as blackboards, where highly trained teachers demand peak performance from our students, where every 8-year-old can point to a book and say, "I can read it myself."

By the year 2000, the single most critical thing we can do is to give every single American who wants it the chance to go to college. We must make 2 years of college just as universal in 4 years as a high school education is today. And we can do it. We can do it, and we should cut taxes to do it.

I propose a $1,500-a-year tuition tax credit for Americans, a HOPE scholarship for the first 2 years of college to make the typical community college education available to every American. I believe every working family ought also to be able to deduct up to $10,000 in college tuition costs per year for education after that. I believe the families of this country ought to be able to save money for college in a tax-free IRA, save it year-in and year-out, withdraw it for college education without penalty. We should not tax middle income Americans for the money they spend on college. We'll get the money back down the road many times over.

I want to say here, before I go further, that these tax cuts and every other one I mention tonight are all fully paid for in my balanced budget plan, line by line, dime by dime, and they focus on education.

Now, one thing so many of our fellow Americans are learning is that education no longer stops on graduation day. I have proposed a new "GI bill" for American workers, a

$2,600 grant for unemployed and underemployed Americans so that they can get the training and the skills they need to go back to work at better paying jobs, good high-skilled jobs for a good future.

But we must demand excellence at every level of education. We must insist that our students learn the old basics we learned and the new basics they have to know for the next century. Tonight let us set a clear national goal: All children should be able to read on their own by the third grade. When 40 percent of our 8-year-olds cannot read as well as they should, we have to do something. I want to send 30,000 reading specialists and national service corps members to mobilize a volunteer army of one million reading tutors for third graders all across America. They will teach our young children to read.

Let me say to our parents: You have to lead the way. Every tired night you spend reading a book to your child will be worth it many times over. I know that Hillary and I still talk about the books we read to Chelsea when we were so tired we could hardly stay awake. We still remember them, and more important, so does she. But we're going to help the parents of this country make every child able to read for himself or herself by the age of 8, by the third grade. Do you believe we can do that? Will you help us do that? [Applause] Thank you.

We must give parents, all parents, the right to choose which public school their children will attend and to let teachers form new charter schools with a charter they can keep only if they do a good job. We must keep our schools open late so that young people have someplace to go and something to say yes to and stay off the street.

We must require that our students pass tough tests to keep moving up in school. A diploma has to mean something when they get out. We should reward teachers that are doing a good job, remove those who don't measure

up, but in every case, never forget that none of us would be here tonight if it weren't for our teachers. I know I wouldn't. We ought to lift them up, not tear them down.

We need schools that will take our children into the next century. We need schools that are rebuilt and modernized with an unprecedented commitment from the National Government to increase school construction and with every single library and classroom in America connected to the information superhighway by the year 2000.

Now, folks, if we do these things, every 8-year-old will be able to read, every 12-year-old will be able to log in on the Internet, every 18-year-old will be able to go to college, and all Americans will have the knowledge they need to cross that bridge to the 21st century.

I want to build a bridge to the 21st century in which we create a strong and growing economy to preserve the legacy of opportunity for the next generation, by balancing our budget in a way that protects our values and ensuring that every family will be able to own and protect the value of their most important asset, their home.

Tonight let us proclaim to the American people, we will balance the budget. And let us also proclaim, we will do it in a way that preserves Medicare, Medicaid, education, the environment, the integrity of our pensions, the strength of our people.

Now, last year when the Republican Congress sent me a budget that violated those values and principles, I vetoed it. And I would do it again tomorrow. I could never allow cuts that devastate education for our children, that pollute our environment, that end the guarantee of health care for those who are served under Medicaid, that end our duty or violate our duty to our parents through Medicare. I just couldn't do that. As long as I'm President, I'll never let it happen. And it doesn't matter if they try again, as they did before, to use the blackmail threat of a shutdown of the Federal Government to force these things on the American people. We didn't let it happen before. We won't let it happen again.

Of course, there is a better answer to this dilemma. We could have the right kind of balanced budget with a new Congress, a Democratic Congress.

I want to balance the budget with real cuts in Government, in waste. I want a plan that invests in education, as mine does, in technology, and yes, in research, as Christopher Reeve so powerfully reminded us we must do.

And my plan gives Americans tax cuts that will help our economy to grow. I want to expand IRA's so that young people can save tax-free to buy a first home. Tonight I propose a new tax cut for homeownership that says to every middle income working family in this country, if you sell your home, you will not have to pay a capital gains tax on it ever, not ever. I want every American to be able to hear those beautiful words, "Welcome home."

Let me say again, every tax cut I call for tonight is targeted, it's responsible, and it is paid for within my balanced budget plan. My tax cuts will not undermine our economy, they will speed economic growth.

We should cut taxes for the family sending a child to college, for the worker returning to college, for the family saving to buy a home or for long-term health care, and a $500-per-child credit for middle income families raising their children who need help with child care and what the children will do after school. That is the right way to cut taxes: pro-family, pro-education, pro-economic growth.

Now, our opponents have put forward a very different plan, a risky $550 billion tax scheme that will force them to ask for even bigger cuts in Medicare, Medicaid, education, and the environment than they passed and I vetoed last year. But even then they will not cover the costs of their scheme, so that even then this plan will explode the deficit, which will increase interest rates by 2 percent, according to their own estimates last year. It will require huge cuts in the very investments we need to grow and to grow together and, at the same time, slow down the economy.

You know what higher interest rates mean? To you it means a higher mortgage payment, a higher car payment, a higher credit card payment. To our economy it means business people will not borrow as much money, invest as much money, create as many new jobs, create as much wealth, raise as many wages. Do we really want to make that same mistake all over again?

Audience members. No-o-o!

The President. Do we really want to stop economic growth again?

Audience members. No-o-o!

The President. Do we really want to start piling up another mountain of debt?

Audience members. No-o-o!

The President. Do we want to bring back the recession of 1991 and '92?

Audience members. No-o-o!

The President. Do we want to weaken our bridge to the 21st century?

Audience members. No-o-o!

The President. Of course we don't. We have an obligation, you and I, to leave our children a legacy of opportunity, not a legacy of debt. Our budget would be balanced today, we would have a surplus today, if we didn't have to make the interest payments on the debt run up in the 12 years before the Clinton/Gore administration took office.

Audience members. Four more years! Four more years! Four more years!

The President. So let me say, this is one of those areas in which I respectfully disagree with my opponent. I don't believe we should bet the farm, and I certainly don't believe we should bet the country. We should stay on the right track to the 21st century.

Opportunity alone is not enough. I want to build an America in the 21st century in which all Americans take personal responsibility for themselves, their families, their communities, and their country. I want our Nation to take responsibility to make sure that every single child can look out the window in the morning and see a whole community getting up and going to work.

We want these young people to know the thrill of the first paycheck, the challenge of starting that first business, the pride in following in a parent's footsteps. The welfare reform law I signed last week gives America a chance, but not a guarantee, to have that kind of new beginning, to have a new social bargain with the poor, guaranteeing health care, child care, and nutrition for the children but requiring able-bodied parents to work for the income.

Now, I say to all of you, whether you supported the law or opposed it, but especially to those who supported it, we have a responsibility, we have a moral obligation to make sure the people who are being required to work have the opportunity to work. We must make sure the jobs are there. There should be one million new jobs for welfare recipients by the year 2000. States under this law can now take the money that was spent on the welfare check and use it to help businesses provide paychecks. I challenge every State to do it soon.

I propose also to give businesses a tax credit for every person hired off welfare and kept employed. I propose to offer private job placement firms a bonus for every welfare recipient they place in a job who stays in it. And more important, I want to help communities put welfare recipients to work right now, without delay, repairing schools, making their neighborhoods clean and safe, making them shine again. There's lots of work to be done out there. Our cities can find ways to put people to work and bring dignity and strength back to these families.

My fellow Americans, I have spent an enormous amount of time with our dear friend, the late Ron Brown, and with Secretary Kantor and others, opening markets for America around the world. And I'm proud of every one we opened. But let us never forget, the greatest untapped market for American enterprise is right here in America, in the inner cities, in the rural areas, who have not felt this recovery. With investment and business and jobs, they can become our partners in the future. And it's a great opportunity we ought not to pass up.

I propose more empowerment zones like the one we have right here in Chicago to draw business into poor neighborhoods. I propose more community development banks, like the South Shore Bank right here in Chicago, to help people in those neighborhoods start their own small businesses. More jobs, more incomes, new markets for America right here at home making welfare reform a reality. [Applause]

Now, folks, you cheered—and I thank you—but the Government can only do so much. The private sector has to provide most of these jobs. So I want to say again, tonight I challenge every business person in America who has ever complained about the failure of the welfare system to try to hire somebody off welfare and try hard. [Applause] Thank you. After all, the welfare system you used to complain about is not here anymore. There is no more "who's to blame" on welfare. Now the only question is what to do. And we all have a responsibility, especially those who have criticized what was passed and who have asked for a change and who have the ability to give poor people a chance to grow and support their families. I want to build a bridge to the 21st century that ends the permanent under class, that lifts up the poor and ends their isolation, their exile. And they're not forgotten anymore. [Applause] Thank you.

Audience members. Four more years! Four more years! Four more years!

The President. I want to build a bridge to the 21st century where our children are not killing other children anymore, where children's lives are not shattered by violence at home or in the schoolyard, where a generation of young people are not left to raise themselves on the streets.

With more police and punishment and prevention, the crime rate has dropped for 4 years in a row now. But we cannot rest, because we know it's still too high. We cannot rest until crime is a shocking exception to our daily lives, not news as usual. Will you stay with me until we reach that good day? [Applause]

My fellow Americans, we all owe a great debt to Sarah and Jim Brady, and I'm glad they took their wrong turn and wound up in Chicago. I was glad to see that. It is to them we owe the good news that 60,000 felons, fugitives, and stalkers couldn't get handguns because of the Brady bill. But not a single hunter in Arkansas or New Hampshire or Illinois or anyplace else missed a hunting season.

But now I say we should extend the Brady bill, because anyone who has committed an act of domestic violence against a spouse or a child should not buy a gun. And we must ban those cop-killer bullets. They are designed for one reason only, to kill police officers. We asked the police to keep us safe. We owe it to them to help keep them safe while they do their job for us.

We should pass a victims' rights constitutional amendment because victims deserve to be heard; they need to know when an assailant is released. They need to know these things, and the only way to guarantee them is through a constitutional amendment.

We have made a great deal of progress. Even the crime rate among young people is finally coming down. So it is very, very painful to me that drug use among young people is up. Drugs nearly killed my brother when he was a young man, and I hate them. He fought back. He's here tonight with his wife, his little boy is here,

and I'm really proud of him. But I learned something—I learned something in going through that long nightmare with our family. And I can tell you, something has happened to some of our young people; they simply don't think these drugs are dangerous anymore, or they think the risk is acceptable. So beginning with our parents, and without regard to our party, we have to renew our energy to teach this generation of young people the hard, cold truth: Drugs are deadly; drugs are wrong; drugs can cost you your life.

General Barry McCaffrey, the four-star general who led our fight against drugs in Latin America, now leads our crusade against drugs at home: stopping more drugs at our borders, cracking down on those who sell them, and most important of all, pursuing a national antidrug strategy whose primary aim is to turn our children away from drugs. I call on Congress to give him every cent of funding we have requested for this strategy and to do it now.

There is more we will do. We should say to parolees: We will test you for drugs; if you go back on them, we will send you back to jail. We will say to gangs: We will break you with the same antiracketeering law we used to put mob bosses in jail. You're not going to kill our kids anymore or turn them into murderers before they're teenagers. My fellow Americans, if we're going to build that bridge to the 21st century we have to make our children free, free of the vise grip of guns and gangs and drugs, free to build lives of hope.

I want to build a bridge to the 21st century with a strong American community, beginning with strong families, an America where all children are cherished and protected from destructive forces, where parents can succeed at home and at work. Everywhere I've gone in America, people come up and talk to me about their struggle with the demands of work and their desire to do a better job with their children. The very first person I ever saw fight that battle was here with me 4 years ago, and tonight I miss her very, very much. My irrepressible, hard-working, always optimistic mother did the best she could for her brother and me, often against very stiff odds. I learned from her just how much love and determination can overcome. But from her and from our life, I also learned that no parent can do it alone. And no parent should have to. She had the kind of help every parent deserves, from our neighbors, our friends, our teachers, our pastors, our doctors, and so many more.

You know, when I started out in public life with a lot of my friends from the Arkansas delegation down here, there used to be a saying from time to time that every man who runs for public office will claim that he was born in a log cabin he built with his own hands. [Laughter] Well, my mother knew better. And she made sure I did, too. Long before she even met Hillary, my mother knew it takes a village, and she was grateful for the support she got.

As Tipper Gore and Hillary said on Tuesday, we have, all of us in our administration, worked hard to support families in raising their children and succeeding at work. But we must do more. We should extend the family and medical leave law to give parents some time off to take their children to regular doctor's appointments or attend those parent-teacher conferences at school. That is a key determination of their success. We should pass a flex-time law that allows employees to take their overtime pay in money or in time off, depending on what's better for their family.

The FDA has adopted new measures to reduce advertising and sales of cigarettes to children. The Vice President spoke so movingly of it last night. But let me remind you, my fellow Americans, that is very much an issue in this election because that battle is far from over and the two candidates have different views. I pledge to America's parents that I will see this effort all the way through.

Working with the entertainment industry, we're giving parents the V-chip. TV shows are being rated for content so parents will be able to make a judgment about whether their small children should see them. And 3 hours of quality children's programming every week, on every network, are on the way.

The Kennedy-Kassebaum law says every American can keep his or her health insurance if they have to change jobs, even if someone in their family has been sick. That is a very important thing. But tonight we should spell out the next steps. The first thing we ought to do is to extend the benefits of health care to people who are unemployed. I propose in my balanced budget plan, paid for, to help unemployed families keep their health insurance for up to 6 months. A parent may be without a job, but no child should be without a doctor. And let me say again, as the First Lady did on Tuesday, we should protect mothers and newborn babies from being forced out of the hospital in less than 48 hours.

We respect the individual conscience of every American on the painful issue of abortion but believe as a matter of law that this decision should be left to a woman, her conscience, her doctor, and her God. But abortion should not only be safe and legal, it should be rare. That's why I helped to establish and support a national effort to reduce out-of-wedlock teen pregnancy, and that is why we must promote adoption.

Last week the minimum wage bill I signed contained a $5,000 credit to families who adopt children, even more if the children have disabilities. It put an end to racial discrimination in the adoption process. It was a good thing for America. My fellow Americans, already there are tens of thousands of children out there who need a good home with loving parents. I hope more of them will find it now.

I want to build a bridge to the 21st century with a clean and safe environment. We are making our food safer from pesticides. We're protecting our drinking water and our air from poisons. We saved Yellowstone from mining. We established the largest national park south of Alaska in the Mojave Desert in California. We are working to save the precious Florida Everglades. And when the leaders of this Congress invited the polluters into the back room to roll back 25 years of environmental protections that both parties had always supported, I said no.

But we must do more. Today, 10 million children live within just 4 miles of a toxic waste dump. We have cleaned up 197 of those dumps in the last 3 years, more than in the previous 12 years combined. In the next 4 years, we propose to clean up 500 more, two-thirds of all that are left and the most dangerous ones. Our children should grow up next to parks, not poison.

We should make it a crime even to attempt to pollute. We should freeze the serious polluter's property until they clean up the problems they create. We should make it easier for families to find out about toxic chemicals in their neighborhoods so they can do more to protect their own children. These are the things that we must do to build that bridge to the 21st century.

My fellow Americans, I want to build a bridge to the 21st century that makes sure we are still the nation with the world's strongest defense, that our foreign policy still advances the values of our American community in the community of nations. Our bridge to the future must include bridges to other nations, because we remain the world's indispensable nation to advance prosperity, peace, and freedom and to keep our own children safe from the dangers of terror and weapons of mass destruction.

We have helped to bring democracy to Haiti and peace to Bosnia. Now the peace signed on the White House lawn between the Israelis and the Palestinians must embrace more of Israel's neighbors. The deep desire for peace that Hillary and I felt when we walked the streets of Belfast and Derry must become real for all the people of Northern Ireland. And Cuba must finally join the community of democracies.

Nothing in our lifetime has been more heartening than when people of the former Soviet Union and Central Europe broke the grip of communism. We have aided their progress, and I am proud of it. And I will continue our strong partnership with a democratic Russia. And we will bring some of Central Europe's new democracies into NATO so that they will never question their own freedom in the future.

Our American exports are at record levels. In the next 4 years, we have to break down even more barriers to them, reaching out to Latin America, to Africa, to other countries in Asia, making sure that our workers and our products, the world's finest, have the benefit of free and fair trade.

In the last 4 years, we have frozen North Korea's nuclear weapons program. And I am proud to say that tonight there is not a single Russian nuclear missile pointed at an American child. Now we must enforce and ratify without delay measures that further reduce nuclear arsenals, banish poison gas, and ban nuclear tests once and for all.

We have made investments, new investments, in our most important defense asset, our magnificent men and women in uniform. By the year 2000, we also will have increased funding to modernize our weapons systems by 40 percent. These commitments will make sure that our military remains the best trained, best equipped fighting force in the entire world. We are developing a sensible national missile defense, but we must not, not now, not by the year 2000, squander $60 billion on an unproved, ineffective Star Wars program that could be obsolete tomorrow.

We are fighting terrorism on all fronts with a three-pronged strategy. First, we are working to rally a world coalition with zero tolerance for terrorism. Just this month, I signed a law imposing harsh sanctions on foreign companies that invest in key sectors of the Iranian and Libyan economies. As long as Iran trains, supports, and protects terrorists, as long as Libya refuses to give up the people who blew up Pan Am 103, they will pay a price from the United States.

Second, we must give law enforcement the tools they need to take the fight to terrorists. We need new laws to crack down on money laundering and to prosecute and punish those who commit violent acts against American citizens abroad, to add chemical markers or taggants to gunpowder used in bombs so we can crack the bombmakers, to extend the same power police now have against organized crime to save lives by tapping all the phones that terrorists use. Terrorists are as big a threat to our future, perhaps bigger, than organized crime. Why should we have two different standards for a common threat to the safety of America and our children? We need, in short, the laws that Congress refused to pass. And I ask them again, please, as an American, not a partisan matter, pass these laws now.

Third, we will improve airport and air travel security. I have asked the Vice President to establish a commission and report back to me on ways to do this. But now we will install the most sophisticated bomb-detection equipment in all our major airports. We will search every airplane flying to or from America from another nation, every flight, every cargo hold, every cabin, every time.

My fellow Democrats and my fellow Americans, I know that in most election seasons foreign policy is not a matter of great interest in the debates in the barbershops and the cafes of America, on the plant floors and at the bowling alleys. But there are times, there are times when only America can make the difference between war and peace, between freedom and repression, between life and death. We cannot save all the world's children, but we can save many of them. We cannot become the world's policeman, but where our values and our interests are at stake and where we can make a difference, we must act and we must lead. That is our job, and we are better, stronger, and safer because we are doing it.

My fellow Americans, let me say one last time, we can only build our bridge to the 21st century if we build it together and if we're willing to walk arm in arm across that bridge together. I have spent so much of your time that you gave me these last 4 years to be your President worrying about the problems of Bosnia, the Middle East, Northern Ireland, Rwanda, Burundi. What do these places have in common? People are killing each other and butchering children because they are different from one another. They share the same piece of land, but they are different from one another. They hate their race, their tribe, their ethnic group, their religion.

We have seen the terrible, terrible price that people pay when they insist on fighting and killing their neighbors over their differences. In our own country, we have seen America pay a terrible price for any form of discrimination. And we have seen us grow stronger as we have steadily let more and more of our hatreds and our fears go, as we have given more and more of our people the chance to live their dreams.

That is why the flame of our Statue of Liberty, like the Olympic flame carried all across America by thousands of citizen heroes, will always, always burn brighter than the fires that burn our churches, our synagogues, our mosques—always.

Look around this hall tonight—and to our fellow Americans watching on television, you look around this hall tonight—there is every conceivable difference here among the people who are gathered. If we want to build that bridge to the 21st century we have to be willing to say loud and clear: If you believe in the values of the

Constitution, the Bill of Rights, the Declaration of Independence, if you're willing to work hard and play by the rules, you are part of our family and we're proud to be with you. [Applause] You cheer now, because you know this is true. You know this is true. When you walk out of this hall, think about it. Live by it.

We still have too many Americans who give in to their fears of those who are different from them. Not so long ago, swastikas were painted on the doors of some African-American members of our Special Forces at Fort Bragg. Folks, for those of you who don't know what they do, the Special Forces are just what the name says: they are special forces. If I walk off this stage tonight and call them on the telephone and tell them to go halfway around the world and risk their lives for you and be there by tomorrow at noon, they will do it. They do not deserve to have swastikas on their doors.

So look around here, look around here: Old or young, healthy as a horse or a person with a disability that hasn't kept you down, man or woman, Native American, native born, immigrant, straight or gay, whatever, the test ought to be, I believe in the Constitution, the Bill of Rights, and the Declaration of Independence; I believe in religious liberty; I believe in freedom of speech; I believe in working hard and playing by the rules; I'm showing up for work tomorrow; I'm building that bridge to the 21st century. That ought to be the test.

My fellow Americans, 68 nights from tonight the American people will face once again a critical moment of decision. We're going to choose the last President of the 20th century and the first President of the 21st century. But the real choice is not that. The real choice is whether we will build a bridge to the future or a bridge to the past, about whether we believe our best days are still out there or our best days are behind us, about whether we want a country of people all working together or one where you're on your own.

Let us commit ourselves this night to rise up and build the bridge we know we ought to build all the way to the 21st century. Let us have faith, American faith that we are not leaving our greatness behind. We're going to carry it right on with us into that new century, a century of new challenge and unlimited promise. Let us, in short, do the work that is before us, so that when our time here is over, we will all watch the sun go down, as we all must, and say truly, we have prepared our children for the dawn.

My fellow Americans, after these 4 good, hard years, I still believe in a place called Hope, a place called America.

Thank you, God bless you, and good night.

Note: The President spoke at 9 P.M. at United Center. In his remarks, he referred to actor Christopher Reeve, who was paralyzed in an equestrian accident; and Sarah Brady, head of Hand Gun Control, Inc., wife of former White House press secretary James S. Brady, who was wounded in the 1981 assassination attempt on President Ronald Reagan.

10. Second Inaugural Address January 20, 1997

From: The White House, Office of the Press Secretary

My fellow citizens: At this last presidential inauguration of the 20th century, let us lift our eyes toward the challenges that await us in the next century. It is our great good fortune that time and chance have put us not only at the edge of a new century, in a new millennium, but on the edge of a bright new prospect in human affairs—a moment that will define our course, and our character, for decades to come.

We must keep our old democracy forever young. Guided by the ancient vision of a promised land, let us set our sights upon a land of new promise.

The promise of America was born in the 18th century out of the bold conviction that we are all created equal. It was extended and preserved in the 19th century, when our nation spread across the continent, saved the union, and abolished the awful scourge of slavery.

Then, in turmoil and triumph, that promise exploded onto the world stage to make this the American Century.

And what a century it has been. America became the world's mightiest industrial power; saved the world from tyranny in two world wars and a long cold war; and time and again, reached out across the globe to millions who, like us, longed for the blessings of liberty.

Along the way, Americans produced a great middle class and security in old age; built unrivaled centers of learning and opened public schools to all; split the atom and explored the heavens; invented the computer and the microchip; and deepened the wellspring of justice by making a revolution in civil rights for African Americans and all minorities, and extending the circle of citizenship, opportunity and dignity to women.

Now, for the third time, a new century is upon us, and another time to choose. We began the 19th century with a choice, to spread our nation from coast to coast. We began the 20th century with a choice, to harness the Industrial Revolution to our values of free enterprise, conservation, and human decency. Those choices made all the difference. At the dawn of the 21st century a free people must now choose to shape the forces of the Information Age and the global society, to unleash the limitless potential of all our people, and, yes, to form a more perfect union.

When last we gathered, our march to this new future seemed less certain than it does today. We vowed then to set a clear course to renew our nation.

In these four years, we have been touched by tragedy, exhilarated by challenge, strengthened by achievement. America stands alone as the world's indispensable nation. Once again, our economy is the strongest on Earth. Once again, we are building stronger families, thriving communities, better educational opportunities, a cleaner environment. Problems that once seemed destined to deepen now bend to our efforts: our streets are safer and record numbers of our fellow citizens have moved from welfare to work.

And once again, we have resolved for our time a great debate over the role of government. Today we can declare: Government is not the problem, and government is not the solution. We—the American people—we are the solution. (Applause.) Our founders understood that well and gave us a democracy strong enough to endure for centuries, flexible enough to face our common challenges and advance our common dreams in each new day.

As times change, so government must change. We need a new government for a new century—humble enough not to try to solve all our problems for us, but strong enough to give us the tools to solve our problems for ourselves; a government that is smaller, lives within its means, and does more with less. Yet where it can stand up for our values and interests in the world, and where it can give Americans the power to make a real difference in their everyday lives, government should do more, not less. The preeminent mission of our new government is to give all Americans an opportunity—not a guarantee, but a real opportunity—to build better lives. (Applause.)

Beyond that, my fellow citizens, the future is up to us. Our founders taught us that the preservation of our liberty and our union depends upon responsible citizenship. And we need a new sense of responsibility for a new century. There is work to do, work that government alone cannot do: teaching children to read; hiring people off welfare rolls; coming out from behind locked doors and shuttered windows to help reclaim our streets from drugs and gangs and crime; taking time out of our own lives to serve others.

Each and every one of us, in our own way, must assume personal responsibility—not only for ourselves and our families, but for our neighbors and our nation. (Applause.) Our greatest responsibility is to embrace a new spirit of community for a new century. For any one of us to succeed, we must succeed as one America.

The challenge of our past remains the challenge of our future—will we be one nation, one people, with one common destiny, or not? Will we all come together, or come apart?

The divide of race has been America's constant curse. And each new wave of immigrants gives new targets to old prejudices. Prejudice and contempt, cloaked in the pretense of religious or political conviction are no different. (Applause.) These forces have nearly destroyed our nation in the past. They plague us still. They fuel the fanaticism of terror. And they torment the lives of millions in fractured nations all around the world.

These obsessions cripple both those who hate and, of course, those who are hated, robbing both of what they might become. We cannot, we will not, succumb to the dark impulses that lurk in the far regions of the soul everywhere. We shall overcome them. (Applause.) And we shall replace them with the generous spirit of a people who feel at home with one another.

Our rich texture of racial, religious and political diversity will be a Godsend in the 21st century. Great rewards will come to those who can live together, learn together, work together, forge new ties that bind together.

As this new era approaches we can already see its broad outlines. Ten years ago, the Internet was the mystical province of physicists;

today, it is a commonplace encyclopedia for millions of schoolchildren. Scientists now are decoding the blueprint of human life. Cures for our most feared illnesses seem close at hand.

The world is no longer divided into two hostile camps. Instead, now we are building bonds with nations that once were our adversaries. Growing connections of commerce and culture give us a chance to lift the fortunes and spirits of people the world over. And for the very first time in all of history, more people on this planet live under democracy than dictatorship. (Applause.)

My fellow Americans, as we look back at this remarkable century, we may ask, can we hope not just to follow, but even to surpass the achievements of the 20th century in America and to avoid the awful bloodshed that stained its legacy? To that question, every American here and every American in our land today must answer a resounding "Yes." (Applause.)

This is the heart of our task. With a new vision of government, a new sense of responsibility, a new spirit of community, we will sustain America's journey. The promise we sought in a new land we will find again in a land of new promise. (Applause.)

In this new land, education will be every citizen's most prized possession. Our schools will have the highest standards in the world, igniting the spark of possibility in the eyes of every girl and every boy. And the doors of higher education will be open to all. The knowledge and power of the Information Age will be within reach not just of the few, but of every classroom, every library, every child. Parents and children will have time not only to work, but to read and play together. And the plans they make at their kitchen table will be those of a better home, a better job, the certain chance to go to college.

Our streets will echo again with the laughter of our children, because no one will try to shoot them or sell them drugs anymore. Everyone who can work, will work, with today's permanent under class part of tomorrow's growing middle class. New miracles of medicine at last will reach not only those who can claim care now, but the children and hardworking families too long denied.

We will stand mighty for peace and freedom, and maintain a strong defense against terror and destruction. Our children will sleep free from the threat of nuclear, chemical or biological weapons. Ports and airports, farms and factories will thrive with trade and innovation and ideas. And the world's greatest democracy will lead a whole world of democracies.

Our land of new promise will be a nation that meets its obligations—a nation that balances its budget, but never loses the balance of its values. (Applause.) A nation where our grandparents have secure retirement and health care, and their grandchildren know we have made the reforms necessary to sustain those benefits for their time. (Applause.) A nation that fortifies the world's most productive economy even as it protects the great natural bounty of our water, air, and majestic land.

And in this land of new promise, we will have reformed our politics so that the voice of the people will always speak louder than the din of narrow interests—regaining the participation and deserving the trust of all Americans. (Applause.)

Fellow citizens, let us build that America, a nation ever moving forward toward realizing the full potential of all its citizens. Prosperity and power—yes, they are important, and we must maintain them. But let us never forget: The greatest progress we have made, and the greatest progress we have yet to make, is in the human heart. In the end, all the world's wealth and a thousand armies are no match for the strength and decency of the human spirit. (Applause.)

Thirty-four years ago, the man whose life we celebrate today spoke to us down there, at the other end of this Mall, in words that moved the conscience of a nation. Like a prophet of old, he told of his dream that one day America would rise up and treat all its citizens as equals before the law and in the heart. Martin Luther King's dream was the American Dream. His quest is our quest: the ceaseless striving to live out our true creed. Our history has been built on such dreams and labors. And by our dreams and labors we will redeem the promise of America in the 21st century.

To that effort I pledge all my strength and every power of my office. I ask the members of Congress here to join in that pledge. The American people returned to office a President of one party and a Congress of another. Surely, they did not do this to advance the politics of petty bickering and extreme partisanship they plainly deplore. (Applause.) No, they call on us instead to be repairers of the breach, and to move on with America's mission.

America demands and deserves big things from us—and nothing big ever came from being small. (Applause.) Let us remember the timeless wisdom of Cardinal Bernardin, when facing the end of his own life. He said: "It is wrong to waste the precious gift of time, on acrimony and division." Fellow citizens, we must not waste the precious gift of this time. For all of us are on that same journey of our lives, and our journey, too, will come to an end. But the journey of our America must go on.

And so, my fellow Americans, we must be strong, for there is much to dare. The demands of our time are great and they are different. Let us meet them with faith and courage, with patience and a grateful and happy heart. Let us shape the hope of this day into the noblest chapter in our history. Yes, let us build our bridge. (Applause.) A bridge wide enough and strong enough for every American to cross over to a blessed land of new promise.

May those generations whose faces we cannot yet see, whose names we may never know, say of us here that we led our beloved land into a new century with the American Dream alive for all her children; with the American promise of a more perfect union a reality for all her people; with America's bright flame of freedom spreading throughout all the world.

From the height of this place and the summit of this century, let us go forth. May God strengthen our hands for the good work ahead—and always, always bless our America. (Applause.)

11. State of the Union Address February 4, 1997

Public Papers of the Presidents of the United States: William J. Clinton, 1997. Vol. 1. Washington, D.C.: U.S. Government Printing Office, pages 109–117

Thank you. Thank you very much. Mr. Speaker, Mr. Vice President, members of the 105th Congress, distinguished guests, my fellow Americans:

I think I should start by saying thanks for inviting me back.

I come before you tonight with a challenge as great as any in our peacetime history—and a plan of action to meet that challenge, to prepare our people for the bold new world of the 21st century.

We have much to be thankful for. With four years of growth, we have won back the basic strength of our economy. With crime and welfare rolls declining, we are winning back our optimism, the enduring faith that we can master any difficulty. With the Cold War receding and global commerce at record levels, we are helping to win an unrivaled peace and prosperity all across the world.

My fellow Americans, the state of our union is strong, but now we must rise to the decisive moment, to make a nation and a world better than any we have ever known.

The new promise of the global economy, the Information Age, unimagined new work, life-enhancing technology—all these are ours to seize. That is our honor and our challenge. We must be shapers of events, not observers, for if we do not act, the moment will pass and we will lose the best possibilities of our future.

We face no imminent threat, but we do have an enemy. The enemy of our time is inaction.

So tonight I issue a call to action—action by this Congress, action by our states, by our people to prepare America for the 21st century; action to keep our economy and our democracy strong and working for all our people; action to strengthen education and harness the forces of technology and science; action to build stronger families and stronger communities and a safer environment; action to keep America the world's strongest force for peace, freedom and prosperity; and above all, action to build a more perfect union here at home.

The spirit we bring to our work will make all the difference.

We must be committed to the pursuit of opportunity for all Americans, responsibility from all Americans in a community of all Americans. And we must be committed to a new kind of government: not to solve all our problems for us, but to give our people—all our people—the tools they need to make the most of their own lives. And we must work together.

The people of this nation elected us all. They want us to be partners, not partisans. They put us all right here in the same boat. They gave us all oars, and they told us to row. Now, here is the direction I believe we should take.

First, we must move quickly to complete the unfinished business of our country: to balance the budget, renew our democracy, and finish the job of welfare reform.

Over the last four years we have brought new economic growth by investing in our people, expanding our exports, cutting our deficits, creating over 11 million new jobs, a four-year record.

Now we must keep our economy the strongest in the world. We here tonight have an historic opportunity. Let this Congress be the Congress that finally balances the budget. Thank you.

In two days I will propose a detailed plan to balance the budget by 2002. This plan will balance the budget and invest in our people while protecting Medicare, Medicaid, education and the environment. It will balance the budget and build on the vice president's efforts to make our government work better—even as it costs less.

It will balance the budget and provide middle-class tax relief to pay for education and health care, to help to raise a child, to buy and sell a home.

Balancing the budget requires only your vote and my signature. It does not require us to rewrite our Constitution. I believe, I believe it is both unnecessary, unwise to adopt a balanced budget amendment that could cripple our country in time of economic crisis and force unwanted results such as judges halting Social Security checks or increasing taxes.

Let us at least agree we should not pass any measure, no measure should be passed that threatens Social Security. We don't need, whatever your view on that, we all must concede we don't need a constitutional amendment, we need action. Whatever our differences, we should balance the budget now, and then, for the long-term health of our society, we must agree to a bipartisan process to preserve Social Security and reform Medicare for the long run, so that these fundamental programs will be as strong for our children as they are for our parents.

And let me say something that's not in my script tonight. I know this is not going to be easy. But I really believe one of the reasons the American people gave me a second term was to take the tough decisions in the next four years that will carry our country through the next 50 years.

I know it is easier for me than for you to say or do. But another reason I was elected is to support all of you, without regard to party, to give you what is necessary to join in these decisions. We owe it to our country and to our future.

Our second piece of unfinished business requires us to commit ourselves tonight, before the eyes of America, to finally enacting bipartisan campaign finance reform.

Now, Senators McCain and Feingold, Representatives Shays and Meehan have reached across party lines here to craft tough and fair reform. Their proposal would curb spending, reduce the role of special interests, create a level playing field between challengers and incumbents, and ban contributions from non-citizens, all corporate sources, and the other large soft-money contributions that both parties receive.

You know and I know that this can be delayed, and you know and I know that delay will mean the death of reform.

So let's set our own deadline. Let's work together to write bipartisan campaign finance reform into law and pass McCain-Feingold by the day we celebrate the birth of our democracy, July the 4th.

There is a third piece of unfinished business. Over the last four years we moved a record two and a quarter million people off the welfare roles. Then last year Congress enacted landmark welfare reform legislation demanding that all able-bodied recipients assume the responsibility of moving from welfare to work. Now each and every one of us has to fulfill our responsibility, indeed our moral obligation, to make sure that people who now must work can work. And now we must act to meet a new goal: two million more people off the welfare rolls by the year 2000.

Here is my plan:

Tax credits and other incentives for businesses that hire people off welfare;

Incentives for job placement firms in states to create more jobs for welfare recipients;

Training, transportation and child care to help people go to work.

Now I challenge every state—turn those welfare checks into private sector paychecks. I challenge every religious congregation, every community nonprofit, every business to hire someone off welfare. And I'd like to say especially to every employer in our country who ever criticized the old welfare system, you can't blame that old system anymore; we have torn it down. Now, do your part. Give someone on welfare the chance to go to work.

Tonight I am pleased to announce that five major corporations—Sprint, Monsanto, UPS, Burger King and United Airlines—will be the first to join in a new national effort to marshal America's businesses large and small to create jobs so that people can move from welfare to work.

We passed welfare reform. All of you know I believe we were right to do it. But no one can walk out of this chamber with a clear conscience unless you are prepared to finish the job.

And we must join together to do something else, too, something both Republican and Democratic governors have asked us to do: to restore basic health and disability benefits when misfortune strikes immigrants who came to this country legally, who work hard, pay taxes, and obey the law. To do otherwise is simply unworthy of a great nation of immigrants.

Now, looking ahead, the greatest step of all, the high threshold to the future we must now cross, and my number one priority for the next four years, is to ensure that all Americans have the best education in the world. Thank you.

Let's work together to meet these three goals: every eight-year-old must be able to read, every 12-year-old must be able to log on to the Internet, every 18-year-old must be able to go to college, and every adult American must be able to keep on learning for a lifetime.

My balanced budget makes an unprecedented commitment to these goals—$51 billion next year—but far more than money is required. I have a plan, a call to action for American education based on these 10 principles:

First, a national crusade for education standards—not federal government standards, but national standards, representing what all our students must know to succeed in the knowledge economy of the 21st century. Every state and school must shape the curriculum to reflect these standards and train teachers to lift students up to them. To help schools meet the standards and measure their progress, we will lead an effort over the next two years to develop national tests of student achievement in reading and math.

Tonight I issue a challenge to the nation. Every state should adopt high national standards, and by 1999, every state should test every 4th grader in reading and every 8th grader in math to make sure these standards are met.

Raising standards will not be easy, and some of our children will not be able to meet them at first. The point is not to put our children down, but to lift them up. Good tests will show us who needs help, what changes in teaching to make, and which schools need to improve. They can help us end social promotion, for no child should move from grade school to junior high or junior high to high school until he or she is ready.

Last month our secretary of education, Dick Riley, and I visited northern Illinois, where 8th grade students from 20 school districts, in a project aptly called First in the World, took the third International Math and Science Study.

That's a test that reflects the world-class standards our children must meet for the new era. And those students in Illinois tied for first in the world in science and came in second in math. Two of them, Kristen Tanner and Chris Getsla, are here tonight along with their teacher, Sue Winski. They're up there with the first lady, and they prove that when we aim high and challenge our students, they will be the best in the world. Let's give them a hand. Stand up, please.

Second, to have the best schools, we must have the best teachers. Most of us in this chamber would not be here tonight without the help of those teachers. I know that I wouldn't be here.

For years many of our educators, led by North Carolina's governor, Jim Hunt, and the National Board for Professional Teaching Standards, have worked very hard to establish nationally accepted credentials for excellence in teaching.

Just 500 of these teachers have been certified since 1995. My budget will enable 100,000 more to seek national certification as master teachers. We should reward and recognize our best teachers. And as we reward them, we should quickly and fairly remove those few who don't measure up, and we should challenge more of our finest young people to consider teaching as a career.

Third, we must do more to help all our children read. Forty percent—40 percent—of our 8-year-olds cannot read on their own. That's why we have just launched the America Reads initiative, to build a citizen army of one million volunteer tutors to make sure every child can read independently by the end of the 3rd grade. We will use thousands of AmeriCorps volunteers to mobilize this citizen army. We want at least 100,000 college students to help.

And tonight I'm pleased that 60 college presidents have answered my call, pledging that thousands of their work-study students will serve for one year as reading tutors.

This is also a challenge to every teacher and every principal.

You must use these tutors to help your students read. And it is especially a challenge to

our parents. You must read with your children every night.

This leads to the fourth principle: Learning begins in the first days of life. Scientists are now discovering how young children develop emotionally and intellectually from their very first days and how important it is for parents to begin immediately talking, singing, even reading to their infants. The first lady has spent years writing about this issue, studying it. And she and I are going to convene a White House conference on early learning and the brain this spring to explore how parents and educators can best use these startling new findings.

We already know we should start teaching children before they start school. That's why this balanced budget expands Head Start to one million children by 2002. And that is why the vice president and Mrs. Gore will host their annual family conference this June on what we can do to make sure that parents are an active part of their children's learning all the way through school.

They've done a great deal to highlight the importance of family in our life, and now they're turning their attention to getting more parents involved in their children's learning all the way through school. I thank you, Mr. Vice President, and I thank you especially, Tipper, for what you're doing.

Fifth, every state should give parents the power to choose the right public school for their children. Their right to choose will foster competition and innovation that can make public schools better. We should also make it possible for more parents and teachers to start charter schools, schools that set and meet the highest standards and exist only as long as they do.

Our plan will help America to create 3,000 of these charter schools by the next century, nearly seven times as there are in the country today, so that parents will have even more choices in sending their children to the best schools.

Sixth, character education must be taught in our schools. We must teach our children to be good citizens. And we must continue to promote order and discipline; supporting communities that introduce school uniforms, impose curfews, enforce truancy laws, remove disruptive students from the classroom, and have zero tolerance for guns and drugs in schools.

Seventh, we cannot expect our children to raise themselves up in schools that are literally falling down. With the student population at an all-time high, and record numbers of school buildings falling into disrepair, this has now become a serious national concern. Therefore, my budget includes a new initiative: $5 billion to help communities finance $20 billion in school construction over the next four years.

Eighth, we must make the 13th and 14th years of education—at least two years of college—just as universal in America by the 21st century as a high school education is today, and we must open the doors of college to all Americans.

To do that, I propose America's Hope Scholarship, based on Georgia's pioneering program—two years of a $1,500 tax credit for college tuition, enough to pay for the typical community college. I also propose a tax deduction of up to $10,000 a year for all tuition after high school, an expanded IRA you can withdraw from tax free for education, and the largest increase in Pell Grant scholarship in 20 years.

Now this plan will give most families the ability to pay no taxes on money they save for college tuition. I ask you to pass it and give every American who works hard the chance to go to college.

Ninth, in the 21st century we must expand the frontiers of learning across a lifetime. All our people, of whatever age, must have the chance to learn new skills.

Most Americans live near a community college. The roads that take them there can be paths to a better future. My GI bill for America's workers will transform the confusing tangle of federal training programs into a simple skill grant to go directly into eligible workers' hands.

For too long this bill has been sitting on that desk there, without action. I ask you to pass it now. Let's give more of our workers the ability to learn and to earn for a lifetime.

Tenth, we must bring the power of the Information Age into all our schools.

Last year I challenged America to connect every classroom and library to the Internet by the year 2000, so that for the first time in our history, children in the most isolated rural town, the most comfortable suburbs, the poorest inner-city schools will have the same access to the same universe of knowledge.

That is my plan—a call to action for American education. Some may say that it is unusual for a president to pay this kind of attention to education. Some may say it is simply because the president and his wonderful wife have been obsessed with this subject for more years than they can recall. That is not what is driving these proposals. We must understand the significance of this endeavor.

One of the greatest sources of our strength throughout the Cold War was a bipartisan foreign policy. Because our future was at stake, politics stopped at the water's edge. Now I ask you, and I ask all our nation's governors, I ask parents, teachers and citizens all across America, for a new nonpartisan commitment to education, because education is a critical national security issue for our future and politics must stop at the schoolhouse door.

To prepare America for the 21st century, we must harness the powerful forces of science and technology to benefit all Americans. This is the first State of the Union carried live in video over the Internet, but we've only begun to spread the benefits of a technology revolution that should become the modern birthright of every citizen.

Our effort to connect every classroom is just the beginning. Now we should connect every hospital to the Internet so that doctors can instantly share data about their patients with the best specialists in the field.

And I challenge the private sector tonight to start by connecting every children's hospital as soon as possible so that a child in bed can stay in touch with school, family and friends. A sick child need no longer be a child alone.

We must build the second generation of the Internet so that our leading universities and national laboratories can communicate in speeds a thousand times faster than today to develop new medical treatments, new sources of energy, new ways of working together. But we cannot stop there.

As the Internet becomes our new town square, a computer in every home: a teacher of all subjects, a connection to all cultures. This will no longer be a dream, but a necessity. And over the next decade, that must be our goal.

We must continue to explore the heavens, pressing on with the Mars probes and the International Space Station, both of which will have practical applications for our everyday living.

We must speed the remarkable advances in medical science. The human genome project is now decoding the genetic mysteries of life. American scientists have discovered genes linked to breast cancer and ovarian cancer and medication that stops a stroke in progress and begins to reverse its effects, and treatments that dramatically lengthen the lives of people with HIV and AIDS.

Since I took office, funding for AIDS research at the National Institutes of Health has increased dramatically to $1.5 billion. With new resources, NIH will now become the most powerful discovery engine for an AIDS vaccine, working with other scientists, to finally end the threat of AIDS. Thank you. Remember that every year, every year we move up the discovery of an AIDS vaccine we'll save mil-lions of lives around the world. We must reinforce our commitment to medical science.

To prepare America for the 21st century we must build stronger families. Over the past four years the Family and Medical Leave Law has helped millions of Americans to take time off to be with their families.

With new pressures on people and the way they work and live, I believe we must expand family leave so that workers can take time off for teacher conferences and a child's medical checkup. We should pass flex time so workers can choose to be paid for overtime in income or trade it in for time off to be with their families.

We must continue—we must continue, step by step, to give more families access to affordable quality health care. Forty million Americans still lack health insurance. Ten million children still lack health insurance. Eighty percent of them have working parents who pay taxes. That is wrong.

My—my balanced budget will extend health coverage to up to 5 million of those children. Since nearly half of all children who lose their insurance do so because their parents lose or change a job, my budget will also ensure that people who temporarily lose their jobs can still afford to keep their health insurance. No child should be without a doctor just because a parent is without a job.

My Medicare plan modernizes Medicare, increases the life of the trust fund to 10 years, provides support for respite care for the many families with loved ones afflicted with Alzheimer's, and, for the first time, it would fully pay for annual mammograms.

Just as we ended drive-through deliveries of babies last year, we must now end the dangerous and demeaning practice of forcing women home from the hospital only hours after a mastectomy.

I ask your support for bipartisan legislation to guarantee that a woman can stay in the hospital for 48 hours after a mastectomy. With us tonight is Dr. Kristen Zarfos, a Connecticut surgeon whose outrage at this practice spurred a national movement and inspired this legislation. I'd like her to stand so we can thank her for her efforts. Dr. Zarfos, thank you.

In the last four years, we have increased child support collections by 50 percent. Now we should go further and do better by making it a felony for any parent to cross a state line in an attempt to flee from this, his or her most sacred obligation.

Finally, we must also protect our children by standing firm in our determination to ban the advertising and marketing of cigarettes that endanger their lives.

To prepare America for the 21st century, we must build stronger communities. We should start with safe streets. Serious crime has dropped five years in a row. The key has been community policing. We must finish the job of putting 100,000 community police on the streets of the United States.

We should pass the Victims' Rights Amendment to the Constitution, and I ask you to mount a full-scale assault on juvenile crime, with legislation that declares war on gangs with new prosecutors and tougher penalties, extends the Brady bill so violent teen criminals will not be able to buy handguns, requires child safety locks on handguns to prevent unauthorized use, and helps to keep our schools open after hours, on weekends and in the summer so our young people will have someplace to go and something to say yes to.

This balanced budget includes the largest anti-drug effort ever—to stop drugs at their source; punish those who push them; and teach our young people that drugs are wrong, drugs are illegal, and drugs will kill them. I hope you will support it.

Our growing economy has helped to revive poor urban and rural neighborhoods, but we must do more to empower them to create the conditions in which all families can flourish and to create jobs through investment by business and loans by banks.

We should double the number of empowerment zones. They've already brought so much hope to communities like Detroit, where the unemployment rate has been cut in half in four years. We should restore contaminated urban land and buildings to constructive use. We should expand the network of community development banks.

And together, we must pledge tonight that we will use this empowerment approach, including private sector tax incentives, to renew our capital city so that Washington is a great place to work and live—and once again the proud face America shows the world!

We must protect our environment in every community. In the last four years, we cleaned up 250 toxic waste sites, as many as in the previous 12. Now we should clean up 500 more so that our children grow up next to parks, not poison. I urge to pass my proposal to make big polluters live by a simple rule: If you pollute our environment, you should pay to clean it up.

In the last four years, we strengthened our nation's safe food and clean drinking water laws; we protected some of America's rarest, most beautiful land in Utah's Red Rocks region; created three new national parks in the California desert; and began to restore the Florida Everglades.

Now we must be as vigilant with our rivers as we are with our lands. Tonight I announce that this year I will designate 10 American Heritage Rivers to help communities alongside them revitalize their waterfronts and clean up pollution in the rivers, proving once again that we can grow the economy as we protect the environment.

We must also protect our global environment, working to ban the worst toxic chemicals and to reduce the greenhouse gases that challenge our health even as they change our climate.

Now, we all know that in all of our communities some of our children simply don't have what they need to grow and learn in their own homes or schools or neighborhoods. And that means the rest of us must do more, for they are our children, too. That's why President Bush, General Colin Powell, former Housing Secretary Henry Cisneros will join the vice president and me to lead the President's Summit of Service in Philadelphia in April.

Our national service program, AmeriCorps, has already helped 70,000 young people to work their way through college as they serve America. Now we intend to mobilize millions of Americans to serve in thousands of ways. Citizen service is an American responsibility which all Americans should embrace. And I ask your support for that endeavor.

I'd like to make just one last point about our national community. Our economy is measured in numbers and statistics. And it's very important. But the enduring worth of our nation lies in our shared values and our soaring spirit. So instead of cutting back on our modest efforts to support the arts and humanities I believe we should stand by them and challenge our artists, musicians, and writers, challenge our museums, libraries, and theaters.

We should challenge all Americans in the arts and humanities to join with their fellow citizens to make the year 2000 a national celebration of the American spirit in every community, a celebration of our common culture in the century that is past and in the new one to come in a new millennium so that we can remain the world's beacon not only of liberty but of creativity long after the fireworks have faded.

To prepare America for the 21st century we must master the forces of change in the world and keep American leadership strong and sure for an uncharted time.

Fifty years ago, a farsighted America led in creating the institutions that secured victory in the Cold War and built a growing world economy. As a result, today more people than ever embrace our ideals and share our interests.

Already we have dismantled many of the blocks and barriers that divided our parents' world. For the first time, more people live under democracy than dictatorship including every nation in our own hemisphere but one, and its day, too, will come.

Now we stand at another moment of change and choice, and another time to be farsighted, to bring America 50 more years of security and prosperity.

In this endeavor, our first task is to help to build for the very first time an undivided, democratic Europe. When Europe is stable, prosperous, and at peace, America is more secure.

To that end, we must expand NATO by 1999, so that countries that were once our adversaries can become our allies. At the special NATO summit this summer, that is what we will begin to do. We must strengthen NATO's Partnership for Peace with non-member allies. And we must build a stable partnership between NATO and a democratic Russia.

An expanded NATO is good for America, and a Europe in which all democracies define their future not in terms of what they can do to each other, but in terms of what they can do together for the good of all—that kind of Europe is good for America.

Second, America must look to the East no less than to the West.

Our security demands it. Americans fought three wars in Asia in this century.

Our prosperity requires it. More than 2 million American jobs depend upon trade with Asia. There, too, we are helping to shape an Asia Pacific community of cooperation, not conflict.

Let our—let our progress there not mask the peril that remains. Together with South Korea, we must advance peace talks with North Korea and bridge the Cold War's last divide. And I call on Congress to fund our share of the agreement under which North Korea must continue to freeze and then dismantle its nuclear weapons program.

We must pursue a deeper dialogue with China for the sake of our interests and our ideals. An isolated China is not good for America. A China playing its proper role in the world is. I will go to China, and I have invited China's president to come here, not because we agree on everything, but because engaging China is the best way to work on our common challenges, like ending nuclear testing, and to deal frankly with our fundamental differences, like human rights.

The American people must prosper in the global economy. We've worked hard to tear down trade barriers abroad so that we can create good jobs at home. I'm proud to say that today America is once again the most competitive nation and the No. 1 exporter in the world.

Now we must act to expand our exports, especially to Asia and Latin America, two of the fastest-growing regions on earth, or be left behind as these emerging economies forge new ties with other nations. That is why we need the authority now to conclude new trade agreements that open markets to our goods and services even as we preserve our values.

We need not shrink from the challenge of the global economy. After all, we have the best workers and the best products. In a truly open market, we can out-compete anyone, anywhere on earth.

But this is about more than economics. By expanding trade, we can advance the cause of freedom and democracy around the world. There is no better example of this truth than Latin America where democracy and open markets are on the march together. That is why I will visit there in the spring to reinforce our important ties.

We should all be proud that America led the effort to rescue our neighbor, Mexico, from its economic crisis. And we should all be proud that last month Mexico repaid the United States, three full years ahead of schedule, with half a billion dollar profit to us.

America must continue to be an unrelenting force for peace. From the Middle East to Haiti, from Northern Ireland to Africa, taking reasonable risks for peace keeps us from being drawn into far more costly conflicts later. With American leadership, the killing has stopped in Bosnia. Now the habits of peace must take hold.

The new NATO force will allow reconstruction and reconciliation to accelerate. Tonight I ask Congress to continue its strong support of our troops. They are doing a remarkable job there for America, and America must do right by them.

Fifth, we must move strongly against new threats to our security. In the past four years, we agreed to ban—we led the way to a worldwide agreement to ban nuclear testing.

With Russia, we dramatically cut nuclear arsenals and we stopped targeting each other's citizens. We are acting to prevent nuclear materials from falling into the wrong hands, and to rid the world of land mines.

We are working with other nations with renewed intensity to fight drug traffickers and to stop terrorists before they act and hold them fully accountable if they do.

Now we must rise to a new test of leadership—ratifying the Chemical Weapons Convention. Make no mistake about it, it will make our troops safer from chemical attack. It will help us to fight terrorism. We have no more important obligations, especially in the wake of what we now know about the Gulf War.

This treaty has been bipartisan from the beginning, supported by Republican and Democratic administrations, and Republican and Democratic members of Congress, and already approved by 68 nations. But if we do not act by April the 29th, when this convention goes into force—with or without us—we will lose the chance to have Americans leading and enforcing this effort. Together we must make the Chemical Weapons Convention law so that at last we can begin to outlaw poisoned gas from the earth.

Finally, we must have the tools to meet all these challenges. We must maintain a strong and ready military. We must increase funding for weapons modernization by the year 2000. And we must take good care of our men and women in uniform. They are the world's finest.

We must also renew our commitment to America's diplomacy and pay our debts and dues to international financial institutions like the World Bank—and to a reforming United Nations. Every dollar—every dollar we devote to preventing conflicts, to promoting democracy, to stopping the spread of disease and starvation brings a sure return in security and savings. Yet international affairs spending today is just 1 percent of the federal budget, a small fraction of what America invested in diplomacy to choose leadership over escapism at the start of the cold war.

If America is to continue to lead the world, we here who lead America simply must find the will to pay our way. A farsighted America moved the world to a better place over these last 50 years. And so it can be for another 50 years. But a shortsighted America will soon find its words falling on deaf ears all around the world.

Almost exactly 50 years ago in the first winter of the Cold War President Truman stood before a Republican Congress and called upon our country to meet its responsibilities of leadership. This was his warning. He said, "If we falter, we may endanger the peace of the world, and we shall surely endanger the welfare of this nation."

That Congress, led by Republicans like Senator Arthur Vandenburg, answered President Truman's call. Together, they made the commitments that strengthened our country for 50 years. Now let us do the same. Let us do what it takes to remain the indispensable nation, to keep America strong, secure and prosperous for another 50 years.

In the end, more than anything else, our world leadership grows out of the power of our example here at home, out of our ability to remain strong as one America.

All over the world people are being torn asunder by racial, ethnic and religious conflicts that fuel fanaticism and terror. We are the world's most diverse democracy, and the world looks to us to show that it is possible to live and advance together across those kinds of differences. America has always been a nation of immigrants.

From the start, a steady stream of people in search of freedom and opportunity have left their own lands to make this land their home. We started as an experiment in democracy fueled by Europeans. We have grown into an experiment in democratic diversity fueled by openness and promise.

My fellow Americans, we must never, ever believe that our diversity is a weakness; it is our greatest strength.

Americans speak every language, know every country. People on every continent can look to us and see the reflection of their own great potential, and they always will, as long as we strive to give all our citizens, whatever their background, an opportunity to achieve their own greatness.

We're not there yet. We still see evidence of a biting bigotry and intolerance in ugly words and awful violence, in burned churches and bombed buildings. We must fight against this in our country and in our hearts.

Just a few days before my second inauguration, one of our country's best-known pastors, Reverend Robert Schuller, suggested that I read Isaiah 58:12. Here's what it says: "Thou shalt raise up the foundations of many generations, and thou shalt be called the repairer of the breach, the restorer of paths to dwell in."

I placed my hand on that verse when I took the oath of office, on behalf of all Americans, for no matter what our differences in our faiths, our backgrounds, our politics, we must all be repairers of the breach.

I want to say a word about two other Americans who show us how. Congressman Frank Tejeda was buried yesterday, a proud American whose family came from Mexico. He was only 51 years old. He was awarded the Silver Star, the Bronze Star and the Purple Heart fighting for his country in Vietnam. And he went on to serve Texas and America fighting for our future here in this chamber.

We are grateful for his service and honored that his mother, Lillie Tejeda, and his sister, Mary Alice, have come from Texas to be with us here tonight. And we welcome you. Thank you.

Gary Locke, the newly-elected governor of Washington state, is the first Chinese-American governor in the history of our country. He's the proud son of two of the millions of Asian American immigrants who strengthened America with their hard work, family values and good citizenship.

He represents the future we can all achieve. Thank you, governor, for being here. Please stand up.

Reverend Schuller, Congressman Tejeda, Governor Locke, along with Kristen Tanner and Chris Getsla, Sue Winski and Dr. Kristen Zarfos—they're all Americans from different roots whose lives reflect the best of what we can become when we are one America.

We may not share a common past, but we surely do share a common future. Building one America is our most important mission, the foundation for many generations of every other strength we must build for this new century. Money cannot buy it, power cannot compel it, technology cannot create it. It can only come from the human spirit.

America is far more than a place; it is an idea—the most powerful idea in the history of nations, and all of us in this chamber, we are now the bearers of that idea, leading a great people into a new world.

A child born tonight will have almost no memory of the 20th century. Everything that child will know about America will be because of what we do now to build a new century. We don't have a moment to waste.

Tomorrow there will be just over 1,000 days until the year 2000. One thousand days to prepare our people. One thousand days to work together. One thousand days to build a bridge to a land of new promise.

My fellow Americans, we have work to do. Let us seize those days and the century.

Thank you. God bless you. And God bless America.

12. *Clinton v. Jones* 520 U.S. 681 (1997)

From: Cornell Law School. The Legal Information Institute. Available online. URL: http://supct.law.cornell.edu/supct/html/95-1853.ZS.html. Accessed June 2004

WILLIAM JEFFERSON CLINTON, PETITIONER v. PAULA CORBIN JONES On Writ of Certiorari to the United States Court of Appeals for the Eighth Circuit May 27, 1997

Justice Stevens delivered the opinion of the Court.

This case raises a constitutional and a prudential question concerning the Office of the President of the United States. Respondent, a private citizen, seeks to recover damages from the current occupant of that office based on actions allegedly taken before his term began. The President submits that in all but the most exceptional cases the Constitution requires federal courts to defer such litigation until his term ends and that, in any event, respect for the office warrants such a stay. Despite the force of the arguments supporting the President's submissions, we conclude that they must be rejected.

Petitioner, William Jefferson Clinton, was elected to the Presidency in 1992, and re-elected in 1996. His term of office expires on January 20, 2001. In 1991 he was the Governor of the State of Arkansas. Respondent, Paula Corbin Jones, is a resident of California. In 1991 she lived in Arkansas, and was an employee of the Arkansas Industrial Development Commission.

On May 6, 1994, she commenced this action in the United States District Court for the Eastern District of Arkansas by filing a complaint naming petitioner and Danny Ferguson, a former Arkansas State Police officer, as defendants. The complaint alleges two federal claims, and two state law claims over which the federal court has jurisdiction because of the diverse citizenship of the parties. As the case comes to us, we are required to assume the truth of the detailed—but as yet untested—factual allegations in the complaint.

Those allegations principally describe events that are said to have occurred on the afternoon of May 8, 1991, during an official conference held at the Excelsior Hotel in Little Rock, Arkansas. The Governor delivered a speech at the conference; respondent—working as a state employee—staffed the registration desk. She alleges that Ferguson persuaded her to leave her desk and to visit the Governor in a business suite at the hotel, where he made "abhorrent" sexual advances that she vehemently rejected. She further claims that her superiors at work subsequently dealt with her in a hostile and rude manner, and changed her duties to punish her for rejecting those advances. Finally, she alleges that after petitioner was elected President, Ferguson defamed her by making a statement to a reporter that implied she had accepted petitioner's alleged overtures, and that various persons authorized to speak for the President publicly branded her a liar by denying that the incident had occurred.

Respondent seeks actual damages of $75,000, and punitive damages of $100,000. Her complaint contains four counts. The first charges that petitioner, acting under color of state law, deprived her of rights protected by the Constitution, in violation of Rev. Stat. §1979, 42 U.S.C. § 1983. The second charges that petitioner and Ferguson engaged in a conspiracy to violate her federal rights, also actionable under federal law. See Rev. Stat. §1980, 42 U.S.C. § 1985. The third is a state common law claim for intentional infliction of emotional distress, grounded primarily on the incident at the hotel. The fourth count, also based on state law, is for defamation, embracing both the comments allegedly made to the press by Ferguson and the statements of petitioner's agents. Inasmuch as the legal sufficiency of the claims has not yet been challenged, we assume, without deciding, that each of the four counts states a cause of action as a matter of law. With the exception of the last charge, which arguably may involve conduct within the outer perimeter of the President's official responsibilities, it is perfectly clear that the alleged misconduct of petitioner was unrelated to any of his official duties as President of the United States and, indeed, occurred before he was elected to that office.

In response to the complaint, petitioner promptly advised the District Court that he intended to file a motion to dismiss on grounds of Presidential immunity, and requested the court to defer all other pleadings and motions until after the immunity issue was resolved. Relying on our cases holding that immunity questions should be decided at the earliest possible stage of the litigation, 858 F. Supp. 902, 905 (ED Ark. 1994), our recognition of the "'singular importance of the President's duties,'" *id.*, at 904 (quoting *Nixon* v. *Fitzgerald*, 457 U.S. 731, 751 (1982)), and the fact that the question did not require any analysis of the allegations of the complaint, 858 F. Supp., at 905, the court granted the request. Petitioner thereupon filed a motion "to dismiss . . . without prejudice and to toll any statutes of limitation [that may be applicable] until he is no longer President, at which time the plaintiff may refile the instant suit." Record, Doc. No. 17. Extensive submissions were made to the District Court by the parties and the Department of Justice.

The District Judge denied the motion to dismiss on immunity grounds and ruled that discovery in the case could go forward, but ordered any trial stayed until the end of petitioner's Presidency. 869 F. Supp. 690 (ED Ark. 1994). Although she recognized that a "thin majority" in *Nixon* v. *Fitzgerald*, 457 U.S. 731 (1982), had held that "the President has absolute immunity from civil damage actions arising out of the execution of official duties of office," she was not convinced that "a President has absolute immunity from civil causes of action arising prior to assuming the office." She was, however, persuaded by some of the reasoning in our opinion in *Fitzgerald* that deferring the trial if one were required would be appropriate. 869 F. Supp., at 699–700. Relying in part on the fact that respondent had failed to bring her complaint until two days before the 3-year period of limitations expired, she concluded that the public interest in avoiding litigation that might hamper the President in conducting the duties of his office outweighed any demonstrated need for an immediate trial. *Id.*, at 698–699.

Both parties appealed. A divided panel of the Court of Appeals affirmed the denial of the motion to dismiss, but because it regarded the order postponing the trial until the President leaves office as the "functional equivalent" of a grant of temporary immunity, it reversed that order. 72 F. 3d 1354, 1361, n. 9, 1363 (CA8 1996). Writing for the majority, Judge Bowman

explained that "the President, like all other government officials, is subject to the same laws that apply to all other members of our society," *id.*, at 1358, that he could find no "case in which any public official ever has been granted any immunity from suit for his unofficial acts," *ibid.*, and that the rationale for official immunity "is inapposite where only personal, private conduct by a President is at issue," *id.*, at 1360. The majority specifically rejected the argument that, unless immunity is available, the threat of judicial interference with the Executive Branch through scheduling orders, potential contempt citations, and sanctions would violate separation of powers principles. Judge Bowman suggested that "judicial case management sensitive to the burdens of the presidency and the demands of the President's schedule," would avoid the perceived danger. *Id.*, at 1361.

In dissent, Judge Ross submitted that even though the holding in *Fitzgerald* involved official acts, the logic of the opinion, which "placed primary reliance on the prospect that the President's discharge of his constitutional powers and duties would be impaired if he were subject to suits for damages," applies with equal force to this case. 72 F. 3d, at 1367. In his view, "unless exigent circumstances can be shown," all private actions for damages against a sitting President must be stayed until the completion of his term. *Ibid.* In this case, Judge Ross saw no reason why the stay would prevent respondent from ultimately obtaining an adjudication of her claims.

In response to the dissent, Judge Beam wrote a separate concurrence. He suggested that a prolonged delay may well create a significant risk of irreparable harm to respondent because of an unforeseeable loss of evidence or the possible death of a party. *Id.*, at 1363–1364. Moreover, he argued that in civil rights cases brought under §1983 there is a "public interest in an ordinary citizen's timely vindication of . . . her most fundamental rights against alleged abuse of power by government officials." *Id.*, at 1365. In his view, the dissent's concern about judicial interference with the functioning of the Presidency was "greatly overstated." *Ibid.* Neither the involvement of prior presidents in litigation, either as parties or as witnesses, nor the character of this "relatively uncomplicated civil litigation," indicated that the threat was serious. *Id.*, at 1365–1366. Finally, he saw "no basis for staying discovery or trial of the claims against Trooper Ferguson." *Id.*, at 1366.

The President, represented by private counsel, filed a petition for certiorari. The Solicitor General, representing the United States, supported the petition, arguing that the decision of the Court of Appeals was "fundamentally mistaken" and created "serious risks for the institution of the Presidency." In her brief in opposition to certiorari, respondent argued that this "one of a kind case is singularly inappropriate" for the exercise of our certiorari jurisdiction because it did not create any conflict among the Courts of Appeals, it "does not pose any conceivable threat to the functioning of the Executive Branch," and there is no precedent supporting the President's position.

While our decision to grant the petition expressed no judgment concerning the merits of the case, it does reflect our appraisal of its importance. The representations made on behalf of the Executive Branch as to the potential impact of the precedent established by the Court of Appeals merit our respectful and deliberate consideration.

It is true that we have often stressed the importance of avoiding the premature adjudication of constitutional questions. That doctrine of avoidance, however, is applicable to the entire Federal Judiciary, not just to this Court, cf. *Arizonans for Official English* v. *Arizona*, 520 U.S. ___ (1997), and comes into play after the court has acquired jurisdiction of a case. It does not dictate a discretionary denial of every certiorari petition raising a novel constitutional

question. It does, however, make it appropriate to identify two important constitutional issues not encompassed within the questions presented by the petition for certiorari that we need not address today.

First, because the claim of immunity is asserted in a federal court and relies heavily on the doctrine of separation of powers that restrains each of the three branches of the Federal Government from encroaching on the domain of the other two, see, *e.g.*, *Buckley* v. *Valeo*, 424 U.S. 1, 122 (1976), it is not necessary to consider or decide whether a comparable claim might succeed in a state tribunal. If this case were being heard in a state forum, instead of advancing a separation of powers argument, petitioner would presumably rely on federalism and comity concerns, as well as the interest in protecting federal officials from possible local prejudice that underlies the authority to remove certain cases brought against federal officers from a state to a federal court, see 28 U.S.C. § 1442(a); *Mesa* v. *California*, 489 U.S. 121, 125–126 (1989). Whether those concerns would present a more compelling case for immunity is a question that is not before us.

Second, our decision rejecting the immunity claim and allowing the case to proceed does not require us to confront the question whether a court may compel the attendance of the President at any specific time or place. We assume that the testimony of the President, both for discovery and for use at trial, may be taken at the White House at a time that will accommodate his busy schedule, and that, if a trial is held, there would be no necessity for the President to attend in person, though he could elect to do so.

Petitioner's principal submission—that "in all but the most exceptional cases," Brief for Petitioner i, the Constitution affords the President temporary immunity from civil damages litigation arising out of events that occurred before he took office—cannot be sustained on the basis of precedent.

Only three sitting Presidents have been defendants in civil litigation involving their actions prior to taking office. Complaints against Theodore Roosevelt and Harry Truman had been dismissed before they took office; the dismissals were affirmed after their respective inaugurations. Two companion cases arising out of an automobile accident were filed against John F. Kennedy in 1960 during the Presidential campaign. After taking office, he unsuccessfully argued that his status as Commander in Chief gave him a right to a stay under the Soldiers' and Sailors' Civil Relief Act of 1940, 50 U. S. C. App. §§501–525. The motion for a stay was denied by the District Court, and the matter was settled out of court. Thus, none of those cases sheds any light on the constitutional issue before us.

The principal rationale for affording certain public servants immunity from suits for money damages arising out of their official acts is inapplicable to unofficial conduct. In cases involving prosecutors, legislators, and judges we have repeatedly explained that the immunity serves the public interest in enabling such officials to perform their designated functions effectively without fear that a particular decision may give rise to personal liability. We explained in *Ferri* v. *Ackerman*, 444 U.S. 193 (1979):

"As public servants, the prosecutor and the judge represent the interest of society as a whole. The conduct of their official duties may adversely affect a wide variety of different individuals, each of whom may be a potential source of future controversy. The societal interest in providing such public officials with the maximum ability to deal fearlessly and impartially with the public at large has long been recognized as an acceptable justification for official immunity. The point of immunity for such officials is to forestall an atmosphere of intimidation that would conflict with their

resolve to perform their designated functions in a principled fashion." *Id.*, at 202–204.

That rationale provided the principal basis for our holding that a former President of the United States was "entitled to absolute immunity from damages liability predicated on his official acts," *Fitzgerald*, 457 U. S., at 749. See *id.*, at 752 (citing *Ferri* v. *Ackerman*). Our central concern was to avoid rendering the President "unduly cautious in the discharge of his official duties." 457 U.S., at 752, n. 32.

This reasoning provides no support for an immunity for *unofficial* conduct. As we explained in *Fitzgerald*, "the sphere of protected action must be related closely to the immunity's justifying purposes." *Id.*, at 755. Because of the President's broad responsibilities, we recognized in that case an immunity from damages claims arising out of official acts extending to the "outer perimeter of his authority." *Id.*, at 757. But we have never suggested that the President, or any other official, has an immunity that extends beyond the scope of any action taken in an official capacity. See *id.*, at 759 (Burger, C. J., concurring) (noting that "a President, like Members of Congress, judges, prosecutors, or congressional aides—all having absolute immunity—are not immune for acts outside official duties"); see also *id.*, at 761, n. 4.

Moreover, when defining the scope of an immunity for acts clearly taken *within* an official capacity, we have applied a functional approach. "Frequently our decisions have held that an official's absolute immunity should extend only to acts in performance of particular functions of his office." *Id.*, at 755. Hence, for example, a judge's absolute immunity does not extend to actions performed in a purely administrative capacity. See *Forrester* v. *White*, 484 U.S. 219, 229–230 (1988). As our opinions have made clear, immunities are grounded in "the nature of the function performed, not the identity of the actor who performed it." *Id.*, at 229.

Petitioner's effort to construct an immunity from suit for unofficial acts grounded purely in the identity of his office is unsupported by precedent.

We are also unpersuaded by the evidence from the historical record to which petitioner has called our attention. He points to a comment by Thomas Jefferson protesting the subpoena *duces tecum* Chief Justice Marshall directed to him in the Burr trial, a statement in the diaries kept by Senator William Maclay of the first Senate debates, in which then Vice President John Adams and Senator Oliver Ellsworth are recorded as having said that "the President personally [is] not . . . subject to any process whatever," lest it be "put. . . . in the power of a common Justice to exercise any Authority over him and Stop the Whole Machine of Government," and to a quotation from Justice Story's Commentaries on the Constitution. None of these sources sheds much light on the question at hand.

Respondent, in turn, has called our attention to conflicting historical evidence. Speaking in favor of the Constitution's adoption at the Pennsylvania Convention, James Wilson—who had participated in the Philadelphia Convention at which the document was drafted—explained that, although the President "is placed [on] high," "not a single privilege is annexed to his character; far from being above the laws, he is amenable to them in his private character as a citizen, and in his public character by impeachment." 2 J. Elliot, Debates on the Federal Constitution 480 (2d ed. 1863) (emphasis omitted). This description is consistent with both the doctrine of presidential immunity as set forth in *Fitzgerald*, and rejection of the immunity claim in this case. With respect to acts taken in his "public character"—that is official acts—the President may be disciplined principally by impeachment, not by private lawsuits for damages. But he is otherwise subject to the laws for his purely private acts.

In the end, as applied to the particular question before us, we reach the same conclusion about these historical materials that Justice Jackson described when confronted with an issue concerning the dimensions of the President's power. "Just what our forefathers did envision, or would have envisioned had they foreseen modern conditions, must be divined from materials almost as enigmatic as the dreams Joseph was called upon to interpret for Pharaoh. A century and a half of partisan debate and scholarly speculation yields no net result but only supplies more or less apt quotations from respected sources on each side. . . . They largely cancel each other." *Youngstown Sheet & Tube Co. v. Sawyer*, 343 U.S. 579, 634–635 (1952) (concurring opinion).

Petitioner's strongest argument supporting his immunity claim is based on the text and structure of the Constitution. He does not contend that the occupant of the Office of the President is "above the law," in the sense that his conduct is entirely immune from judicial scrutiny. The President argues merely for a postponement of the judicial proceedings that will determine whether he violated any law. His argument is grounded in the character of the office that was created by Article II of the Constitution, and relies on separation of powers principles that have structured our constitutional arrangement since the founding.

As a starting premise, petitioner contends that he occupies a unique office with powers and responsibilities so vast and important that the public interest demands that he devote his undivided time and attention to his public duties. He submits that—given the nature of the office—the doctrine of separation of powers places limits on the authority of the Federal Judiciary to interfere with the Executive Branch that would be transgressed by allowing this action to proceed.

We have no dispute with the initial premise of the argument. Former presidents, from

George Washington to George Bush, have consistently endorsed petitioner's characterization of the office. After serving his term, Lyndon Johnson observed: "Of all the 1,886 nights I was President, there were not many when I got to sleep before 1 or 2 a.m., and there were few mornings when I didn't wake up by 6 or 6:30." In 1967, the Twenty-fifth Amendment to the Constitution was adopted to ensure continuity in the performance of the powers and duties of the office; one of the sponsors of that Amendment stressed the importance of providing that "at all times" there be a President "who has complete control and will be able to perform" those duties. As Justice Jackson has pointed out, the Presidency concentrates executive authority "in a single head in whose choice the whole Nation has a part, making him the focus of public hopes and expectations. In drama, magnitude and finality his decisions so far overshadow any others that almost alone he fills the public eye and ear." *Youngstown Sheet & Tube Co.* v. *Sawyer,* 343 U. S., at 653 (Jackson, J., concurring). We have, in short, long recognized the "unique position in the constitutional scheme" that this office occupies. *Fitzgerald,* 457 U. S., at 749. Thus, while we suspect that even in our modern era there remains some truth to Chief Justice Marshall's suggestion that the duties of the Presidency are not entirely "unremitting," *United States* v. *Burr,* 25 F. Cas. 30, 34 (CC Va. 1807), we accept the initial premise of the Executive's argument.

It does not follow, however, that separation of powers principles would be violated by allowing this action to proceed. The doctrine of separation of powers is concerned with the allocation of official power among the three co-equal branches of our Government. The Framers "built into the tripartite Federal Government . . . a self-executing safeguard against the encroachment or aggrandizement of one branch at the expense of the other." *Buckley* v. *Valeo,* 424 U. S., at 122. Thus, for example, the

Congress may not exercise the judicial power to revise final judgments, *Plaut* v. *Spendthrift Farm, Inc.,* 514 U.S. 211 (1995), or the executive power to manage an airport, see *Metropolitan Washington Airports Authority* v. *Citizens for Abatement of Aircraft Noise, Inc.,* 501 U.S. 252, 276 (1991) (holding that "[i]f the power is executive, the Constitution does not permit an agent of Congress to exercise it"). See *J. W. Hampton, Jr., & Co.* v. *United States,* 276 U.S. 394, 406 (1928) (Congress may not "invest itself or its members with either executive power or judicial power"). Similarly, the President may not exercise the legislative power to authorize the seizure of private property for public use. *Youngstown,* 343 U. S., at 588. And, the judicial power to decide cases and controversies does not include the provision of purely advisory opinions to the Executive, or permit the federal courts to resolve nonjusticiable questions.

Of course the lines between the powers of the three branches are not always neatly defined. See *Mistretta* v. *United States,* 488 U.S. 361, 380–381 (1989). But in this case there is no suggestion that the Federal Judiciary is being asked to perform any function that might in some way be described as "executive." Respondent is merely asking the courts to exercise their core Article III jurisdiction to decide cases and controversies. Whatever the outcome of this case, there is no possibility that the decision will curtail the scope of the official powers of the Executive Branch. The litigation of questions that relate entirely to the unofficial conduct of the individual who happens to be the President poses no perceptible risk of misallocation of either judicial power or executive power.

Rather than arguing that the decision of the case will produce either an aggrandizement of judicial power or a narrowing of executive power, petitioner contends that—as a by product of an otherwise traditional exercise of judicial power—burdens will be placed on the President that will hamper the performance of his official duties. We have recognized that "[e]ven when a branch does not arrogate power to itself . . . the separation of powers doctrine requires that a branch not impair another in the performance of its constitutional duties." *Loving* v. *United States*, 517 U. S. ___, ___ (1996) (slip op., at 8); see also *Nixon* v. *Administrator of General Services*, 433 U.S. 425, 443 (1977). As a factual matter, petitioner contends that this particular case—as well as the potential additional litigation that an affirmance of the Court of Appeals judgment might spawn—may impose an unacceptable burden on the President's time and energy, and thereby impair the effective performance of his office.

Petitioner's predictive judgment finds little support in either history or the relatively narrow compass of the issues raised in this particular case. As we have already noted, in the more than 200-year history of the Republic, only three sitting Presidents have been subjected to suits for their private actions. See *supra*, at 9–10. If the past is any indicator, it seems unlikely that a deluge of such litigation will ever engulf the Presidency. As for the case at hand, if properly managed by the District Court, it appears to us highly unlikely to occupy any substantial amount of petitioner's time.

Of greater significance, petitioner errs by presuming that interactions between the Judicial Branch and the Executive, even quite burdensome interactions, necessarily rise to the level of constitutionally forbidden impairment of the Executive's ability to perform its constitutionally mandated functions. "[O]ur . . . system imposes upon the Branches a degree of overlapping responsibility, a duty of interdependence as well as independence the absence of which 'would preclude the establishment of a Nation capable of governing itself effectively.'" *Mistretta*, 488 U. S., at 381 (quoting *Buckley*, 424 U. S., at 121). As Madison explained, separation of powers does not mean that the branches "ought to have no *partial*

agency in, or no *controul* over the acts of each other." The fact that a federal court's exercise of its traditional Article III jurisdiction may significantly burden the time and attention of the Chief Executive is not sufficient to establish a violation of the Constitution. Two long settled propositions, first announced by Chief Justice Marshall, support that conclusion.

First, we have long held that when the President takes official action, the Court has the authority to determine whether he has acted within the law. Perhaps the most dramatic example of such a case is our holding that President Truman exceeded his constitutional authority when he issued an order directing the Secretary of Commerce to take possession of and operate most of the Nation's steel mills in order to avert a national catastrophe. *Youngstown Sheet & Tube Co.* v. *Sawyer*, 343 U.S. 579 (1952). Despite the serious impact of that decision on the ability of the Executive Branch to accomplish its assigned mission, and the substantial time that the President must necessarily have devoted to the matter as a result of judicial involvement, we exercised our Article III jurisdiction to decide whether his official conduct conformed to the law. Our holding was an application of the principle established in *Marbury* v. *Madison*, 1 Cranch 137 (1803), that "[i]t is emphatically the province and duty of the judicial department to say what the law is." *Id.*, at 177.

Second, it is also settled that the President is subject to judicial process in appropriate circumstances. Although Thomas Jefferson apparently thought otherwise, Chief Justice Marshall, when presiding in the treason trial of Aaron Burr, ruled that a subpoena *duces tecum* could be directed to the President. *United States* v. *Burr*, 25 F. Cas. 30 (No. 14,692d) (CC Va. 1807). We unequivocally and emphatically endorsed Marshall's position when we held that President Nixon was obligated to comply with a subpoena commanding him to produce certain tape recordings of his conversations with his aides. *United States* v. *Nixon* 418 U.S. 683 (1974). As we explained, "neither the doctrine of separation of powers, nor the need for confidentiality of high level communications, without more, can sustain an absolute, unqualified Presidential privilege of immunity from judicial process under all circumstances." *Id.*, at 706.

Sitting Presidents have responded to court orders to provide testimony and other information with sufficient frequency that such interactions between the Judicial and Executive Branches can scarcely be thought a novelty. President Monroe responded to written interrogatories, see Rotunda, Presidents and Ex Presidents as Witnesses: A Brief Historical Footnote, 1975 U. Ill. L. F. 1, 5–6, President Nixon—as noted above—produced tapes in response to a subpoena *duces tecum*, see *United States* v. *Nixon*, President Ford complied with an order to give a deposition in a criminal trial, *United States* v. *Fromme*, 405 F. Supp. 578 (ED Cal. 1975), and President Clinton has twice given videotaped testimony in criminal proceedings, see *United States* v. *McDougal*, 934 F. Supp. 296 (ED Ark. 1996); *United States* v. *Branscum*, No., LRP-CR%96-49 (ED Ark., June 7, 1996). Moreover, sitting Presidents have also voluntarily complied with judicial requests for testimony. President Grant gave a lengthy deposition in a criminal case under such circumstances, R. Rotunda & J. Nowak, Treatise on Constitutional Law §7.1 (2d ed. 1992), and President Carter similarly gave videotaped testimony for use at a criminal trial, *ibid.*

In sum, "[i]t is settled law that the separation of powers doctrine does not bar every exercise of jurisdiction over the President of the United States." *Fitzgerald*, 457 U. S., at 753–754. If the Judiciary may severely burden the Executive Branch by reviewing the legality of the President's official conduct, and if it may direct appropriate process to the President himself, it must follow that the federal courts have power to determine the legality of his unofficial conduct. The burden on the President's time and energy that is a mere by product of such review surely cannot be considered as onerous as the direct burden imposed by judicial review and the occasional invalidation of his official actions. We therefore hold that the doctrine of separation of powers does not require federal courts to stay all private actions against the President until he leaves office.

The reasons for rejecting such a categorical rule apply as well to a rule that would require a stay "in all but the most exceptional cases." Brief for Petitioner i. Indeed, if the Framers of the Constitution had thought it necessary to protect the President from the burdens of private litigation, we think it far more likely that they would have adopted a categorical rule than a rule that required the President to litigate the question whether a specific case belonged in the "exceptional case" subcategory. In all events, the question whether a specific case should receive exceptional treatment is more appropriately the subject of the exercise of judicial discretion than an interpretation of the Constitution. Accordingly, we turn to the question whether the District Court's decision to stay the trial until after petitioner leaves office was an abuse of discretion.

The Court of Appeals described the District Court's discretionary decision to stay the trial as the "functional equivalent" of a grant of temporary immunity. 72 F. 3d, at 1361, n. 9. Concluding that petitioner was not constitutionally entitled to such an immunity, the court held that it was error to grant the stay. *Ibid.* Although we ultimately conclude that the stay should not have been granted, we think the issue is more difficult than the opinion of the Court of Appeals suggests.

Strictly speaking the stay was not the functional equivalent of the constitutional immunity that petitioner claimed, because the District Court ordered discovery to proceed.

Moreover, a stay of either the trial or discovery might be justified by considerations that do not require the recognition of any constitutional immunity. The District Court has broad discretion to stay proceedings as an incident to its power to control its own docket. See, *e.g.*, *Landis v. North American Co.*, 299 U.S. 248, 254 (1936). As we have explained, "[e]specially in cases of extraordinary public moment, [a plaintiff] may be required to submit to delay not immoderate in extent and not oppressive in its consequences if the public welfare or convenience will thereby be promoted." *Id.*, at 256. Although we have rejected the argument that the potential burdens on the President violate separation of powers principles, those burdens are appropriate matters for the District Court to evaluate in its management of the case. The high respect that is owed to the office of the Chief Executive, though not justifying a rule of categorical immunity, is a matter that should inform the conduct of the entire proceeding, including the timing and scope of discovery.

Nevertheless, we are persuaded that it was an abuse of discretion for the District Court to defer the trial until after the President leaves office. Such a lengthy and categorical stay takes no account whatever of the respondent's interest in bringing the case to trial. The complaint was filed within the statutory limitations period—albeit near the end of that period—and delaying trial would increase the danger of prejudice resulting from the loss of evidence, including the inability of witnesses to recall specific facts, or the possible death of a party.

The decision to postpone the trial was, furthermore, premature. The proponent of a stay bears the burden of establishing its need. *Id.*, at 255. In this case, at the stage at which the District Court made its ruling, there was no way to assess whether a stay of trial after the completion of discovery would be warranted. Other than the fact that a trial may consume some of the President's time and attention, there is

nothing in the record to enable a judge to assess the potential harm that may ensue from scheduling the trial promptly after discovery is concluded. We think the District Court may have given undue weight to the concern that a trial might generate unrelated civil actions that could conceivably hamper the President in conducting the duties of his office. If and when that should occur, the court's discretion would permit it to manage those actions in such fashion (including deferral of trial) that interference with the President's duties would not occur. But no such impingement upon the President's conduct of his office was shown here.

We add a final comment on two matters that are discussed at length in the briefs: the risk that our decision will generate a large volume of politically motivated harassing and frivolous litigation, and the danger that national security concerns might prevent the President from explaining a legitimate need for a continuance.

We are not persuaded that either of these risks is serious. Most frivolous and vexatious litigation is terminated at the pleading stage or on summary judgment, with little if any personal involvement by the defendant. See Fed. Rules Civ. Proc. 12, 56. Moreover, the availability of sanctions provides a significant deterrent to litigation directed at the President in his unofficial capacity for purposes of political gain or harassment. History indicates that the likelihood that a significant number of such cases will be filed is remote. Although scheduling problems may arise, there is no reason to assume that the District Courts will be either unable to accommodate the President's needs or unfaithful to the tradition—especially in matters involving national security—of giving "the utmost deference to Presidential responsibilities." Several Presidents, including petitioner, have given testimony without jeopardizing the Nation's security. See *supra*, at 23. In short, we have confidence in the ability of our federal judges to deal with both of these concerns.

If Congress deems it appropriate to afford the President stronger protection, it may respond with appropriate legislation. As petitioner notes in his brief, Congress has enacted more than one statute providing for the deferral of civil litigation to accommodate important public interests. Brief for Petitioner 34–36. See, *e.g.*, 11 U.S.C. § 362 (litigation against debtor stayed upon filing of bankruptcy petition); Soldiers' and Sailors' Civil Relief Act of 1940, 50 U. S. C. App. §§501–525 (provisions governing, *inter alia*, tolling or stay of civil claims by or against military personnel during course of active duty). If the Constitution embodied the rule that the President advocates, Congress, of course, could not repeal it. But our holding today raises no barrier to a statutory response to these concerns.

The Federal District Court has jurisdiction to decide this case. Like every other citizen who properly invokes that jurisdiction, respondent has a right to an orderly disposition of her claims. Accordingly, the judgment of the Court of Appeals is affirmed.

It is so ordered.

13. State of the Union Address January 27, 1998

From: The White House, Office of the Press Secretary

Mr. Speaker, Mr. Vice President, members of the 105th Congress, distinguished guests, my fellow Americans:

Since the last time we met in this chamber, America has lost two patriots and fine public servants. Though they sat on opposite sides of the aisle, Representatives Walter Capps [D, California] and Sonny Bono [R, California] shared a deep love for this House and an unshakable commitment to improving the lives of all our people. In the past few weeks they've

both been eulogized. Tonight, I think we should begin by sending a message to their families and their friends that we celebrate their lives and give thanks for their service to our nation.

For 209 years it has been the president's duty to report to you on the state of the Union. Because of the hard work and high purpose of the American people, these are good times for America. We have more than 14 million new jobs; the lowest unemployment in 24 years; the lowest core inflation in 30 years; incomes are rising; and we have the highest homeownership in history. Crime has dropped for a record five years in a row. And the welfare rolls are at their lowest levels in 27 years. Our leadership in the world is unrivaled. Ladies and gentlemen, the state of our Union is strong.

With barely 700 days left in the 20th century, this is not a time to rest. It is a time to build, to build the America within reach: an America where everybody has a chance to get ahead with hard work; where every citizen can live in a safe community; where families are strong, schools are good and all young people can go to college; an America where scientists find cures for diseases from diabetes to Alzheimer's to AIDS; an America where every child can stretch a hand across a keyboard and reach every book ever written, every painting ever painted, every symphony ever composed; where government provides opportunity and citizens honor the responsibility to give something back to their communities; an America which leads the world to new heights of peace and prosperity.

This is the America we have begun to build; this is the America we can leave to our children—if we join together to finish the work at hand. Let us strengthen our nation for the 21st century.

Rarely have Americans lived through so much change, in so many ways, in so short a time. Quietly, but with gathering force, the ground has shifted beneath our feet as we have moved into an Information Age, a global economy, a truly new world.

For five years now we have met the challenge of these changes as Americans have at every turning point—by renewing the very idea of America: widening the circle of opportunity, deepening the meaning of our freedom, forging a more perfect union.

We shaped a new kind of government for the Information Age. I thank the vice president for his leadership and the Congress for its support in building a government that is leaner, more flexible, a catalyst for new ideas—and most of all, a government that gives the American people the tools they need to make the most of their own lives.

We have moved past the sterile debate between those who say government is the enemy and those who say government is the answer. My fellow Americans, we have found a third way. We have the smallest government in 35 years, but a more progressive one. We have a smaller government, but a stronger nation. We are moving steadily toward an even stronger America in the 21st century: an economy that offers opportunity, a society rooted in responsibility and a nation that lives as a community.

First, Americans in this chamber and across our nation have pursued a new strategy for prosperity: fiscal discipline to cut interest rates and spur growth; investments in education and skills, in science and technology and transportation, to prepare our people for the new economy; new markets for American products and American workers.

When I took office, the deficit for 1998 was projected to be $357 billion, and heading higher. This year, our deficit is projected to be $10 billion, and heading lower. For three decades, six presidents have come before you to warn of the damage deficits pose to our nation. Tonight, I come before you to announce that the federal deficit—once so incomprehensibly large that it had 11 zeroes—will be, simply, zero. I will submit to Congress for 1999 the first balanced budget in 30 years. And if we hold fast to fiscal discipline, we may balance the budget this year—four years ahead of schedule.

You can all be proud of that, because turning a sea of red ink into black is no miracle. It is the product of hard work by the American people, and of two visionary actions in Congress—the courageous vote in 1993 that led to a cut in the deficit of 90 percent and the truly historic bipartisan balanced budget agreement passed by this Congress. Here's the really good news: If we maintain our resolve, we will produce balanced budgets as far as the eye can see.

We must not go back to unwise spending or untargeted tax cuts that risk reopening the deficit. Last year, together we enacted targeted tax cuts so that the typical middle class family will now have the lowest tax rates in 20 years. My plan to balance the budget next year includes both new investments and new tax cuts targeted to the needs of working families: for education, for child care, for the environment.

But whether the issue is tax cuts or spending, I ask all of you to meet this test: Approve only those priorities that can actually be accomplished without adding a dime to the deficit.

Now, if we balance the budget for next year, it is projected that we'll then have a sizable surplus in the years that immediately follow. What should we do with this projected surplus? I have a simple four-word answer: Save Social Security first.

Tonight, I propose that we reserve 100 percent of the surplus—that's every penny of any surplus—until we have taken all the necessary measures to strengthen the Social Security system for the 21st century. Let us say to all Americans watching tonight—whether you're 70 or 50, or whether you just started paying into the system—Social Security will be there when you need it. Let us make this commitment: Social Security first. Let's do that together.

I also want to say that all the American people who are watching us tonight should be invited to join in this discussion, in facing these issues squarely, and forming a true consensus on how we should proceed. We'll start by conducting nonpartisan forums in every region of the country—and I hope that lawmakers of both parties will participate. We'll hold a White House Conference on Social Security in December. And one year from now I will convene the leaders of Congress to craft historic, bipartisan legislation to achieve a landmark for our generation—a Social Security system that is strong in the 21st century.

In an economy that honors opportunity, all Americans must be able to reap the rewards of prosperity. Because these times are good, we can afford to take one simple, sensible step to help millions of workers struggling to provide for their families: We should raise the minimum wage.

The Information Age is, first and foremost, an education age, in which education must start at birth and continue throughout a lifetime. Last year, from this podium, I said that education has to be our highest priority. I laid out a 10-point plan to move us forward and urged all of us to let politics stop at the schoolhouse door. Since then, this Congress, across party lines, and the American people have responded, in the most important year for education in a generation—expanding public school choice, opening the way to 3,000 new charter schools, working to connect every classroom in the country to the Information Superhighway, committing to expand Head Start to a million children, launching America Reads, sending literally thousands of college students into our elementary schools to make sure all our eight-year-olds can read.

Last year I proposed, and you passed, 220,000 new Pell Grant scholarships for deserving students. Student loans, already less expensive and easier to repay, now you get to deduct the interest. Families all over America now can put their savings into new tax-free education IRAs. And this year, for the first two years of college, families will get a $1,500 tax credit—a HOPE Scholarship that will cover the cost of most community college tuition. And for junior and senior year, graduate school and job training, there is a lifetime learning credit. You did that and you should be very proud of it.

And because of these actions, I have something to say to every family listening to us tonight: Your children can go on to college. If you know a child from a poor family, tell her not to give up—she can go on to college. If you know a young couple struggling with bills, worried they won't be able to send their children to college, tell them not to give up—their children can go on to college. If you know somebody who's caught in a dead-end job and afraid he can't afford the classes necessary to get better jobs for the rest of his life, tell him not to give up—he can go on to college. Because of the things that have been done, we can make college as universal in the 21st century as high school is today. And, my friends, that will change the face and future of America.

We have opened wide the doors of the world's best system of higher education. Now we must make our public elementary and secondary schools the world's best as well by raising standards, raising expectations and raising accountability.

Thanks to the actions of this Congress last year, we will soon have, for the very first time, a voluntary national test based on national standards in 4th grade reading and 8th grade math. Parents have a right to know whether their children are mastering the basics. And every parent already knows the key: good teachers and small classes. Tonight, I propose the first ever national effort to reduce class size in the early grades.

My balanced budget will help to hire 100,000 new teachers who have passed a state competency test. Now, with these teachers—listen—with these teachers, we will actually be able to reduce class size in the 1st, 2nd and 3rd grades to an average of 18 students a class, all across America.

If I've got the math right, more teachers teaching smaller classes requires more classrooms. So I also propose a school construction tax cut to help communities modernize or build 5,000 schools.

We must also demand greater accountability. When we promote a child from grade to grade who hasn't mastered the work, we don't do that child any favors. It is time to end social promotion in America's schools.

Last year, in Chicago, they made that decision—not to hold our children back, but to lift them up. Chicago stopped social promotion, and started mandatory summer school, to help students who are behind to catch up. I propose to help other communities follow Chicago's lead. Let's say to them: Stop promoting children who don't learn, and we will give you the tools to make sure they do.

I also ask this Congress to support our efforts to enlist colleges and universities to reach out to disadvantaged children, starting in the 6th grade, so that they can get the guidance and hope they need so they can know that they, too, will be able to go on to college.

As we enter the 21st century, the global economy requires us to seek opportunity not just at home, but in all the markets of the world. We must shape this global economy, not shrink from it. In the last five years, we have led the way in opening new markets, with 240 trade agreements that remove foreign barriers to products bearing the proud stamp "Made in the USA." Today, record high exports account for fully one-third of our economic growth. I want to keep them going, because that's the way to keep America growing and to advance a safer, more stable world.

All of you know whatever your views are that I think this a great opportunity for America. I know there is opposition to more comprehensive trade agreements. I have listened carefully and I believe that the opposition is rooted in two fears: first, that our trading partners will have lower environmental and labor standards which will give them an unfair advantage in our market and do their own people no favors, even if there's more business; and, second, that if we have more trade, more of our workers will lose their jobs and have to start over. I think we should seek to advance worker and environmental standards around the world. I have made it abundantly clear that it should be a part of our trade agenda. But we cannot influence other countries' decisions if we send them a message that we're backing away from trade with them.

This year, I will send legislation to Congress, and ask other nations to join us, to fight the most intolerable labor practice of all—abusive child labor. We should also offer help and hope to those Americans temporarily left behind by the global marketplace or by the march of technology, which may have nothing to do with trade. That's why we have more than doubled funding for training dislocated workers since 1993—and if my new budget is adopted, we will triple funding. That's why we must do more, and more quickly, to help workers who lose their jobs for whatever reason.

You know, we help communities in a special way when their military base closes. We ought to help them in the same way if their factory closes. Again, I ask the Congress to continue its bipartisan work to consolidate the tangle of training programs we have today into one single G.I. Bill for Workers, a simple skills grant so people can, on their own, move quickly to new jobs, to higher incomes and brighter futures.

We all know in every way in life change is not always easy, but we have to decide whether we're going to try to hold it back and hide from it or reap its benefits. And remember the big picture here: While we've been entering into hundreds of new trade agreements, we've been creating millions of new jobs. So this year we will forge new partnerships with Latin America, Asia and Europe. And we should pass the new African Trade Act—it has bipartisan support. I will also renew my request for the fast track negotiating authority necessary to open more new markets, create more new jobs, which every president has had for two decades.

You know, whether we like it or not, in ways that are mostly positive, the world's economies are more and more interconnected and interdependent. Today, an economic crisis anywhere can affect economies everywhere. Recent months have brought serious financial problems to Thailand, Indonesia, South Korea and beyond.

Now, why should Americans be concerned about this? First, these countries are our customers. If they sink into recession, they won't be able to buy the goods we'd like to sell them. Second, they're also our competitors. So if their currencies lose their value and go down, then the price of their goods will drop, flooding our market and others with much cheaper goods, which makes it a lot tougher for our people to compete. And, finally, they are our strategic partners. Their stability bolsters our security.

The American economy remains sound and strong, and I want to keep it that way. But because the turmoil in Asia will have an impact on all the world's economies, including ours, making that negative impact as small as possible is the right thing to do for America—and the right thing to do for a safer world.

Our policy is clear: No nation can recover if it does not reform itself. But when nations are willing to undertake serious economic reform, we should help them do it. So I call on Congress to renew America's commitment to the International Monetary Fund. And I think we should say to all the people we're trying to represent here that preparing for a far-off storm that may reach our shores is far wiser than ignoring the thunder until the clouds are just overhead.

A strong nation rests on the rock of responsibility. A society rooted in responsibility must first promote the value of work, not welfare. We can be proud that after decades of finger-pointing and failure, together we ended the old welfare system. And we're now replacing welfare checks with paychecks.

Last year, after a record four-year decline in welfare rolls, I challenged our nation to move two million more Americans off welfare by the year 2000. I'm pleased to report we have also met that goal, two full years ahead of schedule. This is a grand achievement, the sum of many acts of individual courage, persistence and hope. For 13 years, Elaine Kinslow of Indianapolis, Indiana, was on and off welfare. Today, she's a dispatcher with a van company. She's saved enough money to move her family into a good neighborhood, and she's helping other welfare recipients go to work. Elaine Kinslow and all those like her are the real heroes of the welfare revolution. There are millions like her all across America. And I'm happy she could join the First Lady tonight. Elaine, we're very proud of you. Please stand up.

We still have a lot more to do, all of us, to make welfare reform a success—providing child care, helping families move closer to available jobs, challenging more companies to join our welfare-to-work partnership, increasing child support collections from deadbeat parents who have a duty to support their own children. I also want to thank Congress for restoring some of the benefits to immigrants who are here legally and working hard—and I hope you will finish that job this year.

We have to make it possible for all hard-working families to meet their most important responsibilities. Two years ago, we helped guarantee that Americans can keep their health insurance when they change jobs. Last year, we extended health care to up to 5 million children. This year, I challenge Congress to take the next historic steps.

One hundred sixty million of our fellow citizens are in managed care plans. These plans save money and they can improve care. But medical decisions ought to be made by medical doctors, not insurance company accountants. I urge this Congress to reach across the aisle and write into law a Consumer Bill of Rights that says this: You have the right to know all your medical options, not just the cheapest. You have the right to choose the doctor you want for the care you need. You have the right to emergency room care, wherever and whenever you need it. You have the right to keep your medical records confidential. Traditional care or managed care, every American deserves quality care.

Millions of Americans between the ages of 55 and 65 have lost their health insurance. Some are retired; some are laid off; some lose their coverage when their spouses retire. After a lifetime of work, they are left with nowhere to turn. So I ask the Congress: Let these hard-working Americans buy into the Medicare system. It won't add a dime to the deficit—but the peace of mind it will provide will be priceless.

Next, we must help parents protect their children from the gravest health threat that they face: an epidemic of teen smoking, spread by multimillion-dollar marketing campaigns. I challenge Congress: Let's pass bipartisan, comprehensive legislation that improve public health, protect our tobacco farmers, and change the way tobacco companies do business forever. Let's do what it takes to bring teen smoking down. Let's raise the price of cigarettes by up to $1.50 a pack over the next 10 years, with penalties on the tobacco industry if it keeps marketing to our children. Tomorrow, like every day, 3,000 children will start smoking, and 1,000 will die early as a result. Let this Congress be remembered as the Congress that saved their lives.

In the new economy, most parents work harder than ever. They face a constant struggle to balance their obligations to be good workers—and their even more important obligations to be good parents. The Family and Medical Leave Act was the very first bill I was privileged to sign into law as president in 1993. Since then, about 15 million people have taken advantage of it, and I've met a lot of them all across this country. I ask you to extend that law to cover 10 million more workers, and to give parents time off when they have to go see their children's teachers or take them to the doctor.

Child care is the next frontier we must face to enable people to succeed at home and at work. Last year, I co-hosted the very first White House Conference on Child Care with one of our foremost experts, America's First Lady. From all corners of America, we heard the same message, without regard to region or income or political affiliation: We've got to raise the quality of child care. We've got to make it safer. We've got to make it more affordable.

So here's my plan: Help families to pay for child care for a million more children. Scholarships and background checks for child care workers, and a new emphasis on early learning. Tax credits for businesses that provide child care for their employees. And a larger child care tax credit for working families. Now, if you pass my plan, what this means is that a family of four with an income of $35,000 and high child care costs will no longer pay a single penny of federal income tax.

I think this is such a big issue with me because of my own personal experience. I have often wondered how my mother, when she was a young widow, would have been able to go away to school and get an education and come back and support me if my grandparents hadn't been able to take care of me. She and I were really very lucky. How many other families have never had that same opportunity? The truth is, we don't know the answer to that question. But we do know what the answer should be: Not a single American family should have to choose between the job they need and the child they love.

A society rooted in responsibility must provide safe streets, safe schools and safe neighborhoods. We pursued a strategy of more police, tougher punishment, smarter prevention, with crime-fighting partnerships with local law enforcement and citizen groups, where the rubber hits the road. I can report to you tonight that it's working. Violent crime is down, robbery is down, assault is down, burglary is down—for five years in a row, all across America. We need to finish the job of putting 100,000 more police on our streets.

Again, I ask Congress to pass a juvenile crime bill that provides more prosecutors and probation officers, to crack down on gangs and guns and drugs, and bar violent juveniles from buying guns for life. And I ask you to dramatically expand our support for after-school programs. I think every American should know that most juvenile crime is committed between the hours of 3:00 in the afternoon and 8:00 at night. We can keep so many of our children out of trouble in the first place if we give them someplace to go other than the streets, and we ought to do it.

Drug use is on the decline. I thank General McCaffrey for his leadership. And I thank this Congress for passing the largest antidrug budget in history. I ask you to join me in a groundbreaking effort to hire 1,000 new border patrol agents and to deploy the most sophisticated available new technologies to help close the door on drugs at our borders.

Police, prosecutors, and prevention programs, as good as they are, they can't work if

our court system doesn't work. Today there are a large number of vacancies in the federal courts. Here is what the Chief Justice of the United States wrote: Judicial vacancies cannot remain at such high levels indefinitely without eroding the quality of justice. I simply ask the United States Senate to heed this plea, and vote on the highly qualified judicial nominees before you, up or down.

We must exercise responsibility not just at home, but around the world. On the eve of a new century, we have the power and the duty to build a new era of peace and security. But, make no mistake about it, today's possibilities are not tomorrow's guarantees. America must stand against the poisoned appeals of extreme nationalism. We must combat an unholy axis of new threats from terrorists, international criminals and drug traffickers. These 21st century predators feed on technology and the free flow of information and ideas and people. And they will be all the more lethal if weapons of mass destruction fall into their hands.

To meet these challenges, we are helping to write international rules of the road for the 21st century, protecting those who join the family of nations and isolating those who do not. Within days, I will ask the Senate for its advice and consent to make Hungary, Poland, and the Czech Republic the newest members of NATO. For 50 years, NATO contained communism and kept America and Europe secure. Now these three formerly communist countries have said yes to democracy. I ask the Senate to say yes to them—our new allies.

By taking in new members and working closely with new partners, including Russia and Ukraine, NATO can help to assure that Europe is a stronghold for peace in the 21st century.

Next, I will ask Congress to continue its support for our troops and their mission in Bosnia. This Christmas, Hillary and I traveled to Sarajevo with Senator and Mrs. Dole and a bipartisan congressional delegation. We saw children playing in the streets, where two years ago they were hiding from snipers and shells. The shops are filled with food; the cafes were alive with conversation. The progress there is unmistakable—but it is not yet irreversible. To take firm root, Bosnia's fragile peace still needs the support of American and allied troops when the current NATO mission ends in June. I think Senator Dole actually said it best. He said, "This is like being ahead in the 4th quarter of a football game. Now is not the time to walk off the field and forfeit the victory."

I wish all of you could have seen our troops in Tuzla. They're very proud of what they're doing in Bosnia. And we're all very proud of them. One of those brave soldiers is sitting with the First Lady tonight—Army Sergeant Michael Tolbert. His father was a decorated Vietnam vet. After college in Colorado, he joined the Army. Last year, he led an infantry unit that stopped a mob of extremists from taking over a radio station that is a voice of democracy and tolerance in Bosnia. Thank you very much, Sergeant, for what you represent.

In Bosnia and around the world, our men and women in uniform always do their mission well. Our mission must be to keep them well-trained and ready, to improve their quality of life, and to provide the 21st century weapons they need to defeat any enemy.

I ask Congress to join me in pursuing an ambitious agenda to reduce the serious threat of weapons of mass destruction. This year, four decades after it was first proposed by President Eisenhower, a comprehensive nuclear test ban is within reach. By ending nuclear testing we can help to prevent the development of new and more dangerous weapons and make it more difficult for non-nuclear states to build them.

I'm pleased to announce four former Chairmen of the Joint Chiefs of Staff—Generals John Shalikashvili, Colin Powell and David Jones, and Admiral William Crowe—have endorsed this treaty. And I ask the Senate to approve it this year.

Together, we also must confront the new hazards of chemical and biological weapons, and the outlaw states, terrorists and organized criminals seeking to acquire them. Saddam Hussein has spent the better part of this decade, and much of his nation's wealth, not on providing for the Iraqi people, but on developing nuclear, chemical and biological weapons—and the missiles to deliver them. The United Nations weapons inspectors have done a truly remarkable job, finding and destroying more of Iraq's arsenal than was destroyed during the entire Gulf War. Now Saddam Hussein wants to stop them from completing their mission.

I know I speak for everyone in this chamber, Republicans and Democrats, when I say to Saddam Hussein: You cannot defy the will of the world. And when I say to him: You have used weapons of mass destruction before; we are determined to deny you the capacity to use them again.

Last year, the Senate ratified the Chemical Weapons Convention to protect our soldiers and citizens from poison gas. Now we must act to prevent the use of disease as a weapon of war and terror. The Biological Weapons Convention has been in effect for 23 years now. The rules are good, but the enforcement is weak. We must strengthen it with a new international inspection system to detect and deter cheating.

In the months ahead, I will pursue our security strategy with old allies in Asia and Europe, and new partners from Africa to India and Pakistan, from South America to China. And from Belfast, to Korea to the Middle East, America will continue to stand with those who stand for peace.

Finally, it's long past time to make good on our debt to the United Nations. More and more, we are working with other nations to achieve common goals. If we want America to lead, we've got to set a good example. As we see so clearly in Bosnia, allies who share our goals can also share our burdens. In this new era, our freedom and independence are actually enriched, not weakened, by our increasing interdependence with other nations. But we have to do our part.

Our founders set America on a permanent course toward "a more perfect union." To all of you I say it is a journey we can only make together—living as one community. First, we have to continue to reform our government— the instrument of our national community. Everyone knows elections have become too expensive, fueling a fundraising arms race. This year, by March 6th, at long last the Senate will actually vote on bipartisan campaign finance reform proposed by Senators [John] McCain [R, Arizona] and [Russell] Feingold [D, Wisconsin]. Let's be clear: A vote against McCain and Feingold is a vote for soft money and for the status quo. I ask you to strengthen our democracy and pass campaign finance reform this year.

At least equally important, we have to address the real reason for the explosion in campaign costs—the high cost of media advertising. To the folks watching at home, those were the groans of pain in the audience. I will formally request that the Federal Communications Commission act to provide free or reduced-cost television time for candidates who observe spending limits voluntarily. The airwaves are a public trust, and broadcasters also have to help us in this effort to strengthen our democracy.

Under the leadership of Vice President Gore, we've reduced the federal payroll by 300,000 workers, cut 16,000 pages of regulation, eliminated hundreds of programs and improved the operations of virtually every government agency. But we can do more. Like every taxpayer, I'm outraged by the reports of abuses by the IRS. We need some changes there—new citizen advocacy panels, a stronger taxpayer advocate, phone lines open 24 hours a day, relief for innocent taxpayers. Last year, by an overwhelming bipartisan margin, the House of Representatives passed sweeping IRS reforms. This bill must not now languish in the Senate. Tonight I ask the Senate: follow the House, pass the bipartisan package as your first order of business.

I hope to goodness before I finish I can think of something to say, "follow the Senate" on, so I'll be out of trouble.

A nation that lives as a community must value all its communities. For the past five years, we have worked to bring the spark of private enterprise to inner city and poor rural areas—with community development banks, more commercial loans in the poor neighborhoods, cleanup of polluted sites for development. Under the continued leadership of the vice president, we propose to triple the number of empowerment zones, to give business incentives to invest in those areas. We should also give poor families more help to move into homes of their own, and we should use tax cuts to spur the construction of more low-income housing.

Last year, this Congress took strong action to help the District of Columbia. Let us renew our resolve to make our capital city a great city for all who live and visit here. Our cities are the vibrant hubs of great metropolitan areas. They are still the gateways for new immigrants, from every continent, who come here to work for their own American Dreams. Let's keep our cities going strong into the 21st century. They're a very important part of our future.

Our communities are only as healthy as the air our children breathe, the water they drink, the Earth they will inherit. Last year, we put in place the toughest-ever controls on smog and soot. We moved to protect Yellowstone, the Everglades, Lake Tahoe. We expanded every community's right to know about the toxins that threaten their children. Just yesterday, our food safety plan took effect, using new science to protect consumers from dangers like *E. coli* and salmonella.

Tonight, I ask you to join me in launching a new Clean Water Initiative, a far-reaching effort to clean our rivers, our lakes, our coastal waters for our children.

Our overriding environmental challenge tonight is the worldwide problem of climate change, global warming, the gathering crisis that requires worldwide action. The vast majority of scientists have concluded unequivocally that if we don't reduce the emission of greenhouse gases, at some point in the next century we'll disrupt our climate and put our children and grandchildren at risk. This past December, America led the world to reach a historic agreement committing our nation to reduce greenhouse gas emissions through market forces, new technologies, energy efficiency. We have it in our power to act right here, right now. I propose $6 billion in tax cuts and research and development to encourage innovation, renewable energy, fuel-efficient cars, energy-efficient homes.

Every time we have acted to heal our environment, pessimists have told us it would hurt the economy. Well, today our economy is the strongest in a generation, and our environment is the cleanest in a generation. We have always found a way to clean the environment and grow the economy at the same time. And when it comes to global warming, we'll do it again.

Finally, community means living by the defining American value—the ideal heard round the world that we are all created equal. Throughout our history, we haven't always honored that ideal and we've never fully lived up to it. Often it's easier to believe that our differences matter more than what we have in common. It may be easier, but it's wrong.

What we have to do in our day and generation to make sure that America becomes truly one nation—what do we have to do? We're becoming more and more and more diverse. Do you believe we can become one nation? The answer cannot be to dwell on our differences, but to build on our shared values. We all cherish family and faith, freedom and responsibility. We all want our children to grow up in a world where their talents are matched by their opportunities.

I've launched this national initiative on race to help us recognize our common interests and to bridge the opportunity gaps that are keeping us from becoming one America. Let us begin by recognizing what we still must overcome. Discrimination against any American is un-American. We must vigorously enforce the laws that make it illegal. I ask your help to end the backlog at the Equal Employment Opportunity Commission. Sixty thousand of our fellow citizens are waiting in line for justice, and we should act now to end their wait.

We also should recognize that the greatest progress we can make toward building one America lies in the progress we make for all Americans, without regard to race. When we open the doors of college to all Americans, when we rid all our streets of crime, when there are jobs available to people from all our neighborhoods, when we make sure all parents have the child care they need, we're helping to build one nation.

We, in this chamber and in this government, must do all we can to address the continuing American challenge to build one America. But we'll only move forward if all our fellow citizens—including every one of you at home watching tonight—is also committed to this cause.

We must work together, learn together, live together, serve together. On the forge of common enterprise Americans of all backgrounds can hammer out a common identity. We see it today in the United States military, in the Peace Corps, in AmeriCorps. Wherever people of all races and backgrounds come together in a shared endeavor and get a fair chance, we do just fine. With shared values and meaningful opportunities and honest communication and citizen service, we can unite a diverse people in freedom and mutual respect. We are many; we must be one.

In that spirit, let us lift our eyes to the new millennium. How will we mark that passage? It just happens once every thousand years. This year, Hillary and I launched the White House Millennium Program to promote America's creativity and innovation, and to preserve our heritage and culture into the 21st century. Our culture lives in every community, and every community has places of historic value that tell our stories as Americans. We should protect them. I am proposing a public-private partnership to advance our arts and humanities, and to celebrate the millennium by saving American's treasures, great and small.

And while we honor the past, let us imagine the future. Think about this—the entire store of human knowledge now doubles every five years. In the 1980s, scientists identified the gene causing cystic fibrosis—it took nine years. Last year, scientists located the gene that causes Parkinson's Disease—in only nine days. Within a decade, "gene chips" will offer a road map for prevention of illnesses throughout a lifetime. Soon we'll be able to carry all the phone calls on Mother's Day on a single strand of fiber the width of a human hair. A child born in 1998 may well live to see the 22nd century.

Tonight, as part of our gift to the millennium, I propose a 21st Century Research Fund for pathbreaking scientific inquiry—the largest funding increase in history for the National Institutes of Health, the National Science Foundation, the National Cancer Institute.

We have already discovered genes for breast cancer and diabetes. I ask you to support this initiative so ours will be the generation that finally wins the war against cancer, and begins a revolution in our fight against all deadly diseases.

As important as all this scientific progress is, we must continue to see that science serves humanity, not the other way around. We must prevent the misuse of genetic tests to discriminate against any American. And we must ratify the ethical consensus of the scientific and religious communities, and ban the cloning of human beings.

We should enable all the world's people to explore the far reaches of cyberspace. Think of this—the first time I made a State of the Union speech to you, only a handful of physicists used the World Wide Web. Literally, just a handful of people.

Now, in schools, in libraries, homes and businesses, millions and millions of Americans surf the Net every day. We must give parents the tools they need to help protect their children from inappropriate material on the Internet. But we also must make sure that we protect the exploding global commercial potential of the Internet. We can do the kinds of things that we need to do and still protect our kids.

For one thing, I ask Congress to step up support for building the next generation Internet. It's getting kind of clogged, you know. And the next generation Internet will operate at speeds up to a thousand times faster than today.

Even as we explore this inner space in a new millennium we're going to open new frontiers in outer space. Throughout all history, humankind has had only one place to call home—our planet Earth. Beginning this year, 1998, men and women from 16 countries will build a foothold in the heavens—the international space station. With its vast expanses, scientists and engineers will actually set sail on an unchartered sea of limitless mystery and unlimited potential.

And this October, a true American hero, a veteran pilot of 149 combat missions and one, five-hour space flight that changed the world, will return to the heavens. Godspeed, [Senator] John Glenn [D, Ohio]. John, you will carry with you America's hopes. And on your uniform, once again, you will carry America's flag, marking the unbroken connection between the deeds of America's past and the daring of America's future.

Nearly 200 years ago, a tattered flag, its broad stripes and bright stars still gleaming through the smoke of a fierce battle, moved Francis Scott Key to scribble a few words on the back of an envelope—the words that became our national anthem. Today, that Star Spangled Banner, along with the Declaration of Independence, the Constitution and the Bill of Rights, are on display just a short walk from here. They are America's treasures and we must also save them for the ages.

I ask all Americans to support our project to restore all our treasures so that the generations of the 21st century can see for themselves the images and the words that are the old and continuing glory of America; an America that has continued to rise through every age, against every challenge, of people of great works and greater possibilities, who have always, always found the wisdom and strength to come together as one nation—to widen the circle of opportunity, to deepen the meaning of our freedom, to form that "more perfect union." Let that be our gift to the 21st century.

14. The Articles of Impeachment for President Clinton December 12, 1998

From: Facts On File, Inc. *Landmark Documents in American History*

U.S. House Committee Backs Impeachment Articles Against President Clinton in Lewinsky Scandal

Text of Articles of Impeachment

Resolution impeaching William Jefferson Clinton, President of the United States, for high crimes and misdemeanors.

Resolved, that William Jefferson Clinton, President of the United States, is impeached for high crimes and misdemeanors, and that the following articles of impeachment be exhibited to the United States Senate:

Articles of impeachment exhibited by the House of Representatives of the United States of America in the name of itself and of the people of the United States of America, against William Jefferson Clinton, President of the United States of America, in maintenance and support of its impeachment against him for high crimes and misdemeanors.

Article I

In his conduct while President of the United States, William Jefferson Clinton, in violation of his constitutional oath faithfully to execute the office of President of the United States and, to the best of his ability, preserve, protect, and defend the Constitution of the United States, and in violation of his constitutional duty to take care that the laws be faithfully executed, has willfully corrupted and manipulated the judicial process of the United States for his personal gain and exoneration, impeding the administration of justice, in that:

On August 17, 1998, William Jefferson Clinton swore to tell the truth, the whole truth, and nothing but the truth before a Federal grand jury of the United States. Contrary to that oath, William Jefferson Clinton willfully provided perjurious, false and misleading testimony to the grand jury concerning one or more of the following: (1) the nature and details of his relationship with a subordinate Government employee; (2) prior perjurious, false and misleading testimony he gave in a Federal civil rights action brought against him; (3) prior false and misleading statements he allowed his attorney to make to a Federal judge in that civil rights action; and (4) his corrupt efforts to influence the testimony of witnesses and to impede the discovery of evidence in that civil rights action.

In doing this, William Jefferson Clinton has undermined the integrity of his office, has brought disrepute on the Presidency, has betrayed his trust as President, and has acted in a manner subversive of the rule of law and justice, to the manifest injury of the people of the United States.

Wherefore, William Jefferson Clinton, by such conduct, warrants impeachment and trial, and removal from office and disqualification to hold and enjoy any office of honor, trust or profit under the United States.

Article II

In his conduct while President of the United States, William Jefferson Clinton, in violation of his constitutional oath faithfully to execute the office of President of the United States and, to the best of his ability, preserve, protect, and defend the Constitution of the United States, and in violation of his constitutional duty to take care that the laws be faithfully executed, has willfully corrupted and manipulated the judicial process of the United States for his personal gain and exoneration, impeding the administration of justice, in that:

(1) On December 23, 1997, William Jefferson Clinton, in sworn answers to written questions asked as part of a Federal civil rights action brought against him, willfully provided perjurious, false and misleading testimony in response to questions deemed relevant by a Federal judge concerning conduct and proposed conduct with subordinate employees.

(2) On January 17, 1998, William Jefferson Clinton swore under oath to tell the truth, the whole truth, and nothing but the truth in a deposition given as part of a Federal civil rights action brought against him. Contrary to that oath, William Jefferson Clinton willfully pro-

vided perjurious, false and misleading testimony in response to questions deemed relevant by a Federal judge concerning the nature and details of his relationship with a subordinate Government employee, his knowledge of that employee's involvement and participation in the civil rights action brought against him, and his corrupt efforts to influence the testimony of that employee.

In all of this, William Jefferson Clinton has undermined the integrity of his office, has brought disrepute on the Presidency, has betrayed his trust as President, and has acted in a manner subversive of the rule of law and justice, to the manifest injury of the people of the United States.

Wherefore, William Jefferson Clinton, by such conduct, warrants impeachment and trial, and removal from office and disqualification to hold and enjoy any office of honor, trust or profit under the United States.

Article III

In his conduct while President of the United States, William Jefferson Clinton, in violation of his constitutional oath faithfully to execute the office of President of the United States and, to the best of his ability, preserve, protect, and defend the Constitution of the United States, and in violation of his constitutional duty to take care that the laws be faithfully executed, has prevented, obstructed, and impeded the administration of justice, and has to that end engaged personally, and through his subordinates and agents, in a course of conduct or scheme designed to delay, impede, cover up, and conceal the existence of evidence and testimony related to a Federal civil rights action brought against him in a duly instituted judicial proceeding.

The means used to implement this course of conduct or scheme included one or more of the following acts:

(1) On or about December 17, 1997, William Jefferson Clinton corruptly encouraged a witness in a Federal civil rights action brought against him to execute a sworn affidavit in that proceeding that he knew to be perjurious, false and misleading.

(2) On or about December 17, 1997, William Jefferson Clinton corruptly encouraged a witness in a Federal civil rights action brought against him to give perjurious, false and misleading testimony if and when called to testify personally in that proceeding.

(3) On or about December 28, 1997, William Jefferson Clinton corruptly engaged in, encouraged, or supported a scheme to conceal evidence that had been subpoenaed in a Federal civil rights action brought against him.

(4) Beginning on or about December 7, 1997, and continuing through and including January 14, 1998, William Jefferson Clinton intensified and succeeded in an effort to secure job assistance to a witness in a Federal civil rights action brought against him in order to corruptly prevent the truthful testimony of that witness in that proceeding at a time when the truthful testimony of that witness would have been harmful to him.

(5) On January 17, 1998, at his deposition in a Federal civil rights action brought against him, William Jefferson Clinton corruptly allowed his attorney to make false and misleading statements to a Federal judge characterizing an affidavit, in order to prevent questioning deemed relevant by the judge. Such false and misleading statements were subsequently acknowledged by his attorney in a communication to that judge.

(6) On or about January 18 and January 20–21, 1998, William Jefferson Clinton related a false and misleading account of events relevant to a Federal civil rights action brought against him to a potential witness in that proceeding, in order to corruptly influence the testimony of that witness.

(7) On or about January 21, 23 and 26, 1998, William Jefferson Clinton made false and misleading statements to potential witnesses in a Federal grand jury proceeding in order to corruptly influence the testimony of those witnesses. The false and misleading statements made by William Jefferson Clinton were repeated by the witnesses to the grand jury, causing the grand jury to receive false and misleading information.

In all of this, William Jefferson Clinton has undermined the integrity of his office, has brought disrepute on the Presidency, has betrayed his trust as President, and has acted in a manner subversive of the rule of law and justice, to the manifest injury of the people of the United States.

Wherefore, William Jefferson Clinton, by such conduct, warrants impeachment and trial, and removal from office and disqualification to hold and enjoy any office of honor, trust or profit under the United States.

Article IV

Using the powers and influence of the office of President of the United States, William Jefferson Clinton, in violation of his constitutional oath faithfully to execute the office of President of the United States and, to the best of his ability, preserve, protect, and defend the Constitution of the United States, and in disregard of his constitutional duty to take care that the laws be faithfully executed, has engaged in conduct that resulted in misuse and abuse of his high office, impaired the due and proper administration of justice and the conduct of lawful inquiries, and contravened the authority of the legislative branch and the truth-seeking purpose of a coordinate investigative proceeding in that, as President, William Jefferson Clinton, refused and failed to respond to certain written requests for admission and willfully made perjurious, false and misleading sworn statements in response to certain written requests for admission propounded to him as part of the impeachment inquiry authorized by the House of Representatives of the Congress of the United States.

William Jefferson Clinton, in refusing and failing to respond, and in making perjurious, false and misleading statements, assumed to himself functions and judgments necessary to the exercise of the sole power of impeachment vested by the Constitution in the House of Representatives and exhibited contempt for the inquiry.

In doing this, William Jefferson Clinton has undermined the integrity of his office, has brought disrepute on the Presidency, has betrayed his trust as President, and has acted in a manner subversive of the rule of law and justice, to the manifest injury of the people of the United States.

Wherefore, William Jefferson Clinton, by such conduct, warrants impeachment and trial, and removal from office and disqualification to hold and enjoy any office of honor, trust or profit under the United States.

15. State of the Union Address January 19, 1999

From: The White House, Office of the Press Secretary

Mr. Speaker, Mr. Vice President, members of Congress, honored guests, my fellow Americans: Tonight, I have the honor of reporting to you on the State of the Union.

Let me begin by saluting the new Speaker of the House, and thanking him, especially tonight, for extending an invitation to two special guests sitting in the gallery with Mrs. Hastert: Lyn Gibson and Wei Ling Chestnut are the widows of the two brave Capitol Hill police officers who gave their lives to defend freedom's house.

Mr. Speaker, at your swearing-in, you asked us all to work together in a spirit of civility and bipartisanship. Mr. Speaker, let's do exactly that.

Tonight, I stand before you to report that America has created the longest peacetime economic expansion in our history—with nearly 18 million new jobs, wages rising at more than twice the rate of inflation, the highest home ownership in history, the smallest welfare rolls in 30 years, and the lowest peacetime unemployment since 1957.

For the first time in three decades, the budget is balanced. From a deficit of $290 billion in 1992, we had a surplus of $70 billion last year. And now we are on course for budget surpluses for the next 25 years.

Thanks to the pioneering leadership of all of you, we have the lowest violent crime rate in a quarter century and the cleanest environment in a quarter century. America is a strong force for peace from Northern Ireland to Bosnia to the Middle East.

Thanks to the leadership of Vice President Gore, we have a government for the Information Age. Once again, a government that is a progressive instrument of the common good, rooted in our oldest values of opportunity, responsibility and community; devoted to fiscal responsibility; determined to give our people the tools they need to make the most of their own lives in the 21st century—a 21st century government for 21st century America.

My fellow Americans, I stand before you tonight to report that the state of our union is strong.

America is working again. The promise of our future is limitless. But we cannot realize that promise if we allow the hum of our prosperity to lull us into complacency. How we fare as a nation far into the 21st century depends upon what we do as a nation today.

So with our budget surplus growing, our economy expanding, our confidence rising, now is the moment for this generation to meet our historic responsibility to the 21st century.

Our fiscal discipline gives us an unsurpassed opportunity to address a remarkable new challenge—the aging of America. With the number of elderly Americans set to double by 2030, the baby boom will become a senior boom. So first, and above all, we must save Social Security for the 21st century.

Early in this century, being old meant being poor. When President Roosevelt created Social Security, thousands wrote to thank him for eliminating what one woman called the "stark terror of penniless, helpless old age." Even today, without Social Security, half our nation's elderly would be forced into poverty.

Today, Social Security is strong. But by 2013, payroll taxes will no longer be sufficient to cover monthly payments. By 2032, the trust fund will be exhausted and Social Security will be unable to pay the full benefits older Americans have been promised.

The best way to keep Social Security a rock-solid guarantee is not to make drastic cuts in benefits, not to raise payroll tax rates, not to drain resources from Social Security in the name of saving it. Instead, I propose that we make an historic decision to invest the surplus to save Social Security.

Specifically, I propose that we commit 60 percent of the budget surplus for the next 15 years to Social Security, investing a small portion in the private sector, just as any private or state government pension would do. This will earn a higher return and keep Social Security sound for 55 years.

But we must aim higher. We should put Social Security on a sound footing for the next 75 years. We should reduce poverty among elderly women, who are nearly twice as likely to be poor as our other seniors. And we should eliminate the limits on what seniors on Social Security can earn.

Now, these changes will require difficult but fully achievable choices over and above the dedication of the surplus. They must be made on a bipartisan basis. They should be made this year. So let me say to you tonight, I reach out my hand to all of you in both Houses, in both parties, and ask that we join together in saying to the American people: We will save Social Security now.

Now, last year we wisely reserved all of the surplus until we knew what it would take to save Social Security. Again, I say, we shouldn't spend any of it—not any of it—until after Social Security is truly saved. First things first.

Second, once we have saved Social Security, we must fulfill our obligation to save and improve Medicare. Already, we have extended the life of the Medicare trust fund by 10 years—but we should extend it for at least another decade. Tonight, I propose that we use one out of every $6 in the surplus for the next 15 years to guarantee the soundness of Medicare until the year 2020.

But, again, we should aim higher. We must be willing to work in a bipartisan way and look at new ideas, including the upcoming report of the bipartisan Medicare Commission. If we work together, we can secure Medicare for the next two decades and cover the greatest growing need of seniors—affordable prescription drugs.

Third, we must help all Americans, from their first day on the job—to save, to invest, to create wealth. From its beginning, Americans have supplemented Social Security with private pensions and savings. Yet, today, millions of people retire with little to live on other than Social Security. Americans living longer than ever simply must save more than ever.

Therefore, in addition to saving Social Security and Medicare, I propose a new pension initiative for retirement security in the 21st century.

I propose that we use a little over 11 percent of the surplus to establish universal savings accounts—USA accounts—to give all Americans the means to save. With these new accounts Americans can invest as they choose and receive funds to match a portion of their savings, with extra help for those least able to save. USA accounts will help all Americans to share in our nation's wealth and to enjoy a more secure retirement. I ask you to support them.

Fourth, we must invest in long-term care. I propose a tax credit of $1,000 for the aged, ailing or disabled, and the families who care for them. Long-term care will become a bigger and bigger challenge with the aging of America, and we must do more to help our families deal with it.

I was born in 1946, the first year of the baby boom. I can tell you that one of the greatest concerns of our generation is our absolute determination not to let our growing old place an intolerable burden on our children and their ability to raise our grandchildren. Our economic success and our fiscal discipline now give us an opportunity to lift that burden from their shoulders, and we should take it.

Saving Social Security, Medicare, creating USA accounts—this is the right way to use the surplus. If we do so—if we do so—we will still have resources to meet critical needs in education and defense. And I want to point out that this proposal is fiscally sound. Listen to this: If we set aside 60 percent of the surplus for Social Security and 16 percent for Medicare, over the next 15 years, that saving will achieve the lowest level of publicly held debt since right before World War I, in 1917.

So with these four measures—saving Social Security, strengthening Medicare, establishing the USA accounts, supporting long-term care—we can begin to meet our generation's historic responsibility to establish true security for 21st century seniors.

Now, there are more children from more diverse backgrounds in our public schools than at any time in our history. Their education must provide the knowledge and nurture the creativity that will allow our entire nation to thrive in the new economy.

Today we can say something we couldn't say six years ago: With tax credits and more affordable student loans, with more work-study grants and more Pell grants, with education IRAs and the new HOPE Scholarship tax cut that more than five million Americans will receive this year, we have finally opened the doors of college to all Americans. With our support, nearly every state has set higher academic standards for public schools, and a voluntary national test is being developed to measure the progress of our students. With over $1 billion in discounts available this year, we are well on our way to our goal of connecting every classroom and library to the Internet.

Last fall, you passed our proposal to start hiring 100,000 new teachers to reduce class size in the early grades. Now I ask you to finish the job.

You know, our children are doing better. SAT scores are up; math scores have risen in nearly all grades. But there's a problem. While our 4th graders outperform their peers in other countries in math and science, our 8th graders are around average, and our 12th graders rank near the bottom. We must do better. Now, each year the national government invests more than $15 billion in our public schools. I believe we must change the way we invest that money, to support what works and to stop supporting what does not work.

First, later this year, I will send to Congress a plan that, for the first time, holds states and school districts accountable for progress and rewards them for results. My Education Accountability Act will require every school district receiving federal help to take the following five steps.

First, all schools must end social promotion. No child should graduate from high school with a diploma he or she can't read. We do our children no favors when we allow them to pass from grade to grade without mastering the material.

But we can't just hold students back because the system fails them. So my balanced budget triples the funding for summer school and after-school programs, to keep a million children learning.

Now, if you doubt this will work, just look at Chicago, which ended social promotion and made summer school mandatory for those who don't master the basics. Math and reading scores are up three years running—with some of the biggest gains in some of the poorest neighborhoods. It will work, and we should do it.

Second, all states and school districts must turn around their worst-performing schools—or shut them down. That's the policy established in North Carolina by Governor Jim Hunt. North Carolina made the biggest gains in test scores in the nation last year. Our budget includes $200 million to help states turn around their own failing schools.

Third, all states and school districts must be held responsible for the quality of their teachers. The great majority of our teachers do a fine job. But in too many schools, teachers don't have college majors—or even minors—in the subjects they teach. New teachers should be required to pass performance exams, and all teachers should know the subjects they're teaching. This year's balanced budget contains resources to help them reach higher standards.

And to attract talented young teachers to the toughest assignments, I recommend a sixfold increase in our program for college scholarships for students who commit to teach in the inner cities and isolated rural areas and Indian communities. Let us bring excellence in every part of America.

Fourth, we must empower parents, with more information and more choices. In too many communities, it's easier to get information on the quality of the local restaurants than on the quality of the local schools. Every school district should issue report cards on every school. And parents should be given more choices in selecting their public schools.

When I became President, there was just one independent public charter school in all America. With our support, on a bipartisan basis, today there are 1,100. My budget assures that early in the next century, there will be 3,000.

Fifth, to assure that our classrooms are truly places of learning, and to respond to what teachers have been asking us to do for years, we should say that all states and school districts must both adopt and implement sensible discipline policies.

Now, let's do one more thing for our children. Today, too many of our schools are so old they're falling apart, or so over-crowded students are learning in trailers. Last fall, Congress missed the opportunity to change that. This year, with 53 million children in our schools, Congress must not miss that opportunity again. I ask you to help our communities build or modernize 5,000 schools.

If we do these things—end social promotion; turn around failing schools; build modern ones; support qualified teachers; promote innovation, competition and discipline—then we will begin to meet our generation's historic responsibility to create 21st century schools.

Now, we also have to do more to support the millions of parents who give their all every day at home and at work. The most basic tool of all is a decent income. So let's raise the minimum wage by a dollar an hour over the next two years. And let's make sure that women and men get equal pay for equal work by strengthening enforcement of equal pay laws.

That was encouraging, you know. There was more balance on the seats. I like that. Let's give them a hand. That's great.

Working parents also need quality child care. So, again this year, I ask Congress to support our plan for tax credits and subsidies for working families, for improved safety and quality, for expanded after-school programs. And our plan also includes a new tax credit for stay-at-home parents, too. They need support, as well.

Parents should never have to worry about choosing between their children and their work. Now, the Family and Medical Leave Act—the very first bill I signed into law—has now, since 1993, helped millions and millions of Americans to care for a newborn baby or an ailing relative without risking their jobs. I think it's time, with all the evidence that it has been so little burdensome to employers, to extend Family Leave to 10 million more Americans working for smaller companies. And I hope you will support it.

Finally on the matter of work, parents should never have to face discrimination in the workplace. So I want to ask Congress to prohibit companies from refusing to hire or promote workers simply because they have children. That is not right.

America's families deserve the world's best medical care. Thanks to bipartisan federal support for medical research, we are now on the verge of new treatments to prevent or delay diseases from Parkinson's to Alzheimer's, to arthritis to cancer. But as we continue our advances in medical science, we can't let our medical system lag behind. Managed care has literally transformed medicine in America— driving down costs, but threatening to drive down quality as well.

I think we ought to say to every American: You should have the right to know all your medical options—not just the cheapest. If you need a specialist, you should have the right to see one. You have a right to the nearest emergency care if you're in an accident. These are things that we ought to say. And I think we ought to say, you should have a right to keep your doctor during a period of treatment, whether it's a pregnancy or a chemotherapy treatment, or anything else. I believe this.

Now, I've ordered these rights to be extended to the 85 million Americans served by Medicare, Medicaid, and other federal health programs. But only Congress can pass a patients' bill of rights for all Americans. Now, last year, Congress missed that opportunity and we must not miss that opportunity again. For the sake of our families, I ask us to join together across party lines and pass a strong, enforceable patients' bill of rights.

As more of our medical records are stored electronically, the threats to all our privacy increase. Because Congress has given me the authority to act if it does not do so by August, one way or another, we can all say to the American people, we will protect the privacy of medical records and we will do it this year.

Now, two years ago, the Congress extended health coverage to up to five million children. Now, we should go beyond that. We should make it easier for small businesses to offer health insurance. We should give people between the ages of 55 and 65 who lose their health insurance the chance to buy into Medicare. And we should continue to ensure access to family planning.

No one should have to choose between keeping health care and taking a job. And, therefore, I especially ask you tonight to join hands to pass the landmark bipartisan legislation—proposed by Senators Kennedy and Jeffords, Roth and Moynihan—to allow people with disabilities to keep their health insurance when they go to work.

We need to enable our public hospitals, our community, our university health centers to provide basic, affordable care for all the millions of working families who don't have any insurance. They do a lot of that today, but much more can be done. And my balanced budget makes a good down payment toward that goal. I hope you will think about them and support that provision.

Let me say we must step up our efforts to treat and prevent mental illness. No American should ever be afraid—ever—to address this disease. This year, we will host a White House Conference on Mental Health. With sensitivity, commitment and passion, Tipper Gore is leading our efforts here, and I'd like to thank her for what she's done. Thank you. Thank you.

As everyone knows, our children are targets of a massive media campaign to hook them on cigarettes. Now, I ask this Congress to resist the tobacco lobby, to reaffirm the FDA's authority to protect our children from tobacco, and to hold tobacco companies accountable while protecting tobacco farmers.

Smoking has cost taxpayers hundreds of billions of dollars under Medicare and other programs. You know, the states have been right about this—taxpayers shouldn't pay for the cost of lung cancer, emphysema and other smoking-related illnesses—the tobacco companies should. So tonight I announce that the Justice Department is preparing a litigation plan to take the tobacco companies to court—and with the funds we recover, to strengthen Medicare.

Now, if we act in these areas—minimum wage, family leave, child care, health care, the safety of our children—then we will begin to meet our generation's historic responsibility to strengthen our families for the 21st century.

Today, America is the most dynamic, competitive, job-creating economy in history. But we can do even better—in building a 21st century economy that embraces all Americans.

Today's income gap is largely a skills gap. Last year, the Congress passed a law enabling workers to get a skills grant to choose the training they need. And I applaud all of you here who were part of that. This year, I recommend a five-year commitment in the new system so that we can provide, over the next five years, appropriate training opportunities for all Americans who lose their jobs, and expand rapid response teams to help all towns which have been really hurt when businesses close. I hope you will support this.

Also, I ask your support for a dramatic increase in federal support for adult literacy, to mount a national campaign aimed at helping the millions and millions of working people who still read at less than a 5th grade level. We need to do this.

Here's some good news: In the past six years, we have cut the welfare rolls nearly in half. Two years ago, from this podium, I asked five companies to lead a national effort to hire people off welfare. Tonight, our Welfare to Work Partnership includes 10,000 companies who have hired hundreds of thousands of people. And our balanced budget will help another 200,000 people move to the dignity and pride of work. I hope you will support it.

We must do more to bring the spark of private enterprise to every corner of America—to build a bridge from Wall Street to Appalachia to the Mississippi Delta, to our Native American communities—with more support for community development banks, for empowerment zones, for 100,000 more vouchers for affordable housing. And I ask Congress to support our bold new plan to help businesses raise up to $15 billion in private sector capital to bring jobs and opportunities to our inner cities and rural areas—with tax credits, loan guarantees, including the new American Private Investment Company, modeled on the Overseas Private Investment Company.

For years and years and years, we've had this OPIC, this Overseas Private Investment Corporation, because we knew we had untapped markets overseas. But our greatest untapped markets are not overseas—they are right here at home. And we should go after them.

We must work hard to help bring prosperity back to the family farm. As this Congress knows very well, dropping prices and the loss of foreign markets have devastated too many family farms. Last year, the Congress provided substantial assistance to help stave off a disaster in American agriculture. And I am ready to work with lawmakers of both parties to create a farm safety net that will include crop insurance reform and farm income assistance. I ask you to join with me and do this. This should not be a political issue. Everyone knows what an economic problem is going on out there in rural America today, and we need an appropriate means to address it.

We must strengthen our lead in technology. It was government investment that led to the creation of the Internet. I propose a 28 percent increase in long-term computing research.

We also must be ready for the 21st century from its very first moment, by solving the so-called Y2K computer problem.

We had one member of Congress stand up and applaud. And we may have about that ratio out there applauding at home, in front of their television sets. But remember, this is a big, big problem. And we've been working hard on it. Already, we've made sure that the Social Security checks will come on time. But I want all the folks at home listening to this to know that we need every state and local government, every business, large and small, to work with us to make sure that this Y2K computer bug will be remembered as the last headache of the 20th century, not the first crisis of the 21st.

For our own prosperity, we must support economic growth abroad. You know, until recently, a third of our economic growth came from exports. But over the past year and a half, financial turmoil overseas has put that growth at risk. Today, much of the world is in recession, with Asia hit especially hard. This is the most serious financial crisis in half a century. To meet it, the United States and other nations have reduced interest rates and strengthened the International Monetary Fund. And while the turmoil is not over, we have worked very hard with other nations to contain it.

At the same time, we have to continue to work on the long-term project, building a global financial system for the 21st century that promotes prosperity and tames the cycle of boom and bust that has engulfed so much of Asia. This June I will meet with other world leaders to advance this historic purpose. And I ask all of you to support our endeavors.

I also ask you to support creating a freer and fairer trading system for 21st century America.

I'd like to say something really serious to everyone in this chamber in both parties. I think trade has divided us, and divided Americans outside this chamber, for too long. Somehow we have to find a common ground on which business and workers and environmentalists and farmers and government can stand together. I believe these are the things we ought to all agree on. So let me try.

First, we ought to tear down barriers, open markets, and expand trade. But at the same time, we must ensure that ordinary citizens in all countries actually benefit from trade—a trade that promotes the dignity of work, and the rights of workers, and protects the environment. We must insist that international trade organizations be more open to public scrutiny, instead of mysterious, secret things subject to wild criticism.

When you come right down to it, now that the world economy is becoming more and more integrated, we have to do in the world what we spent the better part of this century doing here at home. We have got to put a human face on the global economy.

We must enforce our trade laws when imports unlawfully flood our nation. I have already informed the government of Japan that if that nation's sudden surge of steel imports into our country is not reversed, America will respond.

We must help all manufacturers hit hard by the present crisis with loan guarantees and other incentives to increase American exports by nearly $2 billion. I'd like to believe we can achieve a new consensus on trade, based on these principles. And I ask the Congress again to join me in this common approach and to give the President the trade authority long used—and now overdue and necessary—to advance our prosperity in the 21st century.

Tonight, I issue a call to the nations of the world to join the United States in a new round of global trade negotiations to expand exports of services, manufacturers and farm products. Tonight I say we will work with the International Labor Organization on a new initiative to raise labor standards around the world. And this year, we will lead the international community to conclude a treaty to ban abusive child labor everywhere in the world.

If we do these things—invest in our people, our communities, our technology, and lead in the global economy—then we will begin to meet our historic responsibility to build a 21st century prosperity for America.

You know, no nation in history has had the opportunity and the responsibility we now have to shape a world that is more peaceful, more secure, more free. All Americans can be proud that our leadership helped to bring peace in Northern Ireland. All Americans can be proud that our leadership has put Bosnia on the path to peace. And with our NATO allies, we are pressing the Serbian government to stop its brutal repression in Kosovo—to bring those responsible to justice, and to give the people of Kosovo the self-government they deserve.

All Americans can be proud that our leadership renewed hope for lasting peace in the Middle East. Some of you were with me last December as we watched the Palestinian National Council completely renounce its call for the destruction of Israel. Now I ask Congress to provide resources so that all parties can implement the Wye Agreement—to protect Israel's security, to stimulate the Palestinian economy, to support our friends in Jordan. We must not, we dare not, let them down. I hope you will help.

As we work for peace, we must also meet threats to our nation's security—including increased dangers from outlaw nations and terrorism. We will defend our security wherever we are threatened, as we did this summer when we struck at Osama bin Laden's network of terror. The bombing of our embassies in Kenya and Tanzania reminds us again of the risks faced every day by those who represent America to the world. So let's give them the support they need, the safest possible workplaces, and the resources they must have so America can continue to lead.

We must work to keep terrorists from disrupting computer networks. We must work to prepare local communities for biological and chemical emergencies, to support research into vaccines and treatments.

We must increase our efforts to restrain the spread of nuclear weapons and missiles, from Korea to India and Pakistan. We must expand our work with Russia, Ukraine, and the other former Soviet nations to safeguard nuclear materials and technology so they never fall into the wrong hands. Our balanced budget will increase funding for these critical efforts by almost two-thirds over the next five years.

With Russia, we must continue to reduce our nuclear arsenals. The START II treaty and the framework we have already agreed to for START III could cut them by 80 percent from their Cold War height.

It's been two years since I signed the Comprehensive Test Ban Treaty. If we don't do the right thing, other nations won't either. I ask the Senate to take this vital step: Approve the treaty now, to make it harder for other nations to develop nuclear arms, and to make sure we can end nuclear testing forever.

For nearly a decade, Iraq has defied its obligations to destroy its weapons of terror and the missiles to deliver them. America will continue to contain Saddam—and we will work for the day when Iraq has a government worthy of its people.

Now, last month, in our action over Iraq, our troops were superb. Their mission was so flawlessly executed that we risk taking for granted the bravery and the skill it required. Captain Jeff Taliaferro, a 10-year veteran of the Air Force, flew a B-1B bomber over Iraq as we attacked Saddam's war machine. He's here with us tonight. I'd like to ask you to honor him and all the 33,000 men and women of Operation Desert Fox.

It is time to reverse the decline in defense spending that began in 1985. Since April, together we have added nearly $6 billion to maintain our military readiness. My balanced budget calls for a sustained increase over the next six years for readiness, for modernization, and for pay and benefits for our troops and their families.

We are the heirs of a legacy of bravery represented in every community in America by millions of our veterans. America's defenders today still stand ready at a moment's notice to go where comforts are few and dangers are many, to do what needs to be done as no one else can. They always come through for America. We must come through for them.

The new century demands new partnerships for peace and security. The United Nations plays a crucial role, with allies sharing burdens America might otherwise bear alone. America needs a strong and effective U.N. I want to work with this new Congress to pay our dues and our debts.

We must continue to support security and stability in Europe and Asia—expanding NATO and defining its new missions; maintaining our alliance with Japan, with Korea, without our other Asian allies; and engaging China.

In China, last year, I said to the leaders and the people what I'd like to say again tonight: Stability can no longer be bought at the expense of liberty. But I'd also like to say again

to the American people: It's important not to isolate China. The more we bring China into the world, the more the world will bring change and freedom to China.

Last spring, with some of you, I traveled to Africa, where I saw democracy and reform rising, but still held back by violence and disease. We must fortify African democracy and peace by launching Radio Democracy for Africa, supporting the transition to democracy now beginning to take place in Nigeria, and passing the African Trade and Development Act.

We must continue to deepen our ties to the Americas and the Caribbean; our common work to educate children, fight drugs, strengthen democracy and increase trade. In this hemisphere, every government but one is freely chosen by its people. We are determined that Cuba, too, will know the blessings of liberty.

The American people have opened their hearts and their arms to our Central American and Caribbean neighbors who have been so devastated by the recent hurricanes. Working with Congress, I am committed to help them rebuild. When the First Lady and Tipper Gore visited the region, they saw thousands of our troops and thousands of American volunteers. In the Dominican Republic, Hillary helped to rededicate a hospital that had been rebuilt by Dominicans and Americans, working side-by-side. With her was someone else who has been very important to the relief efforts.

You know, sports records are made and, sooner or later, they're broken. But making other people's lives better, and showing our children the true meaning of brotherhood—that lasts forever. So, for far more than baseball, Sammy Sosa, you're a hero in two countries tonight. Thank you.

So I say to all of you, if we do these things—if we pursue peace, fight terrorism, increase our strength, renew our alliances—we will begin to meet our generation's historic responsibility to build a stronger 21st century America in a freer, more peaceful world.

As the world has changed, so have our own communities. We must make them safer, more livable and more united. This year, we will reach our goal of 100,000 community police officers—ahead of schedule and under budget. The Brady Bill has stopped a quarter million felons, fugitives and stalkers from buying handguns. And, now, the murder rate is the lowest in 30 years and the crime rate has dropped for six straight years.

Tonight, I propose a 21st century crime bill to deploy the latest technologies and tactics to make our communities even safer. Our balanced budget will help put up to 50,000 more police on the street, in the areas hardest hit by crime—and then to equip them with new tools, from crime-mapping computers to digital mug shots.

We must break the deadly cycle of drugs and crime. Our budget expands support for drug testing and treatment, saying to prisoners: If you stay on drugs, you have to stay behind bars. And to those on parole: If you want to keep your freedom, you must stay free of drugs.

I ask Congress to restore the five-day waiting period for buying a handgun—and extend the Brady Bill to prevent juveniles who commit violent crimes from buying a gun.

We must do more to keep our schools the safest places in our communities. Last year, every American was horrified and heartbroken by the tragic killings in Jonesboro, Paducah, Pearl, Edinboro, Springfield. We were deeply moved by the courageous parents now working to keep guns out of the hands of children and to make other efforts so that other parents don't have to live through their loss.

After she lost her daughter, Suzann Wilson of Jonesboro, Arkansas, came here to the White House with a powerful plea. She said, "Please, please, for the sake of your children, lock up your gun. Don't let what happened in Jonesboro happen in your town." It's a message she is passionately advocating every day.

Suzann is here with us tonight, with the First Lady. I'd like to thank her for her courage and her commitment. Thank you.

In memory of all the children who lost their lives to school violence, I ask you to strengthen the Safe and Drug-Free School Act, to pass legislation to require child trigger locks, to do everything possible to keep our children safe.

A century ago, President Theodore Roosevelt defined our "great, central task" as "leaving this land even a better land for our descendants than it is for us." Today, we're restoring the Florida Everglades, saving Yellowstone, preserving the red rock canyons of Utah, protecting California's redwoods and our precious coasts. But our most fateful new challenge is the threat of global warming. 1998 was the warmest year ever recorded. Last year's heat waves, floods and storms are but a hint of what future generations may endure if we do not act now.

Tonight I propose a new clean air fund to help communities reduce greenhouse and other pollution, and tax incentives and investments to spur clean energy technology. And I want to work with members of Congress in both parties to reward companies that take early, voluntary action to reduce greenhouse gases.

All our communities face a preservation challenge, as they grow and green space shrinks. Seven thousand acres of farmland and open space are lost every day. In response, I propose two major initiatives: First, a $1-billion Livability Agenda to help communities save open space, ease traffic congestion, and grow in ways that enhance every citizen's quality of life. And second, a $1-billion Lands Legacy Initiative to preserve places of natural beauty all across America—from the most remote wilderness to the nearest city park.

These are truly landmark initiatives, which could not have been developed without the visionary leadership of the Vice President, and I want to thank him very much for his commitment here.

Now, to get the most out of your community, you have to give something back. That's why we created AmeriCorps—our national service program that gives today's generation a chance to serve their communities and earn money for college.

So far, in just four years, 100,000 young Americans have built low-income homes with Habitat for Humanity, helped to tutor children with churches, worked with FEMA to ease the burden of natural disasters, and performed countless other acts of service that have made America better. I ask Congress to give more young Americans the chance to follow their lead and serve America in AmeriCorps.

Now, we must work to renew our national community as well for the 21st century. Last year the House passed the bipartisan campaign finance reform legislation sponsored by Representatives Shays and Meehan and Senators McCain and Feingold. But a partisan minority in the Senate blocked reform. So I'd like to say to the House: Pass it again, quickly. And I'd like to say to the Senate: I hope you will say yes to a stronger American democracy in the year 2000.

Since 1997, our Initiative on Race has sought to bridge the divides between and among our people. In its report last fall, the Initiative's Advisory Board found that Americans really do want to bring our people together across racial lines.

We know it's been a long journey. For some, it goes back to before the beginning of our Republic; for others, back since the Civil War; for others, throughout the 20th century. But for most of us alive today, in a very real sense, this journey began 43 years ago, when a woman named Rosa Parks sat down on a bus in Alabama, and wouldn't get up. She's sitting down with the First Lady tonight, and she may

get up or not, as she chooses. We thank her. Thank you, Rosa.

We know that our continuing racial problems are aggravated, as the Presidential Initiative said, by opportunity gaps. The initiative I've outlined tonight will help to close them. But we know that the discrimination gap has not been fully closed either. Discrimination or violence because of race or religion, ancestry or gender, disability or sexual orientation, is wrong, and it ought to be illegal. Therefore, I ask Congress to make the Employment Non-Discrimination Act and the Hate Crimes Prevention Act the law of the land.

Now, since every person in America counts, every American ought to be counted. We need a census that uses modern scientific methods to do that.

Our new immigrants must be part of our One America. After all, they're revitalizing our cities, they're energizing our culture, they're building up our economy. We have a responsibility to make them welcome here; and they have a responsibility to enter the mainstream of American life. That means learning English and learning about our democratic system of government. There are now long waiting lines of immigrants that are trying to do just that. Therefore, our budget significantly expands our efforts to help them meet their responsibility. I hope you will support it.

Whether our ancestors came here on the Mayflower, on slave ships, whether they came to Ellis Island or LAX in Los Angeles, whether they came yesterday or walked this land a thousand years ago—our great challenge for the 21st century is to find a way to be One America. We can meet all the other challenges if we can go forward as One America.

You know, barely more than 300 days from now, we will cross that bridge into the new millennium. This is a moment, as the First Lady has said, "to honor the past and imagine the future."

I'd like to take just a minute to honor her. For leading our Millennium Project, for all she's done for our children, for all she has done in her historic role to serve our nation and our best ideals at home and abroad, I honor her.

Last year, I called on Congress and every citizen to mark the millennium by saving America's treasures. Hillary has traveled all across the country to inspire recognition and support for saving places like Thomas Edison's Invention Factory or Harriet Tubman's home. Now we have to preserve our treasures in every community. And tonight, before I close, I want to invite every town, every city, every community to become nationally recognized "millennium community," by launching projects that save our history, promote our arts and humanities, prepare our children for the 21st century.

Already, the response has been remarkable. And I want to say a special word of thanks to our private sector partners and to members in Congress of both parties for their support. Just one example: Because of you, the Star-Spangled Banner will be preserved for the ages. In ways large and small, as we look to the millennium we are keeping alive what George Washington called "the sacred fire of liberty."

Six years ago, I came to office in a time of doubt for America, with our economy troubled, our deficit high, our people divided. Some even wondered whether our best days were behind us. But across this country, in a thousand neighborhoods, I have seen—even amidst the pain and uncertainty of recession—the real heart and character of America. I knew then that we Americans could renew this country.

Tonight, as I deliver the last State of the Union address of the 20th century, no one anywhere in the world can doubt the enduring resolve and boundless capacity of the American people to work toward that "more perfect union" of our founders' dream.

We're now at the end of a century when generation after generation of Americans answered the call to greatness, overcoming Depression, lifting up the dispossessed, bringing down barriers to racial prejudice, building the largest middle class in history, winning two world wars and the "long twilight struggle" of the Cold War. We must all be profoundly grateful for the magnificent achievement of our forbearers in this century.

Yet, perhaps, in the daily press of events, in the clash of controversy, we don't see our own time for what it truly is—a new dawn for America.

A hundred years from tonight, another American President will stand in this place and report on the State of the Union. He—or she—he or she will look back on a 21st century shaped in so many ways by the decisions we make here and now. So let it be said of us then that we were thinking not only of our time, but of their time; that we reached as high as our ideals; that we put aside our divisions and found a new hour of healing and hopefulness; that we joined together to serve and strengthen the land we love.

My fellow Americans, this is our moment. Let us lift our eyes as one nation, and from the mountaintop of this American Century, look ahead to the next one—asking God's blessing on our endeavors and on our beloved country.

Thank you and good evening.

16. State of the Union Address January 27, 2000

Public Papers of the Presidents of the United States: William J. Clinton, 2000. Vol. 1. Washington, D.C.: U.S. Government Printing Office, pages 129–140

Mr. Speaker, Mr. Vice President, members of Congress, honored guests, my fellow Americans:

We are fortunate to be alive at this moment in history. [Applause.] Never before has our nation enjoyed, at once, so much prosperity and social progress with so little internal crisis and so few external threats. Never before have we had such a blessed opportunity—and, therefore, such a profound obligation—to build the more perfect union of our founders' dreams.

We begin the new century with over 20 million new jobs; the fastest economic growth in more than 30 years; the lowest unemployment rates in 30 years; the lowest poverty rates in 20 years; the lowest African American and Hispanic unemployment rates on record; the first back-to-back budget surpluses in 42 years. And next month, America will achieve the longest period of economic growth in our entire history. [Applause.]

We have built a new economy.

And our economic revolution has been matched by a revival of the American spirit: crime down by 20 percent, to its lowest level in 25 years; teen births down seven years in a row; adoptions up by 30 percent; welfare rolls cut in half to their lowest levels in 30 years.

My fellow Americans, the state of our union is the strongest it has ever been. [Applause.]

As always, the real credit belongs to the American people. [Applause.] My gratitude also goes to those of you in this chamber who have worked with us to put progress over partisanship.

Eight years ago, it was not so clear to most Americans there would be much to celebrate in the year 2000. Then our nation was gripped by economic distress, social decline, political gridlock. The title of a best-selling book asked: "America: What Went Wrong?"

In the best traditions of our nation, Americans determined to set things right. We restored the vital center, replacing outmoded ideologies with a new vision anchored in basic, enduring values: opportunity for all, responsibility from all, a community of all Americans. We reinvented government, transforming it into a catalyst for new ideas that stress both opportunity and responsibility, and give our people the tools they need to solve their own problems.

With the smallest federal work force in 40 years, we turned record deficits into record surpluses, and doubled our investment in education. We cut crime, with 100,000 community police and the Brady law, which has kept guns out of the hands of half a million criminals. [Applause.]

We ended welfare as we knew it—[applause]—requiring work while protecting health care and nutrition for children, and investing more in child care, transportation, and housing to help their parents go to work. We've helped parents to succeed at home and at work, with family leave, which 20 millions Americans have now used to care for a newborn child or a sick loved one. We've engaged 150,000 young Americans in citizen service through AmeriCorps, while helping them earn money for college.

In 1992, we just had a road map; today, we have results. [Applause.]

But even more important, America again has the confidence to dream big dreams. But we must not let this confidence drift into complacency. For we, all of us, will be judged by the dreams and deeds we pass on to our children. And on that score, we will be held to a high standard, indeed, because our chance to do good is so great.

My fellow Americans, we have crossed the bridge we built to the 21st century. Now, we must shape a 21st century American revolution—of opportunity, responsibility and community. We must be now, as we were in the beginning, a new nation.

At the dawn of the last century, Theodore Roosevelt said, "the one characteristic more essential than any other is foresight. . . . it should be the growing nation with a future that takes the long look ahead." So, tonight, let us take our long look ahead—and set great goals for our nation.

To 21st century America, let us pledge these things: Every child will begin school ready to learn and graduate ready to succeed. [Applause.] Every family will be able to succeed at home and at work, and no child will be raised in poverty. [Applause.] We will meet the challenge of the aging of America. We will assure quality, affordable health care, at last, for all Americans. [Applause.]

We will make America the safest big country on Earth. [Applause.] We will pay off our national debt for the first time since 1835. [Applause.] We will bring prosperity to every American community. We will reverse the course of climate change and leave a safer, cleaner planet. America will lead the world toward shared peace and prosperity, and the far frontiers of science and technology. And we will become at last what our founders pledged us to be so long ago—one nation, under God, indivisible, with liberty and justice for all. [Applause.]

These are great goals, worthy of a great nation. We will not reach them all this year. Not even in this decade. But we will reach them. Let us remember that the first American Revolution was not won with a single shot; the continent was not settled in a single year. The lesson of our history—and the lesson of the last seven years—is that great goals are reached step by step, always building on our progress, always gaining ground.

Of course, you can't gain ground if you're standing still. And for too long this Congress has been standing still on some of our most pressing national priorities. So let's begin tonight with them.

Again, I ask you to pass a real patients' bill of rights. [Applause.] I ask you to pass common-sense gun safety legislation. [Applause.] I ask you to pass campaign finance reform. [Applause.] I ask you to vote up or down on judicial nominations and other important appointees. [Applause.] And, again I ask you—

I implore you—to raise the minimum wage. [Applause.]

Now, two years ago—let me try to balance the seesaw here—[laughter]—two years ago, as we reached across party lines to reach our first balanced budget, I asked that we meet our responsibility to the next generation by maintaining our fiscal discipline. Because we refused to stray from that path, we are doing something that would have seemed unimaginable seven years ago. We are actually paying down the national debt. [Applause.]

Now, if we stay on this path, we can pay down the debt entirely in 13 just years now and make America debt-free for the first time since Andrew Jackson was President in 1835. [Applause.]

In 1993, we began to put our fiscal house in order with the Deficit Reduction Act, which you'll all remember won passages in both Houses by just a single vote. Your former colleague, my first Secretary of the Treasury, led that effort and sparked our long boom. He's here with us tonight. Lloyd Bentsen, you have served America well, and we thank you. [Applause.]

Beyond paying off the debt, we must ensure that the benefits of debt reduction go to preserving two of the most important guarantees we make to every American—Social Security and Medicare. [Applause.] Tonight, I ask you to work with me to make a bipartisan down payment on Social Security reform by crediting the interest savings from debt reduction to the Social Security Trust Fund so that it will be strong and sound for the next 50 years. [Applause.]

But this is just the start of our journey. We must also take the right steps toward reaching our great goals. First and foremost, we need a 21st century revolution in education, guided by our faith that every single child can learn. [Applause.] Because education is more important than ever, more than ever the key to our children's future, we must make sure all our children have that key. That means quality pre-school and after-school, the best trained teachers in the classroom, and college opportunities for all our children. [Applause.]

For seven years now, we've worked hard to improve our schools, with opportunity and responsibility—investing more, but demanding more in turn. Reading, math, college entrance scores are up. Some of the most impressive gains are in schools in very poor neighborhoods.

But all successful schools have followed the same proven formula: higher standards, more accountability, and extra help so children who need it can get it to reach those standards. I have sent Congress a reform plan based on that formula. It holds states and school districts accountable for progress, and rewards them for results. Each year, our national government invests more than $15 billion in our schools. It is time to support what works and stop supporting what doesn't. [Applause.]

Now, as we demand more from our schools, we should also invest more in our schools. [Applause.] Let's double our investment to help states and districts turn around their worst-performing schools, or shut them down. Let's double our investments in after-school and summer school programs, which boost achievement and keep people off the streets and out of trouble. [Applause.] If we do this, we can give every single child in every failing school in America—everyone—the chance to meet high standards.

Since 1993, we've nearly doubled our investment in Head Start and improved its quality. Tonight, I ask you for another $1 billion for Head Start, the largest increase in the history of the program. [Applause.]

We know that children learn best in smaller classes with good teachers. For two years in a row, Congress has supported my plan to hire 100,000 new qualified teachers to lower class size in the early grades. I thank you for that, and I ask you to make it three in a row. [Applause.] And to make sure all teachers know

the subjects they teach, tonight I propose a new teacher quality initiative—to recruit more talented people into the classroom, reward good teachers for staying there, and give all teachers the training they need. [Applause.]

We know charter schools provide real public school choice. When I became President, there was just one independent public charter school in all America. Today, thanks to you, there are 1,700. I ask you now to help us meet our goal of 3,000 charter schools by next year. [Applause.]

We know we must connect all our classrooms to the Internet, and we're getting there. In 1994, only 3 percent of our classrooms were connected. Today, with the help of the Vice President's E-rate program, more than half of them are. And 90 percent of our schools have at least one Internet connection. [Applause.]

But we cannot finish the job when a third of all our schools are in serious disrepair. Many of them have walls and wires so old, they're too old for the Internet. So tonight, I propose to help 5,000 schools a year make immediate and urgent repairs; and again, to help build or modernize 6,000 more, to get students out of trailers and into high-tech classrooms. [Applause.]

I ask all of you to help me double our bipartisan Gear-Up program, which provides mentors for disadvantaged young people. If we double it, we can provide mentors for 1.4 million of them. [Applause.] Let's also offer these kids from disadvantaged backgrounds the same chance to take the same college test-prep courses wealthier students use to boost their test scores. [Applause.]

To make the American Dream achievable for all, we must make college affordable for all. For seven years, on a bipartisan basis, we have taken action toward that goal: larger Pell grants, more affordable student loans, education IRAs, and our HOPE scholarships, which have already benefitted 5 million young people.

Now, 67 percent of high school graduates are going on to college. That's up 10 percent since 1993. Yet millions of families still strain to pay college tuition. They need help. [Applause.] So I propose a landmark $30-billion college opportunity tax cut—a middle class tax deduction for up to $10,000 in college tuition costs. [Applause.] The previous actions of this Congress have already made two years of college affordable for all. It's time to make four years of college affordable for all. [Applause.] If we take all these steps, we'll move a long way toward making sure every child starts school ready to learn and graduates ready to succeed.

We need a 21st century revolution to reward work and strengthen families, by giving every parent the tools to succeed at work and at the most important work of all—raising children. That means making sure every family has health care and the support to care for aging parents, the tools to bring their children up right, and that no child grows up in poverty.

From my first days as President, we've worked to give families better access to better health care. In 1997, we passed the Children's Health Insurance Program—CHIP—so that workers who don't have coverage through their employers at least can get it for their children. So far, we've enrolled 2 million children; we're well on our way to our goal of 5 million.

But there are still more than 40 million of our fellow Americans without health insurance—more than there were in 1993. Tonight I propose that we follow Vice President Gore's suggestion to make low income parents eligible for the insurance that covers their children. [Applause.] Together with our children's initiative—think of this—together with our children's initiative, this action would enable us to cover nearly a quarter of all the uninsured people in America.

Again, I want to ask you to let people between the ages of 55 and 65—the fastest growing group of uninsured—buy into Medicare. [Applause.] And this year I propose to give them a tax credit to make that choice an affordable one. I hope you will support that, as well. [Applause.]

When the baby boomers retire, Medicare will be faced with caring for twice as many of our citizens; yet, it is far from ready to do so. My generation must not ask our children's generation to shoulder our burden. We simply must act now to strengthen and modernize Medicare.

My budget includes a comprehensive plan to reform Medicare, to make it more efficient and competitive. And it dedicates nearly $400 billion of our budget surplus to keep Medicare solvent past 2025. [Applause.] And, at long last, it also provides funds to give every senior a voluntary choice of affordable coverage for prescription drugs. [Applause.]

Lifesaving drugs are an indispensable part of modern medicine. No one creating a Medicare program today would even think of excluding coverage for prescription drugs. Yet more than three in five of our seniors now lack dependable drug coverage which can lengthen and enrich their lives. Millions of older Americans who need prescription drugs the most pay the highest prices for them. In good conscience, we cannot let another year pass without extending to all our seniors this lifeline of affordable prescription drugs. [Applause.]

Record numbers of Americans are providing for aging or ailing loved ones at home. It's a loving, but a difficult and often very expensive choice. Last year, I proposed a $1,000 tax credit for long-term care. Frankly, it wasn't enough. This year, let's triple it, to $3,000. [Applause.] But this year, let's pass it. [Applause.]

We also have to make needed investments to expand access to mental health care. I want to take a moment to thank the person who led our first White House Conference on Mental

Health last year, and who for seven years has led all our efforts to break down the barriers to decent treatment of people with mental illness. Thank you, Tipper Gore. [Applause.]

Taken together, these proposals would mark the largest investment in health care in the 35 years since Medicare was created—the largest investment in 35 years. That would be a big step toward assuring quality health care for all Americans, young and old. And I ask you to embrace them and pass them. [Applause.]

We must also make investments that reward work and support families. Nothing does that better than the Earned Income Tax Credit—the EITC. [Applause.] The "E" in the EITC is about earning, working, taking responsibility and being rewarded for it. In my very first address to you, I asked Congress to greatly expand this credit; and you did. As a result, in 1998 alone, the EITC helped more than 4.3 million Americans work their way out of poverty toward the middle class. That's double the number in 1993.

Tonight, I propose another major expansion of the EITC: to reduce the marriage penalty, to make sure it rewards marriage as it rewards work—(applause)—and also, to expand the tax credit for families that have more than two children. It punishes people with more than two children today. [Applause.] Our proposal would allow families with three or more children to get up to $1,100 more in tax relief. These are working families; their children should not be in poverty. [Applause.]

We also can't reward work and family unless men and women get equal pay for equal work. [Applause.] Today, the female unemployment rate is the lowest it has been in 46 years. Yet, women still only earn about 75 cents for every dollar men earn. We must do better, by providing the resources to enforce present equal pay laws; training more women for high-paying, high-tech jobs; and passing the Paycheck Fairness Act. [Applause.]

Many working parents spend up to a quarter—a quarter—of their income on child care. Last year, we helped parents provide child care for about 2 million children. My child care initiative, before you now, along with funds already secured in welfare reform, would make child care better, safer and more affordable for another 400,000 children. I ask you to pass that. They need it out there—[Applause.]

For hard-pressed middle-income families, we should also expand the child care tax credit. And I believe strongly we should take the next big step and make that tax credit refundable for low-income families. [Applause.] For people making under $30,000 a year, that could mean up to $2,400 for child care costs. You know, we all say we're pro-work and pro-family. Passing this proposal would prove it. [Applause.]

Tens of millions of Americans live from paycheck to paycheck. As hard as they work, they still don't have the opportunity to save. Too few can make use of IRAs and 401-K plans. We should do more to help all working families save and accumulate wealth. That's the idea behind the Individual Development Accounts, the IDAs. I ask you to take that idea to a new level, with new Retirement Savings Accounts that enable every low- and moderate-income family in America to save for retirement, a first home, a medical emergency, or a college education. I propose to match their contributions, however small, dollar for dollar, every year they save. And I propose to give a major new tax credit to any small business that will provide a meaningful pension to its workers. Those people ought to have retirement as well as the rest of us. [Applause.]

Nearly one in three American children grows up without a father. These children are five times more likely to live in poverty than children with both parents at home. Clearly, demanding and supporting responsible fatherhood is critical to lifting all children out of poverty. We've doubled child support collections since 1992. And I'm proposing to you tough new measures to hold still more fathers responsible.

But we should recognize that a lot of fathers want to do right by their children, but need help to do it. Carlos Rosas of St. Paul, Minnesota, wanted to do right by his son, and he got the help to do it. Now he's got a good job and he supports his little boy. My budget will help 40,000 more fathers make the same choices Carlos Rosas did. I thank him for being here tonight. [Applause.] Stand up, Carlos. Thank you. [Applause.]

If there is any single issue on which we should be able to reach across party lines, it is in our common commitment to reward work and strengthen families, similar to what we did last year. We came together to help people with disabilities keep their health insurance when they go to work. And I thank you for that. Thanks to overwhelming bipartisan support from this Congress, we have improved foster care. We've helped those young people who leave it when they turn 18, and we have dramatically increased the number of foster care children going into adoptive homes. I thank all of you for all of that. [Applause.]

Of course, I am forever grateful to the person who has led our efforts from the beginning, and who's worked so tirelessly for children and families for 30 years now: my wife, Hillary. And I thank her. [Applause.]

If we take the steps I've just discussed, we can go a long, long way toward empowering parents to succeed at home and at work, and ensuring that no child is raised in poverty. We can make these vital investments in health care, education, support for working families, and still offer tax cuts to help pay for college, for retirement, to care for aging parents, to reduce the marriage penalty. We can do these things without forsaking the path of fiscal discipline that got us to this point here tonight.

Indeed, we must make these investments and these tax cuts in the context of a balanced budget that strengthens and extends the life of Social Security and Medicare and pays down the national debt. [Applause.]

Crime in America has dropped for the past seven years—that's the longest decline on record—thanks to a national consensus we helped to forge on community police, sensible gun safety laws, and effective prevention. But nobody—nobody here, nobody in America—believes we're safe enough. So again, I ask you to set a higher goal. Let's make this country the safest big country in the world. [Applause.]

Last fall, Congress supported my plan to hire, in addition to the 100,000 community police we've already funded, 50,000 more, concentrated in high-crime neighborhoods. I ask your continued support for that.

Soon after the Columbine tragedy, Congress considered common-sense gun legislation, to require Brady background checks at the gun shows, child safety locks for new handguns, and a ban on the importation of large-capacity ammunition clips. With courage—and a tie-breaking vote by the Vice President—[applause]—the Senate faced down the gun lobby, stood up for the American people, and passed this legislation. But the House failed to follow suit.

Now, we have all seen what happens when guns fall into the wrong hands. Daniel Mauser was only 15 years old when he was gunned down at Columbine. He was an amazing kid—a straight-A student, a good skier. Like all parents who lose their children, his father Tom has borne unimaginable grief. Somehow he has found the strength to honor his son by transforming his grief into action. Earlier this month, he took a leave of absence from his job to fight for tougher gun safety laws. I pray that his courage and wisdom will at long last move this Congress to make common-sense gun legislation the very next order of business. [Applause.]

Tom Mauser, stand up. We thank you for being here tonight. [Applause.] Tom. Thank you, Tom. [Applause.]

We must strengthen our gun laws and enforce those already on the books better. [Applause.] Federal gun crime prosecutions are up 16 percent since I took office. But we must do more. I propose to hire more federal and local gun prosecutors and more ATF agents to crack down on illegal gun traffickers and bad-apple dealers. And we must give them the enforcement tools that they need, tools to trace every gun and every bullet used in every gun crime in the United States. I ask you to help us do that. [Applause.]

Every state in this country already requires hunters and automobile drivers to have a license. I think they ought to do the same thing for handgun purchases. [Applause.] Now, specifically, I propose a plan to ensure that all new handgun buyers must first have a photo license from their state showing they passed the Brady background check and a gun safety course, before they get the gun. I hope you'll help me pass that in this Congress. [Applause.]

Listen to this—listen to this. The accidental gun rate—the accidental gun death rate of children under 15 in the United States is nine times higher than in the other 25 industrialized countries combined. Now, technologies now exist that could lead to guns that can only be fired by the adults who own them. I ask Congress to fund research into smart gun technology, to save these children's lives. [Applause.] I ask responsible leaders in the gun industry to work with us on smart guns, and other steps to keep guns out of the wrong hands, to keep our children safe.

You know, every parent I know worries about the impact of violence in the media on their children. I want to begin by thanking the entertainment industry for accepting my challenge to put voluntary ratings on TV programs and video and Internet games. But, frankly, the ratings are too numerous, diverse and confusing to be really useful to parents. So tonight, I ask the industry to accept the First Lady's challenge to develop a single voluntary rating system for all children's entertainment that is easier for parents to understand and enforce. [Applause.] The steps I outline will take us well on our way to making America the safest big country in the world.

Now, to keep our historic economic expansion going—the subject of a lot of discussion in this community and others—I believe we need a 21st century revolution to open new markets, start new businesses, hire new workers right here in America—in our inner cities, poor rural areas, and Native American reservations. [Applause.]

Our nation's prosperity hasn't yet reached these places. Over the last six months, I've traveled to a lot of them, joined by many of you, and many far-sighted business people, to shine a spotlight on the enormous potential in communities from Appalachia to the Mississippi Delta, from Watts to the Pine Ridge Reservation. Everywhere I go, I meet talented people eager for opportunity, and able to work. Tonight I ask you, let's put them to work. [Applause.] For business, it's the smart thing to do. For America, it's the right thing to do. And let me ask you something—if we don't do this now, when in the wide world will we ever get around to it? [Applause.]

So I ask Congress to give businesses the same incentives to invest in America's new markets they now have to invest in markets overseas. [Applause.] Tonight, I propose a large New Markets tax credit and other incentives to spur $22 billion in private-sector capital to create new businesses and new investments in our inner cities and rural areas. [Applause.]

Because empowerment zones have been creating these opportunities for five years now, I also ask you to increase incentives to invest in them and to create more of them. [Applause.]

And let me say to all of you again what I have tried to say at every turn—this is not a Democratic or a Republican issue. Giving people a chance to live their dreams is an American issue. [Applause.]

Mr. Speaker, it was a powerful moment last November when you joined Reverend Jesse Jackson and me in your home state of Illinois, and committed to working toward our common goal, by combining the best ideas from both sides of the aisle. I want to thank you again, and to tell you, Mr. Speaker, I look forward to working with you. This is a worthy, joint endeavor. Thank you. [Applause.]

I also ask you to make special efforts to address the areas of our nation with the highest rates of poverty—our Native American reservations and the Mississippi Delta. My budget includes $110-million initiative to promote economic development in the Delta, and a billion dollars to increase economic opportunity, health care, education and law enforcement for our Native American communities. [Applause.] In this new century—we should begin this new century by honoring our historic responsibility to empower the first Americans. [Applause.] And I want to thank tonight the leaders and the members from both parties who've expressed to me an interest in working with us on these efforts. They are profoundly important.

There's another part of our American community in trouble tonight—our family farmers. When I signed the Farm Bill in 1996, I said there was great danger it would work well in good times, but not in bad. Well, droughts, floods, and historically low prices have made these times very bad for the farmers. We must work together to strengthen the farm safety net, invest in land conservation, and create some new markets for them by expanding our programs for bio-based fuels and products. Please, they need help—let's do it together. [Applause.]

Opportunity for all requires something else today—having access to a computer and knowing how to use it. That means we must close the digital divide between those who've got the tools and those who don't. [Applause.]

Connecting classrooms and libraries to the Internet is crucial, but it's just a start. My budget ensures that all new teachers are trained to teach 21st century skills, and it creates technology centers in 1,000 communities to serve adults. This spring, I'll invite high-tech leaders to join me on another New Markets tour, to close the digital divide and open opportunity for our people.

I want to thank the high-tech companies that already are doing so much in this area. I hope the new tax incentives I have proposed will get all the rest of them to join us. This is a national crusade. We have got to do this, and do it quickly. [Applause.]

Now, again I say to you, these are steps, but step by step, we can go a long way toward our goal of bringing opportunity to every community.

To realize the full possibilities of this economy, we must reach beyond our own borders, to shape the revolution that is tearing down barriers and building new networks among nations and individuals, and economies and cultures: globalization. It's the central reality of our time.

Of course, change this profound is both liberating and threatening to people. But there's no turning back. And our open, creative society stands to benefit more than any other—if we understand, and act on, the realities of interdependence. We have to be at the center of every vital global network, as a good neighbor and a good partner. We have to recognize that we cannot build our future without helping others to build theirs.

The first thing we have got to do is to forge a new consensus on trade. Now, those of us who believe passionately in the power of open trade, we have to ensure that it lifts both our living standards and our values, never tolerating abusive child labor or a race to the bottom in the environment and worker protection. But others must recognize that open markets and rule-based trade are the best engines we know of for raising living standards, reducing global poverty and environmental destruction, and assuring the free flow of ideas.

I believe as strongly tonight as I did the first day I got here, the only direction forward for America on trade—the only direction for America on trade is to keep going forward. I ask you to help me forge that consensus. [Applause.]

We have to make developing economies our partners in prosperity. That's why I would like to ask you again to finalize our groundbreaking African and Caribbean Basin trade initiatives. [Applause.]

But globalization is about more than economics. Our purpose must be to bring together the world around freedom and democracy and peace, and to oppose those who would tear it apart. Here are the fundamental challenges I believe America must meet to shape the 21st century world.

First, we must continue to encourage our former adversaries, Russia and China, to emerge as stable, prosperous, democratic nations. Both are being held back today from reaching their full potential: Russia by the legacy of communism, an economy in turmoil, a cruel and self-defeating war in Chechnya; China by the illusion that it can buy stability at the expense of freedom.

But think how much has changed in the past decade: 5,000 former Soviet nuclear weapons taken out of commission; Russian soldiers actually serving with ours in the Balkans; Russian people electing their leaders for the first time in a thousand years; and in China, an economy more open to the world than ever before.

Of course, no one, not a single person in this chamber tonight, can know for sure what direction these great nations will take. But we do know for sure that we can choose what we do. And we should do everything in our power to increase the chance that they will choose wisely, to be constructive members of our global community.

That's why we should support those Russians who are struggling for a democratic, prosperous future; continue to reduce both our nuclear arsenals; and help Russia to safeguard weapons and materials that remain.

And that's why I believe Congress should support the agreement we negotiated to bring China into the WTO, by passing Permanent Normal Trade Relations with China as soon as possible this year. [Applause.]

I think you ought to do it for two reasons. First of all, our markets are already open to China; this agreement will open China's markets to us. [Applause.] And, second, it will plainly advance the cause of peace in Asia and promote the cause of change in China. No, we don't know where it's going. All we can do is decide what we're going to do. But when all is said and done, we need to know we did everything we possibly could to maximize the chance that China will choose the right future. [Applause.]

A second challenge we've got is to protect our own security from conflicts that pose the risk of wider war and threaten our common humanity. We can't prevent every conflict or stop every outrage. But where our interests are at stake and we can make a difference, we should be, and we must be, peacemakers.

We should be proud of our role in bringing the Middle East closer to a lasting peace; building peace in Northern Ireland; working for peace in East Timor and Africa; promoting reconciliation between Greece and Turkey and in Cyprus; working to defuse these crises between India and Pakistan; in defending human rights and religious freedom. And we should be proud of the men and women of our

Armed Forces and those of our allies who stopped the ethnic cleansing in Kosovo, enabling a million people to return to their homes. [Applause.]

When Slobodan Milosevic unleashed his terror on Kosovo, Captain John Cherrey was one of the brave airmen who turned the tide. And when another American plane was shot down over Serbia, he flew into the teeth of enemy air defenses to bring his fellow pilot home. Thanks to our Armed Forces' skill and bravery, we prevailed in Kosovo without losing a single American in combat. [Applause.] I want to introduce Captain Cherrey to you. We honor Captain Cherrey, and we promise you, Captain, we'll finish the job you began. Stand up so we can see you. [Applause.]

A third challenge we have is to keep this inexorable march of technology from giving terrorists and potentially hostile nations the means to undermine our defenses. Keep in mind, the same technological advances that have shrunk cell phones to fit in the palms of our hands can also make weapons of terror easier to conceal and easier to use.

We must meet this threat by making effective agreements to restrain nuclear and missile programs in North Korea; curbing the flow of lethal technology to Iran; preventing Iraq from threatening its neighbors; increasing our preparedness against chemical and biological attack; protecting our vital computer systems from hackers and criminals; and developing a system to defend against new missile threats—while working to preserve our ABM missile treaty with Russia. We must do all these things.

I predict to you, when most of us are long gone, but some time in the next 10 to 20 years, the major security threat this country will face will come from the enemies of the nation state: the narco-traffickers and the terrorists and the organized criminals, who will be organized together, working together, with increasing access to ever-more sophisticated chemical and biological weapons.

And I want to thank the Pentagon and others for doing what they're doing right now to try to help protect us and plan for that, so that our defenses will be strong. I ask for your support to ensure they can succeed. [Applause.]

I also want to ask you for a constructive bipartisan dialogue this year to work to build a consensus which I hope will eventually lead to the ratification of the Comprehensive Nuclear Test Ban Treaty. [Applause.]

I hope we can also have a constructive effort to meet the challenge that is presented to our planet by the huge gulf between rich and poor. We cannot accept a world in which part of humanity lives on the cutting edge of a new economy, and the rest live on the bare edge of survival. I think we have to do our part to change that—with expanded trade, expanded aid, and the expansion of freedom.

This is interesting—from Nigeria to Indonesia, more people got the right to choose their leaders in 1999 than in 1989, when the Berlin Wall fell. We've got to stand by these democracies—including, and especially tonight, Colombia, which is fighting narco-traffickers, for its own people's lives and our children's lives. I have proposed a strong two-year package to help Colombia win this fight. I want to thank the leaders in both parties in both Houses for listening to me and the President of Colombia about it. We have got to pass this. I want to ask your help. A lot is riding on it. And it's so important for the long-term stability of our country, and for what happens in Latin America.

I also want you to know I'm going to send you new legislation to go after what these drug barons value the most—their money. And I hope you'll pass that as well. [Applause.]

In a world where over a billion people live on less than a dollar a day, we also have got to do our part in the global endeavor to reduce the debts of the poorest countries, so they can invest in education, health care and economic growth. That's what the Pope and other religious leaders have urged us to do. And last year, Congress made a down payment on America's share. I ask you to continue that. I thank you for what you did, and ask you to stay the course. [Applause.]

I also want to say that America must help more nations to break the bonds of disease. Last year in Africa, 10 times as many people died from AIDS as were killed in wars—10 times. The budget I give you invests $150 million more in the fight against this and other infectious killers. And today, I propose a tax credit to speed the development of vaccines for diseases like malaria, TB and AIDS. I ask the private sector and our partners around the world to join us in embracing this cause. We can save millions of lives together, and we ought to do it. [Applause.]

I also want to mention our final challenge, which, as always, is the most important. I ask you to pass a national security budget that keeps our military the best-trained and best-equipped in the world, with heightened readiness and 21st century weapons; which raises salaries for our servicemen and women; which protects our veterans; which fully funds the diplomacy that keeps our soldiers out of war; which makes good on our commitment to pay our U.N. dues and arrears. I ask you to pass this budget. [Applause.]

I also want to say something, if I might, very personal tonight. The American people watching us at home, with the help of all the commentators, can tell from who stands and who sits, and who claps and who doesn't, that there's still modest differences of opinion in this room. [Laughter.] But I want to thank you for something, every one of you. I want to thank you for the extraordinary support you have given—Republicans and Democrats alike—to our men and women in uniform. I thank you for that. [Applause.]

I also want to thank, especially, two people. First, I want to thank our Secretary of Defense, Bill Cohen, for symbolizing our bipartisan commitment to national security. Thank you, sir. [Applause.] Even more, I want to thank his wife, Janet, who, more than any other American citizen, has tirelessly traveled this world to show the support we all feel for our troops. Thank you, Janet Cohen. I appreciate that. Thank you. [Applause.]

These are the challenges we have to meet so that we can lead the world toward peace and freedom in an era of globalization.

I want to tell you that I am very grateful for many things as President. But one of the things I'm grateful for is the opportunity that the Vice President and I have had to finally put to rest the bogus idea that you cannot grow the economy and protect the environment at the same time. [Applause.]

As our economy has grown, we've rid more than 500 neighborhoods of toxic waste, ensured cleaner air and water for millions of people. In the past three months alone, we've helped preserve 40 million acres of roadless lands in the national forests, created three new national monuments.

But as our communities grow, our commitment to conservation must continue to grow. Tonight, I propose creating a permanent conservation fund, to restore wildlife, protect coastlines, save natural treasures, from the California redwoods to the Florida Everglades. [Applause.]

This Lands Legacy endowment would represent by far the most enduring investment in land preservation ever proposed in this House. I hope we can get together with all the people with different ideas and do this. This is a gift we should give to our children and our grandchildren for all time, across party lines. We can make an agreement to do this. [Applause.]

Last year, the Vice President launched a new effort to make communities more liberal— livable—[laughter]—liberal, I know. [Laughter and applause.] Wait a minute, I've got a punch-line now. That's this year's agenda; last year was livable, right? [Laughter.] That's what Senator Lott is going to say in the commentary afterwards. [Laughter.] To make our communities more livable. This is big business. This is a big issue. What does that mean? You ask anybody that lives in an unlivable community, and they'll tell you. They want their kids to grow up next to parks, not parking lots; the parents don't have to spend all their time stalled in traffic when they could be home with their children.

Tonight, I ask you to support new funding for the following things, to make American communities for liberal—livable. [Laughter and applause.] I've done pretty well with this speech, but I can't say that. [Applause.]

One, I want you to help us to do three things. We need more funding for advanced transit systems. [Applause.] We need more funding for saving open spaces in places of heavy development. [Applause.] And we need more funding—this ought to have bipartisan appeal—we need more funding for helping major cities around the Great Lakes protect their waterways and enhance their quality of life. We need these things and I want you to help us. [Applause.]

The greatest environmental challenge of the new century is global warming. The scientists tell us the 1990s were the hottest decade of the entire millennium. If we fail to reduce the emission of greenhouse gases, deadly heat waves and droughts will become more frequent, coastal areas will flood, and economies will be disrupted. That is going to happen, unless we act.

Many people in the United States—some people in this chamber—and lots of folks around the world still believe you cannot cut greenhouse gas emissions without slowing economic growth. In the Industrial Age that may well have been true. But in this digital economy, it is not true anymore. New technologies

make it possible to cut harmful emissions and provide even more growth.

For example, just last week, automakers unveiled cars that get 70 to 80 miles a gallon—the fruits of a unique research partnership between government and industry. And before you know it, efficient production of bio-fuels will give us the equivalent of hundreds of miles from a gallon of gasoline.

To speed innovation in these kind of technologies, I think we should give a major tax incentive to business for the production of clean energy, and to families for buying energy-saving homes and appliances and the next generation of super-efficient cars when they hit the showroom floor. I also ask the auto industry to use the available technologies to make all new cars more fuel-efficient right away.

And I ask this Congress to do something else. Please help us make more of our clean energy technology available to the developing world. That will create cleaner growth abroad and a lot more new jobs here in the United States of America. [Applause.]

In the new century, innovations in science and technology will be the key not only to the health of the environment, but to miraculous improvements in the quality of our lives and advances in the economy. Later this year, researchers will complete the first draft of the entire human genome, the very blueprint of life. It is important for all our fellow Americans to recognize that federal tax dollars have funded much of this research, and that this and other wise investments in science are leading to a revolution in our ability to detect, treat, and prevent disease.

For example, researchers have identified genes that cause Parkinson's, diabetes, and certain kinds of cancer—they are designed precision therapies that will block the harmful effect of these genes for good. Researchers already are using this new technique to target and destroy cells that cause breast cancer. Soon, we may be able to use it to prevent the onset of Alzheimer's. Scientists are also working on an artificial retina to help many blind people to see—and listen to this—microchips that would actually directly stimulate damaged spinal cords in a way that could allow people now paralyzed to stand up and walk. [Applause.]

These kinds of innovations are also propelling our remarkable prosperity. Information technology only includes 8 percent of our employment, but now it counts for a third of our economic growth—along with jobs that pay, by the way, about 80 percent above the private sector average. Again, we ought to keep in mind, government-funded research brought supercomputers, the Internet, and communications satellites into being. Soon researchers will bring us devices that can translate foreign languages as fast as you can talk; materials 10 times stronger than steel at a fraction of the weight; and—this is unbelievable to me—molecular computers the size of a tear drop with the power of today's fastest supercomputers.

To accelerate the march of discovery across all these disciplines in science and technology, I ask you to support my recommendation of an unprecedented $3 billion in the 21st Century Research Fund, the largest increase in civilian research in a generation. We owe it to our future. [Applause.]

Now, these new breakthroughs have to be used in ways that reflect our values. First and foremost, we have to safeguard our citizens' privacy. Last year, we proposed to protect every citizen's medical record. This year, we will finalize those rules. We've also taken the first steps to protect the privacy of bank and credit card records and other financial statements. Soon I will send legislation to you to finish that job. We must also act to prevent any genetic discrimination whatever by employers or insurers. I hope you will support that. [Applause.]

These steps will allow us to lead toward the far frontiers of science and technology. They will enhance our health, the environment, the economy in ways we can't even imagine today. But we all know that at a time when science, technology and the forces of globalization are bringing so many changes into all our lives, it's more important than ever that we strengthen the bonds that root us in our local communities and in our national community.

No tie binds different people together like citizen service. There's a new spirit of service in America—a movement we've tried to support with AmeriCorps, expanded Peace Corps, unprecedented new partnerships with businesses, foundations, community groups. Partnerships, for example, like the one that enlisted 12,000 companies which have now moved 650,000 of our fellow citizens from welfare to work. Partnerships to battle drug abuse, AIDS, teach young people to read, save America's treasures, strengthen the arts, fight teen pregnancy, prevent violence among young people, promote racial healing. The American people are working together.

But we should do more to help Americans help each other. First, we should help faith-based organizations to do more to fight poverty and drug abuse, and help people get back on the right track, with initiatives like Second Chance Homes that do so much to help unwed teen mothers. Second, we should support Americans who tithe and contribute to charities, but don't earn enough to claim a tax deduction for it. [Applause.] Tonight, I propose new tax incentives that would allow low- and middle-income citizens who don't itemize to get that deduction. It's nothing but fair, and it will get more people to give. [Applause.]

We should do more to help new immigrants to fully participate in our community. That's why I recommend spending more to teach them civics and English. And since everybody in our community counts, we've got to make sure everyone is counted in this year's census. [Applause.]

Within 10 years—just 10 years—there will be no majority race in our largest state of California. In a little more than 50 years, there will be no majority race in America. In a more interconnected world, this diversity can be our greatest strength. Just look around this chamber. Look around. We have members in this Congress from virtually every racial, ethnic, and religious background. And I think you would agree that America is stronger because of it. [Applause.]

You also have to agree that all those differences you just clapped for all too often spark hatred and division even here at home. Just in the last couple of years, we've seen a man dragged to death in Texas just because he was black. We saw a young man murdered in Wyoming just because he was gay. Last year, we saw the shootings of African Americans, Asian Americans, and Jewish children just because of who they were. This is not the American way, and we must draw the line. [Applause.]

I ask you to draw that line by passing without delay the Hate Crimes Prevention Act and the Employment Non-Discrimination Act. [Applause.] And I ask you to reauthorize the Violence Against Women Act. [Applause.]

Finally tonight, I propose the largest-ever investment in our civil rights laws for enforcement, because no American should be subjected to discrimination in finding a home, getting a job, going to school, or securing a loan. Protections in law should be protections in fact. [Applause.]

Last February, because I thought this was so important, I created the White House Office of One America to promote racial reconciliation. That's what one of my personal heroes, Hank Aaron, has done all his life. From his days as our all-time home run king to his recent acts of healing, he has always brought people together. We should follow his example, and we're honored to have him with us tonight. Stand up, Hank Aaron. [Applause.]

I just want to say one more thing about this, and I want every one of you to think about this the next time you get mad at one of your colleagues on the other side of the aisle. This fall, at the White House, Hillary had one of her millennium dinners, and we had this very distinguished scientist there, who is an expert in this whole work in the human genome. And he said that we are all, regardless of race, genetically 99.9 percent the same.

Now, you may find that uncomfortable when you look around here. [Laughter] But it is worth remembering. We can laugh about this, but you think about it. Modern science has confirmed what ancient faiths has always taught: the most important fact of life is our common humanity. Therefore, we should do more than just tolerate our diversity—we should honor it and celebrate it. [Applause.]

My fellow Americans, every time I prepare for the State of the Union, I approach it with hope and expectation and excitement for our nation. But tonight is very special, because we stand on the mountain top of a new millennium. Behind us we can look back and see the great expanse of American achievement; and before us we can see even greater, grander frontiers of possibility. We should, all of us, be filled with gratitude and humility for our present progress and prosperity. We should be filled with awe and joy at what lies over the horizon. And we should be filled with absolute determination to make the most of it.

You know, when the framers finished crafting our Constitution in Philadelphia, Benjamin Franklin stood in Independence Hall and he reflected on the carving of the sun that was on the back of a chair he saw. The sun was low on the horizon. So he said this—he said, "I've often wondered whether that sun was rising or setting. Today," Franklin said, "I have the happiness to know it's a rising sun." Today, because each succeeding generation of Americans has kept the fire of freedom burning brightly, lighting those frontiers of possibility, we all still bask in the glow and the warmth of Mr. Franklin's rising sun.

After 224 years, the American revolution continues. We remain a new nation. And as long as our dreams outweigh our memories, America will be forever young. That is our destiny. And this is our moment.

Thank you, God bless you, and God bless America. [Applause.]

17. Farewell Address to the Nation January 18, 2001

Public Papers of the Presidents of the United States: William J. Clinton, 2000. Vol. 3. Washington, D.C.: U.S. Government Printing Office, pages 2,952–2,953

My fellow citizens, tonight is my last opportunity to speak to you from the Oval Office as your President. I am profoundly grateful to you for twice giving me the honor to serve, to work for you and with you to prepare our Nation for the 21st century.

And I'm grateful to Vice President Gore, to my Cabinet Secretaries, and to all those who have served with me for the last 8 years.

This has been a time of dramatic transformation, and you have risen to every new challenge. You have made our social fabric stronger, our families healthier and safer, our people more prosperous. You, the American people, have made our passage into the global information age an era of great American renewal.

In all the work I have done as President—every decision I have made, every executive action I have taken, every bill I have proposed and signed—I've tried to give all Americans the tools and conditions to build the future of our dreams in a good society with a strong economy, a cleaner environment, and a freer, safer, more prosperous world.

I have steered my course by our enduring values: opportunity for all, responsibility from all, a community of all Americans. I have sought to give America a new kind of Government, smaller, more modern, more effective, full of ideas and policies appropriate to this new time, always putting people first, always focusing on the future.

Working together, America has done well. Our economy is breaking records with more than 22 million new jobs, the lowest unemployment in 30 years, the highest homeownership ever, the longest expansion in history. Our families and communities are stronger. Thirty-five million Americans have used the family leave law; 8 million have moved off welfare. Crime is at a 25-year low. Over 10 million Americans receive more college aid, and more people than ever are going to college. Our schools are better. Higher standards, greater accountability, and larger investments have brought higher test scores and higher graduation rates. More than 3 million children have health insurance now, and more than 7 million Americans have been lifted out of poverty. Incomes are rising across the board. Our air and water are cleaner. Our food and drinking water are safer. And more of our precious land has been preserved in the continental United States than at any time in a 100 years.

America has been a force for peace and prosperity in every corner of the globe. I'm very grateful to be able to turn over the reins of leadership to a new President with America in such a strong position to meet the challenges of the future.

Tonight I want to leave you with three thoughts about our future.

First, America must maintain our record of fiscal responsibility. Through our last four budgets we've turned record deficits to record surpluses, and we've been able to pay down $600 billion of our national debt—on track to be debt-free by the end of the decade for the first time since 1835. Staying on that course will bring lower interest rates, greater prosperity, and the opportunity to meet our big challenges. If we choose wisely, we can pay down the debt, deal with the retirement of the baby boomers, invest more in our future, and provide tax relief.

Second, because the world is more connected every day, in every way, America's security and prosperity require us to continue to lead in the world. At this remarkable moment in history, more people live in freedom than ever before. Our alliances are stronger than ever. People all around the world look to America to be a force for peace and prosperity, freedom and security. The global economy is giving more of our own people and billions around the world the chance to work and live and raise their families with dignity. But the forces of integration that have created these good opportunities also make us more subject to global forces of destruction, to terrorism, organized crime and narcotrafficking, the spread of deadly weapons and disease, the degradation of the global environment.

The expansion of trade hasn't fully closed the gap between those of us who live on the cutting edge of the global economy and the billions around the world who live on the knife's edge of survival. This global gap requires more than compassion; it requires action. Global poverty is a powder keg that could be ignited by our indifference.

In his first Inaugural Address, Thomas Jefferson warned of entangling alliances. But in our times, America cannot and must not disentangle itself from the world. If we want the world to embody our shared values, then we must assume a shared responsibility.

If the wars of the 20th century, especially the recent ones in Kosovo and Bosnia, have taught us anything, it is that we achieve our aims by defending our values and leading the forces of freedom and peace. We must embrace boldly and resolutely that duty to lead—to stand with our allies in word and deed and to put a human face on the global economy, so that expanded trade benefits all peoples in all nations, lifting lives and hopes all across the world.

Third, we must remember that America cannot lead in the world unless here at home we weave the threads of our coat of many colors into the fabric of one America. As we become ever more diverse, we must work harder to unite around our common values and our common humanity. We must work harder to overcome our differences, in our hearts and in our laws. We must treat all our people with fairness and dignity, regardless of their race, religion, gender, or sexual orientation, and regardless of when they arrived in our country—always moving toward the more perfect Union of our Founders' dreams.

Hillary, Chelsea, and I join all Americans in wishing our very best to the next President, George W. Bush, to his family and his administration, in meeting these challenges, and in leading freedom's march in this new century.

As for me, I'll leave the Presidency more idealistic, more full of hope than the day I arrived, and more confident than ever that America's best days lie ahead.

My days in this office are nearly through, but my days of service, I hope, are not. In the years ahead, I will never hold a position higher or a covenant more sacred than that of President of the United States. But there is no title I will wear more proudly than that of citizen.

Thank you. God bless you, and God bless America.

SELECTED BIBLIOGRAPHY

Adler, David Gray, Michael A. Genovese, and Thomas E. Cronin, eds. *The Presidency and the Law: The Clinton Legacy.* Lawrence: University Press of Kansas, 2002.

Albright, Madeleine. *Madame Secretary: A Memoir.* New York: Warner Books, 2003.

Aldrich, Gary. *Unlimited Access: An FBI Agent inside the Clinton White House.* Lanham, N.Y.: Regnery Publishing, 1998.

Baker, Peter. *The Breach: Inside the Impeachment and Trial of William Jefferson Clinton.* New York: Scribner, 2000.

Barber, Benjamin R. *The Truth of Power: Intellectual Affairs in the Clinton White House.* Boulder, Colo.: Westview, 2001.

Berman, William C. *From the Center to the Edge: The Politics and Policies of the Clinton Presidency.* Lanham, Md.: Rowman & Littlefield, 2001.

Blumenthal, Sidney. *The Clinton Wars.* New York: Farrar, Straus and Giroux, 2003.

Bovard, James. *Feeling Your Pain: The Explosion and Abuse of Government Power in the Clinton-Gore Years.* New York: St. Martin's Press, 2000.

Brock, David. *The Seduction of Hillary Rodham.* New York: Free Press, 1996.

Brummett, John. *Highwire: From the Backroads to the Beltway, the Education of Bill Clinton.* New York: Hyperion, 1994.

Brune, Lester H. *The United States and Post-Cold War Interventions: Bush and Clinton in Somalia, Haiti, and Bosnia, 1992–1998.* Claremont, Calif.: Regina Books, 1998.

Burns, James MacGregor. *Dead Center: Clinton-Gore Leadership and the Perils of Moderation.* New York: Scribner, 1999.

Busby, Robert. *Defending the American Presidency: Clinton and the Lewinsky Scanda.* New York: Palgrave, 2001.

Campbell, Colin, and Bert A. Rockman, eds. *The Clinton Legacy.* New York: Chatham House, 2000.

———. *The Clinton Presidency: First Appraisals.* Chatham, N.J.: Chatham House, 1996.

Christopher, Warren. *In the Stream of History: Shaping Foreign Policy for a New Era.* Stanford, Calif.: Stanford University Press, 1998.

Cimbala, Stephen J. *Clinton and Post-Cold War Defense.* Westport, Conn: Praeger, 1996.

Clinton, Hillary Rodham. *Dear Socks, Dear Buddy.* New York: Simon & Schuster, 1998.

———. *It Takes a Village and Other Lessons Children Teach Us.* New York: Simon & Schuster, 1996.

———. *Living History.* New York: Simon & Schuster, 2003.

Cohen, Richard. *Changing Course in Washington: Clinton and the New Congress.* New York: Macmillan, 1994.

Conason, Joe. *The Hunting of the President: The Ten-Year Campaign to Destroy Bill and Hillary Clinton.* New York: Thomas Dunne Books, 2000.

Daalder, Ivo H., and Michael E. O'Hanlon. *Winning Ugly: NATO's War to Save Kosovo.* Washington, D.C.: Brookings Institution Press, 2000.

Denton, Robert E. *The 1992 Presidential Campaign: A Communication Perspective.* Westport, Conn.: Praeger, 1994.

Denton, Robert E., and Rachel L. Holloway. *The Clinton Presidency: Images, Issues, and Communication Strategies.* Westport, Conn.: Praeger, 1996.

———. *Images, Scandal, and Communication Strategies of the Clinton Presidency*. Westport, Conn.: Praeger, 2003.

Dover, E. D. *The Presidential Election of 1996: Clinton's Incumbency and Television*. Westport, Conn.: Praeger, 1998.

Doyle, William. *Inside the Oval Office: The White House Tapes from FDR to Clinton*. New York: Kodansha America, 1999.

Drew, Elizabeth. *Finding His Voice: Clinton's Ambitious & Turbulent First Year*. New York: Simon & Schuster, 1994.

———. *On the Edge: The Clinton Presidency*. New York: Simon & Schuster, 1994.

———. *Showdown: The Struggle between the Gingrich Congress and the Clinton White House*. New York: Simon & Schuster, 1996.

———. *Whatever It Takes: The Real Struggle for Political Power in America*. New York: Viking, 1997.

Dumas, Ernest. *The Clintons of Arkansas*. Fayetteville: University of Arkansas Press, 1993.

Germond, Jack, and Jules Witcover. *Mad as Hell: Revolt at the Ballot Box 1992*. New York: Warner Books, 1993.

Greenberg, Stanley B. *Middle Class Dreams: The Politics and Power of the New American Majority*. New York: Times Books, 1995.

Guinier, Lani. *Lift Every Voice: Turning a Civil Rights Setback into a New Vision of Social Justice*. New York: Simon & Schuster, 1998.

Hacker, Jacob S. *The Road to Nowhere: The Genesis of President Clinton's Plan for Health Security*. Princeton, N.J.: Princeton University Press, 1997.

Halberstam, David. *War in a Time of Peace: Bush, Clinton, and the Generals*. New York: Scribner, 2001.

Hayden, Joseph M. *Covering Clinton: The President and the Press in the 1990's*. Westport, Conn.: Praeger, 2001.

Hendrickson, Ryan C. *The Clinton Wars: The Constitution, Congress, and War Powers*. Nashville, Tenn.: Vanderbilt University Press, 2002.

Henrickson, Thomas H. *Clinton's Foreign Policy in Somalia, Bosnia, Haiti, and North Korea*. Stanford, Calif.: Stanford University Press, 1996.

Herrnson, Paul S., and Dilys M. Hill. *The Clinton Presidency: The First Term, 1992–96*. New York: St. Martin's Press, 1999.

Hohenberg, John. *The Bill Clinton Story: Winning the Presidency*. Syracuse, N.Y.: Syracuse University Press, 1994.

———. *Reelecting Bill Clinton: Why America Chose a "New" Democrat*. Syracuse, N.Y.: Syracuse University Press, 1997.

Holbrooke, Richard. *To End a War*. New York: Random House, 1998.

Hubbell, Webb. *Friends in High Places: Our Journey from Little Rock to Washington, D.C.* New York: W. Morrow, 1997.

Hyland, William G. *Clinton's World: Remaking American Foreign Policy*. Westport, Conn.: Praeger, 1999.

Isikoff, Michael. *Uncovering Clinton: A Reporter's Story*. New York: Crown Publishers, 1999.

Johnson, Haynes. *The Best of Times: America in the Clinton Years*. New York: Harcourt Brace, 2001.

Johnson, Haynes, and David S. Broder. *The System: The American Way of Politics at the Breaking Point*. Boston: Little, Brown, 1996.

Jones, Bryan D. *The New American Politics: Reflections of Political Change and the Clinton Administration*. Boulder, Colo.: Westview, 1995.

Jones, Charles O. *Clinton and Congress, 1993–1996: Risk, Restoration, and Reflection*. Norman: University of Oklahoma Press, 1999.

Kaplan, Leonard V., and Beverly I. Moran. *Aftermath: The Clinton Impeachment and the Presidency in the Age of Political Spectacle*. New York: New York University Press, 2000.

Kelley, Virginia. *Leading with My Heart*. New York: Simon & Schuster, 1994.

Klein, Joe. *The Natural: The Misunderstood Presidency of Bill Clinton*. New York: Doubleday, 2001.

Kumar, Martha Joynt, and Terry Sullivan. *The White House World: Transitions, Organization, and Office*

Operations. College Station: Texas A&M University Press, 2003.

Kuntz, Phil. *The Starr Evidence.* New York: Simon & Schuster, 1998.

———. *The Starr Report.* New York: Simon & Schuster, 1998.

Kurtz, Howard. *Spin Cycle: Inside the Clinton Propaganda Machine.* New York: Free Press, 1998.

Kuypers, Jim A. *Presidential Crisis Rhetoric and the Press in the Post-Cold War World.* Westport, Conn.: Praeger, 1997.

Laham, Nicholas. *A Lost Cause: Bill Clinton's Campaign for National Health Insurance.* Westport, Conn.: Praeger, 1996.

Lasater, Martin. *The Changing of the Guard: President Clinton and the Security of Taiwan.* Boulder, Colo.: Westview, 1995.

Levy, Peter B. *Encyclopedia of the Clinton Presidency.* Westport, Conn.: Greenwood, 2001.

Lippmann, Thomas W. *Madeleine Albright and the New American Diplomacy.* Boulder, Colo.: Westview, 2000.

Lowi, Theodore J., and Benjamin Ginsberg. *Democrats Return to Power: Politics and Policy in the Clinton Era.* Chicago: W.W. Norton, 1994.

Lyons, Gene. *Fools for Scandal: How the Media Invented Whitewater.* New York: Franklin Square Press, 1996.

Maraniss, David. *The Clinton Enigma: A Four-and-a-Half-Minute Speech Reveals This President's Entire Life.* New York: Simon & Schuster, 1998.

———. *First in His Class.* New York: Simon & Schuster, 1995.

McLoughlin, Merrill. *The Impeachment and Trial of President Clinton.* New York: Random House, 1999.

Morris, Dick. *Behind the Oval Office.* New York: Random House, 1997.

———. *Behind the Oval Office: Getting Reelected against All Odds.* Los Angeles: Renaissance Books, 1999.

Morris, Irwin L. *Votes, Money, and the Clinton Impeachment.* Boulder, Colo.: Westview, 2002.

Morris, Roger. *Partners in Power: The Clintons & Their America.* New York: Henry Holt, 1996.

Morton, Andrew. *Monica's Story.* New York: St. Martin's Press, 1999.

Pilon, Roger. *The Rule of Law in the Wake of Clinton.* Washington, D.C.: Cato Institute, 2000.

Pomper, Gerald M., Walter Dean Burnham, Anthony Corrado, Marjorie Randon Hershey, Marion R. Just, Scott Keeter, Wilson Carey McWilliams, and William G. Mayer. *The Election of 1996: Reports and Interpretations.* New York: Chatham House, 1997.

Posner, Richard A. *An Affair of State: The Investigation, Impeachment, and Trial of President Clinton.* Cambridge, Mass.: Harvard University Press, 1999.

Radcliffe, Donnie. *Hillary Rodham Clinton: A First Lady for Our Time.* New York: Warner Books, 1993.

Reich, Robert B. *Locked in the Cabinet.* New York: Vintage, 1998.

Renshon, Stanley A. *The Clinton Presidency: Campaigning, Governing and the Psychology of Leadership.* Boulder, Colo.: Westview, 1995.

———. *High Hopes: The Clinton Presidency and the Politics of Ambition.* New York: New York University Press, 1996.

Rozell, Mark J., and Clyde Wilcox. *The Clinton Scandal and the Future of American Government.* Georgetown, Md.: Georgetown University Press, 2000.

Rubinstein, Alvin H., Albina Shayevich, and Boris Zlotnikov. *The Clinton Foreign Policy Reader: Presidential Speeches with Commentary.* Armonk, N.Y.: M.E. Sharpe, 2000.

Schier, Steven E. *The Postmodern Presidency: Bill Clinton's Legacy in U.S. Politics.* Pittsburgh, Pa.: Pittsburgh University Press, 2000.

Schmidt, Susan. *Truth at Any Cost: Ken Starr and the Unmaking of Bill Clinton.* New York: HarperCollins Publishers, 2000.

Sheehy, Gail. *Hillary's Choice*. New York: Random House, 1999.

Sigal, Leon D. *Disarming Strangers: Nuclear Diplomacy with North Korea*. Princeton, N.J.: Princeton University Press, 1998.

Skocpol, Theda. *Boomerang: Clinton's Health Security Effort and the Turn against Government in U.S. Politics*. Chicago: W.W. Norton, 1996.

Starr, Kenneth. *The Starr Evidence: Including the Complete Text of the Grand Jury Testimony of President Clinton and Monica Lewinsky*. New York: Public Affairs, 1998.

———. *The Starr Report: The Findings of Independent Counsel Kenneth W. Starr on President Clinton and the Lewinsky Affair*. New York: Public Affairs, 1998.

Stephanopoulos, George. *All Too Human: A Political Education*. Chicago: Little, Brown, 1999.

Stewart, James B. *Blood Sport: The President & His Adversaries*. New York: Simon & Schuster, 1996.

Talbott, Strobe. *The Russia Hand: A Memoir of Presidential Diplomacy*. New York: Random House, 2002.

Toobin, Jeffrey. *A Vast Conspiracy: The Real Story of the Sex Scandal That Nearly Brought Down a President*. New York: Random House, 1999.

Walden, Gregory S. *On Best Behavior: The Clinton Administration and Ethics in Government*. Indianapolis, Ind.: Hudson Institute, 1995.

Waldman, Michael. *POTUS Speaks: Finding the Words That Defined the Clinton Presidency*. New York: Simon & Schuster, 2000.

Waldman, Steven. *The Bill: How the Adventures of Clinton's National Service Bill Reveal What Is Corrupt, Comic, Cynical—and Noble—about Washington*. New York: Viking, 1995.

Walker, Martin. *The President We Deserve: Bill Clinton, His Rise, Falls, and Comebacks*. New York: Crown Publishers, 1996.

Woodward, Bob. *The Agenda: Inside the Clinton White House*. New York: Simon & Schuster, 1994.

———. *The Choice*. New York: Simon & Schuster, 1996.

———. *Shadow: Five Presidents and the Legacy of Watergate*. New York: Simon & Schuster, 1999.

INDEX

᭜

Boldface page numbers indicate primary discussions. *Italic* page numbers indicate illustrations. Page numbers followed by *c* indicate an item in the chronology.